1985

James C. Edwards

FURMAN UNIVERSITY

Douglas M. MacDonald

FURMAN UNIVERSITY

OCCASIONS FOR PHILOSOPHY

Second Edition

Prentice-Hall, Inc., Englewood Cliffs, N.J. 07632

Library of Congress Cataloging in Publication Data
Main entry under title:

Occasions for philosophy.

     1. Philosophy—Addresses, essays, lectures.   2. Life—
Addresses, essays, lectures.   I. Edwards, James C.,
[date]   II. MacDonald, Douglas M. [date]
B29.025   1985   100   84-9839
ISBN 0-13-629262-3

Editorial/production supervisor: *Edith Riker*
Cover designer: *Diane Saxe*
Manufacturing buyer: *Ron Chapman*

Printed in the United States of America

10   9   8   7   6   5   4   3   2   1

ISBN 0-13-629262-3 01

Prentice-Hall International, Inc., *London*
Prentice-Hall of Australia Pty. Limited, *Sydney*
Editora Prentice-Hall do Brasil, Ltda., *Rio de Janeiro*
Prentice-Hall Canada Inc., *Toronto*
Prentice-Hall of India Private Limited, *New Delhi*
Prentice-Hall of Japan, Inc., *Tokyo*
Prentice-Hall of Southeast Asia Pte. Ltd., *Singapore*
Whitehall Books Limited, *Wellington, New Zealand*

This book is dedicated to Martha and to Willis

CONTENTS

ACKNOWLEDGMENTS

Since we began to teach philosophy at Furman University in 1970 our students have been constant in their superior abilities, in their demands for excellence, and in their charities to strugglers. Their enthusiasm for learning has, time and again, challenged us to think anew and has shamed us when we were tempted to settle for easy half-truths or apparently profound obscurities. It is because of these students, and particularly because of a special few, who know who they are, that this anthology exists. . . .

Certain individuals and groups have aided us very directly in this endeavor. A grant from the W. K. Kellogg Foundation to Furman University provided the initial opportunity to redesign our introductory philosophy course, and a grant from Furman's Research and Professional Growth Committee provided a summer's freedom in which to consolidate our thought into this anthology. Our grateful thanks to both groups. The Kellogg grant enabled us to bring to Furman as a consultant J. B. Schneewind, Provost of Hunter College, CUNY; and his insights and suggestions are acknowledged with gratitude. . . . The academic administration . . . has been consistently supportive of our efforts; thanks to them all.

Finally, we wish to acknowledge the debts—of every variety—implied in our dedications. "Whereof one cannot speak, thereof must one be silent."

James C. Edwards
Douglas M. MacDonald

January 1978

NOTE
TO THE
SECOND EDITION

The years since January 1978, when we sent off to Prentice-Hall the first edition of this book, have brought enormous changes to each of us, but one thing at least remains the same: our joy in teaching philosophy to the students of Furman University. Part of this has to do with philosophy itself, of course, which—given its unlimited opportunities for discussion, rethinking, and flat-out admissions of ignorance—must be the best of all subjects to teach. But part of it certainly has to do with the students we have taught. To be sure, not all of them have enthusiastically welcomed our preoccupations and our demands, like all teachers we have sometimes encountered incomprehension, discomfort, even anger. (Indeed, like all teachers, we secretly cherish some of those who fought us every step of the way, sure that we were scoundrels out to undermine their faith or their political loyalties, or that we were merely shameless purveyors of useless gabble—for which they usually had a less polite term.) Nevertheless, in every class there has been the indispensable heaven of those who have taken themselves and us seriously enough to try out thinking for themselves; these have been willing to undertake the activity of philosophy. We are grateful to these men and women, as we are grateful to the college that gives them (and us) shelter.

A book's revision is just that: a re-vision, a looking-again; it is not a new book. This second edition remains, therefore, deeply indebted to all those already acknowledged in the first, and we are pleased now to renew our thanks to them.

In the meantime, however, others have come forward to help—or, to put it better, perhaps—have been fully recognized by us to be our helpers, and it is appropriate that we add their names to those in our original dedication: L. D. Johnson (1916-1981); Emily and Creighton Edwards; Phyllis Watts; Ruby N. Morgan; and Jane S. Chew.

James C. Edwards
Douglas M. MacDonald

INTRODUCTION

Another introductory philosophy anthology? Yes, for what we believe are very good reasons.

Three main sorts of introductory philosophy courses, with textbooks to match, are found in American universities today. There are, first of all, historical introductions, which study representative great philosophers in historical sequence, hoping to introduce the student to philosophy through its historical dialectic. Then there are "problems" courses, which isolate a number of major philosophical issues—usually in epistemology, metaphysics, and values theory—and deploy around these some readings from classical and contemporary philosophers. While both sorts of courses can sometimes serve as excellent introductions to philosophy, they have more frequently been charged with a glaring defect—a lack of perceived connection between the material read and the lives of the students and teachers who read it. Students often leave such courses with the distinct (if unfounded) impression that what philosophers have written is of little use to "real" life, that the problems philosophers worry about are not, for all their difficulty and historical patina, problems that ought to concern any thinking person. The problems of philosophy are historical curiosities, and the study of philosophy is the dusty unwrapping of these thought-mummies.

The concern for freshness and clear human interest in introductory philosphy courses is sharpened since such courses are usually taught as part of the general education sequence of a college curriculum. At most schools the student's general education requirements are met by taking a certain number and distribution of the introductory courses of various academic departments, philosophy among them; so introductory philosophy courses are thereby asserted to be relevant to the student's general education as well as being introductory of the discipline *per se.* But are they? Does a straightforward introduction, whether historical or problems-oriented, contribute most significantly to the general education of the student who will, in all likelihood, never take another philosophy course?

Spurred by such questions, a third type of introductory philosophy course has recently arisen. Its avowed aim has been *relevance,* bridging the gap between the student's concerns and the traditional concerns of philosophers. Anthologies have been produced that include standard philosophical pieces alongside readings from contemporary political statements, pop psychology, the new religions, and the like. ("Immanuel Kant, say hello to Carlos Castaneda.") But large problems still remain. In the first place, the philosophical interest of the "bridge" material is frequently negligible. Furthermore, the connections between such material and the included philosophy selections are often either very slight or else buried too deep for the beginning student to appreciate. And third, today's guru is tomorrow's blank look; a course that seeks relevance the easy way courts very swift obsolescence. How can one demonstrate some connections between philosophy and a student's very real and immediate human concerns without the fluff and strained relevance one finds in the pop texts and courses?

We intend that this anthology serve as the basis for a course that is both an introduction to *philosophy* and a signficant part of the student's general education. We believe that an introductory philosophy course, especially one that claims to serve the purposes of general education, ought to exhibit clear connections with issues fundamental to any thoughtful human life; and in selecting topics and readings we have tried to show that philosophical reflection does have a substantial (indeed, essential) place in such a life. We do this, not by including bits of ephemeral nonphilosophical material, but by showing what powerful philosophers have had to say on issues that are of perennial human interest no matter what the political, social, and aesthetic climate—issues like death and the threat it poses to life's meaning, the nature and significance of our varied personal relations, the possibility of religious belief. Such issues are of intrinsic concern to any thoughtful person, and philosophers have had much interesting and useful to say about them.

We wish to emphasize our concern with *doing philosophy.* All the selections in this book have substantial philosophical content; their authors are among the finest classical and contemporary thinkers: Plato, Aristotle, Aquinas, Kierkegaard, James, and Nagel. As is clear from the first section, we model a first encounter with philosophy on the figure of Socrates. Our selections are analytical and critical, not constructive and speculative. In an introductory course students respond best to the challenge of critically investigating their own presuppositions, and for that task there could hardly be a better model than Socrates. Rather than scatter-shoot, we have included relatively few major topics, with deeper analysis of each. Philosophy is argument; so we have, as best we can, arranged our selections dialectically. And we have tried to leave each issue with the student; philosophy shouldn't end with the course.

So, here is our anthology. We, of course, think it is a good book; but the proof of the pudding is in the eating. Teaching philosophy well is enormously difficult, but its rewards are commensurate with its difficulty. If this book in any way mitigates the difficulty without diminishing the rewards, it will have justified itself. We wish it, and you, well.

CHAPTER ONE
PHILOSOPHY
AND THE
SOCRATIC MODEL

What is philosophy? According to one philosopher it is the attempt "to understand how things in the broadest possible sense of the term hang together in the
broadest possible sense of the term";[1] for another it is "a battle against the bewitchment of our intelligence by means of language."[2] The trouble with such
definitions is that they are either so vague as to be almost meaningless or so specific
as to exclude what some other philosophers consider to be vital to the subject. The
specification of the nature of philosophy is itself a major philosophical task; thus
we will not begin this book by trying to capture the essence of philosophy in a
single, all-inclusive verbal definition. Rather, in this first section of readings
philosophy is defined *ostensively*, that is, it is demonstrated by example, not by a
discussion. By presenting one exemplary philosopher—Socrates—we intend to
introduce the aims, techniques, and values specific to philosophical activity itself.

What, then, do we see the philosopher Socrates doing? We see him talking and
talking and talking. But rather than being idle chatter, the Socratic dialogues are
conversations with a man who is intelligent, rational, playful, and unwilling to
accept another's opinions at face value. In the *Euthyphro,* for example, we see
Socrates conversing with a man who believes himself to be the paradigm of piety, a
man who is so sure of his righteousness that he is willing to prosecute his own
father. In his dialogue with the self-satisfied Euthyphro, Socrates himself is *never*
satisfied: He tries repeatedly to make Euthyphro define what he means by "piety"

1

and to make him assess the arguments on which his self-righteousness rests. Socrates shows himself to be a skeptic of a sort; but his critical questioning of received opinion is not an end in itself; it is a means to truth. While much of Scorates' philosophical activity is destructive, he sees the razing of illusion as the necessary first step in attaining wisdom.

The *Euthyphro* ends on a disquieting note; the discussion concludes practically where it began. Is this also a characteristic of philosophical investigation—that it goes nowhere? Perhaps the message (albeit unintended) of the *Euthyphro* is that philosophy is unimportant to the discovery of public truth; perhaps, even more radically, public truth is itself an illusion, and we are thrown back on opinions, of which those of one person are just as good as those of another. Or perhaps the message of the dialogue is just that truth is always difficult to grasp and that its attainment requires a great deal more persistence and intellectual integrity than Euthyphro offers.

The *Apology*, ostensibly the story of Socrates' trial for treason, is also his defense of the philosophical life itself. Then, as now, many people saw philosophy as corrosive of the social framework essential to their contentment; the *Apology* forces us to consider whether philosophy has any real virtue for the individual or for society. In his defense Socrates urges that we have arguments for our beliefs, actions, and attitudes; that we be willing to examine and reexamine our life to discover whether its structure has justification. He forcefully opposes any form of intellectual dogmatism. For him philosophy is an *activity,* not a body of sterile doctrine—an activity appropriate to all of one's life. Without philosophy, an individual is condemned to live in illusion, condemned not to know the true sense of his or her life. A society without philosophers is like a city of slaves; it is a prisoner of ignorance, prejudice, tradition, and passion.

For Socrates, the activity of philosophy is integral to being fully human; merely having a human body doesn't guarantee having a genuinely human life. The distinction of human beings is *autonomy,* one's control of one's own life. Animals cannot be autonomous; their actions are controlled either by innate behavioral mechanisms or by reinforced environmental patterns. They are in bondage to their genes and their habitats. We human beings seem to be able to determine for ourselves (at least some of) our actions. We can, it appears, *reason* about what we are to do; we can direct our behavior internally, not always have it imposed from without. Autonomy, however, is something to be won; if we don't struggle, we will still be ruled externally by ignorance, tradition, and illusion. For Socrates, philosophy is the way to autonomy, the way to a life that is distinctively human.

Furthermore, philosophical autonomy has an important social dimension. A person's actions are based (consciously or unconsciously) on beliefs that he or she holds—about the nature of the world, about morality, about religion—and in our social contacts it doesn't take us long to realize just how diverse these beliefs are. Since our lives don't always allow us the luxury of ignoring these diversities, disagreement and conflict arise; and these disputes can be resolved by force, bribery, or rational persuasion. Physical force has always been an effective way of getting people to change their actions, if not their minds; and much of modern advertising is a form of bribery. ("Want a date this Saturday night? Use our toothpaste and . . .") But these forms of persuasion are not respecters of the person; they externally compel assent. A person's beliefs and actions are changed, not by compulsion for truth, but by *fear*—fear of pain, fear of not being loved.

The Socratic appeal to reason, on the other hand, is a recognition of personal autonomy. It asks us to believe only that for which there are good reasons, and it encourages us to give up those beliefs which we cannot rationally support. Neither is easy; for as difficult as it often is to specify good reasons for our beliefs, it is even harder to abandon those cherished propositions for which we have been unable to find a rational basis. Yet, hard or easy, the Socratic ideal is an ideal worthy of the *individual;* it fully allows for autonomy. We want to be allowed to make up our own mind; simple justice demands that we allow others the same. If we care about autonomy, then the Socratic conception of philosophical activity seems to be essential to us in our desire for individual freedom and for a just basis of social cooperation.

The Socratic model of the philosopher, the person committed to the critical examination of his life, shapes this book. The selections raise issues vital to any thoughtful, sensitive person; the intent is not to raise senseless questions or to criticize for the sake of criticism, but to provoke us into truth. But truth is hard to get, and very easy to confuse with other things. It is sometimes, for instance, confused with rhetorical skill and argumentative facility.

> Just as a vagrant accused of stealing a carrot from a field stands before a comfortably seated judge who keeps up an elegant flow of queries, comments, and witticisms while the accused is unable to stammer a word, so truth stands before an intelligence which is concerned with the elegant manipulation of opinions.[3]

Caveat: The study of philosophy often seems to help one in the elegant manipulation of opinions; it is rare that it actually gives one the truth.

A final word of caution: The Socratic model of philosophy requires the criticism of beliefs, attitudes, and actions. As much as Socrates was critical of others, he was, ironically, even more critical of himself. He was never more sincere than when he proclaimed to Athens his own ignorance. We would be poor students of Socrates if we were to accept his critical model of philosophy uncritically. Although the Socratic model certainly shapes this book, the selections by Drengson and Nietzsche raise—in very different ways—some hard questions about this conception of philosophy and about Socrates' use of it.

What, then, is philosophy? Surely, in part, philosophy is what Socrates did, and what, after his example, we now do. For philosophy is, finally, something that is *done;* we do not study philosophical texts to try to emulate point by point the great philosophers like Socrates. Rather, the texts in which we encounter him and his descendents are *occasions* for philosophy, for *our* philosophy, the reflective examination of our own life here and now.

NOTES

1. Wilfrid Sellars, *Science, Perception and Reality* (London: Routledge and Kegan Paul, 1963), p. 1.

2. Ludwig Wittgenstein, *Philosophical Investigations,* trans. G. E. M. Anscombe (Oxford: Basil Blackwell, 1953), sec. 109.

3. Simone Weil, *Selected Essays 1934-1943,* trans. Sir Richard Rees (London: Oxford University Press, 1965), p. 13.

EUTHYPHRO

Plato

Characters

Socrates
Euthyphro

Scene—The Hall of the King

EUTHYPHRO: What in the world are you doing here in the king's hall, Socrates? Why have you left your haunts in the Lyceum? You surely cannot have a suit before him, as I have.

SOCRATES: The Athenians, Euthyphro, call it an indictment, not a suit.

EUTH.: What? Do you mean that someone is prosecuting you? I cannot believe that you are prosecuting anyone yourself.

SOCR.: Certainly I am not.

EUTH.: Then is someone prosecuting you?

SOCR.: Yes.

EUTH.: Who is he?

SOCR.: I scarcely know him myself, Euthyphro; I think he must be some unknown young man. His name, however, is Meletus, and his district Pitthis, if you can call to mind any Meletus of that district—a hook-nosed man with lanky hair and rather a scanty beard.

EUTH.: I don't know him, Socrates. But tell me, what is he prosecuting you for?

SOCR.: What for? Not on trivial grounds, I think. It is no small thing for so young a man to have formed an opinion on such an important matter. For he, he says, knows how the young are corrupted, and who are their corrupters. He must be a wise man who, observing my ignorance, is going to accuse me to the state, as his mother, of corrupting his friends. I think that he is the only one who begins at the right point in his political reforms; for his first care is to make the young men as good as possible, just as a good farmer will take care of his young plants first, and, after he has done that, of the others. And so Meletus, I suppose, is first clearing us away who, as he says, corrupt the young men growing up; and then,

From *Euthyphro, Apology, Crito,* trans. F. J. Church (Indianapolis: The Library of Liberal Arts, Bobbs-Merrill, 1956), pp. 1-20. Reprinted by permission of the publisher.

EUTH.:   when he has done that, of course he will turn his attention to the older men, and so become a very great public benefactor. Indeed, that is only what you would expect when he goes to work in this way.

EUTH.:   I hope it may be so, Socrates, but I fear the opposite. It seems to me that in trying to injure you, he is really setting to work by striking a blow at the foundation of the state. But how, tell me, does he say that you corrupt the youth?

SOCR.:   In a way which sounds absurd at first, my friend. He says that I am a maker of gods; and so he is prosecuting me, he says, for inventing new gods and for not believing in the old ones.

EUTH.:   I understand, Socrates. It is because you say that you always have a divine guide. So he is prosecuting you for introducing religious reforms; and he is going into court to arouse prejudice against you, knowing that the multitude are easily prejudiced about such matters. Why, they laugh even at me, as I were out of my mind, when I talk about divine things in the assembly and tell them what is going to happen; and yet I have never foretold anything which has not come true. But they are resentful of all people like us. We must not worry about them; we must meet them boldly.

SOCR.:   My dear Euthyphro, their ridicule is not a very serious matter. The Athenians, it seems to me, may think a man to be clever without paying him much attention, so long as they do not think that he teaches his wisdom to others. But as soon as they think that he makes other people clever, they get angry, whether it be from resentment, as you say, or for some other reason.

EUTH.:   I am not very anxious to test their attitude toward me in this matter.

SOCR.:   No, perhaps they think that you are reserved, and that you are not anxious to teach your wisdom to others. But I fear that they may think that I am; for my love of men makes me talk to everyone whom I meet quite freely and unreservedly, and without payment. Indeed, if I could I would gladly pay people myself to listen to me. If then, as I said just now, they were only going to laugh at me, as you say they do at you, it would not be at all an unpleasant way of spending the day—to spend it in court, joking and laughing. But if they are going to be in earnest, then only prophets like you can tell where the matter will end.

EUTH.:   Well, Socrates, I dare say that nothing will come of it. Very likely you will be successful in your trial, and I think that I shall be in mine.

SOCR.:   And what is this suit of yours, Euthyphro? Are you suing, or being sued?

EUTH.:   I am suing.

SOCR.:   Whom?

EUTH.:   A man whom people think I must be mad to prosecute.

SOCR.:   What? Has he wings to fly away with?

EUTH.:   He is far enough from flying; he is a very old man.

SOCR.:   Who is he?

EUTH.:   He is my father.

SOCR.:   Your father, my good man?

EUTH.:   He is indeed.

SOCR.:   What are you prosecuting him for? What is the accusation?

EUTH.:   Murder, Socrates.

SOCR.:   Good heavens, Euthyphro! Surely the multitude are ignorant of what is right. I take it that it is not everyone who could rightly do what you are doing; only a man who was already well advanced in wisdom.

EUTH.:   That is quite true, Socrates.

SOCR.:   Was the man whom your father killed a relative of yours? But, of course, he was. You would never have prosecuted your father for the murder of a stranger?

EUTH.:   You amuse me, Socrates. What difference does it make whether the murdered man were a relative or a stranger? The only question that you have to ask is, did the murderer kill justly or not? If justly, you must let him alone; if unjustly, you must indict him for murder, even though he share your hearth and sit at your table. The pollution is the same if you associate with such a man, knowing what he has done, without purifying yourself and him too, by bringing him to justice. In the present case the murdered man was a poor laborer of mine, who worked for us on our farm in Naxos. While drunk he got angry with one of our slaves and killed him. My father therefore bound the man hand and foot and threw him into a ditch, while he sent to Athens to ask the priest what he should do. While the messenger was gone, he entirely neglected the man, thinking that he was a murderer, and that it would be no great matter, even if he were to die. And that was exactly what happened; hunger and cold and his bonds killed him before the messenger returned. And now my father and the rest of my family are indignant with me because I am prosecuting my father for the murder of this murderer. They assert that he did not kill the man at all; and they say that, even if he had killed him over and over again, the man himself was a murderer, and that I ought not to concern myself about such a person because it is impious for a son to prosecute his father for murder. So little, Socrates, do they know the divine law of piety and impiety.

SOCR.:   And do you mean to say, Euthyphro, that you think that you understand divine things and piety and impiety so accurately that, in such a case as you have stated, you can bring your father to justice without fear that you yourself may be doing something impious?

EUTH.:   If I did not understand all these matters accurately, Socrates, I should not be worth much—Euthyphro would not be any better than other men.

SOCR.:   Then, my dear Euthyphro, I cannot do better than become your pupil and challenge Meletus on this very point before the trial begins. I should say that I had always thought it very important to have knowledge about divine things; and that now, when he says that I offend by speaking carelessly about them, and by introducing reforms, I have become your pupil. And I should say, "Meletus, if you acknowledge Euthyphro to be wise in these matters and to hold the correct belief, then think the same of me and do not put me on trial; but if you do not, then bring a suit, not against me, but against my master, for corrupting his elders—namely, myself whom he corrupts by his teaching, and his own father whom he corrupts by admonishing and punishing him." And if I did not succeed in persuading him to release me from the suit or to indict you in my place, then I could repeat my challenge in court.

EUTH.:   Yes, by Zeus! Socrates, I think I should find out his weak points if he were to try to indict me. I should have a good deal to say about him in court long before I spoke about myself.

SOCR.:   Yes, my dear friend, and knowing this I am anxious to become your pupil. I see that Meletus here, and others too, seem not to notice you at all, but he sees through me without difficulty and at once prosecutes me for impiety. Now, therefore, please explain to me what you were so confident just now that you knew. Tell me what are righteousness and sacrilege with respect to murder and everything else. I suppose that piety is the same in all actions, and that impiety is always the opposite of piety, and retains its identity, and that, as impiety, it always has the same character, which will be found in whatever is impious.

EUTH.: Certainly, Socrates, I suppose so.

SOCR.: Tell me, then, what is piety and what is impiety?

EUTH.: Well, then, I say that piety means prosecuting the unjust individual who has committed murder or sacrilege, or any other such crime, as I am doing now, whether he is your father or your mother or whoever he is; and I say that impiety means not prosecuting him. And observe, Socrates, I will give you a clear proof, which I have already given to others, that it is so, and that doing right means not letting off unpunished the sacrilegious man, whosoever he may be. Men hold Zeus to be the best and the most just of the gods; and they admit that Zeus bound his own father, Cronos, for wrongfully devouring his children; and that Chronos, in his turn, castrated his father for similar reasons. And yet these same men are incensed with me because I proceed against my father for doing wrong. So, you see, they say one thing in the case of the gods and quite another in mine.

SOCR.: Is not that why I am being prosecuted, Euthyphro? I mean, because I find it hard to accept such stories people tell about the gods? I expect that I shall be found at fault because I doubt those stories. Now if you who understand all these matters so well agree in holding all those tales true, and I suppose that I must yield to your authority. What could I say when I admit myself that I know nothing about them? But tell me, in the name of friendship, do you really believe that these things have actually happened?

EUTH.: Yes, and more amazing things, too, Socrates, which the multitude do not know of.

SOCR.: Then you really believe that there is war among the gods, and bitter hatreds, and battles, such as the poets tell of, and which the great painters have depicted in our temples, notably in the pictures which cover the robe that is carried up to the Acropolis at the great Panathenaic festival? Are we to say that these things are true, Euthyphro?

EUTH.: Yes, Socrates, and more besides. As I was saying, I will report to you many other stories about divine matters, if you like, which I am sure will astonish you when you hear them.

SOCR.: I dare say. You shall report them to me at your leisure another time. At present please try to give a more definite answer to the question which I asked you just now. What I asked you, my friend, was, What is piety? and you have not explained it to me to my satisfaction. You only tell me that what you are doing now, namely, prosecuting your father for murder, is a pious act.

EUTH.: Well, that is true, Socrates.

SOCR.: Very likely. But many other actions are pious, are they not, Euthyphro?

EUTH.: Certainly.

SOCR.: Remember, then, I did not ask you to tell me one or two of all the many pious actions that there are; I want to know what is characteristic of piety which makes all pious actions pious. You said, I think, that there is one characteristic which makes all pious actions pious, and another characteristic which makes all impious actions impious. Do you not remember?

EUTH.: I do.

SOCR.:   Well, then, explain to me what is this characteristic, that I may have it to turn to, and to use as a standard whereby to judge your actions and those of other men, and be able to say that whatever action resembles it is pious, and whatever does not, is not pious.

EUTH.:   Yes, I will tell you that if you wish, Socrates.

SOCR.:   Certainly I do.

EUTH.:   Well, then, what is pleasing to the gods is pious, and what is not pleasing to them is impious.

SOCR.:   Fine, Euthyphro. Now you have given me the answer that I wanted. Whether what you say is true, I do not know yet. But, of course, you will go on to prove that it is true.

EUTH.:   Certainly.

SOCR.:   Come, then, let us examine our statement. The things and the men that are pleasing to the gods are pious, and the things and the men that are displeasing to the gods are impious. But piety and impiety are not the same; they are as opposite as possible—was not that what we said?

EUTH.:   Certainly.

SOCR.:   And it seems the appropriate statement?

EUTH.:   Yes, Socrates, certainly.

SOCR.:   Have we not also said, Euthyphro, that there are quarrels and disagreements and hatreds among the gods?

EUTH.:   We have.

SOCR.:   But what kind of disagreement, my friend, causes hatred and anger? Let us look at the matter thus. If you and I were to disagree as to whether one number were more than another, would that make us angry and enemies? Should we not settle such a dispute at once by counting?

EUTH.:   Of course.

SOCR.:   And if we were to disagree as to the relative size of two things, we should measure them and put an end to the disagreement at once, should we not?

EUTH.:   Yes.

SOCR.:   And should we not settle a question about the relative weight of two things by weighing them?

EUTH.:   Of course.

SOCR.:   Then what is the question which would make us angry and enemies if we disagreed about it, and could not come to a settlement? Perhaps you have not an answer ready; but listen to mine. Is it not the question of the just and unjust, of the honorable and the dishonorable, of the good and the bad? Is it not questions about these matters which make you and me and everyone else quarrel, when we do quarrel, if we differ about them and can reach no satisfactory agreement?

EUTH.:   Yes, Socrates, it is disagreements about these matters.

SOCR.:   Well, Euthyphro, the gods will quarrel over these things if they quarrel at all, will they not?

EUTH.:   Necessarily.

SOCR.:   Then, my good Euthyphro, you say that some of the gods think one thing just, the others another; and that what some of them hold to be honorable or good, others hold to be dishonorable or evil. For there would not have been quarrels among them if they had not disagreed on these points, would there?

EUTH.:   You are right.

SOCR.:   And each of them loves what he thinks honorable, and good, and just; and hates the opposite, does he not?

EUTH.: Certainly.

SOCR.: But you say that the same action is held by some of them to be just, and by others to be unjust; and that then they dispute about it, and so quarrel and fight among themselves. Is it not so?

EUTH.: Yes.

SOCR.: Then the same thing is hated by the gods and loved by them; and the same thing will be displeasing and pleasing to them.

EUTH.: Apparently.

SOCR.: Then, according to your account, the same thing will be pious and impious.

EUTH.: So it seems.

SOCR.: Then, my good friend, you have not answered my question. I did not ask you to tell me what action is both pious and impious; but it seems that whatever is pleasing to the gods is also displeasing to them. And so, Euthyphro, I should not be surprised if what you are doing now in punishing your father is an action well pleasing to Zeus, but hateful to Cronos and Uranus, and acceptable to Hephaestus, but hateful to Hera; and if any of the other gods disagree about it, pleasing to some of them and displeasing to others.

EUTH.: But on this point, Socrates, I think that there is no difference of opinion among the gods; they all hold that if one man kills another unjustly, he must be punished.

SOCR.: What, Euthyphro? Among mankind, have you never heard disputes whether a man ought to be punished for killing another man unjustly, or for doing some other unjust deed?

EUTH.: Indeed, they never cease from these disputes, especially in courts of justice. They do all manner of unjust things; and then there is nothing which they will not do and say to avoid punishment.

SOCR.: Do they admit that they have done something unjust, and at the same time deny that they ought to be punished, Euthyphro?

EUTH.: No, indeed, that they do not.

SOCR.: Then it is not the case that there is nothing which they will not do and say. I take it, they do not dare to say or argue that they must not be punished if they have done something unjust. What they say is that they have not done anything unjust, is it not so?

EUTH.: That is true.

SOCR.: Then they do not disagree over the question that the unjust individual must be punished. They disagree over the question, who is unjust, and what was done and when, do they not?

EUTH.: That is true.

SOCR.: Well, is not exactly the same thing true of the gods if they quarrel about justice and injustice, as you say they do? Do not some of them say that the others are doing something unjust, while the others deny it? No one, I suppose, my dear friend, whether god or man dares to say that a person who has done something unjust must not be punished.

EUTH.: No, Socrates, that is true, by and large.

SOCR.: I take it, Euthyphro, that the disputants, whether men or gods, if the gods do disagree, disagree over each separate act. When they quarrel about any act, some of them say that it was just, and others that it was unjust. Is it not so?

EUTH.: Yes.

SOCR.: Come, then, my dear Euthyphro, please enlighten me on this point. What proof have you that all the gods think that a laborer who has been imprisoned for murder by the master of the man whom he has murdered, and who dies from his imprisonment before the master has had time to learn from the religious authorities what he should do, dies unjustly? How do you know that it is just for a son to indict his father and to prosecute him for the murder of such a man? Come, see if you can make it clear to me that the gods necessarily agree in thinking that this action of yours is just; and if you satisfy me, I will never cease singing your praises for wisdom.

EUTH.: I could make that clear enough to you, Socrates; but I am afraid that it would be a long business.

SOCR.: I see you think that I am duller than the judges. To them, of course, you will make it clear that your father has committed an unjust action, and that all the gods agree in hating such actions.

EUTH.: I will indeed, Socrates, if they will only listen to me.

SOCR.: They will listen if they think that you are a good speaker. But while you were talking, it occured to me to ask myself this question: suppose that Euthyphro were to prove to me as clearly as possible that all the gods think such a death unjust, how has he brought me any nearer to understanding what piety and impiety are? This particular act, perhaps, may be displeasing to the gods, but then we have just seen that piety and impiety cannot be defined in that way; for we have seen that what is displeasing to the gods is also pleasing to them. So I will let you off on this point, Euthyphro; and all the gods shall agree in thinking your father's action wrong and in hating it, if you like. But shall we correct our definition and say that whatever all the gods hate is impious, and whatever they all love is pious; while whatever some of them love, and others hate, is either both or neither? Do you wish us now to define piety and impiety in this manner?

EUTH.: Why not Socrates?

SOCR.: There is no reason why I should not, Euthyphro. It is for you to consider whether that definition will help you to teach me what you promised.

EUTH.: Well, I should say that piety is what all the gods love, and that impiety is what they all hate.

SOCR.: Are we to examine this definition, Euthyphro, and see if it is a good one? Or are we to be content to accept the bare statements of other men or of ourselves without asking any questions? Or must we examine the statements?

EUTH.: We must examine them. But for my part I think that the definition is right this time.

SOCR.: We shall know that better in a little while, my good friend. Now consider this question. Do the gods love piety because it is pious, or is it pious because they love it?

EUTH.: I do not understand you, Socrates.

SOCR.: I will try to explain myself: we speak of a thing being carried and carrying, and being led and leading, and being seen and seeing; and you understand that all such expressions mean different things, and what the difference is.

EUTH.: Yes, I think I understand.

SOCR.: And we talk of a thing being loved, of a thing loving, and the two are different?

EUTH.: Of course.

SOCR.: Now tell me, is a thing which is being carried in a state of being carried because it is carried, or for some other reason?

EUTH.:   No, because it is carried.

SOCR.:   And a thing is in a state of being led because it is led, and of being seen because it is seen?

EUTH.:   Certainly.

SOCR.:   Then a thing is not seen because it is in a state of being seen: it is in a state of being seen because it is seen; and a thing is not led because it is in a state of being led: it is in a state of being led because it is led; and a thing is not carried because it is in a state of being carried: it is in a state of being carried because it is carried. Is my meaning clear now, Euthyphro? I mean this: if anything becomes or is affected, it does not become because it is in a state of becoming; it is in a state of becoming because it becomes; and it is not affected because it is in a state of being affected: it is in a state of being affected because it is affected. Do you not agree?

EUTH.:   I do.

SOCR.:   Is not that which is being loved in a state either of becoming or of being affected in some way by something?

EUTH.:   Certainly.

SOCR.:   Then the same is true here as in the former cases. A thing is not loved by those who love it because it is in a state of being loved; it is in a state of being loved because they love it.

EUTH.:   Necessarily.

SOCR.:   Well, then, Euthyphro, what do we say about piety? Is it not loved by all the gods, according to your definition?

EUTH.:   Yes.

SOCR.:   Because it is pious, or for some other reason?

EUTH.:   No, because it is pious.

SOCR.:   Then it is loved by the gods because it is pious; it is not pious because it is loved by them?

EUTH.:   It seems so.

SOCR.:   But, then, what is pleasing to the gods is pleasing to them, and is in a state of being loved by them, because they love it?

EUTH.:   Of course.

SOCR.:   Then piety is not what is pleasing to the gods, and what is pleasing to the gods is not pious, as you say, Euthyphro. They are different things.

EUTH.:   And why, Socrates?

SOCR.:   Because we are agreed that the gods love piety because it is pious, and that it is not pious because they love it. Is not this so?

EUTH.:   Yes.

SOCR.:   And that what is pleasing to the gods because they love it, is pleasing to them by reason of this same love, and that they do not love it because it is pleasing to them.

EUTH.:   True.

SOCR.:   Then, my dear Euthyphro, piety and what is pleasing to the gods are different things. If the gods had loved piety because it is pious, they would also have loved what is pleasing to them because it is pleasing to them; but if what is pleasing to them had been pleasing to them because they loved it, then piety, too, would have been piety because they loved it. But now you see that they are opposite things, and wholly different from each other. For the one is of a sort to be loved because it is loved, while the other is loved because it is of a sort to be loved. My question, Euthyphro, was, What is piety? But it turns out that you have not explained to me the essential character of piety; you have been content to mention an effect which belongs to it—namely, that all the gods love it. You have not yet told me what its essential character is. Do not, if you please, keep from me what piety is; begin again and tell me that. Never mind whether the gods love it, or whether it has other effects: we shall not differ on that point. Do your best to make clear to me what is piety and what is impiety.

EUTH.: But, Socrates, I really don't know how to explain to you what is in my mind. Whatever statement we put forward always somehow moves round in a circle, and will not stay where we put it.

SOCR.: I think that your statements, Euthyphro, are worthy of my ancestor Daedalus. If they had been mine and I had set them down, I dare say you would have made fun of me, and said that it was the consequence of my descent from Daedalus that the statements which I construct run away, as his statues used to, and will not stay where they are put. But, as it is, the statements are yours, and the joke would have no point. You yourself see that they will not stay still.

EUTH.: Nay, Socrates, I think that the joke is very much in point. It is not my fault that the statement moves round in a circle and will not stay still. But you are the Daedalus, I think; as far as I am concerned, my statements would have stayed put.

SOCR.: Then, my friend, I must be a more skillful artist than Daedalus; he only used to make his own works move, while I, you see, can make other people's works move, too. And the beauty of it is that I am wise against my will. I would rather that our statements had remained firm and immovable than have all the wisdom of Daedalus and all the riches of Tantalus to boot. But enough of this. I will do my best to help you to explain to me what piety is, for I think that you are lazy. Don't give in yet. Tell me, do you not think that all piety must be just?

EUTH.: I do.

SOCR.: Well, then, is all justice pious, too? Or, while all piety is just, is a part only of justice pious, and the rest of it something else?

EUTH.: I do not follow you, Socrates.

SOCR.: Yet you have the advantage over me in your youth no less than your wisdom. But, as I say, the wealth of your wisdom makes you complacent. Exert yourself, my good friend: I am not asking you a difficult question. I mean the opposite of what the poet said, when he wrote:

"You shall not name Zeus the creator, who made all things: for where there is fear there also is reverence."

Now I disagree with the poet. Shall I tell you why?

EUTH.: Yes.

SOCR.: I do not think it true to say that where there is fear, there also is reverence. Many people who fear sickness and poverty and other such evils seem to me to have fear, but no reverence for what they fear. Do you not think so?

EUTH.: I do.

SOCR.: But I think that where there is reverence there also is fear. Does any man feel reverence and a sense of shame about anything, without at the same time dreading and fearing the reputation of wickedness?

EUTH.: No, certainly not.

SOCR.: Then, though there is fear wherever there is reverence, it is not correct to say that where there is fear there also is reverence. Reverence does not always accompany fear; for fear, I take it, is wider than reverence. It is part of fear, just as the odd is a part of number, so that where you have the odd you must also have number, though where you have number you do not necessarily have the odd. Now I think you follow me?

EUTH.: I do.

SOCR.: Well, then, this is what I meant by the question which I asked you. Is there always piety where there is justice? Or, though there is always justice where there is piety, yet there is not always piety where there is justice, because piety is only a part of justice? Shall we say this, or do you differ?

EUTH.: No, I agree. I think that you are right.

SOCR.: Now observe the next point. If piety is a part of justice, we must find out, I suppose, what part of justice it is? Now, if you had asked me just now, for instance, what part of number is the odd, and what number is an odd number, I should have said that whatever number is not even is an odd number. Is it not so?

EUTH.: Yes.

SOCR.: Then see if you can explain to me what part of justice is piety, that I may tell Meletus that now that I have been adequately instructed by you as to what actions are righteous and pious, and what are not, he must give up prosecuting me unjustly for impiety.

EUTH.: Well, then , Socrates, I should say that righteousness and piety are that part of justice which has to do with the careful attention which ought to be paid to the gods; and that what has to do with the careful attention which ought to be paid to men is the remaining part of justice.

SOCR.: And I think that your answer is a good one, Euthyphro. But there is one little point about which I still want to hear more. I do not yet understand what the careful attention is to which you refer. I suppose you do not mean that the attention which we pay to the gods is like the attention which we pay to other things. We say, for instance, do we not, that not everyone knows how to take care of horses, but only the trainer of horses?

EUTH.: Certainly.

SOCR.: For I suppose that the skill that is concerned with horses is the art of taking care of horses.

EUTH.: Yes.

SOCR.: And not everyone understands the care of dogs, but only the huntsman.

EUTH.: True.

SOCR.: For I suppose that the huntsman's skill is the art of taking care of dogs.

EUTH.: Yes.

SOCR.: And the herdsman's skill is the art of taking care of cattle.

EUTH.: Certainly.

SOCR.: And you say that piety and righteousness are taking care of the gods, Euthyphro?

EUTH.: I do.

SOCR.: Well, then, has not all care the same object? Is it not for the good and benefit of that on which its bestowed? For instance, you see that horses are benefited and improved when they are cared for by the art which is concerned with them. Is it not so?

EUTH.: Yes, I think so.

SOCR.: And dogs are benefited and improved by the huntsman's art, and cattle by the herdsman's, are they not? And the same is always true. Or do you think care is ever meant to harm that which is cared for?

EUTH.: No, indeed; certainly not.

SOCR.:	But to benefit it?
EUTH.:	Of course.
SOCR.:	Then is piety, which is our care for the gods, intended to benefit the gods, or to improve them? Should you allow that you make any of the gods better when you do a pious action?
EUTH.:	No indeed; certainly not.
SOCR.:	No, I am quite sure that that is not your meaning, Euthyphro. It was for that reason that I asked you what you meant by the careful attention which ought to be paid to the gods. I thought that you did not mean that.
EUTH.:	You were right, Socrates. I do not mean that.
SOCR.:	Good. Then what sort of attention to the gods will piety be?
EUTH.:	The sort of attention, Socrates, slaves pay to their masters.
SOCR.:	I understand; then it is a kind of service to the gods?
EUTH.:	Certainly.
SOCR.:	Can you tell me what result the art which serves a doctor serves to produce? Is it not health?
EUTH.:	Yes.
SOCR.:	And what result does the art which serves a shipwright serve to produce?
EUTH.:	A ship, of course, Socrates.
SOCR.:	The result of the art which serves a builder is a house, is it not?
EUTH.:	Yes.
SOCR.:	Then tell me, my good friend: What result will the art which serves the gods serve to produce? You must know, seeing that you say that you know more about divine things than any other man.
EUTH.:	Well, that is true, Socrates.
SOCR.:	Then tell me, I beg you, what is that grand result which the gods use our services to produce?
EUTH.:	There are many notable results, Socrates.
SOCR.:	So are those, my friend, which a general produces. Yet it is easy to see that the crowning result of them all is victory in war, is it not?
EUTH.:	Of course.
SOCR.:	And, I take it, the farmer produces many notable results; yet the principal result of them all is that he makes the earth produce food.
EUTH.:	Certainly.
SOCR.:	Well, then, what is the principal result of the many notable results which the gods produce?
EUTH.:	I told you just now, Socrates, that accurate knowledge of all these matters is not easily obtained. However, broadly I say this: if any man knows that his words and actions in prayer and sacrifice are acceptable to the gods, that is what is pious; and it preserves the state, as it does private families. But the opposite of what is acceptable to the gods is sacrilegious, and this it is that undermines and destroys everything.
SOCR.:	Certainly, Euthyphro, if you had wished, you could have answered my main question in far fewer words. But you are evidently not anxious to teach me. Just now, when you were on the very point of telling me what I want to know, you stopped short. If you had gone on then, I should have learned from you clearly enough by this time what piety is. But now I am asking you questions, and must follow wherever you lead me; so tell me, what is it that you mean by piety and impiety? Do you not mean a science of prayer and sacrifice?
EUTH.:	I do.

SOCR.: To sacrifice is to give to the gods, and to pray is to ask of them, is it not?

EUTH.: It is, Socrates.

SOCR.: Then you say that piety is the science of asking of the gods and giving to them?

EUTH.: You understand my meaning exactly, Socrates.

SOCR.: Yes, for I am eager to share your wisdom, Euthyphro, and so I am all attention; nothing that you say will fall to the ground. But tell me, what is this service of the gods? You say it is to ask of them, and to give to them?

EUTH.: I do.

SOCR.: Then, to ask rightly will be to ask of them what we stand in need of from them, will it not?

EUTH.: Naturally.

SOCR.: And to give rightly will be to give back to them what they stand in need of from us? It would not be very skillful to make a present to a man of something that he has no need of.

EUTH.: True, Socrates.

SOCR.: Then piety, Euthyphro, will be the art of carrying on business between gods and men?

EUTH.: Yes, if you like to call it so.

SOCR.: But I like nothing except what is true. But tell me, how are the gods benefited by the gifts which they receive from us? What they give is plain enough. Every good thing that we have is their gift. But how are they benefited by what we give them? Have we the advantage over them in these business transactions to such an extent that we receive from them all the good things we possess, and we give them nothing in return?

EUTH.: But do you suppose, Socrates, that the gods are benefited by the gifts which they receive from us?

SOCR.: But what *are* these gifts, Euthyphro, that we give the gods?

EUTH.: What do you think but honor and praise, and, as I have said, what is acceptable to them.

SOCR.: Then piety, Euthyphro, is acceptable to the gods, but it is not profitable to them nor loved by them?

EUTH.: I think that nothing is more loved by them.

SOCR.: Then I see that piety means that which is loved by the gods.

EUTH.: Most certainly.

SOCR.: After that, shall you be surprised to find that your statements move about instead of staying where you put them? Shall you accuse me of being the Daedalus that makes them move, when you yourself are far more skillful than Daedalus was, and make them go round in a circle? Do you not see that our statement has come round to where it was before? Surely you remember that we have already seen that piety and what is pleasing to the gods are quite different things. Do you not remember?

EUTH.: I do.

SOCR.: And now do you not see that you say that what the gods love is pious? But does not what the gods love come to the same thing as what is pleasing to the gods?

EUTH.: Certainly.

SOCR.: Then either our former conclusion was wrong or, if it was right, we are wrong now.

EUTH.: So it seems.

SOCR.:   Then we must begin again and inquire what piety is. I do not mean to give in until I have found out. Do not regard me as unworthy; give your whole mind to the question, and this time tell me the truth. For if anyone knows it, it is you; and you are a Proteus whom I must not let go until you have told me. It cannot be that you would ever have undertaken to prosecute your aged father for the murder of a laboring man unless you had known exactly what piety and impiety are. You would have feared to risk the anger of the gods, in case you should be doing wrong, and you would have been afraid of what men would say. But now I am sure that you think that you know exactly what is pious and what is not; so tell me, my good Euthyphro, and do not conceal from me what you think.

EUTH.:   Another time, then, Socrates. I am in a hurry now, and it is time for me to be off.

SOCR.:   What are you doing, my friend! Will you go away and destroy all my hopes of learning from you what is pious and what is not, and so of escaping Meletus? I meant to explain to him that now Euthyphro has made me wise about divine things, and that I no longer in my ignorance speak carelessly about them or introduce reforms. And then I was going to promise him to live a better life for the future.

THE APOLOGY

Plato

Characters

Socrates
Meletus

Scene—The Court of Justice

SOCRATES: I do not know what impression my accusers have made upon you, Athenians. But I do know that they nearly made me forget who I was, so persuasive were they. And yet they have scarcely spoken one single word of truth. Of all their many falsehoods, the one which astonished me most was their saying that I was a clever speaker, and that you must be careful not to let me deceive you. I thought that it was most shameless of them not to be ashamed to talk in that way. For as soon as I open my mouth they will be refuted, and I shall prove that I am not a clever speaker in any way at all—unless, indeed, by a clever speaker they mean someone who speaks the truth. If that is their meaning, I agree with them that I am an orator not to be compared with them. My accusers, I repeat, have said little or nothing that is true, but from me you shall hear the whole truth. Certainly you will not hear a speech,

From *Euthyphro, Apology, Crito,* trans. F. J. Church (Indianapolis: The Library of Liberal Arts, Bobbs-Merrill, 1956), pp. 21-49. Reprinted by permission of the publisher.

Athenians, dressed up, like theirs, with fancy words and phrases. I will say to you what I have to say, without artifice, and I shall use the first words which come to mind, for I believe that what I have to say is just, so let none of you expect anything else. Indeed, my friends, it would hardly be right for me, at my age, to come before you like a schoolboy with his concocted phrases. But there is one thing, Athenians, which I do most earnestly beg and entreat of you. Do not be surprised and do not interrupt with shouts if in my defense I speak in the same way that I am accustomed to speak in the market place, at the tables of the money-changers, where many of you have heard me, and elsewhere. The truth is this: I am more than seventy, and this is the first time that I have ever come before a law court; thus your manner of speech here is quite strange to me. If I had really been a stranger, you would have forgiven me for speaking in the language and the manner of my native country. And so now I ask you to grant me what I think I have a right to claim. Never mind the manner of my speech—it may be superior or it may be inferior to the usual manner. Give your whole attention to the question, whether what I say is just or not? That is what is required of a good judge, as speaking the truth is required of a good orator.

I have to defend myself, Athenians, first against the older false accusations of my old accusers, and then against the more recent ones of my present accusers. For many men have been accusing me to you, and for very many years, who have not spoken a word of truth; and I fear them more than I fear Anytus and his associates, formidable as they are. But, my friends, the others are still more formidable, since they got hold of most of you when you were children and have been more persistent in accusing me untruthfully, persauding you that there is a certain Socrates, a wise man, who speculates about the heavens, who investigates things that are beneath the earth, and who can make the worse argument appear the stronger. These men, Athenians, who spread abroad this report are the accusers whom I fear; for their hearers think that persons who pursue such inquiries never believe in the gods. Besides they are many, their attacks have been going on for a long time, and they spoke to you when you were most ready to believe them, since you were all young, and some of you were children. And there was no one to answer them when they attacked me. The most preposterous thing of all is that I do not even know their names: I cannot tell you who they are except when one happens to be a comic poet. But all the rest who have persuaded you, from motives of resentment and prejudice, and sometimes, it may be, from conviction, are hardest to cope with. For I cannot call any one of them forward in court to cross-examine him. I have, as it were, simply to spar with shadows in my defense, and to put questions which there is no one to answer. I ask you, therefore, to believe that, as I say, I have been attacked by two kinds of accusers—first, by Meletus and his associates, and, then, by those older ones of whom I have spoken. And, with your leave, I will defend myself first against my old accusers, since you heard their accusations first, and they were much more compelling than my present accusers are.

Well, I must make my defense, Athenians, and try in the short time allowed me to remove the prejudice which you have been so long a time acquiring. I hope that I may manage to do this, if it be best for you and for me, and that my defense may be successful; but I am quite aware of the nature of my task, and I know that it is a difficult one. Be the outcome, however, as is pleasing to god, I must obey the law and make my defense.

Let us begin from the beginning, then, and ask what is the accusation that has given rise to the prejudice against me, on which Meletus relied when he brought his indictment. What is the prejudice which my enemies have been spreading about me? I must assume that they are formally accusing me, and read their indictment. It would run somewhat in this fashion: "Socrates is guilty of engaging in inquiries into things beneath the earth and in the heavens, of making the weaker argument appear the stronger, and of teaching others these same things." That is what they say. And in the comedy of Aristophanes you yourselves saw a man called Socrates swinging around in a basket and saying that he walked on air, and sputtering a great deal of nonsense about matters of which I understand nothing at all. I do not mean to disparage that kind of knowledge if there is anyone who is wise about these matters. I trust Meletus may never be able to prosecute me for that. But the truth is, Athenians, I have nothing to do with these matters, and almost all of you are yourselves my witnesses of this. I beg all of you who have ever heard me discussing, and they are many, to inform your neighbors and tell them if any of you have ever heard me discussing such matters at all. That will show you that the other common statements about me are as false as this one.

But the fact is that not one of these is true. And if you have heard that I undertake to educate men, and make money by so doing, that is not true either, though I think that it would be a fine thing to be able to educate men, as Gorgias of Leontini, and Prodicus of Ceos, and Hippias of Elis do. For each of them, my friends, can go into any city, and persuade the young men to leave the society of their fellow citizens, with any of whom they might associate for nothing, and to be only too glad to be allowed to pay money for the privilege of associating with themselves. And I believe that there is another wise man from Paros residing in Athens at this moment. I happened to meet Callias, the son of Hipponicus, a man who has spent more money on sophists than everyone else put together. So I said to him (he has two sons), "Callias, if your two sons had been foals or calves, we could have hired a trainer for them who would have trained them to excel in doing what they are naturally capable of. He would have been either a groom or a farmer. But whom do you intend to take to train them, seeing that they are men? Who understands the excellence which a man and citizen is capable of attaining? I suppose that you must have thought of this, because you have sons. Is there such a person or not?" "Certainly there is," he replied. "Who is he," said I, "and where does he come from, and what is his fee?" "Evenus, Socrates," he replied, "from Paros, five minae." Then I thought that Evenus was a fortunate person if he really understood this art and could teach so cleverly. If I had possessed knowledge of that kind, I should have been conceited and disdainful. But, Athenians, the truth is that I do not possess it.

Perhaps some of you may reply: "But, Socrates, what is the trouble with you? What has given rise to these prejudices against you? You must have been doing something out of the ordinary. All these rumors and reports of you would never have arisen if you had not been doing something different from other men. So tell us what it is, that we may not give our verdict arbitrarily." I think that that is a fair question, and I will try to explain to you what it is that has raised these prejudices against me and given me this reputation. Listen, then. Some of you, perhaps, will think that I am joking, but I assure you that I will tell you the whole truth. I have gained this reputation, Athenians, simply by reason of a certain wisdom. But by what kind of wisdom? It is by just that wisdom which is perhaps human wisdom. In that, it may be, I am really wise. But the men of whom I was speaking just now must be wise in a wisdom which is greater than human wisdom, or else I cannot describe it, for certainly I know nothing of it myself, and if any man says that I do, he lies and speaks to arouse prejudice against me. Do not interrupt me with shouts, Athenians, even if you think that I am boasting. What I am going to say is not my own statement. I will tell you who says it, and he is worthy of your respect. I will bring the god of Delphi to be the witness of my wisdom, if it is wisdom at all, and of its nature. You remember Chaerephon. From youth upwards he was my comrade; and also a partisan of your democracy, sharing your recent exile and returning with you. You remember, too, Chaerephon's character—how impulsive he was in carrying through whatever he took in hand. Once he went to Delphi and ventured to put this question to the oracle—I entreat you again, my friends, not to interrupt me with your shouts—he asked if there was anyone who was wiser than I. The priestess answered that there was no one. Chaerephon himself is dead, but his brother here will witness to what I say.

Now see why I tell you this. I am going to explain to you how the prejudice against me has arisen. When I heard of the oracle I began to reflect: What can the god mean by this riddle? I know very well that I am not wise, even in the smallest degree. Then what can he mean by saying that I am the wisest of men? It cannot be that he is speaking falsely, for he is a god and cannot lie. For a long time I was at a loss to understand his meaning. Then, very reluctantly, I turned to investigate it in this manner: I went to a man who was reputed to be wise, thinking that there, if anywhere, I should prove the answer wrong, and meaning to point out to the oracle its mistake, and to say, "You said that I was the wisest of men, but this man is wiser than I am." So I examined the man— I need not tell you his name, he was a politician—but this was the result, Athenians. When I conversed with him I came to see that, though a great many persons, and most of all he himself, thought that he was wise, yet he was not wise. Then I tried to prove to him that he was not wise, though he fancied that he was. By so doing I made him indignant, and many of the bystanders. So when I went away, I thought to myself, "I am wiser than this man: neither of us knows anything that is really worth knowing, but he thinks that he has knowledge when he has not, while I, having no knowledge, do not think that I have. I seem, at any rate, to be a little wiser than he is on this point: I do not think that I know what I do not know." Next I went to another man who was reputed to be still wiser than the last, with exactly the same result. And there again I made him, and many other men, indignant.

Then I went on to one man after another, realizing that I was arousing indignation every day, which caused me much pain and anxiety. Still I thought that I must set the god's command above everything. So I had to go to every man who seemed to possess any knowledge, and investigate the meaning of oracle. Athenians, I must tell you the truth; I swear, this was the result of the investigation which I made at the god's command: I found that the men whose reputation for wisdom stood highest were nearly the most lacking in it, while others who were looked down on as common people were much more intelligent. Now I must describe to you the wanderings which I undertook, like Herculean labors, to prove the oracle irrefutable. After the politicians, I went to the poets, tragic, dithyrambic, and others, thinking that there I should find myself manifestly more ignorant than they. So I took up the poems on which I thought that they had spent most pains, and asked them what they meant, hoping at the same time to learn something from them. I am ashamed to tell you the truth, my friends, but I must say it. Almost any one of the bystanders could have talked about the works of these poets better than the poets themselves. So I soon found that it is not by wisdom that the poets create their works, but by a certain instinctive inspiration, like soothsayers and prophets, who say many fine things, but understand nothing of what they say. The poets seemed to me to be in a similar situation. And at the same time I perceived that, because of their poetry, they thought that they were the wisest of men in other matters too, which they were not. So I went away again, thinking that I had the same advantage over the poets that I had over the politicians.

Finally, I went to the artisans, for I knew very well that I possessed no knowledge at all worth speaking of, and I was sure that I should find that they knew many fine things. And in that I was not mistaken. They knew what I did not know, and so far they were wiser than I. But, Athenians, it seemed to me that the skilled artisans had the same failing as the poets. Each of them believed himself to be extremely wise in matters of the greatest importance because he was skillful in his own art: and this presumption of theirs obscured their real wisdom. So I asked myself, on behalf of the oracle, whether I would choose to remain as I was, without either their wisdom or their ignorance, or to possess both, as they did. And I answered to myself and to the oracle that it was better for me to remain as I was.

From this examination, Athenians, has arisen much fierce and bitter indignation, and as a result a great many prejudices about me. People say that I am "a wise man." For the bystanders always think that I am wise myself in any matter wherein I refute another. But, gentlemen, I believe that the god is really wise, and that by this oracle he meant that human wisdom is worth little or nothing.

I do not think that he meant that Socrates was wise. He only made use of my name, and took me as an example, as though he would say to men, "He among you is the wisest who, like Socrates, knows that his wisdom is really worth nothing at all." Therefore I still go about testing and examining every man whom I think wise, whether he be a citizen or a stranger, as the god has commanded me. Whenever I find that he is not wise, I point out to him, on the god's behalf, that he is not wise. I am so busy in this pursuit that I have never had leisure to take any part worth mentioning in public matters or to look after my private affairs. I am in great poverty as the result of my service to the god.

Besides this, the young men who follow me about, who are the sons of wealthy persons and have the most leisure, take pleasure in hearing men cross-examined. They often imitate me among themselves; then they try their hands at cross-examining other people. And, I imagine, they find plenty of men who think that they know a great deal when in fact they know little or nothing. Then the persons who are cross-examined get angry with me instead of with themselves, and say that Socrates is an abomination and corrupts the young. When they are asked, "Why, what does he do? What does he teach?" they do not know what to say. Not to seem at a loss, they repeat the stock charges against all philosophers, and allege that he investigates things in the air and under the earth, and that he teaches people to disbelieve in the gods, and to make the worse argument appear the stronger. For, I suppose, they would not like to confess the truth, which is that they are shown up as ignorant pretenders to knowledge that they do not possess. So they have been filling your ears with their bitter prejudices for a long time, for they are ambitious, energetic, and numerous; and they speak vigorously and persuasively against me. Relying on this Meletus, Anytus, and Lycon have attacked me. Meletus is indignant with me on behalf of the poets. Anytus on behalf of the artisans and politicians, and Lycon on behalf of the orators. And so, as I said at the beginning, I shall be surprised if I am able, in the short time allowed me for my defense, to remove from your minds this prejudice which has grown so strong. What I have told you, Athenians, is the truth: I neither conceal nor do I suppress anything, trivial or important. Yet I know that it is just this outspokenness which rouses indignation. But that is only a proof that my words are true, and that the prejudice against me, and the causes of it, are what I have said. And whether you investigate them now or hereafter, you will find that they are so.

What I have said must suffice as my defense against the charges of my first accusers. I will try next to defend myself against Meletus, that "good patriot," as he calls himself, and my later accusers. Let us assume that they are a new set of accusers, and read their indictment, as we did in the case of the others. It runs thus: Socrates is guilty of corrupting the youth, and of believing not in the gods whom the state believes in, but in other new divinities. Such is the accusation. Let us examine each point in it separately. Meletus says that I am guilty of corrupting the youth. But I say, Athenians, that he is guilty of playing a solemn joke by casually bringing men to trial, and pretending to have a solemn interest in matters to which he has never given a moment's thought. Now I will try to prove to you that this is so.

Come here, Meletus. Is it not a fact that you think it very important that the young should be as good as possible?

MELETUS: It is.

SOCRATES: Come, then, tell the judges who improve them. You care so much, you must know. You are accusing me, and bringing me to trial, because, as you say, you have discovered that I am the corrupter of the youth. Come now, reveal to the gentlemen who improves them. You see, Meletus, you have nothing to say; you are silent. But don't you think that this is shameful? Is not your silence a conclusive proof of what I say—that you have never cared? Come, tell us, my good man, who makes the young better?

MEL.: The laws.

SOCR.: That, my friend, is not my question. What man improves the young, who begins by knowing the laws?

MEL.: The judges here, Socrates.

SOCR.: What do you mean, Meletus? Can they educate the young and improve them?

MEL.: Certainly.

SOCR.: All of them? Or only some of them?

MEL.: All of them.

SOCR.: By Hera, that is good news! Such a large supply of benefactors! And do the members of the audience here improve them, or not?

MEL.: They do.

SOCR.: And do the councilors?

MEL.: Yes.

SOCR.: Well, then, Meletus, do the members of the assembly corrupt the young or do they again all improve them?

MEL.: They, too, improve them.

SOCR.: Then all the Athenians, apparently, make the young into good men except me, and I alone corrupt them. Is that your meaning?

MEL.: Certainly, that is my meaning.

SOCR.: You have discovered me to be most unfortunate. Now tell me: do you think that the same holds good in the case of horses? Does one man do them harm and everyone else improve them? On the contrary, is it not one man only, or a very few—namely, those who are skilled with horses—who can improve them, while the majority of men harm them if they use them and have anything to do with them? Is it not so, Meletus, both with horses and with every other animal? Of course it is, whether you and Anytus say yes or no. The young would certainly be very fortunate if only one man corrupted them, and everyone else did them good. The truth is, Meletus, you prove conclusively that you have never thought about the young in your life. You exhibit your carelessness in not caring for the very matters about which you are prosecuting me.

Now be so good as to tell us, Meletus, is it better to live among good citizens or bad ones? Answer, my friend. I am not asking you at all a difficult question. Do not the bad harm their associates and the good do them good?

MEL.: Yes.

SOCR.: Is there anyone who would rather be injured than benefited by his companions? Answer, my good man; you are obliged by the law to answer. Does anyone like to be injured?

MEL.: Certainly not.

SOCR.: Well, then, are you prosecuting me for corrupting the young and making them worse, voluntarily or involuntarily?

MEL.: For doing it voluntarily.

SOCR.: What, Meletus? Do you mean to say that you, who are so much younger than I, are yet so much wiser that I that you know that bad citizens always do evil, and that good citizens do good, to those with whom they come in contact, while I am so extraordinarily ignorant as not to know that, if I make any of my companions evil, he will probably injure me in some way? And you allege that I do this voluntarily? You will not make me believe that, nor anyone else either, I should think. Either I do not corrupt the young at all or, if I do, I do so involuntarily, so that you are lying in either case. And if I corrupt them involuntarily, the law does not call upon you to prosecute me for an error which is involuntary, but to take me aside privately and reprove and educate me. For, of course, I shall cease from doing wrong involuntarily, as soon as I know that I have been doing wrong. But you avoided associating with me and educating me; instead you bring me up before the court, where the law sends persons, not for education, but for punishment.

The truth is, Athenians, as I said, it is quite clear that Meletus has never cared at all about these matters. However, now tell us, Meletus, how do you say that I corrupt the young? Clearly, according to your indictment, by teaching them not to believe in the gods the state believes in, but other new divinities instead. You mean that I corrupt the young by that teaching, do you not?

MEL.: Yes, most certainly I mean that.

SOCR.: Then in the name of these gods of whom we are speaking, explain yourself a little more clearly to me and to these gentlemen here. I cannot understand what you mean. Do you mean that I teach the young to believe in some gods, but not in the gods of the state? Do you accuse me of teaching them to believe in strange gods? If that is your meaning, I myself believe in some gods, and my crime is not that of complete atheism. Or do you mean that I teach other people not to believe in them either?

MEL.: I mean that you do not believe in the gods in any way whatever.

SOCR.: You amaze me, Meletus! Why do you say that? Do you mean that I believe neither the sun nor the moon to be gods, like other men?

MEL.: I swear he does not, judges. He says that the sun is a stone, and the moon earth.

SOCR.: My dear Meletus, do you think that you are prosecuting Anaxagoras? You must have a very poor opinion of these men, and think them illiterate, if you imagine that they do not know that the works of Anaxagoras of Clazomenae are full of these doctrines. And so young men learn these things from me, when they can often buy them in the theater for a drachma at most, and laugh at Socrates were he to pretend that these doctrines, which are very peculiar doctrines, too, were his own. But please tell me, do you really think that I do not believe in the gods at all?

MEL.: Most certainly I do. You are a complete atheist.

SOCR.: No one believes that, Meletus, not even you yourself. It seems to me, Athenians, that Meletus is very insolent and reckless, and that he is prosecuting me simply out of insolence, recklessness, and youthful bravado. For he seems to be testing me, by asking me a riddle that has no answer. "Will this wise Socrates," he says to himself, "see that I am joking and contradicting myself? Or shall I deceive him and everyone else who hears me?" Meletus seems to me to contradict himself in his indictment: it is as if he were to say, "Socrates is guilty of not believing in the gods, but believes in the gods." This is joking.

Now, my friends, let us see why I think that this is his meaning. You must answer me, Meletus, and you, Athenians, must remember the request which I made to you at the start, and not interrupt me with shouts if I talk in my usual manner.

Is there any man, Meletus, who believes in the existence of things pertaining to men and not in the existence of men? Make him answer the question, gentlemen, without these interruptions. Is there any man who believes in the existence of horsemanship and not in the existence of horses? Or in flute playing and not in flute players? There is not, my friend. If you will not answer, I will tell both you and the judges. But you must answer my next question. Is there any man who believes in the existence of divine things and not in the existence of divinities?

MEL.: There is not.

SOCR.: I am very glad that these gentlemen have managed to extract an answer from you. Well then, you say that I believe in divine things, whether they be old or new, and that I teach others to believe in them. At any rate, according to your statement, I believe in divine things. That you have sworn in your indictment. But if I believe in divine things, I suppose it follows necessarily that I believe in divinities. Is it not so? It is. I assume that you grant that, as you do not answer. But do we not believe that divinities are either gods themselves or the children of the gods? Do you admit that?

MEL.: I do.

SOCR.: Then you admit that I believe in divinities Now, if these divinities are gods, then, as I say, you are joking and asking a riddle, and asserting that I do not believe in the gods, and at the same time that I do, since I believe in divinities. But if these divinities are the illegitimate children of the gods, either by the nymphs or by other mothers, as they are said to be, then, I ask, what man could believe in the existence of the children of the gods, and not in the existence of the gods? That would be as absurd as believing in the existence of the offspring of horses and asses, and not in the existence of horses and asses. You must have indicted me in this manner, Meletus, either to test me or because you could not find any act of injustice that you could accuse me of with truth. But you will never contrive to persuade any man with any sense at all that a belief in divine things and things of the gods does not necessarily involve a belief in divinities, and in the gods.

But in truth, Athenians, I do not think that I need say very much to prove that I have not committed the act of injustice for which Meletus is prosecuting me. What I have said is enough to prove that. But be assured it is certainly true, as I have already told you, that I have aroused much indignation. That is what will cause my condemnation if I am condemned; not Meletus nor Anytus either, but that prejudice and resentment of the multitude which have been the destruction of many good men before me, and I think will be so again. There is no prospect that I shall be the last victim.

Perhaps someone will say: "Are you not ashamed, Socrates, of leading a life which is very likely now to cause your death?" I should answer him with justice, and say: "My friend, if you think that a man of any worth at all ought to reckon the chances of life and death when he acts, or that he ought to think of anything but whether he is acting justly or unjustly, and as a good or a bad man would act, you are mistaken. According to you, the demigods who died at Troy would be foolish, and among them Achilles, who thought nothing of danger when the alternative was disgrace. For when his mother—and she was a goddess—addressed him, when he was resolved to slay Hector, in this fashion, 'My son, if you avenge the death of your comrade Patroclus and slay Hector, you will die yourself, for fate awaits you next after Hector.' When he heard this, he scorned danger and death; he feared much more to live a coward and not to avenge his friend. 'Let me punish the evildoer and afterwards die,' he said, 'that I may not remain here by the beaked ships jeered at, encumbering the earth.'" Do you suppose that he thought of danger or of death? For this, Athenians, I believe to be the truth. Whatever a man's station is, whether he has chosen it of his own will, or whether he has been placed at it by his commander, there it is his duty to remain and face the danger without thinking of death or of any other thing except disgrace.

When the generals whom you chose to command me, Athenians, assigned me my station durng the battles of Potideae, Amphipolis, and Delium, I remained where they stationed me and ran the risk of death, like other men. It would be very strange conduct on my part if I were to desert my station now from fear of death or of any other thing when the god has commanded me—as I am persuaded that he has done—to spend my life in searching for wisdom, and in examining myself and others. That would indeed be a very strange thing. Then certainly I might with justice be brought to trial for not believing in the gods, for I should be disobeying the oracle, and fearing death and thinking myself wise when I was not wise. For to fear death, my friends, is only to think ourselves wise without really being wise, for it is to think that we know what we do not know. For no one knows whether death may not be the greatest good that can happen to man. But men fear it as if they knew quite well that it was the greatest of evils. And what is this but that shameful ignorance of thinking that we know what we do not know? In this matter, too, my friends, perhaps I am different from the multitude. And if I were to claim to be at all wiser than others, it would be because, not knowing very much about the other world, I do not think I know. But I do know very well that it is evil and disgraceful to do an unjust act, and to disobey my superior, whether man or god. I will never do what I know to be evil, and shrink in fear from what I do not know to be good or evil. Even if you acquit me now, and do not listen to Anytus' argument that, if I am to be acquitted, I ought never to have been brought to trial at all, and that, as it is, you are bound to put me to death because, as he said, if I escape, all your sons will be utterly corrupted by practicing what Socrates teaches. If you were therefore to say to me, "Socrates, this time we will not listen to Anytus. We will let you go, but on the condition that you give up this investigation of yours, and philosophy. If you are found following these pursuits again, you shall die." I say, if you offered to let me go on these terms, I should reply: "Athenians, I hold you in the highest regard and affection, but I will be persuaded by the god rather than you. As long as I have breath and strength I will not give up philosophy and exhorting you and declaring the truth to every one of you whom I meet, saying, as I am accustomed, 'My good friend, you are a citizen of Athens, a city which is very great and very famous for its wisdom and power—are you not ashamed of caring so much for the making of money and for fame and prestige, when you neither think nor care about wisdom and truth and the improvement of your soul?'" If he disputes my words and says that he does care about these things, I shall not at once release him and go away: I shall question him and cross-examine him and test him. If I think that he has not attained excellence, though he says that he has, I shall reproach him for undervaluing the most valuable things, and overvaluing those that are less valuable. This I shall do to everyone whom I meet, young or old, citizen or stranger, but especially to citizens, since they are more closely related to me. This, you must recognize, the god has commanded me to do. And I think that no greater good has ever befallen you in the state than my service to the god. For I spend my whole life in going about and persuading you all to give your first and greatest care to the improvement of your souls, and not till you have done that to think of your bodies or your wealth. And I tell you that wealth does not bring excellence, but that wealth, and every other good thing which men have, whether in public or in private, comes from excellence. If then I corrupt the youth by this teaching, these things must be harmful. But if any man says that I teach anything else, there is nothing in what he says. And therefore, Athenians, I say, whether you are persuaded by Anytus or not, whether you acquit me or not, I shall not change my way of life; no, not if I have to die for it many times.

Do not interrupt me, Athenians, with your shouts. Remember the request which I made to you, and do not interrupt my words. I think that it will profit you to hear them. I am going to say something more to you, at which you may be inclined to protest, but do not do that. Be sure that if you put me to death, I who am what I have told you that I am, you will do yourselves more harm than me. Meletus and Anytus can do me no harm: that is impossible, for I am sure it is not allowed that a good man be injured by a worse. He may indeed kill me, or drive me into exile, or deprive me of my civil rights. Perhaps Meletus and others think those things great evils. But I do not think so. I think it is a much greater evil to do what he is doing now, and to try to put a man to death unjustly. And now, Athenians, I am not arguing in my own defense at all, as you might expect me to do, but rather in yours in order you may not make a mistake about the gift of the god to you by condemning me. For if you put me to death, you will not easily find another who, if I may use a ludicrous comparison, clings to the state as a sort of gadfly to a horse that is large and well-bred but rather sluggish because of its size, so that it needs to be aroused. It seems to me that the god has attached me like that to the state, for I am constantly alighting upon you at every point to arouse, persuade, and reproach each of you all day long. You will not easily find anyone else, my friends, to fill my place; and if you are persuaded by me, you will spare my life. You are indignant, as drowsy persons are when they are awakened, and, of course, if you are persuaded by Anytus, you could easily kill me with a single blow, and then sleep on undisturbed for the rest of your lives, unless the god in his care for you sends another to arouse you. And you may easily see that it is the god who has given me to your city; for it is not human, the way in which I have neglected all my own interests and allowed my private affairs to be neglected for so many years, while occupying myself unceasingly in your interests, going to each of you privately, like a father or an elder brother, trying to persuade him to care for human excellence. There would have been a reason for it, if I had gained any advantage by this, or if I had been paid for my exhortations; but you see yourselves that my accusers, though they accuse me of everything else without shame, have not had the shamelessness to say that I ever either exacted or demanded payment. To that they have no witness. And I think that I have sufficient witness to the truth of what I say—my poverty.

Perhaps it may seem strange to you that, though I go about giving this advice privately and meddling in others' affairs, yet I do not venture to come forward in the assembly and advise the state. You have often heard me speak of my reason for this, and in many places: it is that I have a certain divine guide, which is what Meletus has caricatured in his indictment. I have had it from childhood. It is a kind of voice which, whenever I hear it, always turns me back from something which I was going to do, but never urges me to act. It is this which forbids me to take part in politics. And I think it does well to forbid me. For, Athenians, it is quite certain that, if I had attempted to take part in politics, I should have perished at once and long ago without doing any good either to you or to myself. And do not be indignant with me for telling the truth. There is no man who will preserve his life for long, either in Athens or elsewhere, if he firmly opposes the multitude, and tries to prevent the commission of much injustice and illegality in the state. He who would really fight for justice must do so as a private citizen, not as a political figure, if he is to preserve his life, even for a short time.

I will prove to you that this is so by very strong evidence, not by mere words, but by what you value more—actions. Listen, then, to what has happened to me, that you may know that there is no man who could make me consent to commit an unjust act from the fear of death, but that I would perish at once rather than give way. What I am going to tell you may be commonplace in the law court; nevertheless, it is true. The only office that I ever held in the state, Athenians, was that of councilor. When you wished to try the ten admirals who did not rescue their men after the battle of Arginusae as a group, which was illegal, as you all came to think afterwards, the executive committee was composed of members of the tribe Antiochis, to which I belong. On that occasion I alone of the committee members opposed your illegal action and gave my vote against you. The orators were ready to impeach me and arrest me; and you were clamoring and urging them on with your shouts. But I thought that I ought to face the danger, with law and justice on my side, rather than join with you in your unjust proposal, from fear of imprisonment or death. That was when the state was democratic. When the oligarchy came in, The Thirty sent for me, with four others, to the council-chamber, and ordered us to bring Leon the Salaminian from Salamis, that they might put him to death. They were in the habit of frequently giving similar orders to many others, wishing to implicate as many as possible in their crimes. But then I again proved, not by mere words, but by my actions, that, if I may speak bluntly, I do not care a straw for death; but that I do care very much indeed about not doing anything unjust or impious. That government with all its power did not terrify me into doing anything unjust. When we left the council-chamber, the other four went over to Salamis and brought Leon across to Athens; I went home. And if the rule of The Thirty had not been overthrown soon afterwards, I should very likely have been put to death for what I did then. Many of you will be my witnesses in this matter.

Now do you think that I could have remained alive all these years if I had taken part in public affairs, and had always maintained the cause of justice like a good man, and had held it a paramount duty, as it is, to do so? Certainly not, Athenians, nor could any other man. But throughout my whole life, both in private and in public, whenever I have had to take part in public affairs, you will find I have always been the same and have never yielded unjustly to anyone; no, not to those whom my enemies falsely assert to have been my pupils. But I was never anyone's teacher. I have never withheld myself from anyone, young or old, who was anxious to hear me converse while I was making my investigation; neither do I converse for payment, and refuse to converse without payment. I am ready to ask questions of rich and poor alike, and if any man wishes to answer me, and then listen to what I have to say, he may. And I cannot justly be charged with causing these men to turn out good or bad, for I never either taught or professed to teach any of them any knowledge whatever. And if any man asserts that he ever learned or heard anything from me in private which everyone else did not hear as well as he, be sure that he does not speak the truth.

Why is it, then, that people delight in spending so much time in my company? You have heard why, Athenians. I told you the whole truth when I said that they delight in hearing me examine persons who think that they are wise when they are not wise. It is certainly very amusing to listen to. And, as I have said, the god had commanded me to examine men, in oracles and in dreams and in every way in which the divine will was ever declared to man. This is the truth, Athenians, and if it were not the truth, it would be easily refuted. For if it were really the case that I have already corrupted some of the young men, and am now corrupting others, surely some of them, finding as they grew older that I had given them bad advice in their youth, would have come forward today to accuse me and take their revenge. Or if they were unwilling to do so themselves, surely their relatives, their fathers or brothers, or others, would, if I had done them any harm, have remembered it and taken their revenge. Certainly I see many of them in court. Here is Crito, of my own district and of my own age, the father of Critobulus; here is Lysanias of Sphettus, the father of Aeschines; here is also Antiphon of Cephisus, the father of Epigenes. Then here are others whose brothers have spent their time in my company—Nicostratus, the son of Theozotides and brother of Theodotus—and Theodotus is dead, so he at least cannot entreat his brother to be silent; here is Paralus, the son of Demodocus and the brother of Theages; here is Adeimantus, the son of Ariston, whose brother is Plato here; and Aeantodorus, whose brother is Aristodorus. And I can name many others to you, some of whom Meletus ought to have called as witnesses in the course of his own speech; but if he forgot to call them then, let him call them now—I will yield the floor to him—and tell us if he has any such evidence. No, on the contrary, my friends, you will find all these men ready to support me, the corrupter who has injured their relatives, as Meletus and Anytus call me. Those of them who have been already corrupted might perhaps have some reason for supporting me, but what reason can their relatives have who are grown up, and who are uncorrupted, except the reason of truth and justice—that they know very well that Meletus is lying, and that I am speaking the truth?

Well, my friends, this, and perhaps more like this, is pretty much all I have to offer in my defense. There may be some one among you who will be indignant when he remembers how, even in a less important trial than this, he begged and entreated the judges, with many tears, to acquit him, and brought forward his children and many of his friends and relatives in court in order to appeal to your feelings; and then finds that I shall do none of these things, though I am in what he would think the supreme danger. Perhaps he will harden himself against me when he notices this; it may make him angry, and he may cast his vote in anger. If it is so with any of you—I do not suppose that it is, but in case it should be so—I think that I should answer him reasonably if I said: "My friend, I have relatives, too, for, in the words of Homer, I am 'not born of oak or a rock' but of flesh and blood." And so, Athenians, I have relatives, and I have three sons, one of them nearly grown up, and the other two still children. Yet I will not bring any of them forward before you and implore you to acquit me. And why will I do none of these things? It is not from arrogance, Athenians, nor because I lack respect for you—whether or not I can face death bravely is another question—but for my own good name, and for your good name, and for the good name of the whole state. I do not think it right, at my age and with my reputation, to do anything of that kind. Rightly or wrongly, men have made up their minds that in some way Socrates is different from the multitude of men. And it will be shameful if those of you who are thought to excel in wisdom, or in bravery, or in any other excellence, are going to act in this fashion. I have often seen men of reputation behaving in an extraordinary way at their trial, as if they thought it a terrible fate to be killed, and as though they expected to live forever if you did not put them to death. Such men seem to me to bring shame upon the state, for any stranger would suppose that the best and most eminent Athenians, who are selected by their fellow citizens to hold office, and for other honors, are no better than women. Those of you, Athenians, who have any reputation at all ought not to do these things, and you ought not to allow us to do them. You should show that you will be much more ready to condemn men who make the state ridiculous by these pathetic performances than men who remain quiet.

But apart from the question of reputation, my friends, I do not think that it is right to entreat the judge to acquit us, or to escape condemnation in that way. It is our duty to each and persuade him. He does not sit to give away justice as a favor, but to pronounce judgment; and he has sworn, not to favor any man whom he would like to favor, but to judge according to law. And, therefore, we ought not to encourage you in the habit of breaking your oaths; and you ought not to allow yourselves to fall into this habit, for then neither you nor we would be acting piously. Therefore, Athenians, do not require me to do these things, for I believe them to be neither good nor just nor pious; especially, do not ask me to do them today when Meletus is prosecuting me for impiety. For were I to be successful and persuade you by my entreaties to break your oaths, I should be clearly teaching you to believe that there are no gods, and I should be simply accusing myself by my defense of not believing in them. But, Athenians, that is very far from the truth. I do believe in the gods as no one of my accusers believes in them; and to you and to the god I commit my cause to be decided as is best for you and for me.

(He is found guilty by 281 votes to 220.)

I am not indignant at the verdict which you have given, Athenians, for many reasons. I expected that you would find me guilty; and I am not so much surprised at that as at the numbers of the votes. I certainly never thought that the majority against me would have been so narrow. But now it seems that if only thirty votes had changed sides, I should have escaped. So I think that I have escaped Meletus, as it is; and not only have I escaped him, for it is perfectly clear that if Anytus and Lycon had not come forward to accuse me, too, he would not have obtained the fifth part of the votes, and would have had to pay a fine of a thousand drachmae.

So he proposes death as the penalty. Be it so. And what alternative penalty shall I propose to you, Athenians? What I deserve, of course, must I not? What then do I deserve to pay or to suffer for having determined not to spend my life in ease? I neglected the things which most men value, such as wealth, and family interests, and military commands, and public oratory, and all the civic appointments, and social clubs, and political factions, that there are in Athens; for I thought that I was really too honest a man to preserve my life if I engaged in these affairs. So I did not go where I should have done no good either to you or to myself. I went, instead, to each one of you privately to do him, as I say, the greatest of benefits, and tried to persuade him not to think of his affairs until he had thought of himself and tried to make himself as good and wise as possible, nor to think of the affairs of Athens until he had thought of Athens herself; and to care for other things in the same manner. Then what do I deserve for such a life? Something good, Athenians, if I am really to propose what I deserve; and something good which it would be suitable for me to receive. Then what is a suitable reward to be given to a poor benefactor who requires leisure to exhort you? There is no reward, Athenians, so suitable for him as receiving free meals in the prytaneum. It is a much more suitable reward for him than for any of you who has won a victory at the Olympic games with his horse or his chariots. Such a man only makes you seem happy, but I make you really happy; he is not in want, and I am. So if I am to propose the penalty which I really deserve, I propose this—free meals in the prytaneum.

Perhaps you think me stubborn and arrogant in what I am saying now, as in what I said about the entreaties and tears. It is not so, Athenians. It is rather that I am convinced that I never wronged any man voluntarily, though I cannot persuade you of that, since we have conversed together only a little time. If there were a law at Athens, as there is elsewhere, not to finish a trial of life and death in a single day, I think that I could have persuaded you; but now it is not easy in so short a time to clear myself of great prejudices. But when I am persuaded that I have never wronged any man, I shall certainly not wrong myself, or admit that I deserve to suffer any evil, or propose any evil for myself as a penalty. Why should I? Lest I should suffer the penalty which Meletus proposes when I say that I do not know whether it is a good or an evil? Shall I choose instead of it something which I know to be an evil, and propose that as a penalty? Shall I propose imprisonment? And why should I pass the rest of my days in prison, the slave of successive officials? Or shall I propose a fine, with imprisonment until it is paid? I have told you why I will not do that. I should have to remain in prison, for I have no money to pay a fine with. Shall I then propose exile? Perhaps you would agree to that. Life would indeed be very dear to me if I were unreasonable enough to expect that strangers would cheerfully tolerate my discussions and arguments when you who are my fellow citizens cannot endure them, and have found them so irksome and odious to you that you are seeking now to be relieved of them. No, indeed, Athenians, that is not likely. A fine life I should lead for an old man if I were to withdraw from Athens and pass the rest of my days in wandering from city to city, and continually being expelled. For I know very well that the young men will listen to me wherever I go, as they do here. If I drive them away, they will persuade their elders to expel me; if I do not drive them away, their fathers and other relatives will expel me for their sakes.

Perhaps someone will say, "Why cannot you withdraw from Athens, Socrates, and hold your peace?" It is the most difficult thing in the world to make you understand why I cannot do that. If I say that I cannot hold my peace because that would be to disobey the god, you will think that I am not in earnest and will not believe me. And if I tell you that no greater good can happen to a man than to discuss human excellence every day and the other matters about which you have heard me arguing and examining myself and others, and that an unexamined life is not worth living, then you will believe me still less. But that is so, my friends, though it is not easy to persuade you. And, what is more, I am not accustomed to think that I deserve anything evil. If I had been rich, I would have proposed as large a fine as I could pay: that would have done me no harm. But I am not rich enough to pay a fine unless you are willing to fix it at a sum within my means. Perhaps I could pay you a mina, so I propose that. Plato here, Athenians, and Crito, and Critobulus, and Apollodorus bid me propose thirty minae, and they guarantee its payment. So I propose thirty minae. Their security will be sufficient to you for the money.

(He is condemned to death.)

You have not gained very much time, Athenians, and at the price of the slurs of those who wish to revile the state. And they will say that you put Socrates, a wise man, to death. For they will certainly call me wise, whether I am wise or not, when they want to reproach you. If you had waited for a little while, your wishes would have been fulfilled in the course of nature; for you see that I am an old man, far advanced in years, and near to death. I am saying this not to all of you, only to those who have voted for my death. And to them I have something else to say. Perhaps, my friends, you think that I have been convicted because I was wanting in the arguments by which I could have persuaded you to acquit me, if I had thought it right to do or to say anything to escape punishment. It is not so. I have been convicted because I was wanting, not in arguments, but in impudence and shamelessness—because I would not plead before you as you would have liked to hear me plead, or appeal to you with weeping and wailing, or say and do many other things which I maintain are unworthy of me, but which you have been accustomed to from other men. But when I was defending myself, I thought that I ought not to do anything unworthy of a free man because of the danger which I ran, and I have not changed my mind now. I would very much rather defend myself as I did, and die, than as you would have had me do, and live. Both in a lawsuit and in war, there are some things which neither I nor any other man may do in order to escape from death. In battle, a man often sees that he may at least escape from death by throwing down his arms and falling on his knees before the pursuer to beg for his life. And there are many other ways of avoiding death in every danger if a man is willing to say and to do anything. But, my friends, I think that it is a much harder thing to escape from wickedness than from death, for wickedness is swifter than death. And now I, who am old and slow, have been overtaken by the slower pursuer: and my accusers, who are clever and swift, have been overtaken by the swifter pursuer—wickedness. And now I shall go away, sentenced by you to death; they will go away, sentenced by truth to wickedness and injustice. And I abide by this award as well as they. Perhaps it was right for these things to be so. I think that they are fairly balanced.

And now I wish to prophesy to you, Athenians, who have condemned me. For I am going to die, and that is the time when men have most prophetic power. And I prophesy to you who have sentenced me to death that a far more severe punishment than you have inflicted on me will surely overtake you as soon as I am dead. You have done this thing, thinking that you will be relieved from having to give an account of your lives. But I say that the result will be very different. There will be more men who will call you to account, whom I have held back, though you did not recognize it. And they will be harsher toward you than I have been, for they will be younger, and you will be more indignant with them. For if you think that you will restrain men from reproaching you for not living as you should, by putting them to death, you are very much mistaken. That way of escape is neither possible nor honorable. It is much more honorable and much easier not to suppress others, but to make yourselves as good as you can. This is my parting prophesy to you who have condemned me.

With you who have acquitted me I should like to discuss this thing that has happened, while the authorities are busy, and before I go to the place where I have to die. So, remain with me until I go: there is no reason why we should not talk with each other while it is possible. I wish to explain to you, as my friends, the meaning of what has happened to me. An amazing thing has happened to me, judges—for I am right in calling you judges. The prophetic guide has been constantly with me all through my life till now, opposing me even in trivial matters if I were not going to act rightly. And now you yourselves see what has happened to me—a thing which might be thought, and which is sometimes actually reckoned, the supreme evil. But the divine guide did not oppose me when I was leaving my house in the morning, nor when I was coming up here to the court, nor at any point in my speech when I was going to say anything; though at other times it has often stopped me in the very act of speaking. But now, in this matter, it has never once opposed me, either in my words or my actions. I will tell you what I believe to be the reason. This thing that has come upon me must be a good; and those of us who think that death is an evil must needs be mistaken. I have a clear proof that that is so; for my accustomed guide would certainly have opposed me if I had not been going to meet with something good.

And if we reflect in another way, we shall see that we may well hope that death is a good. For the state of death is one of two things: either the dead man wholly ceases to be and loses all consciousness or, as we are told, it is a change and a migration of the soul to another place. And if death is the absence of all consciousness, and like the sleep of one whose slumbers are unbroken by any dreams, it will be a wonderful gain. For if a man had to select that night in which he slept so soundly that he did not even dream, and had to compare with it all the other nights and days of his life, and then had to say how many days and nights in his life he had spent better and more pleasantly than this night, I think that a private person, nay, even the Great King of Persia himself, would find them easy to count, compared with the others. If that is the nature of death, I for one count it a gain. For then it appears that all time is nothing more than a single night. But if death is a journey to another place, and what we are told is true—that all who have died are there— what good could be greater than this, my judges? Would a journey not be worth taking, at the end of which, in the other world, we should be delivered from the pretended judges here and should find the true judges who are said to sit in judgment below, such as Minos and Rhadamanthus and Aeacus and Triptolemus, and the other demigods who were just in their own lives? Or what would you not give to converse with Orpheus and Musaeus and Hesiod and Homer? I am willing to die many times if this be true. And for my own part I should find it wonderful to meet there Palamedes, and Ajax the son of Telamon, and the other men of old who have died through an unjust judgment, and to compare my experiences with theirs. That I think would be no small pleasure. And, above all, I could spend my time in examining those who are there, as I examine men here, and in finding out which of them is wise, and which of them thinks himself wise when he is not wise. What would we not give, my judges, to be able to examine the leader of the great expedition against Troy, or Odysseus, or Sisyphus, or countless other men and women whom we could name? It would be an inexpressible happiness to converse with them and to live with them and to examine them. Assuredly there they do not put men to death for doing that. For besides the other ways in which they are happier than we are, they are immortal, at least if what we are told is true.

And you too, judges, must face death hopefully, and believe this one truth, that no evil can happen to a good man, either in life or after death. His affairs are not neglected by the gods; and what has happened to me today has not happened by chance. I am persuaded that it was better for me to die now, and to be released from trouble; and that was the reason why the guide never turned me back. And so I am not at all angry with my accusers or with those who have condemned me to die. Yet it was not with this in mind that they have accused me and condemned me, but meaning to do me an injury. So far I may blame them.

Yet I have one request to make of them. When my sons grow up, punish them, my friends, and harass them in the same way that I have harassed you, if they seem to you to care for riches or for any other thing more than excellence; and if they think that they are something when they are really nothing, reproach them, as I have reproached you, for not caring for what they should, and for thinking that they are something when really they are nothing. And if you will do this, I myself and my sons will have received justice from you.

But now the time has come, and we must go away—I to die, and you to live. Which is better is known to the god alone.

THE VIRTUE OF SOCRATIC IGNORANCE

Alan R. Drengson

We think of the world, and our place in it, in terms of what we know, and in terms of what we think we know. Our libraries are filled with the fruits of our "knowledge explosion," but contain scant mention of our ignorance. Our preoccupation with knowledge in both the abstract and the concrete often prevents us from realizing ignorance close at hand, and this failure prevents us from being aware of the open and unsettled character of much of human life. It is difficult to characterize ignorance because it seems a negative thing, and yet our ignorance, as much as our knowledge, defines or limits our world for us. Our tendency to lack awareness of ignorance has been observed before. Socrates said that it was his awareness of ignorance, his own and others', that made him the wisest person in ancient Greece. This was an extraordinary thing to say, considering that we normally think that wisdom is related to, and grows out of, great knowledge. But consider, how much knowledge does one need in order to be wise? Taken in one way the quest for knowledge is a pursuit with no end in sight.

In a certain sense, then, wisdom does not result from just *any* knowledge. Nor can it depend on complete knowledge, for our ignorance is vast, and will always be larger than all that we can know at any given time. If we assume that the known and the unknown—which is defined by the questions we can now ask— is all there is, then we will fail to appreciate the extent of our ignorance. However, it is from the vastness of our ignorance that both our sense of wonder and sense of the sacred grow. The dialectical interplay of ignorance and knowledge promote the process of dialogue, whereas a focus on knowledge alone would soon end it. Such a focus would prevent the development of the understanding necessary for life and for virtuous action. It was such an understanding that was at the heart of Socrates' claim to wisdom.

Although we might not pay much attention to our ignorance in this Socratic mode, we do in a way recognize the importance of it. We attest to this by spending vast amounts to combat what we take to be ignorance. As sin is to the preacher, so ignorance is to the teacher. Ignorance is to be combatted by knowledge. Here is the text; our students are ignorant of all it contains; thus we must teach them. We must overcome their ignorance. But, is all lack of knowledge worthy of attention? Of course, we would say it is not. One cannot learn everything. Even human languages are beyond the mastery of any one person. Hence, ignorance as a lack of knowledge *per se* cannot be banished.

Not all ignorance is a defect or a sin of omission, then. Moreover, in some cases it is wise *not* to pursue and test certain kinds of knowledge, e.g., how to destroy the earth's ecosystems. Not all knowledge is good. We think ignorance is something to be combatted in some cases, but not in all. So ignorance is not quite like evil and sin. The former is often viewed as a wholly negative thing, whereas evil and sin are regarded as something negative which positively exists.

From *American Philosophical Quarterly,* 18, no. 3 (July 1981), 237-242 (revised by A. R. D.).

As can be seen from what we have said so far, ignorance is something we are inclined to think is wholly negative, a lack of something, namely knowledge. In fact, many dictionaries define it in just such a way. In this sense it is a lack which cannot be made up, since our knowledge can never be complete. If we must overcome this lack of knowledge in order to be wise, we can never be wise; and, unless we are aware of our ignorance, our knowledge might seem complete; then we will be blinded by what we know. This seems a muddle.

As a result of the foregoing considerations we are forced to conclude that wisdom is not the result of gaining just any knowledge whatsoever. It must be related to something that we need to know. The central question is, what do we need to know in order to live wisely? The apparent answer is that the knowledge we must seek is a practical knowledge of what our particular excellence is *as* humans, and also of what we are as individuals. But before this investigation can begin in earnest, we must first come to realize our own lack of practical knowledge, our own ignorance.

Socrates might have reasoned in some such a way, and he had the simple faith that such practical knowledge and wisdom can be attained. It is possible for each of us to know how to act rightly, to know how to care for the soul, how to act virtuously, and how to perfect or realize the excellence that is distinctively human. For him this excellence found its expression in philosophizing and in right action. He claimed that he found the key to wisdom in his awareness of his ignorance. For Socrates then, realizing one's ignorance is the beginning of wisdom and understanding.

Other philosophers and other traditions have recognized the importance of insight into ignorance. Consider the following as illustrative but by no means exhaustive examples. For Plato the prisoners in the cave represent the state of ignorance in ordinary life which results from thinking that the whole of reality is revealed through the senses alone. Humans are thus in the dark, looking at shadows of reality, without knowing their own blind spots. For Plato, as for Socrates, ignorance is the source of wrongdoing. For Lao Tzu accumulated learning of all sorts of facts and theories renders intelligence almost helpless; dispensing with this type of learning brings freedom from the ignorance that specialized learning often becomes. For Spinoza ignorance of the ways of the universe and of the ways of passion keeps humans in bondage. For the Buddhists the principal explanation for the arising of Karma, Samsara, and suffering is ignorance. For Western Enlightenment philosophers ignorance was seen as the source of superstition and as counter to progress. For twentieth-century liberals ignorance is part of the mix of poverty and disease that breeds conflicts, war and human suffering. It is something to be eliminated through systems of education.

As noted earlier, ignorance is often defined as a lack of knowledge; as such the solution to problems arising from ignorance would seem to be to gain knowledge. If we think of these problems as like a disease, then knowledge will be seen as a cure. However, as we have seen, ignorance in this sense is not simply a lack of knowledge, but is a lack of knowledge of a certain sort.

So far we have spoken in general terms, and if we are to advance our inquiry we must consider in more detail the interplay between ignorance and knowledge. In so doing we will perhaps recognize distinctions that have thus far been blurred. We will do this, and we will also consider the kinds of ignorance that are relevant to our inquiry. In the process we hope to shed light on the virtue that Socratic ignorance is.

In the first place then, we have ignorant ignorance. We are ignorant of our ignorance. This is the state in which Socrates claimed to find many of the citizens of Athens. When we do not know that we are ignorant, then we are in the most undesirable state, for we will not even know enough to begin to investigate. If we think that we know the ends of human life, but are actually ignorant of them, then realizing these ends will be at best a matter of chance. At worst, our assumptions to know might lead us to act consistently in ways contrary to realizing these ends and our own excellence.

Now it is difficult to realize one's ignorance in this way. Socrates thought it so difficult that he saw his special mission that of a gadfly to harass the "sleeping" citizens of Athens. He says in the *Apology* that they needed to be stung awake to their own ignorance. It is only when humans acutely feel their ignorance that they can pass through the disorienting fire of a dialogue which enables them to abandon false opinions. Only then are we ready to enter that inquiry which is aimed at knowledge of our areté, the knowledge which, for Socrates, is necessary if we are to act wisely. This knowledge is something we each must realize for ourselves, for it is not merely information. It is nothing less than knowledge of oneself as an agent, as a subject. It is knowledge of one's soul. It is not theory, nor is it belief. The right life and virtuous action are both grounded in this knowledge of, and care for, the soul. Our insight into this is an immediate personal knowing that arises out of the conditions of the questioning that Socratic dialogue is. Thus we reach Socratic ignorance, by turns humble, then ironic. We are awakened from our slumber by the stinging questions philosophy asks. Although we might formerly have acted with conviction, we did not know our actions were right. Just as Euthyphro was convinced he knew that he was acting piously by prosecuting his own father, so we too might have believed that we generally acted virtuously. We each think that we know what virtuous action is. We do not knowingly do evil, but because we are ignorant of our ignorance, we think we know what we do not.

The test that we do not know is that when pressed we cannot say, e.g., what piety is; we can only cite examples of specific pious acts. But his diversity of acts is not so far an account of piety. They do not by themselves tell us what it is. We cannot say precisely what it is that makes them pious. Once we exhaust our initial views and fail to properly characterize piety, then we reach the state of knowing we are ignorant; this is Socratic ignorance. For Socrates we are now in a position to find out what we need to know. Our inquiry can go on. We can begin to philosophize in a constructive way, for until now our efforts have been negative. This knowledge that we need is neither theoretic nor speculative. It is a practical knowing in which we are aware of and come to understand the unity of virtue in the soul and in action.

This practical knowing has the feature of being self-reflexive, for such an agent acts with the full awareness that he/she acts virtuously. This self-reflexive knowledge is grounded in knowledge of the soul, and a feature of its excellence in action is practical, intelligent awareness. Hence, its excellence is expressed as intelligent action which grows out of the open wakefulness to which Socratic philosophizing leads, when it frees us from our claims to know, from our prejudices, beliefs, opinions, erroneous habits of thought and the like, when it frees us, that is, from the ignorance of our ignorance. What Socrates leaves unsaid is something that is realized only by each of us through our own insight. The teacher can only bring us to the condition from which we can clearly understand. This is why Socrates also called himself a midwife, as one who helps those pregnant with knowledge to give birth to it within themselves.

Of course, before the dawning of this awareness one might have acted in the right ways. One might have known what one needed to know, but one might have been ignorant that one knew this. Socrates suggests that no one can teach this to us. It is not the form of knowledge that can be passed along, as we have already noted. In the *Meno,* e.g., it is said that all learning is a form of remembering; virtue cannot be taught. One way in which to understand this is to say that all along we know, e.g., that the care of the soul is at the center of all goodness; but we do not know that we know this. In many ways confusion and conflict give rise to self-induced ignorance, or to self-deception. It is not that someone has purposefully misled us on these matters, nor are they hidden from us in the world or in the stars. For these matters are with *us.* However, our preoccupation with the objects of the world, and our confused passions obscure our knowing capacity. Nonetheless, virtuous action and the knowing agent are inseparable, and virtuous action requires knowledge of one's self in relationships and in actions. We must know fully what and why we are doing, and this requires that we not merely think about the action, but realize its significance for us.[1]

For Socrates, then, once we realize our ignorance and begin to search in earnest for understanding, we slowly come to see that this understanding can only be drawn out of ourselves. When we are pregnant with it, the midwife helps us to give birth; for no one else can give birth for us in this way. In this process we begin to sense that we have known many of these things all along, for in this birth process we meet ourselves—as if for the first time. Of course, we have been seeing the reflections of ourselves in our actions all our lives. We just did not realize the significance of what was there before us all of the time.

As with Plato's prisoner who leaves the cave, so too with us as we philosophize, the objects of our world have a familiarity that becomes increasingly clarified as inquiry frees our perceptions of the obscurity of erroneous beliefs. Thus one progresses from ignorant ignorance, to Socratic ignorance and then to the awareness that one has known in a way, but has been ignorant of this knowledge in and of the soul. The awareness that our actions are expressions of the self, however obscured by confusion, conflict, ignorance, and acquired beliefs, leads us to seek the self-knowledge which penetrates these veils of ignorance that obscure our intelligence. Once these veils are lifted our capacities for intelligent observation and understanding function properly. Now we know we act rightly, for our actions are grounded in the solid confidence that is aware of its own knowing process; this is not inferential but immediate.[2]

For Socrates virtuous action requires this kind of receptive, open, full awareness. The way to this for Socrates is through inquiry, a continuous examination of life. Thus in a sense the philosopher is a virtuoso of concepts. He/she is attached to no rigid theory. He/she uses this mastery or virtuosity to transcend the limits of theory and belief.

But philosophy, as the word implies, is no disinterested study; for Socrates it was an activity which faces death and uncertainty fully prepared for anything, for the philosopher expects nothing.[3] The mind is freed of its useless clutter by this activity. As Socrates remarked, "to philosophize is to be prepared to die." With death fast approaching he engaged in philosophizing. For him this activity is full living itself. Through it, and in it, we are able to live fearlessly. Instead of sinking into fear and moroseness while awaiting death, Socrates actually paid attention to the process of dying, reporting to his friends what the hemlock was doing to his body. Thus, for Socrates philosophy was not a luxury, nor an activity to be pursued only by a few in their idleness. He saw it as a realization of human excellence. Neither animal nor divine, the human spirit is able to move between divine intelligence and animal awareness. The examined life is one in which this is brought to flower out of our own need as a love for that which we lack, viz. wisdom. If one is human, then to live in this Socratic manner is to live wisely. This is the completion of the fully human life.

We have been discussing the features of the dialectical interplay of ignorance and knowledge. Clearly what transcends this play is wisdom. For, if it is possible to act wisely, this means that wisdom can arise through our awareness of this interplay, but it cannot arise out of our ignorance of ignorance. Wisdom grows out of seeing the unending dialectic of ignorance and knowledge in a whole way, as this is related to human life. Once we recognize the futility of trying to have perfect knowledge in the form of an account or theory that covers *all* possibilities, then we are able to grasp the possibility of wisdom. Wisdom, for Socrates, arises in the fully awake action that philosophy is.

As a result of the broad topography of the interplay of ignorance and knowledge we have sketched so far, we can see that there are forms of ignorance of particular concern to Socrates. In summary, we note that these are the following: ignorance of our actions, ignorance of our unique situations, ignorance of our relationships, ignorance of what to do, how to do it and why, and most importantly ignorance of self. Ignorance of self is the ignorance from which all other forms of ignorant action spring. Looking at these other forms of ignorance without realizing this can lead us to inquire, but full understanding of the former is dependent on self-knowledge. The expert can have detailed knowledge of tree leaves and not know the forest as a biotic unity. We need to know not only trees and forest, but also ourselves within the forest of our ecological interactions. Only then is the activity of wise forestry possible. To leave the human subject out of the picture is to fail to have truly objective knowledge. Objective knowledge is not knowledge of objects independent of the knower, but is knowledge of the knower and the object of knowledge in relationship, in action, in dynamic reciprocal process.

This knowledge of self and object, which embraces both ignorance and knowledge, is the source of our deepest spiritual values. Knowledge as a mere collection of information, unrelated to knowers and to their ignorance, is not a form of knowledge that brings wisdom. It can, however, bring arrogance and pride. Awareness of our ignorance, on the other hand, can awaken humility and compassion.

We said of the example of the forest that sound forestry is based on a wisdom that transcends the narrow knowledge of the expert. To be sure, for Socrates life is like an art or craft, that is, both develop when there is insight and creativity, but these arise in the context of practice. They grow out of a maturing skill. Just as a craft can be learned and perfected, so too life can be lived in an increasingly skillful way. However, the master of life is not the expert who is the product of a highly specialized and narrow training. In the latter sense, there are no experts on how to live. There are no specialists who can judge for each and every one of us what is the right course of action. Socrates' vision focuses out attention on the mature, responsible human who integrates both his/her divine and animal elements. Philosophizing for Socrates gives us the whole understanding that makes this possible. Thus philosophy is not something in which we engage to find a final view to live by for the rest of our lives. Life is filled with uncertainty and change and human limitations require an ongoing practice focused on the proper care of the soul. This practice is what gives unity through time to our virtuous actions regardless of the diversity of our contexts and conditions.

Despite the confusing diversity of actions which are virtuous, then, Socrates holds that virtue itself is one. For example, although we can cite numerous cases of courageous acts, Socrates would ask us what it is that unifies these acts beyond the fact that they are all called courageous. What is it that makes them courageous? It is not just the external features of the situation, nor alone what is done. As noted earlier, the soul, or psyche also must be considered. Socrates, convinced of the unity of virtues, would have us look to the soul and to our practice for that which unifies many instances of virtuous acts. The unity that virtue is, is not to be found in some abstract timeless form, nor in some arbitrary definition, but is to be found here in the soul and in our practice. Thus Socrates refocused the attention of philosophy from the heavens to the heart. We are now to intensely inquire to know how we should live, for without this knowledge all other knowledge pursuits are pointless, perhaps even dangerous. Every craft and every art has an end, whether politics, poetry, or carpentry, in short all of our practices in which there is a settled order and a tradition. Now knowing the purpose of the craft is tantamount to not knowing what we are doing. Similarly not knowing the seat of virtue is akin to being purposeless in life. This we can know only if we know ourselves and what constitutes proper care of the soul. It is because Socrates taught this that he is said by Cornford to have discovered the knowing subject.[4]

Thus for Socrates virtue is one in the soul. It is its own reward, for it is the expression and development of one's excellence *as* human. The care of the soul is the development of its virtue that comes through this knowing process that Socratic inquiry is. The many virtues are one, since they flow from the same excellence in the well- cared-for soul. Furthermore, in this oneness all virtues are forms of knowing. The virtues, whether justice, courage, temperance, and the like, are all expressions in action in diverse contexts of what the virtuous person is, and of her/his knowledge of the good. Courage is this knowledge in the face of danger. Justice is this knowledge in the context of social interactions and resolution of conflicts. And so on.

For Socrates, then, the question must always be, "Does the act detract from the care of the soul, does it damage my excellence or the excellence of another, or does it improve us?" His conviction is that no harm can come to a truly good person from outside, for only his/her own ignorance and lack of authenticity can harm the soul. Thus care of the soul requires an integral knowledge and a practice that is a continuous development of its excellence. This excellence is nothing less than its capacity for awareness, for understanding, for intelligent discernment.[5] Only through this do we find balance, harmony, integration and *eudaemonia.* It is from such care of the soul, through inquiry and open learning, that understanding arises and justice and goodness flow into our acts. Only then do we become completely capable of contributing to the health of our society. Only then is our life a full human life worth living.

The knowing of the subject, then, is a self-knowing in which we know ourselves transparently in action. This knowing and our actions are one. In this sense, Socrates was his philosophy. He and his philosophizing were one. He is the paradigm Sage of the way of philosophy for Western humanist traditions. He exemplifies the person free from attachments to wealth, position, views, and the passions. He finds and exemplifies his teaching as the activity it is, aimed as it is at knowing the full value *in* human life, by knowing the human subject. His form of inquiry dissolves the inner stance of self-image rationalizations that stand between us and unified action. His dialectical movement beyond knowledge and ignorance is a movement to nondiscursive knowing or wisdom. Subject and virtuous action form a conscious unity through which we become wise.[6] In dissolving our pretenses to know we first become aware that we know nothing. The virtue of this Socratic ignorance is that it brings us to the humble awareness from which intelligent and virtuous action become possible. Once this happens the adventure of life intensifies with all of its mysteries, its joys, its sorrows and satisfactions. In this adventure philosophy is the active meeting of life receptive to all of its enigmas and unknowns, for only this inquiry that philosophy is takes us beyond the limits of our complacent knowledge, to the realization of our own ignorance. This philosophical activity is the dialogue that itself makes communion possible, and it flourishes and promotes the community in which this spirit is kept alive. Hence, we continue the Socratic tradition when we come together to dialogue and to seek communion through our inquiries.

Thus we see that for Socrates philosophy was a labor of love, a serious leisure activity out of which comes our deepest insights and our wisdom.[7] The hazard of professional philosophy is that it will turn philosophizing into intellectual work and that alone. Without insight or wisdom, and with a concentration on techniques and methods of discursive reasoning, philosophy easily degenerates into endless theorizing which becomes either purely formal, or gives way to debate and to futile skepticism. Either extreme represents the imbalance to which concentration on intellect alone can lead. For Socrates philosophizing must engage the whole person. For him what is left unsaid in dialogue is as important, and often more so, than what is actually said. The insights that philosophizing leads us to come in the illuminating silence that results from our inquiry. This direct, immediate knowing is a clear, simple perception of being itself as it works intelligently through us. For Socrates, wise action ultimately means acting in this self-illuminating and illuminated way.

The virtue of Socratic ignorance, then, is that it makes our dialogue possible. As we have seen, it also makes possible that action which realizes the virtue through which the intelligence of the soul is tuned to its highest excellence.[8]

NOTES

1. Courage, e.g., cannot be fully defined in terms of a specific action in a specific context without mention of the agent, for the same action done in the same context by two different agents, might in the one case be brave and in the other not.

2. This immediate knowing is in some respects analogous to the continuous sensitive awareness of the martial artist (or gymnast) which enables him/her to respond instantly to the slightest change in resistance or direction of movement. This is something that the artist develops, and it is dependent upon becoming more aware, more fully able to pay complete attention to what is going on, at the same time as he/she is able to broaden his/her awareness of the whole scene. This awareness of both detail and perspective is necessary in acute situations when engagement involves attacks that might come from any of several directions. At some stage in the learning of a martial art practice involves cultivating this ability to handle several attackers at one time; this is possible only with the kind of total awareness we are here trying to describe.

3. "Philosophy," we hardly need to remind ourselves, means literally the *love* and pursuit of wisdom.

4. See F. M. Cornford's book *Before and After Socrates* (Cambridge,1960).

5. Socrates has been said to intellectualize virtue, but this claim is not consistent with his character. He obeyed his inner voice. He was a passionate man, who admitted his passions and his erotic attractions. This acceptance and open acknowledgment disarmed the passions of their sway over his intelligence, but it did not deprive his life of eros. Socrates did not live disinterestedly, and he was not indifferent to right action. His commitments and his moral insights transcended mere intellectual theorizing. For Socrates, then, knowing is not disinterested. He thought it arises from our deepest needs as humans.

6. Socrates said that those who do wrong do so out of ignorance. This is said to be paradoxical. However, this remark can be understood as the observation that there are no bad persons, only bad actions, only ignorant acts, and these harm the agent far more than they harm others; the deepest harm is not physical but spiritual. In spiritual harm we must be participants. Thus when we act greedily, greed is the same for us all. There are many greedy actions, but greed as a state of the soul is the same for us all. This we know, and if we are not self-reflectively aware of our greed it will continue to have a hold over us. The enemy is not the other person, but the greed or the ambition in which we all tend to be caught up. In the absence of knowing this, our ignorance ensures that we will be enslaved by these vices. Thus we have no recourse but to philosophize as Socrates did, if we are to be free to act virtuously.

7. By "leisure" we do not ean "idleness." We emphasize leisure to stress that philosophy, in the sense we are discussing, is part of one's whole life and is not merely an occupation one does for eight hours, five days a week and then forgets the rest of the time. Philosophy as this Socratic activity is one with our settled life. It is a way of life in the sense of total commitment and practice.

8. An earlier version of this paper was read as the Presidential address at the Northwest Conference on Philosophy meetings on November 30, 1979, held at Oregon State University in Corvallis, Oregon.

REFERENCES

I. Primary Sources. Plato's *Apology* served as the major primary source for this paper. In addition, other dialogues by Plato that were important include the following: *Crito, Euthyphro, Phaedo, Meno, Symposium,* and *Republic.* Comments by Aristotle, Xenophon, and Aristophanes provided valuable perspectives.
II. Secondary Sources. The following books are some of the better commentaries available on Socrates and the historical backgrounds and influence of Socratism. Some are especially good on the Sophists, e.g., Versényi and Guthrie, others emphasize the influence of Socrates on Western traditions, e.g., Spidgelberg and Sauvage.
CORNFORD, F. M.,   *Before and after Socrates* (Cambridge: Cambridge University Press, 1960).
GUTHRIE, W. K. C.,   *Socrates* (Cambridge: Cambridge University Press, 1971).
SAUVAGE, MICHELINE,   *Socrates as the Conscience of Man* (New York: Harper and Brothers, 1960).
SPIDGELBERG, H.,   *The Socratic Enigma* (New York: Bobbs-Merrill, 1964).
TAYLOR, A. E.,   *Socrates:* The *Man and His Thought* (New York: Doubleday Anchor, 1953).
VERSÉNYI, TASZEO,   *Socratic Humanism* (New Haven: Yale University Press, 1963).
VLASTOS, GREGORY (ed.),   *The Philosophy of Socrates: A Collection of Critical Essays* (New York: Anchor Books, 1971).

THE PROBLEM OF SOCRATES

Friedrich Nietzsche

1

Concerning life, the wisest men of all ages have judged alike: it is *no good*. Always and everywhere one has heard the same sound from their mouths—a sound full of doubt, full of melancholy, full of weariness of life, full of resistance to life. Even Socrates said, as he died: "To live—that means to be sick a long time: I owe

Asclepius the Savior a rooster." Even Socrates was tired of it. What does that evidence? What does it evince? Formerly one would have said (–oh, it has been said, and loud enough, and especially by our pessimists): "At least something of all this must be true! The consensus of the sages evidences the truth." Shall we still talk like that today? *May* we? "At least something must be *sick* here," *we* retort. These wisest men of all ages–they should first be scrutinized closely. Were they all perhaps shaky on their legs? late? tottery? decadents? Could it be that wisdom appears on earth as a raven, inspired by a little whiff of carrion?

2

This irreverent thought that the great sages are *types of decline* first occurred to me precisely in a case where it is most strongly opposed by both scholarly and un-scholarly prejudice: I recognized Socrates and Plato to be symptoms of degenera-tion, tools of the Greek dissolution, pseudo-Greek, anti-Greek (*Birth of Tragedy*, 1872). The consensus of the sages–I comprehended this ever more clearly–proves least of all that they were right in what they agreed on: it shows rather that they themselves, these wisest men, agreed in some *physiological* respect, and hence adopted the same negative attitude to life–*had to* adopt it. Judgments, judgments of value, concerning life, for it or against it, can, in the end, never be true: they have value only as symptoms, they are worthy of consideration only as symptoms; in themselves such judgments are stupidities. One must by all means stretch out one's fingers and make the attempt to grasp this amazing finesse, *that the value of life cannot be estimated.* Not by the living, for they are an interested party, even a bone of contention, and not judges; not by the dead, for a different reason. For a philosopher to see a problem in the value of life is thus an objection to him, a ques-tion mark concerning his wisdom, an un-wisdom. Indeed? All these great wise men–they were not only decadents but not wise at all? But I return to the problem of Socrates.

3

In origin, Socrates belonged to the lowest class: Socrates was plebs. We know, we can still see for ourselves, how ugly he was. But ugliness, in itself an objection, is among the Greeks almost a refutation. Was Socrates a Greek at all? Ugliness is often enough the expression of a development that has been crossed, *thwarted* by crossing. Or it appears as *declining* development. The anthropoligists among the criminol-ogists tell us that the typical criminal is ugly: *monstrum in fronte, monstrum in animo.* But the criminal is a decadent. Was Socrates a typical criminal? At least that would not be contradicted by the famous judgment of the physiognomist which sounded so offensive to the friends of Socrates. A foreigner who knew about faces once passed through Athens and told Socrates to his face that he *was* a *monstrum*–that he harbored in himself all the bad vices and appetites. And Socrates merely answered: "You know me, sir!"

4

Socrates' decadence is suggested not only by the admitted wantonness and anarchy of his instincts, but also by the hypertrophy of the logical faculty and that *sarcasm of the rachitic* which distinguishes him. Nor should we forget those auditory hallucinations which, as "the *daimonion* of Socrates," have been interpreted religiously. Everything in him is exaggerated, *buffo*, a caricature, everything is at the same time concealed, ulterior, subterranean. I seek to comprehend what idiosyncrasy begot that Socratic equation of reason, virtue, and happiness: that most bizarre of all equations, which, moreover, is opposed to all the instincts of the earlier Greeks.

5

With Socrates, Greek taste changes in favor of dialectics. What really happened there? Above all, a *noble* taste is thus vanquished; with dialectics the plebs come to the top. Before Socrates, dialectic manners were repudiated in good society: they were considered bad manners, they were compromising. The young were warned against them. Furthermore, all such presentations of one's reasons were distrusted. Honest things, like honest men, do not carry their reasons in their hands like that. It is indecent to show all five fingers. What must first be proved is worth while. Wherever authority still forms part of good bearing, where one does not give reasons but commands, the dialectician is a kind of buffon: one laughs at him, one does not take him seriously. Socrates was a buffoon who *got himself taken seriously:* what really happened there?

6

One choosen dialectic only when one has no other means. One knows that one arouses mistrust with it, that it is not very persuasive. Nothing is easier to erase than a dialectical effect: the experience of every meeting at which there are speeches proves this. It can only be *self-defense* for those who no longer have other weapons. One must have to *enforce* one's right: until one reaches that point, one makes no use of it. The Jews were dialecticians for that reason; Reynard the Fox was one—and Socrates too?

7

Is the irony of Socrates an expression of revolt? Of plebian *ressentiment*? Does he, as one oppressed, enjoy his own ferocity in the knife-thrusts of his syllogisms? Does he *avenge* himself on the noble people whom he fascinates? As a dialectician, one holds a merciless tool in one's hand; one can become a tyrant by means of it; one compromises those one conquers. The dialectician leaves it to his opponent to prove that he is no idiot: he makes one furious and helpless at the same time. The dialectician renders the intellect of this opponent powerless. Indeed? Is dialectic only a form of *revenge* in Socrates?

8

I have given to understand how it was that Socrates could repel: it is therefore all the more necessary to explain his fascination. That he discovered a new kind of *agon*,[1] that he became its first fencing master for the noble circles of Athens, is one point. He fascinated by appealing to the agonistic impulse of the Greeks—he introduced a variation into the wrestling match between young men and youths. Socrates was also a great *erotic*.

9

But Socrates guessed even more. He saw *through* his noble Athenians; he comprehended that his own case, his idiosyncrasy, was no longer exceptional. The same kind of degeneration was quietly developing everywhere: old Athens was coming to an end. And Socrates understood that all the world *needed* him—his means, his cure, his personal artifice of self-preservation. Everywhere the instincts were in anarchy; everywhere one was within five paces of excess: *monstrum in animo* was the general danger. "The impulses want to play the tyrant; one must invent a *counter-tyrant* who is stronger." When the physiognomist had revealed to Socrates who he was—a cave of bad appetites—the great master of irony let slip another word which is the key to his character. "This is true," he said, "but I mastered them all." *How* did Socrates become master over *himself*? His case was, at bottom, merely the extreme case, only the most striking instance of what was then beginning to be a universal distress: no one was any longer master over himself, the instincts turned *against* each other. He fascinated, being this extreme case; his awe-inspiring ugliness proclaimed him as such to all who could see: he fascinated, of course, even more as an answer, a solution, an apparent *cure* of this case.

10

When one finds it necessary to turn *reason* into a tyrant, as Socrates did, the danger cannot be slight that something else will play the tyrant. Rationality was then hit upon as the savior; neither Socrates nor his "patients" had any choice about being rational: it was *de rigeur*, it was their last resort. The fanaticism with which all Greek reflection throws itself upon rationality betrays a desperate situation; there was danger, there was but one choice: either to perish or—to be *absurdly rational*. The moralism of the Greek philosophers from Plato on is pathologically conditioned; so is their esteem of dialectics. Reason-virtue-happiness, that means merely that one must imitate Socrates and counter the dark appetites with a permanent daylight—the daylight of reason. One must be clever, clear, bright at any price: any concession to the instincts, to the unconscious, leads *downward*.

11

I have given to understand how it was that Socrates fascinated: he seemed to be a physician, a savior. Is it necessary to go on to demonstrate the error in his faith in "rationality at any price"? It is a self-deception on the part of philosophers and moralists if they believe that they are extricating themselves from decadence when they merely wage war against it. Extrication lies beyond their strength: what they choose as a means, as salvation, is itself but another expression of decadence; they change its expression, but they do not get rid of decadence itself. Socrates was a misunderstanding; *the whole improvement-morality, including the Christian, was a misunderstanding.* The most blinding daylight; rationality at any price; life, bright, cold, cautious, conscious, without instinct, in opposition to the instincts— all this too was a mere disease, another disease, and by no means a return to "virtue," to "health," to happiness. To *have* to fight the instincts—that is the formula of decadence: as long as life is *ascending*, happiness equals instinct.

12

Did he himself still comprehend this, this most brilliant of all self-outwitters? Was this what he said to himself in the end, in the *wisdom* of his courage to die? Socrates *wanted* to die: not Athens, but he himself chose the hemlock; he forced Athens to sentence him. "Socrates is no physician," he said softly to himself; "here death alone is the physician. Socrates himself has merely been sick a long time."

NOTE

1. "Contest."

CHAPTER TWO
PHILOSOPHY, EDUCATION, AND THE LIBERAL ARTS

In the first section of this text we met Euthyphro, a man who claimed to know the nature of piety. Upon closer examination by Socrates, however, Euthyphro was shown to have only a shallow conception of piety and its proper place in life. Just as piety plays a dominant role in Euthyphro's life, education plays an important role in our own. During an average lifetime of seventy years, most of us spend at least sixteen years, approximately twenty-three percent of our lives, in formal education. Like Euthyphro, we probably believe we understand what education is and what value it brings to our lives. Have we ever stopped, however, to consider it reflectively, to articulate and defend the role of education in a rational life plan? Probably not.

For the first sixteen years of our lives, education is mandatory. Our compulsory-education laws leave a young person no alternative but to be in school. When one is left no option, the natural tendency is simply to do what is required, not to examine that requirement or investigate its possible justification. Moreover, most young people, lacking intellectual maturity, have not developed a rational life plan to provide them with the perspective necessary to define for themselves the nature and value of education. In our culture, the choice of whether to go to college is typically the first occasion for considering formal education as a living option. A young person must not only decide whether to continue formal schooling past high school; he or she must also decide what sort of higher education—a technical school, a professional education like forestry, or a liberal arts degree—is worth pursuing. In many cases, however, these choices are not made through rational reflection. Instead, parental and peer-group pressures combine to make higher education another requirement, not an option to be chosen autonomously.

As a result of these pressures, many students matriculate at a college and spend at least four years there, investing large amounts of time, effort, and money. They pursue a degree without any deep understanding of what they are pursuing, or why. In the process they become masters at playing the educational game. Note-taking skills are honed to a razor edge; test-taking and writing papers are just hurdles on the way to a degree. The student becomes adept at "psyching" his teachers—finding out what they want and giving it to them in the required form. Information is gathered, memorized, and regurgitated on final exams. Like rats learning to run a maze, students become skilled at performing the required tasks; many, if not most, graduate untouched and unchanged by their exposure to college. From their point of view, one more hurdle has been cleared; now it is time to move on to the more important things in life. The sad fact is that students and society are frequently under the illusion that in this process *education* has taken place.

If students were to encounter Socrates, and were asked to pause in their frantic pursuit of grades and a degree long enough to offer a rational justification of their activities, many would probably assert that higher education is a means to an end. The end at which many aim is success in one's work: the high-paying job, and the material pleasures that our consumer society provides. Perhaps a few would reject the goal of material rewards and would claim instead that college is a means to a humanly satisfying vocation.

Yet nagging doubts may undermine these instrumental justifications of higher education. In years past there was a direct correlation between the amount of higher education one received and the financial rewards that one obtained. In today's economic world, this correlation may not always hold true. Many "blue collar" workers now earn as much as college graduates. Although a college degree may provide one with a passport to a meaningful vocation, it is far from certain that upon graduation a student will obtain employment in his or her chosen profession. It is not unknown for a college graduate (or the holder of a Ph.D. degree) to work as a store clerk, waiter, or taxi driver, simply because he or she could not find employment in a chosen profession.

Such uncomfortable facts shake the foundations of instrumental justifications of higher education and ought to provide educators and students with an occasion to examine critically the nature and value of higher education. The articles in this section begin such an examination by raising and trying to answer the following questions. What is a Liberal Arts education? What role should it play in the life of a person who comes under its influence? How does it foster a fuller and more satisfactory, if not materially richer, life? Moreover, are instrumental lines of reasoning appropriate means of justifying the time, effort, and money that we invest in education? Finally, are there widespread presuppositions about education, presuppositions linked to powerful societal forces, that threatened the very nature of liberal education? If we are content to leave these fundamental questions unexamined, we are—like Euthyphro—condemning ourselves to a superficial understanding of an ideal that occupies a significant and enduring place in our lives.

FOUR KINDS OF MINDS

Walter Kaufmann

1

There are visionaries and scholastics. This distinction is essential for an understanding of the humanities as well as the natural and social sciences. No diagnosis of the ills of higher education should ignore this basic contrast.

Visionaries are loners. Alienated from the common sense of their time, they see the world differently and make sustained attempts to spell out their vision. Usually, they find existing languages inadequate, and often they encounter serious problems of communication.

Scholastics travel in schools, take pride in their rigor and professionalism, and rely heavily on their consensus or their common "know-how." They are usually hostile to contemporary visionaries, especially in their own field, but swear by some visionaries of the past.

In religion the visionaries are often called prophets and the scholastics priests. In philosophy and literature, history and the arts, there are no traditional terms for the two types, but sometimes the visionaries are called geniuses.

In science we have long had the contrast between the popular image of the mad scientist as a visionary and the positivists' very different notion of what it means to be scientific. In *The Structure of Scientific Revolutions* (1962) Thomas Kuhn has shown, in effect, how both visionaries and "normal" scientists function in the history of science. He described "normal science" as "puzzle-solving" within an accepted framework and then dealt with the emergence of scientific discoveries that lead to changes of world views. He did not deal primarily with human types and did not disparage what he called normal. On the contrary, he tried to show how needful the work of the industrious toilers is. The impact of his book has been immense.

More than a generation earlier, in 1918, Albert Einstein had delivered a brief address on the occasion of Max Planck's sixtieth birthday. By dividing the scholastic camp in two, he had recognized three types. There are those who "take to science out of a joyful sense of their superior intellectual power," people for whom science is a kind of "sport" that allows them to satisfy their ambition, while many others enter the temple of science "for purely utilitarian purposes. Were an angel of the Lord to come and drive all the people belonging to these two categories

From *The Future of the Humanities,* (New York: Reader's Digest Press, 1977), pp. 1-46.

out of the temple," a few people would still be left, including Planck—"and that is why we love him."

This typology, unlike Kuhn's, is far from being value-free. It may even appear to be completely different from Kuhn's contrast and irrelevant to our purposes. For Einstein dealt with the psychological motives of research, although his address was later included in *Mein Weltbild*, and then also in several English collections of his essays, under the title "Principles of Research." But whatever *his* motive may have been, he left no doubt that his third type, the few like Planck, corresponds to our visionaries. For after conceding that it might be difficult in some cases to draw the line, he went on to say that he felt sure of one thing: "If the types we have just expelled were the only types there were, the temple would never have existed, any more than one can have a wood consisting of nothing but creepers."

Understandably, Einstein's typology did not have any very great immediate impact. It was not worked out in detail, and the disparagement of "creepers" could hardly have made it very popular. . . .

Before we decide whether to keep our typology value-free, let us trace back the fundamental contrast beyond Einstein, to Goethe. Goethe was not only the greatest German poet but also a remarkable scientist. In his *Doctrine of Colors* (*Farbenlehre*, 1810), which he himself considered as important as any of his works, he argued against Newton. Even those who have no doubt that *Einstein* scored against Newton generally take for granted that Goethe did not, and that Goethe's *Doctrine of Colors* can be safely ignored. Yet this work has merits that are quite independent of the question whether Goethe or Newton was right about colors.

Goethe pioneered a humanistic approach to science. In his beautifully written preface he said:

> We compare the Newtonian color theory with an old castle that was initially planned by its builder with youthful haste, but by and by amplified by him and furnished in accordance with the needs of the time and circumstances and, in the course of skirmishes and hostilities, fortified and secured more and more.

Goethe went on to describe how the castle was gradually enlarged as one "added towers, baywindows, and battlements," as well as ever so many other features. All the while

> one venerated the old castle because it had never been conquered, because it had repulsed so many attacks, frustrated so many enemies, and retained its virginity. This claim, this reputation still endures. Nobody notices that the old building has become uninhabitable.

Surprisingly, perhaps, it was by no means Goethe's central purpose to show that his own doctrine was true and Newton's false, nor even to replace the "old castle" with his own edifice.

If we should succeed by the use of our utmost power and skill to reduce this bastille [that is, to bring off a scientific revolution] and to gain a free space, it is by no means our intention to cover it up and molest it again right away with a new building. We prefer to use it in order to present a series of beautiful forms.

The third part is therefore devoted to historical investigations and preliminaries. If we said above that the history of man shows us man, one could now claim that the history of science is science itself. One cannot gain pure recognition of what one possesses until one knows what others have possessed before us. One will not truly and honestly enjoy the advantages of one's own time if one does not know how to appreciate the advantages of the past. But to write a history of the doctrine of color . . . was impossible as long as the Newtonian doctrine held the field. For no aristocratic conceit has ever looked down with as much intolerable arrogance upon those who did not belong to the same guild, as the Newtonian school has always condemned everything that was achieved before or beside it.

What concerns us here is not Goethe's quarrel with Newton, who was, like Goethe, one of the greatest visionaries of all time, but rather Goethe's critique of the Newtonian school—of the scholastics. In 1829 he returned to this theme in a short essay that was published only posthumously, in 1833, under the title "Analysis and Synthesis":

A false hypothesis is better than none at all, for that it is false does no harm at all; but when it fortifies itself, when it is accepted universally and becomes a kind of creed that nobody may doubt, that nobody may investigate, that is the disaster of which centuries suffer.

The Newtonian doctrine could be presented; even in his own time its defects were urged against it, but the man's other great merits and his position in the social and scholarly world did not allow contradiction to gain any standing. The French especially are to be blamed more than anyone else for the spread and ossification of this doctrine. In the nineteenth century they should therefore make up for this mistake by favoring a fresh analysis of this intricate and frozen hypothesis.

Goether introduced so many pertinent themes in unforgettable images that it seemed best to let him speak at some length. (Translations in this book are always mine.) Here is an archvisionary putting his case against scholasticism—prompted not by pique but by concern for the freedom of the human spirit. He pioneered a new humanistic discipline, the history of science, and rejected the dogmatic faith in cumulative progress that was widely shared until Kuhn's *Structure of Scientific Revolutions* called it into question more than a century and a half later. Of course, the theme of discontinuity and the insight that science is a human endeavor alongside poetry and music, history and philosophy, art and religion, were prominent in Hegel's thought as well as Nietzsche's; but in the English-speaking world they have gained ground only since World War II.

Legions of professors and students in the humanities have accepted "science" as a model while still sharing the positivistic faith in cumulative progress. But Goethe knew that his own scientific discoveries were not altogether different from his work as a poet; both involved vision; and the history of science, as he conceived it, placed science in a human context. . . .

2

My contrast of visionaries and scholastics represents a variation on an old theme. It can be developed in one of two ways. We can follow Einstein's lead and think of the visionaries as a few people including Planck—as well as Einstein and Goethe, Beethoven and Michelangelo, Plato and Moses. These visionaries did not yield to anyone in craftsmanship. If we contrast people of this type with scholastics who, by definition, do not have great visions of their own, the dichotomy becomes somewhat Manichaean, with all good on one side.

To avoid that, one could expand the category of the visionaries to include crackpots. One could insist that both visionaries and scholastics can be "good" or "bad." Visionaries can have fixed ideas that they back up with ingenious arguments; they can be obsessional or paranoiac and often are both; even the greatest visionaries sometimes are of this type at least some of the time—Newton, for example—and most people of this type lack Newton's genius.

One could even go further and insist that people with distinctive world views are quite common in asylums, that hallucinations are visions of a sort, and that Goethe and his kind represent no more than one type of visionary and a very small minority of the whole class. The virtue of this approach is that it is by no means Manichaean or simplistic. Its disadvantage is that it encumbers us with types that are of no great interest in connection with the future of the humanities.

Of course, there is a multitude of human types, and a scholastic might have a great time noting subclasses and making fine distinctions. For our purposes, however, it will be most fruitful to stick to the definitions given at the outset. Sustained attempts to spell out a distinctive vision—and that is part of my definition—require a mastery of technique. Those who have visions but lack the power to articulate them in a sustained way are of no concern to us here. It follows that what distinguishes the scholastic from the visionary is not rigor but reliance on consensus and the lack of a distinctive vision.

It does not follow that all visionaries are "good," all scholastics "bad." Not every distinctive vision is plausible, beautiful, or fruitful. And it may require the concerted efforts of a great many scholastics to work out the details of a vision before we can judge its value.

Nietzsche was right when he said in a posthumously published note: "The first adherents prove nothing *against* a doctrine." Freud had ample reasons to agree with that, and yet, for all of his dissatisfaction with his followers, he needed them to test his theories. He was a visionary; he did make a sustained attempt to spell out his vision; and he kept testing it by both continued self-analysis and his analysis of patients, as well as a good deal of reading. But he knew that all this was not enough; he also needed scholastics.

In sum, many visionaries do have fixed ideas that are not particularly fruitful; and many scholastics are by no means unimaginative drudges but perform tasks that are badly needed. The great visionary whose technical virtuosity compels our wonder does not have to be considered a mixed type. But there are intermediate types—scholastics who belong to a school and rely on its consensus but who also try to spell out some perceptions of their own. The size of this perception may vary, but in those who are not visionaries it falls short of a comprehensive vision that amounts to an alternative to the consensus. What people of this type see is often merely a new way of supporting the consensus of their school. In Einstein's words, it may be "a pretty ticklish job" in some cases to draw the line, but generally people of this type are best considered as scholastics. So far, then, we have two fundamental types.

3

Some periods are more scholastic than others. Scholasticism prevails whenever the leading figures in a field are to be found at schools, at colleges or universities.

Originally, the term "scholastics" referred to medieval philosophers who taught at schools, belonged to schools of thought, prized subtlety and rigor, and depended heavily on a consensus that they did not question. In many ways most twentieth-century philosophers—and professors in other fields as well—resemble them.

In the seventeenth and eighteenth centuries, however, the most memorable philosophers were visionaries who neither taught nor belonged to any school of thought; notably Francis Bacon, Hobbes, and Descartes; Spinoza, Locke, and Leibniz; Berkeley, Hume, and Rousseau. Kant was the first great modern philosopher who was a professor.

Kant was a visionary, but nobody could have known it until he was fifty-seven and had held a chair for eleven years. In many ways he was as timid as his vision was bold, and he had a terrible time trying to communicate his vision in a book. When he finally did, his prose looked like a parody of scholasticism. He seemed anxious to be more pedantic than the German schoolmen of his century and the scholastics of the Middle Ages. But his German successors quickly adopted his manner, and soon Hegel perfected the parody. In the nineteenth century most philosophers were professors, and many tried to write like Kant and Hegel. In our own time, many philosophers and literary critics, as well as some social scientists still do; for example, Jean-Paul Sartre in his philosophical tomes.

If we could only classify Kant and Hegel as scholastics, we would avoid a dichotomy in which all genius is on one side. In defense of such a move one could point out that both at times supported a consensus. Yet we cannot begin to understand either of these men until we see how each had a distinctive and exceptionally comprehensive vision that was importantly different from any consensus of their time. Neither of them relied on the agreement of professional colleagues or on a method shared by fellow workers in the field. Both were loners and spent their most creative years on a sustained attempt to spell out their visions.

Their scholastic critics and interpreters often fail to understand that Kant and Hegel felt sure they were right not so much on account of one or another argument but rather because they thought that they could see how all the major parts of their philosophies were connected and supported one another. It was partly for this reason that Kant did not take kindly to the well-meant suggestion that he might attenuate his moral rigorism to make his ethic gentler and a little more humane. The rigorism was required by what Hegel, a generation later, would have called "the system."

In the nineteenth century there were still a few major philosophers who were not professors of philosophy: John Stuart Mill and Nietzsche, for example. But in the twentieth century philosophy as well as the study of art, music, and religion, literature, and history became almost wholly academic. Since World War II ever more artists and poets, composers and novelists, have become academics, too. And most professors are scholastics.

4

It may seem to be an inevitable consequence of higher education for the masses that almost all the teachers have to be scholastics. The more students one tries to educate reasonably well, the more teachers one needs, and visionaries are rare.

Moreover, most visionaries require a good deal of solitude to retain a firm hold on their distinctive vision, and they generally prefer their creative work to teaching large numbers of students. Conversely, when they do immerse themselves in academic life and try to get along with large numbers of colleagues and students, they tend to become more and more scholastic.

A visionary could hardly feel at home in the academic milieu, as Spinoza knew when he declined an invitation to become a professor at Heidelberg, as Nietzsche found out before he resigned his chair of classical philology at Basel, and as Wittgenstein found out at Cambridge University. Those who neither decline nor resign are tempted constantly to make concessions to the prevalent scholasticism.

The consensus of the scholastics differs drastically from one school to another but is usually intolerant because one cannot concentrate on playing a game well if the rules are questioned continually. The visionary calls into question the whole framework within which the scholastics are trying to solve various puzzles. Or, to develop Einstein's metaphor, the visionary marks for chopping down the trees on which the creepers climb and thrive.

"Creepers" is a term with disparaging overtones that suggests the hostility of a great visionary to a caste he did not love. Synonyms have different associations but are hardly friendlier: "climbers," for example, or "ramblers." The German word Einstein used was *Schlingpflanzen*—plants that coil around trees like giant snakes that suffocate or crush their prey. *Schlingen* also means devouring greedily, and Einstein's total image shows how he thought of the creepers or climbers as parasites.

It is no wonder then that the scholastics should feel threatened by the visionaries—excepting those on whom they depend for their sustenance. The hostility is mutual. And it would be utterly unrealistic to suppose that visionaries generally are like Einstein. His charm and his humanity were as extraordinary as his genius.

The visionaries whom a school might consider hiring or promoting are almost always of an altogether different order of magnitude. Those who play the games favored by a given department, abide by the rules, and play exceptionally well can be judged highly competent. Those who disdain some of the rules or engage in altogether different enterprises, while considering the games played by the department with indifference or contempt, may simply be unsound, undisciplined, and incompetent. It is much less likely that one or another of these people has a vision that it would be worthwhile adding to one's offerings. The odds are against that. The safest procedure in hiring and promotions is to stick to what one knows well and can judge.

If a department is very broad-minded and eager to present its students with two or more alternatives, it will still be safer not to take a chance on visionaries. The obvious thing to do is to hire scholastics who belong to another school of thought and are recommended as highly competent representatives of that school. As a result, teachers who question the consensus of the dominant schools of thought in college departments are not likely to be hired or promoted unless they belong to rival schools of thought that have gained a wide following and therefore also respectability. Visionaries, being loners, do not stand much of a chance in academia.

To quote the conclusion of a short poem, "The Academic Zoo," from my *Cain and Other Poems*:

> Whatever spins web or cocoon
> is welcome, however jejune.
>> Butterfly
>> need not apply.

For the reasons given, this is not surprising. But it is startling at times to see how scholastics bury their own prophet under appreciations of the kind he loathed; how little feeling they show, more often than not, for his spirit; and how oblivious they are as a rule to his opinion of the games they play.

That Wittgenstein is a striking case in point is well known. Kierkegaard is another. It is not enough to note that most of those who write about him, or who translate him, appear to have no feeling for his mordant humor. Nor is it sufficient to imagine how he might have satirized the parsons and professors who contribute to the literature about him. Naturally, our university presses, who bear the brunt of scholarly publishing, must accept solid and stolid studies about Kierkegaard that he himself would have detested, provided only that such manuscripts are truly scholarly—as Kierkegaard was not. But suppose for a moment that Kierkegaard had submitted *The Concept of Dread* or *The Sickness unto Death*, or any number of his other books, to a good university press. They would certainly have been rejected.

Anyone as innovative, eccentric, and provocative as Kierkegaard could hardly hope to "make it" in the academic world. That is as true in our time as it was in Kierkegaard's. But even in the case of Kierkegaard, which is particularly glaring, few of the scholastics who have gathered round him seem to have much sense of that.

This contrast between visionaries and "creepers" is surely one of the most pervasive features of the life—or is it the death?—of the spirit. It is the curse of religion and one of the staples of humanities departments. William Butler Yeats, perhaps the greatest poet in the English language in this century, dealt with it in a twelve-line poem called

The Scholars

Bald heads forgetful of their sins,
Old, learned, respectable bald heads
Edit and annotate the lines
That young men, tossing on their beds,
Rhymed out in love's despair . . .
All think what other people think . . . .

This is not Yeats at his best, and he dulls the point by contrasting the old and young. If that were all, I should not dwell on the point here. A cynic might even suggest that this is not such a bad occupation for the old. But today most scholastics are young, and most of them make sure that their students and readers "think what other people think."

Those who have never been upset by all this do not know the poverty of higher education. It is easy to shut one's eyes to it and dwell on what looks good, or to laugh at the farce and drown in resignation. Yet all this is *not* inevitable. The dualistic typology presented so far is inadequate. We have to introduce a third type.

5

Socrates was no scholastic. He was a loner and questioned the common sense of his time. Yet he did not try to spell out a vision of his own. He made a point of not being a visionary and of being, in effect, an antischolastic. He examined the faith and morals of his time, ridiculed claims to knowledge that were based on an uncritical reliance on consensus, and exerted himself to show how ignorant, confused, and credulous most people are—including the most famous teachers, politicians, and popular oracles. Thus *Socrates embodied a third type.*

The most striking feature of this type is its concentration on criticism. But if I spoke of *critics*, visionaries, and scholastics, this might invite the misapprehension that most so-called critics who write about art and music, literature and films, exemplify this type. In fact, some are scholastics, and most of them are journalists.

Journalism is a profession, like teaching; and if we think of journalists in this sense, they are obviously not all of one type. But it may be useful to define *the journalist as a fourth type*, in line with the literal meaning of the term. So understood, the journalist writes for the day, for instant consumption, knowing that his wares have to be sold now or never because they will be stale tomorrow. He has no time for extensive research and no taste for the scholastic's rigor. Footnotes are not for him, while scholastics frequently discover when they check their sources once more to add footnotes that their facts require some correction. Hence scholastics, no less than visionaries, often feel contempt for journalists.

In his stage directions, near the beginning of Act IV of *The Doctor's Dilemma*, Bernard Shaw describes a journalist as

> a cheerful, affable young man who is disabled for ordinary business pursuits by a congenital erroneousness which renders him incapable of describing accurately anything he sees, or understanding or reporting accurately anything he hears. As the only employment in which these defects do not matter is journalism . . . , he has perforce become a journalist. . . .

If possible, Byron was even nastier in "English Bards and Scotch Reviewers" (lines 976ff.) when he spoke of

> A monthly scribbler of some low lampoon,
> Condemn'd to drudge, the meanest of the mean,
> And furbish falsehoods for a magazine, . . .
> Himself a living libel on mankind.

In Nietzsche's recurrent polemics against journalism we encounter another motif that is as important for the future of the humanities now as it was in his time. On January 16, 1872, he delivered the first of six public lectures in Basel, "On the Future of Our Educational Institutions." Near the end of this lecture he contrasted "the journalist, the servant of the moment," with the genius whom he called rather romantically "the redeemer from the moment." The theme sounded here at the beginning of Nietzsche's career is varied a year later in the brilliant title of his *Untimely Meditations.*

What is at stake for Nietzsche is his own vision of the philosopher as "a man of tomorrow and the day after tomorrow" who must stand "in contradiction to his today" (*Beyond Good and Evil*, section 212). Philosophers, he goes on to say, should be "the bad conscience of their time." And then Socrates is described as an exemplary philosopher who was a ruthless critic of his age.

Our concern here is with the humanities, whose point it is, at least in part, to provide us with perspectives on our time. This theme will have to be developed at length later on, but it must be introduced at the outset because in this way the ethos of the humanities is diametrically opposed to that of the journalist as a type. But for the present let us return to Shaw.

Shaw made an important point, though I take exception to "congenital erroneousness." The attitude in question is not really congenital but inculcated.

I remember being interviewed for a student newspaper when I was an undergraduate, newly arrived from Nazi Germany. I was appalled by what struck me as utterly pointless inaccuracies and especially the young man's defense of his placing in quotes all sorts of statements I had not made. He assured me that quotation marks made things more interesting and that it was important to break up a story every now and then with quotes.

The ethos of the journalist as a type, alongside the visionary, scholastic, and Socratic type, is to provide copy that looks interesting and readable at first blush but is not expected to stand up on close examination, much less a few years later. This ethos is widespread enough to be worth discussing here; and many of us also know people who exemplify this ethos in conversation.

Many professors in the humanities as well as the sciences consider it an important part of their job to wean their students from this dirty habit and housebreak them. In this respect many scholastic and Socratic teachers are at one.

When we read stories in even the best of newspapers about events that we have personally witnessed, we find almost always that there are many inaccuracies and that the reporter's or the editor's attitude was not far different from that of the undergraduate journalist. Having read Shaw, one is frequently reminded of his comments. But people who make lists of the leading intellectuals of their society and end up largely with the names of people who either edit or contribute frequently to journals are not thinking of reporters . . . .

Journalism and scholasticism may seem to be opposites. The scholastic values rigor and being sound, the journalist speed and being interesting. Yet there are journalistic scholastics—professors who write for journals, which may range all the way from *The New Yorker* to so-called scholarly journals. And what, it may be asked, is wrong with that?

Nothing. Not all people who are journalists by profession belong to the type under consideration here; much less do all people who sometimes write for journals. What matters is the ethos.

Those who make a living writing for a journal can have the highest standards of accuracy, though this would be sure to make their life very hard. And some who never write for journals have very little intellectual integrity. Moreover, sometimes—although much more rarely than most people seem to think—speed is indeed of the essence, and a report must be published in a hurry without time for much checking and double-checking.

What needs to be noted is that the ethos of those who do not care how the things they fashion in a hurry will stand up in thirty years is very different from that of a historian like Thucydides who had the ambition to create "a possession for all time," or a philosopher like Nietzsche who hoped to be "born posthumously." Many scholastics write on timely topics for scholarly journals, making a great show of rigor, although they have no hope whatsoever that their publications might endure for thirty years, or even ten; and upon close inspection the rigor is often merely apparent and the wares are as shoddy as at first glance they seemed solid.

The journalistic orientation poses an immense threat to the future of the humanities. Some old-fashioned humanists felt that whatever was not worth reading ten times was not worth reading at all. They concentrated on books that had survived for centuries, and they ignored what seemed ephemeral—often even science, because it kept changing. The predilection of journalistic teachers for what is "news" and their concern with the latest fads endangers the conservation of the greatest works of the human spirit. More and more students graduate from college having read a lot of recent articles and books that but a short while later are as dated and forgotten as are most of last year's headlines. Meanwhile, even art historians rarely know the Bible.

6

It should be clear why I speak of the Socratic type and not of critics. If we spoke of critics, we would have to distinguish at least two types: the Socratic and the journalistic critic. These two are plainly antithetical.

Socrates insisted that his wisdom consisted in his awareness of his ignorance, while most of those considered wise in his time claimed to know what in fact they did not know. It was part of his mission, as he himself defined it according to the *Apology*, to expose the ignorance of those who were considered wise and the spuriousness of their claim to knowledge.

The journalist, as defined here, claims to know what he does not know—and in some cases even what he knows not to be so, as when he places statements in quotation marks because that looks more interesting. Socrates maintained that even the most pious and defensible beliefs could never justify confusions or bad arguments. What he impressed upon posterity, by way of some of Plato's works in which he appears as a character, was the need for intellectual integrity. But when we examine his own arguments closely, we find that he often fell short of his own standards, sometimes because he enjoyed making fools of others.

What I mean by the Socratic type is the type committed to the rigorous examination of the faith and morals of the time, giving pride of place to those convictions which are widely shared and rarely questioned. Reliance on consensus and prestigious paradigms are prime targets. There may be an element of perversity in all this. However that may be, for people of this type it is a point of honor to swim against the stream.

There have been many famous visionaries, and scholastics as well as journalists come in large numbers. But Socrates may have been the only very famous exemplar of the unalloyed Socratic type. Later teachers of this kind have found no Plato. Teachers who have no vision of their own and do not write are often fondly and admiringly remembered by their students without attaining lasting fame.

It is crucially important to recognize this type as a viable alternative to the visionary and scholastic. Most teachers will never achieve lasting fame in any case, and many, after due reflection on the main alternatives, might well opt for this ethos.

Moreover, the Socratic tendency has appeared in a variety of blends. . . . For our purposes it will be quite sufficient to distinguish four kinds of minds, provided we recall that pure types are the exception. Moreover, one might suppose that while journalists and visionaries can be found in many fields, only philosophers can be scholastic or Socratic. . . . Philosophers have no monopoly on either type. The Socratic probing of the faith and morals of the age and the Socratic ridicule of the most celebrated oracles—including those it is not fashionable to attack—are not by any means prerogatives of the philosophers. To be sure, philosophy could contribute a great deal along this line, but so can novelists and poets, artists and teachers in other fields—as well as men and women who are by profession journalists.

7

Recognition of these four types could make a tremendous difference in higher education. It is pointless to criticize scholastics for not being visionaries. Such criticism is sterile and can hardly produce innovation. Moreover, a faculty consisting largely of visionaries would be a nightmare. But one can fault a faculty for being insufficiently Socratic and for not communicating the Socratic ethos to its students.

It is essential for us to realize that being a scholastic is not the only respectable alternative to being a great visionary. The Socratic option is not often spelled out clearly, but when something of the sort is done, the scholastics sometimes plead that this is not their job.

This is a very curious notion. Its obvious meaning is: This is not what we get paid for. There is some truth in that.

Academic freedom developed in the nineteenth century in Germany, where the professors were civil servants, paid by the state. They were granted "academic" freedom, meaning that they were free to teach their subject matter as they wished, provided they refrained from questioning the faith, morals, and politics of their society. Their freedom was thus strictly academic; and being Socratic was emphatically not what they were paid for.

In a sense, then, the retort that this is not our job is true. But only the meanest hirelings will be content—or should be content—to tailor their conception of their task as professors to the wishes of the state or those from whom the money comes with which they happen to be paid. More than almost anybody else, tenured professors can define their own job, and they are in an excellent position to persuade society of their conception of their task. Actually, it is the professors to whom we owe the current prestige of the scholastic conception. It is the professors who have sold this conception to the public, without ever reflecting deeply on alternatives.

The claim that the cultivation of a Socratic ethos is not their job must be met with the following questions. First: Is the job worth doing? And then, if it is worth doing: Is there any other group that is better qualified by training and position to do it? And finally, if there is not: Are we doing something so much more important that it would be irresponsible of us to take on this job?

Let us try to answer all three questions, beginning with the first: Is the job worth doing? The best approach to it is concrete and historical.

8

Through the first third of this century, Germany was a model of higher education and professionalism. Many Americans went to German universities to obtain a Ph.D., and the American graduate schools, which are still with us in the last third of the century, were developed in the German image. In the 1920s physicists from all over the world went to Göttingen to study there.

In the 1930s the German universities became the perfect paradigm of the moral bankruptcy of pure professionalism. Most of the leading German scholars failed to question the faith, morals, and politics of their society. After all, that was not their job. It was not what they got paid for. And their students, taught by internationally famous scholars, were even more uncritically enthusiastic about the new faith, morals, and politics of the Nazi state than their less educated fellow citizens. The students had never been taught to apply to faith, morals, and politics the standards of conscientiousness of which scholastics are so proud. On the contrary, they had been taught a kind of two-world doctrine, and faith and morals—or in one word, values—were believed to be immune against critical scrutiny. The domain of values had become a refuge for prejudice and passion.

The two dominant Western philosophies of the 1920s—existentialism and positivism—are still dominant half a century later. Although they may seem to be diametrically opposite and their partisans see them as antithetical, both schools agree in their profoundly, but extremely unprofound, anti-Socratic ethos. Both confine reason to the world of facts and leave the realm of faith, morals, and politics to emotion, passion, and irrational decisons.

This anti-Socratic ethos need not put on philosophic airs. Legions of professors who would never call themselves positivists or existentialists still share the consensus that their job is to teach their specialty, and that academic competence and excellence depend on more and ever more specialization. Our modern scholastics often insist that faith and morals are best left to preachers. But on reflection this makes no sense. What special expertise do preachers have? Why should we listen to them? Where scholars fear to tread, demagogues rush in.

Socrates' job needs doing. The conflicting faiths, moral codes, and ideologies of our time badly need thoughtful examination. No group is better qualified and in a better position to do this job than the tenured faculties of colleges and universities. If they have no time for the Socratic task, it is idle to hope that the job will be done well elsewhere.

9

The question remains whether the job actually done by most professors teaching the humanities is more important. If so, it might still be the lesser evil to leave Socrates' job undone. People who are not professors might well say that the very question is ridiculous and that what most professors teaching the humanities are doing is downright trivial by comparison. But people who are not scholars may not be reliable judges of what is trivial and what is not.

It seems reasonable to distinguish form and content at this point. The content of much work in the humanities *is*, I think, trivial compared to the Socratic undertaking; but the discipline acquired in the course of such work can nevertheless be invaluable. This is an important point that will require more attention in the chapter "Vision Can Be Taught, But. . . ."

The question facing us is not whether it would be better for all professors to be scholastics or for all of them to be Socratic. Since World War II our faculties have become more and more scholastic, and the question is whether we can afford the extinction of the Socratic ethos. I am arguing that we cannot, but his obviously does not commit me to the notion that it would be best if this were the only type represented on our faculties. Those who plead against the extinction of whales are not implying that it would be best if there were nothing but whales in the oceans.

Of course, my interest in the survival of the Socratic type is prompted by a deep concern not for mere variety but for the future of the humanities. The point is not that it would be a great pity if we had one type less than we used to have; it is rather that *the humanities require a mix in which the Socratic type is an indispensable ingredient.*

One might compare the Socratic ethos to salt or pepper, suggesting that without it the diet becomes flat and tasteless, although a diet of nothing but salt or pepper would be worse. But this image is misleading in many ways. As the example of Germany shows, what is at stake is not a mere matter of taste. Nor is it enough to leaven a large faculty with one or two Socratic teachers. We need many.

It does not follow that each should abandon his own field to become what poor polemicists occasionally call "a self-appointed critic of the age." As if this were a calling to which one could also be appointed by someone else! In any case a Socratic teacher does not sit in judgment on a throne above the contest. The Socratic ethos is to probe and question. And it would be well if some of those appointed to professorships felt that it was part of their job to do this, each in his own field.

In whose field are values, faiths, moral codes, and ideologies? If they did not lean over backwards to eschew Socrates' heritage, professors of philosophy and religion, literature and art, history as well as politics and economics, sociology and anthropology, would surely find themselves confronted with such topics in their own fields. Without taking time out to master computers or gain some other newly fashionable expertise, they could explore with their students some especially compelling alternatives to current fashions. In the process they might ask how various orthodoxies of our time look from the outside, how well grounded our common sense and all sorts of scholastic as well as nonacademic consensuses are, and what might be said for and against each alternative.

To be exhaustive is, of course, impossible, but students could be trained in the examination of a few particularly interesting and important alternatives. They could also be taught to look for alternatives. They could be imbued with a Socratic ethos.

Socratic teachers do not have to be visionaries. They do not need to develop views of their own. Teaching social philosophy, for example, a Socratic teacher might begin by having the students read Dostoevsky's "Grand Inquisitor," then Tolstoy's *My Religion*, T. S. Eliot's *The Idea of a Christian Society*, and Milton's *Areopagitica*. The students would be confronted with powerful and eloquent statements of radically divergent views. They would be free, of course, to agree with any of the authors read but would soon discover that they could not very well agree with many of them. They would be led to question the views presented to them—as well as their own views and the common sense of their parents, their friends, their society.

Teaching comparative religion or the history of philosophy, a Socratic teacher might exert himself to bring to life each view—each vision—that is studied, lending it his own voice, and confront the students with a series of challenges.

The Socratic ethos is critical, but in many courses it would be implemented best by teachers who excel at sympathetic understanding. Precisely those lacking a powerful vision of their own that requires detailed development might find a sense of fulfillment in bringing to life the visions of others. But the point would not be purely histrionic or aesthetic. The central motive would be to question our orthodoxies and the students' views now from this point of view and now from that—and to question each of these alternative points of view from the others. A strenuous task? Yes. A rewarding and exciting one that the students would both enjoy and profit from? Yes. A task for which one needs to be a visionary? No. A task that one could *learn* to perform? Yes.

By way of contrast, a scholastic teacher who was a Thomist might assign selections from the writings of St. Thomas, supplemented by some Maritain and some contemporary Thomists. A Marxist might assign selections from Karl Marx and Frederich Engels, Lenin, and some contemporary Marxists. An analytical philosopher might look for an anthology or two of recent articles by analytical philosophers. In a seminar a scholastic might choose parts of one major work and supplement that with some recent articles discussing it.

A journalistic teacher would choose readings that have been much in the news of late: *The Greening of America* (1970) perhaps in the early seventies, but certainly no longer in the mid-seventies. The issues, too, would be picked in accordance with current fashion.

Actually, a Socratic teacher might also choose a fashionable text, but only to show what was wrong with it. In fact, any text can be studied scholastically, Socratically, or journalistically. The scholastic will teach one approach and—deliberately or unwittingly—try to indoctrinate the students, if only regarding the right way of doing things. The journalist will be most concerned to be interesting, exciting, and up to date—and will leave the students with nothing much worth remembering. The Socratic teacher will stress the need for critical evaluation of alternatives and continued self-examination.

Each of the three types can be exciting or boring, and a great deal depends on a teacher's personality. Most teachers certainly teach their students very little, if anything, that is remembered ten years later, and some teachers are loved for little more than their enthusiasm. Some professors are frustrated actors, and a few of these teach literature and spend a fair amount of time reading parts of plays to their students, taking all the parts. It would serve no purpose to expand our typology to accommodate this type. Yet teachers of this kind may open the eyes of some of their students to Shakespeare or Molière, or even to plays or poetry in general.

10

Visionaries are not necessarily particularly good teachers. They often come to feel that they have no time for the views of others—especially views that they consider obviously inferior to their own—and when they do discuss rival positions their heart isn't in it. As long as their vision is maturing, they may be excellent at taking students along on their voyages of discovery. But once they have spelled out their own positions, they are frequently far less effective teachers than are younger men and women who have no positions to defend. . . .

Of course, one could design an educational system that would make things easier for visionaries. Until well after World War II there was relatively little room for discussion in the German universities. German professors gave lectures, and the German word for lectures is *Vorlesungen*, which means readings. German professors read their works in progress to their students. This gave them an opportunity to present their vision, or what the philosophers called their system. The students had no opportunity to raise questions, nor were the lectures coordinated with discussions of reading assignments. This method of teaching would have been highly problematic even if most of the professors had been visionaries. It was thoroughly authoritarian and did not foster a critical spirit.

Moreover, even professiors who did have a system were not necessarily visionaries. To quote from "The Academic Zoo" once more:

> Most birds soar through the ether, but
> since peacocks cannot fly they strut.

When the Nazis came to power in 1933, a student who later emigrated to the United States and became a famous philosopher was writing his doctoral dissertation in Berlin under the supervision of a Jewish professor who decided to accept a call to the University of Istanbul. The student had to ask another professor at the University of Berlin to serve as one of his examiners. Herr Geheimrat Professor

Dr. Maier has no claim to fame except for his role in this story. Before the student could be examined by the Herr Geheimrat, he had to master "Herr Geheimrat's system." Since this could not be done quickly by way of the lectures, the student took private lessons with one of Herr Geheimrat's assistants. Whenever he asked her a question, she would answer: "In Herr Geheimrat's system everything meshes with everything, and you cannot understand any part until you understand the whole." When the student finally was ready to take his exam, Herr Geheimrat did precisely what he would have done if Kierkegaard had invented the whole story. He died. And his system died with him.

The Socratic ethos stands opposed to this sort of vanity, but it may be thought to foster relativism. In fact, it does not. It nurtures a critical spirit and immunizes students against the facile notion that any view is as good, or bad, as any other. Students are taught to distinguish clearly untenable views from the few positions that appear to be defensible.

Socrates' heirs reject relativism no less than dogmatism; they aim to show how most views are untenable. But they are not committed to refuting all views or to finding all they reject equally bad. Some solutions of a problem are more confused and inconsistent than others; some are only slightly flawed; and one, or perhaps two or three, may be acceptable. It is worth remembering that Socrates had standards for which he was quite willing to die, and he was far from supposing that any norm or argument or book is every bit as good as any other.

The students of a Socratic teacher will realize that he is neither a relativist nor a dogmatist, and that he does not consider it his mission in life to teach them "the Truth." Instead they learn to avoid all sorts of mistakes, and a Socratic teacher should be able to quote the words of Socrates at the end of Plato's *Theaetetus*:

> If you should ever conceive again . . . your budding thoughts should be better as a result of this scrutiny; but if you remain barren, you will be gentler and kinder to your companions, having the good sense not to fancy that you know what you do not know. . . .

Why, then, has the Socratic teacher become a rarity? One might suppose that scholastics would appreciate the Socratic rigor. They do—as long as it stops short of their consensus, their know-how and know-what.

This should not surprise us, and yet it is strange when one recalls how during the first half of the twentieth century "Socratic" was a term of praise for teachers, especially in the United States, and Socrates' hyperbolic claim that "the un-examined life is not worth living" was one of the most popular slogans in the academic world. What happened?

11

In the United States the turning point coincided with the McCarthy period after World War II when it became politically unsafe to question the consensus. It became ever safer to become increasingly scholastic. Sad to say, most academics are timid conformists. Many go into teaching because schools provide a sheltered atmosphere and more security than is to be found anywhere else. Having finished school, they do not want to leave. If possible, this last point applied even more in the United Kingdom than in the United States. Yet the growth of scholasticism is worldwide, and this explanation is insufficient.

In the Communist world the Socratic ethos had no place in any case and was never tolerated in the universities. In the rest of the world the most crucial fact was that after World War II higher education was extended to far greater numbers of students than ever before. It ceased to be a privilege to which a few were entitled, and became highly competitive. Rather suddenly, masses of new teachers were needed, and in the process academia became infinitely more professional, scholastic, and anti-Socratic.

Students became more concerned about examinations, and professors about publications. Neither had much time left for Socratic questioning. It is no accident that Socrates did not prepare his students to take tests, and that he did not publish anything. It does not follow that one could not devise Socratic essay questions for examination, and books can certainly breathe a Socratic spirit. But it is easy to see why most tests were un-Socratic and based on a consensus, and why the masses of new teachers published scholastic articles.

Not being visionaries, they could not spell out in print a vision of their own. And since they did not see much, it is not surprising that so many of them took to writing lengthy papers on small points. The old German doctoral dissertation became the model for scholarly publications. It was supposed to be a contribution to knowledge, nothing Socratic. And since most teachers could not make any large contribution, microscopism grew by leaps and bounds.

This development is ubiquitous throughout academia. A few brief illustrations will show what we are up against.

In the 1950s most philosophy departments in the United States had two standard courses that were required of all philosophy majors and a boon to students interested in taking no more than a little philosophy. One dealt with ancient philosophy, the other with modern philosophy, from Descartes to Kant. Gradually, this sequence has disappeared at most colleges and universities. More and more professors came to feel that they lacked expert knowledge to cover so much ground; and the papers they must publish to obtain professional advancement could at most deal with a single problem in one book by one philosopher. Moreover, almost all philosophical journals came to prefer nonhistorical articles. Increasingly, people became more interested in the future than in the past. By 1970, anyone teaching a course that dealt with three or four philosophers was likely to be asked whether it would not be better to devote a whole course to one of them, and more specifically to one or at most two works by him. The historical courses still offered have become more and more unhistorical, and Socratic comparisons of different views together with the questioning of our present common sense has given way to ever more technical discussions of ever smaller points.

Once this development has gained momentum, the Socratic critic is experienced as a threat by the scholastics whose consensus he is calling into question. They feel much less menaced by scholastics of another school of thought, for the ethos of other scholastics is much more like their own.

What we encounter in other fields is very similar. In literature departments the so-called new criticism has had its day, but it served as the vanguard of a microscopic and anti-Socratic professional orientation. One ceased to care about poets or novelists as human beings, about their world views or their perhaps withering critiques of their society—or, by extension, ours—and instead of this one traced their imagery or details of their diction. Not to see the forest for the trees in it became a virtue, and the study of a single leaf came to be thought of as superior still.

In religion two examples from a single department may suffice. One professor had begun his career with a book on the relevance of the Hebrew prophets, but in the last years before his retirement he got grants for studies of weights and measures in the Bible. A younger colleague whose first book had dealt with Martin Buber and the I-Thou relationship turned to analysis of arguments about the old scholastic arguments for God's existence.

Of course, it does not follow that the early books were better than the later articles. There is a great deal to be said for careful craftsmanship. But the change of orientation remains striking.

One could multiply examples from all humanities departments. One could even say that they are doing their best to cease to be humanities. They have come to eschew the study of humanity and the critical examination of our values, faith, and moral notions.

Something important has been lost. It would be silly to claim that many people used to do superbly what hardly any do at all today. I am not trying to eulogize the dead past. The question is what we should attempt in the future.

12

It can hardly be denied that the prestige of the scholastics has grown enormously since World War II while that of the Socratic ethos has declined. Yet there is room for conflicting interpretations. Some observers would say that the humanities are dying, perhaps even that they are committing suicide. Others would insist that respectability depends on being scientific, or that progress does, and that the notion of humanities departments as an equal branch besides social science, and natural science departments is antiquated. Either way the humanities would have no future.

The most relevant questions, however, are rarely asked. Diagnosticians have often operated with highly misleading categories, as if the question confronting a professor were whether he wished to be a prophet and thus a fraud or a hard-working professional who contributes to progress in his discipline by finding his models in the sciences. There is some presumption among scholastics that whatever is of interest to people outside one's specialty can hardly be respectable and must be journalistic. Being unable to follow the papers published by mathematicians, one tries to publish articles that will be almost equally incomprehensible to all but a few colleagues. One simply fails to ask what alternatives are available, what kind of progress has actually been made since World War II, whether Socrates' job needs doing, and who is to do it.

The typology offered here should permit a better diagnosis. In the sciences, too, there are a few visionaries and legions of scholastics. Humanities professors, disclaiming visionary and prophetic powers, have modeled themselves not on the great scientists—nor would it make much sense to try to be an Einstein or a Newton—but on scientific scholastics, with dubious success. In the process much of their work has become trivial. It is arguable that the work of most humanities professors has always been trivial, and that it is only the numbers of the teachers and the volume of their publications that have mushroomed. But what has increased no less is the presumption, the loss of self-perception, the delusions of grandeur about progress, about a revolution in philosophy, and about working on the frontiers of knowledge.

The agencies and the foundations that give grants to professors have for the most part swallowed this bombast. After all, they must rely on the expert advice of professors. Applicants for grants have long learned that a project that layment can understand is not likely to be funded, any more than a paper that laymen could read is likely to be printed in a professional journal. The way to demonstrate one's competence is to be technical. By the time one has one's doctorate, all this is second nature. Again, the dissertation is the paradigm.

When one is asked what one is working on, it is embarrassing to give an answer to a colleague that would not have stood up when one was working on a doctor's thesis or that would not do when one applies for a foundation grant. A Socratic answer would be a ridiculous as a visionary reply. The thing to do is to mention something small and technical, and what makes the best impression is a topic so refined that the questioner could not possibly hope to understand it short of a lengthy explanation—and perhaps not even then.

Thus thousands of professors were thriving while the humanities were dying. Only in the late 1960s was there a brief revolt.

13

The revolt was led by students who noted the desiccation and dehumanization of the humanities and social sciences. They could hardly be blamed for not grasping very well what had happened. Their demand for "relevance" was understandable, but their interpretation of that slogan was for the most part very crude and anti-intellectual. They spoke much of unmasking the establishment, but never succeeded because the fiendish conspiracy that they wished to expose did not exist. But without realizing it, they did unmask the conformism and timidity of many professors who, lacking any clear conception of their calling, aimed to please.

It would lead too far afield at this point to attempt any detailed analysis of the students' claims, the professors' reactions, and the changes made as a result. But one way in which a great many professors aimed to please ought to be mentioned. They became "relevant" in their spare time, orating about morals and politics without professional constraints, without professional rigor, without professional conscience. The point was to demonstrate a *social* conscience and to show that one's heart was in the right place—or rather on the left. But the conviction that the realm of faith, morals, and politics was the domain of passion and emotion was not questioned, and many scholastics saw nothing wrong in principle with the students' inference that the best way to demonstrate the depth of one'e emotion and to bring about results was to use force.

It would have been a miracle if the changes brought about in this way had happened to be wise. It is no wonder that so many of them were extremely ill considered. Understandably, there was a protest against excessive emphasis on examinations and on publications. The result in many places was a drastic lowering of standards and a further decline of the humanities. In some universities in Europe faculty ranks were swelled with young mediocrities who, as was soon discovered, but too late to remedy the situation, left no openings for brilliant students. Elsewhere, from Berlin to Adelaide, faculty as well as students argued that political tests were more important for faculty appointments than academic qualifications. For the students a great many requirements were dropped, including not only a lot of examinations but also so-called distribution requirements that had formerly prevented at least extremes of specialization. In the wake of the revolts, specialization at the graduate level increased more than ever.

The more and more popular option of writing papers instead of taking examinations would make more sense if students were required to learn how to write. Most of them do not know how, and most of their teachers do not know how to write either, except articles for scholarly journals that are not meant to be comprehensible to anyone but a few colleagues with the same specialty.

To some extent the student revolutions were directed against some of the evils of scholasticism. But in the absence of any halfway adequate diagnosis of the situation—lacking the very concept of scholasticism, not to speak of the Socratic ethos—the rebels only made scholasticism worse.

14

The notion that the humanities are dying of desiccation and inanition may seem questionable. There is wide agreement—a consensus—that specialization is good and that only fellow specialists can judge the work being done. And scholastics are often very enthusiastic about the work of their peers and friends. Frogs approve of croaking.

It is idle to pit metaphors against each other or to debate the merits of what is being done. But it is important to note what is *not* being done.

Some scholastics are unquestionably very good at what they do, and if you ask other scholastics they will testify to that. But there are also many things that they either do not do or do badly; for example, three.

First, they do not cultivate Socrates' ethos. When they deal at all with faith and substantive moral and political questions, they usually do it after hours, often emotionally and usually irresponsibly. Owing to their two-world doctrine, they seem to have checked their reason and professional conscience at the gate before entering this realm.

Second, the scholastics generally lack the category of the You, of the human being who has dimensions (in Shylock's phrase). When they write about visionaries this usually leads to farcical misunderstandings. Typically, the scholastic has no sense of context, least of all the human context, from which sentences and concepts gain their meaning, nor do scholastics realize that the context precludes many meanings. Whether St. Thomas quotes Scripture or a modern scholastic analyzes a text by Kant or by some poet or perhaps a picture, the spectacle is basically the same. One deals with a helpless object that can be used and not with a You, a human document that confronts and challenges us. (This point will be developed in the next chapter.) It is exceedingly ironical that many scholastics took up the slogan of the student rebels who claimed that "the establishment" had no respect for persons and dehumanized us, with realizing how they themselves were advancing this process and dehumanizing the humanities as well as their students.

Third, the scholastics generally lack perspective and fail to see *larger* contexts. Their lack of a historical sense and their inability to see the historical context of their own school and of its point of view are merely examples of this. Their attitude toward their specialty furnishes another crucial illustration.

At a conference on Machiavelli or on philosophy of language it is no longer startling to find that even top scholars who specialize in political theory or theory of knowledge and who have read and taught the basic materials cannot follow the lectures and discussions because they revolve around some recent articles that are never identified and summarized. This is no longer felt to be a lack of basic courtesy; it is widely considered an essential ingredient of professionalism. The scholastics fail to see how such practices facilitate an uncritical reliance on a narrow consensus. They disparage attempts to make things clear for those who do not share the same specialty, although such attempts are really invaluable because they force us to step back sufficiently to see the context of our specialty and to become aware of our assumptions. When trying to explain something to fellow scholars in another field, or to any intelligent and critical person, one generally learns a great deal. In their serious work, scholastics prefer to address only those who agree with them on essentials. As a result we are losing a whole dimension of discourse.

Some scholastics dabble in journalism after hours, writing things that can be understood by specialists in other fields and by educated laymen. But these excursions do not have the same importance either in their own eyes or in fact as their attempts to make contributions to their specialties. Thus their writing in this vein is of a piece with the sophomoric notion that interdisciplinary courses should be relegated to the sophomore level, as if only highly specialized work could be serious.

In fact, many of the problems most important for humanity . . . demand an interdisciplinary approach. Those who deal with them only from the point of view of their specialty, whether that should be French literature, physiology, or linguistic philosophy, confine themselves to triviality. Those who really wish to work on the frontiers of knowledge must cross the frontiers of their departments.

15

. . . My typology is not designed to classify children or applicants for college admissions, any more than soldiers, politicians, or neurotics. I have not yet discussed the conditions that might favor the development of visionaries, but it is worth noting that great visionaries have hardly ever been children of visionaries. Journalists are surely made and not born. I have commented on four types but concentrated on two, the scholastic and the Socratic. Neither of these two is innate or hereditary, and whether we get large numbers of either of these types depends on the education we offer.

Both types are encountered on the faculties of colleges and universities. Since World War II, higher education in most countries has produced unprecedented numbers of scholastics, and scholastic college teachers have increased by leaps and bounds while the percentage of Socratic teachers has decreased to the point where this type might become extinct. During the same period insufficient thought has been given to the questions whether this development is desirable and inevitable. I have tried to show in some detail that it is neither desirable nor inevitable.

One could expand this typology to make it more generally applicable. The term "visionary" could be retained, but instead of "scholastics" one might in that case speak of "technicians," and instead of the "Socratic type" one might after all speak of "critics," making it clear that what is meant is not the caste of professional reviewers. Then one could say that for certain jobs one needs technicians, while for some others it is desirable to find people with some vision, and for yet others those with a critical talent. Still, it would be pernicious, I think, to try to classify people along these lines before they embark on higher education and to push them into this channel or that. The point of my typology is not to make it easier to push people around but rather to make them aware of alternatives to enable them to choose this path or that with their eyes open.

Obviously, good technicians are preferable to bad critics. Yet André Gide had a point when he said in his journal for *The Counterfeiters:* "To disturb is my function. The public always prefers to be reassured. There are those whose job this is. There are only too many."

If most professors were like Gide, or if they were visionaries, our problems would be very different from what they are now. Anyone contemplating the future of the humanities today must start with the realization that scholasticism has become prevalent, and that for legions of professors their work is, in Einstein's phrase, a kind of "sport," if not a game, or a racket.

Perhaps another metaphor will prove more helpful. Most humanities professors are engaged in the analysis of a few chess moves, often moves by players who are not much better than *they* are. A few scholastics are very good at such analyses, and now and then one actually succeeds in discovering a new move.

For playing a whole game, life is felt to be too short. But it is arguable that life is too short to spend one's time analyzing a few chess moves or even to devote one's most creative hours to playing chess. If some people wish to spend their lives that way, let them be; but when this way of life is held up to generations of students as the best way of developing their talents, it is time to ask if this is not a death in life. With all due respect for the finest players and the most brilliant analysts, the enterprises at which they excel are not the greatest of which human beings are capable. If these are the only role models that we present to our students, higher education ceases to be humanistic or humane.

The idea behind my topology is not to ring variations on the contrast between visionaries and technicians. My intent is even less to lament the dearth of visionaries. The point is more nearly to show how threadbare and pernicious this dualistic scheme is, and how the Socratic type represents a viable alternative. The scholastic notion that for young academics who are not great visionaries there is only one respectable alternative is wrong and harmful.

Of course, not every teacher is cut out to be another Socrates; but neither will everyone become another Bobby Fischer. If the highest peaks of excellence are out of our reach, we still have a choice between ideals. What we desperately need is more reflection on alternatives. For a long time we have bred mainly two types, the scholastic and the journalistic.

WORK, LABOUR, AND UNIVERSITY EDUCATION

Peter Herbst

The central idea of this paper is to apply a distinction of Hannah Arendt's[1] to the educational scene; the distinction is between work and labour. The thesis is briefly that education is work rather than labour, and that to educate well is to work, as well as to teach people to work. Some critical conclusions will then be drawn about contemporary education and some unflattering remarks made about contemporary universities.

From *The Philosophy of Education,* ed. R. S. Peters, © Oxford University Press, 1973 (pp. 58-74). Reprinted by permission of the author and Oxford University Press.

A revised version of a paper, first written in 1967 as a contribution to a symposium on education in the Australian National University.

The work-labour distinction may be interpreted as an application of certain theories in the philosophy of action. The relevant investigations have mainly occupied continental philosophers, existentialists, and phenomenologists for instance. The Marxists and neo-Wittgensteinians have also contributed. The theme of these philosophers is that human actions are subject to certain characteristic defects which make them less characteristically actions and which make the agents less characteristically human. Such defects are variously called alienation, bad faith, viscosity, anomie, and so on. People who elect life-styles which involve them in habitually defective action are sometimes said to lack authenticity, or to be de-humanized.

Roughly speaking, work is conceived to be a species of unalienated action, labour is activity tending to alienation. (It must be conceded from the outset that the distinction between work and labour cannot be made very sharp. More than one criterion for distinguishing them will need to be introduced, and there will be cases which will answer to one criterion, but not to another.)

Work and labour have this in common, that they consume the time and energies of people, and that, being directed to a purpose, they may be done more or less quickly, or more or less competently, or more or less conscientiously, and so on. Also, and for these reasons, both work and labour tend to exclude other human pursuits. They call for a certain discipline or self-direction, and so, whether you work, or whether you labour at a task, you cannot at the same time make love or engage in sport.

Both work and labour are commonly directed to production, though not everything which is produced is a commodity, or a negotiable possession. For present purposes we must subsume the provision of services, and the tasks of planning, administration, and exchange under the heading of production, even though, in an obvious sense, much labour is quite unproductive. An instance is the labour which is expended in the service of the war-industry.

The products of work are works. I am sorry that the only available English word is so weak and colourless. I shall use the Latin word 'opus' instead. The opus, as I conceive it, is the point of the workman's work; if the opus is well done, he has not worked in vain. I shall argue that in order to work well, a workman needs to love or value that at which he works and if so, he aims at good workmanship. The excellence of an opus will be sharply distinguished from its instrumental goodness, and in particular, from its propensity to procure satisfaction for consumers. At the same time it is not denied that in objects which belong to a telic species, what counts as their excellence may depend on their telos. For instance, because a chair may be defined as something for sitting on, being comfortable is a virtue in chairs.

The satisfaction of consumers is not a measure of the excellence of a product. This seems pretty evident, particularly if the consumers themselves have been exposed to sales talk. Thus efficient advertising induces consumers positively to prefer shoddy to good workmanship, and sometimes, to regard all goods as being made purely for consumption, so that, unlovely and unmemorable, they will have served their turn, if, by being consumed, they perish.

Palmström, a creation of the German poet Morgenstern , did not share this attitude. He had a handkerchief of such exquisite beauty and workmanship, that, meaning to blow his nose in it, he was overawed by its grandeur. The handkerchief was re-folded, the nose betrayed. I mention him because he illustrates the mistaken idea that if the telos of an opus is not utilitarian satisfaction, the object must become a mere museum piece.

Labour is toil, labour is hardship. It is the price which we pay for whatever advantages the rewards of labour will buy. A typist who neither understands nor cares for the material which she is typing, is hired to work in an office. She accepts the inconvenience of having to perform an uncongenial task for the sake of keeping body and soul together and for the sake of the activities and amusements which her wages and her social contacts at work bring within her reach. If she could obtain these advantages without having to type, that would be better, but typing is better than foregoing the advantages. It is a ledger-calculation.

Labour may in some circumstances cause us to have pleasurable experiences, and very commonly, it puts us into a position to buy pleasures. But, if it is not justified puritanically, as the *aspera* which are involved in the pursuit of *astra*, it must be justified by the pleasures or satisfactions to which it is a means. Work need not similarly cause or give us pleasure; congenial work on the contrary *is* a pleasure. The pleasure consists in doing the work, not in some consequence, or state of mind, produced by the work. The pleasure of labour on the other hand (if any) is always extrinsic to it.

The view of happiness on which the argument relies is Aristotelian. Happiness *consists in* activities: it is not compounded of pleasures which are *produced by* activities. Activities conceived as pleasure-producers are labour. Activities conceived as happiness-constituents are work.

Labour is contingently related to its product. Artifacts of the same kind may be produced by radically different productive processes. Human labour may be made more productive, more efficient, by being aided or even supplanted by machines. The process of production and the product are conceptually distinct. Many process-workers do not even know to what product their labour contributes: the finished artifact is no concern of theirs.

Work is non-contingently related to its product. The description of the process and the description of the product are part of a single conceptual scheme. The excellences of the product may be described in terms of workmanship, the productive work as aiming at these excellences.[2] Education is a case in hand. To be educated, is to bear the marks of having been through the educational process. Thus finished product and productive processes are correlatively understood.

The adequacy of work and the excellence of its product are *judged* together. If the unified conceptual scheme is abandoned, this advantage is lost and the point of the work is no longer clear. It is then, poor thing, fed into the machine of means and ends and justified by the calculus of satisfactions. The ironic outcome is that the workman comes to hate his work, or in bad faith, to invent a myth in order to persuade himself that he likes it, and thus its fruits are mortgaged, even before they have been gathered. The workman then becomes a labourer.

A simple, but perhaps not over-simple account of unalienated action is that the aims and purposes of the agent, as a person, accord with the general telos of his enterprise. Unalienated work is a case in hand; there has to be some enterprise in which an opus of a certain kind is produced, subject to standards of excellence for *that kind* of work, and such that the workman desires to produce that kind of work under a description such that these standards of excellence are appropriate, which he endorses in any case.

The view that work, unlike labour, must have a point which the workman can endorse, and a purpose with which he can associate himself, has been apparently bypassed by some doctrines, recently orthodox, in the philosophy of action. The position which I have in mind is that any performance or activity may be described in indefinitely many ways of which none is more basic or more revealing than another, and it is held that the frustration of not being free to do as one purposes is avoided, provided that one endorses what one does under some description which one's exertions will bear. Thus, for instance, since much labour is correctly described as making money and most labourers are keen on making money, it seems that, except through their failure to make money, they cannot be frustrated.

The theory of multiple descriptions is also used to deflect the point of the remark that the frustration of labour arises as much from the absence of standards of excellence to which the labourer can aspire, as from the lack of a real object in labouring. In certain situations, especially under conditions of modern advertising, there may be a performance which is a bad way of earning money but a good way of building a house, or a good way of achieving promotion in a university but a bad way of teaching pupils. Here again it will be argued that if the labourer really wants money and promotion, then he can take a pride of workmanship in his endeavours, provided that they are adequately described as successful money-getting or promotion-earning. Thus, according to this relativist thesis, conceptions of skill and excellence of workmanship vary with different descriptions of the same activity, and the labourer will not go without reward if he conceptualizes his activities under some description under which they come out well.

These arguments seem to be nothing better than sophistries. It is clearly wrong to say that people *care* about making money or achieving status; they *desire* these things. The concept of care connects with the idea that there are some things which we cherish, and to which we devote ourselves. We care for things lovingly, or tenderly, or devotedly, but except in bad faith we pursue our interests quite unsentimentally.

The workman then *cares* for his opus, and he will have a reason for proceeding thus rather than thus, in terms of the qualities and excellences at which he aims in the finished product. Thus his performance bears a description under which it is a condition of quality in his product, there being a description of his product under which he wants to make it, and to make it well.

Now it is not evident that these conditions can be met by activities of which the point is money-making, or some such other extrinsic end. The money which a man earns is not his product, but rather what he gets in exchange for his product. Money is not an opus. One lot of money differs from another lot of money only by way of more or less; money does not bear the marks of craftsmanship. Similarly, the activities which are addressed to the task of money-making have the qualities and excellences of which they are capable only relative to some opus which is saleable, or some purpose from the pursuit of which an income happily results.

Let us meet the critics of our viewpoint who proceed from the theory of multiple descriptions by experimenting with an example. Consider a man who, being a devoted builder, has conceptions of excellence in houses, and under these conceptions cares about what and how he builds. Incidentally, he wants to earn a living out of building. Now let us attempt to invert the example. Thus we get a man who, being a devoted money-getter, has conceptions of excellence in money-getting, and under these conceptions cares for the sums of money which he makes, and for what he does by way of getting them. Incidentally, what he does by way of money-getting is house-building.

Now it makes sense to suppose that a man builds houses, no matter whether well or badly, in order to obtain money, but it does not make the same sense to suppose that a man makes money, no matter whether well or badly, in order to obtain a house. The only interpretation which we can place on that suggestion is that he makes money in order to be in a position to *buy* a house, and if so, he had better do well at money-making, because the house of his choice may turn out expensive.

There seems to be a confusion between constitution and instrumentality in the arguments of the cynics. Good workmanship is constitutive of a good work, but (with good luck) only a means of obtaining rewards. Good workmanship on the other hand is as little constitutive of rewards as it is instrumental to a well-made opus. By these tests not all descriptions under which a man may be said to be acting when he makes something come out equal. For instance "earning a living," "making a reputation for himself," "earning promotion," "serving his company," "doing his duty," cannot be descriptions of work, while "building a house," "composing a quartet," "working at a philosophical problem," and "educating a student" may serve as work descriptions proper. A workman is one who avowably acts under such a description.

Universities, despite the composition of their councils, are, by and large, self-governing institutions still, but more than the armed forces, or the institutionalized professions, the pressures of society affect them everywhere. Governments hold the purse-strings; they do not find it difficult to persuade universities to volunteer research in areas deemed useful, nor do they hesitate to encourage subject-areas and educational techniques to produce students who will accept the roles envisaged by the official planners. The media and the politicians, not to mention the representatives of business interests and the trade unions, are forever admonishing universities not to abuse their positions of privilege, but to shoulder their social responsibilities, and to assist in the accomplishment of some task which, at the time, is conceived to be essential to progress, or to the country's well-being (or to that of the nation, mankind, society, or some other likely recipient of people's fundamental loyalties). The funds and the support which universities receive from the public purse are insufficient for their needs, however, and thus they must seek the assistance of industry, and trade, and the professions to enable them to branch out into areas of research on which their prestige depends. It seems likely that funds would no longer be readily available if the interests of learning and the interests of the donors came to be in serious conflict. Situations in which the consciences of individual university teachers conflict with the interests of a donor are now increasingly common, especially in the ecological field. The results will need to be studied.

Some university people feel slightly guilty about the pursuit of learning: the image of the ivory tower puts them on the defensive. In such a mood they are anxious to stress the continuity of their outlook with that of society at large, and they become active in organizations to which the idea of thought, directed to the telos of truth, is alien, but in which they can prove themselves good fellows.

The attachment of some university teachers to their institutions, and to the traditions and ideals of universities, is often only partial. Take a department in a vocational branch of university teaching: law, for instance. Some of its most distinguished members are fully functioning members of their profession, perhaps on temporary loan to a university. The department as a whole has its moorings at least as much in chambers and in the law-courts as in the cloisters, it invites distinguished counsel, judges, and attorneys general for talks and dinners: in return its members sit on committees which make them influential in the profession, and are allowed to appear in an advisory capacity on various bodies designed to solve the legal problems of governments, banks, trade unions, and public corporations. The interests of the legal profession, however, are no more guaranteed to coincide with the interests of the students in acquiring an education than the interests of General Motors are guaranteed to accord with those of the American nation. Thus for a teacher who has the education of his students at heart (as distinct from their careers) there may be a tension, a case of divided loyalties. The students themselves undoubtedly often feel this tension, and the disinterested desire to emerge as educated men and women struggles with the desire for a meal ticket. What it is to receive an education remains to be discussed below.

The professions and the institutions to whose service students are destined have influence, not only through their members or nominees on university councils, grants commissions, research foundations and such bodies which control universities and their work, but also because they have it in their power to employ or to reject graduates. This power is great, and to many, fearful.

Thus, for many reasons, and not least, because it is a universal tendency for people to rationalize the pressures upon them and to contrive an ideology designed to make these pressures bearable, universities reflect the ethos of the societies in which they operate, even where this ethos is incompatible with the enterprise of teaching and research. That seems to be the present situation in the technologically advanced affluent societies of the western world. Some remarks about this ethos are called for.

To begin with a cliché: we live in a society of consumers. It is true, the pundits and the politicians are forever exhorting us to production, and seem to regard the indefinite expansion of production as the greatest good, but production is conceived of as a mere correlative of consumption. We produce either what we anticipate that we will consume, or we produce the means of accelerated production, machines, that is to say. Sometimes we even produce the means of accelerated consumption, as in the advertising industry. Society as a whole is here conceived to be acting on the supposition that consumption is the only worth-while human function, and that the indefinite expansion of the production-consumption cycle, together with the unhampered freedom to produce and consume, are the only worth-while ends of action.

The greater part of our political energy is devoted to economic matters, to welfare, the enhancement of the standard of living, the expansion of output, the procurement of "jobs," and the provision of common services which otherwise would have to be purchased by the individual. To this we must add our preoccupation with stability and security, the protection of our vast and infinitely complex system of production, administration, commerce, and organized consumption against organic imbalances, and against internal and external foes. The question whether the ideological emphasis in our society is on production or consumption is bound up with whether we are concerned with the health and stability of the system, growth-rates for instance, employment opportunities and the avoidance of slumps, or whether, concerned to advertise the benefits of the system, we point to the bonanza of an indefinitely rising "standard of living." It seems clear that, despite the emphasis on growth-rates, few believe in production for its own sake. Our consciences are ruffled when the alleged needs of the stability of the system cause us to dump foodstuffs in the sea, even without the thought of the starving millions of Bangla Desh.

To consume a commodity is so to put it to use that in the process it disappears or perishes. Thus a commodity is given in exchange for a service or a satisfaction. Not all consumer commodities are as ephemeral as food: some, the so-called durable consumer goods, are consumed slowly. There are also consumer services (banking, for instance); and there are those objects which are not, in any obvious way, consumed at all, but which are produced, bought, sold, and disposed of as if they were consumer goods. I mean "desirable residences," gardens, jewels, and the palpable artifacts of learning and art (books, paintings, stereo, etc.).

It has been remarked that the central ethos of capitalist production is puritanism, that is, justification by achievement wrought from self-sacrifice, self-discipline, frugality, and labour. Paradoxically enough, the central ethos of capitalist consumption is utilitarianism,[3] that is, the doctrine that the discipline and toil of the productive process can only by justified by the personal satisfactions of the consumers. Since the most successful producers acquire wealth, they also become major consumers, and thus we have that grotesque historical joke, the tycoon who practises frugality in luxury, and who pursues his pleasures in the same spirit of grim determination in which he approaches his managerial role. The puritan ethos is irreducibly individualistic, no man can hope to win merit for another, none can assuage his conscience through the sacrifices or exertions of another man. The utilitarian ethos on the other hand is social and impersonal. Any man may glean satisfactions from consuming a commodity, no matter who produced it, and society as a whole is conceived to be in a state of well-being if the majority is happy, that is, according to that idology, if the level of consumption is high.

The early philosophers and economists who set the intellectual tone of our system of production saw one thing very clearly: the destiny of a consumer-good is to be consumed, and there is no point in consuming it unless one derives some pleasure or satisfaction from doing so. Thus we produce in order that we may consume, and we consume for the sake of the satisfactions to be derived from doing so; thus our satisfactions alone are an end, and everything else, the goods themselves, the productive process of which they are the fruit, and the labour which is expended in the process are but means. Viewed from this standpoint nothing has intrinsic value but human satisfactions, and the best life is that in which the capacity for consumption is maximized, and the opportunities do not lag behind.

From our point of view the crucial thing about the consumer ideology is its indifference to the opus, the work which a workman makes. Since the opus is conceived to be a mere means, a cog in a process of which the end-product is pleasure or satisfaction, there are no conceptions of excellence for it as such; its goodness becomes a relational property; to be good it must be such that out of its consumption the consumers derive satisfactions. Thus art is debased to amusement, literature to journalism, the serious and rational debate of public issues to image-building and gimmickry, and that part of learning which is not a mere service industry for trade, industry, government, or the professions is made to provide a cultural varnish for the young barbarians whom the system needs and nourishes.

The labourer is a social being.[4] He subserves the "needs of society," and, if properly socialized, conceives of himself as subserving these needs. If society cannot consume his products, he has laboured in vain. If his products are not good to consume, or if they are inefficiently produced, or produced at too great a cost to society, he has laboured badly. Labourers, as I here conceive them, include some of the most highly paid men in the kingdom, and most of our society consists of labourers.

The things which we value or love engage our interest: we care about them and they concern us. We cannot *care* about what touches us only through its effects or its potential uses. A key for instance, common and undistinguished, is unlikely to be something about which we care, even if it puts a fortune within our reach. The attitudes of interest, concern, or care depend on the intrinsic properties of an object. If an object touches us only because we can use it, or because we want what it will bring about, then we do not care about it as such. Our attitude to it will then be commercial. That which is treated exclusively as a means, commercially that is to say, is thereby degraded if it is degradable. The time-honoured example is a prostitute. Even if no money changes hands, the girl's dignity is undermined if, viewing her only as an instrument of sexual gratification, we do not care whether she be happy or unhappy, religious or atheistical, interested in mountaineering or politics, and so on. In the commercial state of mind we do not even care whether she like or abominates her partner, nor will we be concerned about her subsequent fate.

The consumer's society degrades whatever it touches, work, nature, art, its own history and traditions, and the creations of men of genius. Work (being confused with labour) is but toil, the process of production is distinct from and merely instrumental to the product; it is the product and, beyond it, a satisfaction which are desired, not the process. Since the process of producing is troublesome, we abandon it with relief and turn to its natural counter-pole, which is play (or fun as the newspapers now call it). This increasingly becomes the really serious business of our lives; besides, it has the advantage of opening up quite unlimited new opportunities for consumption.

The ideological producer for consumption, despite his rockets to the moon, is the world's most unambitious creature and also the most destructive. All, or nearly all, the immense array of ingenious and amazing objects to the manufacture of which his intelligence is harnessed are made for consumption. At the same time, as the opportunities for consumption magnify, so does the consumer's appetite, until, as things stand now, the earth itself stands in danger of being devoured. He destroys the beauty of nature, the animal kingdom is expended for his satisfaction, he destroys whole cultures and traditions to stimulate trade, and finally he destroys men themselves. I do not mean in warfare only, which is nothing peculiar to our times, but by a process of depersonalization which results from being made a means to an end.

It is time we returned to the universities. Universities do not fit in well in a consumer's society. I do not mean that the structure and fabric of a university cannot survive in such a society; that would clearly be wrong. Universities are growing still. They receive unprecedented attention from the mighty, and a degree has become a passport to worldly success as never before.

Nevertheless universities do not flourish in a consumer's society without suffering a sea change. The ethos of a university has in the past been principally an ethos of work, and the objects to the achievement of which universities used to be committed were conceived as of intrinsic worth. These objects were twofold, namely the pursuit of learning (or inquiry as I propose to call it) and the education of the young. They seem to me to be the proper aims of universities still. Unfortunately they are in danger of being lost. If they are lost, it will not be as a result of an open change, but imperceptibly, ostensibly under the old ethos still. They will be lost, like liberty in a society grown totalitarian in the defence of liberty. Even in 1984, the academic credo affirming the pursuit of learning and the education of the young will be intoned. But it seems that the pursuit of learning will be transmuted into the pursuit of skills and know-how, and that education will become training or instruction. It seems probable that the matter of education will increasingly be parcelled out into one or other of two broad categories, on the one hand essential knowledge, that is, knowledge which is good for some socially acceptable purpose, and luxury knowledge, a sort of prestigious top-dressing on the other. It is possible even that the pursuit of luxury knowledge will altogether disappear from the syllabus, and that activities which fall within its sphere will become extra-curricular. There will be concerts, exhibitions, poetry-readings, and meditation-sessions, and these will be calculated to perform a function in that parcel of life which is now called leisure.

We are sufficiently imbued with the ethos of our era for the thought that universities are primarily for the service of society to be natural to us. Thus we conceive of our role in terms of the satisfaction of social needs. We provide society with trained men for the professions, with experts to advise government and industry, and we produce persons with cultural graces to dignify our voracity. When we think of university expansion, we naturally look at the market to see what graduates it will absorb, and we plan research training as immediately addressed to social needs.

Thus we become a factory for making a certain kind of equipment which society needs, people as well as computers. But perhaps this account of the matter may strike you as too pessimistic. There is a current development which seems to belie it; I mean the expansion of research in universities, and the prestige which it enjoys.

Research is surely work. Many of us, perhaps a majority, regard it as the real business of universities, and think of the advancement of knowledge as the ultimate aim. Teaching is viewed as a slightly inferior activity, necessary, alas, both because society demands it and for the perpetuation of academic institutions, but an imposition on a true man of learning. Adapting Plato's famous simile, academic people have to earn a place in the sun of pure research by a temporary sojourn in the cave of education. They do their duty, earn their release, and go off on sabbatical leave.

There are few images as appealing as the image of ourselves adding to the sum of human knowledge. Knowledge seems to us like a vast impersonal edifice, to which, by the sheer exercise of our industry and wit, we can add a brick. What could be a more enduring monument than this? Our knowledge is not and cannot be consumed, neither could it conceivably have accrued from some activity generically different from inquiry. It is therefore non-contingently related to the activity from which it results. Our claims to knowledge are tested by the tools of logic and the resources of experiment and these alone provide the tests of workmanship.

This image is pretty, but it does more than justice to most contemporary academic research. There is a sense of course in which all knowledge is enduring. Copies of our monographs and journals will continue to accumulate in our libraries at an ever-expanding rate, but much of this work is undertaken as labour rather than work.

The idea that work may be undertaken in the spirit of labour presents no difficulty. Analogously a puritan may debauch himself in the spirit of duty, and an intending lover may trade his affections in the spirit of a ledger-clerk. In each case the conception which the agent has of his act ill accords with its point, and this argues confusion or self-deception on his part. The agent does not know what he is about: he acts katatelically.

Research-labourers do research katatelically, though not necessarily without results, if "results" are a kind of pay-off to society or to some interest represented in it. (Discoveries of genuine interest to intellectuals are not excluded.) A research-labourer works in the spirit of labour. He puts his highly trained labour-force at the disposal of society or its agencies. He works in its interests, and conceives that to be its point. The beneficiaries generally reward him, but not from love of the intellectual enterprise. The beneficiaries use him, even as he will presently use his students, or prepare them for social use after they have obtained their "qualification." The beneficiaries accept useful results, whether or not they have accrued from intellectually reputable work. They know what they want: unfortunately he generally does not.

Inquiry absorbs a man. It is an extension of his personality. Roughly, if a man is content to engage in a piece of research from nine to five as a job, he will not engage in it as inquiry. The workman is involved in his work. The sort of involvement which I have in mind is not unlike what is called commitment. One cannot change one's work as one can change one's job. The workman who is deprived of his work is deprived *tout court.*

Research, it seems, has become a sort of independent empire. There is indeed a myth that people who have gone through the research-mill make good university teachers, and if the function of a good university teacher is simply to train people in the techniques of research, it may not be a myth entirely. The belief that research produces good teachers adds to our notion of its utility.

Research begets research. Much of it is addressed to the expansion of the research-culture, which nobody, not even the research workers, regards as intrinsically valuable. We tend the dog, clip its fur, polish its teeth, publish its pedigree, and enter it for every available dog-show, but we are not really fond of animals.

Now we come to teaching. This presents us with our thorniest problem. It is in our attitudes to students that we most clearly show whether we accept or reject the ethos of consumption. Our traditions demand that we should educate our students. Education is one of the excellences of which human beings are capable, and just as the excellence of a painting cannot be defined in terms of its monetary value or in terms of its social usefulness, so also the state of being educated cannot be defined in careerist or social-utility terms.

An educated student is one in whom certain potentialities are developed, including the potentiality for work in a certain field. Students are intelligent or stupid before they enroll, but good teachers develop their intelligence and teach them to use it, to apply it, to delight in its exercise. An educated man is sensitive perceptive, daring in imagination, subtle in distinction, lucid and powerful in reasoning, and articulate. An educated student understands the enterprise of inquiry. This may take the form of reflection, discussion, or internal dialectic, it need not consist in writing articles. For instance, the preparation of a creative lecture is also part of the enterprise. Often the kind of inquiry which most obviously lends itself to publication is from the point of education, infertile. For this reason, among others, the greater part of our journal literature is almost at birth embedded in the sedimentary deposits of the academy, and will never be looked at again.

The education of a student is an end in itself, and the making of him is our noblest work. This work requires no further justification, and by attempting to justify it further, in terms of the values of the consumer society, we only succeed in undermining it.

We educate students by working with them in a field or discipline. One cannot do everything at once, and a certain concentration in a field ensures that work is done in depth and discourages superficiality. But the field is never more than the locus in which the work of education is accomplished. Competence in a field is not the aim of education, but only one of its expedients. The emphasis on a field as against the potentialities which work in a field makes actual is inimical to the enterprise of education.

The consumer mentality makes education well-nigh impossible. First a relatively mild and engaging variant, the idea that it is our task to equip students to earn a livelihood, or to make a position for themselves in society. If a teacher is fond of his students, he will not wish them to come to grief in life, and thus he may skimp their education in order to increase their value in the market.

The more insidious forms of consumer education mould the student, not in his own material interests but in the alleged interests of society. The student and his skills are debased into a means for the achievement of social ends. The student becomes a capital investment. He is there for the performance of certain kinds of labour which will procure satisfactions for his fellow citizens, and the teachers are there in order to train him in the skills which will make him a useful instrument in procuring these satisfactions. *He* ceases to matter, provided only that he performs the part which the diviners of social needs have cast for him. The diviners of social needs are roughly men in authority, with their academic advisers.

The replacement of education by instruction is a serious matter. It naturally goes hand in hand with the abandonment of any real interest in students or their maturation, which in turn is the inevitable result of the mass-production techniques which are now being forced on us. Instruction is a practical enterprise in which a set skill, or a standard quota of information is imparted for a purpose. The point of instruction is to suit the subject to a task. Thus soldiers are instructed in the use of weapons, and trainee-policemen are instructed in their duties. Instruction is standardized, uncritical, undialectical, and it discourages speculation about ends and means alike. Some university courses seem to be almost pure instruction. All available teaching time is parcelled out into segments each of which is devoted to imparting some particular item of information, or to allow time for the practice of some particular skill. Directives to tutors are printed in detailed cyclostyled sheets; these ensure that all tutorials will operate in parallel. The student is there to absorb this material. He contributes nothing and his intellect remains unengaged. The teachings of some psychologists have aggravated this state of affairs.

Education is a dialectical enterprise, critical, discursive, and largely idiosyncratic on the teacher's and the student's side alike. It is true that education presupposes the mastery of some skills and the possession of some information. These are ancillary to education. In the consumer's society, however, they tend to replace it. One cannot educate a student well at a distance. Education is a meeting of two intellects, and therefore of two persons, and this requires a common life. But in the contemporary academy the teacher is becoming ever more inaccessible. Many students do not even know their lecturers by name.

The students who are subjected to this sort of pseudo-education are not fully conscious of what is happening, but they are dimly aware that they are being used for purposes not of their own choosing. Many feel cheated. They came to the university for an education, and find themselves being moulded for the purposes of a society of which the official representatives often strike them as unadmirable. "Society" speaks to them through members of the establishment.

The view that their teachers lack capacity, or knowledge, or skill is not essential to this state of mind, and it is not the principal cause of discontent. On the contrary, student disaffection is often associated with a sense of inferiority. Students feel that their teacher's interest in them is inauthentic. The jargon-word "alienation" is not easily banished from one's lips.

To sum up, the danger in modern universities is that students will be regarded as capital equipment and that by being "instructed" they will be conditioned to take their place in the technical, commercial, or administrative machinery of a society which recognizes no values but consumption. They will therefore be made ready for being used. When that happens, the university will have played a part in the production of highly skilled and (unless there is an oversupply) extremely precious labourers, but it will not have taught them to work, albeit both their well-being and that of society depends on their capacity for action, which, in the productive field, is work. Neither is the producing of such young men and women anything but labour, and thus some of the most imaginative and ingenious men and women in the land are reduced to the status of labourers. Thus, given the tedious absurdities of the research-empire, especially in subjects which are insecure in their standing and seek to prove that they too are hard-headed and "scientific," the university and its *raison d'etre* pass each other by.

The idea that universities should subserve social needs, as these are understood in the dominant ideology, has been disparaged in this essay, and the traditional values of men of learning have been defended in opposition to ideological, economic, and political demands. Society, in so far as it can be said to have judgment and articulation, is a poor judge of its own needs, and universities sacrifice a good to promote an evil if they think themselves committed to the utilitarian objectives (or the ideologically inspired projects) which worldly spokesmen advocate. The consumer's ethos does not serve its exponents well. By undermining the human personality, it deprives people of the power of happiness. True, it provides us with the technical means of abolishing the miseries of disease and want, but it also destroys that capacity for love and care, and that freedom of the spirit, which vouchsafe fulfilment, and which are a condition of the enjoyment of worldly things. We do no service to society by making ourselves into its servants.

A society is not better than the persons who compose it. If by education we produce men and women of excellence, we have no need of a higher aim.

NOTES

1. Hannah Arendt, *The Human Condition* (Chicago: University of Chicago Press, 1958), chs. 3 and 4.

2. The view that work does not play a part in the *causation* of opera (assuming its intelligibility) is not expressed here, and must not be ascribed to the author.

3. The popular, not the "philosophical" variant is intended.

4. A thesis of Mrs. Arendt's.

REASON, HIGHER LEARNING, AND THE GOOD SOCIETY

Henry Aiken

The aim of this essay is critical and constructive. I mean to attack views of education and of the good society widely prevalent in our culture, particularly in our institutions of so-called higher learning, i.e., the colleges and universities, and, more recently, the institutes for advanced study. But the point of view I shall call in question goes deeper and extends more widely. It involves a conception of higher learning, accepted by virtually the whole society in which we live and the civilization of which we are a part, and this in turn reflects conceptions of knowledge, of human nature, and of human values and attainments, to be found in the writings of formative thinkers of our entire western tradition as far back as Plato. In some considerable part, the break down of our civilization is evidence of the errors—I should call them philosophical—inherent in this point of view which I call "rationalism." Unlike some others, however, I do not believe that the whole aim of Educators concerned with liberal education is to try to shore up the ruins of the rationalist tradition. Here, in my judgment, we would do well to let the dead bury their dead. What is worthy of survival—and of course much is—in the West has developed in spite of and against the grain of the rationalist tradition. What should be saved must be set free from the bonds in which it has hitherto been tied. In fact, what is most worthy of survival belongs to an unofficial, almost an underground

From *Perspectives in Education, Religion, and Arts.* Howard Kiefer and Milton K. Munitz, ed. (Albany, N.Y.: State University of New York Press, 1970), pp. 43-72.

culture, that has grown up in spite of the attempts of rationalists to destroy or else to conceal it.

As these last sentences suggest, I shall not be merely critical, but shall offer in later sections some more positive suggestions about education and the good society. But the bases for them will emerge gradually through my dialectical oppositions to rationalism.

I. The Ideology of Rationalism

In speaking of the "ideology" of rationalism, I do not use the word "ideology" itself in a pejorative sense. Accordingly, I do not mean that rationalism is wicked or a form of "false consciousness," simply because it is an ideology; some ideologies, kept within bounds, may be quite benign. Nor does it seem to me possible for a society with continuous traditions, or a people with a sense of its own identity, to persist without some form of ideology. Ideologies, which are in part the products of philosophical ideas and points of view, are semi-systems of ideals, principles, standards, aspirations, along with their supporting over-beliefs about the world, the nature of man, his history and his destiny, his capacities and limitations, his institutions and forms of life. Such over-beliefs, moreover, may be either scientific or wildly speculative, explicit or implicit, literal-minded or figurative. What makes them ideological, as I use the term, are (a) their active social roles, and (b) the fact that their roles are social. The social roles of ideological attitudes and beliefs are active and practical in the sense that they serve as determinants and conditions of action, as mental sets, attitudes, presuppositions, assumptions that guide not only action but thought conceived as symbolic action and as a preparation for actions that are overt and explicit. As ideological, however, such roles are not selected by individuals at their own pleasure; rather, they are ingrained in the whole institutional life of a society or people or social class. And for a society, they form a large part of its lore, its prevailing intellectual and social history, what it conceives to be its traditions. Inevitably they are also ingrained in its basic educational practices and institutions; its teachers tend to follow it; its administrators expound it, its students assimilate it; and students and teachers who oppose "the system" are usually in one way or another opposed to its ideology. I am convinced that many of the so-called "drop-outs" from our own contemporary institutions of higher learning are in fact people disaffected with the ideology of rationalism. Hence, even if one wants merely to understand the sources of disquiet, of disaffection and revolt, in our contemporary universities one must look to the rationalist ideology that animates much of our established culture.

Just because rationalism as an ideology is a pervasive set of social attitudes and beliefs, it cannot be ascribed *in toto* to any particular philosopher or even to a certain philosophical succession. Plato, I am persuaded, is preeminent among the philosophical progenitors of the rationalist ideology, but I do not, save for purposes of reference and illustration identify rationalism with Plato's philosophy. Likewise, the great succession of Continental rationalists, from Descartes to Leibniz, have also had considerable formative influence upon the ideology of rationalism. But they did not, so to say, write its constitution. And no doubt rationalism betrays, or caricatures, the thought of these great thinkers at one point or another. Sometimes indeed it betrays some of their deeper intentions. Furthermore, one can find, as one would expect if my view of the matter is right, evidences of rationalism in the thought of many philosophers, historians, men of letters, who are, or think they are, opposed to major aspects of Plato's or Descartes' thought, or who are, or think they are, simply preoccupied with different questions. Although in the text books the theory of knowledge called "empiricism" is commonly set in opposition to rationalist theories of knowledge, many empiricists hold views about knowledge and its place in human affairs that are virtually paradigms of what I here understand by rationalism.

The following outline of rationalism as an ideology is intended merely as a rough, though I hope serviceable, sketch. Let us begin by noticing a fact or two about the term rationalism itself. As an *"ism"* word, rationalism in its ordinary use refers primarily to a cluster of attitudes, points of view, ways of taking things. It stands to reason and rationality as evolutionism stands to evolution or historicism to history. In short, it is not only a theory about reason and rationality, though it indeed involves such a theory, but also it is a perspective upon human experience and conduct which ascribes to reason and rationality a central and controlling place in our scheme of things. The rationalist, it is plain, not merely defends reason against its detractors: plenty of people, myself included, would wish to do this against irrationalists, mystagogues, and obscurantists. The rationalist also asserts the supremacy of reason as a human faculty, the fundamentality of its norms, and its sufficiency as an organon for thought and action. In Santayana's phrase, the rationalist is committed, symptomatically and above all else, to something he envisages as "the life of reason."

But there is a second aspect of the use of the term "rationalism" in most quarters. Some "ism" words are mainly pejorative, or are conceived by people who employ them pejoratively. Thus "historicism" is, for most people, Karl Popper for instance, a bugaboo, a scapegoat, a kind of original sin philosophically and ideologically. In a primarily rationalist tradition and culture rationalism is, not unnaturally, a word with a halo around it, as one discovers when one attacks the points of view associated with it. And when one avows oneself to be an antirationalist, one automatically declares oneself to be a deviant, a kind of drop-out from the prevailing culture. So be it.

As here conceived the principal doctrines or contentions of rationalism and rationalists are as follows:[1]

1. First of all, rationalism is a doctrine about man and his culture. Man, for the rationalist, is par excellence the rational animal. It is rationality which distinguishes him from other creatures. And it is rationality which is his salient gift, his most precious faculty. The classical rationalists of course conceived of exercise of reason

teleologically as man's own distinctive and proper end. But they also conceived it in quasi-administrative terms, as the faculty which properly coordinates and controls all other human faculties, activities, and affairs. It is, or ought to be, the master of the passions and emotions. If certain other ends are also inherent in human nature, reason not only discovers the means to their realization, but, where they conflict, it is empowered and entitled to reorient and harmonize them in various appropriate ways. Finally, not only is human rationality thus conceived immanent within human nature, so that all men, unless perverted or deprived in some way, strive, at first unconsciously, and then more and more consciously, to become rational animals; but also the principles of rationality are, both in thought and in action, to be regarded eternalistically as unamenable to change.[2] Its norms, whose paradigms of course are the norms of logic and exact science, are not only universalistic but universal rules of order to which every man is at all times beholden. Questions of genesis, history, social or psychological context, have nothing to do with and are always strictly irrelevant to questions of rationality. Nor is it merely that rational standards and claims are formulated ahistorically; it is also, and more saliently so, that no meta-descriptive account of them, which suggests that they are really subject to change, is acceptable. Such an account is not an account of rationality in history but only of fallible human meta-beliefs about it or else of vagaries in the practices of historical individuals and societies.

Certain important consequences concerning human nature follow at once. The rationalist views, or tends to view, man's faculties as forming a kind of hierarchy and, so to say, the internal political economy of a human life as properly a sort of artistocracy. Here, however, there is considerable room for variation within the rationalist tradition. In the view of some rationalists, rationality, though exhibited most saliently, in the work of the logician and scientist, may also be present in some implicit fashion in art and poetry, or in religious thought. In short, some rationalists are, as we may call them, "inclusivists" and informalists who seek to find in every sphere of activity redemptive and entitling evidences of rationality. From their point of view, although a poet may be a less perfect example of the rational animal than a logician, a rational poet is superior to a nonrational or irrational one. Others are "exclusivists" or rigorists who limit rationality strictly to logical and scientific thought. From their point of view, any activity, such as painting or sculpture, perhaps even morality and religion, which is found to be (from the preferred point of view) essentially nonrational, is *ipso facto* below the salt of essentially *human* aspiration. And poets, musicians, ministers, *et al.* are not in their characteristic work acting as human beings.

2. Taking classical rationalism again as a preliminary point of reference, we are to view man's good as complex. His complete good consists in the fulfillment of his whole nature, including his basic appetitive and emotional drives. Usually the rationalists have envisaged man's complete good as a harmony. Each propensity or power being fulfilled only to the extent that it does not impair fulfillment of the rest. Such a harmony, however, is minimal, for it envisages nothing more than a mutual compatibility or consistency. Maximally, the fulfilled propensities would be

a form of a kind of consortium, each of which provided a positive reinforcement or support for the rest. Thus a man whose hunger and whose sexual impulses are adequately satisfied is so far enabled to devote his energies more fully to his proper work as a rational being than one who is continually hungery or sexually deprived. Man's highest good, however, consists alone in the exercise of his rational faculty.

On this point, again, rationalists have not always taken precisely the same view of what this good involves. In part this is owing to variant theories of human cognition; in part also it is owing to different views about the degrees of worth to be ascribed to several objects or levels of knowledge; and finally, it is owing to different views about the diversity of intellectual capacity among men.

The following broad tendencies may be noted here. Among classical rationalists, who conceive of at least the higher forms of knowledge in terms of a direct intellectual intuition of the object known, the exercise of reason, in its higher, theoretical reaches, is essentially contemplative. However, among modern rationalist theories of knowledge, for which scientific knowledge serves as a paradigm, the cognitive role assigned to intuition has continually declined. Knowledge is now viewed in verificationist terms, and one who knows is one who is able to, or knows how to verify the propositions and theories that he is said to know. In another way, scientific knowledge which is now conceived in terms of controlled inquiry and explanation does not consist in intuitive perceptions of the thing known, but rather in an ability to offer satisfactory explanations of it. Thus, knowing that certain propositions are true or probable depends essentially upon skills necessary to knowing how to explain that which one knows, and this in particular involves both powers of logico-mathematical formulation and manipulation for the statement and organization of theories and skills required for the performance of controlled experiments and observations required for their verification.[3]

It is no accident that all forms of rationalism which view theoretical science as the paradigm of human knowledge also tend to assign to the most exact and certain of the sciences the place of highest intrinsic value in the hierarchy of cognitive disciplines. Correspondingly, the scientists who possess this knowledge and the skills pertaining thereto, are regarded as individuals of the highest dignity and authority among those who know. Such persons, moreover, tend to be viewed by rationalists as paradigms of human excellence generally, to be emulated wherever possible, to be deferred to where not. In classical times this meant that philosophers were the most examplary of men, not just because they loved wisdom but because the knowledge they aspired to possess was the highest, most perfect of all. Such a view with some variations prevailed down through the time of Descartes and Spinoza. It is notable, however, that John Locke regarded his own philosophical activity in less exalted terms, and since Locke rationalists have tended to demote philosophy, at best, to a subordinate place in the hierarchy of cognitive disciplines. Nowadays, as we know, few professional philosophers love wisdom and those who do love it occupy an even lower place in the hierarchy than their colleagues.

In passing it is also worth remarking that so-called rational theology, which during the middle ages surpassed even philosophy as an intellectual discipline, has fallen to a position even lower than philosophy in the modern rationalist hierarchy. In fact the general view among rationalists, nowadays, appears to be that rational theology is a contradiction in terms, and that among theologians, semantical atheists who repudiate "God-talk" altogther are by all odds the most reputable. In mentioning the theologians, here, let me add, my aim is merely to remove a possible objection to this part of my synopsis of rationalism. Remembering Plato and Aristotle, as well as the Medieval philosophers and theologians, it is arguable that some thinkers who belong to the rationalist tradition have assigned priority to philosophy or theology, not only because it was considered to be the most exact and perfect of all forms of knowledge, but also because the object of philosophical or theological study is the highest of all forms of being. And certainly many rationalists have taken such a view. But this does not require a serious qualification of my account of rationalism as an ideology. On the contrary, it serves indirectly to reinforce that account. For upon discovering that knowledge of God or the good is neither clear nor exact, at least from a scientific point of view, rationalists do not conclude that there are forms of knowledge that surpass the sciences in value and authority, and knowers who possess a higher dignity than the scientists. On the contrary, they conclude that such forms of knowledge, if knowledge they be, are of much lower value, and those who profess it of much less distinction as knowers.

In our universities, at the present time, such is precisely the prevailing view. In general, the sciences most highly esteemed are mathematics and the exact physical sciences; and theologians who at least try to be rational in their investigations occupy places of far less intellectual prestige than their colleagues. And if, in some academic circles, philosophy has to some extent recouped its losses, this is due largely, or entirely, to the rise of mathematical logic and to its widespread use among analytical philosophers and in particular among philosophers of science.[4]

A word must now be said about the attitudes of rationalists regarding the abilities of men to achieve man's highest good. It is of course not enough simply to say that man's highest good consists in the possession of exact, scientific knowledge. For if there are men who have little scientific ability, and if therefore they are highly imperfect and inadequate rational animals (and indeed to that extent imperfect and inadequate human beings) then the conclusion likely to be drawn is that man's highest good is simply beyond their grasp, or else is available to them only in a diminshed or diluted form. And if it is believed, as Plato and Aristotle for example plainly did believe, that such ability is relatively rare, or restricted to particular races or classes of men, then the basis for certain forms of elitism is already prepared.

Here again however, we must proceed with caution. And though, rationalism is, as I am convinced, inherently elitist, just to the extent that its view of the highest good is not accessible or else is accessible only in a diminished form to many, or most, men, it does not follow that rationalism is thereby committed, for example, to elitist political ideologies in the ordinary sense. There are many elites and accordingly many kinds of elitism, just as there are many views of the diversity of human abilities. Moreover, there are, within rationalist theories of knowledge, countervailing tendencies which to some extent offset its proneness to elitism.

Let me speak of the latter. In the first place, modern rationalists have increasingly stressed the public, objective, impersonal, and impartial character of scientific inquiry and knowledge. Such knowledge therefore is accessible in some degree to anyone who can master the skills required for scientific analysis, experimentation, and observation. Hence, questions of race, color, wealth, social class, or political power are wholly irrelevant to an individual's ability to share in the scientific enterprise or to enjoy the benefits of a scientific education. Indeed, it is commonly argued that the scientific community is a perfect democracy, a society of equals, each of whom is free to confute his fellow, if he can, and everyone is pledged to subordinate his judgment to the immanent consensus of qualified scientific observers or judges. But of course a scientific consensus is at best an ideal one, since no member of the scientific community, at any given time, has the time, energy, or relevant knowledge necessary to test the theories of his peers. And in fact the amount of faith actually required to keep the enterprise of empirical science going has become, in our time, exponential.

In brief, the equalitarian and democratic tendencies implied by modern rationalist doctrines of knowledge are both in principle and in fact restrictive. Perhaps the least misleading analogy here is the *institution* of science and the restrictive democracy of ancient Athens. In principle, anyone who possesses the necessary aptitudes and can acquire the requisite skills for performing the appropriate intellectual operations, is free to enter the scientific establishment. Even so, such a principle is by definition restrictive.[5] Here we shall discount restrictions that are owing to historical social factors, which are generally regarded by rationalists as accidental rather than essential. Even so it is impossible to ignore the great native differences in scientific aptitude. Bertrand Russell, himself a great liberal as well as a rationalist, has said somewhere that the difference in intellectual capacity between an Einstein and an ordinary man is hardly less great than the difference in this regard between an ordinary man a chimpanzee. Russell has often been given to hyperboles, but I think we all get the point: A great number of human beings, even under optimum conditions, cannot be expected to understand clearly, not to say make contributions to, the most advanced forms of exact science. And if intellectual power, not to say rationality itself, is measured primarily in terms of the ability to do exact science, then it may be taken for granted that scientific institutions and especially those concerned with the so-called higher learning, provide little basis or support for principles of extensive human equality and general social or political democracy. And from the standpoint of society as a whole, any rationalist ideology preoccupied with the greatest possible realization of man's highest good, itself conceived essentially in terms of scientific understanding, is bound to that extent to be elitist and hence undemocratic.

No doubt such a conception of rationalism as a general ideology is too simplistic, though I think that it is well to have it in the record before its lines are softened. With this understanding, several important qualifications of it may now be introduced. From Plato on down, rationalists have generally emphasized that there should be equal opportunity among the members of society to receive as much intellectual training as possible, and so to fulfill whatever powers they may have for realizing man's distinctive or highest good. Secondly, many rationalists, including Plato, have argued that *high* intellectual capacity (again conceived in terms of rationalist assumptions) may not be required for the creditable performance of other jobs essential to any tolerable, not to say good, society. Moreover, such jobs both presuppose and realize some measure of intellectual power. In the performance of such jobs, imaginatively conceived and understood, men of relatively low intelligence (once more conceived in rationalist terms) thus realize their own limits of man's highest good. More important, however, rationalism need not ignore the common requirements for citizenship and, still more important, for moral respect. On these scores, rationalists often argue that the essential thing is not high intelligence but simple intelligence, not perfect rationality but essential rationality. Citizenship may be intellectually less demanding than set theory or nuclear physics, but every chump above the level of a chimp can qualify for the citizen's bit. So the basic forms of social and political life in a rationalist utopia (which as a utopia aspires only to the not-impossible) might still be conceived in quite boradly equalitarian and democratic terms. As for moral respect, which the rationalist is disposed to conceive—at least by analogy—in law-like terms, this is the respect due any individual in terms that are essentially "human." And all that being human requires, from this point of view, is a medium of the power to perform the operations essential to scientific understanding. What I must respect in the case of every featherless biped that can qualify as human in his essential rationality, not the degree of his brilliance as a potential mathematician or physicist or logician.

3. We have now to consider, also only schematically, the rationalist approach to the ideal of the good society. Broadly speaking, it follows from the rationalist conceptions of man, his nature and good. I have already remarked upon rationalism's fundamental view concerning the moral relations among men. Something more must now be said about rationalist approaches to morality. This is a sticky wicket. To begin with, as I have said, the ground of *moral* rights and responsibilities for most rationalists is human rationality itself. But now this thesis must itself be qualified. Here we may distinguish a strong or exclusivist rationalism in ethics from a weaker or inclusivist rationalism. Strong or exclusivist rationalism maintains that the sole basis of moral regard or concern should be man's nature as a rational being. This may be taken to imply that the fundamental human right to respect for the rationality of the individual: his capacity, that is to say, for scientific understanding and judgment. All other human rights are derived from or justified in terms of this right. Thus, if the fundamental right is a right to respect for the rational faculty of every individual who possesses it, it follows, since every faculty exists not simply to be possessed as a latent power but to be exercised in practice and in act, that each individual has a right (a) to respect for those opinions which are rationally arrived at and which therefore fall within the range of his intellectual competence and (b) to as much education as his natural powers permit. Other rights, accordingly, could be justified as conditions of these primary rights of rational beings as such. Thus, for example, the rights to life, security, the satisfaction of natural appetites or drives, liberty, and so on might be justified in terms of their utility in

relation to the life of reason which is the life of knowledge. But it must be added at once, exclusivist rationalism does not acknowledge any independent human right to any of these other putative goods or satisfactions.

It is not clear that any great moral philosopher has been an exponent of exclusivist rationalism, though some Kantians appear to have come very close to such a view. However, Kant himself (as I understand him) contended that although each rational being has a right to be regarded as an end unto himself, he is, to himself, not merely a rational being but also one who desires happiness. And for present purposes this may be taken to include the satisfaction of his natural desires. Hence, it could be argued that Kant's own view implied that although the right to exercise and develop one's rational faculty is the absolutely unconditional and primary human right, there is another right, that is, the right to pursue one's happiness which, although secondary to the right to regard and respect as a rational being and conditional upon one's being a rational being (non-rational beings, that is, cannot claim a right to pursue happiness) is *not* dependent upon its utility as a means to the life of reason itself.

The Greeks generally talked less of rights and duties than of goods and virtues. However, a weak or inclusivist rationalism may be easily derived from the classical rationalist conception of man's complete good. From this inclusivist point of view, one could readily argue that although man's primary, or in cases of conflict, prior, rights pertain to his essential rationality, his other fundamental propensities provide the basis of rights which, as such, need not be defended on utilitarian grounds as causal conditions of the exercise and enjoyment of the rights of rational beings. These rights pertain only to *rational* beings, but, on this condition, though secondary or lower, they deserve respect. The rights pertaining to rationality always take precedence. But where no problem of conflict exists, they provide the basis of moral claims by individuals both upon society itself and upon its members.

There remains another position open to rationalists which is of considerable interest both on its own account and in the light of certain developments in the institutional life of modern science. The rationalist may begin by returning to the basic premise of his notion of the good life, namely, that man's highest good consists in the pursuit and enjoyment of knowledge, and that the exemplary form of human knowledge is exact positive science. He then may argue that the rights of men as functioning *rational* beings are not a result of their native endowment of judgment and understanding, which is virtually nil. Man is through and through a social being, and his rationality, both in potency and in act, is a social achievement. And the more exact and systematic human knowledge becomes, the more evident is this fact. Both the advancement of learning and its transmission through the educational process are increasingly products of corporate institutional activities. To be sure, the collective fund of human knowledge is acquired, saved, and transmitted through the work of men. Nevertheless, the individual scholar, scientist, and teacher of science, remains, so to say, the legatee and trustee of a corporate fund of knowledge. And his rights and his dignity as a rational animal derive entirely from his ability to fill these roles. In short, the scientist as such is a truly anonymous public servant whose goals, standards, and works belong entirely to the social institutions which he serves.

In times past, to be sure, the advancement of learning was, or appeared to be, largely the work of independent scholars and inquirers, and the transmission of the skills and powers essential to this advancement was a far more loosely organized social enterprise than it has become in our own time. Accordingly, the progress of human knowledge was intermittent, spotty, and uncertain. Now the reverse is true. The exponential enlargement of human learning is itself a direct function of the development of modern institutions of controlled experimental inquiry. These corporate bodies, with their own indispensable divisions of labor, involve sharply differentiated and stratified intellectual responsibilities and prerogatives. In the great scientific laboratories, for example, section heads, laboratory technicians, secretarial aides, and the rest are in practice organized in a quasi-platonic manner, under the direction of administrative "guardians" who at once set the goals for inquiry and determine the rights of various classes of scientific workers. And even in universities, where the organization is looser than in industrial research corporations, stratifications remain and individual freedom of inquiry, except among tenured professors, is severely limited. And the freedom of teachers to teach what they please, as they please, is perhaps even more restricted by departmental and university needs and by corporate standards of objectivity and truth.

If, then, the highest of human goods is the advancement of knowledge, then in the modern world that good must be regarded, progressively and ideally, as the collective achievement of a highly organized and stratified institution or hierarchy of institutions. And if the society of scientific inquirers and scholars is still viewed, as it commonly is by rationalists, as a paradigm of the rational and hence good society itself, then rationalism is to that extent increasingly committed to a corporatist, rather than an individualist or contractualist conception of the ideal social system. This suggests also that old-fashioned libertarian notions of free thought and inquiry should be radically qualified, if indeed not replaced altogether, in ways that take account of the real social conditions of scientific research. Indeed, one can readily imagine that, from a rationalist point of view, the free-lance inquirer who investigates whatever he pleases in accordance with whatever procedures and standards of truth and meaning he may consider appropriate is to be viewed as intellectually irresponsible and hence socially undesirable.

To a certain extent, in fact, such a view already prevails in practice within the universities and scientific institutes, if not yet in the society at large. This is evidenced by the fact that, as a number of leading sociologists, including Daniel Bell and Lewis Coser, have suggested, the old individualist ideal of the intellectual, along with those of his progenitors, the philosophe and the general man of letters, have now been replaced by those of the academician and the scholar. And though the free-floating intellectual still exists, he tends to be regarded by professional scholars as, at best, a "journalist," and at worst, as an incompetent meddler in affairs that are not his concern.

In sum, then, corporatist or institutionalist rationalism, as it may be called, tends increasingly to view the rights of men as rational beings as entirely a function of their potentialities as participants in the collective work of scientific research and education. The *fundamental* right, however, belongs to the enterprise of science itself and to the research and academic institutions to which that enterprise is entrusted. Accordingly, freedom of inquiry, so far as the individual is concerned, is a derivative freedom, at once justified in terms of his institutional roles and limited by the appropriate rules that govern them. The fundamental respect that is due man, the rational being, is thus a respect for the self-determining and the self-correcting corporate enterprise of science as a whole. Accordingly, the correlative rights of individual men, as rational beings, are essentially social rights which that enterprise, through its appropriate qualified representatives, should determine.

Modern rationalist ideologies, I believe, are increasingly a cross between what I have called inclusive rationalism and corporate rationalism. Undoubtedly this is responsible for some of the profound tensions which now exist within the primary institution concerned with the advancement and transmission of human knowledge in modern societies: the university itself. On the one side, there remains an ideal of a society of human individuals in whom certain inalienable rights to respect and nurture are invested. According to this ideal each individual is to be entirely free to inquire, to think, to express himself as he sees fit, subject only to the inner checks within his conscience of right reason. Because the multiversity, as Clark Kerr has dubbed it, is not only a "science factory," but also a kind of republic in its own right, complete with facilities that minister not only to the student's scientific development but also (if incidentally) to his artistic, religious, and moral nurture, as well as his basic bodily needs for shelter, food, and sexual gratification, it can indeed be viewed to a certain extent, microcosmically, as an inclusive rationalist's modern paradigm of the good society itself.[6]

At the same time, there can be no doubt that the multiversity, however diversified its activities, however pluralistic its internal organization, remains a corporate institution which (with a qualification presently to be observed) not only seeks to advance and transmit knowledge but which, through its own governing bodies, its various departments and schools, its area studies and research projects, establishes the rules and principles in terms of which the advancement and transmission of knowledge are in practice to be understood. Here of course it is impossible to describe what all this means from the standpoints of the several groups which constitute the multiversity: the administration, the faculty, the student body, and the great miscellany of workers that perform the tasks necessary to the operation of the physical plant, the housekeeping and dining facilities, the stores, and the extracurricular facilities essential to the life of the institution and its communities. In his interesting book, *Bureaucracy in Higher Education*, Dean Herbert Stroup, himself a professional sociologist, has illuminatingly described the organization of offices in the modern American university as a cross between two systems or types of hierarchy: (a) the scalar, and (b) the functional.[7] From this account, it is clear that the hierarchical organization of the university itself cannot be understood in terms of simplistic analogies provided by the pyramidal hierarchies to be found in some military or business organizations (though even there, one suspects the hierarchies are not as simplistic as they may appear to the casual observer). Nonetheless, the importance of the integral hierarchies of the university, which also pervade its structures of formal instruction and research, cannot be minimized. One simple way of testing this fact is to compare the modern university with Paul Goodman's quasi-medieval ideal of a university as an anarchist community of more or less independent scholars and students who gather together, for the time being, for whatever intellectual and personal companionship and mutual illumination their friendly company may afford. Goodman's ideal, relative to what exists, is admittedly utopian. Nor is it a utopia to which modern academicians generally aspire. Only the so-called "free universities" that have sprung up in the shadows of the multiversity bear any analogy to the Goodmanian ideal. And from any modern rationalist's point of view, they are accordingly thoroughly subversive.

Before bringing this résumé of the drift of rationalism as an ideology to a close, two further points remains to be made. Both concern the institutions of education, and in particular the institutions of higher learning. In the first place, as Plato, the archetypal rationalist, long ago foresaw, the educational system is for the rationalist ideology the indispensable feeder institution to the good society or polis. In an era of advanced scientific technology such as our own, in which every other institution from industry to government, from business to the so-called media, from Madison Avenue image makers and advertisers to city planners, depends continually and essentially upon the achievements and products of modern science, there is scarcely a human activity that is not directly dependent upon or vitally affected by the educational system. Indeed, what is called "self-defense" is itself now largely dependent upon the establishments of scientific education. Modern national societies such as our own, have in this regard out-Platonized Plato himself.

But the Platonic analogy goes still deeper. For just as in the *Republic*, the state and the educational system are, in effect, one and the same, the educators serving as guardians and the guardians as educators, so in our own national society, the government and the educational system are similarly intertwined. Hence, as it now becomes impossible within the university to separate what President Perkins of Cornell calls the "missions" of research and teaching from that of public service—which in practice means primarily service in and to the federal government—so it becomes increasingly difficult, even in a formal congressional system like our own, to separate the "leaders" of the academy from those who at once implement and determine the working policies of the state. Without a cooperative educational system, including in particular the universities, the state quite simply could neither sustain nor defend itself. And without the interlocking ties to the state and its government, the whole educational system itself would disintegrate. To be sure, this need not mean that the proximate aims of the state are indistinguishable from those of the educational system, though in practice they overlap increasingly. Nor does it mean that the educational system, again including the universities in particular, is a mere pawn of the nation-state or of its government. Rather, it means, that the destinies of the state and the educational system, and in particular the university, conceived as the primary institution for the propagation and advancement of scientific learning, are mutually indispensable to one another.

The second main point concerns the role of the educational system generally, and the university in particular, in relation not simply to the concerns of the nation-state but to the society as a whole. Here I shall adopt for the sake of discussion the point of view of the inclusive rationalist who, while envisaging the corporate advancement of scientific knowledge as man's highest good, also accepts the notion of a common social good which includes satisfaction of the noncognitive propensities of men. In the *Republic* Plato does not always keep steadily in view the complete good of the community, and so he sometimes overstresses, or appears to overstress, the role of education in the polis as a whole. In a way Plato, its founder, fell in love with Academy. However, the enlightened rationalist acknowledges that the educational system, no matter how indispensable, is merely a necessary, not a sufficient institution for a tolerable, not to say, a good society. Furthermore, the inclusive rationalist insists on not only the necessity of ministering to the needs of all members of society (and not merely those which show promise of intellectual distinction and hence usefulness to the state), but of serving them all in depth, as whole men who have needs that cannot be the immediate concern of education, including educational institutions as far-flung in their activities and roles as the multiversity. Education, no matter how encompassing the activities of its own institutions may be, moves toward different goals than do government or economy. There are also many lower-order cultural activities that have different proximate goals from those of the educational system, no matter how broadly gauged. For example, art, literature, music, and dance, as well as the newer "media," as they are called, are intended in part at least not as contributions to learning but rather as sources of consummatory satisfaction or pleasure. Their aim, as Bernard Berenson used to say, is immediately "life-enhancing." And just because of this they must not be tied too closely to activities that are concerned with learning and teaching. The proper complaint against academic art is simply that it is a bore. And rationalists, no more than other people, are not obliged to approve of boredom. Thus, while the university should cultivate (in moderation) all of the arts, it should distinguish between the work of the teacher and the apprentice on the one side, and the mature, creative artist and his audience on the other, even though in practice both, or all, of these groups may in fact overlap.

The rationalist himself may be the first to insist that an educational system whose concern is with the advancement and propagation of knowledge cannot be all things to all men, however much the universities may tend to become microcosmic societies and social systems in their own right. Education cannot be all, because learning cannot be all. Man is indeed, as Ralph Barton Perry used to put it, the "docile" animal, by which he meant that animal that learns from his experience. However, docility is not manhood, only its condition. And when we become "men"—as, one may hope, we are always becoming from the moment of birth—we seek, rightly and rightfully, to use our acquired skills and abilities to make and form and act and do things which, as such, are not the learner's immediate business—nor yet, therefore, the teacher's. A society dominated by its teachers and learners is a society committed to the ideal that learning is man's only, or primary good. And this is not true. Such a society, ironically, makes a fetish of immaturity.

II

It is evident from the preceding remarks that we have been passing implicitly from the description of rationalism as an ideology, including its sense in its more inclusive forms of the role of education, toward its critique. Let us now bring that critique into the open.

I shall begin by saying something about the fundamental weaknesses of rationalism as an ideology, even at its best, and hence the radical errors to which, at that best, its view of man, society, and education are prone. This is also a critique of an ever more deeply ingrained tradition in our whole Western culture with which, in my judgment, it is necessary to make a final and radical break. Of necessity, I shall have to deal with these difficult matters in a very summary and superficial fashion which may make it appear that I am more dogmatic, as well as surer of my ground, than I am. The following remarks are thus to be viewed as challenges and as explorations, rather than as finished positions.

Bluntly: although rationality is indeed one essential dimension of a tolerable human nature, it is by no means the only propensity that on the one side distinguishes man from other creatures: nor does it form *the* basis of his highest good.

Consider how much is either left out or misconceived when man's rational faculty is viewed as his unique, controlling, and highest human endowment. For example, man is also uniquely the religious animal, the being capable of grasping his own mortality, and of making something beyond his own individual existence a matter of ultimate concern. This is something that escapes the rational animal as such. Secondly (and here I am not interested in questions of priority or rank), man is the communal animal, capable of friendship, comradeship, and the forms of love sometimes grouped under the heading of agape. Man, if you will, is the animal that loves; he is therefore the animal that reciprocates and needs reciprocity. At the same time, man is also the self-perfecting, self-overcoming, and self-transcending being. And this, not only in the religious or social or intellectual dimension, but in the widest sense, in the ethical or moral dimension. Now, however, another ideal comes more distinctly into view: the ideal of self-determination, of self-control, of what Kant called "giving onself the law." The very notion of morality is impossible apart from the ideal of the individual as an autonomous agent, who assumes responsibility for his own conduct, his own principles, his own comportment. In fact, apart from such a view of man, free personal relations among men, including above all the relations of contract and personal loyalty and love, can scarcely exist.

But the moment the word "person" is introduced, a whole dimension of human character comes into view which cannot be adequately comprehended by the notion of rationality. In fact rationality itself is but one of the forms which this dimension of character normally takes. Man is, inventively, the role-playing, the acting, and not merely the active animal. In large part his cultural and spiritual life, indeed his entire mental life itself is a matter of role-playing and of acting. Clearly role-playing involves the capacity to follow rules, and the attitudes attendant thereto. The role-playing requires the ability to subordinate his interests, feelings, indeed his whole "subjective" personality, as it is sometimes called, to the role itself. But it requires much more; in most cases it also requires the capacity for identification which is sometimes called empathy. And since the mode of identification is in this case freely imaginative, it is not something that can be fully understood in terms of rule-governed activities and practices: it is, in fact, to the latter what the actual, open-ended, dialogical and speculative use of language is to rules of grammar and of usage.

Summarily we may say that man is or should be distinctively the animal capable of living the life of the mind. This, among other things, means the power to turn or to transform every motion, every bodily change, every purely behavioral process into an action, a passion, an event, an occasion. Or if this sounds insufferably loose and romantic, we may say more exactly that man is the creature whose own bodily processes, changes, and motions have no *being* for him save in so far as he can relate them to mental events, developments, actions.

But such a conception of man is not adequately conveyed by the notion of the rational animal. In fact I should be prepared to argue that the rationalist misconceives the life of the mind, and that his reductivist view of knowledge is itself symptomatic of that misconception. His own fault, curiously, is itself a failure of understanding and of knowledge. In consequence he at once misconceives and misrepresents man's good, high as well as complete, and as a result the forms of social life and of education required for both endurable- and well-being. Worse, he has an inadequate understanding of rationality itself. Rationality in fact must be saved from the ideology of rationalism.

In saying this, let me add that I do not object to the view, which my friend Frankena (in conversation) considers very rationalistic indeed, that the task of education, as such, being concerned with learning is therefore concerned with knowledge. For I conceive the proximate aim of all learning to be some form of knowledge, and knowledge to be the achievement which learning, and hence education itself, can bestow. My objections to rationalism are (a) that it woefully narrows both the proper range of human knowledge and hence the proper forms of learning education, and (b) that even when that range is extended as far as it legitimately may be, there is still much more to the life of the mind than the idea of knowledge adequately comprehends.

To take the last point first, we want and ought to do more with our minds than seek knowledge. We want and ought, for one thing, simply to exercise them. Physical exercise is a pleasure, but so is mental exercise. Study, inquiry, analysis can be intrinsic goods even for those who do not succeed very far in advancing learning. But the point is more extensive. I am not proposing a bill of rights, educational or otherwise, for intellectual failures. The great romantics, however much they may have overstated or misrepresented their own aspirations, recognized above all the incomparable values and virtues of what they called the imagination. Every form of cultural and mental life yields satisfactions as well as achievements which are more and less than cognitive. And the value of these achievements is often mixed: it is intrinsic to the satisfaction or to the act as well as instrumental to other ends.

I am aware that many inclusive rationalists doubtless mean to do justice to the "lower" pleasures and to the satisfactions afforded by the body. I am not talking of them here, though the rationalist's hierarchies strike me as absurd. I am not, in short, talking about the plainly *mental* values inherent in sensory experience, or in the affective gratifications which sensation may yield, important as they may be. What is here in view is the entire incomparable life of the constructive imagination, whose aim at least in part, is not to inform us about what is or ought to be but to offer envisagements of what might be and to fashion symbolic forms to which questions of literal fact are not determining. Nothing is more indispensable to the domains of literature and indeed of all art than the tropes, in which the mind finds a great part of its own inner life and happiness. Their loss, or worse their repudiation among literal-minded "cognitivists," concerned exclusively with describing or explaining what is the case, entails not only for themselves but for societies and educational systems which view them as exemplary, a terrible constriction of the whole life of the human spirit and a ghastly depletion of man's capacity for refreshment and self-renewal.

But if the rationalist misunderstands the mind he so greatly prizes, no less does he foolishly disenfranchise familiar ranges of human cognition. This is all the more perverse, since from his point of view, knowledge itself is the proper end and achievement of the human mind. Here, let me emphasize, I do not mean to dwell simply upon the nonempirical elements in scientific understanding itself: that is, its essential dependence upon mathematics and logic, its involvement in contra-factual or subjunctive modes of understanding, and the sophisticated perceptual and motor drills and skills required for experimental inquiries and confirmations. The issue now concerns forms of knowledge that are *not* merely dimensions or vehicles of scientific inquiry or conditions of the cognitive achievements which it affords.

In such a paper as this it is perhaps most useful to proceed by reference to domains of activity that the modern rationalist, at least, generally concedes to lie outside of the scope of positive science itself. Most important is the understanding of ordinary language and symbolic forms themselves. The rationalist often appears to take linguistic understanding for granted. And in fact the great rationalists have often treated language as little more than an auxiliary device for communicating ideas and beliefs, perceptions and understandings already acquired and possessed in some other way. Here I can do no more than remind you of a truth, tersely stated by one of the greatest of modern rationalists, C. S. Peirce, namely, that "thought and expression are one," and that without the intelligent use of language as well as other modes of expression there could be no thought and no knowledge of any sort. Language is essential not to communication only, but also to the very formation of scientific propositions, theories, and doctrines. It is also indispensable to that dialogue of the soul with itself in terms of which Socrates conceived self-knowledge. Without it, in fact, the life of the mind would shrivel virtually to nothing. But the knowledge achieved by anyone who knows how to use any natural language (together with its attendant symbolisms) properly and hence discriminately is a knowledge of an enormously varied range of forms of expression (and thought) that serve to articulate and to guide corresponding forms of life. To know how to read and to speak a natural language is automatically to know what it is to participate in all such correlative ways of life.

Of course such understandings may be jammed, confused, impoverished by a prevailing rationalist ideology or culture. But they cannot entirely be destroyed by it. Men who know what it means to love God may be hobbled by a misguided semantics or theory of knowledge, or an ontology beset by preconceptions about "what there is." But the language they learn, and the knowledge thereby acquired, permit no further hobbling. Likewise, those who know what is said when the moralist, or the poet, or the politician says his bit, know and learn more than any rationalist ideology can undo. If an atheist learns the King's English he automatically learns in spite of himself what it means to pray. And if a Platonist learns the marvelous language of his forebearers, he learns more than tendentious Plato could try to make him unlearn.

I need go no further. Knowledge of a natural language continues a basic human culture in its own right, an ability to achieve many things that the rationalist always misunderstands or falsifies. Let me be more specific. The person who learns how to read the Bible, knows also what it can be to know or love God. The person who knows how to read Hamlet knows what it is to understand and appreciate a work of art. The individual who knows what a "person" is knows at the same time what it means to assume or to be assigned a role, along with the responsibilities and rights that pertain thereto. And the person who knows how we address another as "you" or "thou," knows what communication and fraternity, what contract and community are. Overstating the point in order to make it, I say: language is all. Or if it is not (and it is not), a statement of what the knower of a language really knows suffices both to confute and to enlarge the understanding of anyone who fancies himself to be a rationalist.

Of course the knowledge of a language makes possible many forms of achievement that are *not* intrinsically cognitive. Thus, giving an order, though it indeed presupposes and involves a considerable range of cognitive skills—including knowing how to give an order—is not itself a cognitive achievement. Not everything we do with words, by a very long shot, is to articulate or communicate something we know, even in the very widest sense of the term. Nor is every successful verbal expression or communication intended to convey a cognition. Yet one of the major ranges (or system of ranges) of human utterance is indeed cognitive. And cognition, in one form or another, is the proximate goal of a very great part of human expression and thought. In fact, my main intention in mentioning the centrality of the knowledge required for the use of a natural language is not only to show what other things are presupposed by linguistic skills, but to first of all set the stage for a review of the gamut of essentially cognitive activities for which the knowledge of a natural language prepares us:

(A) Understanding of a (natural) language makes possible, and is essential to, all forms of theoretical knowledge which the rationalist himself most saliently emphasizes; that is to say, general knowledge of matters of fact, and, no less important, those systematic bodies of such knowledge which comprise a theory or, more broadly, a science.

(B) Furthermore, it makes possible the basic modes of the formal knowledge that comprise logic and mathematics. And because the conditions of this sort of knowledge are not exactly the same as those required for general factual knowledge, or of the sorts embodied in the empirical sciences, the adequate understanding of a language at least introduces the user to the differential conditions required for formal logical understanding and for empirical knowledge.

(C) Understanding the roles and functions of a natural language also enables us to grasp the forms of knowledge concerned with the life of conduct and of action. In so doing it introduces us to the principles and ranges of practical reason. Here I must simply state what I believe to be the truth, that although these forms of knowledge do indeed involve and presuppose empirical factual knowledge, practical understanding is not reducible to the latter. In fact one of the ways of bringing out the differences between the latter and the knowledge involved in matters of action is through the sorts of desultory linguistic study to which so-called ordinary language philosophers have so usefully devoted themselves since the Second World War.

(C_1) Among the forms of knowledge essential to the life of action are first of all those comprised under the headings of want, desire, and interest. Rational action would be impossible if individuals could not know, or come to know, *what* they desire. And I consider it a very grave error on the part of philosophers in the tradition of Hume to set human knowledge generally in contrast or opposition to those forms of deliberation and action that determine, inform, and issue from desire. Knowing what one wants is a distinctive and often difficult human achievement, rendered all the more difficult by philosophies which systematically deny it cognitive status as such. But knowing what one wants also presupposes another preliminary form of knowledge to which Stuart Hampshire, among others, has called attention in his recent book, *The Freedom of the Individual.* This is the knowledge of the kinds of possibility which I shall here call "human" in order to distinguish them from logical or physical possibilities. Here I have space only to mention the knowledge of possible objectives as well as possible lines of action which one could pursue, or institute, if one chose to do so. This sort of knowledge, let me add, is an indispensable phase of that range of human understanding we call self-knowledge.

(C_2) Of course knowing what one wants, or could do if one wanted to, is only a part of what one needs to know in order to understand oneself or in order to engage in rational action. Here we may simply follow Kant in making a general but indispensable distinction between the knowledge of what is wanted or desired and the knowledge of what is good and right, of what ought to be and to be done (including what *ought* to be affirmed and said). All the same, I believe Kant to be mistaken in certain fundamental particulars as to the nature of the latter forms of knowledge. But again there is space here only to set out the barest mention of what I take to be the correct view. First is the knowledge derived from and dependent upon the employment of public standards and grading systems. Participation in such routine collective enterprises as various as going to market, getting an academic degree, passing an examination, or returning a bad egg to the waiter, all essentially involve both the knowledge of standards and the ability to apply them. Knowing what is good and bad is in very large part knowledge of just this sort. But it should be stressed here that one has not learned all that is involved and required in distinguishing between the good and the bad unless one also knows what it is to be involved in a grading situation, to perform grading operations, and not least to establish *and to modify* the standards by which things may be graded. By analogical extension, we move by stages from the simple knowledge of grades and of things as graded, to the knowledge—also essentially public and impersonal—involved in the understanding of institutions and the forms of activity essential or proper to them. Here in particular I have in mind the knowledge of what particular institutions and forms of activity are for, the ends they serve—in terms of which alone they are distinguished from one another as institutions. Here indeed, at a distance, there is much to be learned from the classical rationalist, and especially Plato himself. Among such forms of activity are the various arts and crafts, and indeed all the various disciplines whose principles must be known if one is to engage in or to obtain a competence in them. In many instances, it may be added, such knowledge would be difficult or impossible to acquire without formal instruction of some sort. For, also involved in full knowledge of a discipline is the understanding of its various offices, and of the distinctive responsibilities and rights pertaining thereto. All this knowledge is also entirely public and impersonal, although it has aspects which again radically distinguish it from the sorts of knowledge that are usually called scientific. Where Plato and Aristotle went radically wrong is in supposing that institutions and hence their constitutions are unalterable. Full knowledge of an institution entails a grasp of its history and hence its possibilities and directions of change.

(C_3) But of course no man is merely a bundle of stations and duties, and only the mythological organization man has solved the problems about what he should do with himself when he knows the institutions, the activities, and the responsibilities and rights pertaining thereto, in which his life is entangled. And if we use the term "ethics" in referring to the codes of right action which such institutional activities involve, then let us reserve the term "moral," here, for responsibilities and problems of conduct not covered by such codes. This way of putting the matter, however, may be misleading, for I do not mean to suggest that morality is simply what is left over after, so to say, we have done our various ethical sums and received the grades we truly deserve. In particular there are problems of "personal relations," which I conceive of as distinctively and crucially *moral* problems, that cannot be settled by appeal to any institutional or disciplinary principles whatever. Nonetheless, for each individual there *is* such a thing as moral knowledge—that is to say, the knowledge of what "I" ought to aim at and to do. And, correlatively, there is an irreducibly first-personal knowledge of moral responsibilities or obligations. This knowledge, as I have argued elsewhere, may itself be (and be called) objective. But this, precisely, does not entail that such knowledge is of the sort acquired by following either the public routines of the positive sciences or the lines of activity which our public stations and duties impose upon us. Objectivity is *not* the special or exclusive prerogative of public or of institutional life, not to mention the form of institutional life of which "science" is the inadequate summary name.

(C₄) But it is essential now to say something about philosophical knowledge. As I conceive it, morality is concerned with problems of personal relations and hence with problems of conduct concerned essentially with what we, as human beings, ought to do in our dealings with persons (including ourselves). But if all of us, *as moral beings*, are more and less than systems of stations and duties, so also are we as individual human beings more than persons. Our selves encompass and are not encompassed by our various personae; we also encompass and are not encompassed by our personalities as moral agents. I agree with Professor Frankena, although for different reasons, that what he calls the good life includes more than the moral life. But from my point of view the moral life and the moral problems which it involves are an inalienable part of the good, or at least the tolerable, life. Nor, on the other hand, do I conceive the good or tolerable life in terms either of ends set by our interests or desires, or even of their harmonious or inclusive satisfaction. For a tolerable life would involve, among other things, living or trying to live up to one's moral responsibilities, being able, as we say suggestively, to live with oneself. But a good life encompasses more than a life both of satisfied desires and of good conscience in the moral sense. For a good life must, in principle, provide some fulfillment or satisfaction of every range and dimension of the self. And this includes the fulfillment of those responsibilities which one sets oneself, simply as such, but which go beyond the range of personal relations. Here, for purposes of discussion, let me invoke the useful Protestant notion of the vocation or calling. Thus conceived, an individual self becomes involved, by stages, in a *life* and in a destiny that is peculiarly and poignantly his own. And the knowledge or understanding of that life, and of the vocation or vocations it commits him to is achieved only by many stages, not all of them moral. No one, I should argue, can finally know my vocation but me (and God, if God there be). Others may offer advice, which may and doubtless should be gratefully listened to—on occasion. But the knowledge their advice is based on or may embody is not, as such, the knowledge of what I am finally to be and to become. For it remains general and impersonal, a knowledge of human character and human nature, which, again, is at once both more and much less than a knowledge of myself.

What has this to do with philosophy? In the end quite simply everything. For if morality concerns the problems of first-personal relations among self-determining persons, philosophy concerns the problems faced by the would-be self-governing self in its great confrontations with its total environment and in its developing and cumulative efforts to discover for itself those modes of self-identification out of which it can make a life. The philosopher, who by definition seeks not just the wisdom of life in general (if such there be) but the wisdom of and for his own life, is driven precisely to raise all the limiting questions which the establishmentarian, the bureaucrat, and the functionary do not answer because they have neither a need nor a duty to ask them. For the latter, in fact, such questions are precisely meaningless, without point, silly. For the philosopher (and, of course, in some fashion everyone of us is a philosopher) however, they and his efforts to answer them are in a way his very life. And, conversely, his life is a series of *agones:* struggles, or arguments with himself whose ever-unfinished and unfinishable end is precisely that positive freedom to which (among others) Socrates and Spinoza, the great idealists, and, in our time, the existentialists, have all in one way or another aspired. This is why the dialogical form adopted by Plato, and recurrently employed and readapted by many philosophers since his time, seems so naturally to be the classical literary genre for the presentation of philosophical problems. It is also why, at a certain stage, it becomes necessary for the philosopher to move, as Kant for one so conspicuously did, from analysis to dialectic. For analysis offers only the elucidation of a distinctive form of words or symbols and its corresponding form of activity and life. Dialectic, however, is required when one moves beyond the principles that govern it to their ever unstable places in one's own scheme of things and hence to the claims they may rightly make upon one's own encompassing being.

Thus conceived, there can be strictly no such thing as *the* philosophy of science, *the* philosophy of art, or *the* philosophy of education, but only philosophies of science, art, and education. And these themselves become philosophies, or rather partial philosophies, only when they are eventually brought into dialectical relation to the other "philosophies of x" which concern one's life.

The analytic stages of philosophical inquiry do, or can, yield bona fide public knowledge, though properly conceived this can never be a purely empirical knowledge, precisely because the "object" to be known is not a pattern of physical change but a form of thought and action, a system not of phenomena, but of principles, rules, methods. But the philosopher, again, can never content himself with analysis; for having discovered, as he thinks, what the principles governing a form of activity are, he must then go on to ask normative questions about them which in the final instance are essentially first-personal. And if the answers he comes to are illuminating to others, this is only because they have asked analogous questions for themselves and find themselves involved in corresponding predicaments of their own. But each of us must finally discover the "essential facts" for himself.

Much more would have to be said of course to turn this rude sketch into a convincing portrait. If I am right, however, philosophical knowledge or understanding, like moral knowledge, can never aspire to become part of the cumulative, public knowledge which the rationalist so exclusively prizes and indeed regards as the paradigm form of human knowledge itself. But this means that philosophy, like morality (let me now add), like religion, literature and the arts, and indeed like all the humanities, when they go to fundamentals, presents educational problems, and particularly for formal educational institutions such as the school, the college, and the university, which are essentially different from those presented by the sciences.[8]

But before saying anything about these problems by way of a conclusion, let me express my own commitment to the humanities, not just as indispensable parts of a liberal education and of a decent or free life, but also therefore, as inalienable activities of a decent, properly free society. Or, rather, it is just because they are, as I view them, inalienable functions of a free life and a free society, that any tolerable system of public education must make them central features of its curriculum. And indeed, it is only when the sciences themselves are taught and learned in a liberal and philosophical spirit that they themselves become proper parts of that liberal education which is indispensable to free men and a free society. I will go further: Until the humanities, properly conceived, are again regarded as the very heartland of such an education, and a humanistic spirit is made to prevail throughout the whole educational system—especially and increasingly throughout its institutions of higher learning—that system and those institutions will remain inadequate to their occasions. Worse, when, as now, they are regarded as incidental studies, cultural adornments to be satisfied mainly in the form of a meager and haphazard distribution requirement, or else are viewed like the sciences themselves as specialties for a few unchosen spirits who haven't the wits to do proper science, the educational system becomes a positive impediment to personal and social freedom.

Nothing could be educationally more subversive from the standpoint of a free society than a system of higher learning dominanted by the aspirations—wholly legitimate of course in their own way—of positive science and scientific technology, i.e., of the spirit of rationalism. And in fact it is precisely in the closed and totalitarian society that the institutions of higher learning become nothing but institutes of science and technology. Make no mistake: in the Soviet Union, for example, the exact physical sciences, and the forms of education that serve them, flourish as well or better than they do in so-called free societies. It is the humanities, and philosophy in particular that must go underground, if they are to exist at all in the totalitarian state. I have no doubt that there are true philosophers in the Soviet Union, just as I have no doubt that there are true philosophers wherever individual men ask limiting questions, however secretly, about "the system." And just to the extent that philosophers exist, the system is already broken, whether its masters know it or not. In a tolerable society, however, the system is broken in public.

But now a word must be said about the problems which philosophy in particular and the humanities in general present to the educator and especially to the formal educational institution. One may ask whether philosophy, as I conceive it, can be taught at all. And if in some sense it can be taught, the question remains whether it can be properly taught within the university. Let me say at once that no problems of special difficulty arise—up to a point at least—so long as one confines oneself to the history of philosophy and to the analytical philosophical preliminaries and prolegomena. Intellectual history generally requires skills which are no doubt beyond the reach of the ordinary political or social historian. Still, formal courses in intellectual history and in the history of philosophy, conceived as a branch of intellectual history, are taught, and well taught—up to a point—in many contemporary universities. Similarly, excellent courses in so-called analytical and linguistic philosophy are given in many universities and colleges. And the same is true of other humanistic studies.

It is also arguable that the only way in which philosophy can be taught is through its history. And the same may be said of other humanistic studies, including literature, the arts, and religion. I should argue, however, that the historian as such can never finally penetrate the heart of a philosophical work, any more than he can penetrate the heart of a work of literature, a musical composition, or a bible. And the reason is simply this: the matters to which such a work addresses itself are philosophical problems, and that if one has no philosophical impulses of one's own one cannot understand finally what it is all about, any more than a musicologist with a tin ear can understand what a string quartet is all about. Understanding here presupposes the possibility of first-personal appreciation, which requires a direct individual engagement and involvement with the object. In the case of philosophy, however, there is in a sense no "object" at all, but only a series of meditations which the reader or listener is permitted, for his own edification and use, to overhear. Or, to vary the figure, it is only the internal dialogue which the reader carries on with the philosophical work which is the true philosophical object. And until the historian is ready and able to conduct such a dialogue with Spinoza or Hume or Hegel or Wittgenstein he is inadequate to the work he seeks to study and to understand as a work of *philosophy.*

In philosophy, as such, the following stages can be regarded in principle as forms of learning. First of all is the task of learning how to read a philosophical work. This requires a grasp of its intention as a search for clarification and self-control on the part of its author. And this means that one must come to know what such searches and what results are to be expected from them. Here one learns and comes to know only by doing, that is, by entering directly and freely into the philosophical enterprise itself. This involves, for the reader, impersonating the philosopher one reads or listens to by asking or coming to ask his questions and struggling toward the answers he seeks and sometimes finds. But to read philosophically requires not only impersonation but, as I have already suggested, a continuing dialogical relationship on the reader's part to the work, to its questions and answers: that is to say, a questioning of the point and significance of the questions themselves, a demand for their further clarification, and a continuing struggle to make the questions one's own, or else, as is sometimes the case, to see why one must repudiate them along with their answers. As Moore once said, a large part of learning philosophy is learning what questions to ask. Another large part consists in learning what questions not to ask, what are merely pseudo-questions or show-questions that have no significance for one's life. Said Peirce in one of his profoundest *dicta,* "Dismiss make-believe!" But dismissing make-believe often takes a bit of doing. Moreover, one sometimes finds, as I have done, that one begins by making believe and ends by asking in dead earnest. Each person must finally dismiss his own make-believe. There is a sense in which the playfulness of Socrates is an essential part of his ultimate seriousness. Just because philosophy is, in part, a search for significant questions, it requires a touch of the child's play at raising questions. The question, Why? begins as a game, and ends, sometimes, as the puzzle of a life-time.

No doubt philosophy can, by various forms of indirection, imitation, and emulation, be learned. And no doubt the philosopher is, and must be, a supreme example of the autodidact. The question rather is whether anyone else can teach a man philosophy but the man himself. Here the answers are of great difficulty and my suggestions are made with diffidence.

Confining myself now to the ultimate aspirations of philosophers, rather than to the analytical preliminaries, I think one must say, first of all, that all philosophical learning and hence teaching must be at once informal and dialogical. And if, on occasion, the philosophical teacher "lectures," as I am doing here, he must try to impersonate his pupils by trying to anticipate their questions, by raising their difficulties, and by conveying the sense of struggle—the agony, if you will—involved in all genuine philosophical reflection. Socrates remains, in my view, the archetypal philosophical teacher, that is, one who teaches by asking leading questions, and then by forcing his "pupils" to question and requestion their own successive answers. All philosophical teaching is indeed a kind of spiritual midwifery. The philosopher does not and cannot teach by telling or even, finally, by explaining. Or rather, all his tellings and explainings are at best leading and exemplary. But even these will misfire without a plentiful and continual dose of the irony, including the self-mockery, of which Socrates was so great a master.

Now I must bring these remarks to a head and close. I do not mean to suggest that Socrates is the ideal teacher; in many spheres of learning his way of teaching is either impossible or immensely inefficient. There is a place for the pedagogue who teaches by telling and explaining, by formal demonstrations, and the rest. What I do contend is that philosophical education and the forms of learning and teaching possible and proper to it, is an indispensable part of any education that pretends to be liberal and that aims at the cultivation of free men and free minds for a free society.

What does all this really come to? It means, I think, that there is not and can never be an "objective" paradigm case of the philosopher, or a philosophical problem, even, indeed, of a philosophical activity. Philosophy is not a science, but neither is it an art. Philosophers want discipline, but not entrance into a discipline. There are, and can be, no principles of philosophy, in the way that there are, say, principles of logic or of physics. Philosophical principles, like moral ones, are at best or worst first-personal precepts, even when, on occasion, the first person happens to be not singular but plural. Philosophy in short is the indispensable free activity of the liberal mind and the free man. Its possibility is also a condition and a token of the free or tolerable society. And philosophical education, accordingly, must be an indispensable ingredient in any system of higher education proper to a free society.

One may go a step further. The informality of philosophical study, and hence of philosophical learning and teaching; its playfulness and seriousness; its imitativeness and its refusal to put up with imitation; its exemplars and undercutting of all exemplars and leaders; and finally, its aspiration to go beyond study to mature acts of self-commitment and self-creation offers, not a model for the good society or the good life, but a necessary dimension or aspect of a tolerable society and an endurable human life. Accordingly, it is because rationalism so totally perverts the philosophical spirit and aspiration that it must be exorcised not only from academic philosophy itself, but also, and for deeper, more fundamental reasons, from the implicit ideologies both of the university and of our contemporary polis in America. Or it must be exorcised if the American university is to be a truly liberal institution of higher education and if the American polis is to be, or to aspire to be, a society fit for free men.

As it is, I am bound to say, it is entirely problematic whether American universities—deeply interpenetrated as they are by the spirit of rationalism and the American social system, and overwhelmed as the latter is by the cant and by all the status symbols of a rationalist ideology—are very much better fitted than their "totalitarian" counter-parts to be the objects of a philosopher's piety and love.

NOTES

1. From time to time I will mention variant forms of rationalism. My purpose in so doing is in part to make it clear that rationalism, like all living ideologies, is not a static but a historically developing point of view.

2. It is on this point of course that Hegel differs from ordinary rationalists, as it is, also, a major reason for their disdain for his philosophy.

3. Henceforth it is these latter conceptions of the powers essential to scientific thought and understanding which will be emphasized.

4. Let me add that in my opinion it is largely owing to the pervasive influence of rationalism as an ideology both within the universities generally and also within academic departments of philosophy that existentialism has had little or no impact upon professional philosophy, despite the great interest of students in it. For a similar reason, the so-called informalist linguistic and analytical philosophy that stems from the work of the later Wittgenstein may now be seen for what it always had been: a mere episode in the history of academic philosophy in the twentieth century.

5. In practice, of course, there are *de facto* limitations which always make such a principle still more restrictive. For apart from the question of native ability, there is the problem of utilizable ability—of what, in view of their early nurture or "background" (economic, social, educational, psychological), individuals can manage to accomplish. In any actual, historical society, the working abilities of men so far as potential scientific understanding is concerned, vary and doubtless will continue to vary enormously. Many, perhaps most, men in actual societies, and certainly in our own, would be unable to make use of the sort of training Plato envisaged for the philosophers (guardians in the *Republic*). And it is for this reason that scientifically oriented educators, such as James Bryant Conant, have argued that the ideal of a university education for everyone is impractical, even in a society which could afford it.

6. Let me emphasize that I am aware that important qualifications of such a conception would have to be made in any full account, since a multiversity is precisely not a complete polis, and doubtless should not be permitted to become one. Even for the rationalist it remains merely *one* highly complex and indispensable institution within a still more inclusive and complex social system. I am also aware that most rationalists would themselves insist that there are

corporate responsibilities which the multiversity cannot, and doubtless should not, assume in relation either to its individual factuty members or to its students.

7. The former, exemplified in certain military and business organizations, is pyramidal, involving chains and levels of authority and responsibility, that begin with the trustees and run down through the various offices of the president, the deans, department heads, professors, assistants, and so on. The latter, or functional type, is a class structure whose rights and duties are established by various specific functions or roles essential to the activities and the work of the university as a whole. It is in terms of this structure that the familiar distinctions between students, faculty, and administration are conceived, as well as the divisions of the faculties themselves into schools and departments, and the so-called liberal arts departments are arranged in the well-known trivium of natural sciences, social sciences, and humanities.

8. Of course, this as it stands won't do either.

CHAPTER THREE
PHILOSOPHY
AND THE
MORAL LIFE

We live in a world of brilliant colors and subtle shadings. The deep blue of an October sky or the bright green of a spring leaf are unmistakable, of course, but what about the color of the sea on a sunny day? Is it blue, or is it green, or is it somehow both at once?

Our world is morally colored, too. We confront there good and evil, right and wrong; and sometimes, as with the colors of leaf or sky, we can all agree about the good or evil that we see. In other instances, as with the sea, two persons may call the moral colors quite differently; and such differing moral perceptions raise personal and philosophical problems of great difficulty. Consider the following situation, for example.

The war, now in its third bloody year, is not going well for the Allies. After the lightning advances of the first year, the enemy seems in firm command of his captured territory. His industrial strength is growing daily, as is the morale of his people, and his army is rested and well equipped. In another six months a counteroffensive by the Allies will be out of the question. If something is to be done to avoid total defeat, it must be done quickly.

In preparation for a counteroffensive, Allied agents have infiltrated enemy-occupied territory; patient months have been spent compiling maps of enemy fortification, recruiting and training resistance fighters, creating an effective spy network, and making detailed plans for insurrection and sabotage. In a few days all will be ready. In the meantime, of course, the enemy has not been idle in his efforts to unmask Allied agents and resistance leaders. But now has come some extraordinary luck for the Allies: Resistance forces have captured the director of enemy counterintelligence, a man notorious for both his skill and his barbaric tactics, a man known to the partisans as "the Butcher." As head of the Allied intelligence group, you are parachuted into occupied territory to interrogate him.

You are taken to the house where the Butcher is being held under tight security, and there you are greeted and briefed by the leader of the group that captured him.

"The Butcher is ours now," he says. "He is a dead man. You, my friend, may question him as you wish. You may beat him; you may burn him with cigarettes; you may pull out his fingernails. We don't care. You do whatever you wish, whatever works. But this much is sure: He was a dead man from the minute we stopped his car; he will never leave this house alive."

You walk downstairs to a dark basement. There, tied in a straight chair, sits the Butcher. His bruised face and bandaged head show that the questioning so far—futile, all of it—has not been gentle. As you approach he opens his eyes and smiles.

"I know you," he says. "And you know me. How many hours have we spent reading each other's files and thinking each other's thoughts? Listen. I have a proposition for you.

"I know what you are planning, this counteroffensive. I have already read your mind and taken steps to stop you. We know the names of some of your best agents; we know the location of most of your weapons and supplies; we know the details of some of your attack plans. We are ready for you. I am your enemy, you know, but you also know I am an honorable man. I do not lie to another officer and gentleman. So believe me: Your plans are in trouble.

"I do not wish to die, but these men who hold me will kill me if they can. Here is my offer. Give me your solemn word—I know you are an honorable man too—give me your word as an officer and a gentleman that my life will be spared, and I will tell you, right now, what we know and what I have ordered done to spoil your plans. If you act immediately you can hide your agents, move your supplies, and alter your tactics. Otherwise, your efforts will surely fail. Give me your word, promise me safety, and I will tell you; if you refuse, then I will die with the knowledge you need. Pleading and torture will do you no good. Only give me your word . . . ."

There is the offer. The Butcher is right: You do need to know what he knows. You cannot risk pulling out all your agents or changing all your plans. There simply isn't time. If these things are known, as the Butcher says, then the sabotage *will* probably fail, thus putting at high risk the Allied counteroffensive. But you cannot honestly give him your word, of course. You cannot sincerely promise him safety when you *know* that the resistance leader is waiting upstairs to kill him. If you promise, it will be a lie. And if you don't promise, the whole Allied war effort will be in jeopardy.

What would *you* do? Would you lie, or would you turn and climb out of that basement? That, of course, is a moral question, perhaps for you a difficult one, perhaps not. The philosophical question here—difficult for *anyone*—is: How should one *decide* such a moral question?

Socratic philosophy maintains that the unexamined life is not worth living. As we saw in his encounter with Euthyphro, Socrates insists that we investigate *why* we do what we do, that we seek *appropriate structures of justification* for our actions. Thus, to live that examined life, we cannot simply follow parents' rules, religious tradition, or social custom; we must think for ourselves, achieve our autonomy as rational beings. When we face a moral choice—luckily, most of them are not as difficult as the one just described—we must choose between good and evil. Choosing well—that is, autonomously—presupposes that we can tell the difference. But how *do* we tell the difference between good and evil? Socrates would put the philosophical question this way: What is the good life for a human being? More recent philosophers have discussed the matter in terms of *right and wrong actions,* rather than good and evil lives, and have put the question thus: What makes an action right to do?

Philosophers have proposed quite different answers to this question. One answer identifies the rightness of an action as a function of the goodness of its consequences. If the consequences of an action are *good* consequences, then the action is right to do; if they are not, then it is not right to do. For example, if lying to the Butcher has good consequences (innocent lives saved, the enemy defeated, and so on), then telling that lie is the right thing to do. If that lie has bad consequences, then it is not right to tell it.

This view—it is unusually called *consequentialism,* for obvious reasons—has a certain stark simplicity to commend it, but many questions remain to be answered: What makes *good* consequences *good*? Do *all* the consequences of a right action have to be good, or just *most* of them? Is rightness determined by *actual* consequences or by *likely* or *intended* ones? Are all the *effects* of an action thereby *consequences* of it? If consequences determine the rightness of an action, does this mean that an action might be right at one time (or for one person) and yet wrong at another (or for another)? And if consequences determine rightness, does this mean that *any* action—even murder or slavery—might be right, given the appropriate circumstances?

Troubled by such questions, some philosophers have formulated another answer, which argues that the rightness (or wrongness) of an action is something inherent in that kind of action itself, not something determined by external considerations like its consequences. If it is right to tell the truth, then it is *always* right, even to the Butcher. How, they ask, can moral rightness—absolute, necessary—depend upon some contingency? Right is simply right, and wrong wrong, come hell or high water. But this approach—typically called *deontology,* after *deon,* the Greek word for *duty*—is troubled by its own questions. How can one tell which actions belong on which side of the right/wrong barrier? What is it that makes an action so absolutely right or so absolutely wrong? Don't circumstances always alter cases? And doesn't deontology approach fanaticism? Isn't its insistence upon the absoluteness of right and wrong a reversion to a childish approach to morality, an attempt to avoid the gray areas that make adult moral life so trying?

In this chapter you will study the writings of both consequentialists and deontologists. First you will look at the most familiar form of consequentialist moral philosophy, the *utilitarianism* of Jeremy Bentham and John Stuart Mill. Then attention will turn to deontology, and you will read selections from the greatest of such moral philosophers, Immanuel Kant. In both instances you will also be furnished essays that raise critical questions about these moral philosophies.

You will see that neither consequentialism nor deontology can be easily dismissed. Each has its powerful philosophical advocates, and, more important, each captures something of our common moral experience. In the insistence that moral thinking pay close attention to the circumstances of agent and action we hear the voice of the consequentialist, just as we do in the reformer's plea that we act "for the greatest good of the greatest number." Likewise, in the promptings of conscience that justice to the individual cannot be forfeited not matter what the gains to the social whole, we recognize the claims of deontology. Each moral philosophy has its point; yet the two remain fundamentally opposed, antithetical images of moral thought and life. Since Socratic wisdom abhors such a contradiction between basic viewpoints, seeing it as a sign that at least one of them is mistaken, one cannot be both a consequentialist and a deontologist. Hence we face the question: By which of these compelling visions shall we live?

So we see that the difficulties of the moral life are not all moral. To live well, not only must we fight our own sloth, cowardice, and lapses of judgment; we must also confront fundamental philosophical disputes about the nature of moral action itself. Here we recognize both the inescapability of philosophy and its urgency. We must live, after all. We do choose this rather than that, and we believe—hope—that we are choosing rightly. But are we sure? Certainly we cannot be until we have wrestled with the philosophical issues at the bottom of our lives. And what then? Can we be sure that they will submit to our struggle, that the answers we need will come crystal clear? Certainly not. The promise of Socratic philosophy is not the promise of easy victory; perhaps, as with Socrates himself, our efforts will be lifelong. But that is no cause for despair, since in those efforts we came for the first time fully alive, building human souls for our human bodies.

CONSEQUENTIALISM

THE GOOD AS PLEASURE

Jeremy Bentham

The principle of utility.   Nature has placed mankind under the governance of two sovereign masters, *pain* and *pleasure*. It is for them alone to point out what

From Jeremy Bentham, *An Introduction to the Principles of Morals and Legislation,* chapters 1, 2, 4, and 10 (London: to come 1823).

we ought to do, as well as to determine what we shall do. On the one hand the standard of right and wrong, on the other the chain of causes and effects, are fastened to their throne. They govern us in all we do, in all we say, in all we think; every effort we can make to throw off our subjection, will serve but to demonstrate and confirm it. In words a man may pretend to abjure their empire: but in reality he will remain subject to it all the while. The *principle of utility* recognizes the subjection, and assumes it for the foundation of that system, the object of which is to rear the fabric of felicity by the hands of reason and of law. Systems which attempt to question it, deal in sounds instead of sense, in caprice instead of reason, in darkness instead of light.

But enough of metaphor and declamation: it is not by such means that moral science is to be improved.

The principle of utility is the foundation of the present work; it will be proper therefore at the outset to give an explicit and determinate account of what is meant by it. By the principle of utility is meant that principle which approves or disapproves of every action whatsoever, according to the tendency which it appears to have to augment or diminish the happiness of the party whose interest is in question; or what is the same thing in other words, to promote or to oppose that happiness. I say of every action whatsoever; and therefore not only of every action of a private individual, but of every measure of government.

By utility is meant that property in any object, whereby it tends to produce benefit, advantage, pleasure, good, or happiness (all this in the present case comes to the same thing) or (what comes again to the same thing) to prevent the happening of mischief, pain, evil, or unhappiness to the party whose interest is considered: if that party be the community in general, then the happiness of the community: if a particular individual, then the happiness of that individual.

The interest of the community is one of the most general expressions that can occur in the phraseology of morals: no wonder that the meaning is often lost. When it has a meaning, it is this. The community is a fictitious *body,* composed of the individual persons who are considered as constituting as it were its *members.* The interest of the community then is, what?—the sum of the interests of the several members who compose it.

It is in vain to talk of the interest of the community, without understanding what is the interest of the individual. A thing is said to promote the interest, or to be *for* the interest, of an individual, when it tends to add to the sum total of his pleasures: or, what comes to the same thing, to diminish the sum total of his pains.

An action then may be said to be comfortable to the principle of utility, or, for shortness' sake, to utility (meaning with respect to the community at large) when the tendency it has to augment the happiness of the community is greater than any it has to diminish it.

A measure of government (which is but a particular kind of action, performed by a particular person or persons) may be said to be conformable to or dictated by the principle of utility, when in like manner the tendency which it has to augment the happiness of the community is greater than any which it has to diminish it. . . .

Of an action that is comfortable to the principle of utility, one may always say either that it is one that ought to be done, or at least that it is not one that ought not to be done. One may also say, that it is right it should be done; at least that it is not wrong it should be done: that it is a right action; at least that it is not a wrong action. When thus interpreted, the words *ought,* and *right* and *wrong,* and others of that stamp, have a meaning: when otherwise, they have none.

Principles adverse to that of utility.   If the principle of utility be a right principle to be governed by, and that in all cases, it follows from what has been just observed, that whatever principle differs from it in any case must necessarily be a wrong one. To prove any other principle, therefore, to be a wrong one, there needs no more than just to show it to be what it is, a principle of which the dictates are in some point or other different from those of the principle of utility: to state it is to confute it.

A principle may be different from that of utility in two ways: 1. By being constantly opposed to it: this is the case with a principle which may be termed the principle of *asceticism.* 2. By being sometimes opposed to it, and sometimes not, as it may happen: this is the case with another, which may be termed the principle of *sympathy* and *antipathy.*

By the principle of asceticism I mean that principle, which, like the principle of utility, approves or disapproves of any action, according to the tendency which it appears to have to augment or diminish the happiness of the party whose interest is in question; but in an inverse manner: approving of actions in as far as they tend to diminish his happiness; disapproving of them in as far as they tend to augment it. . . .

The principle of asceticism seems originally to have been the reverie of certain hasty speculators, who having perceived, or fancied, that certain pleasures, when reaped in certain circumstances, have, at the long run, been attended with pains more than equivalent to them, took occasion to quarrel with everything that offered itself under the name of pleasure. Having then got thus far, and having forgot the point which they set out from, they pushed on, and went so much further as to think it meritorious to fall in love with pain. Even this, we see, is at bottom but the principle of utility misapplied.

The principle of utility is capable of being consistently pursued; and it is but tautology to say, that the more consistently it is pursued, the better it must ever be for humankind. The principle of asceticism never was, nor never can be, consistently pursued by any living creature. Let but one tenth part of the inhabitants of this earth pursue it consistently, and in a day's time they will have turned it into a hell.

Among principles adverse to that of utility, that which at this day seems to have most influence in matters of government, is what may be called the principle of sympathy and antipathy. By the principle of sympathy and antipathy, I mean that principle which approves or disapproves of certain actions, not on account of their tending to augment the happiness, nor yet on account of their tending to diminish the happiness of the party whose interest is in question, but merely because a man finds himself disposed to approve or disapprove of them: holding up that approbation or disapprobation as a sufficient reason for itself, and disclaiming the necessity of looking out for any extrinsic ground. Thus far in the general department of morals; and in the particular department of politics, measuring out the quantum (as well as determining the ground) of punishment, by the degree of the disapprobation.

It is manifest, that this is rather a principle in name than in reality; it is not a positive principle of itself, so much as a term employed to signify the negation of all principle. What one expects to find in a principle is something that points out some external consideration, as a means of warranting and guiding the internal sentiments of approbation and disapprobation; this expectation is but ill fulfilled by a proposition, which does neither more nor less than hold up each of those sentiments as a ground and standard for itself.

In looking over the catalogue of human actions (says a partisan of this principle) in order to determine which of them are to be marked with the seal of disapprobation, you need but to take counsel of your own feelings: whatever you find in yourself a propensity to condemn, is wrong for that very reason. For the same reason it is also meet for punishment: in what proportion it is adverse to utility, or whether it be adverse to utility at all, is a matter that makes no difference. In that same *proportion* also it is meet for punishment; if you hate much, punish much; if you hate little, punish little; punish as you hate. If you hate not at all, punish not at all; the fine feelings of the soul are not to be overborne and tyrannized by the harsh and rugged dictates of political utility.

The various systems that have been formed concerning the standard of right and wrong, may all be reduced to the principle of sympathy and antipathy. One account may serve for all of them. They consist all of them in so many contrivances for avoiding the obligation of appealing to any external standard, and for prevailing upon the reader to accept of the author's sentiment or opinion as a reason for itself.

The hedonistic calculus.   Pleasures, then, and the avoidance of pains, are the *ends* which the legislator has in view: it behooves him therefore to understand their *value.* Pleasures and pains are the *instruments* he has to work with: it behooves him therefore to understand their force, which is again, in other words, their value.

To a person considered *by himself,* the value of a pleasure or pain considered *by itself,* will be greater or less, according to the four following circumstances:

1. Its *intensity.*
2. Its *duration.*
3. Its *certainty* or *uncertainty.*
4. Its *propinquity* or *remoteness.*

These are the circumstances which are to be considered in estimating a pleasure or a pain considered each of them by itself. But when the value of any pleasure or pain is considered for the purpose of estimating the tendency of any *act* by which it is produced, there are two other circumstances to be taken into the account; these are,

5. Its *fecundity,* or the chance it has of being followed by sensations of the *same* kind: that is, pleasures, if it be a pleasure: pains, if it be a pain.
6. Its *purity,* or the chance it has of *not* being followed by sensations of the *opposite* kind: that is, pains, if it be a pleasure: pleasures, if it be a pain.

These two last, however, are in strictness scarcely to be deemed properties of the pleasures or the pain itself; they are not, therefore, in strictness to be taken into the account of the value of that pleasure or that pain. They are in strictness to be deemed properties only of the act, or other event, by which such pleasure or pain has been produced; and accordingly are only to be taken into the account of the tendency of such act or such event.

To a *number* of persons, with reference to each of whom the value of a pleasure or a pain is considered, it will be greater or less, according to seven circumstances: to wit, the six preceding ones: viz.

1. Its *intensity.*
2. Its *duration.*
3. Its *certainty* or *uncertainty.*
4. Its *propinquity* or *remoteness.*
5. Its *fecundity.*
6. Its *purity.*

And one other; to wit:

7. Its *extent;* that is, the number of persons to whom it *extends;* or (in other words) who are affected by it.

To take an exact account then of the general tendency of any act, by which the interests of a community are affected, proceed as follows. Begin with any one person of those whose interests seem most immediately to be affected by it: and take an account,

1. Of the value of each distinguishable *pleasure* which appears to be produced by it in the *first* instance.
2. Of the value of each *pain* which appears to be produced by it in the *first* instance.
3. Of the value of each pleasure which appears to be produced by it *after* the first. This constitutes the *fecundity* of the first *pleasure* and the *impurity* of the first *pain.*
4. Of the value of each *pain* which appears to be produced by it after the first. This constitutes the *fecundity* of the first *pain,* and the *impurity* of the first *pleasure.*
5. Sum up all the values of all the *pleasures* on the one side, and those of all the *pains* on the other. The balance, if it be on the side of pleasure, will give the *good* tendency of the act upon the whole, with respect to the interests of that *individual* person; if on the side of pain, the *bad* tendency of it upon the whole.

6. Take an account of the *number* of persons whose interests appear to be concerned; and repeat the above process with respect to each. *Sum up* the numbers expressive of the degrees of *good* tendency, which the act has, with respect to each individual, in regard to whom the tendency of it is *good* upon the whole: do this again with respect to each individual, in regard to whom the tendency of it is *bad* upon the whole. Take the *balance;* which, if on the side of *pleasure,* will give the general *good tendency* of the act, with respect to the total number or community of individuals concerned; if on the side of *pain,* the general *evil tendency,* with respect to the same community.

It is not to be expected that this process should be strictly pursued previously to every moral judgment, or to every legislative or judicial operation. It may, however, be always kept in view: and as near as the process actually pursued on these occasions approaches to it, so near will such process approach to the character of an exact one.

Motives.   With respect to goodness and badness, as it is with everything else that is not itself either pain or pleasure, so is it with motives. If they are good or bad, it is only on account of their effects: good, on account of their tendency to produce pleasure, or avert pain: bad, on account of their tendency to produce pain, or avert pleasure. Now the case is, that from one and the same motive, and from every kind of motive, may proceed actions that are good, others that are bad, and others that are indifferent. . . .

It appears then that there is no such thing as any sort of motive which is a bad one in itself: nor, consequently, any such thing as a sort of motive which in itself is exclusively a good one. And as to their effects, it appears too that these are sometimes bad, at other times either indifferent or good, and this appears to be the case with every sort of motive. *If any sort of motive then is either good or bad on the score of its effects, this is the case only on individual occasions, and with individual motives;* and this is the case with one sort of motive as well as with another. *If any sort of motive then can, in consideration of its effects, be termed with any propriety a bad one,* it can only be with reference to the balance of all the effects it may have had of both kinds within a given period, that is, of its most usual tendency.

What then? (it will be said) are not lust, cruelty, avarice, bad motives? Is there so much as any one individual occasion, in which motives like these can be otherwise than bad? No, certainly: and yet the proposition, that there is no one *sort* of motive but what will on many occasions be a good one, is nevertheless true. The fact is, that these are names which, if properly applied, are never applied but in the cases where the motives they signify happen to be bad. The names of these motives, considered apart from their effects, are sexual desire, displeasure, and pecuniary interest. To sexual desire, when the effects of it are looked upon as bad, is given the name of lust. Now lust is always a bad motive. Why? Because if the case be such, that the effects of the motive are not bad, it does not go, or at least ought not to go, by the name of lust. The case is, then, that when I say, "Lust is a bad motive," it is a proposition that merely concerns the import of the word lust; and which would be false if transferred to the other word used for the same motive, sexual desire. Hence we see the emptiness of all those rhapsodies of common-place morality, which consist in the taking of such names as lust, cruelty, and avarice, and branding them with marks of reprobation: applied to the *thing,* they are false; applied to the *name,* they are true indeed, but nugatory. Would you do a real service to mankind, show them the cases in which sexual desire *merits* the name of lust; displeasure, that of cruelty, and pecuniary interest, that of avarice.

UTILITARIANISM

John Stuart Mill

Chapter I: General Remarks

There are few circumstances among those which make up the present condition of human knowledge, more unlike what might have been expected, or more significant of the backward state in which speculation on the most important subjects still lingers, than the little progress which has been made in the decision of the contro-versy respecting the criterion of right and wrong. From the dawn of philosophy, the question concerning the *summum bonum,* or, what is the same thing, concerning the foundation of morality, has been accounted the main problem in speculative thought, has occupied the most gifted intellects, and divided them into sects and schools, carrying on a vigorous warfare against one another. And after more than two thousand years the same discussions continue, philosophers are still ranged under the same contending banners, and neither thinkers nor mankind at large seem nearer to being unanimous on the subject, than when the youth Socrates listened to the old Protagoras, and asserted (if Plato's dialogue be grounded on a real conver-sation) the theory of utilitarianism against the popular morality of the so-called sophist.

It is true that similar confusion and uncertainty, and in some cases similar discordance, exist respecting the first principles of all the sciences, not excepting that which is deemed the most certain of them, mathematics; without much impairing, generally indeed without impairing at all, the trustworthiness of the conclusions of those sciences. An apparent anomaly, the explanation of which is, that the detailed doctrines of a science are not usually deducted from, nor depend for their evidence upon, what are called its first principles. Were it not so, there would be no science more precarious, or whose conclusions were more insuffici-ently made out, than algebra; which derives none of its certainty from what are commonly taught to learners as its elements, since these, as laid down by some of its most eminent teachers, are as full of fictions as English law, and of mysteries as theology. The truths which are ultimately accepted as the first principles of a science, are really the last results of metaphysical analysis, practised on the elemen-

From *Utilitarianism* (London: Parker, Son, and Bourn, 1863), chapters 1, 2, and 4.

tary notions with which the science is conversant; and their relation to the science is not that of foundations to an edifice, but of roots to a tree, which may perform their office equally well though they be never dug down to and exposed to light. But though in science the particular truths precede the general theory, the contrary might be expected to be the case with a practical art, such as morals or legislation. All action is for the sake of some end, and rules of action, it seems natural to suppose, must take their whole character and colour from the end to which they are subservient. When we engage in a pursuit, a clear and precise conception of what we are pursuing would seem to be the first thing we need, instead of the last we are to look forward to. A test of right and wrong must be the means, one would think, of ascertaining what is right or wrong, and not a consequence of having already ascertained it.

The difficulty is not avoided by having recourse to the popular theory of a natural faculty, a sense or instinct, informing us of right and wrong. For—besides that the existence of such a moral instinct is itself one of the matters in dispute—those believers in it who have any pretensions to philosophy, have been obliged to abandon the idea that it discerns what is right or wrong in the particular case in hand, as our other senses discern the sight or sound actually present. Our moral faculty, according to all those of its interpreters who are entitled to the name of thinkers, supplies us only with the general principles of moral judgments; it is a branch of our reason, not of our sensitive faculty; and must be looked to for the abstract doctrines of morality, not for perception of it in the concrete. The intuitive, no less than what may be termed the inductive, school of ethics, insists on the necessity of general laws. They both agree that the morality of an individual action is not a question of direct perception, but of the application of a law to an individual case. They recognize also, to a great extent, the same moral laws; but differ as to their evidence, and the source from which they derive their authority. According to the one opinion, the principles of morals are evident *à priori,* requiring nothing to command assent, except that the meaning of the terms be understood. According to the other doctrine, right and wrong, as well as truth and falsehood, are questions of observation and experience. But both hold equally that morality must be deduced from principles; and the intuitive school affirm as strongly as the inductive, that there is a science of morals. Yet they seldom attempt to make out a list of the *a priori* principles which are to serve as the premises of the science; still more rarely do they make any effort to reduce those various principles to one first principle, or common ground of obligation. They either assume the ordinary precepts of morals as of *à priori* authority, or they lay down as the common groundwork of those maxims, some generality much less obviously authoritative than the maxims themselves, and which has never succeeded in gaining popular acceptance. Yet to support their pretensions there ought either to be some one fundamental principle or law, at the root of all morality, or if there be several, there should be a determinate order of precedence among them; and the one principle, or the rule for deciding between the various principles when they conflict, ought to be self-evident.

To inquire how far the bad effects of this deficiency have been mitigated in practice, or to what extent the moral beliefs of mankind have been vitiated or made uncertain by the absence of any distinct recognition of an ultimate standard, would imply a complete survey and criticism of past and present ethical doctrine. It would, however, be easy to show that whatever steadiness or consistency these moral beliefs have attained, has been mainly due to the tacit influence of a standard not recognised. Although the non-existence of an acknowledged first principle has made ethics not so much a guide as a consecration of men's actual sentiments, still, as men's sentiments, both of favour and of aversion, are greatly influenced by what they suppose to be the effects of things upon their happiness, the principle of utility, or as Bentham latterly called it, the greatest happiness principle, has had a large share in forming the moral doctrines even of those who most scornfully reject its authority. Nor is there any school of thought which refuses to admit that the influence of actions on happiness is a most material and even predominant consideration in many of the details of morals, however unwilling to acknoweldge it as the fundamental principle of morality, and the source of moral obligation. I might go much further, and say that to all those *à priori* moralists who deem it necessary to argue at all, utilitarian arguments are indispensable. It is not my present purpose to criticise these thinkers; but I cannot help referring, for illustration, to a systematic treatise by one of the most illustrious of them, the *Metaphysics of Ethics,* by Kant. This remarkable man, whose system of thought will long remain one of the landmarks in the history of philosophical speculation, does, in the treatise in question, lay down a universal first principle as the origin and ground of moral obligation; it is this:—"So act, that the rule on which thou actest would admit of being adopted as a law by all rational beings." But when he begins to deduce from this precept any of the actual duties of morality, he fails, almost grotesquely, to show that there would be any contradiction, any logical (not to say physical) impossibility, in the adoption by all rational beings of the most outrageously immoral rules of conduct. All he shows is that the *consequences* of their universal adoption would be such as no one would choose to incur.

On the present occasion, I shall, without further discussion of the other theories, attempt to contribute something toward the understanding and appreciation of the Utilitarian or Happiness theory, and toward such proof as it is susceptible of. It is evident that this cannot be proof in the ordinary and popular meaning of the term. Questions of ultimate ends are not amenable to direct proof. Whatever can be proved to be good, must be so by being shown to be a means to something admitted to be good without proof. The medical art is proved to be good by its conducing to health; but how is it possible to prove that health is good? The art of music is good, for the reason, among others, that it produces pleasure; but what proof is it possible to give that pleasure is good? If, then, it is asserted that there is a comprehensive formula, including all things which are in themselves good, and that whatever else is good, is not so as an end, but as a mean, the formula may be accepted or rejected, but is not a subject of what is commonly understood by proof. We are not, however, to infer that its acceptance or rejection must depend on blind impulse, or arbitrary choice. There is a larger meaning of the word proof, in which this question is as amenable to it as any other of the disputed questions of philosophy. The subject is within the cognisance of the rational faculty; and neither does that faculty deal with it solely in the way of intuition. Considerations may be presented capable of determining the intellect either to give or withhold its assent to the doctrine; and this is equivalent to proof.

We shall examine presently of what nature are these considerations; in what manner they apply to the case, and what rational grounds, therefore, can be given for accepting or rejecting the utilitarian formula. But it is a preliminary condition of rational acceptance or rejection, that the formula should be correctly understood. I believe that the very imperfect notion ordinarily formed of its meaning, is the chief obstacle which impedes its reception; and that could it be cleared, even from only the grosser misconceptions, the question would be greatly simplified, and a large proportion of its difficulties removed. Before, therefore, I attempt to enter into the philosophical grounds which can be given for assenting to the utilitarian standard, I shall offer some illustrations of the doctrine itself; with the view of showing more clearly what it is, distinguishing it from what it is not, and disposing of such of the practical objections to it as either originate in, or are closely connected with, mistaken interpretations of its meaning. Having thus prepared the ground, I shall afterwards endeavour to throw such light as I can upon the question, considered as one of philosophical theory.

Chapter II: What Utilitarianism Is

A passing remark is all that needs be given to the ignorant blunder of supposing that those who stand up for utility as the test of right and wrong, use the term in that restricted and merely colloquial sense in which utility is opposed to pleasure. An apology is due to the philosophical opponents of utilitarianism, for even the momentary appearance of confounding them with any one capable of so absurd a misconception; which is the more extraordinary, inasmuch as the contrary accusation, of referring everything to pleasure, and that too in its grossest form, is another of the common charges against utilitarianism: and, as has been pointedly remarked by an able writer, the same sort of persons, and often the very same persons, denounce the theory "as impracticably dry when the word utility precedes the word pleasure, and as too practicably voluptuous when the word pleasure precedes the word utility." Those who know anything about the matter are aware that every writer, from Epicurus to Bentham, who maintained the theory of utility, meant by it, not something to be contradistinguished from pleasure, but pleasure itself, together with exemption from pain; and instead of opposing the useful to the agreeable or the ornamental, have always declared that the useful means these, among other things. Yet the common herd, including the herd of writers, not only in newspapers and periodicals, but in books of weight and pretension, are perpetually falling into this shallow mistake. Having caught up the word utilitarian, while knowing nothing whatever about it but its sound, they habitually express by it the rejection, or the neglect, of pleasure in some of its forms; of beauty, of ornament, or of amusement. Nor is the term thus ignorantly misapplied solely in disparagement, but occasionally in compliment; as though it implied superiority to frivolity and the mere pleasures of the moment. And this perverted use is the only one in which the word is popularly known, and the one from which the new generation are acquiring their sole notion of its meaning. Those who introduced the word, but who had for many years discontinued it as a distinctive appellation, may well feel themselves called to resume it, if by doing so they can hope to contribute anything toward rescuing it from this utter degradation.[1]

The creed which accepts as the foundation of morals, Utility, or the Greatest Happiness Principle, holds that actions are right in proportion as they tend to promote happiness, wrong as they tend to produce the reverse of happiness. By happiness is intended pleasure, and the absence of pain; by unhappiness, pain, and the privation of pleasure. To give a clear view of the moral standard set up by the theory, much more requires to be said; in particular, what things it includes in the ideas of pain and pleasure; and to what extent this is left an open question. But these supplementary explanations do not affect the theory of life on which this theory of morality is grounded—namely, that pleasure, and freedom from pain, are the only things desirable as ends; and that all desirable things (which are as numerous in the utilitarian as in any other scheme) are desirable either for the pleasure inherent in themselves, or as means to the promotion of pleasure and the prevention of pain.

Now, such a theory of life excites in many minds, and among them in some of the most estimable in feeling and purpose, inveterate dislike. To suppose that life has (as they express it) no higher end than pleasure—no better and nobler object of desire and pursuit—they designate as utterly mean and grovelling; as a doctrine worthy only of swine, to whom the followers of Epicurus were, at a very early period, contemptuously likened; and modern holders of the doctrine are occasionally made the subject of equally polite comparisons by its German, French, and English assailants.

When thus attacked, the Epicureans have always answered, that it is not they, but their accusers, who represent human nature in a degrading light; since the accusation supposes human beings to be capable of no pleasures except those of which swine are capable. If this supposition were true, the charge could not be gainsaid, but would then be no longer an imputation; for if the sources of pleasure were precisely the same to human beings and to swine, the rule of life which is good enough for the one would be good enough for the other. The comparison of the Epicurean life to that of beasts is felt as degrading, precisely because a beast's pleasures do not satisfy a human being's conception of happiness. Human beings have faculties more elevated than the animal appetites, and when once made conscious of them, do not regard anything as happiness which does not include their gratification. I do not, indeed, consider the Epicureans to have been by any means faultless in drawing out their scheme of consequences from the utilitarian principle.

To do this in any sufficient manner, many Stoic, as well as Christian elements require to be included. But there is no known Epicurean theory of life which does not assign to the pleasures of the intellect, of the feelings and imagination, and of the moral sentiments, a much higher value as pleasures than to those of mere sensation. It must be admitted, however, that utilitarian writers in general have placed the superiority of mental over bodily pleasures chiefly in the greater permanency, safety, uncostliness, etc., of the former—that is, in their circumstantial advantages rather than in their intrinsic nature. And on all these points utilitarians have fully proved their case; but they might have taken the other, and, as it may be called, higher ground, with entire consistency. It is quite compatible with the principle of utility to recognise the fact, that some *kinds* of pleasure are more desirable and more valuable than others. It would be absurd that while, in estimating all other things, quality is considered as well as quantity, the estimation of pleasures should be supposed to depend on quantity alone.

If I am asked, what I mean by difference of quality in pleasures, or what makes one pleasure more valuable than another, merely as a pleasure, except its being greater in amount, there is but one possible answer. Of two pleasures, if there be one to which all or almost all who have experience of both give a decided preference, irrespective of any feeling of moral obligation to prefer it, that is the more desirable pleasure. If one of the two is, by those who are competently acquainted with both, placed so far above the other that they prefer it, even though knowing it to be attended with a greater amount of discontent, and would not resign it for any quantity of the other pleasure which their nature is capable of, we are justified in ascribing to the preferred enjoyment a superiority in quality, so far out-weighing quantity as to render it, in comparison, of small account.

Now it is an unquestionable fact that those who are equally acquainted with, and equally capable of appreciating and enjoying, both, do give a most marked preference to the manner of existence which employs their higher faculties. Few human creatures would consent to be changed into any of the lower animals, for a promise of the fullest allowance of a beast's pleasures; no intelligent human being would consent to be a fool, no instructed person would be an ignoramus, no person of feeling and conscience would be selfish and base, even though they should be persuaded that the fool, the dunce, or the rascal is better satisfied with his lot than they are with theirs. They would not resign what they possess more than he for the most complete satisfaction of all the desires which they have in common with him. If they ever fancy they would, it is only in cases of unhappiness so extreme, that to escape from it they would exchange their lot for almost any other, however undesirable in their own eyes. A being of higher faculties requires more to make him happy, is capable probably of more acute suffering, and certainly accessible to it at more points, than one of an inferior type; but in spite of these liabilities, he can never really wish to sink into what he feels to be a lower grade of existence. We may give what explanation we please of this unwillingness; we may attribute it to pride, a name which is given indiscriminately to some of the most and to some of the least estimable feelings of which mankind are capable: we may refer it to the love of liberty and personal independence, an appeal to which was with the Stoics one of the most effective means for the inculcation of it; to the love of power, or to the love of excitement, both of which do really enter into and contribute to it: but its most appropriate appellation is a sense of dignity, which all human beings possess in one form or another, and in some, though by no means in exact, proportion to their higher faculties, and which is so essential a part of the happiness of those in whom it is strong, that nothing which conflicts with it could be, otherwise than momentarily, an object of desire to them. Whoever supposes that this preference takes place at a sacrifice of happiness—that the superior being, in anything like equal circumstances, is not happier than the inferior—confounds the two very different ideas, of happiness, and content. It is indisputable that the being whose capacities of enjoyment are low, has the greatest chance of having them fully satisfied; and a highly endowed being will always feel that any happiness which he can look for, as the world is constituted, is imperfect. But he can learn to bear its imperfections, if they are at all bearable; and they will not make him envy the being who is indeed unconscious of the imperfections, but only because he feels not at all the good which those imperfections qualify. It is better to be a human being dissatisfied than a pig satisfied; better to be Socrates dissatisfied than a fool satisfied. And if the fool, or the pig, are of a different opinion, it is because they only know their own side of the question. The other party to the comparison knows both sides.

It may be objected, that many who are capable of the higher pleasures, occasionally, under the influence of temptation, postpone them to the lower. But this is quite compatible with a full appreciation of the intrinsic superiority of the higher. Men often, from infirmity of character, make their election for the nearer good, though they know it to be the less valuable; and this no less when the choice is between two bodily pleasures, than when it is between bodily and mental. They pursue sensual indulgences to the injury of health, though perfectly aware that health is the greater good. It may be further objected, that many who begin with youthful enthusiasm for everything noble, as they advance in years sink into indolence and selfishness. But I do not believe that those who undergo this very common change, voluntarily choose the lower description of pleasures in preference to the higher. I believe that before they devote themselves exclusively to the one, they have already become incapable of the other. Capacity for the nobler feelings is in most natures a very tender plant, easily killed, not only by hostile influences, but by mere want of sustenance; and in the majority of young persons it speedily dies away if the occupations to which their position in life has devoted them, and the society into which it has thrown them, are not favourable to keeping that higher capacity in exercise. Men lose their high aspirations as they lose their intellectual tastes, because they have not time or opportunity for indulging them; and they addict themselves to inferior pleasures, not because they deliberately prefer them, but because they are either the only ones to which they have access, or the only ones which they are any longer capable of enjoying. It may be questioned whether any one who has remained equally susceptible to both classes of pleasures, ever knowingly and calmly preferred the lower; though many, in all ages, have broken down in an ineffectual attempt to combine both.

From this verdict of the only competent judges, I apprehend there can be no appeal. On a question which is the best worth having of two pleasures, or which of two modes of existence is the most grateful to the feelings, apart from its moral attributes and from its consequences, the judgment of those who are qualified by knowledge of both, or, if they differ, that of the majority among them, must be admitted as final. And there needs be the less hesitation to accept this judgment respecting the quality of pleasures, since there is no other tribunal to be referred to even on the question of quantity. What means are there of determining which is the acutest of two pains, or the intensest of two pleasurable sensations, except the general suffrage of those who are familiar with both? Neither pains nor pleasures are homogeneous, and pain is always heterogeneous with pleasure. What is there to decide whether a particular pleasure is worth purchasing at the cost of a particular pain, except the feelings and judgment of the experienced? When, therefore, those feelings and judgment declare the pleasures derived from the higher faculties to be preferable *in kind,* apart from the question of intensity, to those of which the animal nature, disjoined from the higher faculties, is susceptible, they are entitled on this subject to the same regard.

I have dwelt on this point, as being a necessary part of a perfectly just conception of Utility or Happiness, considered as the directive rule of human conduct. But it is by no means an indispensable condition to the acceptance of the utilitarian standard; for that standard is not the agent's own greatest happiness, but the greatest amount of happiness altogether; and if it may possibly be doubted whether a noble character is always the happier for its nobleness, there can be no doubt that it makes other people happier, and that the world in general is immensely a gainer by it. Utilitarianism, therefore, could only attain its end by the general cultivation of nobleness of character, even if each individual were only benefited by the nobleness of others, and his own, so far as happiness is concerned, were a sheer deduction from the benefit. But the bare enunciation of such an absurdity as this last, renders refutation superfluous.

According to the Greatest Happiness Principle, as above explained, the ultimate end, with reference to and for the sake of which all other things are desirable (whether we are considering our own good or that of other people), is an existence exempt as far as possible from pain, and as rich as possible in enjoyments, both in point of quantity and quality; the test of quality, and the rule for measuring it against quantity, being the preference felt by those who in their opportunities of experience, to which must be added their habits of self-consciousness and self-observation, are best furnished with the means of comparison. This, being, according to the utilitarian opinion, the end of human action, is necessarily also the standard of morality; which may accordingly be defined, the rules and precepts for human conduct, by the observance of which an existence such as has been described might be, to the greatest extent possible, secured to all mankind; and not to them only, but, so far as the nature of things admits, to the whole sentient creation.

Against this doctrine, however, arises another class of objectors, who say that happiness, in any form, cannot be the rational purpose of human life and action; because, in the first place, it is unattainable: and they contemptuously ask, what right hast thou to be happy? a question which Mr. Carlyle clenches by the addiction, What right, a short time ago, hast thou even *to be*? Next, they say, that men can do *without* happiness; that all noble human beings have felt this, and could not have become noble but by learning the lesson of Entsagen, or renunciation; which lesson, thoroughly learnt and submitted to, they affirm to be the beginning and necessary condition of all virtue.

The first of these objections would go to the root of the matter were it well founded; for if no happiness is to be had at all by human beings, the attainment of it cannot be the end of morality, or of any rational conduct. Though, even in that case, something might still be said for the utilitarian theory; since utility includes not solely the pursuit of happiness, but the prevention or mitigation of unhappiness; and if the former aim be chimerical, there will be all the greater scope and more imperative need for the latter, so long at least as mankind think fit to live, and do not take refuge in the simultaneous act of suicide recommended under certain conditions by Novalis. When, however, it is thus positively asserted to be impossible that human life should be happy, the assertion, if not something like a verbal quibble, is at least an exaggeration. If by happiness be meant a continuity of highly pleasurable excitement, it is evident enough that this is impossible. A state of exalted pleasure lasts only moments, or in some cases, and with some intermissions, hours or days, and is the occasional brilliant flash of enjoyment, not its permanent and steady flame. Of this the philosophers who have taught that happiness is the end of life were as fully aware as those who taunt them. The happiness which they meant was not a life of rapture; but moments of such, in an existence made up of few and transitory pains, many and various pleasures, with a decided predominance of the active over the passive, and having as the foundation of the whole, not to expect more from life than it is capable of bestowing. A life thus composed, to those who have been fortunate enough to obtain it, has always appeared worthy of the name of happiness. And such an existence is even now the lot of many, during some considerable portion of their lives. The present wretched education, and wretched social arrangements, are the only real hindrance to its being attainable by almost all.

The objectors perhaps may doubt whether human beings, if taught to consider happiness as the end of life, would be satisfied with such a moderate share of it. But great numbers of mankind have been satisfied with much less. The main constitutents of a satisfied life appear to be two, either of which by itself is often found sufficient for the purpose: tranquillity, and excitement. With much tranquillity, many find that they can be content with very little pleasure: with much excitement, many can reconcile themselves to a considerable quantity of pain. There is assuredly no inherent impossibility in enabling even the mass of mankind to unite both; since the two are so far from being incompatible that they are in natural alliance, the prolongation of either being a preparation for, and exciting a wish for, the other. It is only those in whom indolence amounts to a vice, that do not desire excitement after an interval of repose: it is only those in whom the need of excitement is a disease, that feels the tranquillity which follows excitement dull and insipid, instead of pleasurable in direct proportion to the excitement which preceded it. When people who are tolerably fortunate in their outward lot do not find in life sufficient enjoyment to make it valuable to them, the cause generally is, caring for nobody but themselves. To those who have neither public nor private affections, the excitements of life are much curtailed, and in any case dwindle in value as the time approaches when all selfish interests must be terminated by death: while those who leave after them objects of personal affection, and especially those who have also cultivated a fellow-feeling with the collective interests of mankind, retain as lively an interest in life on the eve of death as in the vigour of youth and health. Next to selfishness, the principal cause which makes life unsatisfactory is want of mental cultivation. A cultivated mind—I do not mean that of a philosopher, but any mind to which the fountains of knowledge have been opened, and which has been taught, in any tolerable degree, to exercise its faculties—finds sources of inexhaustible interest in all that surrounds it; in the objects of nature, the achievements of art, the imaginations of poetry, the incidents of history, the ways of mankind, past and present, and their prospects in the future. It is possible, indeed, to become indifferent to all this, and that too without having exhausted a thousandth part of it; but only when one has had from the beginning no moral or human interest in these things, and has sought in them only the gratification of curiosity.

Now there is absolutely no reason in the nature of things why an amount of mental culture sufficient to give an intelligent interest in these objects of contemplation, should not be the inheritance of every one born in a civilised country. As little is there an inherent necessity that any human being should be a selfish egotist, devoid of every feeling or care but those which center in his own miserable individuality. Something far superior to this is sufficiently common even now, to give ample earnest of what the human species may be made. Genuine private affections, and a sincere interest in the public good, are possible, though in unequal degrees, to every rightly brought up human being. In a world in which there is so much to interest, so much to enjoy, and so much also to correct and improve, every one who has this moderate amount of moral and intellectual requisites is capable of an existence which may be called enviable; and unless such a person, through bad laws, or subjection to the will of others, is denied the liberty to use the sources of happiness within his reach, he will not fail to find this enviable existence, if he escape the positive evils of life, the great sources of physical and mental suffering—such as indigence, disease, and the unkindness, worthlessness, or premature loss of objects of affection. The main stress of the problem lies, therefore, in the contest with these calamities, from which it is a rare good fortune entirely to escape; which as things now are, cannot be obviated, and often cannot be in any material degree mitigated. Yet no one whose opinion deserves a moment's consideration can doubt that most of the great positive evils of the world are in themselves removable, and will, if human affairs continue to improve, be in the end reduced within narrow limits. Poverty, in any sense implying suffering, may be completely extinguished by the wisdom of society, combined with the good sense and providence of individuals. Even the most intractable of enemies, disease, may be indefinitely reduced in dimensions by good physical and moral education, and proper control of noxious influences; while the progress of science holds out a promise for the future of still more direct conquests over this detestable foe. And every advance in that direction relieves us from some, not only of the chances which cut short our own lives, but, what concerns us still more, which deprive us of those in whom our happiness is wrapt up. As for vicissitudes of fortune, and other disappointments connected with wordly circumstances, these are principally the effect either of gross imprudence, of ill-regulated desires, or of bad or imperfect social institutions. All the grand sources, in short, of human suffering are in a great degree, many of them almost entirely, conquerable by human care and effort; and though their removal is grievously slow—though a long succession of generations will perish in the breach before the conquest is completed, and this world becomes all that, if will and knowledge were not wanting, it might easily be made—yet every mind sufficiently intelligent and generous to bear a part, however small and unconspicuous, in the endeavour, will draw a noble enjoyment from the contest itself, which he would not for any bribe in the form of selfish indulgence consent to be without.

And this leads to the true estimation of what is said by the objectors concerning the possibility, and the obligation, of learning to do without happiness. Unquestionably it is possible to do without happiness; it is done involuntarily by nineteen-twentieths of mankind, even in those parts of our present world which are least deep in barbarism; and it often has to be done voluntarily by the hero or the martyr, for the sake of something which he prizes more than his individual happiness. But this something, what is it, unless the happiness of others, or some of the requisites of happiness? It is noble to be capable of resigning entirely one's own portion of happiness, or chances of it: but, after all, this self-sacrifice must be for some end; it is not its own end; and if we are told that its end is not happiness, but virtue, which is better than happiness, I ask, would the sacrifice be made if the hero or martyr did not believe that it would earn for others immunity from similar sacrifices? Would it be made if he thought that his renunciation of happiness for himself would produce no fruit for any of his fellow creatures, but to make their lot like his, and place them also in the condition of persons who have renounced happiness? All honour to those who can abnegate for themselves the personal enjoyment of life, when by such renunciation they contribute worthily to increase the amount of happiness in the world; but he who does it, or professes to do it, for any other purpose, is no more deserving of admiration than the ascetic mounted on his pillar. He may be an inspiring proof of what men *can* do, but assuredly not an example of what they *should*.

Though it is only in a very imperfect state of the world's arrangements that any one can best serve the happiness of others by the absolute sacrifice of his own, yet so long as the world is in that imperfect state, I fully acknowledge that the readiness to make such a sacrifice is the highest virtue which can be found in man. I will add, that in this condition of the world, paradoxical as the assertion may be, the conscious ability to do without happiness gives the best prospect of realising such happiness as is attainable. For nothing except that consciousness can raise a person above the chances of life, by making him feel that, let fate and fortune do their worst, they have not power to subdue him: which, once felt, frees him from excess of anxiety concerning the evils of life, and enables him, like many a Stoic in the worst times of the Roman Empire, to cultivate in tranquillity the sources of satisfaction accessible to him, without concerning himself about the uncertainty of their duration, any more than about their inevitable end.

Meanwhile, let utilitarians never cease to claim the morality of self devotion as a possession which belongs by as good a right to them, as either to the Stoic or to the Transcendentalist. The utilitarian morality does recognise in human beings the power of sacrificing their own greatest good for the good of others. It only refuses to admit that the sacrifice is itself a good. A sacrifice which does not increase, or tend to increase, the sum total of happiness, it considers as wasted. The only self-renunciation which it applauds, is devotion to the happiness, or to some of the means of happiness, of others; either of mankind collectively, or of individuals within the limits imposed by the collective interests of mankind.

I must again repeat, what the assailants of utilitarianism seldom have the justice to acknowledge, that the happiness which forms the utilitarian standard of what is right in conduct, is not the agent's own happiness, but that of all concerned. As between his own happiness and that of others, utilitarianism requires him to be as strictly impartial as a disinterested and benevolent spectator. In the golden rule of Jesus of Nazareth, we read the complete spirit of the ethics of utility. To do as you would be done by, and to love your neighbour as yourself, constitute the ideal perfection of utilitarian morality. As the means of making the nearest approach to this ideal, utility would enjoin, first, that laws and social arrangements should place the happiness, or (as speaking practically it may be called) the interest, of every individual, as nearly as possible in harmony with the interest of the whole; and secondly, that education and opinion, which have so vast a power over human character, should so use that power as to establish in the mind of every individual an indissoluble association between his own happiness and the good of the whole; especially between his own happiness and the practice of such modes of conduct, negative and positive, as regard for the universal happiness prescribes; so that not only he may be unable to conceive the possibility of happiness to himself, consistently with conduct opposed to the general good, but also that a direct impulse to promote the general good may be in every individual one of the habitual motives of action, and the sentiments connected therewith may fill a large and prominent place in every human being's sentient existence. If the impugners of the utilitarian morality represented it to their own minds in this its true character, I know not what recommendation possessed by any other morality they could possibly affirm to be wanting to it; what more beautiful or more exalted developments of human nature any other ethical system can be supposed to foster, or what springs of action, not accessible to the utilitarian, such systems rely on for giving effect to their mandates.

The objectors to utilitarianism cannot always be charged with representing it in a discreditable light. On the contrary, those among them who entertain anything like a just idea of its disinterested character, sometimes find fault with its standard as being too high for humanity. They say it is exacting too much to require that people shall always act from the inducement of promoting the general interests of society. But this is to mistake the very meaning of a standard of morals, and confound the rule of action with the motive of it. It is the business of ethics to tell us what are our duties, or by what test we may know them; but no system of ethics requires that the sole motive of all we do shall be a feeling of duty; on the contrary, ninety-nine hundredths of all our actions are done from other motives, and rightly so done, if the rule of duty does not condemn them. It is the more unjust to utilitarianism that this particular misapprehension should be made a ground of objection to it, inasmuch as utilitarian moralists have gone beyond almost all others in affirming that the motive has nothing to do with the morality of the action, though much with the worth of the agent. He who saves a fellow-creature from drowning does what is morally right, whether his motive be duty, or the hope of being paid for his trouble; he who betrays the friend that trusts him, is guilty of a crime, even if his object be to serve another friend to whom he is under greater obligation. But to speak only of actions done from the motive of duty, and in direct obedience to principle: it is a misapprehension of the utilitarian mode of thought, to conceive it as implying that people should fix their minds upon so wide a generality as the world, or society at large. The great majority of good actions are intended not for the benefit of the world, but for that of individuals, of which the good of the world is made up; and the thoughts of the most virtuous man need not on these occasions travel beyond the particular persons concerned, except so far as is necessary to assure himself that in benefiting them he is not violating the rights, that is, the legitimate and authorised expectations, of any one else. The multiplication of happiness is, according to the utilitarian ethics, the object of virtue: the occasions on which any person (except one in a thousand) has it in his power to do this on an extended scale, in other words to be a public benefactor, are but exceptional; and on these occasions alone is he called on to consider public utility; in every other case, private utility, the interest or happiness of some few persons, is all he has to attend to. Those alone the influence of whose actions extends to society in general, need concern themselves habitually about so large an object. In the case of abstinences indeed—of things which people forbear to do from moral considerations, though the consequences in the particular case might be beneficial—it would be unworthy of an intelligent agent not to be consciously aware that the action is of a class which, if practised generally, would be generally injurious, and that this is the ground of the obligation to abstain from it. The amount of regard for the public interest implied in this recognition, is no greater than is demanded by every system of morals, for they all enjoin to abstain from whatever is manifestly pernicious to society.

The same considerations dispose of another reproach against the doctrine of utility, founded on a still grosser misconception of the purpose of a standard of morality, and of the very meaning of the words right and wrong. It is often affirmed that utilitarianism renders men cold and unsympathising; that it chills their moral feelings toward individuals; that it makes them regard only the dry and hard consideration of the consequences of actions, not taking into their moral esti-mate the qualities from which those actions emanate. If the assertion means that they do not allow their judgment respecting the rightness or wrongness of an action to be influenced by their opinion of the qualities of the person who does it, this is a complaint not against utilitarianism, but against having any standard of morality at all; for certainly no known ethical standard decides an action to be good or bad because it is done by a good or a bad man, still less because done by an amiable, a brave, or a benevolent man, or the contrary. These considerations are relevant, not to the estimation of actions, but of persons; and there is nothing in the utilitarian theory inconsistent with the fact that there are other things which interest us in persons besides the rightness and wrongness of their actions. The Stoics, indeed, with the paradoxical misuse of language which was part of their system, and by which they strove to raise themselves above all concern about anything but virtue, were fond of saying that he who has that has everything; that he, and only he, is rich, is beautiful, is a king. But no claim of this description is made for the virtuous man by the utilitarian doctrine. Utilitarians are quite aware that there are other desirable possessions and qualities besides virtue, and are perfectly willing to allow to all of them their full worth. They are also aware that a right action does not necessarily indicate a virtuous character, and that actions which are blamable, often proceed from qualities entitled to praise. When this is apparent in any particular case, it modifies their estimation, not certainly of the act, but of the agent. I grant that they are, notwithstanding, of opinion, that in the long run the best proof of a good character is good actions; and resolutely refuse to consider any mental dis-position as good, of which the predominant tendency is to produce bad conduct. This makes them unpopular with many people; but it is an unpopularity which they must share with every one who regards the distinction between right and wrong in a serious light; and the reproach is not one which a conscientious utilitarian need be anxious to repel.

If no more be meant by the objection than that many utilitarians look on the morality of actions, as measured by the utilitarian standard, with too exclusive a regard, and do not lay sufficient stress upon the other beauties of character which go toward making a human being lovable or admirable, this may be admitted. Utilitarians who have cultivated their moral feelings, but not their sympathies nor their artistic perceptions, do fall into this mistake; and so do all other moralists under the same conditions. When can be said in excuse for other moralists is equally available for them, namely, that, if there is to be any error, it is better that it should be on that side. As a matter of fact, we may affirm that among utilitarians as among adherents of other systems, there is every imaginable degree of rigidity and of laxity in the application of their standard; some are even puritanically rigorous, while others are as indulgent as can possibly be desired by sinner or by sentimentalist. But on the whole, a doctrine which brings prominently forward the interest that mankind have in the repression and prevention of conduct which violates the moral law, is likely to be inferior to no other in turning the sanctions of opinion against such violations. It is true, the question, What does violate the moral law? is one on which those who recognise different standards of morality are likely now and then to differ. But difference of opinion on moral questions was not first introduced into the world by utilitarnism, while that doctrine does supply, if not always an easy, at all events a tangible and intelligible mode of deciding such differences.

It may not be superfluous to notice a few more of the common misapprehensions of utilitarian ethics, even those which are so obvious and gross that it might appear impossible for any person of candour and intelligence to fall into them; since persons, even of considerable mental endowment, often give themselves so little trouble to understand the bearings of any opinion against which they entertain a prejudice, and men are in general so little conscious of this voluntary ignorance as a defect, that the vulgarest misunderstandings of ethical doctrines are continually met with in the deliberate writings of persons of the greatest pretensions both to high principle and to philosophy. We not uncommonly hear the doctrine of utility inveighed against as a *godless* doctrine. If it be necessary to say anything at all against so mere an assumption, we may say that the question depends upon what idea we have formed of the moral character of the Deity. If it be a true belief that God desires, above all things, the happiness of his creatures, and that this was his purpose in their creation, utility is not only not a godless doctrine, but more profoundly religious than any other. If it be meant that utilitarianism does not recognise the revealed will of God as the supreme law of morals, I answer, that a utilitarian who believes in the perfect goodness and wisdom of God, necessarily believes that whatever God has thought fit to reveal on the subject of morals, must fulfil the requirements of utility in a supreme degree. But others besides utilitarians have been of opinion that the Christian revelation was intended, and is fitted, to inform the hearts and minds of mankind with a spirit which should enable them to find for themselves what is right, and incline them to do it when found, rather than to tell them, except in a very general way, what it is; and that we need a doctrine of ethics, carefully followed out, to *interpret* to us the will of God. Whether this opinion is correct or not, it is superfluous here to discuss; since whatever aid religion, either natural or revealed, can afford to ethical investigation, is as open to the utilitarian moralist as to any other. He can use it as the testimony of God to the usefulness or hurtfulness of any given course of action, by as good a right as others can use it for the indication of a transcendental law, having no connection with usefulness or with happiness.

Again, Utility is often summarily stigmatised as an immoral doctrine by giving it the name of Expediency, and taking advantage of the popular use of that term to contrast it with Principle. But the Expedient, in the sense in which it is opposed to the Right, generally means that which is expedient for the particular interest of the agent himself; as when a minister sacrifices the interests of his country to keep himself in place. When it means anything better than this, it means that which is expedient for some immediate object, some temporary purpose, but which violates a rule whose observance is expedient in a much higher degree. The Expedient, in this sense, instead of being the same thing with the useful, is a branch of the hurtful. Thus, it would often be expedient, for the purpose of getting over some momentary embarrassment, or attaining some object immediately useful to ourselves or others, to tell a lie. But inasmuch as the cultivation in ourselves of a sensitive feeling on the subject of veracity, is one of the most useful, and the enfeeblement of that feeling one of the most hurtful, things to which our conduct can be instrumental; and inasmuch as any, even unintentional, deviation from truth, does that much toward weakening the trustworthiness of human assertion, which is not only the principal support of all present social well-being, but the insufficiency of which does more than any one thing that can be named to keep back civilisation, virtue, everything on which human happiness on the largest scale depends; we feel that the violation, for a present advantage, of a rule of such transcendant expediency, is not expedient, and that he who, for the sake of a convenience to himself or to some other individual, does what depends on him to deprive mankind of the good, and inflict upon them the evil, involved in the greater or less reliance which they can place in each other's word, acts the part of one of their worst enemies. Yet that even this rule, sacred as it is, admits of possible exceptions, is acknowledged by all moralists; the chief of which is when the withholding of some fact (as of information from a malefactor, or of bad news from a person dangerously ill) would save an individual (especially an individual other than oneself) from great and unmerited evil, and when the withholding can only be effected by denial. But in order that the exception may not extend itself beyond the need, and may have the least possible effect in weakening reliance on veracity, it ought to be recognised, and, if possible, its limits defined; and if the principle of utility is good for anything, it must be good for weighing these conflicting utilities against one another, and marking out the region within which one or the other preponderates.

Again, defenders of utility often find themselves called upon to reply to such objections as this—that there is not time, previous to action, for calculating and weighing the effects of any line of conduct on the general happiness. This is exactly as if any one were to say that it is impossible to guide our conduct by Christianity, because there is not time, on every occasion on which anything has to be done, to read through the Old and New Testaments. The answer to the objection is, that there has been ample time, namely, the whole past duration of the human species. During all that time, mankind have been learning by experience the tendencies of actions; on which experience all the prudence, as well as all the morality of life, are dependent. People talk as if the commencement of this course of experience had hitherto been put off, and as if, at the moment when some man feels tempted to meddle with the property or life of another, he had to begin considering for the first time whether murder and theft are injurious to human happiness. Even then I do not think that he would find the question very puzzling; but, at all events, the matter is now done to his hand. It is truly a whimsical supposition that, if mankind were agreed in considering utility to be the test of morality, they would remain without any agreement as to what *is* useful, and would take no measures for having their notions on the subject taught to the young, and enforced by law and opinion. There is no difficulty in proving any ethical standard whatever to work ill, if we suppose universal idiocy to be conjoined with it; but on any hypothesis short of that, mankind must by this time have acquired positive beliefs as to the effects of some actions on their happiness; and the beliefs which have thus come down are the rules of morality for the multitude, and for the philosopher until he has succeeded in finding better. That philosophers might easily do this, even now, on many subjects; that the received code of ethics is by no means of divine right; and that mankind have still much to learn as to the effects of actions on the general happiness, I admit, or rather, earnestly maintain. The corollaries from the principle of utility, like the precepts of every practical art, admit of indefinite improvement, and, in a progressive state of the human mind, their improvement is perpetually going on. But to consider the rules of morality as improvable, is one thing; to pass over the intermediate generalisations entirely, and endeavour to test each individual action directly by the first principle, is another. It is a strange notion that the acknowledgement of a first principle is inconsistent with the admission of secondary ones. To inform a traveller respecting the place of his ultimate destination, is not to forbid the use of landmarks and direction-posts on the way. The proposition that happiness is the end and aim of morality, does not mean that no road ought to be laid down to that goal, or that persons going thither should not be advised to take one direction rather than another. Men really ought to leave off talking a kind of nonsense on this subject, which they would neither talk nor listen to on other matters of practical concernment. Nobody argues that the art of navigation is not founded on astronomy, because sailors cannot wait to calculate the National Almanack. Being rational creatures, they go to sea with it ready calculated; and all rational creatures go out upon the sea of life with their minds made up on the common questions of right and wrong, as well as on many of the far more difficult questions of wise and foolish. And this, as long as foresight is a human quality, it is to be presumed they will continue to do. Whatever we adopt as the fundamental principle of morality, we require subordinate principles to apply it by; the impossibility of doing without them, being common to all systems, can afford no argument against any one in particular; but gravely to argue as if no such secondary principles could be had, and as if mankind had remained till now, and always must remain, without drawing any general conclusions from the experience of human life, is as high a pitch, I think, as absurdity has ever reached in philosophical controversy.

The remainder of the stock arguments against utilitarianism mostly consist in laying to its charge the common infirmities of human nature, and the general difficulties which embarrass conscientious persons in shaping their course through life. We are told that a utilitarian will be apt to make his own particular case an exception to moral rules, and, when under temptation, will see a utility in the breach of a rule, greater than he will see in its observance. But is utility the only creed which is able to furnish us with excuses for evil doing, and means of cheating our own conscience? They are afforded in abundance by all doctrines which recognise as a fact in morals the existence of conflicting considerations; which all doctrines do, that have been believed by sane persons. It is not the fault of any creed, but of the complicated nature of human affairs, that rules of conduct cannot be so framed as to require no exceptions, and that hardly any kind of action can safely be laid down as either always obligatory or always condemnable. There is no ethical creed which does not temper the rigidity of its laws, by giving a certain latitude, under the moral responsibility of the agent, for accommodation to peculiarities of circumstances; and under every creed, at the opening thus made, self-deception and dishonest casuistry get in. There exists no moral system under which there do not arise unequivocal cases of conflicting obligation. These are the real difficulties, the knotty points both in the theory of ethics, and in the conscientious guidance of personal conduct. They are overcome practically, with greater or with less success, according to the intellect and virtue of the individual; but it can hardly be pretended that any one will be the less qualified for dealing with them, from possessing an ultimate standard to which conflicting rights and duties can be referred. If utility is the ultimate source of moral obligations, utility may be invoked to decide between them when their demands are incompatible. Though the application of the standard may be difficult, it is better than none at all: while in other systems, the moral laws all claiming independent authority, there is no common umpire entitled to interfere between them; their claims to precedence one over another rest on little better than sophistry, and unless determined, as they generally are, by the unacknowledged influence of considerations of utility, afford a free scope for the action of personal desires and partialities. We must remember that only in these cases of conflict between secondary principles is it requisite that first principles should be appealed to. There is no case of moral obligation in which some secondary principle is not involved; and if only one, there can seldom be any real doubt which one it is, in the mind of any person by whom the principle itself is recognised.

Chapter IV: Of What Sort of Proof the Principle of Utility is Susceptible

It has already been remarked, that questions of ultimate ends do not admit of proof, in the ordinary acceptation of the term. To be incapable of proof by reasoning is common to all first principles; to the first premises of our knowledge, as well as to those of our conduct. But the former, being matters of fact, may be the subject of a direct appeal to the faculties which judge of fact—namely, our senses, and our internal consciousness. Can an appeal be made to the same faculties on questions of practical ends? Or by what other faculty is cognisance taken of them?

Questions about ends are, in other words, questions what things are desirable. The utilitarian doctrine is, that happiness is desirable, and the only thing desirable, as an end; all other things being only desirable as means to that end. What ought to be required of this doctrine—what conditions is it requisite that the doctrine should fulfil—to make good its claim to be believed?

The only proof capable of being given that an object is visible, is that people actually see it. The only proof that a sound is audible, is that people hear it: and so of the other sources of our experience. In like manner, I apprehend, the sole evidence it is possible to produce that anything is desirable, is that people do actually desire it. If the end which the utilitarian doctrine proposes to itself were not, in theory and in practice, acknowledged to be an end, nothing could ever convince any person that it was so. No reason can be given why the general happiness is desirable, except that each person, so far as he believes it to be attainable, desires his own happiness. This, however, being a fact, we have not only all the proof which the case admits of, but all which it is possible to require, that happiness is a good: that each person's happiness is a good to that person, and the general happiness, therefore, a good to the aggregate of all persons. Happiness has made out its title as *one* of the ends of conduct, and consequently one of the criteria of morality.

But it has not, by this alone, proved itself to be the sole criterion. To do that, it would seem, by the same rule, necessary to show, not only that people desire happiness, but that they never desire anything else. Now it is palpable that they do desire things which, in common language, are decidedly distinguished from happiness. They desire, for example, virtue, and the absence of vice, no less really than pleasure and the absence of pain. The desire of virtue is not as universal, but it is as authentic a fact, as the desire of happiness. And hence the opponents of the utilitarian standard deem that they have a right to infer that there are other ends of human action besides happiness, and that happiness is not the standard of approbation and disapprobation.

But does the utilitarian doctrine deny that people desire virtue, or maintain that virtue is not a thing to be desired? The very reverse. It maintains not only that virtue is to be desired, but that it is to be desired disinterestedly, for itself. Whatever may be the opinion of utilitarian moralists as to the original conditions by which virtue is made virtue; however they may believe (as they do) that actions and dispositions are only virtuous because they promote another end than virtue; yet this being granted, and it having been decided, from considerations of this description, what *is* virtuous, they not only place virtue at the very head of the things which are good as means to the ultimate end, but they also recognise as a psychological fact the possibility of its being, to the individual, a good in itself, without looking to any end beyond it; and hold, that the mind is not in a right state, not in a state conformable to Utility, not in the state most conducive to the general happiness, unless it does love virtue in this manner—as a thing desirable in itself, even although, in the individual instance, it should not produce those other desirable consequences which it tends to produce, and on account of which it is held to be virtue. This opinion is not, in the smallest degree, a departure from the Happiness principle. The ingredients of happiness are very various, and each of them is desirable in itself, and not merely when considered as swelling an aggregate. The principle of utility does not mean that any given pleasure, as music, for instance, or any given exemption from pain, as for example health, is to be looked upon as means to a collective something termed happiness, and to be desired on that account. They are desired and desirable in and for themselves; besides being means, they are a part of the end. Virtue, according to the utilitarian doctrine, is not naturally and originally part of the end, but it is capable of becoming so; and in those who love it disinterestedly it has become so, and is desired and cherished, not as a means to happiness, but as a part of their happiness.

To illustrate this further, we may remember that virtue is not the only thing, originally a means, and which if it were not a means to anything else, would be and remain indifferent, but which by association with what it is a means to, comes to be desired for itself, and that too with the utmost intensity. What, for example, shall we say of the love of money? There is nothing originally more desirable about money than about any heap of glittering pebbles. Its worth is solely that of the things which it will buy; the desires for other things than itself, which it is a means of gratifying. Yet the love of money is not only one of the strongest moving forces of human life, but money is, in many cases, desired in and for itself; the desire to possess it is often stronger than the desire to use it, and goes on increasing when all the desires which point to ends beyond it, to be compassed by it, are falling off. It may, then, be said truly, that money is desired not for the sake of an end, but as part of the end. From being a means to happiness, it has come to be itself a principal ingredient of the individual's conception of happiness. The same may be said of the majority of the great objects of human life—power, for example, or fame; except that to each of these there is a certain amount of immediate pleasure annexed, which has at least the semblance of being naturally inherent of fame, is the immense aid they give to the attainment of in them; a thing which cannot be said of money. Still, however, the strongest natural attraction, both of power and our other wishes; and it is the strong association thus generated between them and all our objects of desire, which gives to the direct desire of them the intensity it often assumes, so as in some characters to surpass in strength all other desires. In these cases the means have become a part of the end, and a more important part of it than any of the things which they are means to. What was once desired as an instrument for the attainment of happiness, has come to be desired for its own sake. In being desired for its own sake it is, however, desired as *part* of happiness. The person is made, or thinks he would be made, happy by its mere possession; and is made unhappy by failure to obtain it. The desire of it is not a different thing from the desire of happiness, any more than the love of music, or the desire of health. They are included in happiness. They are some of the elements of which the desire of happiness is made up. Happiness is not an abstract idea, but a concrete whole; and these are some of its parts. And the utilitarian standard sanctions and approves their being so. Life would be a poor thing, very ill provided with sources of happiness, if there were not this provision of nature, by which things originally indifferent, but conducive to, or otherwise associated with, the satisfaction of our primitive desires, become in themselves sources of pleasure more valuable than the primitive pleasures, both in permanency, in the space of human existence that they are capable of covering, and even in intensity.

Virtue, according to the utilitarian conception, is a good of this description. There was no original desire of it, or motive to it, save its conduciveness to pleasure, and especially to protection from pain. But through the association thus formed, it may be felt a good in itself, and desired as such with as great intensity as any other good; and with this difference between it and the love of money, of power, or of fame, that all of these may, and often do, render the individual noxious to the other members of the society to which he belongs, whereas there is nothing which makes him so much a blessing to them as the cultivation of the disinterested love of virtue. And consequently, the utilitarian standard, while it tolerates and approves those other acquired desires, up to the point beyond which they would be more injurious to the general happiness than promotive of it, enjoins and requires the cultivation of the love of virtue up to the greatest strength possible, as being above all things important to the general happiness.

It results from the preceding considerations, that there is in reality nothing desired except happiness. Whatever is desired otherwise than as a means to some end beyond itself, and ultimately to happiness, is desired as itself a part of happiness, and is not desired for itself until it has become so. Those who desire virtue for its own sake, desire it either because the consciousness of it is a pleasure, or because the consciousness of being without it is a pain, or for both reasons united; as in truth the pleasure and pain seldom exist separately, but almost always together, the same person feeling pleasure in the degree of virtue attained, and pain in not having attained more. If one of these gave him no pleasure, and the other no pain, he would not love or desire virtue, or would desire it only for the other benefits which it might produce to himself or to persons whom he cared for.

We have now, then, an answer to the question, of what sort of proof the principle of utility is susceptible. If the opinion which I have now stated is psychologically true—if human nature is so constituted as to desire nothing which is not either a part of happiness or a means of happiness, we can have no other proof, and we require no other, that these are the only things desirable. If so, happiness is the sole end of human action, and the promotion of it the test by which to judge of all human conduct; from whence it necessarily follows that it must be the criterion of morality, since a part is included in the whole.

And now to decide whether this is really so; whether mankind do desire nothing for itself but that which is a pleasure to them, or of which the absence is a pain; we have evidently arrived at a question of fact and experience, dependent, like all similar questions, upon evidence. It can only be determined by practiced self-consciousness and self-observation, assisted by observation of others. I believe that these sources of evidence, impartially consulted, will declare that desiring a thing and finding it pleasant, aversion to it and thinking of it as painful, are phenomena entirely inseparable, or rather two parts of the same phenomenon; in strictness of language, two different modes of naming the same psychological fact: that to think of an object as desirable (unless for the sake of its consequences), and to think of it as pleasant, are one and the same thing; and that to desire anything, except in proportion as the idea of it is pleasant, is a physical and metaphysical impossibility.

So obvious does this appear to me, that I expect it will hardly be disputed: and the objection made will be, not that desire can possibly be directed to anything ultimately except pleasure and exemption from pain, but that the will is a different thing from desire; that a person of confirmed virtue, or any other person whose purposes are fixed, carries out his purposes without any thought of the pleasure he has in contemplating them, or expects to derive from their fulfillment; and persists in acting on them, even though these pleasures are much diminished, by changes in his character or decay of his passive sensibilities, or are out-weighed by the pains which the pursuit of the purposes may bring upon him. All this I fully admit, and have stated it elsewhere, as positively and emphatically as any one. Will, the active phenomenon, is a different thing from desire, the state of passive sensibility, and though originally an offshoot from it, may in time take root and detach itself from the parent stock; so much so, that in the case of an habitual purpose, instead of willing the thing because we desire it, we often desire it only because we will it. This, however, is but an instance of that familiar fact, the power of habit, and is nowise confined to the case of virtuous actions. Many indifferent things, which men originally did from a motive of some sort, they continue to do from habit. Sometimes this is done unconsciously, the consciousness coming only after the action: at other times with conscious volition, but volition which has become habitual, and is put in operation by the force of habit, in opposition perhaps to the deliberate preference, as often happens with those who have contracted habits of vicious or hurtful indulgence. Third and last comes the case in which the habitual act of will in the individual instance is not in contradiction to the general intention prevailing at other times, but in fulfillment of it; as in the case of the person of confirmed virtue, and of all who pursue deliberately and consistently any determinate end. The distinction between will and desire thus understood is an authentic and highly important psychological fact; but the fact consists solely in this—that will, like all other parts of our constitution, is amenable to habit, and that we may will from habit what we no longer desire for itself, or desire only because we will it. It is not the less true that will, in the beginning, is entirely produced by desire; including in that term the repelling influence of pain as well as the attractive one of pleasure. Let us take into consideration, no longer the person who has a confirmed will to do right, but him in whom that virtuous will is still feeble, conquerable by temptation, and not to be fully relied on; by what means can it be strengthened? How can the will to be virtuous, where it does not exist in sufficient force, be implanted or awakened? Only by making the person *desire* virtue—by making him think of it in a pleasurable light, or of its absence in a painful one. It is by associating the doing right with pleasure, or the doing wrong with pain, or by eliciting and impressing and bringing home to the person's experience the pleasure naturally involved in the one or the pain in the other, that it is possible to call forth that will to be virtuous, which, when confirmed, acts without any thought of either pleasure or pain. Will is the child of desire, and passes out of the dominion of its parent only to come under that of habit. That which is the result of habit affords no presumption of being intrinsically good; and there would be no reason for wishing that the purpose of virtue should become independent of pleasure and pain, were it not that the influence of the pleasurable and painful associations which prompt to virtue is not sufficiently to be depended on for unerring constancy of action until it has acquired the support of habit. Both in feeling and in conduct, habit is the only thing which imparts certainty; and it is because of the importance to others of being able to rely absolutely on one's feelings and conduct, and to oneself of being able to rely on one's own, that the will to do right ought to be cultivated into this habitual independence. In other words, this state of the will is a means to good, not intrinsically a good; and does not contradict the doctrine that nothing is a good to human beings but in so far as it is either itself pleasurable, or a means of attaining pleasure or averting pain.

But if this doctrine be true, the principle of utility is proved. Whether it is or not must now be left to the consideration of the thoughtful reader.

NOTE

1. The author of this essay has reason for believing himself to be the first person who brought the word utilitarian into use. He did not invent it, but adopted it from a passing expression in Mr. Galt's *Annals of the Parish*. After using it as a designation for several years, he and others abandoned it from a growing dislike to anything resembling a badge or watchword of sectarian distinction. But as a name for one single opinion, not a set of opinions—to denote the recognition of utility as a standard, not any particular way of applying it—the term supplies a want in the language, and offers, in many cases, a convenient mode of avoiding tiresome circumlocution.

MORALITY AND PESSIMISM

Stuart Hampshire

I shall examine a current of moral ideas which was partly philosophical and partly something less precise, a movement in public consciousness. British utilitarianism was a school of moral thought, and a school also of general philosophy, which set out to do good in the world, even though it was only a philosophy; and it may even be judged to have succeeded in large part over many years in this aim. It is certainly

From Stuart Hampshire, *Private and Public Morality,* (Cambridge, England: Cambridge University Press, 1978), pp. 1-22.

not easy, and perhaps it is not possible, to calculate the real effect upon men's lives of any new system of moral ideas and of any new philosophy. But the utilitarian philosophy brought new interests into the study of political economy: into the theory and practice of public administration: into the rhetoric, and into the pro- grammes, of movements of political and social reform in Britain. Indeed the utilitarian philosophy became part of the ordinary furniture of the minds of those enlightened persons, who would criticise institutions, not from the standpoint of one of the Christian churches, but from a secular point of view. As represented by Sidgwick at Cambridge, and in the minds of liberal and radical social reformers everywhere, the utilitarian philosophy was until quite recently a constant support for progressive social policies. Even the rare and strange adaptation of utilitarian- ism, which appeared in the last chapter of G. E. Moore's *Principia Ethica,* pointed toward liberal and improving policies: at least it did in the minds of Keynes, of Leonard Woolf, and of others whose lives were seriously influenced by Moore. Moore himself wrote of his own moral conclusions as prescribing the aims of social policy, and, like Mill, he was marking the target of social improvements. The utilitarian philosophy, before the First World War and for many years after it— perhaps even until 1939—was still a bold, innovative, even a subversive doctrine, with a record of successful social criticism behind it. I believe that it is losing this role, and that it is now an obstruction.

Utilitarianism has always been a comparatively clear moral theory, with a simple core and central notion, easily grasped and easily translated into practical terms. Its essential instruction goes like this: when assessing the value of institu- tions, habits, conventions, manners, rules, and laws, and also when considering the merits of individual actions or policies, turn your attention to the actual or probable states of mind of the persons who are, or will be, affected by them: that is all you need to consider in your assessments. In a final analysis, nothing else counts but the states of mind, and perhaps, more narrowly, the states of feeling, of persons; or, more generously in Bentham and G. E. Moore, of sentient creatures. Anything else that one might consider, in the indefinite range of natural and man- made things, is to be reckoned as mere machinery, as only a possible instrument for producing the all-important—literally all-important—states of feeling. From this moral standpoint, the whole machinery of the natural order, other than states of mind, just is machinery, useful or harmful in proportion as it promotes or prevents desired states of feeling.

For a utilitarian, the moral standpoint, which is to govern all our actions, places men at the very center of the universe, with their states of feeling as the source of all value in the world. If the species perished, to the last man, or if the last men became impassible and devoid of feeling, things would become cold and indifferent and neutral, from the moral point of view; whether this or that other unfeeling species survived or perished, plants, stars, and galaxies, would then be of no consequence. Destruction of things is evil only in so far as it is, or will be, felt as a loss by sentient beings; and the creation of things, and the preservation of species, are to be aimed at and commended only in so far as sentient beings are, or will be, emotionally and sentimentally interested in the things created and preserved.

This doctrine may reasonably be criticised in two contrary ways: first, as involving a kind of arrogance in the face of nature, an arrogance that is intelligible only if the doctrine is seen as a residue of the Christian account of this species' peculiar relation to the Creator. Without the Christian story it seems to entail a strangely arbitrary narrowing of moral interest. Is the destruction, for instance, of a species in nature to be avoided, as a great evil, only or principally because of the loss of the pleasure that human beings may derive from the species? May the natural order to be formed by human beings for their comfort and pleasure without any restriction other than the comfort and pleasure of future human beings? Perhaps there is no rational procedure for answering these questions. But it is strange to answer them with a confident 'Yes'. On the other hand the doctrine that only our feelings are morally significant may be thought, on the contrary, to belittle men: for it makes morality, the system of rights, duties and obligations, a kind of psychical engineering, which shows the way to induce desired or valued states of mind. This suggests, as a corollary, that men might be trained, moulded, even bred, with a view to their experiencing the kinds of feeling that alone lend value to their morally neutral surroundings. With advancing knowledge states of the soul might be controlled by chemical means, and the valuable experiences of the inner life may be best prolonged and protected by a medical technique. So the original sense of the sovereign importance of human beings, and of their feelings, has been converted by exaggeration into its opposite; a sense that these original ends of action are, or may soon become, comparatively manageable problems in applied science.

From the standpoint of philosophy, in a full, old-fashioned sense of that word, we have moved, slowly, stage by stage, in the years since 1914, into a different world of thought from that which most of Leslie Stephen's contemporaries inhabited: and by a 'world of thought' here I mean the set of conditioning assumptions which any European, who thought in a philosophical way about morality, would have in mind before he started to think, assumptions that he probably would not examine one by one, and that he would with difficulty make explicit to himself. One such assumption was that, even if the transcendental claims of Christianity have been denied, any serious thought about morality must acknowledge the absolute exceptionalness of men, the unique dignity and worth of this species among otherwise speechless, inattentive things, and their uniquely open future; how otherwise can morality have its overriding claims? A second assumption, explicit in J. S. Mill, and unchallenged by his utilitarian successors, was that both emotional sensitiveness, and intelligence in the calculation of consequences, can be expected to multiply and increase, as moral enlightenment spreads and as standards of education improve, into an indefinite and open future. In this open future there will be less avoidable waste of human happiness, less unconsidered destruction of positive and valued feelings, as the human sciences develop and superstitions become weaker and softer. The story of the past—this is the assumption—is essentially the story of moral waste, of a lack of clear planning and contrivance, of always repeated losses of happiness because no one methodically added the emotional gains and losses, with a clear head and undistracted by moral prejudices. The modern utilitarian policy-makers will be careful social economists, and their planning mistakes will be progressively corrigible ones; so there is no reason why there should not be a steadily rising balance of positive over negative feelings in all societies that have a rational computational morality. A new era of development is possible, the equivalent in morality of high technology in production.

This implicit optimism has been lost, not so much because of philosophical arguments but perhaps rather because of the hideous face of political events. Persecutions, massacres, and wars have been coolly justified by calculations of the long range benefit to mankind; and political pragmatists, in the advanced countries, using cost-benefit analyses prepared for them by gifted professors, continue to burn and destroy. The utilitarian habit of mind has brought with it a new abstract cruelty in politics, a dull, destructive political righteousness: mechanical, quantitative thinking, leaden academic minds setting out their moral calculations in leaden abstract prose, and more civilised and more superstitious people destroyed because of enlightened calculations that have proved wrong. Suppose a typical situation of political decision, typical, that is, of the present, and likely to be typical of the immediate future; an expert adviser has to present a set of possible policies between which a final choice has to be made; advantages and disadvantages of various outcomes are to be calculated, and a balance is to be struck. The methods of calculation may be quite sophisticated, and very disparate items may appear in the columns of gain and loss. The death of groups of persons may, for example, be balanced as a loss against a very considerable gain in amenity to be handed down to posterity; or a loss of liberty among one group may be balanced against a very great relief from poverty for another. Such calculations are the every day stuff of political decisions, and they seem to require a common measure that enables qualitatively unrelated effects to be held in balance. The need to calculate in this manner, and to do so convincingly, plainly becomes greater as the area of government decision is widened, and as the applied social sciences render remote effects more computable.

Given that the vast new powers of government are in any case going to be used, and given that remote and collateral effects of policies are no longer utterly incalculable, and therefore to be neglected, a common measure to strike a balance is certain to be asked for and to be used; and apparently incommensurable interests will be brought together under this common measure. The utilitarian doctrine, insisting that there is a common measure of those gains and losses, which superficially seem incommensurable, is in any case called into being by the new conditions of political calculation. Any of the original defects in the doctrine will now be blown up, as a photograph is blown up, and made clearly visible in action.

For Machiavelli and his contemporaries, a political calculation was still a fairly simple computation of intended consequences, not unlike the stratagems of private intrigue. He and his contemporaries had no thought that a political calculation might issue in a plan for the future of a whole society or nation, with all kinds of dissimilar side-effects allowed for, and fed into the computation. Computation by a common measure now seems the most orthodox way to think in politics, although this kind of computation had originally been almost scandalous. At first the scandal and surprise lingered around the notion that moral requirements, and moral outrages, could be represented as commensurable gains and losses along a single scale. Yet now those who talk about being responsible in political decision believe that the moral issues must be represented on a common scale, if they are to be counted at all. How can the future of an advanced society be reasonably discussed and planned, if not on this assumption? To others, and particularly to many of the young in America and in Europe, who would not quote Burke, it seems now obvious that the large-scale computations in modern politics and social planning bring with them a coarseness and grossness of moral feeling, a blunting of sensibility, and a suppression of individual discrimination and gentleness, which are a price that they will not pay for the benefits of clear calculation. Their point is worth considering: perhaps it can be given a philosophical basis.

Allow me to go back to the beginnings of moral theory: as a non-committal starting-point, it may be agreed that we all assess ourselves, and other people, as having behaved well or badly, on a particular occasion, or for a tract of time, or taking a life-time as a whole. We similarly assess courses of action, and even whole ways of life, that are open to us before we make a decision. The more fundamental and overriding assessments, in relation to which all other assessments of persons are subsidiary and conditional, we call moral assessments, just because we count them as unconditional and overriding. The goodness or badness imputed may be imputed as a characteristic of persons, or of their actions, their decisions and their policies, or of their character and their dispositions, or of their lives and ways of life. Let me take the assessment of persons as the starting-point. When we assess ourselves or others in some limited role or capacity, as performing well or ill in that role or capacity, the assessment is not fundamental and unconditional; the assessment gives guidance only to someone who wants to have that role or to act in that capacity, or who wants to make use of someone who does. But if we assess persons as good or bad without further qualification or limitation, merely as human beings, and similarly also their decisions, policies, characters, dispositions, ways of life, as being good or bad without qualification, then our assessments have unconditional implications in respect of what should and should not be done, and of what people should, and should not be like, of their character, dispositions and way of life. A human being has the power to reflect on what kind of person he wants to be, and to try to act accordingly, within the limits of his circumstances. His more considered practical choices, and the conflicts that accompany them, will show what he holds to be intrinsically worth pursuing, and will therefore reveal his fundamental moral beliefs.

I believe that all I have so far said about this starting-point of moral philosophy is non-committal between different theories, and is innocent and unquestion-begging, and will be, or ought to be, accepted by moral philosophers of quite different persuasions, including the utilitarians. I believe this, because the various classical moral philosophies can all be formulated within this non-committal frame-work. Each moral philosophy singles out some ultimate ground or grounds for unconditional praise of persons, and prescribes the ultimate grounds for preferring one way of life to another. This is no less true of a utilitarian ethics than of any other; the effectively beneficent and happy man is accounted by a utilitarian more praiseworthy and admirable than any other type of man, and his useful life is thought the best kind of life that anyone could have, merely in virtue of its useful-ness, and apart from any other characteristics it may have. The utilitarian phi-losophy picks out its own essential virtues very clearly, and the duties of a utilitarian are not hard to discern, even though they may on occasion involve diffi-cult computations.

But there is one feature of familiar moralities which utilitarian ethics famously repudiates, or at least makes little of. There are a number of different moral pro-hibitions, apparent barriers to action, which a man acknowledges and which he thinks of as more or less insurmountable, except in abnormal, painful and improb-able circumstances. One expects to meet these prohibitions, barriers to action, in certain quite distinct and clearly marked areas of action; these are the taking of human life, sexual relations, family duties and obligations, and the administration of justice according to the laws and customs of a given society. There are other areas in which strong barriers are to be expected; but these are, I think, the central and obvious ones. A morality is, at the very least, the regulation of the taking of life and the regulation of sexual relations, and it also includes rules of distributive and corrective justice: family duties: almost always duties of friendship: also rights and duties in respect of money and property. When specific prohibitions in these areas are probed and challenged by reflection, and the rational grounds for them looked for, the questioner will think that he is questioning a particular morality specified by particular prohibitions. But if he were to question the validity of any prohibitions in these areas, he would think of himself as challenging the claims of morality itself; for the notion of morality requires that there be some strong barriers against the taking of life, against some varieties of sexual and family relations, against some forms of trial and punishment, some taking of property, and against some distributions of rewards and benefits.

Moral theories of the philosophical kind are differentiated in part by the different accounts that they give of these prohibitions: whether the prohibitions are to be thought of as systematically connected or not: whether they are absolute prohibitions or to be thought of as conditional. Utilitarians always had, and still have, very definite answers: first, they *are* systematically connected, and, secondly, they are to be thought of as not absolute, but conditional, being dependent for their validity as prohibitions upon the beneficial consequences of observing them. Plainly there is no possibility of proof here, since this is a question in ethics, and not in logic or in the experimental sciences. But various reasons for rejecting the utilitarian position can be given.

All of us sometimes speak of things that cannot be done, or that must be done, and that are ruled out as impossible by the nature of the case: also there are things that one must do, that one cannot not do, because of the nature of the case. The signs of necessity in such contexts mark the unqualified, unweakened, barrier to action, while the word 'ought', too much discussed in philosophical writing, conveys a weakened prohibition or instruction. The same contrast appears in the context of empirical statements, as in the judgments 'The inflation ought to stop soon' and 'The inflation must stop soon'. The modal words 'must' and 'ought' preserve a constant relation in a number of different types of discourse, of which moral argument is only one, not particularly conspicuous, example: he who in a shop says to the salesman 'The coat must cover my knees', alternatively, 'The coat ought to cover my knees', speaks of a need or requirement and of something less: he who, looking at the mathematical puzzle, says 'This must be the way to solve it', alternatively 'This ought to be the way to solve it', speaks of a kind of rational necessity, and of something less: examples of 'ought' as the weaker variant of 'must' could be indefinitely prolonged into other types of contexts. So 'He must help him' is the basic, unmodified judgment in the context of moral discussion or reflection, and 'He ought to help him' is its weakened variant, as it is in all other contexts. To learn what a man's moral beliefs are entails learning what he thinks that he must not do, at any cost or at almost any cost.

The range of the utterly forbidden types of conduct amongst Stephen's friends would differ significantly, but not greatly, from the range of the forbidden and the impossible that would be acknowledged in this room. Social anthropologists may record fairly wide variations in the range of the morally impossible, and also, I believe, some barriers that are very general, though not quite universal; and historians similarly. For example, in addition to certain fairly specific types of killing, certain fairly specific types of sexual promiscuity, certain takings of property, there are also types of disloyalty and of cowardice, particularly disloyalty to friends, which are very generally, almost universally, forbidden and forbidden absolutely: they are forbidden as being intrinsically disgraceful and unworthy, and as being, just for these reasons, ruled out: ruled out because they would be disgusting, or disgraceful, or shameful, or brutal, or inhuman, or base, or an outrage.

In arguing against utilitarians I must dwell a little on these epithets usually associated with morally impossible action, on a sense of disgrace, of outrage, of horror, of baseness, of brutality, and most important, a sense that a barrier, assumed to be firm and almost insurmountable, has been knocked over, and a feeling that, if this horrible, or outrageous, or squalid, or brutal, action is possible, then anything is possible and nothing is forbidden, and all restraints are threatened. Evidently these ideas have often been associated with impiety, and with a belief that God, or the Gods, have been defied, and with a fear of divine anger. But they need not have these associations with the supernatural, and they may have, and often have had, a secular setting. In the face of the doing of something that must not be done, and that is categorically excluded and forbidden morally, the fear that one may feel is fear of human nature. A relapse into a state of nature seems a real possibility: or perhaps seems actually to have occurred, unless an alternative morality with new restraints is clearly implied when the old barrier is crossed. This fear of human nature, and sense of outrage, when a barrier is broken down, is an aspect of respect for morality itself rather than for any particular morality and for any particular set of prohibitions.

The notion of the morally impossible—'I cannot leave him now: it would be quite impossible'. 'Surely you understand that I *must* help him'—is distinct. A course of conduct is ruled out ('You cannot do that'), because it would be inexcusably unjust, or dishonest, or humilating, or treacherous, or cruel, or ungenerous, or harsh. These epithets, specifying why the conduct is impossible, mark the vices characteristically recognised in a particular morality. In other societies, at other places and times, other specific epithets might be more usually associated with outrage and morally impossible conduct: but the outrage or shock, and the recognition of impossibility, will be the same in cases where the type of conduct rejected, and the reasons for the rejection, are rather different.

The utilitarian will not deny these facts, but he will interpret them differently. Shock, he will say, is the primitive, pre-rational reaction; after rational reflection the strength of feeling associated with a prohibition can be, and ought to be, proportional to the estimated harm of the immediate and remote consequences; and he will find no more in the signs of necessity and impossibility than an emphasis on the moral rules which have proved to be necessary protections against evil effects. The signs of necessity are signs that there is a rule. But the rational justification of there being a rule is to be found in the full consequences of its observance, and not in non-rational reactions of horror, disgust, shame, and other emotional repugnances.

But I believe that critical reflection may leave the notion of absolutely forbidden, because absolutely repugnant, conduct untouched. There may in many cases be good reflective reasons why doing such things, assuming such a character, may be abhorrent, and excluded from the range of possible conduct; there may be reflective reasons, in the sense that one is able to say why the conduct is impossible as destroying the ideal of a way of life that one aspires to and respects, as being, for example, utterly unjust or cruel or treacherous or corruptly dishonest. To show that these vices are vices, and unconditionally to be avoided, would take one back to the criteria for the assessment of persons as persons, and therefore to the whole way of life that one aspires to as the best way of life. A reflective, critical scrutiny of moral claims is compatible, both logically and psychologically, with an overriding concern for a record of un-monstrous and respectworthy conduct, and of action that has never been mean or inhuman; and it may follow an assessment of the worth of persons which is not to be identified only with a computation of consequences and effects.

There is a model of rational reflection which depends upon a contrast between the primitive moral response of an uneducated man, and of an uneducated society, and the comparatively detached arguments of the sophisticated moralist, who discounts his intuitive responses as being prejudices inherited from an uncritical past. Conspicuous in the philosophical radicals, in John Stuart Mill, and in the

Victorian free-thinkers generally, this model in turn depended upon the idea that primitive, pre-scientific men are usually governed by strict moral taboos, and that in the future intellectually evolved, and scientifically trained, men will be emancipated from these bonds, and will start again with clear reasoning about consequences. The word 'taboo', so often used in these contexts, shows the assumption of moral progress from primitive beginnings, and suggests a rather naive contrast between older moralities and the open morality of the future; empirical calculation succeeds *a priori* prejudice, and the calculation of consequences is reason.

But reflection may discover a plurality of clear and definite moral injunctions; injunctions about the taking of life, about sexual relations, about the conduct of parents toward children and of children toward parents, about one's duties in times of war, about the conditions under which truth must be told and under which it may be concealed, about rights of property, about duties of friendship, and so on over the various aspects and phases of a normal span of life. Such injunctions need not be inferrable from a few basic principles, corresponding to the axioms of a theory. The pattern that they form can have a different type of unity. Taken together, a full set of such injunctions, prohibiting types of conduct in types of circumstance, describes in rough and indeterminate outline, an attainable and recognisable way of life, aspired to, respected and admired: or at least the minimum general features of a respectworthy way of life. And a way of life is not identified and characterised by one distinct purpose, such as the increase of general happiness, or even by a set of such distinct purposes. The connection between the injunctions, the connection upon which a reasonable man reflects, is to be found in the coherence of a single way of life, distinguished by the characteristic virtues and vices recognised within it.

A way of life is a complicated thing, marked out by many details of style and manner, and also by particular activities and interests, which a group of people of similar dispositions in a similar social situation may share; so that the group may become an imitatable human type who transmit many of their habits and ideals to their descendents, provided that social change is not too rapid.

In rational reflection one may justify an intuitively accepted and unconditional prohibition, as a common, expected feature of a recognisable way of life which on other grounds one values and finds admirable: or as a necessary preliminary condition of this way of life. There are rather precise grounds in experience and in history for the reasonable man to expect that certain virtues, which he admires and values, can only be attained at the cost of certain others, and that the virtues typical of several different ways of life cannot be freely combined, as he might wish. Therefore a reasonable and reflective person will review the separate moral injunctions, which intuitively present themselves as having force and authority, as making a skeleton of an attainable, respectworthy and preferred way of life. He will reject those that seem likely in practice to conflict with others that seem more closely part of, or conditions of, the way of life that he values and admires, or that seem irrelevant to this way of life.

One must not exaggerate the degree of connectedness that can be claimed for the set of injunctions that constitute the skeleton of a man's morality. For example, it is a loose, empirical connection that reasonably associates certain sexual customs with the observation of certain family duties, and certain loyalties to the state or country with the recognition of certain duties in respect of property, and in time of war. The phrase 'way of life' is vague and is chosen for its vagueness. The unity of a single way of life, and the compatibility in practice of different habits and dispositions, are learnt from observation, direct experience and from psychology and history; we know that human nature naturally varies, and is deliberately variable, only within limits; and that not all theoretically compatible achievements and enjoyments are compatible in normal circumstances. A reasonable man may envisage a way of life, which excludes various kinds of conduct as impossible, without excluding a great variety of morally tolerable ways of life within this minimum framework. The moral prohibitions constitute a kind of grammar of conduct, showing the elements out of which any fully respectworthy conduct, as one conceives it, must be built.

The plurality of absolute prohibitions, and the looseness of their association with any one way of life, which stresses a certain set of virtues, is to be contrasted with the unity and simplicity of utilitarian ethics. One might interpret the contrast in this way: to the utilitarian it is certain that all reasonable purposes are parts of a single purpose in a creature known to be governed by the pleasure principle or by a variant of it. The anti-utilitarian replies: nothing is certain in the *theory* of morality: but, at a pre-theoretical level, some human virtues fit together as virtues to form a way of life aspired to, and some monstrous and brutal acts are certainly vicious in the sense that they undermine and corrupt this way of life; and we can explain why they are, and what makes them so, provided that we do not insist upon either precision or certainty or simplicity in the explanation.

The absolute moral prohibitions, which I am defending, are not to be identified with Kant's categorical moral injunctions; for they are not to be picked out by the logical feature of being universal in form. Nor are they prescriptions that must be affirmed, and that cannot be questioned or denied, just because they are principles of rationality, and because any contrary principles would involve a form of contradiction. They are indeed judgments of unconditional necessity, in the sense that they imply that what must be done is not necessary because it is a means to some independently valued end, but because the action is a necessary part of a way of life and ideal of conduct. The necessity resides in the nature of the action itself, as specified in the fully explicit moral judgment. The principal and proximate grounds for claiming that the action must, or must not, be performed are to be found in the characterisation of the action offered within the prescription; and if the argument is pressed further, first a virtue or vice, and then a whole way of life will have to be described.

But still a number of distinctions are needed to avoid misunderstandings. First, he who says, for example, 'You must not give a judgment about this until you have heard the evidence', or 'I must stand by my friend in this crisis', claiming an absolute, and unconditional, necessity to act just so on this occasion, is not claiming an overriding necessity so to act in all circumstances and situations. He has so far not generalised at all, as he would have generalised if he were to add 'always' or 'in all circumstances.' The immediate grounds for the necessity of the action or abstention are indicated in the judgment itself. These particular actions, which are cases of the general type 'respecting evidence' and 'standing by friends', are said to be necessary on this occasion in virtue of having just this character, and in virtue of their being this type of action. In other painful circumstances, and on other occasions, other unconditional necessities, with other grounds, might be judged to have overriding claims.

In a situation of conflict, two necessities may be felt to be stringent, and even generally inescapable, and the agent's further reflection may confirm his first feeling of their stringency. Yet in the circumstances of conflict he has to make a choice, and to bring himself to do one of the normally forbidden things, in order to avoid doing the other. He may finally recognise one overriding necessity, even though he would not be ready to generalise it to other circumstaces. The necessity that is associated with types of action—e.g., not to betray one's friends—is absolute and unconditional, in the sense that it is not relative to, or conditional upon, some desirable external end: but it is liable occasionally to conflict with other necessities.

A second distinction must be drawn: from the fact that a man thinks that there is nothing other than X which he can decently do in a particular situation it does not follow that it is intuitively obvious to him that he must do X. Certainly he may have reached the conclusion immediately and without reflection; but he might also have reached the very same conclusion after weighing a number of arguments for and against. A person's belief that so-and-so must be done, and that he must not act in any other way, may be the outcome of the calculation of the consequences of not doing the necessary thing: always provided that he sees the avoidance of bringing about these consequences as something that is imposed on him as a necessity in virtue of the character of the situation. The reason for the necessity of the action sometimes is to be found in its later consequences, rather than in the nature and quality of the action evident at the time of action. In every case there will be a description of the action that shows the immediate ground for the necessity, usually by indicating the virtue or vice involved.

Different men, and different social groups, recognise rather different moral necessities in the same essential areas of moral concern. This is no more surprising, or philosophically disquieting, than the fact that different men, and different social groups, will order the primary virtues of men, and the features of an admirable way of life, differently. That the poverty stricken and the destitute must be helped, just because they suffer, and that a great wrong does not demand a great punishment as retribution, are typical modern opinions about what must be done. Reasoning is associated with these opinions, as it is also with the different orderings of essential virtues; there are no conclusive proofs, or infallible intuitions, which put a stop to the adducing of new considerations. One does not expect that everyone should recognise the same moral necessities; but rather that everyone should recognise some moral necessities, and similar and overlapping ones, in the same, or almost the same areas, of moral concern.

A man's morality, and the morality of a social group, can properly be seen as falling into two parts, first, a picture of the activities necessary to an ideal way of life which is aspired to, and, second, the unavoidable duties and necessities without which even the elements of human worth, and of a respectworthy way of life, are lacking. The two parts are not rationally unconnected. To take the obvious classical examples: a betrayal of friends in a moment of danger, and for the sake of one's own safety, is excluded from the calculation of possibilities; one may lose perhaps everything else, but this cannot be done; the stain would be too great. And one may take public examples: an outrage of cruelty perpetrated upon undefended civilians in war would constitute a stain that would not be erased and would not be balanced against political success.

How would a sceptical, utilitarian friend of Stephen's, a philosophical friend of the utilitarians, respond to these suggestions? Among other objections he would certainly say that I was turning the clock back, suggesting a return to the moral philosophies of the past: absolute prohibitions, elementary decencies, the recognition of a plurality of prohibitions which do not all serve a signle purpose: and with nothing more definite behind them than a form of life aspired to; this is the outline of an Aristotelian ethics: ancient doctrine. Modern utilitarians thought that men have the possibility of indefinite improvement in their moral thinking, and that they were confined and confused by their innate endowments of moral repugnances and emotional admirations. There was a sense of the open future in all their writing. But hope of continuing improvement, if it survives at all now, is now largely without evidence. Lowering the barriers of prohibition, and making rational calculation of consequences the sole foundation of public policies, have so far favoured, and are still favouring, a new callousness in policy, a dullness of sensibility, and sometimes moral despair, at least in respect of public affairs. When the generally respected barriers of impermissible conduct are once crossed, and when no different unconditional barriers, within the same areas of conduct, are put in their place, then the special, apparently superstitious value attached to the preservation of human life will be questioned. This particular value will no longer be distinguished by an exceptionally solemn prohibition; rather it will be assessed on a common scale alongside other desirable things. Yet it is not clear that the taking of lives can be marked and evaluated on a common scale on which increases of pleasure and diminutions of suffering are also measured. This is the suggested discontinuity which a utilitarian must deny.

Moral prohibitions in general, and particularly those that govern the taking of life, the celebration of the dead, and that govern sexual relations and family relations, are artifices that give human lives some distinctive, peculiar, even arbitrary human shape and pattern. They humanise the natural phases of experience, and lend them a distinguishing sense and direction, one among many possible ones. It is natural for men to expect these artificialities, without which their lives would seem to them inhuman. Largely for this reason a purely naturalistic and utilitarian interpretation of duties and obligations, permissions and prohibitions, in these areas, and particularly in the taking of human life, leaves uneasiness. The idea of morality is connected with the idea that taking human life is a terrible act, which has to be regulated by some set of overriding constraints that constitute a morality; and the connection of ideas alleged here is not a vague one. If there were a people who did not recoil from killing, and, what is a distinguishable matter, who seemed to attach no exceptional value to human life, they would be accounted a community of the subhuman; or, more probably, we would doubt whether their words and practices had been rightly interpreted and whether their way of life had been understood. Yet the taking of life does not have any exceptional importance in utilitarian ethics, that is, in an ethics that is founded exclusively on the actual, ascertained desires and sentiments of men (unlike J. S. Mill's); the taking of life is morally significant in so far as it brings other losses with it. For a strict utilitarian (which J. S. Mill was not) the horror of killing is only the horror of causing other losses, principally of possible happiness; in cases where there are evidently no such losses, the horror of killing becomes superstition. And such a conclusion of naturalism, pressed to its limits, does produce a certain vertigo after reflection. It seems that the mainspring of morality has been taken away.

This vertigo is not principally the result of looking across a century of cool political massacres, undertaken with rational aims; it is also a sentiment with a philosophical thought behind it. A consistent naturalism displaces the pre-reflective moral emphasis upon respect for life, and for the preservation of life, on to an exclusive concern for one or other of the expected future products of being alive— happiness, pleasure, the satisfaction of desires. Respect for human life, independent of the use made of it, may seem to utilitarians a survival of a sacramental consciousness, or at least a survival of a doctrine of the soul's destiny, or of the unique relation between God and man. It had been natural to speak of the moral prohibitions against the taking of life as being respect for the sacredness of an individual life; and this phrase has no proper place, it is very reasonably assumed, in the thought of anyone who has rejected belief in supernatural sanctions.

But the situation may be more complicated. The sacredness of life, so called, and the absolute prohibitions against the taking of life, except under strictly defined conditions, may be admitted to be human inventions. Once the human origin of the prohibitions has been recognised, the prohibition against the taking of life, and respect for human life as such, may still be reaffirmed as absolute. They are reaffirmed as complementary to a set of customs, habits and observances, which are understood by reference to their function, and which are sustained, partly because of, partly in spite of, this understanding: I mean sexual customs, family observances, ceremonial treatment of the dead, gentle treatment of those who are diseased and useless, and of the old and senile, customs of war and treatment of prisoners, treatment of convicted criminals, political and legal safeguards for the rights of individuals, and the customary rituals of respect and gentleness in personal dealings. This complex of habits, and the rituals associated with them, are carried over into a secular morality which makes no existential claims that a naturalist would dispute, and which still rejects the utilitarian morality associated with naturalism. The error of the optimistic utilitarian is that he carries the deritualisation of transactions between men to a point at which men not only can, but ought to, use and exploit each other as they use and exploit any other natural objects, as far as this is compatible with general happiness. And at this point, when the mere existence of an individual person by itself has no value, apart from the by-products and uses of the individual in producing and enjoying desirable states of mind, there is no theoretical barrier against social surgery of all kinds. Not only is there no such barrier in theory: but, more important, the non-existence of the barriers is explicitly recognised. The draining of moral significance from ceremonies, rituals, manners and observances, which imaginatively express moral attitudes and prohibitions, leave morality incorporated only in a set of propositions and computations: thin and uninteresting propositions, when so isolated from their base in the observances, and manners, which govern ordinary relations with people, and which always manifest implicit moral attitudes and opinions. The computational morality, on which optimists rely, dismisses the non-propositional and unprogrammed elements in morality altogether, falsely confident that these elements can all be ticketed and brought into the computations.

You may object that I now seem to be arguing for the truth of a doctrine by pointing to the evil consequences of its being disbelieved: this is not my meaning. I have been assuming that prohibitions against killing are primary moral prohibitions; secondly, that the customs and rituals that govern, in different societies, relations between the sexes, marriage, property rights, family relationships, and the celebration of the dead, are primary moral customs; they always disclose the peculiar kind of respect for human life, and occasions for disrespect, which a particular people or society recognises, and therefore their more fundamental moral beliefs and attitudes. Ordinarily a cosmology, or metaphysics, is associated with the morality, and, for Europeans, it has usually been a supernatural cosmology. When the supernatural cosmology is generally rejected, or no longer is taken seriously, the idea that human life has a unique value has to be recognised as a human invention. But it is not an invention from nothing at all: the rituals and manners that govern behavior and respect for persons already express a complex set of moral beliefs and attitudes, and embody a particular way of life. Affirmations of particular rights, duties and obligations, the propositions of a morality, are a development and a correction of this inexplicit morality of ritual and manners.

Each society, each generation within it, and, in the last resort, each reflective individual, accepts, and amends, an established morality expressed in rituals and manners, and in explicit prohibitions; and he will do this, in determining what kind of person he aspires to be and what are the necessary features of a desirable and admirable way of life as he conceives it. If these prohibitions, whatever they are, were no longer observed, and the particular way of life, which depends on them, was lost, and not just amended or replaced, no particular reason would be left to protect human life more than any other natural phenomenon. The different manners of different societies provide, as an element in good manners, for the recognition of differences; so among the more serious moral constraints—serious in the sense that they regulate killing and sexuality and family relationships, and so the conditions of survival of the species—may be the requirement to respect moral differences, at least in certain cases. Provided that there are absolute prohibitions in the same domains with the same function, and provided that their congruence with a desired way of life is grasped, we may without irrationality accept the differences; and there may sometimes be a duty to avoid conflict or to look for compromise in cases of conflict.

Consider the intermediate case between manners in the restricted sense and absolute moral principles: a code of honour of a traditional kind. The different prohibitions of different codes are still recognised as codes of honour; and dishonour incurred in the breach of different disciplines is in each case recognisably dishonour, in virtue of the type of ideal behaviour, and the way of life, that has been betrayed. Prohibitions in other moralities, very different from the moralities of honour, may be similarly diverse in content.

The question cannot be evaded: what is the rational basis for acting as if human life has a peculiar value, quite beyond the value of any other natural things, when one can understand so clearly how different people, for quite different reasons, have come to believe that it has a particular value and to affirm this in their different moralities? Is one not rationally compelled to follow the utilitarians in denying the autonomy of ethics, and the absoluteness of moral prohibitions, if once one comes to understand the social, psychological and other functions which the prohibitions serve? If one reflectively adopts and reaffirms one or other of these moralities, together with its prohibitions, then it may seem that one must be accepting the morality for the sake of its uses and function, rather than for the reasoning associated with it: and this concedes the utilitarian's case.

The conclusion is not necessary. A morality, with its ordering of virtues and its prohibitions, provides a particular ideal of humanity in an ideal way of life; and this moral ideal explains where and why killing is allowed and also for what purposes a man might reasonably give his life; and in this sense it sets its own peculiar value on human life. One cannot doubt that there are causes, largely unknown, that would explain why one particular ideal has a hold upon men at a particular time and place, apart from the reasoning that they would use to defend it. And it seems certain that the repugnances and horror surrounding some moral prohibitions are sentiments that have both a biological and a social function. But the attitude of a reflective man to these repugnances and prohibitions does not for this reason have to be a utilitarian one. One may on reflection respect and reaffirm the prohibitions, and the way of life that they protect, for reasons unconnected with their known or presumed functions: just as one may respect and adopt a code of manners, or a legal system, for reasons that are unconnected with the known functions of such codes and systems in general, and unconnected also with the known causes that brought these particular codes and systems into existence. The reasons that lead a reflective man to prefer one code of manners, and one legal system, to another must be moral reasons; that is, he must find his reasons in some order of priority of interests and activities in the kind of life that he praises and admires and that he aspires to have, and in the kind of person that he wants to become. Reasons for the most general moral choices, which may sometimes be choices among competing moralities, must be found in philosophical reasoning, if they are found at all: that is, in considerations about the relation of men to the natural, or to the supernatural, order.

I will mention one inclining philosophical reason, which has in the past been prominent in moral theories, particularly those of Aristotle and of Spinoza, and which influences me. One may on reflection find a particular set of prohibitions and injunctions, and a particular way of life protected by them, acceptable and respectworthy, partly because this specifically conceived way of life, with its accompanying prohibitions, has in history appeared natural, and on the whole still feels natural, both to oneself and to others. If there are no overriding reasons for rejecting this way of life, or for rejecting some distinguishing features of it, its felt and proven naturalness is one reason among others for accepting it. This reason is likely to influence particularly those who, unlike utilitarians, cannot for other reasons believe that specific states of mind of human beings are the only elements of value in the universe: who, on the contrary, believe that the natural order as a whole is the fitting object of that kind of unconditional interest and respect that is called moral: that the peculiar value to be attached to human life, and the prohibitions against the taking of life, are not dependent on regarding and treating human beings as radically different from other species in some respects that cannot be specified in plain, empirical statements: that the exceptional value attached both to individual lives, and to the survival of the species as a whole, resides in the power of the human mind to begin to understand, and to enjoy, the natural order as a whole, and to reflect upon this understanding and enjoyment: and that, apart from this exceptional power, the uncompensated destruction of any species is always a loss to be avoided.

Among Leslie Stephen's near contemporaries George Eliot and George Henry Lewes had accepted a variant of Spinozistic naturalism close to the doctrine that I have been suggesting. But they still believed in the probability of future moral improvements, once superstitions had gone. Their ethics was still imbued with an optimism that was certainly not shared by Spinoza, and with a sense of an open and unconfined future for the species. Spinoza's own naturalism was quite free from optimism about the historical future. He did not suggest that advanced, highly educated societies will for the first time be governed largely by the dictates of reason, and that human nature will radically change, and that the conflict between reason and the incapacitating emotions will be largely resolved. Rather he suggests an opposing view of history and of the future: that moral progress, in the proper sense of the increasing dominance of gentleness and of reason, is not to be expected except within very narrow limits. He thought that he knew that as psycho-physical organisms persons are so constructed that there must always in most men be recurrences of unreason alongside reason, and that in this respect social and historical change would be superficial in their consequences. This pessimism, or at least lack of optimism, is compatible with a secular doctrine, akin to that of natural law, which represents many of the seemingly natural prohibitions of non-computational morality as more likely to be endorsed than to be superseded by reflection. A naturalist of his persuasion does not foresee a future in which rational computation will by itself replace the various imaginations, unconscious memories and habits, rituals and manners, which have lent substance and content to men's moral ideas, and which have partly formed their various ways of life.

Some of these ways of life, and certainly their complexity and variety, may be respected as an aspect of natural variety: and, like other natural phenomena, they may over the years be studied and explained, at least to some degree explained. From this point of view, that of natural knowledge, the species, if it survives, may perhaps make interesting advances. But this was not the utilitarians' hope; they looked for an historical transformation of human nature, through new moral reasoning, and this has not occurred and is now not to be reasonably expected.

DEONTOLOGY

MORALITY AND THE DEMANDS OF REASON

Immaneul Kant

Nothing can possibly be conceived in the world, or even out of it, which can be called good without qualification, except a *good will.* Intelligence, wit, judgment, and the other *talents* of the mind, however they may be named, or courage, resolution, perseverance, as qualities of temperament, are undoubtedly good and desirable in many respects; but these gifts of nature may also become extremely bad and mischievous if the will which is to make use of them, and which, therefore, constitutes what is called *character,* is not good. It is the same with the *gifts of fortune.* Power, riches, honor, even health, and the general well-being and content-ment with one's condition which is called *happiness,* inspire pride, and often pre-sumption, if there is not a good will to correct the influence of these on the mind, and with this also to rectify the whole principle of acting, and adapt it to its end. The sight of a being who is not adorned with a single feature of a pure and good will, enjoying unbroken prosperity, can never give pleasure to an impartial rational spectator. Thus a good will appears to constitute the indispensable condition even of being worthy of happiness.

There are even some qualities which are of service to this good will itself, and may facilitate its action, yet which have no intrinsic unconditional value, but always presuppose a good will, and this qualifies the esteem that we justly have for them, and does not permit us to regard them as absolutely good. Moderation in the affections and passions, self-control, and calm deliberation are not only good in many respects, but even seem to constitute part of the intrinsic worth of the person; but they are far from deserving to be called good without qualification,

From "Fundamental Principles of Metaphysics of Morals," in *Critique of Practical Reason and Other Works on the Theory of Ethics,* Trans T. K. Abbott (London: Longmans, Green & Co., 1873), pp. 9-10, 12-20, 29-43.

although they have been so unconditionally praised by the ancients. For without the principles of a good will, they may become extremely bad; and the coolness of a villain not only makes him far more dangerous, but also directly makes him more abominable in our eyes than he would have been without it.

A good will is good not because of what it performs or effects, not by its aptness for the attainment of some proposed end, but simply by virtue of the volition—that is, it is good in itself, and considered by itself is to be esteemed much higher than all that can be brought about by it in favor of any inclination, nay, even of the sum-total of all inclinations. Even if it should happen that, owing to special disfavor of fortune, or the niggardly provision of a step-motherly nature, this will should wholly lack power to accomplish its purpose, if with its greatest efforts it should yet achieve nothing, and there should remain only the good will (not, to be sure, a mere wish, but the summoning of all means in our power), then, like a jewel, it would still shine by its own light, as a thing which has its whole value in itself. Its usefulness or fruitlessness can neither add to nor take away anything from this value. It would be, as it were, only the setting to enable us to handle it the more conveniently in common commerce, or to attract to it the attention of those who are not yet connoisseurs, but not to recommend it to true connoisseurs, or to determine its value. . . .

We have then to develop the notion of a will which deserves to be highly esteemed for itself, and is good without a view to anything further, a notion which exists already in the sound natural understanding, requiring rather to be cleared up than to be taught, and which in estimating the value of our actions always takes the first place and constitutes the condition of all the rest. In order to do this, we will take the notion of duty, which includes that of a good will, although implying certain subjective restrictions and hindrances. These, however, far from concealing it or rendering it unrecognizable, rather bring it out by contrast and make it shine forth so much the brighter.

I omit here all actions which are already recognized as inconsistent with duty, although they may be useful for this or that purpose, for with these the question whether they are done *from duty* cannot arise at all, since they even conflict with it. I also set aside those actions which really conform to duty, but to which men have *no* direct *inclination,* performing them because they are impelled thereto by some other inclination. For in this case we can readily distinguish whether the action which agrees with duty is done *from duty* or from a selfish view. It is much harder to make this distinction when the action accords with duty, and the subject has besides a *direct* inclination to it. For example, it is always a matter of duty that a dealer should not overcharge an inexperienced purchaser; and wherever there is much commerce the prudent tradesman does not overcharge, but keeps a fixed price for everyone, so that a child buys of him as well as any other. Men are thus *honestly* served; but this is not enough to make us believe that the tradesman has so acted from duty and from principles of honesty; his own advantage required it; it is out of the question in this case to suppose that he might besides have a direct inclination in favor of the buyers, so that, as it were, from love he should give no advantage to one over another. Accordingly the action was done neither from duty nor from direct inclination, but merely with a selfish view.

On the other hand, it is a duty to maintain one's life; and, in addition, everyone has also a direct inclination to do so. But on this account the often anxious care which most men take for it has no intrinsic worth, and their maxim has no moral import. They preserve their life *as duty requires,* no doubt, but not *because duty requires.* On the other hand, if adversity and hopeless sorrow have completely taken away the relish for life, if the unfortunate one, strong in mind, indignant at his fate rather than desponding or dejected, wishes for death, and yet preserves his life without loving it—not from inclination or fear, but from duty—then his maxim has a moral worth.

To be beneficent when we can is a duty; and besides this, there are many minds so sympathetically constituted that, without any other motive of vanity or self-interest, they find a pleasure in spreading joy around them, and can take delight in the satisfaction of others so far as it is their own work. But I maintain that in such a case an action of this kind, however proper, however amiable it may be, has nevertheless no true moral worth, but is on a level with other inclinations, for example, the inclination to honor, which, if it is happily directed to that which is in fact of public utility and accordant with duty, and consequently honorable, deserves praise and encouragement, but not esteem. For the maxim lacks the moral import, namely, that such actions be done *from duty,* not from inclination. But the case that the mind of that philanthropist was clouded by sorrow of his own, extinguishing all sympathy with the lot of others, and that while he still has the power to benefit others in distress, he is not touched by their trouble because he is absorbed with his own; and now suppose that he tears himself out of this dead insensibility and performs the action without any inclination to it, but simply from duty, then first has his action its genuine moral worth. Further still, if nature has put little sympathy in the heart of this or that man, if he, supposed to be an upright man, is by temperament cold and indifferent to the sufferings of others, perhaps because in respect of his own he is provided with the special gift of patience and fortitude, and supposes, or even requires, that others should have the same—and such a man would certainly not be the meanest product of nature—but if nature had not specially framed him for a philanthropist, would he not still find in himself a source from whence to give himself a far higher worth than that of a good-natured temperament could be? Unquestionably. It is just in this that the moral worth of the character is brought out which is incomparably the highest of all, namely, that he is beneficent, not from inclination, but from duty.

To secure one's own happiness is a duty, at least indirectly; for discontent with one's condition, under a pressure of many anxieties and amidst unsatisfied wants, might easily become a great *temptation to transgression of duty.* But here again, without looking to duty, all men have already the strongest and most intimate inclination to happiness, because it is just in this idea that all inclinations are combined in one total. But the precept of happiness is often of such a sort that it greatly interferes with some inclinations, and yet a man cannot form any definite and certain conception of the sum of satisfaction of all of them which is called happiness. It is not then to be wondered at that a single inclination, definite both as to what it promises and as to the time within which it can be gratified, is often able to overcome such a fluctuating idea, and that a gouty patient, for instance, can choose to enjoy what he likes, and to suffer what he may, since, according to his calculation, on this occasion at least, he has [only] not sacrificed the enjoyment of the present moment to a possibly mistaken expectation of a happiness which is supposed to be found in health. But even in this case, if the general desire for happiness did not influence his will, and supposing that in his particular case health was not a necessary element in this calculation, there yet remains in this, as in all other cases, this law—namely, that he should promote his happiness not from inclination but from duty, and by this would his conduct first acquire true moral worth.

It is in this manner, undoubtedly, that we are to understand those passages of Scripture also in which we are commanded to love our neighbor, even our enemy. For love, as an affection, cannot be commanded, but beneficence for duty's sake may, even though we are not impelled to it by any inclination—nay, are even repelled by a natural and unconquerable aversion. This is *practical* love, and not *pathological*—a love which is seated in the will, and not in the propensions of sense—in principles of action and not of tender sympathy; and it is this love alone which can be commanded.

The second[1] proposition is: That an action done from duty derives its moral worth, *not from the purpose* which is to be attained by it, but from the maxim by which it is determined, and therefore does not depend on the realization of the object of the action, but merely on the *principle of volition* by which the action has taken place, without regard to any object of desire. It is clear from what precedes that the purposes which we may have in view in our actions, or their effects regarded as ends and springs of the will, cannot give to actions any unconditional or moral worth. In what, then, can their worth lie if it is not to consist in the will and in reference to its expected effect? It cannot lie anywhere but in the *principle of the will* without regard to the ends which can be attained by the action. For the will stands between its *a priori* principle, which is formal, and its *a posteriori* spring, which is material, as between two roads, and as it must be determined by something, it follows that it must be determined by the formal principle of volition when an action is done from duty, in which case every material principle has been withdrawn from it.

The third proposition, which is a consequence of the two preceding, I would express thus: *Duty is the necessity of acting from respect for the law.* I may have *inclination* for an object as the effect of my proposed action, but I cannot have *respect* for it just for this reason that it is an effect and not an energy of will. Similarly, I cannot have respect for inclination, whether my own or another's; I can at most, if my own, approve it; if another's, sometimes even love it, that is, look on it as favorable to my own interest. It is only what is connected with my will as a principle, by no means as an effect—what does not subserve my inclination, but overpowers it, or at least in case of choice excludes it from its calculation—in other words, simply the law of itself, which can be an object of respect, and hence a command. Now an action done from duty must wholly exclude the influence of inclination, and with it every object of the will, so that nothing remains which can determine the will except objectively the *law,* and subjectively *pure respect* for this practical law, and consequently the maxim[2] that I should follow this law even to the thwarting of all my inclinations.

Thus the moral worth of an action does not lie in the effect expected from it, nor in any principle of action which requires to borrow its motive from this expected effect. For all these effects—agreeableness of one's condition, and even the promotion of the happiness of others—could have been also brought about by other causes, so that for this there would have been no need of the will of a rational being; whereas it is in this alone that the supreme and unconditional good can be found. The pre-eminent good which we call moral can therefore consist in nothing else than *the conception of law* in itself, *which certainly is only possible in a rational being,* in so far as this conception, and not the expected effect, determines the will. This is a good which is already present in the person who acts accordingly, and we have not to wait for it to appear first in the result.[3]

But what sort of law can that be the conception of which must determine the will, even without paying any regard to the effect expected from it, in order that this will may be called good absolutely and without qualification? As I have deprived the will of every impulse which could arise to it from obedience to any law, there remains nothing but the universal conformity of its actions to law in general, which alone is to serve the will as a principle, that is, I am never to act otherwise than so *that I could also will that my maxim should become a universal law.* Here, now, it is the simple conformity to law in general, without assuming any particular law applicable to certain actions, that serves the will as its principle, and must so serve it if duty is not to be a vain delusion and a chimerical notion. The common reason of men in its practical judgments perfectly coincides with this, and always has in view the principle here suggested. Let the question be, for example: May I when in distress make a promise with the intention not to keep it? I readily distinguish here between the two significations which the question may have: whether it is prudent or whether it is right to make a false promise? The former may undoubtedly often be the case. I see clearly indeed that it is not enough to extricate myself from a present difficulty by means of this subterfuge, but it must be well considered whether there may not hereafter spring from this lie much greater inconvenience than that from which I now free myself, and as, with all my supposed *cunning,* the consequences cannot be so easily foreseen but that credit once lost may be much more injurious to me than any mischief which I seek to avoid at present, it should be considered whether it would not be more *prudent* to act herein according to a universal maxim, and to make it a habit to promise nothing except with the intention of keeping it. But it is soon clear to me that such a maxim will still only be based on the fear of consequences. Now it is a wholly different thing to be truthful from duty, and to be so from apprehension of injurious consequences. In the first case, the very notion of the action already implies a law for me; in the second case, I must first look about elsewhere to see what results may be combined with it which would affect myself. For to deviate from the principle of duty is beyond all doubt wicked; but to be unfaithful to my maxim of prudence may often be very advantageous to me, although to abide by it is certainly safer. The shortest way, however, and an unerring one, to discover the answer to this question whether a lying promise is consistent with duty, is to ask myself, Should I be content that my maxim (to extricate myself from difficulty by a false promise) should hold good as a universal law, for myself as well as for others; and should I be able to say to myself, "Every one may make a deceitful promise when he finds himself in a difficulty from which he cannot otherwise extricate himself?" Then I presently become aware that, while I can will the lie, I can by no means will that lying should be a unviersal law. For with such a law there would be no promises at all, since it would be in vain to allege my intention in regard to my future actions to those who would not believe this allegation, or if they over-hastily did so, would pay me back in my own coin. Hence my maxim, as soon as it should be made a universal law, would necessarily destroy itself.

I do not, therefore, need any far-reaching penetration to discern what I have to do in order that my will may be morally good. Inexperienced in the course of the world, incapable of being prepared for all its contingencies, I only ask myself: Canst thou also will that thy maxim should be a universal law? If not, then it must be rejected, and that not because of a disadvantage accruing from it to myself or even to others, but because it cannot enter as a principle into a possible universal legislation, and reason extorts from me immediate respect for such legislation. I do not indeed as yet *discern* on what this respect is based (this the philosopher may inquire), but at least I understand this—that it is an estimation of the worth which far outweighs all worth of what is recommended by inclination, and that the neces-sity of acting from *pure* respect for the practical law is what constitutes duty, to which every other motive must give place because it is the condition of a will being good *in itself,* and the worth of such a will is above everything. . . .

Everything in nature works according to laws. Rational beings alone have the faculty of acting according *to the conception* of laws—that is, according to principles, that is, have a *will.* Since the deduction of actions from principles requires *reason,* the will is nothing but practical reason. If reason infallibly deter-mines the will, then the actions of such a being which are recognized as objectively necessary are subjectively necessary also, that is, the will is a faculty to choose *that only* which reason independent of inclination recognizes as practically neces-sary, that is, as good. But if reason of itself does not sufficiently determine the will, if the latter is subject also to subjective conditions (particular impulses) which do not always coincide with the objective conditions, in a word, if the will does not *in itself* completely accord with reason (which is actually the case with men), then the actions which objectively are recognized as necessary are subjectively con-tingent, and the determination of such a will according to objective laws is *obliga-tion,* that is to say, the relation of the objective laws to a will that is not thoroughly good is conceived as the determination of the will of a rational being by principles of reason, but which the will from its nature does not of necessity follow.

The conception of an objective principle, in so far as it is obligatory for a will, is called a command (of reason), and the formula of the command is called an Imperative.

All imperatives are expressed by the word *ought* [or *shall*], and thereby indicate the relation of an objective law of reason to a will which from its subjective constitution is not necessarily determined by it (an obligation). They say that something would be good to do or to forbear, but they say it to a will which does not always do a thing because it is conceived to be good to do it. That is practically *good,* however, which determines the will by means of the conceptions of reason, and consequently not from subjective causes, but objectively, that is, on principles which are valid for every rational being as such. It is distinguished from the *pleasant* as that which influences the will only by means of sensation from merely subjective causes, valid only for the sense of this or that one, and not as a principle of reason which holds for every one.[4]

A perfectly good will would therefore be equally subject to objective laws (viz., laws of good), but could not be conceived as *obliged* thereby to act lawfully, because of itself from its subjective constitution it can only be determined by the conception of good. Therefore no imperatives hold for the Divine will, or in general for a *holy* will; *ought* is here out of place because the volition is already of itself necessarily in unison with the law. Therefore imperatives are only formulae to express the relation of objective laws of all volition to the subjective imperfection of the will of this or that rational being, for example, the human will.

Now all *imperatives* command either *hypothetically* or *categorically.* The former represent the practical necessity of a possible action as means to something else that is willed (or at least which one might possibly will). The categorical imperative would be that which represented an action as necessary of itself without reference to another end, that is, as objectively necessary.

Since every practical law represents a possible action as good, and on this account, for a subject who is practically determinable by reason as necessary, all imperatives are formulae determining an action which is necessary according to the principle of a will good in some respects. If now the action is good only as a means *to something else,* then the imperative is *hypothetical;* if it is conceived as good *in itself* and consequently as being necessarily the principle of a will which of itself conforms to reason, then it is *categorical.*

Thus the imperative declares what action possible by me would be good, and presents the practical rule in relation to a will which does not forthwith perform an action simply because it is good, whether because the subject does not always know that it is good, or because, even if it know this, yet its maxim might be opposed to the objective principles of practical reason.

Accordingly the hypothetical imperative only says that the action is good for some purpose, *possible* or *actual.* In the first case it is a *problematical,* in the second an *assertorial* practical principle. The categorical imperative which delcares an action to be objectively necessary in itself without reference to any purpose, that is, without any other end, is valid as an *apodictic* (practical) principle.

Whatever is possible only by the power of some rational being may also be conceived as a possible purpose of some will; and therefore the principles of action as regards the means necessary to attain some possible purpose are in fact infinitely numerous. All sciences have a practical part consisting of problems expressing that some end is possible for us, and of imperatives directing how it may be attained. These may, therefore, be called in general imperatives of *skill.* Here there is no question whether the end is rational and good, but only what one must do in order to attain it. The precepts for the physician to make his patient thoroughly healthy, and for a poisoner to ensure certain death, are of equal value in this respect, that each serves to effect its purpose perfectly. Since in early youth it cannot be known what ends are likely to occur to us in the course of life, parents seek to have their children taught a *great many things,* and provide for their *skill* in the use of means for all sorts of arbitrary ends, of none of which can they determine whether it may not perhaps hereafter be an object to their pupil, but which it is at all events *possible* that he might aim at; and this anxiety is so great that they commonly neglect to form and correct their judgment on the value of the things which may be chosen as ends.

There is *one* end, however, which may be assumed to be actually such to all rational beings (so far as imperatives apply to them, viz., as dependent beings), and, therefore, one purpose which they not merely *may* have, but which we may with certainty assume that they all actually *have* by a natural necessity, and this is *happiness.* The hypothetical imperative which expresses the practical necessity of an action as means to the advancement of happiness is *assertorial.* We are not to present it as necessary for an uncertain and merely possible purpose, but for a purpose which we may presuppose with certainty and *a priori* in every man, because it belongs to his being. Now skill in the choice of means to his own greatest well-being may be called *prudence,* in the narrowest sense. And thus the imperative which refers to the choice of means to one's own happiness, that is, the precept of prudence, is still always *hypothetical;* the action is not commanded absolutely, but only as means to another purpose.

Finally, there is an imperative which commands a certain conduct immediately, without having as its condition any other purpose to be attained by it. This imperative is *categorical.* It concerns not the matter of the action, or its intended result, but its form and the principle of which it is itself a result; and what is essentially good in it consists in the mental disposition, let the consequence be what it may. This imperative may be called that of *morality.* . . .

Now arises the question, how are all these imperatives possible? This question does not seek to know how we can conceive the accomplishment of the action which the imperative ordains, but merely how we can conceive the obligation of the will which the imperative expresses. No special explanation is needed to show how an imperative of skill is possible. Whoever wills the end wills also (so far as reason decides his conduct) the means in his power which are indispensably necessary thereto. This proposition is, as regards the volition, analytical; for in willing an object as my effect there is already thought the causality of myself as an acting cause, that is to say, the use of the means; and the imperative educes from the conception of volition of an end the conception of actions necessary to this end. Synthetical propositions must no doubt be employed in defining the means to a proposed end; but they do not concern the principle, the act of the will, but the object and its realization. For example, that in order to bisect a line on an unerring principle I must draw from its extremities two intersecting arcs; this no doubt is taught by mathematics only in synthetical propositions; but if I know that it is only by this process that the intended operation can be performed, then to say that if I fully will the operation, I also will the action required for it, is an analytical proposition; for it is one and the same thing to conceive something as an effect which I can produce in a certain way, and to conceive myself as acting in this way.

If it were only equally easy to give a definite conception of happiness, the imperatives of prudence would correspond exactly with those of skill, and would likewise be analytical. For in this case as in that, it could be said whoever wills the end wills also (according to the dictate of reason necessarily) the indispensable means thereto which are in his power. But, unfortunately, the notion of happiness is so indefinite that although every man wishes to attain it, yet he never can say definitely and consistently what it is that he really wishes and wills. The reason of this is that all the elements which belong to the notion of happiness are altogether empirical, that is, they must be borrowed from experience, and nevertheless the idea of happiness requires an absolute whole, a maximum of welfare in my present and all future circumstances. Now it is impossible that the most clear-sighted and at the same time most powerful being (supposed finite) should frame to himself a definite conception of what he really wills in this. Does he will riches, how much anxiety, envy, and snares might he not thereby draw upon his shoulders? Does he will knowledge and discernment, perhaps it might prove to be only an eye so much the sharper to show him so much the more fearfully the evils that are now concealed from him and that cannot be avoided, or to impose more wants on his desires, which already give him concern enough? Would he have long life? Who guarantees to him that it would not be a long misery? Would he at least have health? How often has uneasiness of the body restrained from excesses into which perfect health would have allowed one to fall, and so on? In short, he is unable, on any principle, to determine with certainty what would make him truly happy; because to do so he would need to be omniscient. We cannot therefore act on any definite principles to secure happiness, but only on empirical counsels, for example, of regimen, frugality, courtesy, reserve, etc., which experience teaches do, on the average, most promote well-being. Hence, it follows that the imperatives of prudence do not, strictly speaking, command at all, that is, they cannot present actions objectively as practically *necessary;* that they are rather to be regarded as counsels (*consilia*) than precepts (*praecepta*) of reason, that the problem to determine certainly and universally what action would promote the happiness of a rational being is completely insoluble, and consequently no imperative respecting it is possible which should, in the strict sense, command to do what makes happy; because happiness is not an ideal of reason but of imagination, resting solely on empirical grounds, and it is vain to expect that these should define an action by which one could attain the totality of a series of consequences which is really endless. This imperative of prudence would, however, be an analytical proposition if we assume that the means to happiness could be certainly assigned; for it is distinguished from the imperative of skill only by this that in the latter the end is merely *possible,* in the former it is *given;* as, however, both only ordain the means to that which we suppose to be willed as an end, it follows that the imperative which ordains the willing of the means to him who wills the end is in both cases analytical. Thus there is no difficulty in regard to the possibility of an imperative of this kind either.

On the other hand, the question, how the imperative of *morality* is possible, is undoubtedly one, the only one, demanding a solution, as this is not at all hypothetical, and the objective necessity which it presents cannot rest on any hypothesis, as is the case with the hypothetical imperatives. Only here we must never leave out of consideration that we *cannot* make out *by any example,* in other words, empirically, whether there is such an imperative at all; but it is rather to be feared that all those which seem to be categorical may yet be at bottom hypothetical. For instance, when the precept is: Thou shalt not promise deceitfully; and it is assumed that the necessity of this is not a mere counsel to avoid some other evil, so that it should mean: Thou shalt not make a lying promise, lest if it become known thou shouldst destroy thy credit, but that an action of this kind must be regarded as evil in itself, so that the imperative of the prohibition is categorical; then we cannot show with certainty in any example that the will was determined merely by the law, without any other spring of action, although it may appear to be so. For it is always possible that fear of disgrace, perhaps also obscure dread of other dangers, may have a secret influence on the will. Who can prove by experience the non-existence of a cause when all that experience tells us is that we do not perceive it? But in such a case the so-called moral imperative, which as such appears to be categorical and unconditional, would in reality be only a pragmatic precept, drawing our attention to our own interests, and merely teaching us to take these into consideration.

We shall therefore have to investigate *a priori* the possibility of a categorical imperative, as we have not in this case the advantage of its reality being given in experience, so that [the elucidation of] its possibility should be requisite only for its explanation, not for its establishment. In the meantime it may be discerned beforehand that the categorical imperative alone has the purport of a practical law; all the rest may indeed be called *principles* of the will but not laws, since whatever is only necessary for the attainment of some arbitrary purpose may be considered as in itself contingent, and we can at any time be free from the precept if we give up the purpose; on the contrary, the unconditional command leaves the will no liberty to choose the opposite, consequently it alone carries with it that necessity which we require in a law.

Secondly, in the case of this categorical imperative or law of morality, the difficulty (of discerning its possibility) is a very profound one. It is an *a priori* synthetical practical proposition;[5] and as there is so much difficulty in discerning the possibility of speculative propositions of this kind, it may readily be supposed that the difficulty will be no less with the practical.

In this problem we will first inquire whether the mere conception of a categorical imperative may not perhaps supply us also with the formula of it, containing the proposition which alone can be a categorical imperative; for even if we know the tenor of such an absolute command, yet how it is possible will require further special and laborious study, which we postpone to the last section.

When I conceive a hypothetical imperative, in general I do not know beforehand what it will contain until I am given the condition. But when I conceive a categorical imperative, I know at once what it contains. For as the imperative contains besides the law only the necessity that the maxims[6] shall conform to this law, while the law contains no conditions restricting it, there remains nothing but the general statement that the maxim of the action should conform to a universal law, and it is this conformity alone that the imperative properly represents as necessary.[7]

There is therefore but one categorical imperative, namely, this: *Act only on that maxim whereby thou canst at the same time will that it should become a universal law.*

Now if all imperatives of duty can be deduced from this one imperative as from their principle, then, although it should remain undecided whether what is called duty is not merely a vain notion, yet at least we shall be able to show what we understand by it and what this notion means.

Since the universality of the law according to which effects are produced constitutes what is properly called *nature* in the most general sense (as to form)—that is, the existence of things so far as it is determined by general laws—the imperative of duty may be expressed thus: *Act as if the maxim of thy action were to become by thy will a universal law of nature.*

We will now enumerate a few duties, adopting the usual division of them into duties to ourselves and to others, and into perfect and imperfect duties.[8]

1. A man reduced to despair by a series of misfortunes feels wearied of life, but is still so far in possession of his reason that he can ask himself whether it would not be contrary to his duty to himself to take his own life. Now he inquires whether the maxim of his action could become a universal law of nature. His maxim is: From self-love I adopt it as a principle to shorten my life when its longer duration is likely to bring more evil than satisfaction. It is asked then simply whether this principle founded on self-love can become a universal law of nature. Now we see at once that a system of nature of which it should be a law to destroy life by means of the very feeling whose special nature it is to impel to the improvement of life would contradict itself, and therefore could not exist as a system of nature; hence that maxim cannot possibly exist as a universal law of nature, and consequently would be wholly inconsistent with the supreme principle of all duty.

2. Another finds himself forced by necessity to borrow money. He knows that he will not be able to repay it, but sees also that nothing will be lent to him unless he promises stoutly to repay it in a definite time. He desires to make this promise, but he has still so much conscience as to ask himself: Is it not unlawful and inconsistent with duty to get out of a difficulty in this way? Suppose, however, that he resolves to do so, then the maxim of his action would be expressed thus: When I think myself in want of money, I will borrow money and promise to repay it, although I know that I never can do so. Now this principle of self-love or of one's own advantage may perhaps be consistent with my whole future welfare; but the question now is, Is it right? I change then the suggestion of self-love into a universal law, and state the question thus: How would it be if my maxim were a universal law? Then I see at once that it could never hold as a universal law of nature, but would necessarily contradict itself. For supposing it to be a universal law that everyone when he thinks himself in a difficulty should be able to promise whatever he pleases, with the purpose of not keeping his promise, the promise itself would become impossible, as well as the end that one might have in view in it, since no one would consider that anything was promised to him, but would ridicule all such statements as vain pretenses.

3. A third finds in himself a talent which with the help of some culture might make him a useful man in many respects. But he finds himself in comfortable circumstances and prefers to indulge in pleasure rather than to take pains in enlarging and improving his happy natural capacities. He asks, however, whether his maxim of neglect of his natural gifts, besides agreeing with his inclination to indulgence, agrees also with what is called duty. He sees then that a system of nature could indeed subsist with such a universal law, although men (like the South Sea islanders) should let their talents rest and resolve to devote their lives merely to idleness, amusement, and propagation of their species—in a word, to enjoyment; but he cannot possibly *will* that this should be a universal law of nature, or be implanted in us as such by a natural instinct. For, as a rational being, he necessarily wills that his faculties be developed, since they serve him, and have been given him, for all sorts of possible purposes.

4. A fourth, who is in prosperity, while he sees that others have to contend with great wretchedness and that he could help them, thinks: What concerns is it of mine? Let everyone be as happy as Heaven pleases, or as he can make himself; I will take nothing from him nor even envy him, only I do not wish to contribute anything to his welfare or to his assistance in distress! Now no doubt, if such a mode of thinking were a universal law, the human race might very well subsist, and doubtless even better than in a state in which everyone talks of sympathy and good-will, or even takes care occasionally to put it into practice, but, on the other side, also cheats when he can, betrays the rights of men, or otherwise violates them. But although it is possible that a universal law of nature might exist in accordance with that maxim, it is impossible to *will* that such a principle should have the universal validity of a law of nature. For a will which resolved this would contradict itself,

inasmuch as many cases might occur in which one would have need of the love and sympathy of others, and in which, by such a law of nature, sprung from his own will, he would deprive himself of all hope of the aid he desires.

These are a few of the many actual duties, or at least what we regard as such, which obviously fall into two classes on the one principle that we have laid down. We must be *able to will* that a maxim of our action should be a universal law. This is the canon of the moral appreciation of the action generally. Some actions are of such a character that their maxim cannot without contradiction be even *conceived* as a universal law of nature, far from it being possible that we should *will* that it *should* be so. In others, this intrinsic impossibility is not found, but still it is impossible to *will* that their maxim should be raised to the universality of a law of nature, since such a will would contradict itself. It is easily seen that the former violate strict or rigorous (inflexible) duty; the latter only laxer (meritorious) duty. Thus it has been completely shown by these examples how all duties depend as regards the nature of the obligation (not the object of the action) on the same principle.

If now we attend to ourselves on occasion of any transgression of duty, we shall find that we in fact do not will that our maxim should be a universal law, for that is impossible for us; on the contrary, we will that the opposite should remain a universal law, only we assume the liberty of making an *exception* in our own favor or (just for this time only) in favor of our inclination. Consequently, if we considered all cases from one and the same point of view, namely, that of reason, we should find a contradiction in our own will, namely, that a certain principle should be objectively necessary as a universal law, and yet subjectively should not be universal, but admit of exceptions. As, however, we at one moment regard our action from the point of view of a will wholly conformed to reason, and then again look at the same action from the point of view of a will affected by inclination, there is not really any contradiction, but an antagonism of inclination to the precept of reason, whereby the universality of the principle is changed into a mere generality, so that the practical principle of reason shall meet the maxim half way. Now, although this cannot be justified in our own impartial judgment, yet it proves that we do really recognize the validity of the categorical imperative and (with all respect for it) only allow ourselves a few exceptions which we think unimportant and forced from us.

We have thus established at least this much—that if duty is a conception which is to have any import and real legislative authority for our actions, it can only be expressed in categorical, and not at all in hypothetical, imperatives. We have also, which is of great importance, exhibited clearly and definitely for every practical application the content of the categorical imperative, which must contain the principle of all duty if there is such a thing at all. We have not yet, however, advanced so far as to prove *a priori* that there actually is such an imperative, that there is a practical law which commands absolutely of itself and without any other impulse, and that the following of this law is duty. . . .

The will is conceived as a faculty of determining oneself to action *in accordance with the conception of certain laws.* And such a faculty can be found only in rational beings. Now that which serves the will as the objective ground of its self-determination is the *end,* and if this is assigned by reason alone, it must hold for all rational beings. On the other hand, that which merely contains the ground of possibility of the action of which the effect is the end, this is called the *means.* The subjective ground of the desire is the *spring,* the objective ground of the volition is the *motive;* hence the distinction between subjective ends which rest on springs, and objective ends which depend on motives valid for every rational being. Practical principles are *formal* when they abstract from all subjective ends; they are *material* when they assume these, and therefore particular, springs of action. The ends which a rational being proposes to himself at pleasure as *effects* of his actions (material ends) are all only relative, for it is only their relation to the particular desires of the subject that gives them their worth, which therefore cannot furnish principles universal and necessary for all rational beings and for every volition, that is to say, practical laws. Hence all these relative ends can give rise only to hypothetical imperatives.

Supposing, however, that there were something *whose existence* has *in itself* an absolute worth, something which, being *an end in itself,* could be a source of definite laws, then in this and this alone would lie the source of a possible categorical imperative, that is, a practical law.

Now I say: man and generally any rational being *exists* as an end in himself, *not merely as a means* to be arbitrarily used by this or that will, but in all his actions, whether they concern himself or other rational beings, must be always regarded at the same time as an end. All objects of the inclinations have only a conditional worth; for if the inclinations and the wants founded on them did not exist, then their object would be without value. But the inclinations themselves, being sources of want, are so far from having an absolute worth for which they should be desired that, on the contrary, it must be the universal wish of every rational being to be wholly free from them. Thus the worth of any object which is *to be acquired* by our action is always conditional. Beings whose existence depends not on our will but on nature's, have nevertheless, if they are nonrational beings, only a relative value as means, and are therefore called *things;* rational beings, on the contrary, are called *persons,* because their very nature points them out as ends in themselves, that is, as something which must not be used merely as means, and so far therefore restricts freedom of action (and is an object of respect). These, therefore, are not merely subjective ends whose existence has a worth *for us* as an effect of our action, but *objective ends,* that is, things whose existence is an end in itself—an end, moreover, for which no other can be substituted, which they should subserve *merely* as means, for otherwise nothing whatever would possess *absolute worth;* but if all worth were conditioned and therefore contingent, then there would be no supreme practical principle of reason whatever.

If then there is a supreme practical principle or, in respect of the human will, a categorical imperative, it must be one which, being drawn from the conception of that which is necessarily an end for everyone because it is *an end in itself,* constitues an *objective* principle of will, and can therefore serve as a universal practical law. The foundation of this principle is: *rational nature exists as an end in itself.*

Man necessarily conceives his own existence as being so; so far then this is a *subjective* principle of human actions. But every other rational being regards its existence similarly, just on the same rational principle that holds for me;[9] so that it is at the same time an objective principle from which as a supreme practical law all laws of the will must be capable of being deduced. Accordingly the practical imperative will be as follows: *So act as to treat humanity, whether in thine own person or in that of any other, in every case as an end withal, never as means only.* We will now inquire whether this can be practically carried out.

To abide by the previous examples:

First, under the head of necessary duty to oneself: He who contemplates suicide should ask himself whether his action can be consistently with the idea of humanity *as an end in itself.* If he destroys himself in order to escape from painful circumstances, he uses a person merely as *a means* to maintain a tolerable condition up to the end of life. But a man is not a thing, that is to say, something which can be used merely as means, but must in all his actions be always considered as an end in himself. I cannot, therefore, dispose in any way of a man in my own person so as to mutilate him, to damage or kill him. (It belongs to ethics proper to define this principle more precisely, so as to avoid all misunderstanding, for example, as to the amputation of the limbs in order to preserve myself; as to exposing my life to danger with a view to preserve it, etc. This question is therefore omitted here.)

Secondly, as regards necessary duties, or those of strict obligation, toward others: He who is thinking of making a lying promise to others will see at once that he would be using another man *merely as a means,* without the latter containing at the same time the end in himself. For he whom I propose by such a promise to use for my own purposes cannot possibly assent to my mode of acting toward him, and therefore cannot himself contain the end of this action. This violation of the principle of humanity in other men is more obvious if we take in examples of attacks on the freedom and property of others. For then it is clear that he who transgresses the rights of men intends to use the person of others merely as means, without considering that as rational beings ought always to be esteemed also as ends, that is, as beings who must be capable of containing in themselves the end of the very same action.[10]

Thirdly, as regards contingent (meritorious) duties to oneself: It is not enough that the action does not violate humanity in our own person as an end in itself, it must also *harmonize with it.* Now there are in humanity capacities of greater perfection which belong to the end that nature has in view in regard to humanity in ourselves as the subject; to neglect these might perhaps be consistent with the *maintenance* of humanity as an end in itself, but not with the *advancement* of this end.

Fourthly, as regards meritorious duties toward others: The natural end which all men have is their own happiness. Now humanity might indeed subsist although no one should contribute anything to the happiness of others, provided he did not intentionally withdraw anything from it; but after all, this would only harmonize negatively, not positively, with *humanity as an end in itself,* if everyone does not also endeavor, as far as in him lies, to forward the ends of others. For the ends of any subject which is an end in himself ought as far as possible to be *my* ends also, if that conception is to have its *full* effect with me.

This principle that humanity and generally every rational nature is *an end in itself* (which is the supreme limiting condition of every man's freedom of action), is not borrowed from experience, *first,* because it is universal, applying as it does to all rational beings whatever, and experience is not capable of determining anything about them; *secondly,* because it does not present humanity as an end to men (subjectively), that is, as an object which men do of themselves actually adopt as an end; but as an objective end which must as a law constitute the supreme limiting condition of all our subjective ends, let them be what we will; it must therefore spring from pure reason. In fact the objective principle of all practical legislation lies (according to the first principle) in *the rule* and its form of universality which makes it capable of being a law (say, for example, a law of nature); but the *subjective* principle is in the *end;* now by the second principle, the subject of all ends is each rational being inasmuch as it is an end in itself. Hence follows the third practical principle of the will, which is the ultimate condition of its harmony with the universal practical reason, viz., the idea of *the will of every rational being as a universally legislative will.*

On this principle all maxims are rejected which are inconsistent with the will being itself universal legislator. Thus the will is not subject to the law, but so subject that it must be regarded *as itself giving the law,* and on this ground only subject to the law (of which it can regard itself as the author).

NOTES

1. [The first proposition was that to have moral worth an action must be done from duty.]

2. A *maxim* is the subjective principle of volition. The objective principle (*i.e.,* that which would also serve subjectively as a practical principle to all rational beings if reason had full power over the faculty of desire) is the practical *law.*

3. It might be here objected to me that I take refuge behind the word *respect* in an obscure feeling, instead of giving a distinct solution of the question by a concept of the reason. But although respect is a feeling, it is not a feeling *received* through influence, but is *self-wrought* by a rational concept, and, therefore, is specifically distinct from all feelings of the former kind, which may be referred either to inclination or fear. What I recognize immediately as a law for me, I recognize with respect. This merely signifies the consciousness that my will is *subordinate* to a law, without the intervention of other influences on my sense. The immediate determination of the will by the law, and the consciousness of this, is called *respect,* so that this is regarded as an *effect* of the law on the subject, and not as the *cause* of it. Respect is properly the conception of a worth which thwarts my self-love. Accordingly it is something which is considered neither as an object of inclination nor of fear, although it has something analogous to both. The *object* of respect is the *law* only, that is, the law which we impose on *ourselves,* and yet recognize as necessary in itself. As a law, we are subjected to it without consulting self-love; as imposed by us on ourselves, it is a result of our will. In the former aspect it has an analogy to fear, in the latter to inclination. Respect for a person is properly only respect for the law (of honesty, etc.) of which he gives us an example. Since we also look on the improvement of our talents as a duty, we consider that we see in a person of talents, as it were, the *example of a law* (viz. to become like him in this by exercise), and this constitutes our respect. All so-called moral *interest* consists simply in *respect* for the law.

4. The dependence of the desires on sensations is called inclination, and this accordingly always indicates a *want*. The dependence of a contingently determinable will on principles of reason is called an *interest*. This, therefore, is found only in the case of a dependent will which does not always of itself conform to reason; in the Divine will we cannot conceive any interest. But the human will can also *take an interest* in a thing without therefore acting *from interest*. The former signifies the *practical* interest in the action, the latter the *pathological* in the object of the action. The former indicates only dependence of the will on principles of reason in themselves; the second, dependence on principles of reason for the sake of inclination, reason supplying only the practical rules how the requirement of the inclination may be satisfied. In the first case the action interests me; in the second the object of the action (because it is pleasant to me). We have seen in the first section that in an action done from duty we must look not to the interest in the object, but only to that in the action itself, and in its rational principle (viz., the law).

5. I connect the act with the will without presupposing any condition resulting from any inclination, but *a priori*, and therefore necessarily (though only objectively, that is, assuming the idea of a reason possessing full power over all subjective motives). This is accordingly a practical proposition which does not deduce the willing of an action by mere analysis from another already presupposed (for we have not such a perfect will), but connects it immediately with the conception of the will of a rational being, as something not contained in it.

6. A "maxim" is a subjective principle of action, and must be distinguished from the *objective principle*, namely, practical law. The former contains the practical rule set by reason according to the conditions of the subject (often its ignorance or its inclinations), so that it is the principle on which the subject *acts;* but the law is the objective principle valid for every rational being, and is the principle on which it *ought to act*—that is an imperative.

7. [I have no doubt that "den" in the original before "Imperativ" is a misprint for "der," and have translated accordingly. Mr. Semple has done the same. The editions that I have seen agree in reading "den," and Mr. Barni so translates. With this reading, it is the conformity that presents the imperative as necessary.]

8. It must be noted here that I reserve the division of duties for a future *metaphysic of morals;* so that I give it here only as an arbitrary one (in order to arrange my examples). For the rest, I understand by a perfect duty one that admits no exception in favor of inclination, and then I have not merely external but also internal perfect duties. This is contrary to the use of the word adopted in the schools; but I do not intend to justify it here, as it is all one for my purpose whether it is admitted or no. [*Perfect* duties are usually understood to be those which can be enforced by external law; *imperfect*, those which cannot be enforced. They are also called respectively *determinate* and *indeterminate, officia juris* and *officia virtutis.*]

9. This proposition is here stated as a postulate. The ground of it will be found in the concluding section.

10. Let it not be thought that the common: *quod tibi non vis fieri, etc.*, could serve here as the rule or principle. For it is only a deduction from the former, though with several limitations; it cannot be a universal law, for it does not contain the principle of duties to oneself, nor of the duties of benevolence to others (for many a one would gladly consent that others should not benefit him, provided only that he might be excused from showing benevolence to them), nor finally that of duties of strict obligation to one another, for on this principle the criminal might argue against the judge who punishes him, and so on.

ON A SUPPOSED RIGHT TO TELL LIES
FROM BENEVOLENT MOTIVES

Immanuel Kant

In the work called *France,* for the year 1797, Part VI, No. 1, on Political Reactions, by Benjamin Constant, the following passage occurs, page 123:

From *Kant's Critique of Practical Reason and Other Works on the Theory of Ethics,* trans. T. K. Abbott (London: Longmans, Green & Co., 1873).

"The moral principle that it is one's duty to speak the truth, if it were taken singly and unconditionally, would make all society impossible. We have the proof of this in the very direct consequences which have been drawn from this principle by a German philosopher, who goes so far as to affirm that to tell a falsehood to a murderer who asked us whether our friend, of whom he was in pursuit, had not taken refuge in our house, would be a crime."[1]

The French philosopher opposes this principle in the following manner, page 124: "It is a duty to tell the truth. The notion of duty is inseparable from the notion of right. A duty is what in one being corresponds to the right of another. Where there are no rights there are no duties. To tell the truth then is a duty, but only towards him who has a right to the truth. But no man has a right to a truth that injures others." The πρῶτον ψεῦδος here lies in the statement that *"To tell the truth is a duty, but only towards him who has a right to the truth."*

It is to be remarked, first, that the expression "to have a right to the truth" is unmeaning. We should rather say, a man has a right to his own *truthfulness (veracitas),* that is, to subjective truth in his own person. For to have a right objectively to truth would mean that as in *meum* and *tuum* generally, it depends on his *will* whether a given statement shall be true or false, which would produce a singular logic.

Now, the *first* question is whether a man—in cases where he cannot avoid answering *yes* or *no*—has the *right* to be untruthful. The *second* question is whether, in order to prevent a misdeed that threatens him or some one else, he is not actually bound to be untruthful in a certain statement to which an unjust compulsion forces him.

Truth in utterances that cannot be avoided is the formal duty of a man to everyone,[2] however great the disadvantage that may arise from it to him or any other; and although by making a false statement I do no wrong to him who unjustly compels me to speak, yet I do wrong to men in general in the most essential point of duty, so that it may be called a lie (though not in the jurist's sense), that is, so far as in me lies I cause that declarations in general find no credit, and hence that all rights founded on contract should lose their force; and this is a wrong which is done to mankind.

If, then, we define a lie merely as an intentionally false declaration towards another man, we need not add that it must injure another; as the jurists think proper to put in their definition *(mendacium est falsiloquium in praejudicium alterius).* For it always injures another; if not another individual, yet mankind generally, since it vitiates the source of justice. This benevolent lie *may,* however, by *accident (casus)* become punishable even by civil laws; and that which escapes liability to punishment only by accident may be condemned as a wrong even by external laws. For instance, if you have *by a lie* hindered a man who is even now planning a murder, you are legally responsible for all the consequences. But if you have strictly adhered to the truth, public justice can find no fault with you, be the unforeseen consequence what it may. It is possible that whilst you have honestly answered *yes* to the murderer's question, whether his intended victim is in the house, the latter may have gone out unobserved, and so not have come in the way of the murderer, and the deed therefore have not been done; whereas, if you lied and said he was not in the house, and he had really gone out (though unknown to you) so that the murderer met him as he went, and executed his purpose on him, then you might with justice be accused as the cause of his death. For, if you had spoken the truth as well as you knew it, perhaps the murderer while seeking for his enemy in the house might have been caught by neighbours coming up and the deed been prevented. Whoever then *tells a lie*, however good his intentions may be, must answer for the consequences of it, even before the civil tribunal, and must pay the penalty for them, however unforeseen they may have been; because truthfulness is a duty that must be regarded as the basis of all duties founded on contract, the laws of which would be rendered uncertain and useless if even the least exception to them were admitted.

To be *truthful* (honest) in all declarations is therefore a sacred unconditional command of reason, and not to be limited by any expediency.

M. Constant makes a thoughtful and sound remark on the decrying of such strict principles, which it is alleged lose themselves in impracticable ideas, and are therefore to be rejected (p. 123): "In every case in which a principle proved to be true seems to be inapplicable, it is because we do not know the *middle principle* which contains the medium of its application." He adduces (p. 121) the doctrine of *equality* as the first link forming the social chain (p. 121): "namely, that no man can be bound by any laws except those to the formation of which he has contributed. In a very contracted society this principle may be directly applied and become the ordinary rule without requiring any middle principle. But in a very numrous society we must add a new principle to that which we here state. This middle principle is, that the individuals may contribute to the formation of the laws either in their own person or by *representatives*. Whoever would try to apply the first principle to a numerous society without taking in the middle principle would infallibly bring about its destruction. But this circumstance, which would only show the ignorance or incompetence of the lawgiver, would prove nothing against the principle itself." He concludes (p. 125) thus: "A principle recognized as truth must, therefore, never be abandoned, however obviously danger may seem to be involved in it." (And yet the good man himself abandoned the unconditional principle of veracity on account of the danger to society, because he could not discover any middle principle which would serve to prevent this danger; and, in fact, no such principle is to be interpolated here.)

Retaining the names of the persons as they have been here brought forward, "the French philosopher" confounds the action by which one does harm *(nocet)* to another by telling the truth, the admission of which he cannot avoid, with the action by which he does him *wrong (lædit)*. It was merely an *accident (casus)* that the truth of the statement did harm to the inhabitant of the house; it was not a free *deed* (in the juridical sense). For to admit his right to require another to tell a lie for his benefit would be to admit a claim opposed to all law. Every man has not only a right, but the strictest duty to truthfulness in statements which he cannot avoid, whether they do harm to himself or others. He himself, properly speaking, does not *do* harm to him who suffers thereby; but this harm is *caused* by accident. For the man is not free to choose, since (if he must speak at all) veracity is an unconditional duty. The "German philosopher" will therefore not adopt as his principle that proposition (p. 124): "It is a duty to speak the truth, but only to him who has *a right to the truth,*" first on account of the obscurity of the expression, for truth is not a possession the right to which can be granted to one, and refused to another; and next and chiefly, because the duty of veracity (of which alone we are speaking here) makes no distinction between persons towards whom we have this duty, and towards whom we may be free from it; but is an *unconditional duty* which holds in all circumstances.

Now, in order to proceed from a *metaphysic* of *Right* (which abstracts from all conditions of experience) to a principle of *politics* (which applies these notions to cases of experience), and by means of this to the solution of a problem of the latter in accordance with the general principle of right, the philosopher will enunciate: (1) An *Axiom,* that is, an apodictically certain proposition, which follows directly from the definition of external right (harmony of the *freedom* of each with the freedom of all by a universal law). (2) A *Postulate* of external public *law* as the united will of all on the principle of *equality,* without which there could not exist the freedom of all. (3) A *Problem;* how it is to be arranged that harmony may be maintained in a society, however large, on principles of freedom and equality (namely, by means of a representative system); and this will then become a principle of the *political system,* the establishment and arrangement of which will contain enactments which, drawn from practical knowledge of men, have in view only the mechanism of administration of justice, and how this is to be suitably carried out. Justice must never be accommodated to the political system, but always the political system to justice.

"A principle recognized as true (I add, recognized *à priori,* and therefore apodictic) must never be abandoned, however obviously danger may seem to be involved in it," says the author. Only here we must not understand the danger of *doing harm* (accidentally), but of *doing wrong;* and this would happen if the duty of veracity, which is quite unconditional, and constitutes the supreme condition of justice in utterances, were made conditional and subordinate to other considerations; and, although by a certain lie I in fact do no wrong to any person, yet I infringe the principle of justice in regard to all indispensably necessary statements *generally* (I do wrong formally, though not materially); and this is much worse than to commit an injustice to any individual, because such a deed does not presuppose any principle leading to it in the subject. The man who, when asked whether in the statement he is about to make he intends to speak truth or not, does not receive the question with indignation at the suspicion thus expressed towards him that he might be a liar, but who asks permission first to consider possible exceptions, is already a liar *(in potenia),* since he show that he does not recognize veracity as a duty in itself, but reserves exceptions from a rule which in its nature does not admit of exceptions, since to do so would be self-contradictory.

All practical principles of justice must contain strict truths, and the principles here called middle principles can only contain the closer definition of their application to actual cases (according to the rules of politics), and never exceptions from them, since exceptions destroy the universality, on account of which alone they bear the name of principles.

NOTES

1. "J. D. Michaelis, in Göttingen, propounded the same strange opinion even before Kant. That Kant is the philosopher here referred to, I have been informed by the author of this work himself."–K. F. Cramer.

I hereby admit that I have really said this in some place which I cannot now recollect.–I, Kant.

2. I do not wish here to press this principle so far as to say that "falsehood is a violation of duty to oneself." For this principle belongs to Ethics, and here we are speaking only of a duty of justice. Ethics look in this transgression only to the *worthlessness,* the reproach of which the liar draws on himself.

CRITICISM OF KANT'S MORAL PHILOSOPHY

Alasdair MacIntyre

Central to Kant's moral philosophy are two deceptively simple theses: if the rules of morality are rational, they must be the same for all rational beings, in just the way that the rules of arithmetic are; and if the rules of morality are *binding* on all rational beings, then the contingent ability of such beings to carry them out must be unimportant—what is important is their will to carry them out. The project of discovering a rational justification of morality therefore simply *is* the project of discovering a rational test which will discriminate those maxims which are a genuine expression of the moral law when they determine the will from those maxims which are not such an expression. Kant is not of course himself in any doubt as to *which* maxims are in fact the expression of the moral law; virtuous plain men and women did not have to wait for philosophy to tell them in what a good will consisted and Kant never doubted for a moment that the maxims which he had learnt from his own virtuous parents were those which had to be vindicated by a rational test. Thus the content of Kant's morality was conservative in just the way that the content of Kierkegaard's was, and this is scarcely surprising. Although Kant's Lutheran childhood in Konigsberg was a hundred years before Kierkegaard's Lutheran childhood in Copenhagen the same inherited morality marked both men.

Kant then possesses on the one hand a stock of maxims and on the other a conception of what a rational test for a maxim must be. What is this conception and whence is it derived? We can best approach an answer to these questions by considering why Kant rejects two conceptions of such a test which had been widely

From *After Virtue,* pp. 42-45. Copyright 1981, University of Notre Dame Press, Notre Dame, Ind.

influential in the European traditions. On the one hand Kant rejects the view that the test of a proposed maxim is whether obedience to it would in the end lead to the happiness of a rational being. Kant has no doubt that all men do indeed desire happiness; and he has no doubt that the highest good conceivable is that of the individual's moral perfection crowned by the happiness which it merits. But he none the less believes that our *conception* of happiness is too vague and shifting to provide a reliable moral guide. Moreover any precept designed to secure our happiness would be an expression of a rule holding only conditionally; it would instruct to do such-and-such, if and insofar as doing such-and-such would in fact lead to happiness as a result. Whereas Kant takes it to be the case that all genuine expressions of the moral law have an unconditional categorical character. They do not enjoin us hypothetically; they simply enjoin us.

Morality then can find no basis in our desires; but it can find no basis either in our religious beliefs. For the second traditional view which Kant repudiates is that according to which the test of a given maxim or precept is whether it is commanded by God. On Kant's view it can never follow from the fact that God commands us to do such-and-such that we ought to do such-and-such. In order for us to reach such a conclusion justifiably we would also have to know that we always ought to do what God commands. But this last we could not know unless we ourselves possessed a standard of moral judgment independent of God's commandments by means of which we could judge God's deeds and words and so find the latter morally worthy of obedience. But clearly if we possess such a standard, the commandments of God will be redundant.

We can already notice certain large and obvious features of Kant's thought which declare it to be the immediate ancestor of Kierkegaard's. The sphere in which happiness is to be pursued is sharply distinguished from the sphere of morality and both in turn as sharply from that of divine morality and commandment. Moreover the precepts of morality are not only the same precepts as those which were later to constitute the ethical for Kierkegaard; but they are to inspire the same kind of respect. Yet where Kierkegaard had seen the basis of the ethical in choice, Kant sees it in reason.

Practical reason, according to Kant, employs no criterion external to itself. It appeals to no content derived from experience; hence Kant's independent arguments against the use of happiness or the invocation of God's revealed will merely reinforce a position already entailed by the Kantian view of reason's function and powers. It is of the essence of reason that it lays down principles which are universal, categorical, and internally consistent. Hence a rational morality will lay down principles which both can and ought to be held by *all* men, independent of circumstances and conditions, and which could consistently be obeyed by every rational agent on every occasion. The test for a proposed maxim is then easily framed: can we or can we not consistently will that eveyone should always act on it?

How are we to decide whether this attempt to formulate a decisive test for the maxims of morality is successful or not? Kant himself tries to show that such maxims as 'Always tell the truth', 'Always keep promises', 'Be benevolent to those in need' and 'Do not commit suicide' pass his test, while such maxims as 'Only keep promises when it is convenient to you' fail. In fact however, even to approach a semblance of showing this, he has to use notoriously bad arguments, the climax of which is his assertion that any man who wills the maxim 'To kill myself when the prospects of pain outweigh those of happiness' is inconsistent because such willing 'contradicts' an impulse to life implanted in all of us. This is as if someone were to assert that any man who wills the maxim 'Always to keep my hair cut short' is inconsistent because such willing 'contradicts' an impulse to the growth of hair implanted in all of us. But it is not just that Kant's own arguments involve large mistakes. It is very easy to see that many immoral and trivial non-moral maxims are vindicated by Kant's test quite as convincingly—in some cases more convincingly—than the moral maxims which Kant aspires to uphold. So 'Keep all your promises throughout your entire life except one', 'Persecute all those who hold false religious beliefs' and 'Always eat mussels on Mondays in March' will all pass Kant's test, for all can be consistently universalised.

To this one rejoinder may be that if this follows from what Kant said, it cannot be what Kant meant. Certainly and obviously it was not what Kant envisaged, for he himself believed that his test of consistent universalisability had a defining moral content which would have excluded such universal and trivial maxims. Kant believed this because he believed that his formulations of the categorical imperative in terms of universalisability were equivalent to a quite different formulation: 'Always act so as to treat humanity, whether in your own person or in that of others, as an end, and not as a means.'

This formulation clearly does have a moral content, although one that is not very precise, if it is not supplemented by a good deal of further elucidation. What Kant means by treating someone as an end rather than as a means seems to be as follows—as I noticed earlier in using Kant's moral philosophy to highlight a contrast with emotivism. I may propose a course of action to someone either by offering him reasons for so acting or by trying to influence him in non-rational ways. If I do the former I treat him as a rational will, worthy of the same respect as is due to myself, for in offering him reasons I offer him an impersonal consideration for him to evaluate. What makes a reason a good reason has nothing to do with who utters it on a given occasion; and until an agent has decided for himself whether a reason is a good reason or not, he has no reason to act. By contrast an attempt at non-rational suasion embodies an attempt to make the agent a mere instrument of *my* will, without any regard for *his* rationality. Thus what Kant enjoins is what a long line of moral philosophers have followed the Plato of the *Gorgias* in enjoining. But Kant gives us no good reason for holding this position. I can without any inconsistency whatsoever flout it; 'Let everyone except me be treated as a means' may be immoral, but it is not inconsistent and there is not even an inconsistency in willing a universe of egotists all of whom live by this maxim. It might be inconvenient for each if everyone lived by this maxim, but it would not be impossible and to invoke considerations of convenience would in any case be to introduce just that prudential reference to happiness which Kant aspires to eliminate from all considerations of morality.

CHAPTER FOUR
PHILOSOPHY
AND PERSONAL
RELATIONS

Would you, right now, trade your life for the life of Robinson Crusoe, shipwrecked and alone on a desolate island? No matter how unsatisfactory and hassled we feel our present lives to be, very few of us would willingly choose Crusoe's solitary existence. Why? Part of the answer is our awareness of how short a time we would survive outside the complex technologies that provide our food, water, shelter, and other necessities. An even larger part of the answer, however, is our powerful hunger for the company of other people. Human life lived to its fullest is a complex network of personal relations. Many of our greatest joys, as well as our most profound sorrows, would be impossible without relationships binding us to others. What would one's life be like without the possibilities of friendship, love, and sexual union? Hobbes's phrase is perfect: "solitary, poor, nasty, brutish, and short."

How many of us have seriously reflected on the personal relations that give human life its savor? We can, on a moment's consideration, feel their value, but can we truly understand their value to us without first understanding their natures? In this section we have chosen readings that explore in philosophical depth some major forms of the relationships that are essential to our happiness.

One fundamental personal relation is *friendship*. Most of us are friends; we befriend, and we are befriended. When does it mean to be someone's friend? Is friendship, as some maintain, a relationship that can exist only between equals? What could *equality* mean in this context? Is friendship a single specific relationship, or are there various modes of being a friend? We may immediately think that we can make certain demands on friends that we cannot make on strangers or mere acquaintances, but is that so? What are the limits of those demands? Can one ask a friend to lie, to cheat, to break the law? Finally, what exactly does friendship add to human life? In what sense are we potentially more virtuous because we are friends? The selections we have chosen explore some of these large and important questions.

Ours is a society that is constantly talking about *love;* the word is on everyone's lips, from pop singers to preachers and TV pitchmen. What is this love that everyone extols? For many people, the paradigm that comes immediately to mind is romantic love between men and women. But this is to nourish oneself with a one-sided diet of examples; there are many other kinds of love as well. It is unfortunate that love has more often claimed the attention of the poet than of the philosopher, for there are significant philosophical questions to be answered: What are the various kinds of love, and what are their relationships to one another? What is the connection between love and sexual desire? What kind of person must one be to love? Is love a passion, something over which we have no control, or can we rationally choose to grant or withhold our love? The three selections we have included attempt to provide a philosophical basis for answering some of these questions. That raises a further question: Is love analyzed love understood and enriched, or love destroyed?

We do not need to be told that we are sexual beings; our bodies make us well aware of that dominating factor in our existence. To be a sexual being, however, does not require that we understand our sexuality or that we have placed it in proper relationship to other aspects of our lives. Is there such a thing as a purely sexual relationship, and if so, can it be a source of human happiness? Many moralists work with an expression theory of sexual behavior: Sexual relationships are properly the expression of other sorts of relations—love, for example. Must this be so? This raises the issue of the connections between sex and morality. Is there a distinctively sexual morality? Can it be argued that good sex promotes human virtue? The essays by Nagel and Ruddick address these questions and others that are equally important.

The most common long-term relationship among individuals in our society is marriage; it is also an institution under attack from within and without. As commonly understood, marriage is a lifetime commitment: "What God has joined together, let not man put asunder." We know, however, that one in three American marriages ends in divorce. Marriage is also usually considered to demand sexual exclusivity from the partners, but adultery is certainly not uncommon in this society. Is traditional monogamous marriage doomed; more importantly, *ought* it to be doomed? Does marriage add something to the quality of human life that is not to be found in other sorts of personal relations, or is it an institution that inevitably constricts and distorts individuals? The essays of McMurtry and O'Driscoll present a wide range of reasoned opinion on the nature, purpose, and value of marriage.

When Socrates said that the unexamined life is not worth living, part of what he must have meant was that failure to understand those aspects of human life that are the sources of good is to forgo any reasonable chance to attain that good. As we rightfully reject the solitary life of Robinson Crusoe, we also need to recall the character in Sartre's *No Exit* who exclaims, "Hell is—other people." Our personal relations can be sources of good; they can be springs of distress and evil as well. Perhaps philosophical reflection cannot guarantee that our personal relations will yield good rather than evil, but surely a rational investigation of such complex and varied phenomena will heighten our possibilities for fulfillment in these important dimensions of human life.

FRIENDSHIP

FRIENDSHIP AND ITS FORMS

Aristotle

Book VIII

After what we have said, a discussion of friendship would naturally follow, since it is a virtue or implies virtue, and is besides most necessary with a view to living. For without friends no one would choose to live, though he had all other goods; even rich men and those in possession of office and of dominating power are thought to need friends most of all; for what is the use of such prosperity without the opportunity of beneficence, which is exercised chiefly and in its most laudable form towards friends? Or how can prosperity be guarded and preserved without friends? The greater it is, the more exposed is it to risk. And in poverty and in other misfortunes men think friends are the only refuge. It helps the young, too, to keep from error; it aids older people by ministering to their needs and supplementing the activities that are failing from weakness; those in the prime of life it stimulates to noble actions—'two going together'—for with friends men are more able both to think and to act. Again, parent seems by nature to feel it for offspring and offspring for parent, not only among men but among birds and among most animals; it is felt mutually by members of the same race, and especially by men, whence we praise lovers of their fellowmen. We may see even in our travels how near and dear

From "Nichomachean Ethics," trans. W. D. Ross, in *The Oxford Translation of Aristotle,* ed. W. D. Ross, Vol. IX, 1925. Reprinted by permission of Oxford University Press.

every man is to every other. Friendship seems too to hold states together, and law-givers to care more for it than for justice; for unanimity seems to be something like friendship, and this they aim at most of all, and expel faction as their worst enemy; and when men are friends they have no need of justice, while when they are just they need friendship as well, and the truest form of justice is thought to be a friendly quality.

But it is not only necessary but also noble; for we praise those who love their friends, and it is thought to be a fine thing to have many friends; and again we think it is the same people that are good men and are friends.

Not a few things about friendship are matters of debate. Some define it as a kind of likeness and say like people are friends, whence come the sayings 'like to be like', 'birds of a feather flock together', and so on; others on the contrary say 'two of a trade never agree'. On this very question they inquire for deeper and more physical causes, Euripides saying that 'parched earth loves the rain, and stately heaven when filled with rain loves to fall to earth', and Heraclitus that 'it is what opposes that helps' and 'from different tones comes the fairest tune' and 'all things are produced through strife'; while Empedocles, as well as others, expresses the opposite view that like aims at like. The physical problems we may leave alone (for they do not belong to the present inquiry); let us examine those which are human and involve character and feeling, e.g. whether friendship can arise between any two people or people cannot be friends if they are wicked, and whether there is one species of friendship or more than one. Those who think there is only one because it admits of degrees have relied on an inadequate indication; for even things different in species admit of degree. We have discussed this matter previously.

The kinds of friendship may perhaps be cleared up if we first come to know the object of love. For not everything seems to be loved but only the lovable; and this is good, pleasant, or useful; but it would seem to be that by which some good or pleasure is produced that is useful, so that it is the good and the useful that are lovable as ends. Do men love, then, *the* good, or what is good for *them*? These sometimes clash. So too with regard to the pleasant. Now it is thought that each loves what is good for himself, and that the good is without qualification lovable, and what is good for each man is lovable for him; but each man loves not what is good for him but what seems good. This however will make no difference; we shall just have to say this is 'that which seems lovable'. Now there are three grounds on which people love; of the love of lifeless objects we do not use the word 'friendship'; for it is not mutual love, nor is there a wishing of good to the other (for it would surely be ridiculous to wish wine well; if one wishes anything for it, it is that it may keep, so that one may have it oneself); but to a friend we say we ought to wish what is good for his sake. But to those who thus wish good we ascribe only goodwill, if the wish is not reciprocated; goodwill when it *is* reciprocal being friendship. Or must we add 'when it is recognized'? For many people have good-will to those whom they have not seen but judge to be good or useful; and one of these might return this feeling. These people seem to bear goodwill to each other;

but how could one call them friends when they do not know their mutual feelings? To be friends, then, they must be mutually recognized as bearing goodwill and wishing well to each other for one of the aforesaid reasons.

Now these reasons differ from each other in kind; so, therefore, do the corresponding forms of love and friendship. There are therefore three kinds of friendship, equal in number to the things that are lovable; for with respect to each there is a mutual and recognized love, and those who love each other wish well to each other in that respect in which they love one another. Now those who love each other for their utility do not love each other for themselves but in virtue of some good which they get from each other. So too with those who love for the sake of pleasure; it is not for their character that men love ready-witted people, but because they find them pleasant. Therefore those who love for the sake of utility love for the sake of what is good for *themselves,* and those who love for the sake of pleasure do so for the sake of what is pleasant to *themselves,* and not in so far as the other is the person loved but in so far as he is useful or pleasant. And thus these friendships are only incidental; for it is not as being the man he is that the loved person is loved, but as providing some good or pleasure. Such friendships, then, are easily dissolved, if the parties do not remain like themselves; for if the one party is no longer pleasant or useful the other ceases to love him.

Now the useful is not permanent but is always changing. Thus when the motive of the friendship is done away, the friendship is dissolved, inasmuch as it existed only for the ends in question. This kind of friendship seems to exist chiefly between old people (for at that age people pursue not the pleasant but the useful) and, of those who are in their prime or young, between those who pursue utility. And such people do not live much with each other either; for sometimes they do not even find each other pleasant; therefore they do not need such companionship unless they are useful to each other; for they are pleasant to each other only in so far as they rouse in each other hopes of something good to come. Among such friendships people also class the friendship of host and guest. On the other hand the friendship of young people seems to aim at pleasure; for they live under the guidance of emotion, and pursue above all what is pleasant to themselves and what is immediately before them; but with increasing age their pleasures become different. This is why they quickly become friends and quickly cease to be so; their friendship changes with the object that is found pleasant, and such pleasure alters quickly. Young people are amorous too; for the greater part of the friendship of love depends on emotion and aims at pleasure; this is why they fall in love and quickly fall out of love, changing often within a single day. But these people do wish to spend their days and lives together; for it is thus that they attain the purpose of their friendship.

Perfect friendship is the friendship of men who are good, and alike in virtue; for these wish well alike to each other *qua* good, and they are good in themselves. Now those who wish well to their friends for their sake are most truly friends; for they do this by reason of their own nature and not incidentally; therefore their friendship lasts as long as they are good—and goodness is an enduring thing. And each is good without qualification and to his friend, for the good are both good without qualification and useful to each other. So too they are pleasant; for the good are pleasant both without qualification and to each other, since to each his own activities and others like them are pleasurable, and the actions of the good *are* the same or like. And such a friendship is as might be expected permanent, since there meet in it all the qualities that friends should have. For all friendship is for the sake of good or of pleasure—good or pleasure either in the abstract or such as will be enjoyed by him who has the friendly feeling—and is based on a certain resemblance; and to a friendship of good men all the qualities we have named belong in virtue of the nature of the friends themselves; for in the case of this kind of friendship the other qualities also are alike in both friends, and that which is good without qualification is also without qualification pleasant, and these are the most lovable qualities. Love and friendship therefore are found most and in their best form between such men.

But it is natural that such friendships should be infrequent; for such men are rare. Further, such friendship requires time and familiarity; as the proverb says, men cannot know each other till they have 'eaten salt together'; nor can they admit each other to friendship or be friends till each has been found lovable and been trusted by each. Those who quickly show the marks of friendship to each other wish to be friends, but are not friends unless they both are lovable and know the fact; for a wish for friendship may arise quickly, but friendship does not.

This kind of friendship, then, is perfect both in respect of duration and in all other respects, and in it each gets from each in all respects the same as, or something like what, he gives; which is what ought to happen between friends. Friendship for the sake of pleasure bears a resemblance to this kind; for good people too are pleasant to each other. So too does friendship for the sake of utility; for the good are also useful to each other. Among men of these inferior sorts too, friendships are most permanent when the friends get the same thing from each other (e.g. pleasure), and not only that but also from the same source, as happens between ready-witted people, not as happens between lover and beloved. For these do not take pleasure in the same things, but the one in seeing the beloved and the other in receiving attentions from his lover; and when the bloom of youth is passing the friendship sometimes passes too (for the one finds no pleasure in the sight of the other, and the other gets no attention from the first); but many lovers on the other hand are constant, if familiarity has led them to love each other's characters, these being alike. But those who exchange not pleasure but utility in their amour are both less truly friends and less constant. Those who are friends for the sake of utility part when the advantage is at an end; for they were lovers not of each other but of profit.

For the sake of pleasure or utility, then, even bad men may be friends of each other, or good men of bad, or one who is neither good nor bad may be a friend to any sort of person, but for their own sake clearly only good men can be friends; for bad men do not delight in each other unless some advantage come of the relation.

The friendship of the good too and this alone is proof against slander; for it is not easy to trust any one's talk about a man who has long been tested by oneself; and it is among good men that trust and the feeling that 'he would never wrong me' and all the other things that are demanded in true friendship are found. In the other kinds of friendship, however, there is nothing to prevent these evils arising.

For men apply the name of friends even to those whose motive is utility, in which sense states are said to be friendly (for the alliances of states seem to aim at advantage), and to those who love each other for the sake of pleasure, in which sense children are called friends. Therefore we too ought perhaps to call such people friends, and say that there are several kinds of friendship—firstly and in the proper sense that of good men *qua* good, and by analogy the other kinds; for it is in virtue of something good and something akin to what is found in true friendship that they are friends, since even the pleasant is good for the lovers of pleasure. But these two kinds of friendship are not often united, nor do the same people become friends for the sake of utility and of pleasure; for things that are only incidentally connected are not often coupled together.

Friendship being divided into these kinds, bad men will be friends for the sake of pleasure or of utility, being in this respect like each other, but good men will be friends for their own sake, i.e. in virtue of their goodness. These, then, are friends without qualification; the others are friends incidentally and through a resemblance to these.

As in regard to the virtues some men are called good in respect of a state of character, others in respect of an activity, so too in the case of friendship; for those who live together delight in each other and confer benefits on each other, but those who are asleep or locally separated are not performing, but are disposed to perform, the activities of friendship; distance does not break off the friendship absolutely, but only the activity of it. But if the absence is lasting, it seems actually to make men forget their friendship; hence the saying 'out of sight, out of mind'. Neither old people nor sour people seem to make friends easily; for there is little that is pleasant in them, and no one can spend his days with one whose company is painful, or not pleasant, since nature seems above all to avoid the painful and to aim at the pleasant. Those, however, who approve of each other but do not live together seem to be well-disposed rather than actual friends. For there is nothing so characteristic of friends as living together (since while it is people who are in need that desire benefits, even those who are supremely happy desire to spend their days together; for solitude suits such people least of all); but people cannot live together if they are not pleasant and do not enjoy the same things, as friends who are companions seem to do.

The truest friendship, then, is that of the good, as we have frequently said, for that which is without qualification good or pleasant seems to be lovable and desirable, and for each person that which is good or pleasant to him; and the good man is lovable and desirable to the good man for both these reasons. Now it looks as if love were a feeling, friendship a state of character; for love may be felt just as much towards lifeless things, but mutual love involves choice and choice springs from a state of character; and men wish well to those whom they love, for their sake, not as a result of feeling but as a result of a state of character. And in loving a friend men love what is good for themselves; for the good man in becoming a friend becomes a good to his friend. Each, then, both loves what is good for himself, and makes an equal return in goodwill and in pleasantness; for friendship is said to be equality, and both of these are found most in the friendship of the good.

Between sour and elderly people friendship arises less readily, inasmuch as they are less good-tempered and enjoy companionship less; for these are thought to be the greatest marks of friendship and most productive of it. This is why, while young men become friends quickly, old men do not; it is because men do not become friends with those in whom they do not delight; and similarly sour people do not quickly make friends either. But such men may bear goodwill to each other; for they wish one another well and aid one another in need; but they are hardly *friends* because they do not spend their days together nor delight in each other, and these are thought the greatest marks of friendship.

One cannot be a friend to many people in the sense of having friendship of the perfect type with them, just as one cannot be in love with many people at once (for love is a sort of excess of feeling, and it is the nature of such only to be felt towards one person); and it is not easy for many people at the same time to please the same person very greatly, or perhaps even to be good in his eyes. One must, too, acquire some experience of the other person and become familiar with him, and that is very hard. But with a view of utility or pleasure it is possible that many people should please one; for many people are useful or pleasant, and these services take little time.

Of these two kinds that which is for the sake of pleasure is the more like friendship, when both parties get the same things from each other and delight in each other or in the same things, as in the friendships of the young; for generosity is more found in such friendships. Friendship based on utility is for the commercially minded. People who are supremely happy, too, have no need of useful friends, but do need pleasant friends; for they wish to live with *some one* and, though they can endure for a short time what is painful, no one could put up with it continuously, nor even with the Good itself if it were painful to him; this is why they look out for friends who are pleasant. Perhaps they should look out for friends who, being pleasant, are also good, and good for them too; for so they will have all the characteristics that friends should have.

People in positions of authority seem to have friends who fall into distinct classes; some people are useful to them and others are pleasant, but the same people are rarely both; for they seek neither those whose pleasantness is accompanied by virtue nor those whose utility is with a view to noble objects, but in their desire for pleasure they seek for ready-witted people, and their other friends they choose as being clever at doing what they are told, and these characteristics are rarely combined. Now we have said that the *good* man *is* at the same time pleasant and useful; but such a man does not become the friend of one who surpasses him in station, unless he is surpassed also in virtue; if this is not so, he does not establish equality by being proportionally exceeded in both respects. But people who surpass him in both respects are not so easy to find.

However that may be, the aforesaid friendships involve equality; for the friends get the same things from one another and wish the same things for one another, or exchange one thing for another, e.g. pleasure for utility; we have said, however, that they are both less truly friendships and less permanent. But it is from their likeness and their unlikeness to the same thing that they are thought both to be and not to be friendships. It is by their likeness to the friendship of virtue that they seem to be friendships (for one of them involves pleasure and the other utility, and these characteristics belong to the friendship of virtue as well); while it is because the friendship of virtue is proof against slander and permanent, while these quickly change (besides differing from the former in many other respects), that they appear *not* to be friendships; i.e. it is because of their unlikeness to the friendship of virtue. . . .

Should we, then, make as many friends as possible, or—as in the case of hospitality it is thought to be suitable advice, that one should be 'neither a man of many guests nor a man with none'—will that apply to friendship as well; should a man neither be friendless nor have an excessive number of friends?

To friends made with a view to *utility* this saying would seem thoroughly applicable; for to do services to many people in return is a laborious task and life is not long enough for its performance. Therefore friends in excess of those who are sufficient for our own life are superfluous, and hindrances to the noble life; so that we have no need of them. Of friends made with a view to *pleasure,* also, few are enough, as a little seasoning in food is enough.

But as regards *good* friends, should we have as many as possible, or is there a limit to the number of one's friends, as there is to the size of a city? You cannot make a city of ten men, and if there are a hundred thousand it is a city no longer. But the proper number is presumably not a single number, but anything that falls between certain fixed points. So for friends too there is a fixed number—perhaps the largest number with whom one can live together (for that, we found, is thought to be very characteristic of friendship); and that one cannot live with many people and divide oneself up among them is plain. Further, they too must be friends of one another, if they are all to spend their days together; and it is a hard business for this condition to be fulfilled with a large number. It is found difficult, too, to rejoice and to grieve in an intimate way with many people, for it may likely happen that one has at once to be happy with one friend and to mourn with another. Presumably, then, it is well not to seek to have as many friends as possible, but as many as are enough for the purpose of living together; for it would seem actually impossible to be a great friend to many people. This is why one cannot love several people; love is ideally a sort of excess of friendship, and that can only be felt towards one person; therefore great friendship too can only be felt towards a few people. This seems to be confirmed in practice; for we do not find many people who are friends in the comradely way of friendship, and the famous friendships of this sort are always between two people. Those who have many friends and mix intimately with them all are thought to be no one's friend, except in the way proper to fellow-citizens, and such people are also called obsequious. In the way proper to fellow-citizens, indeed, it is possible to be the friend of many and yet not be obsequious but a genuinely good man; but one cannot have with many people the friendship based on virtue and on the character of our friends themselves, and we must be content if we find even a few such.

Do we need friends more in good fortune or in bad? They are sought after in both; for while men in adversity need help, in prosperity they need people to live with and to make the objects of their beneficence; for they wish to do well by others. Friendship, then, is more necessary in bad fortune, and so it is useful friends that one wants in this case; but it is more noble in good fortune, and so we also seek for good men as our friends, since it is more desirable to confer benefits on these and to live with these. For the very presence of friends is pleasant both in good fortune and also in bad, since grief is lightened when friends sorrow with us. Hence one might ask whether they share as it were our burden, or—without that happening—their presence by its pleasantness, and the thought of their grieving with us, make our pain less. Whether it is for these reasons or for some other that our grief is lightened, is a question that may be dismissed; at all events what we have described appears to take place.

But their presence seems to contain a mixture of various factors. The very seeing of one's friends is pleasant, especially if one is in adversity, and becomes a safeguard against grief (for a friend tends to comfort us both by the sight of him and by his words, if he is tactful, since he knows our character and the things that please or pain us); but to see him pained at our misfortunes is painful; for every one shuns being a cause of pain to his friends. For this reason people of a manly nature guard against making their friends grieve with them, and, unless he be exceptionally insensible to pain, such a man cannot stand the pain that ensues for his friends, and in general does not admit fellow-mourners because he is not himself given to mourning; but women and womanly men enjoy sympathisers in their grief, and love them as friends and companions in sorrow. But in all things one obviously ought to imitate the better type of person.

On the other hand, the presence of friends in our *prosperity* implies both a pleasant passing of our time and the pleasant thought of their pleasure at our own good fortune. For this cause it would seem that we ought to summon our friends readily to share our good fortunes (for the beneficent character is a noble one), but summon them to our bad fortunes with hesitation; for we ought to give them as little a share as possible in our evils—whence the saying 'enough is *my* misfortune'. We should summon friends to us most of all when they are likely by suffering a few inconveniences to do us a great service.

Conversely, it is fitting to go unasked and readily to the aid of those in adversity (for it is characteristic of a friend to render services, and especially to those who are in need and have not demanded them; such action is nobler and pleasanter for both persons); but when our friends are prosperous we should join readily in their activities (for they need friends for these too), but be tardy in coming forward to be the objects of their kindness; for it is not noble to be keen to receive benefits. Still, we must no doubt avoid getting the reputation of kill-joys by repulsing them; for that sometimes happens.

The presence of friends, then, seems desirable in all circumstances.

Does it not follow, then, that, as for lovers the sight of the beloved is the thing they love most, and they prefer this sense to the others because on it love depends most for its being and for its origin, so for friends the most desirable thing is living together? For friendship is a partnership, and as a man is to himself, so is he to his friend; now in his own case the consciousness of his being is desirable, and so therefore is the consciousness of his friend's being, and the activity of this consciousness is produced when they live together, so that it is natural that they aim at this. And whatever existence means for each class of men, whatever it is for whose sake they value life, in *that* they wish to occupy themselves with their friends; and so some drink together, others dice together, others join in athletic exercises and hunting, or in the study of philosophy, each class spending their days together in whatever they love most in life; for since they wish to live with their friends, they do and share in those things which give them the sense of living together. Thus the friendship of bad men turns out an evil thing (for because of their instability they unite in bad pursuits, and besides they become evil by becoming like each other), while the friendship of good men is good, being augmented by their companionship; and they are thought to become better too by their activities and by improving each other; for from each other they take the mould of the characteristics they approve—whence the saying 'noble deeds from noble men'. So much, then, for friendship. . . .

FRIENDSHIP

Simone Weil

There is however a personal and human love which is pure and which enshrines an intimation and a reflection of divine love. This is friendship, provided we keep strictly to the true meaning of the word.

Preference for some human being is necessarily a different thing from charity. Charity does not discriminate. If it is found more abundantly in any special quarter, it is because affliction has chanced to provide an occasion there for the exchange of compassion and gratitude. It is equally available for the whole human race,

From *Waiting For God,* trans. Emma Crawfurd. Reprinted by permission of G. P. Putnam's Sons. Copyright 1951 by G. P. Putnam's Sons, pp. 200-208.

inasmuch as affliction can come to all, offering them an opportunity for such an exchange.

Preference for a human being can be of two kinds. Either we are seeking some particular good in him, or we need him. In a general way all possible attachments come under one of these heads. We are drawn toward a thing, either because there is some good we are seeking from it, or because we cannot do without it. Sometimes the two motives coincide. Often however they do not. Each is distinct and quite independent. We eat distasteful food, if we have nothing else, because we cannot do otherwise. A moderately greedy man looks out for delicacies, but he can easily do without them. If we have no air we are suffocated, we struggle to get it, not because we expect to get some advantage from it but because we need it. We go in search of sea air without being driven by any necessity, because we like it. In time it often comes about automatically that the second motive takes the place of the first. This is one of the great misfortunes of our race. A man smokes opium in order to attain to a special condition, which he thinks superior; often, as time goes on, the opium reduces him to a miserable condition which he feels to be degrading; but he is no longer able to do without it. Arnolphe bought Agnès[1] from her adopted mother, because it seemed to him it would be an advantage to have a little girl with him, a little girl whom he would gradually make into a good wife. Later on she ceased to cause him anything but a heart-rending and degrading torment. But with the passage of time his attachment to her had become a vital bond which forced this terrible line from his lips:

"Mais je sens là-dedans qu'il faudra que je crève—"[2]

Harpagon started by considering gold as an advantage. Later it became nothing but the object of a haunting obsession, yet an object of which the loss would cause his death. As Plato says, there is a great difference between the essence of the Necessary and that of the Good.

There is no contradiction between seeking our own good in a human being and wishing for his good to be increased. For this very reason, when the motive which draws us towards anybody is simply some advantage for ourselves, the conditions of friendship are not fulfilled. Friendship is a supernatural harmony, a union of opposites.

When a human being is in any degree necessary to us, we cannot desire his good unless we cease to desire our own. Where there is necessity there is constraint and domination. We are in the power of that of which we stand in need, unless we possess it. The central good for every man is the free disposal of himself. Either we renounce it, which is a crime of idolatry, since it can only be renounced in favour of God, or we desire that the being we stand in need of should be deprived of it.

Any kind of mechanism may join human beings together with bonds of affection which have the iron hardness of necessity. Mother-love is often of such a kind; so at times is paternal love, as in *Le Père Goriot* of Balzac; so is carnal love in its most intense form as in *L'Ecole des Femmes* and in *Phèdre;* so also, very frequently, is the love between husband and wife, chiefly as a result of habit. Filial and fraternal love are more rarely of this nature.

There are moreover degrees of necessity. Everything is necessary in some degree if its loss really causes a decrease of vital energy. (This word is here used in the strict and precise sense which it might have if the study of vital phenomena were as far advanced as that of falling bodies.) When the degree of necessity is extreme, deprivation leads to death. This is the case when all the vital energy of one being is bound up with another by some attachment. In the lesser degrees, deprivation leads to a more or less considerable lessening of energy. Thus a total deprivation of food causes death, whereas a partial deprivation only diminishes the life force. Nevertheless the necessary quantity of food is considered to be that required if a person is not to be weakened.

The most frequent cause of necessity in the bonds of affection is a combination of sympathy and habit. As in the case of avarice or drunkenness, that which was at first a search for some desired good is transformed into a need by the mere passage of time. The difference from avarice, drunkenness and all the vices, however, is that in the bonds of affection the two motives—search for a desired good, and need—can very easily co-exist. They can also be separated. When the attachment of one being to another is made up of need and nothing else it is a fearful thing. Few things in this world can reach such a degree of ugliness and horror. There is always something horrible whenever a human being seeks what is good and only finds necessity. The stories which tell of a beloved being who suddenly appears with a death's head best symbolise this. The human soul possesses a whole arsenal of lies with which to put up a defence against this ugliness and, in imagination, to manufacture sham advantages where there is only necessity. It is for this very reason that ugliness is an evil, because it conduces to lying.

Speaking quite generally, we might say that there is affliction whenever necessity, under no matter what form, is imposed so harshly that the hardness exceeds the capacity for lying of the person who receives the impact. That is why the purest souls are the most exposed to affliction. For him who is capable of preventing the automatic reaction of defence which tends to increase the soul's capacity for lying, affliction is not an evil, although it is always a wounding and in a sense a degradation.

When a human being is attached to another by a bond of affection which contains any degree of necessity, it is impossible that he should wish autonomy to be preserved both in himself and in the other. It is impossible by virtue of the mechanism of nature. It is however made possible by the miraculous intervention of the supernatural. This miracle is friendship.

"Friendship is an equality made of harmony," said the Pythagoreans. There is harmony because there is a supernatural union between two opposites, that is to say necessity and liberty, the two opposites which God combined when he created the world and men. There is equality because each wishes to preserve the faculty of free consent both in himself and in the other.

When anyone wishes to put himself under a human being or consents to be subordinated to him, there is no trace of friendship. Racine's Pylades is not the friend of Orestes. There is no friendship where there is inequality.

A certain reciprocity is essential in friendship. If all good will is entirely lacking on one of the two sides, the other should suppress his own affection, out of respect for the free consent which he should not desire to force. If on one of the two sides there is not any respect for the autonomy of the other, this other must cut the bond uniting them out of respect for himself. In the same way, he who consents to be enslaved cannot gain friendship. But the necessity contained in the bond of affection can exist on one side only, and in this case there is only friendship on one side, if we keep to the strict and exact meaning of the word.

A friendship is tarnished as soon as necessity triumphs, if only for a moment, over the desire to preserve the faculty of free consent on both sides. In all human things, necessity is the principle of impurity. All friendship is impure if even a trace of the wish to please, or the contrary desire to dominate is found in it. In a perfect friendship these two desires are completely absent. The two friends have fully consented to be two and not one, they respect the distance which the fact of being two distinct creatures places between them. Man has the right to desire direct union with God alone.

Friendship is a miracle by which a person consents to view from a certain distance, and without coming any nearer, the very being who is necessary to him as food. It requires the strength of soul that Eve did not have; and yet she had no need of the fruit. If she had been hungry at the moment when she looked at the fruit, and if in spite of that she had remained looking at it indefinitely without taking one step towards it, she would have performed a miracle analogous to that of perfect friendship.

Through this supernatural miracle of respect for human autonomy, friendship is very like the pure forms of compassion and gratitude called forth by affliction. In both cases the contraries which are the terms of the harmony are necessity and liberty, or in other words subordination and equality. These two pairs of opposites are equivalent.

From the fact that the desire to please and the desire to command are not found in pure friendship, it has in it, at the same time as affection, something not unlike a complete indifference. Although it is a bond between two people it is in a sense impersonal. It leaves impartiality intact. It in no way prevents us from imitating the perfection of our Father in heaven who freely distributes sunlight and rain in every place. On the contrary, friendship and this distribution are the mutual conditions one of the other, in most cases at any rate. For, as practically every human being is joined to others by bonds of affection which have in them some degree of necessity, he cannot go towards perfection except by transforming this affection into friendship. Friendship has something universal about it. It consists of loving a human being as we should like to be able to love each soul in particular of all those who go to make up the human race. As a geometrician looks at a particular figure in order to deduce the universal properties of the triangle, so he who knows how to love directs upon a particular human being a love which is universal. The consent to preserve an autonomy within ourselves and in others is essentially of a universal order. As soon as we wish for this autonomy to be respected in more than just one single being we desire it for everyone, for we cease to arrange the order of the world in a circle whose centre is here below. We transport the centre of the circle beyond the heavens.

Friendship does not have this power if the two beings who love each other, through an unlawful use of affection, think they only form one. But then there is not friendship in the true sense of the word. That is what might be called an adulterous union, even though it comes about between husband and wife. There is not friendship were distance is not kept and respected.

The simple fact of having pleasure in thinking in the same way as the beloved being, or in any case the fact of desiring such an agreement of opinion, attacks the purity of the friendship at the same time as its intellectual integrity. It is very frequent. But at the same time pure friendship is rare.

When the bonds of affection and necessity between human beings are not supernaturally transformed into friendship, not only is the affection of an impure and low order, but it is also combined with hatred and repulsion. That is shown very well in *L'Ecole des Femmes* and in *Phèdre*. The mechanism is the same in affections other than carnal love. It is easy to understand this. We hate what we are dependent upon. We become disgusted with what depends on us. Sometimes affection does not only become mixed with hatred and revulsion, it is entirely changed into it. The transformation may sometimes even be almost immediate, so that hardly any affection has had time to show; this is the case when necessity is laid bare almost at once. When the necessity which brings people together has nothing to do with the emotions, when it is simply due to circumstances, hostility often makes its appearance from the start.

When Christ said to his disciples: "Love one another," it was not attachment he was laying down as their rule. As it was a fact that there were bonds between them due to the thoughts, the life and the habits they shared, he commanded them to transform these bonds into friendship, so that they should not be allowed to turn into impure attachment or hatred.

Since, shortly before his death, Christ gave this as a new commandment to be added to the two great commandments of the love of our neighbour and the love of God, we can think that friendship which is pure, like the love of our neighbour, has in it something of a sacrament. Christ perhaps wished to suggest this with reference to Christian friendship when he said: "Where there are two or three gathered together in my name there am I in the midst of them." Pure friendship is an image of that original and perfect friendship which belongs to the Trinity and which is the very essence of God. It is impossible for two human beings to be one while scrupulously respecting the distance which separates them, unless God is present in each of them. The point at which parallels meet is infinity.

NOTES

1. Characters in Molière's *L'Ecole des Femmes.* Harpagon, below, is a character in Molière's *L'Avare.*
2. But I feel in all this that I shall be torn asunder.

LOVE

A CONCEPTUAL INVESTIGATION OF LOVE

W. Newton-Smith

Concepts like love, which we use in describing, explaining and ordering the personal relations of ourselves and others, have received scant attention in the recent Anglo-American philosophical tradition. This contrasts decidedly with philosophical interests on the continent. The difference may be explained in part by the fact that here interests have lain in different areas. More interestingly, perhaps, this difference may reflect disagreement about the connection between such an account and more basic issues in epistemology and the philosophy of mind and about the import of a philosophical account of, say, love. For example, Sartre, when discussing relations with others in *Being and Nothingness,* concludes at the end of something bearing at least a family resemblance to an argument, that it follows from his account of the relation between mind and body that an attempt to love is bound to fail. The acceptance of Sartre's argument would have clear import for someone who regulated his or her sex life according to the principle that sex without love was not permissible. A person who accepted the argument and who was unwilling to adopt a chaste life would seem to be compelled either to violate or to revise his or her principles. Clearly, if one accepts that an account of the relation between mind and body might entail conclusions of this force, one would be interested, to say the least, in working out the entailments.

On a conception of philosophy which has had some currency in the recent Anglo-American tradition such conclusions would not be expected. For, on this view, philosophy is seen as a sort of second-order discipline, which seeks to give a descriptive, and possibly systematic, account of the concepts we employ in dealing with the world. Philosophy presupposes a linguistic practice which it describes and leaves untouched. Within this framework it is highly unlikely that someone would argue that something which we took, at the level of common sense, to be the case was not in fact the case. In the presence of Sartre's strong and counter-intuitive conclusion that love is not possible, it would be argued via paradigm cases that love is indeed possible and that consequently Sartre's account of the relation between mind and body is shown, by *reductio ad absurdum,* to be false. While these few remarks have done justice neither to Sartre nor to the practitioners of this linguistic conception of philosophy, they do suggest an important contrast between these

From *Philosophy and Personal Relations: An Anglo-French Study,* ed. Alan Montefiore (Montreal: McGill-Queen's University Press, 1973), pp. 113-36. Reprinted by permission of the publisher.

An obvious debt of gratitude is owed to all those who participated in the discussions that led to this volume. I would like especially to thank Derek Parfit, Alan Montefiore, and my wife for many stimulating discussions.

traditions with regard to their expectations of the possible fruits of a philosophical account of concepts such as love.

In this paper I will seek both to provide an account of our concept of love and to explore the possible practical bearing of such an account for our thinking and acting in the context of personal relations. The first part of the paper will involve an attempt to determine some of the features which mark the concept off from certain related concepts. Within the confines of this paper, this treatment can only be provided in detail sufficient to suggest the general structure of the concept. A more detailed tracing of the multifarious web of connections will, I hope, come later. In the second part of the paper a number of hypothetical situations in which the protagonists appear to be disagreeing about matters of love will be considered. This will allow us to test the adequacy of the philosophical account of love in terms of its power to account for these disputes. These cases will also be used to determine what relevance the philosophical account might have for us in our personal relations with others. That there may be some practical relevance is suggested by the following considerations.

Any complete account of the state of a relation between persons, as opposed to objects, must take account of what the persons involved take the state of the relationship to be. The state of a personal relationship between business colleagues, Smith and Jones, may be a function more of how Smith sees Jones (i.e. as dishonest) than of how Jones actually is (i.e. honest). Similarly, the practical course of a relationship between Joe and Joel, which they both see as one of love, might be in part a function of what they take love to be or to involve. A philosophical account of love which ruled out one of their ways of thinking of love would then be relevant. Whether this philosophical intervention was for the better is entirely another matter. Rather than defend or amplify this thesis here, it will be left until we consider some hypothetical personal relationships.

Before proceeding further it will be helpful to introduce the following methodological distinctions. As well as speaking of the concept of x, I will talk of someone's conception of x. Someone's conception of x refers to how that person uses the term 'x'. The concept of x refers to those features which anyone's conception of x must possess in order to count as a conception of x at all. This distinction is intended as a device to avoid prejudging the issue concerning the existence of a precise, determinate, public concept of x. That is, different persons might draw the boundaries of their concepts somewhat differently but not so differently that they cannot be said to be speaking of the same thing. For instance, two persons might be said to have the same concept of x in virtue of an agreement about paradigm cases of x but to have slightly different conceptions of x in virtue of making different decisions about borderline cases. I will also speak of someone's picture of x. By this I mean the answer the person would give to the question 'What is x?'. Roughly, then, someone's picture of x is the account he would offer of x. This is intended as a distinction between someone's possessing a certain concept where this is displayed through the correct application of the concept and the person's being able to say in virtue of what features he applies the concept. Someone may possess a concept, x, but have no picture of x at all. If we ask him 'What is x?' he draws a blank or can only point to examples. Someone's picture of x might be a full-blown philosophical analysis of x. It might also be incompatible with the actual use he makes of the concept.

Use will also be made of the following distinction between two sorts of non-contingent truth. If, for example, it should be a necessary truth that *all* cases of love must involve sexual desire, I will speak of a necessary connection between love and sexual desire. And if it should be a necessary truth that *generally* cases of love involve sexual desire I will speak of a g-necessary connection. A particular case lacking a g-necessary feature of x-hood, will count as a case of x only in the presence of some special explanation. Obviously this paper is not the place to enter into a discussion of the nature of necessary truth, and I can here offer no defence of this distinction beyond attempt to display its fruitfulness in application.

I

This study cannot deal with all our uses of 'love'. We speak of loving persons, food, countries, art, hypothetical divine beings, and so on. In this paper I will be interested only in cases where the object of a love is some one or more persons. It would seem fairly clear that this is, as it were, the home territory of the concept of love and that the use of 'love' in conjunction with objects other than persons is best understood as an extension of this use. Having distinguished a kind of love in terms of a kind of object, namely persons, of a love relation, it is necessary to narrow the field of investigation further. And so attention will be confined to cases of love which involve sexuality. For the balance of this paper then, 'love' is to be understood as implying this restriction. 'Sexuality' is used here as a generic term whose species are sexual feelings, desires, acts, and so on. Thus the stipulation excludes from present consideration cases of fraternal love, paternal love, and other cases not involving sexuality.

While this restriction is not intended as a substantial point about love, neither is it purely arbitrary. Rather it is intended to reflect a rough distinction that we do make between kinds of love between persons. Cases of love between persons cluster around certain paradigms. On the one hand we have a group of paradigms which includes Romeo and Juliet, Abelard and Helöise, and Caesar and Cleopatra. Jules and Jim provide another set of paradigms; the heroine of Gorky's *Mother* and the father of the prodigal son still another. It would seem that sexuality can serve as a criterial mark for picking out those cases that cluster around our first set of paradigms. Thus for instance, given a parent that loves a child, the occurrence of a prolonged, active and intense desire for sexual relations with the child on the part of the parent would lead us to regard the love, all things being equal, as not purely maternal. Analogously, the absence of sexuality between two persons of the opposite sex whom we think of as loving each other may incline us to describe the love as platonic or aesthetic. Anyone who thinks that this requirement of sexuality does not capture what is the essential delimiting feature of the romantic paradigms, can regard the requirement as simply a device for selecting a more manageable set of cases for this preliminary investigation.

A brief word about the status of these paradigms is in order. One way of displaying in part what someone's conception of, say, O is, is by displaying what he would regard as paradigm instances of O. While the cases given above would be offered as paradigms by a large number of persons, there is no proper set of paradigms. By this I mean that while the conceptual features of love to be given below rule out certain things as not possibly being paradigms of love, it is possible for different individuals to have different paradigms. In what follows I hope to display what we must think of a relationship in order to think of it as a relationship of love at all. I will suggest that this leaves considerable range for the construction of competing paradigms. This divergence in paradigms leaves room for interesting psychological and sociological investigations in the variations in paradigms from person to person, for instance, or from class to class, or historical era to historical era. And, given the normative aspect of a conception of love, these paradigms take on the character not just of clear examples but of ideals. Some of the consequences of this will be seen in the second half of this paper.

It is not suggested that the sexuality requirement provides any precise distinction. It seems likely that there is not a precise distinction to be marked. For we might wish to allow some feelings of a sexual sort to enter into a case of basically maternal love. And we might allow some aspects of homosexual love in the close relationship between the officer and men of a marine platoon without the relationship ceasing to be basically a fraternal one. However, things are different if the officer is continually wanting to get to bed with one particular soldier. Thus while there may be no precise distinction here, there is nonetheless a distinction. To be any more definite than this would require an exploration of sexuality that cannot be undertaken here.[1]

It might be objected on the basis of certain psychoanalytic theories that all personal relations involve sexuality, and hence sexuality could not be used as the distinguishing feature of a kind of personal relation. The grounds on which such a claim would rest are not uncontroversial. In any event, their acceptance involves the hypothesizing of repressed sexual feelings. This in turn does not invalidate our distinction but rather requires us to draw it in terms of a contrast between repressed and unrepressed sexuality rather than in terms of a contrast between the presence and absence of sexuality. In fact, Freud, in *Civilization and its Discontents,* contrasted aim-inhibited love in which the sexual component is suppressed and sexual love in which it is not suppressed. Freud took this distinction to divide the field roughly as we have done. Thus acceptance of certain psychoanalytic theories would require only the recasting, and not the abandoning, of our sexuality requirement.

The preceding modification would be required if a psychoanalytic theory which claimed that *all* relations involve a form of sexuality was adopted. More plausibly perhaps, it might be argued that in some relationships with no apparent sexuality involved, some form of suppressed sexuality was present. That is, given a psychoanalytic theory of genuine explanatory power, we might want to hypothesize on the basis of, say, some form of aberrant behaviour, the presence of repressed sexuality in a relationship apparently devoid of sexuality. In this case we would have a non-analytic counter-factual to the effect that the removal of repression would lead to explicit sexuality. If such a theory is produced our sexuality requirement will have to be extended to include both explicit and repressed sexuality.

It might also be objected to my sexuality requirement that while instances of courtly love belong with our romantic paradigms, not only was sexuality absent in courtly love relations, it was thought to be incompatible with true (courtly) love. Now evidence of the chastity of courtly lovers is decidedly absent. But in any case, courtly lovers must be thought of as possessing sexual feelings which they set aside. This is implicit in their thinking of themselves as noble for not expressing sexual feelings. There would be no trick to it, and hence no nobility involved, if they simply did not have sexual feelings or inclinations at all.

Having defined the field of investigation, we can now sketch the concepts analytically presupposed in our use of 'love'. An idea of these concepts can be gained by sketching a sequence of relations, the members of which we take as relevant in deciding whether or not some given relationship between persons A and B is one of love. These are not relevant in the sense of being evidence for some further relation 'love' but as being, in part at least, the material of which love consists. The sequence would include at least the following:

1. A knows B (or at least knows something of B)
2. A cares (is concerned) about B
   A likes B
3. A respects B
   A is attracted to B
   A feels affection for B
4. A is committed to B
   A wishes to see B's welfare promoted

The connection between these relations which we will call 'love-comprising relations' or 'LCRs', is not, except for 'knowing about' and possibly 'feels affection for', as tight as strict entailment. While perhaps in certain paradigm cases of love these relations would all be satisfied to a high degree, they are not jointly necessary. In a particular case which we are inclined to regard as one of love, some LCRs may be satisfied to only a low degree or not satisfied at all. For there is no contradiction involved in speaking of, say, love without commitment or love without respect. There would of course be a contradiction involved in asserting that some relationship was one of love while denying that any of the LCRs were satisfied. Thus we have a g-necessary truth that love involves the satisfaction of the LCRs to an as yet unspecified degree.

That the LCRs listed are non-contingently involved in love seems fairly obvious and for that reason not particularly interesting. We would not countenance the claims of A to love B if A had neither met B nor knew anything about B. I will argue below when discussing the limitations of the sorts of reasons A can have for loving B in particular that there are certain sorts of things that A must know about B. The items in group 2 embody the fact that love involves having certain pro-attitudes to the object of the love. Group 3 embodies the condition that the lover sees the object of his love as having in his eyes at least meritorious features. In love it is not just the case that the lover holds the relations of group 2 and 3 to the object of his love, these relations are held to such a degree that the lover is inclined to act on behalf of his beloved in ways that he is not inclined to act for arbitrary strangers or the general run of the mill acquaintances. Suppose that someone has the unhappy choice of saving either his putative beloved or an arbitrary stranger from drowning. If the putative lover elects to save the stranger, then, all things being equal, the relation is not one of love. Acting out of panic or just after a quarrel, among other possibilities, might show that all things were not equal. This feature of love is captured by the items of group 4.

It may seem frivolous to have introduced this thought experiment to prove such an obvious point. However, that the element of commitment is important in marking off love from other related relations can be seen if we vary the parameters in the thought experiment. Suppose the putative lover has to choose between saving his beloved and a group of strangers. In the event of a choice between a single stranger or a large group of strangers, we clearly think that we should opt for the larger number. Does the commitment element entail that the lover place the welfare of his beloved above the welfare of a group of strangers? Or can he call across to her as he saves the strangers, 'I love you, but unfortunately there are more of them'?

A similar dilemma arises if we imagine a putative lover having to choose between his putative beloved and adherence to his ethical or political principles. In fiction anyway, lovers frequently test the devotion of one another by asking if they would steal etc. for their sake. In *Middlemarch,* for example, Rosamund thinks that if Lydgate does in fact love her, he ought to be willing to set aside his moral scruples for her sake. She wants him to withhold large debts owed to the tradesmen in order to sustain her luxurious standard of living. And in Moravia's *Bitter Honeymoon,* Giacome and Simona are portrayed as being in love and as thinking themselves in love. Simona is a committed communist. Giacome describes himself as an 'individualist'. The following interchange takes place:

GIACOME: 'For instance, if a communist government comes to power and I say something against it, you'll inform on me. . . .'
   It was true then, he thought to himself, since she didn't deny it, then she would inform on him. He gripped her arm tighter almost wishing to hurt her. 'The truth is that you don't love me.'
SIMONA: 'I wouldn't have married you except for love.'

These examples are not meant to imply any thesis to the effect that in 'true' love, commitment to the beloved must take preference over all other commitments. The significant conceptual point of the examples is that in the case of love there are these tensions, and this displays the extent to which love involves a commitment.

This marks off love from, for example, relations of just 'liking' or 'being attracted to', where these tensions do not arise. We would not, I think, be tempted to redescribe an apparent relation of liking or being attracted to as not being a relation of liking or being attracted to, just because the protagonists did not tend to place the other party on a par with political or ethical commitments.

It has been suggested that love involves holding the LCRs to the beloved. If someone holds these relations to another, he will hold them to the person under certain descriptions of the person. For a relation to count as one of love these descriptions must be of certain sorts. A's saving his putative beloved, B, from drowning only because she is wearing his watch or has just won the pools, may be incompatible with A's thinking of the relationship as being one of love. Of course motives on a particular isolated occasion are not necessarily conclusive determinants of the kind of relationship one way or the other. But there are general limitations on the sorts of ways in which A thinks of the object of his affections where the ways in question are the grounds of his affection for the person. Very roughly, A must, say, care about B for herself, A must be attracted to B on her own account. That is, not all properties which A sees B as possessing can serve as the grounds for loving B.

Of the descriptions which A sees as applying to B, I will call those which can be the grounds of A's loving B, intrinsic descriptions of B. Descriptions which cannot play this role will be called extrinsic descriptions. Clearly there are some extrinsic and some intrinsic descriptions. Suppose we have an apparent love relation between A and B where B is very wealthy. Suppose B's wealth suddenly evaporates. If A's interest in B should also evaporate, we conclude that, all things being equal, the relation had not been one of love. We might say that A loved not B but B's money. A was interested in B not for her own sake but for the sake of her money. A liked B-the-wealthy-woman and not B *per se*. Of course it is simplistic to speak as I have been doing, as if one isolated incident would lead us to revise our description of a particular personal relation. The complexity of these situations is such that no one incident is likely to be decisive one way or the other. All that is required for the argument is that these incidents give cause to reconsider the descriptions given.

Suppose on the other hand we have an apparent love relation between A and B. A claims to love B largely on account of certain features of her personality and character. But one day, perhaps as the result of some traumatic accident, B undergoes a radical personality transformation. B no longer has those attributes that A loved her for. A, realizing this, can, we suppose, no longer love B. Here we are not so inclined to revise our descriptions of the relation as we were in the case above. We might say that A had indeed loved B but that this was no longer the case as B is no longer the person she once was.

In attempting to draw this distinction I am assuming that it is not a necessary condition of a relationship's being one of love that the lover's attitude to the beloved remain unchanged through all possible changes in the beloved. This question of constancy in love will be taken up later in one of our case studies. The classification of features as extrinsic or intrinsic depends on our attitude to inconstancy, given that the feature in question changed. That is, if A claims to love B in part at least because of her being $\emptyset$, and if A's attitude to B would be negatively affected should B cease to be $\emptyset$ (or, should A cease to see B as being $\emptyset$) then, if we count this inconstancy as evidence against the relationship's having been one of love, $\emptyset$ is an extrinsic property of B; otherwise $\emptyset$ is an intrinsic property. This places no limitations whatsoever on the features which initially attracted A to B. B's money may have been the initial lure. But, if the relationship is to count as one of love, the money cannot be the sustaining feature. In some cases there may be an intimate causal relation between extrinsic and intrinsic factors. In our previous example, B may have been a dynamic capitalist entrepreneur whose personality is intimately bound up with the acquisition of wealth. Financial failure might bring about a personality change. However, only intrinsic factors matter for themselves. The extrinsic factors are relevant only in as much as they are evidence for intrinsic factors.

It was suggested that features of personality and character clearly count as intrinsic and that the state of someone's bank balance was clearly extrinsic. Not all features are so easily classified. Consider the details of the beloved's physical make-up. Traditionally lovers are enraptured with dainty ears, firm thighs, and so on. The general acceptance of these sorts of features as grounds for loving suggests that they are to be counted as intrinsic. But, on the other hand, if the moment the ears thicken or the thighs soften the lover falters, we may well have doubts about his alleged love. This suggests that we consider physical features to be extrinsic ones. Perhaps the most that we can say is that someone might love another solely or chiefly because of his or her physical features but that such cases will not be as near to our paradigms of a love relation as cases in which the beloved is loved solely or chiefly for attributes of his or her personality and character. That is, while physical features can be offered as reasons for loving (indeed our sexuality requirement would entail this), we tend to consider relations, which are not also grounded on regard for aspects of the personality and character of the object of the relation, as lacking certain dimensions. A person having as his chief or only reasons for loving another, regard for their physical attributes, would seem to be regarding the object of his love as being less than a person. Persons are not just bodies, they are at least bodies which think and act.

Any attempt to distinguish between physical characteristics as more extrinsic than features of personality and character is complicated by the problematic status of the role of physical features in determining personality and character. Clearly we identify some personality features via physical features—the look of the eyes, the character of the smile. The possession of some, though certainly not all, personality traits may be tied to the possession of certain physical charactertics. Perhaps some properties, for instance, elegance, while not being entirely physical attributes, can only be possessed by someone with certain physical attributes. I mention this as a question of some interest requiring a detailed consideration which cannot be given here.

That someone might love another for certain of her features suggests a

problem. Suppose someone else should appear who also instantiates these properties. If the possession of these properties is someone's reason for loving one,
reasons being universalizable, he will have equal reason to love the other as well.
Perhaps the second person more perfectly embodies those properties which the
lover previously lauded in the first. According to Gellner,[2] if someone in this kind
of context should divide his affection between the two persons, neither relationship
can be counted as a relationship of love. (We will have reasons to challenge this
assumption later.) In most actual cases the universalizability of reasons will not
require a person, A, to extend his affection to cover both B and C where C is a
second embodiment of those features which A lauded in B. For, often A's reasons
for loving B will involve reference to what B has done for him, to what they have
done together. If A has been socially interacting with B, he is likely to have reasons
of this character and these reasons would not be grounds for loving C as well. However, suppose A falls in love with B from a distance and has no social contact with
B. Even here, one of A's reasons for loving B may be that it was B that first excited
this passion in him. A might recognize that C would have done the same, if he had
first known of C. But, A first met B and B generated the passion. A may now love B
for having been the generator of the passion.

Of course it is possible that reasons of this sort are not among A's reasons for
loving B and that either A does not love B for the reasons he thought he did, or that
A will transfer his affection. I shall argue (part II) that if A extends his affection in
this way, he may nonetheless love both B and C. If A does not think of himself as
having any reasons for loving B that do not equally apply to C, and if A does not
have any inclination to extend his affection to C, this provides us with the grounds
for supposing that A is simply mistaken about his reason for loving. That is, we
would, I think, suppose that there is some present feature of B, or some feature of
B's history or their history together, that was important to A and was part of A's
reasons for loving B whereas the feature in question is not shared by C.

There are two sorts of intriguing and subtle kinds of cases which might seem
to suggest that we have been assuming too readily that there is no problem in
identifying who the object of a love is. The first relates to the suggestion, to be
found in Stendhal, that one never really loves another person but one loves rather
some creation of one's imagination based on, but usually bearing little resemblance
to, the actual person one appears to love. Following Stendhal, I will refer to this
theory as the 'crystallization' theory of love. Stendhal thought of the actual object
of a love as an imaginary creation built on and transforming a few true perceptions
of the apparent object of the love, in a manner analogous to the growth of crystals
on a branch placed in the Salzburg salt mines. Lawrence Durrell, in *Clea,* provides
a model of what I take Stendhal to have in mind. Here Darley is presented as
suddenly realizing that he never loved Justine. He concludes that he loved some
'illusory creation' of his own based on Justine. The revelation comes to him on
Justine's informing him that it was pointless for her to return to him after their
separation, for it was not *her* Darley loved. As the case is presented, Darley thinks

of himself as loving Justine because of certain intrinsic features. But the features do not apply to Justine.

Darley thinks of himself as loving Justine for a sequence $\emptyset_1, \ldots, \emptyset_n$ of features which he takes to apply to Justine. If the following counterfactual is true, the case is easily dealt with. If Darley would feel as strongly about Justine should he come to see that she does not possess the properties in question, he does in fact, all things being equal, love her. He has simply been radically mistaken about her. Perhaps when he discovers what she is really like, his attraction for her will actually increase. Suppose on the other hand, Darley would not think of himself as loving Justine if he came to realize his mistake. In this case he never loved anyone at all and to speak of having loved an 'illusory creation' is, at best, a metaphorical way of saying that he mistakenly thought of himself as loving someone as a result of radically misunderstanding the sort of person she was.

The 'crystallization' theory draws our attention to the notorious fact that we often misapprehend the properties of persons and often act in personal relationships on the basis of our beliefs about persons which are wrong and sometimes radically so. But as a theory to the effect that we never love other persons, it is just wrong. We are not always mistaken about other persons. In many cases the beloved will in fact have some of the properties on the basis of which the lover loves. Even in cases of grave error, the lover may, as I argued above, be said to love in spite of being mistaken.

The other intriguing case concerning the real object of a love arises in psychoanalytic theory. Aberrant behaviour on the part of a person A, who appears to love person B, might be thought explicable in some contexts on the hypothesis that A does not in fact love B but really loves, say, a parental figure. B is a sort of stand-in in an elaborate fantasy. This seems like a misleading description of the case. For, it is towards B and not towards, say, his mother, that A performs the action appropriate in a context of love. Perhaps it is therefore best to say that A does love B while admitting the existence of a causal connection between his attitude towards his mother and his attitude towards B. Perhaps A would not care for B at all if he had not had a certain attitude towards his mother. Or, perhaps A's loving B depends on his thinking of B in ways appropriate to thinking of a mother.

It has been argued that love involves having certain kinds of relations (the LCRs) to some person, and that it also involves thinking of the object of these relations in certain ways. In addition love is essentially reciprocal. Stendhal reports André le Chapelain as writing in his twelfth-century Code of Love 'No one can love unless bidden by the hope of being loved'. It does seem to be a g-necessary truth that if A loves B, A wishes to be loved by B. We can see that this is a conceptual fact and not just a matter of fact about lovers, by seeing what would be involved in imagining a case where A loves B but does not wish to be loved in return. The following situation, drawn with adaptation, from Dickens' *Little Dorrit* seems to provide the sort of case we want. A loves B who is already married to another. A is particularly concerned for the welfare and happiness of B. A knows that B would not be happy loving him. For, if B loved A in return B would suffer extreme guilt feelings at taking on another affection while committed in marriage to another. B has, let us suppose, a loving husband and children. A, being magnanimous, does not reveal his love for B, for fear that the mere revelation would precipitate reciprocated love and subsequent unhappiness for B. In one sense the lover does wish for reciprocated love. He would wish it if all things were equal. But given the circumstances as they are, he does not wish it. No doubt we would countenance the lover's denial of any wish for reciprocated love in the circumstances. But to render this plausible we had to imagine a case where the reciprocated love would be an unhappy love. Other cases can be provided if the lover is imagined to be masochistic or to be involved in some form of self-abasement. In the absence of such a background we would simply fail to understand a denial of a wish for reciprocated love. If someone claims to love another, we understand him as wishing to be loved in return. We do not have to ask, 'And do you wish her to love you?' The inference to a wish for reciprocated love is blocked only if the background is filled out in certain ways. Loving entails, *ceteris paribus*, the desire for reciprocated love.

This essential reciprocity interestingly delimits love from many other concepts used in describing personal relations. A clear case in point is that of worship. A's worshipping B does not, *ceteris paribus*, entail that A wishes to be worshipped by B. Quite the contrary in fact. For, in wishing to be worshipped by B, A would be demeaning B from the elevated position relative to himself, that A accords to B, in thinking of B as an object of worship. Perhaps 'liking' is a more pertinent example for our present purposes. We do not take someone's claim to like another as implying a wish on his part to be liked by the other person. He may or may not. Perhaps we do take him as wishing not to be disliked but this is not the same as wishing to be liked. The reciprocal factor is similarly absent in the case of a commitment outside the context of a love relation (except possibly in the context of a contractual relation). A claim to be committed to my party leader does not imply a wish that he commit himself to me (I may think of myself as a lowly pawn not deserving such a commitment) in the way that a claim to be committed to my beloved does.

It is not suggested that the features of the concept of love which have been given provide anything like a calculus for deciding, objectively, whether or not any given relationship is one of love. The term 'love' has undeniable emotive force. Different individuals may require that the LCRs be satisfied to different degrees before awarding the epithet love to a relationship. It is not uncommon[3] to find the requirements placed so high as to make relationships that count as relationships of love a very rare commodity. The account of love given is intended to display only what one must think of as involved in thinking of a relationship as love. For instance, it is g-necessary that a case of love involves concern. The person who thinks of himself as loving another, and who at sometime sees himself as having failed to act as concern requires, must (g-necessarily) think of himself as having failed. He must see himself as being under a *prima facie* obligation to make excuse. If the person does not see the relation as one of love, he may not see his failure to display concern as anything for which excuse need be made. One does not have an obligation to display to just any acquaintance the sort of concern that loving involves. While we can thus display what is involved in thinking of a relationship under the concept of love, we have no criterial test for 'love' simply because there are no public, objective standards as to the degree of concern, respect, etc., that is required to constitute love. In the case studies that follow we will see something of the consequences of this fact.

II

Case One: Love and Responsibility.   This first case will be constructed around conflicting theories or 'pictures' of love. On one picture of love, a picture most prominent in the romantic tradition, love is seen as a feeling or emotion which simply overcomes one with an all-conquering force. The lover is held to be a victim of his passion. And, if the lover can avoid giving in to his passion, it is not genuine. This picture will be called the involuntaristic one.

I have referred to the above as a 'picture' of love. The reason for so doing is to avoid begging the question that the term is used or could consistently be used by those who would offer this picture in a manner consistent with the picture. For instance, someone might claim that 'red' is the name of a kind of purely private mental impression. It might be argued that no one uses the term in this way and that no one could use a term in this way. In my terminology this could be summed up by saying that this person has an erroneous picture of the concept he in fact possesses.

According to another picture, call this one the 'voluntaristic' picture, love is seen as a deliberate, volitional commitment to another. It is this sort of picture that has at times been appealed to in justifying arranged marriage. The partners once selected and brought together will, it is felt, come to love one another if they make a sincere exercise of will.

We can see how subscribing to one of these pictures can have a practical impact on one's personal relationship. For, on the involuntaristic picture, to be in love is to be in a state of diminished responsibility. Once one is in the grip of love, one may act out of passion in ways that one cannot help. The picture is rarely held in this categorical form. Most commonly on this picture, love is taken as a force, difficult to resist, which comes not of the agent's choice and brings not total absence of responsibility but the diminishing of culpability for acts done out of love. This picture is to be found in the writings of George Sand. Interesting illustrations of the effects of adopting it can be found in the far from simple relations of the Herzens to the Herweghs (and others). Under the sway of George Sand, the protagonists, in what can only be described as an eternal polygon, followed courses of action which they themselves regarded as *prima facie* undesirable, involving as they did considerable unpleasantness for other parties. But acting out of love and seeing love in terms of the involuntaristic picture, they saw themselves as not culpable for these consequences. Or, more accurately, they saw themselves as less culpable than they would have seen themselves if the acts had not been done in the throes of love.

One possible impact of the voluntaristic picture is seen in the context of unobtainable love. In the merry-go-round of relationships in Iris Murdoch's *Bruno's Dream,* one of the protagonists, Lisa, is smitten with love for Miles who is unobtainable. Danby, who is presented as seeing love in an involuntaristic manner, loves Lisa. Lisa emphatically does not love him. However, Lisa, presented as subscribing to a voluntaristic picture, simply decides, when it becomes clear that Miles is indeed unobtainable, to cure herself by taking up with Danby and by coming to love Danby. Of course, when she reveals this to Danby, with his rather more romantic picture of things, he is, to say the least, puzzled and sceptical. Danby thinks that either she loves Miles, and if so cannot volitionally pull off what she is attempting, or that she can pull this off and hence does not love Miles. Lisa thinks of herself as both genuinely and passionately loving Miles and as capable of transferring this sort of affection volitionally to another.

Both of these pictures have some basis in the conceptual facts about love as a look at the LCRs will reveal. For instance, among the LCRs are the relations of respect, affection, and attraction. The involuntaristic picture calls attention to these. One may identify the presence of affection, attraction and respect in terms partly of patterns of volitions. A crude example of this would be concluding that someone is attracted to another because he regularly does things with the intents of being in the presence of this person. But there is a sense in which these feelings are not subject to volitions. For, I cannot here and now decide to feel or not to feel attraction for some given person. I can decide to try and see the girl next door, I cannot decide to be attracted to her. Of course, my deciding to go and see her may be evidence of a degree of attraction. Being attracted involves wanting. I do not decide my wants, I have them and decide on the basis of them to do or not to do various actions. I might decide to give these sorts of feelings the best chance of developing. I focus my attention on the given person, I get to know them intimately, I try to dwell on their good points, and so on. Whether this will lead to attraction, only time will tell. Similarly, I can attempt to put myself in the worst position for the continuation of current feelings of attraction. I join the foreign legion, I associate intimately with other persons, I focus on the given person's worst characteristics and so on. Time and effort may bring success.

Attention to other of the LCRs will bring out the conceptual basis of the voluntaristic picture. For instance, consider commitment. A commitment is something that I can here and now decide to take up. I can promise to commit myself forever to another, I can promise always to be concerned. I cannot, in the same way, promise to be always attracted to another.

On the basis of the account given of love, we can reject any 'picture' which allows only voluntaristic elements or only involuntaristic elements. But granted this, different individuals are free to give different stress to the importance of different LCRs in their conception of love. Someone can give more prominence to the aspects of love involving attraction, than to commitment. This is likely to reveal itself in the selection of paradigms this person would offer. Someone else can give more importance to commitment. There is no conceptual resolution of the question as to which features are more important. The concept is not determinate in this way. We can uncover the features which anyone's conception of love must have in order to be a conception of love at all. However, within these confines one is free to stress passion or commitment.

Case Two: Constancy of Love.   Suppose that Jude and Jan are two persons of the same or opposite sex who have been having an intense affair over a period of time. Mutual declarations of love have been made and all concerned regard the relationship as entirely satisfactory. Until, that is, Jude announces the demise of his love for Jan. The following dialogue ensues:

JAN: 'What do you mean, you don't love me anymore! Have I done anything, said anything?'

JUDE: 'No, it's just that my feelings for you have changed.'

JAN: 'Why? I don't understand. Have I changed in your eyes? Have you changed? What is it?'

JUDE: 'No. It's not anything like that. We're still the same people. It's just that . . . well, the old intensity of feeling just isn't there anymore, that's all.'

JAN: 'You flirt! You never really loved me at all. It's just been an adventure. Look, read this, this is what love is: "Love is not a feeling. Love is put to the test, pain not. One does not say: That was not true pain or it would not have gone off so quickly." '[4]

To this Jude replies with a recitation of 'A Woman's Constancy' and 'The Broken Heart' in which Donne describes 'true' love which flourishes and passes in a single day. Jude adds: 'You admit that there was nothing in my former behaviour and attitude to suggest a lack of love. What has time got to do with it? Love isn't any less true for having been short-lived.'

It may make a difference to Jan whether she (he) decides that Jude did or did not love her. Deciding that it was love may incline her to view the current situation just with regret for the passing of Jude's love. Deciding that Jude never loved may incline her to think of Jude as having operated under false pretences and to see herself as having been trifled with. As we shall see, the various LCRs differ in their temporal aspects. Thus it may be that Jude and Jan are in a sense disagreeing at cross purposes in that they may be operating with conceptions of love that give different stress to the importance of particular LCRs. Some LCRs, like respect and affection, may be imagined to flourish and pass in a relatively short period of time. Some act or feature of a person might call forth feelings of respect or affection. Some later revelations may reveal that things are not as they appeared, thus ending the respect or affection. If the time span is sufficiently long, I think we would allow that affection can simply fade away without there being any particular occurrence which is seen as ending the affection. Perhaps Jude found some things about Jan intriguing which lose their mystery on constant exposure. However, if the time span during which affection is thought to be involved is short enough, we have to think of some things having happened, some realization having occurred, which can be described as the reason for the withdrawal of affection. If an apparent affection begins in the evening and evaporates in the morning and if the person involved cannot point to something real or imagined which serves as a reason for the withdrawal of affection, we would be inclined to view the affection as merely apparent.

Concern and commitment, on the other hand, seem significantly different in this respect from respect and affection. For it would seem that genuine concern or commitment cannot be terminated simply by some revelation about or change in the object of that concern or commitment. We are inclined to accept: 'I felt affection for her so long as I thought she was pure and innocent' but not, 'I was really concerned for her welfare so long as I thought she was pure and innocent.' Being genuinely concerned or committed seems to involve a willingness on my part to extend that concern or commitment to the person even if I have been mistaken about that person with regard to some feature of her that led to the concern, and even if that person ceases to have those features that led me to be concerned or committed to her. I do not want to suggest that there is a total asymmetry between these pairs of relations. But to some extent, one measure of the degree of concern or commitment at a time, is the time it extends and its constancy in the face of alteration. And the measure of affection at a time is more the way it disposes me to act at that time and not through some period of time.

To return to Jude and Jan. It may be that Jude has a picture of love which construes love as just a feeling which can come and go. In declaring his love he did not think of himself as taking on any commitments. If the account of love provided in this paper is at all near the mark, we see that he has failed to see what the concept involves and has possibly misled Jan in his declarations. Or, it may be the case that while Jude and Jan both see that love involves the satisfaction of the LCRs they have different conceptions, Jude giving less stress to affection than commitment than Jan does. As we saw in case 1, there is no conceptual resolution of this sort of difference. Allowing this freedom to legislate within certain bounds does not mean that each conception is equally appropriate. Concepts are tied to forms of life. Just as our concept of love is tied to the fact that we are sexual beings, it is also tied to general facts about social organization. Thus, someone like Donne in opting for a short-range conception of love would appear to be opting for a form of life in which personal relations are diverse, changing and not closely tied to long-term responsibilities. In a society which institutionalizes personal relations and attempts to tie them to long-term responsibilities in the form of children, it is not surprising that many opt for long-range conceptions of love which lay stress on commitment.

Case Three: Multiple Person Love.   Much is made of the particularity of love. It seems commonly felt that if A is in intimate relations with both B and C, whatever the state of that relationship is, it is not one of love. We have this on authority as diverse as André le Chapelain and E. A. Gellner.[5] Apparently proposition 3 of le Chapelain's code of love was: no one can give himself to two loves. I want to consider whether anything in the concept of love rules out multiple person love relations. By a multiple person love relation, or MPLR, I mean some social set-up in which a person is in intimate relations with more than one person, each of whom he *claims* to love. According to Fromm, Jaspers, and other moralists, MPLRs are ruled out as relations of love by the 'very nature (or essence) of love'. This seems rather strong. What we have here in fact is an attempt for normative purposes to enforce a range of paradigms, i.e. those which do not involve MPLRs. I will suggest that there is nothing in the concept of love which rules out MLPRs as relations of love. Any move to rule out the MPLRs will be a legislative one.

No doubt there are severe practical difficulties involved in staging a MPLR. The protagonist in such a situation is apt to find himself spread a little thin if he attempts to provide the sort of concern, interest, commitment, and so on which we take love to involve. In his paper on sexual perversion Nagel has elaborated on some of the complexities involved in staging a multiple person sexual relationship that would approach the paradigms of non-multiple person sexual relations. Such complexities are bound to increase dramatically in any MPLR. But, that it will be difficult to bring off does not show that it is in principle impossible. And there may be those like the carpenter in Agnes Varda's film *Le Bonheur* who find it as easy to do for two persons as for one, what love requires.

Difficulties are most apt to arise if the set-up is not mutual all round. By being mutual all round I mean that each person in the set-up claims to love each other person involved. Suppose Jude thinks of himself as loving both Jan and Joe. Jude, Jan and Joe may be of the same or different sex. Jan and Joe not only loathe each other, they are most unhappy about Jude's divided affection. We may feel that Jude cannot be really concerned for both Jan and Joe if he continues this relationship in a manner which clearly distresses them. But probably all that is required for Jude to be thought of as loving both Jan and Joe is that he be thought of as distressed at their distress. Jude may think, say, that more happiness is to be had all round by this shared affection than by one of them having his whole concern and affection. In any event, to show that love is not so exclusive as to rule out multiple love relationships we need only imagine a set-up that is mutual all round.

For those like Jaspers, who claims in his *Philosophie* that 'He only does love at all who loves one specific person', we might suggest the following thought experiment. Consider that all factors involved in loving, excepting any reference to numbers, are satisfied to a high degree by the pair of persons, A and B, and by the pair, C and D. What grounds could one have for retracting a description of these cases as cases of love when it is discovered that B and D are the same person? The only grounds for ruling out such a case would seem to be an *ad hoc* rule that love is necessarily a one to one relationship. While Jaspers and Fromm are entitled to make up their own rule here, should they wish, it cannot be presented as a fact about the nature or essence of love. Of course, the desirability of multiple love does not follow from its possibility.

I have tried in this paper to sketch some conceptual features of love and to illustrate the role these features, and pictures of these features, play in judgments about personal relations. And if my account of the case studies is at all plausible, coming to accept a philosophical analysis of the concept of love may bear on how we think about our personal relations and may, in affecting how we think about them, affect the state of the relationship itself, though the effects are unlikely to be of a Sartrian magnitude. The variability in possible conceptions of love has ruled out the sort of precise and determinate conceptual relations that philosophers are prone to seek. Because of this indeterminacy, how one must (conceptually) think about love drifts imperceptibly into how one does generally think about love. Crossing this boundary can give rise to the worst sort of arm-chair psychology. But then to shy away from the boundary for fear of crossing is not entirely satisfactory either.

One final, and perhaps pessimistic, note. To show that an analysis of love is relevant to practical dealings in personal relations, would not in any way demonstrate that beneficial results would accrue for the lover or the beloved from the utilization of such knowledge. Ibsenian life lies may be productive of the greater happiness.[6]

NOTES

1. Some beginnings towards such an explication can be found in Thomas Nagel's paper, 'Sexual Perversion', *Journal of Philosophy,* 66, 1969, pp. 5-17.

2. E. A. Gellner, 'Ethics and Logic', *Proceedings of the Aristotelian Society,* 55, 1955, pp. 157-78.

3. In this regard see Erich Fromm's *The Art of Loving,* London, Allen & Unwin, 1957 and José Ortega y Gasset's *On Love . . . Aspects of a Single Theme,* trans. Toby Talbot, London, Jonathan Cape, 1967.

4. L. Wittgenstein, *Zettel,* Berkeley, University of California Press, 1967, p. 89e.

5. Gellner, op. cit., p. 159.

6. Since this paper was written I have come to regard this account of love as in many ways too simplistic.

PERSONAL LOVE AND INDIVIDUAL VALUE

Robert R. Ehman

In this paper, I shall present an interpretation of personal love as our original mode of access to the distinctive value of the individual self. In taking personal love as directed toward and grounded in the individual value of the individual self, I put myself in opposition to the long tradition that maintains that we properly love individuals for their universal attributes and qualities, not for anything pertaining

From *Journal of Value Inquiry,* 10 (summer 1976) pp. 91-105.

to them as mere single individuals. For Plato no good man can fail to love another good man since a good man appreciates and cherishes the good qualities and virtue of other good men and loves them on account of these attributes. The goodness of a person, not the individual person himself, is the primary object of love. The individual has a normative significance only so far as he embodies in his dispositions and actions the common norms of human excellence.

While it is rarely recognized for what it is, this interpretation of personal love is a reduction of it to what it is from the perspective of the impersonal everyday context of practical life in which we measure the human self in terms of its conformity to certain general norms. For Plato, it must be recalled, the individual counts simply in terms of his contribution to the social good; and he is evaluated in functional terms. The mere particularity of the individual's personality is irrelevant; and it provides no proper ground for our evaluation of him. From this point of view, it is impossible not to agree with Heidegger that the Platonic philosophy and the rationalist tradition which fulfills its inner meaning leads directly to the contemporary technological interpretation of man and the world in which everything is reduced to a manipulatable, calculatable object and evaluated in instrumental terms. The authentic individual with a "world" of his own stands beyond the common, public, functional world of everyday and cannot be adequately grasped from the point of view of general norms. So, at least, I shall argue.

The traditional interpretation in fact fails to distinguish a personal love from admiration or approval. The proper attitude toward a person's virtues and excellence is not love but admiration. Admiration ought to be strictly proportional to the excellence of a person's qualities. We properly admire persons for what they do and for what they make of themselves. The norms of admiration are the general norms of everyday functional life; and we admire anyone who fulfills these norms. No good man can fail to admire and approve of another good man, but he does not on this account really love him in a personal sense. There might be something about the most admirable person that repels us or leaves us cold in spite of the fact that we must praise him in the conduct of his everyday life.

From the point of view of the rationalist tradition, a purely personal love is a mere irrational preference without a foundation in objective value. For the rationalist, the objective is found only in the universal; and an objective evaluation or appreciation of an individual must be in terms of universal norms. In order even to begin to appreciate the possibility of the value of an individual personality and to grant validity to a personal love that singles out the individual as its object, it is necessary to put radically into question the supposition that there can be no objective individual values. There appears at the outset no reason to suppose that the universal alone is objective. To be universal is to be applicable to and binding on a class; to be objective is to be valid and binding independently of mere arbitrary whim. Why should the valuation of an individual in his individuality be a matter of mere subjective preference unless the individual himself is a mere subjective appearance? If the individual is an objective reality, why might his individual worth not be objectively valid? For the tradition, the being of an individual depends upon his universal attributes; apart from these, he is nothing. The traditional answer to our question is, then, that the idea that the individual is anything apart from universals is a mere illusion. However, the tradition could never quite decide that this implied that the individual is a mere nexus of universals. If he is more than this, he is real apart from universals and might have a value apart from them, a real, not an illusory, value. However, we need not go this far. In order to hold that the individual might have a real value of his own that is not a universal value, we need not maintain that he has this value independently of all universal attributes. We need only maintain that given all of his universal attributes and values, he has in addition a distinctive value of his own that is more than a mere resultant of the sum of his universal traits. Apart from his virtues and general excellences, he might be worthless, but he nevertheless might have a personal value that is more than the sum of the values of his virtues.

In order to demonstrate that the individual is something on his own account over and above his universal properties and has a value of his own that can be the object of a genuinely personal love or hatred, it is necessary to make intelligible the idea of an individual value. It is only at the human level that anyone would be tempted to affirm a value of this sort; and indeed, the existence of individual values appears to be one of the features that distinguishes the human from "lower" levels of being. Man can in part be understood through an examination of his works; and in exploring a man's individual value, it might be well to begin with the individual value of his most creative works. These are works of art; and it is significant that only man produces art. Classicists and romantics have argued for centuries as to whether there are universal standards for the evaluation of art. For the classicist, there are such standards; and instruction in the creation of and criticism of the arts is a matter of teaching these principles of artistic excellence. For the romantic, on the other hand, the value of a work or art is essentially individual. The classical standards, on his view, serve rather to inhibit creativity than to further the production of outstanding works. For him, art is a product of the genius of the individual; and in his art, the artist creates something as distinctive and individualized as he himself. However, those who affirm the romantic interpretation of art fail to escape from the fundamental classicist assumption that universal norms are needed for objective judgments and evaluations. The romantic's recognition of the significance of the individual does not lead him to a firm conviction of the objective reality of individual value. There is a tendency among those who reject classicism to give up the claim to objectivity in aesthetic judgments. Here we can appreciate the importance of Kant's critique of taste. The thrust of Kant's critique is to attempt to maintain the objectivity of judgments of artistic excellence at the same time that he abandons a classicist postulate of universal norms of artistic judgment and creation.

There might appear at the outset little connection between the problems of the objectivity of judgments of taste and the objectivity and validity of a personal love; but in fact the problem at the root of both is identical. The problem is put in a radical and perspicuous form in Kant's Antinomy of Aesthetic Judgment. For Kant, this antinomy consists in the conflict between the claim for objectivity and universal validity on the part of a judgment of taste and the fact that there are so far as we can know no universal rules or standards for that judgment. Up to this point in his philosophy, Kant remains within the rationalist tradition which holds that objectivity presupposes universal norms and rules; but at this point, Kant is forced by the uniqueness of the values of the aesthetic object to admit an objectivity of judgment apart from norms. In his own solution to the "antinomy" Kant attempts to hold fast to both positions. He argues that there is a rule of aesthetic judgment but that it is not accessible to our "discursive" understanding but only to an "intuitive" understanding. The one grasps the rules of "phenomena"; the other the rules of "the noumenal substrate of nature." Once we recognize that for Kant an intuitive understanding is nothing else than an understanding of an individual as such, we see that what Kant is in fact saying is that the "rule" of the judgment of taste is not in fact a universal rule at all (these are the objects of the discursive understanding) but a "rule" of the organization of the individual as such. The noumenal is the individual as such; the phenomenal, the individual as seen in terms of universals. The "purposiveness" that we apprehend in the aesthetic judgment "without the concept of a purpose" is nothing else than the inner value and organization of the individual as such apart from all teleological functions and general concepts.

For all of its cumbersome terminology, there is a deep insight at the heart of this Kantian view; and that is the insight that in an individual work of art there is really something distinctive, something unique, something original, something creative, something that must be evaluated in its own terms and can never be adequately understood or evaluated simply in terms of general concepts and standards. When we endeavor to evaluate Mozart's *Don Juan,* Van Gogh's *Potato Eaters,* George Eliot's *Middlemarch,* Goethe's *Faust,* we encounter individual values. The value of each work is something distinctive to it and is not a mere function of the application and fulfillment of certain general rules nor is it something that can ever be precisely duplicated in another work. In the end, we cannot *say* what the value of these works is; we cannot fully ground our judgments of them. The judgments are "intuitive" in the sense of an apprehension of an individual "purposiveness" or meaning. In order to apprehend this meaning, we must indeed analyze the work; we must use general concepts and the discursive understanding. But it is not these but the resultant sense of the work itself as an individual whole that finds expression in our ultimate judgment of it. There may be beautiful and even great works in which there are many failings and faults; there may be banal and worthless works which are full of fine insights, craftsmanship, and fulfill all sorts of general norms.

The appreciation of an individual in personal love or hatred is in the same manner an apprehension of a "purposiveness" without the concept of the "purpose." There is a certain order and meaning in the personality of the individual that is his alone, distinctive, unique, original, in some measure creative, and something that must be evaluated in his own terms. When we come face to face with an individual person, the individuality of that person is no more irrelevant than it is in the case of a work of art. In the same manner as a work of art, the individual person comes before us with a value all his own. The "first" thing that we experience when we encounter a work of art is its value; we apprehend it as good or bad, great or trivial prior to a full articulation of it, prior to an attention to all of its detail, even though, of course, that original impression of its value might be modified by further analysis of the work. In the same way, the "first" thing that we apprehend when we encounter another person is his value. We are drawn to him or repelled even before we recognize many of his objective features. The encounter with a person is primarily an encounter with a value and only secondarily an encounter with a set of objective properties. The beginnings of a personal love or hatred are found in every encounter in which the person is more for us than a mere performer of functions, bearer of certain abilities, holder of a certain status. The further analysis of the person's personality only serves to confirm or to modify our original evaluation. The evaluation does not await the analysis.

What is true of the work of art, that it might fulfill the common norms of aesthetic excellence and still be a repellent work, or might fail to fulfill these and be a work of beauty, is true of the human personality; and this explains the fact that we might fail to love "good" men and persist in our love of persons whom we cannot admire. No one can win love as a result of the performance of admirable deeds or the creation of admirable work; and nothing more clearly demonstrates that the person is not simply the agent of actions and works, but something more than this. Personal love perceives the peculiar manner in which a person carries out his actions, creates his works, and "sees" his world. Personal love attends to nuances, to style, to mere "subjective" factors that one overlooks in both moral judgment and in the ordinary judgments of everyday life; it focuses upon the ineffable individuality of the individual. Not that the person's actions and achievements are totally irrelevant. The performance of a certain action might destroy a personal love but not simply because of the nature or value of that action by itself but rather because it puts the whole of the person's personality in another light. The action has a global significance. In art there is the same sort of thing. The least alteration of a work might make it literally a different work with a different value. Not all alterations have this effect, of course, but any might. The mere difference in the manner in which a certain play or musical composition is performed might be sufficient to turn it from a work of greatness to one with little worth. Moreover, the alteration need not in itself be bad or violate a general norm. In the sexual domain too we find cases where a single feature might totally alter the desire. One new line or wrinkle; one small gesture, one awkward movement might end the sexual desire for a person forever. The personal and the sexual evaluation of a person is very exact and very demanding; and it is sensitive to the least nuance, for this might have significance for the whole appearance of the person. In his personal and sexual relations, the ordinary person becomes more alive to subtlety than elsewhere in his life.

The personality of a person is not all there before us as is a portrait or a statue; it unfolds and emerges in time as do musical compositions and stories. However, the portrait or statue presents something of the temporally spread out personality of their subjects. When we see a Rembrandt portrait of an old man, we see something of the life and personal style of that man. On the other side, the moment that we hear the beginning notes of a symphony or read the first few lines of a novel, we gain some apprehension of its style as a whole. There is something of the future in the present. While much is open and indeterminate, the nature of the work is already predelineated. In this same manner, we cannot meet a person without already experiencing something of the person's nature as a whole. He is in a sense "all there" just as he is in a statue or portrait. The past and the future horizons of his life are prefigured in the present appearance. The "look," the manner of speaking, the gestures, the acts of the person not only make manifest his feelings, emotions, attitudes, intentions, but also his individual style of personality. There is a "flavor" of a person in all of the modes in which he appears to us; all of his appearances are in a pregnant sense revelations of *himself.* The appearances indicate more of the person than they directly exhibit. While a person is more than any series of his appearances, still he is there "in person" in and through them. When we encounter and respond emotionally to a person, we do not simply encounter and respond to this or that action or expression but to the personality that discloses itself in them.

In the view that we are presenting, the personality of an individual is not the origin of his actions and meaningful gestures but rather an emergent pattern of these. For this reason, we might appear subject to the criticism that Socrates raised against the interpretation of the soul as the harmony of bodily movements and actions. The central core of a self appears to be the controlling factor in a person's actions, not an emergent by-product of them. However, we are not dealing with a central core in this sense; we are dealing with that which serves as the proper object of a personal love or hatred; and we do not love or hate people for some originating core but rather for the manner and form in which they appear and live their lives. The central core is the agent and originating source of personal being but personal worth derives from the mode in which the powers of the self are used, not from the powers themselves. These might be used otherwise than they are; in themselves, they are valuationally neutral and impersonal; and it is in and through actions and expressions, intentions, and feelings that a person becomes himself. The bare ontological power of agency is simply the possibility of a genuine distinctive selfhood, not the reality of it. The individual self is not an ontological substrate but an achievement of a value.

When we love a person, we transcend the evidence; we implicitly make a "hypothesis" with regard to his personality and live in expectations with regard to the person that might be disappointed. The professed certitude of a personal love is a mere expression of conviction, not of knowledge, for we never know with certitude that the personality that we love is really that of the person before us. There is even a question as to whether a given individual has a single personality.

One might easily envisage an individual beginning to display this or that personality, proceeding to exhibit still another, moving on to a third, and so forth without ever making of the diverse phases of his life a single unity. His life might lack the "purposiveness" needed to constitute a single personality with a single value. His self might be analogous to a novel that the author begins, tears up, begins again, again destroys, again begins but which never actually comes to be as a single unified work. In this case, one might love each of the "personalities" of the person; each might be of unique worth, but because the person never really makes any his own, one's love for him is initially disappointed, again aroused in a different way, and again disappointed. When we think back upon the experience, we find that he never succeeded in becoming a person we could love, even though he began to be such a person again, again, and again. In order to be an object of an authentic love, the person must attain a personality of his own, a single personality.

The idea of a single permanent personality, an "intelligible character" constant through the vicissitudes of time and life, is therefore a postulate of personal love; and it is this to which the romantics give voice when they affirm that all the diverse appearances of our temporal life are appearances of an eternal self. However, the self cannot really be eternal and at the same time be genuinely individual. For how can there be individuals apart from time and space? Does not the individual first begin to exist when it comes to have being in time and space? The eternal is the ideal; and the ideal is always in some measure general. The problem of the ideality of the individual personality comes to the forefront in Nicolai Hartmann's penetrating interpretation of personal love. For Hartmann personal love is not simply love for the concrete empirical individual there before us but for the ideal personality of that individual. The actual individual might more or less fully realize the norm of his own ideal personality. When he falls short, we continue to love him since we love what is constant and transcendent, the ideal personality that is his alone to fulfill. For Hartmann, it is the lover that divines the ideal personality and leads the beloved toward the fulfillment of it. The person himself normally has no inkling of his own ideal.

Hartmann rightly recognizes that love perceives something deeper than any given phenomenal appearance of the beloved. Moreover, he appreciates the fact that the actual self might fail to exhibit a personality for which we can love him. However, in appealing to an ideal personality to justify our love in this case, he raises the radical question as to how the distinctive personality of an individual can be at once ideal and proper to a single individual alone. For Hartmann as for the whole tradition, the ideal is universal, not individual. How, then, can it prescribe for a given individual alone? Hartmann maintains that while others might be able to realize the personality proper to another individual, they ought not to do so. But what is it in the ideal that picks out which individual ought to fulfill a given personality? Hartmann has no answer; and there is no answer. The tradition is correct; the ideal is not individualized. For a personality to be genuinely individual, it must be concrete and real; it must be the actual personality of a temporal-spatial individual. It cannot be *a priori* or eternal, but must emerge or fail to emerge in the course of the actual life of the individual. The distinctive personality of an individual fulfills no ideal norm; and our love for the individual cannot be a love for a norm.

The lover cannot lead the beloved to the fulfillment of his own personality since he has no way of determining this personality prior to the beloved's already having exhibited it. To attempt to impose and ideal personality upon a person is to attempt to mold the person in accordance with our own ideas, not to love him. Love is not creative; it is contemplative and evaluative; it appreciates and cherishes but does not produce what it thereby enjoys. The lover can do much for his beloved; and he aims at his welfare and happiness. But he does not determine the beloved's personality but rather respects and appreciates the personality that the beloved already has. He cherishes the manner in which his beloved does things; he does not want the beloved to do things in another way. When the beloved fails to display the character and personality for which he loves him, when he reveals himself as, as it were, another person, he no longer is able to love him with the same love and perhaps can no longer love him at all. There is nothing "eternal" about love for the very simple reason that there is nothing eternal about the proper object of love. The beloved is ever confirming or disillusioning the lover's vision of his personality and in this manner putting the truth of his love to the test.

When with Hartmann and the romantics, we raise the object of love to an ideal status, we come perilously close to moving back to the classical position that it is not really the individual at all but his ideal qualities that are the proper object of love. In order to hold fast to the individual person as the object of our love, we must give up the certitude of love and be willing to accept disillusionment. We must be willing to affirm that what we thought we loved never really existed rather than saving our love by holding that the object exists in an eternal realm. Moreover, we must give up prescribing for the beloved; we must allow him to constitute himself and must evaluate him for what he is, not for what we wish him to become. There is boundless sadness in disillusioned love; and it is hard to admit that the object, that marvellous person of whom we seemed to catch a glimpse, is mere illusion and not some higher reality. Would that the person had become what we expected, enriched and fulfilled our hopes! But he did not. When we find our love confirmed, there is too an element of surprise. The same personality remains there before us, but its outlines are filled in in unexpected ways. There are new wonders to behold.

The supposition of an ideal individual personality in the end makes just about as much sense as the thesis of an ideal archetype for each work of art. No one would affirm that there is an ideal of Mozart's *Don Juan* or Eliot's *Middlemarch* to which each work more or less conforms and in terms of which the artist's achievement is to be evaluated. To affirm this would be to fail to take seriously the originality of human art and the individuality of the work of art. But the originality and individuality of works of art are simply manifestations of the originality and individuality of the human self. In art the self reveals more clearly than in any other product or any other action its own distinctive individuality, its own world. In personal love, we ought to approach other persons as we approach works of art, with an openness and sensitivity to what is unique and novel in them, and evaluate the person as we do the artwork in its own terms. Personal love and hatred are the authentic responses to the other *par excellence* since it is in them that we open ourselves to, appreciate, and evaluate the other in the depths of his own individual personality.

The individual personality is in a sense the "essence" of the individual person; it is what is invariant and constant in all of his diverse modes of appearance; it is the "purposiveness" (not purpose) of the whole being of the person. When we move from the diverse appearances of the other, his gestures, facial expression, actions, to his personality, we perform a function essentially analogous to what the physicist does when he moves from the diverse visual and tactile appearances of a physical thing to its invariant properties and the physical laws of its behavior. The personality of a person is a sort of "rule" of his behavior but not a rule that can be expressed in a general formula. There is for this reason no "science" of individual personality. Science can at most classify individuals into mere personality types which are totally inadequate to determine a personal love. Personal love perceives deeper than scientific understanding when it comes to a person just as aesthetic taste perceives deeper into a work of art than any general scientific account of its origin or structure can do. The fact that language fails when it comes to stating the grounds of our love or our aesthetic judgments does not so much point up the limits of love or of aesthetic experience as it does the limits of language. In the same manner that one must actually confront a work of art in order properly to evaluate it (imagine assessing a symphony without listening to it or a painting without viewing it!), so we must meet and interact with a person in order to determine our love for him. Here discourse reduces to indicating something beyond words. When we affirm that we love someone for something that he does or says, we mean what we describe to be taken as an epitomization of the person; we are not speaking totally literally.

There is a beautiful romantic idea that there is for each person one other and one alone in all the world that is the proper object of his love. Against this idea, it is easy to raise objections. For it appears to rule out objectivity in our love. If a person is really loveable, all ought to love him, not a single person alone. Moreover, we appear capable of loving many persons; we are not so blind as to be able to appreciate only one. Further, what is true of love ought to be true of hatred too. Is there one and only one person who is a proper object of our hatred? However, in spite of all this, there is a profound insight at the root of this idea. When we love a person, we have the feeling, that he is already, indeed in some sense "eternally," loveable, that he is a priceless value waiting there for us to discover. Moreover, our love is imbued with, "lost," as it were, in its object; and the love for one person is in its own being different from our love for another. There are those who search for a substitute for their beloved mother or first wife, their "first love" or their lost child. While they might succeed in finding another who fulfills the functions that the one did, they can never find another person toward whom they can bear the same love. Love is individualized by its object. The beloved is not interchangeable; and personal love is the deepest experience of the irreplaceability of people. The place of a person whom we love in our lives is not essentially a functional role but a unique value. When we lose someone whom we love (in whatever way), we lose a value that we cannot replace. The same is true of those whom we hate.

Personal love lives in the conviction that the beloved is loveable in his own nature, not merely for us. The value of his personal being appears as an objective value. Those who do not love the person are blind to his value in the eyes of those who do. In this regard, love is altogether different from sexual desire. For desire, it is not the person himself but the person as a participant in a certain form of interaction with our own self that is desirable. The personal being of the sexual object is relevant to desire only so far as he enters into a sexual relationship. For personal love, on the other hand, it is not primarily a mode of relationship with a person, not the person as he is for us, but the person himself that is at issue. Personal love is not essentially, as is sexual desire, a desire to *do* anything with the beloved person. Rather it is primarily an appreciation, a cherishing, a valuing of the person.

In its own meaning, a sexual desire demands a form of reciprocity from the object; it demands an appropriate response. Personal love does not in this manner demand reciprocity. But do we not wish to be loved by those whom we love and can we love those who do not return our love? The idea that love is essentially a demand for love receives its *reductio ad absurdum* at the hands of Sartre. For Sartre, those who love another really project being loved by another; and on this interpretation, it is evident that love can never fulfill its aims. The moment that the beloved returns our love, he simply projects that we love him; and we fail to attain the love that we project. However, this makes no sense at all unless love has in its own nature some other meaning than simply a desire to be loved. For that would be a circular definition. For Sartre, in fact, love means a supreme evaluation, the making of the beloved the end and organizing principle of one's world and existence. The assertion that love is a desire to be loved is not an analysis of the meaning of love itself but rather a cynical interpretation of its actual reality. For Sartre, no one can really love or be loved because no one can transcend the circle of his own self and take an interest in and appreciate another in his own right, as an end in himself, even though this is what love in its own meaning demands. In demonstrating that a love that degenerates into a desire to be loved is futile and vain, Sartre in fact shows that reciprocity, being loved oneself, is not essential to love at all and that it cannot be made essential without making love impossible. The moment that we make our being the object of love a condition of our love, we make our own self rather than the other the focus of our attention, and that is incompatible with a genuine love. In order to be a real object of love, the other need not aggrandize us, need not promote our ends, and need not find us worthy of love. The fact that another is loveable by no means implies that we ourselves are; and even when the other fails to recognize our worth, we might still recognize his. Neither his own attitudes toward us nor any other particular mode of his behavior is a necessary condition in every case of the validity of our love for him. The wish to be loved, even the wish to be justly appreciated, are different from the love of another and neither involves the other. This is not to say that we do not especially wish to be loved by those whom we love since they are important to us. But the sadness over the other's failure to love us does not diminish our love for him but rather presupposes it and is enhanced by it. There is perhaps no greater joy than to be beloved by those whom we really love, but this joy too presupposes the original love that by no means depends upon it.

In maintaining that personal love is a relishing of the value of the other rather than a desire for something from the other, we appear to put ourselves over against the long tradition that interprets love as a desire for some form of *union* with the beloved. Do we not wish to have and to hold the objects of our love? Do we not wish them to be near us? Do we not wish to do things with them? Is love fulfilled in the mere contemplation of the beloved? Does is not require that we in some way live with them? The traditional view comes from failing adequately to distinguish love from mere desire. Union is the aim of sexual desire but not of a genuine love. In personal love, we in some cases wish those whom we love to depart from us and live their own lives apart from us. While this is totally incompatible with sexual desire that seeks the carnal presence of its objects, it is totally compatible with love as we can see from the case of parents and children. When parents send their children out into the world to live their own lives rather than keep them near and at home with them, we do not on this account conclude that they no longer love them; on the contrary, this might itself be an expression of their love. What love desires is that the personality that it cherishes flourish and reach unhindered fulfillment; and it desires to do what it can to forward this end. Genuine love is generous, not possessive; it is ready to sacrifice the joy of living with the beloved when the true inner nature of the beloved beckons him to a distant life. There might appear a conflict in this case between the good of the beloved and that of the lover. For does not the lover find his own good in the presence of the beloved? There is no question but that the departure and distance of the beloved may cause suffering for the lover. But the good of the lover as a lover is not his delight in the presence of the beloved; it is delight in the personal being and freedom of the beloved. The beloved is a part of the happiness of the lover, a "joy of his life," even when his departure from him causes him unhappiness. For the happiness of a lover is not the happiness of possession but happiness in the appreciation of a wondrous value. In the same manner as many other goods and joys, that of being in love might bring about unhappiness and suffering. The enjoyment of any good opens the door to suffering. For not only might we lose the good, it also might not fulfill in every respect our own personal needs and expectations. However, the disappointment in this case presupposes the original joy. The fact that a beloved person causes us pain by departing from us does not mean that he is not a treasure of our life; indeed, the pain presupposes his significance for us. The mother does not love her child the less because his illness, his failure, his death, or his departure cause her grief. The grief presupposes the love and is proportional to it. While love does not necessarily make us happy in the sense of fulfilling our desires, it is nevertheless a joy of our life. For our life is a poorer thing without those whom we love.

There is only one form of union essential to a personal love and that is a cognitive union. Personal love is an appreciation of a personality and therefore requires awareness of it. Once a mother loses touch with her child, she can only love him for what she remembers him to be, not for what he is now, since that she does not know. She cannot keep testing her love to verify it. The love for those who have disappeared from our lives is not essentially other than our love for the dead. Hence, it is necessary to visit, to see, to hear of those whom we love; and love will seek to do this. Parents who love their children and children who love their parents will desire to see each other or in some manner communicate to the other the course of their lives and their personal viewpoints and experiences. The face to face encounter is the privileged mode of experience in this regard; and apart from this, it is impossible to really test a personal love. However, once we have become personally acquainted with a person and gained an insight into his distinctive nature, we might then nourish our love through less direct modes of communication. Letters, pictures, telephone calls may keep the beloved before our mind even though he is distant from us.

For the lover, the beloved is an object of infinite richness and depth and an inexhaustible subject of interest. The lover never tires of hearing of the events and actions of the life of the person whom he loves. The fascination of the lover for the beloved has a counterpart in the fascination of one who is hated for the one who hates him. Here too there is richness of meaning and interest. The attitude of both one who loves and hates must be sharply distinguished from that neutral grey indifference that pervades our impersonal everyday being. In our everyday encounters, we are in a sense interested in the other, but not in him himself, but in his standing and status in comparison with our own. We fear to be outstripped by him and remain on our guard against him. The easy familiarity and politeness of everyday life is a transparent disguise for a jealous watchfulness that intrudes upon an otherwise dull indifference. What we are really concerned about in everyday life is the success of our tasks, especially in competition with others; and the personal is degraded to an object of a jealous and resentful gossip that tears down and never appreciates or understands. The lover does not gossip about his beloved; he does not drag him down to the level of everyday chatter; and against this chatter, he remains discreetly silent out of respect for the value that he cherishes.

In the same manner as sexual relationships, a genuine love is a private affair between one person and another; it is not essentially a public matter; it does not need the stamp of public approval. In this respect the romantics are correct in their insistence that marriage is irrelevant to love and indeed a threat to it inasmuch as it might reduce it to a mere matter of the fulfillment of impersonal institutional duties. For Hegel, on the other side, love requires marriage to provide it with its objective validity and indeed raises it to a higher level by making it the basis of an ethical commitment. For Kierkegaard too, in this as in so much else a genuine Hegelian, love without marriage, indeed even sex without marriage, becomes despairing, meaningless illusion. There is no question but that marriage may be regarded as the institutionalization of love; and the homosexuals who demand the right to marry and the objective recognition of their love are justified to this extent. However, neither sexual desire nor love can be made matters of institutional duty. They must arise spontaneously in the heart of a person. They are direct face to face relationships that cannot be sustained simply by an act of will. One cannot promise to love a person or even sexually satisfy a person since this is not an action but essentially a matter of an emotional response that is not a subject of deliberate control. To make of love or sex a project is to bring it down to the level of an everyday practical affair and to distort it. The "truth" of love is in the inner evaluation of the beloved, not in any institution or obligation.

In order to recognize this, we must not disparage the dimension of emotion, as the tradition does, nor must we overestimate, as do Hegel and Sartre, the importance of the attitudes of others toward us. The other need not become aware of or appprove of our love or our sexual relationships in order for them to be valid. The attitude of outsiders is essentially irrelevant. These personal dimensions of our existence are not their proper concern. There is indeed an ever present need to preserve our personal life from the intrusions of the everyday crowd. It detests what it cannot dictate and control and what is unfamiliar to it. There is nowhere that the dictates of the everyday world are more repressive than in the domains of personal love and sexuality since there are no domains that are essentially more alien to it. The everyday world turns everything into a role and a social status; it attempts to turn the private self into a social self; and there are no more prominent instances of this than the attempt to restrict both love and sex to the family context in which they can be socially recognized and perform a social function. Marriage is indeed socially useful; and the marriage vows give rise to genuine moral obligations. However, while love or sexual desire might serve as motives for marriage, marriage entangles both in relationships and duties that are essentially irrelevant to them. In some cases, a genuine love might require a divorce or motivate against a marriage. Marriage might oppose the aims of love by restricting and hampering the personality of the beloved. There is simply no essential connection between marriage or any other social role and personal love or sexual desire. These might lead to and find fulfillment in modes of relationship that have no recognized place in the crude and narrow world of our everyday functional life.

For Hegel and the tradition, feeling and emotion are blind; and it is through thought alone that we gain genuine insight; and the attitude of the tradition toward both a pure personal love and sexual desire must be understood from the perspective of its disparagement of the emotional dimension of life. However, in fact, emotions are not blind. They are our most primordial modes of the experience of values and "emotional qualities." While thought apprehends the *reasons* for fear, for respect, for anger, for joy, and for grief, it cannot provide us with the direct experience of the threatening, the respectable, the annoying, the joyful or the grievous in their own distinctive natures. For this one must actually undergo the emotions. The radical distinction between the emotional experience of the quality and the rational understanding of the reasons for it comes to the fore when we consider the cases where we experience the quality without finding the reasons. Hence, we might be afraid, angered, overjoyed, even grieved, even though we do not know why. The fact that we find nothing objectively harmful in the object does not always remove our fear. For us, the object remains threatening; and we are motivated to persist in our search for the grounds. The fear is in this case "irrational" but none the less not only might the emotion itself be real (which no one doubts), but the object itself might be really threatening . In the end, it is not rational grounds that justify our believing that an object really has a certain emotional quality; but rather the persistent and universal emotional experience of the presence of the quality. When we again and again find something terrifying, and others do too, it *is* terrifying, whether we can find the reasons or not.

The world as we actually experience it is full of emotional values; things are threatening or reassuring; they are annoying or pleasing; they are delightful or depressing; they are familiar or strange; they are beautiful or ugly; and it is through the corresponding emotions that we come to an awareness of these qualities just as it is through the senses that we come to an awareness of sensory properties. In the absence of emotions, we would be as blind to emotional values as in the absence of sight, we would be to colours. Persons have emotional values too. They too are threatening, annoying, depressing or the reverse. However, they have some distinctive qualities of their own. It is only a person or his work that is worthy of respect; it is only a person or his action with which we can be indignant; it is only a person whom we can love with a personal love. There are, to be sure, other modes of love. In every case love is a cherishing, an appreciation, of the distinctive value of the object. However, it is only in a personal love that the individuality of the object is the proper term of the emotion. In other modes of love, we cherish individuals only for common values. When we love a wine or a horse, we love it as an excellent type of wine or a fine specimen of a horse; we do not love it for being just the particular individual that it is. The individual is essential in a personal love and only in a personal love because it is only at the level of human personality that individuality becomes significant. There are individual values only at the human level.

And it is personal love that provides access to the individual value of the human self. Apart from love and hatred, we might indeed become aware of the other as a mere ontological individual with his own spatial position and own temporal beginning and end, but we could not become aware of him as having a distinctive value all of his own. Thought cannot grasp this value; and it cannot even grasp the reasons for it; nor can mere perception or any other emotion. The importance of personal love for our knowledge of a person is found in this fact; and to reduce personal love either to a blind inner state or to a mere love of common values and virtues is to overlook the distinctive value of each individual self. In the end, there is no authentic relationship with another without a moment of a personal love or hatred since apart from this, we can never really appreciate the other for what he is. In morality, we respect the other as a free being with ends and a "world" of his own, but we never reach an appreciation of the worth of his individual being as such, and of what he alone brings to the world of values. In sexual desire, we desire the other as one with whom we might reciprocally fulfill our sexual potentialities and determine our genuine sexual nature, but here we never perceive the value of the other apart from the sexual context. In personal love, we appreciate and evaluate the other simply as the person he is; and it is in and through our love or hatred that we reveal the value of the individual self as something more than his value in this or that relationship or context, for this or that purpose, in respect to this or that general norm. The self-identical personality of a self, we learn from love and hatred, is no mere substrate of general properties nor a mere subject of feelings and actions, but instead a unique value. The individual human self stands out from others and from nature not so much by reason of what he *is* as by reason of what he is *worth*. The apprehension of the individual self is in the end an appreciation of a value. For an experience of an individual self, we must do more than categorize him; we must do more than merely locate him; we must emotionally respond to him with a love or hatred that penetrates deeper than any category or general norm.

SEX

SEXUAL PERVERSION

Thomas Nagel

There is something to be learned about sex from the fact that we possess a concept of sexual perversion. I wish to examine the concept, defending it against the charge of unintelligibility and trying to say exactly what about human sexuality qualifies it to admit of perversions. Let me make some preliminary comments about the problem before embarking on its solution.

Some people do not believe that the notion of sexual perversion makes sense, and even those who do, disagree over its application. Nevertheless I think it will be widely conceded that, if the concept is viable at all, it must meet certain general conditions. First, if there are any sexual perversions, they will have to be sexual desires or practices that can be plausibly described as in some sense unnatural, though the explanation of this natural/unnatural distinction is of course the main problem. Second, certain practices will be perversions if anything is, such as shoe fetishism, bestiality, and sadism; other practices, such as unadorned sexual intercourse, will not be; about still others there is controversy. Third, if there are perversions, they will be unnatural sexual *inclinations* rather than merely unnatural practices adopted not from inclination but for other reasons. I realize that this is at variance with the view, maintained by some Roman Catholics, that contraception is

From *Journal of Philosophy*, 16, no. 1 (January 16, 1969), pp. 5-17. Reprinted by permission of the author and the editor. My research was supported in part by the National Science Foundation.

a sexual perversion. But although contraception may qualify as a deliberate perversion of the sexual and reproductive functions, it cannot be significantly described as a *sexual* perversion. A sexual perversion must reveal itself in conduct that expresses an unnatural *sexual* preference. And although there might be a form of fetishism focused on the employment of contraceptive devices, that is not the usual explanation for their use.

I wish to declare at the outset my belief that the connection between sex and reproduction has no bearing on sexual perversion. The latter is a concept of psychological, not physiological interest, and it is a concept that we do not apply to the lower animals, let alone to plants, all of which have reproductive functions that can go astray in various ways. (Think of seedless oranges.) Insofar as we are prepared to regard higher animals as perverted, it is because of their psychological, not their anatomical similarity to humans. Furthermore, we do not regard as a perversion every deviation from the reproductive function of sex in humans: sterility, miscarriage, contraception, abortion.

Another matter that I believe has no bearing on the concept of sexual perversion is social disapprobation or custom. Anyone inclined to think that in each society the perversions are those sexual practices of which the community disapproves, should consider all the societies that have frowned upon adultery and fornication. These have not been regarded as unnatural practices, but have been thought objectionable in other ways. What is regarded as unnatural admittedly varies from culture to culture, but the classification is not a pure expression of disapproval or distaste. In fact it is often regarded as a *ground* for disapproval, and that suggests that the classification has an independent content.

I am going to attempt a psychological account of sexual perversion, which will depend on a specific psychological theory of sexual desire and human sexual interactions. To approach this solution I wish first to consider a contrary position, one which provides a basis for skepticism about the existence of any sexual perversions at all, and perhaps about the very significance of the term. The skeptical argument runs as follows:

"Sexual desire is simply one of the appetites, like hunger and thirst. As such it may have various objects, some more common than others perhaps, but none in any sense 'natural.' An appetite is identified as sexual by means of the organs and erogenous zones in which its satisfaction can be to some extent localized, and the special sensory pleasures which form the core of that satisfaction. This enables us to recognize widely divergent goals, activities, and desires as sexual, since it is conceivable in principle that anything should produce sexual pleasure and that a nondeliberate, sexually charged desire for it should arise (as a result of conditioning, if nothing else). We may fail to empathize with some of these desires, and some of them, like sadism, may be objectionable on extraneous grounds, but once we have observed that they meet the criteria for being sexual, there is nothing more to be said on *that* score. Either they are sexual or they are not: sexuality does not admit of imperfection, or perversion, or any other such qualification—it is not that sort of affection."

This is probably the received radical position. It suggests that the cost of defending a psychological account may be to deny that sexual desire is an appetite. But insofar as that line of defense is plausible, it should make us suspicious of the simple picture of appetites on which the skepticism depends. Perhaps the standard appetites, like hunger, cannot be classed as pure appetites in that sense either, at least in their human versions.

Let us approach the matter by asking whether we can imagine anything that would qualify as a gastronomical perversion. Hunger and eating are importantly like sex in that they serve a biological function and also play a significant role in our inner lives. It is noteworthy that there is little temptation to describe as perverted an appetite for substances that are not nourishing. We should probably not consider someone's appetites as *perverted* if he liked to eat paper, sand, wood, or cotton. Those are merely rather odd and very unhealthy tastes: they lack the psychological complexity that we expect of perversions. (Coprophilia, being already a sexual perversion, may be disregarded.) If on the other hand someone liked to eat cookbooks, or magazines with pictures of food in them, and preferred these to ordinary food—or if when hungry he sought satisfaction by fondling a napkin or ashtray from his favorite restaurant—then the concept of perversion might seem appropriate (in fact it would be natural to describe this as a case of gastronomical fetishism). It would be natural to describe as gastronomically perverted someone who could eat only by having food forced down his throat through a funnel, or only if the meal were a living animal. What helps in such cases is the peculiarity of the desire itself, rather than the inappropriateness of its object to the biological function that the desire serves. Even an appetite, it would seem, can have perversions if an addition to its biological function it has a significant psychological structure.

In the case of hunger, psychological complexity is provided by the activities that give it expression. Hunger is not merely a disturbing sensation that can be quelled by eating; it is an attitude toward edible portions of the external world, a desire to relate to them in rather special ways. The method of ingestion: chewing, savoring, swallowing, appreciating the texture and smell, all are important components of the relation, as is the passivity and controllability of the food (the only animals we eat live are helpless mollusks). Our relation to food depends also on our size: we do not live upon it or burrow into it like aphids or worms. Some of these features are more central than others, but any adequate phenomenology of eating would have to treat it as a relation to the external world and a way of appropriating bits of that world, with characteristic affection. Displacements or serious restrictions of the desire to eat could then be described as perversions, if they undermined that direct relation between man and food which is the natural expression of hunger. This explains why it is easy to imagine gastronomical fetishism, voyeurism, exhibitionism, or even gastronomical sadism and masochism. Indeed some of these perversions are fairly common.

If we can imagine perversions of an appetite like hunger, it should be possible to make sense of the concept of sexual perversion. I do not wish to imply that sexual desire is an appetite—only that being an appetite is no bar to admitting of perversions. Like hunger, sexual desire has as its characteristic object a certain relation with something in the external world; only in this case it is usually a person rather than an omelet, and the relation is considerably more complicated. This added complication allows scope for correspondingly complicated perversions.

The fact that sexual desire is a feeling about other persons may tempt us to take a pious view of its psychological content. There are those who believe that sexual desire is properly the expression of some other attitude, like love, and that when it occurs by itself it is incomplete and unhealthy—or at any rate subhuman. (The extreme Platonic version of such a view is that sexual practices are all vain attempts to express something they cannot in principle achieve: this makes them all perversions, in a sense.) I do not believe that any such view is correct. Sexual desire is complicated enough without having to be linked to anything else as a condition for phenomenological analysis. It cannot be denied that sex may serve various functions—economic, social, altruistic—but it also has its own content as a relation between persons, and it is only by analyzing that relation that we can understand the conditions of sexual perversion.

I believe it is very important that the object of sexual attraction is a particular individual, who transcends the properties that make him attractive. When diffeent persons are attracted to a single person for different reasons: eyes, hair, figure, laugh, intelligence—we feel that the object of their desire is nevertheless the same, namely that person. There is even an inclination to feel that this is so if the lovers have different sexual aims, if they include both men and women, for example. Different specific attractive characteristics seem to provide enabling conditions for the operation of a single basic feeling, and the different aims all provide expressions of it. We approach the sexual attitude toward the person through the features that we find attractive, but these features are not the objects of that attitude.

This is very different from the case of an omelet. Various people may desire it for different reasons, one for its fluffiness, another for its mushrooms, another for its unique combination of aroma and visual aspect; yet we do not enshrine the transcendental omelet as the true common object of their affections. Instead we might say that several desires have accidentally converged on the same object: any omelet with the crucial characteristics would do as well. It is not similarly true that any person with the same flesh distribution and way of smoking can be substituted as object for a particular sexual desire that has been elicited by those characteristics. It may be that they will arouse attraction whenever they recur, but it will be a new sexual attraction with a new particular object, not merely a transfer of the old desire to someone else. (I believe this is true even in cases where the new object is unconsciously identified with a former one.)

The importance of this point will emerge when we see how complex a psychological interchange constitutes the natural development of sexual attraction. This would be incomprehensible if its object were not a particular person, but rather a person of a certain *kind.* Attraction is only the beginning, and fulfillment does not consist merely of behavior and contact expression this attraction, but involves much more.

The best discussion of these matters that I have seen appears in part III of Sartre's *Being and Nothingness.*[1] Since it has influenced my own views, I shall say a few things about it now. Sartre's treatment of sexual desire and of love, hate, sadism, masochism, and further attitudes toward others, depends on a general theory of consciousness and the body which we can neither expound nor assume here. He does not discuss perversion, and this is partly because he regards sexual desire as one form of the perpetual attempt of an embodied consciousness to come to terms with the existence of others, an attempt that is as doomed to fail in this form as it is in any of the others, which include sadism and masochism (if not certain of the more impersonal deviations) as well as several nonsexual attitudes. According to Sartre, all attempts to incorporate the other into my world as another subject, i.e., to apprehend him at once as an object for me and as a subject for which I am an object, are unstable and doomed to collapse into one or other of the two aspects. Either I reduce him entirely to an object, in which case his subjectivity escapes the possession or appropriation I can extend to that object; or I become merely an object for him, in which case I am no longer in a position to appropriate his subjectivity. Moreover, neither of these aspects is stable; each is continually in danger of giving way to the other. This has the consequence that there can be no such thing as a *successful* sexual relation, since the deep aim of sexual desire cannot in principle be accomplished. It seems likely, therefore, that the view will not permit a basic distinction between successful or complete and unsuccessful or incomplete sex, and therefore cannot admit the concept of perversion.

I do not adopt this aspect of the theory, nor many of its metaphysical under-pinnings. What interests me is Satre's picture of the attempt. He says that the type of possession that is the object of sexual desire is carried out by "a double reciprocal incarnation" and that this is accomplished, typically in the form of a caress, in the followng way: "I make myself flesh in order to impel the Other to realize *for herself* and *for me* her own flesh, and my caresses cause my flesh to be born for me in so far as it is for the Other *flesh causing her to be born as flesh"* (391; italics Sartre's). The incarnation in question is described variously as a clogging or troubling of consciousness, which is inundated by the flesh in which it is embodied.

The view I am going to suggest, I hope in less obscure language, is related to this one, but it differs from Sartre's in allowing sexuality to achieve its goal on occasion and thus in providing the concept of perversion with a foothold.

Sexual desire involves a kind of perception, but not merely a single percep-tion of its object, for in the paradigm case of mutual desire there is a complex system of superimposed mutual perceptions—not only perceptions of the sexual object, but perceptions of oneself. Moreover, sexual awareness of another involves considerable self-awareness to begin with—more than is involved in ordinary sensory perception. The experience is felt as an assault on oneself by the view (or touch, or whatever) of the sexual object.

Let us consider a case in which the elements can be separated. For clarity we will restrict ourselves initially to the somewhat artificial case of desire at a distance. Suppose a man and a woman, whom we may call Romeo and Juliet, are at opposite ends of a cocktail lounge, with many mirrors on the walls which permit unobserved observation, and even mutual unobserved observation. Each of them is sipping a martini and studying other people in the mirrors. At some point Romeo notices Juliet. He is moved, somehow, by the softness of her hair and the diffidence with which she sips her martini, and this arouses him sexually. Let us say that *X senses Y* whenever *X* regards *Y* with sexual desire. (*Y* need not be a person, and *X*'s apprehension of *Y* can be visual, tactile, olfactory, etc., or purely imaginary; in the present example we shall concentrate on vision.) So Romeo senses Juliet, rather than merely noticing her. At this stage he is aroused by an unaroused object, so he is more in the sexual grip of his body than she of hers.

Let us suppose, however, that Juliet now senses Romeo in another mirror on the opposite wall, though neither of them yet knows that he is seen by the other (the mirror angles provide three-quarter views). Romeo then begins to notice in Juliet the subtle signs of sexual arousal: heavy-lidded stare, dilating pupils, faint flush, et cetera. This of course renders her much more bodily, and he not only notices but senses this as well. His arousal is nevertheless still solitary. But now, cleverly calculating the line of her stare without actually looking her in the eyes, he realizes that it is directed at him through the mirror on the opposite wall. That is, he notices, and moreover senses, Juliet sensing him. This is definitely a new development, for it gives him a sense of embodiment not only through his own reactions but through the eyes and reactions of another. Moreover, it is separable from the initial sensing of Juliet; for sexual arousal might begin with a person's sensing that he is sensed and being assailed by the perception of the other person's desire rather than merely by the perception of the person.

But there is a further step. Let us suppose that Juliet, who is a little slower than Romeo, now senses that he senses her. This puts Romeo in a position to notice, and be aroused by, her arousal at being sensed by him. He senses that she senses that he senses her. This is still another level of arousal, for he becomes conscious of his sexuality through his awareness of its effect on her and of her awareness that this effect is due to him. Once she takes the same step and senses that he senses her sensing him, it becomes difficult to state, let alone imagine, further iterations, though they may be logically distinct. If both are alone, they will presumably turn to look at each other directly, and the proceedings will continue on another plane. Physical contact and intercourse are perfectly natural extensions of this complicated visual exchange, and mutual touch can involve all the complexities of awareness present in the visual case, but with a far greater range of subtlety and acuteness.

Ordinarily, of course, things happen in a less orderly fashion—sometimes in a great rush—but I believe that some version of this overlapping system of distinct sexual perceptions and interactions is the basic framework of any full-fledged sexual relation and that relations involving only part of the complex are significantly incomplete. The account is only schematic, as it must be to achieve generality. Every real sexual act will be psychologically far more specific and detailed, in ways that depend not only on the physical techniques employed and on anatomical details, but also on countless features of the participants' conceptions of themselves and of each other, which become embodied in the act. (It is a familiar enough fact, for example, that people often take their social roles and the social roles of their partners to bed with them.)

The general schema is important, however, and the proliferation of levels of mutual awareness it involves is an example of a type of complexity that typifies human interactions. Consider aggression, for example. If I am angry with someone, I want to make him feel it, either to produce self-reproach by getting him to see himself through the eyes of my anger, and to dislike what he sees—or else to produce reciprocal anger or fear, by getting him to perceive my anger as a threat or attack. What I want will depend on the details of my anger, but in either case it will involve a desire that the object of that anger be aroused. This accomplishment constitutes the fulfillment of my emotion, through domination of the object's feelings.

Another example of such reflexive mutual recognition is to be found in the phenomenon of meaning, which appears to involve an intention to produce a belief or other effect in another by bringing about his recognition of one's intention to produce that effect. (That result is due to H. P. Grice,[2] whose position I shall not attempt to reproduce in detail.) Sex has a related structure: it involves a desire that one's partner be aroused by the recognition of one's desire that he or she be aroused.

It is not easy to define the basic types of awareness and arousal of which these complexes are composed, and that remains a lacuna in this discussion. I believe that the object of awareness is the same in one's own case as it is in one's sexual awareness of another, although the two awarenesses will not be the same, the difference being as great as that between feeling angry and experiencing the anger of another. All stages of sexual perception are varieties of identification of a person with his body. What is perceived is one's own or another's *subjection* to or *immersion* in his body, a phenomenon which has been recognized with loathing by St. Paul and St. Augustine, both of whom regarded "the law of sin which is in my members" as a grave threat to the dominion of the holy will.[3] In sexual desire and its expression the blending of involuntary response with deliberate control is extremely important. For Augustine, the revolution launched against him by his body is symbolized by erection and the other involuntary physical components of arousal. Sartre too stresses the fact that the penis is not a prehensile organ. But mere involuntariness characterizes other bodily processes as well. In sexual desire the involuntary responses are combined with submission to spontaneous impulses: not only one's pulse and secretions but one's actions are taken over by the body; ideally, deliberate control is needed only to guide the expression of those impulses.

This is to some extent also true of an appetite like hunger, but the takeover there is more localized, less pervasive, less extreme. One's whole body does not become saturated with hunger as it can with desire. But the most characteristic feature of a specifically sexual immersion in the body is its ability to fit into the complex of mutual perceptions that we have described. Hunger leads to spontaneous inter-actions with food; sexual desire leads to spontaneous interactions with other persons, whose bodies are asserting their sovereignty in the same way, producing involuntary reactions and spontaneous impulses in *them*. These reactions are perceived, and the perception of them is perceived, and that perception is in turn perceived; at each step the domination of the person by his body is reinforced, and the sexual partner becomes more possessible by physical contact, penetration, and envelopment.

Desire is therefore not merely the perception of a preexisting embodiment of the other, but ideally a contribution to his further embodiment which in turn enhances the original subject's sense of himself. This explains why it is important that the partner be aroused, and not merely aroused, but aroused by the awareness of one's desire. It also explains the sense in which desire has unity and possession as its object: physical possession must eventuate in creation of the sexual object in the image of one's desire, and not merely in the object's recognition of that desire, or in his or her own private arousal. (This may reveal a male bias: I shall say something about that later.)

To return, finally, to the topic of perversion: I believe that various familiar deviations constitute truncated or incomplete versions of the complete configura-tion, and may therefore be regarded as perversions of the central impulse.

In particular, narcissistic practices and intercourse with animals, infants, and inanimate objects seem to be stuck at some primitive version of the first stage. If the object is not alive, the experience is reduced entirely to an awareness of one's own sexual embodiment. Small children and animals permit awareness of the embodiment of the other, but present obstacles to reciprocity, to the recognition by the sexual object of the subject's desire as the source of his (the object's) sexual self-awareness.

Sadism concentrates on the evocation of passive self-awareness in others, but the sadist's engagement is itself active and requires a retention of deliberate control which impedes awareness of himself as a bodily subject of passion in the required sense. The victim must recognize him as the source of his own sexual passivity, but only as the active source. De Sade claimed that the object of sexual desire was to evoke involuntary responses from one's partner, especially audible ones. The inflic-tion of pain is no doubt the most efficient way to accomplish this, but it requires a certain abrogation of one's own exposed spontaneity. All this, incidentally, helps to explain why it is tempting to regard as sadistic an excessive preoccupation with sexual technique, which does not permit one to abandon the role of agent at any stage of the sexual act. Ideally one should be able to surmount one's technique at some point.

A masochist on the other hand imposes the same disability on his partner as the sadist imposes on himself. The masochist cannot find a satisfactory embodiment as the object of another's sexual desire, but only as the object of his control. He is passive not in relation to his partner's passion but in relation to his nonpassive agency. In addition, the subjection to one's body characteristic of pain and physical restraint is of a very different kind from that of sexual excitement: pain causes people to contract rather than dissolve.

Both of these disorders have to do with the second stage, which involves the awareness of oneself as an object of desire. In straightforward sadism and masochism other attentions are substituted for desire as a source of the object's self-awareness. But it is also possible for nothing of that sort to be substituted as in the case of a masochist who is satisfied with self-inflicted pain or of a sadist who does not insist on playing a role in the suffering that arouses him. Greater difficulties of classification are presented by three other categories of sexual activity: elaborations of the sexual act; intercourse of more than two persons; and homosexuality.

If we apply our model to the various forms that may be taken by two-party heterosexual intercourse, none of them seem clearly to qualify as perversions. Hardly anyone can be found these days to inveigh against oral-genital contact, and the merits of buggery are urged by such respectable figures as D. H. Lawrence and Norman Mailer. There may be something vaguely sadistic about the latter technique (in Mailer's writings it seems to be a method of introducing an element of rape), but it is not obvious that this has to be so. In general, it would appear that any bodily contact between a man and a woman that gives them sexual pleasure, is a possible vehicle for the system of multi-level interpersonal awareness that I have claimed is the basic psychological content of sexual interaction. Thus a liberal platitude about sex is upheld.

About multiple combinations, the least that can be said is that they are bound to be complicated. If one considers how difficult it is to carry on two conversations simultaneously, one may appreciate the problems of multiple simultaneous interpersonal perception that can arise in even a small-scale orgy. It may be inevitable that some of the component relations should degenerate into mutual epidermal stimulation by participants otherwise isolated from each other. There may also be a tendency toward voyeurism and exhibitionism, both of which are incomplete relations. The exhibitionist wishes to display his desire without needing to be desired in return; he may even fear the sexual attention of others. A voyeur, on the other hand, need not require any recognition by his object at all: certainly not a recognition of the voyeur's arousal.

It is not clear whether homosexuality is a perversion if that is measured by the standard of the described configuration, but it seems unlikely. For such a classification would have to depend on the possibility of extracting from the system a distinction between male and female sexuality; and much that has been said so far applies equally to men and women. Moreover, it would have to be maintained that there was a natural tie between the type of sexuality and the sex of the body, and also that two sexualities of the same type could not interact properly.

Certainly there is much support for an aggressive-passive distinction between male and female sexuality. In our culture the male's arousal tends to initiate the perceptual exchange, he usually makes the sexual approach, largely controls the course of the act, and of course penetrates whereas the woman receives. When two men or two women engage in intercourse they cannot both adhere to these sexual roles. The question is how essential the roles are to an adequate sexual relation. One relevant observation is that a good deal of deviation from these roles occurs in heterosexual intercourse. Women can be sexually aggressive and men passive, and temporary reversals of role are not uncommon in heterosexual exchanges of reasonable length. If such conditions are set aside, it may be urged that there is something irreducibly perverted in attraction to a body anatomically like one's own. But alarming as some people in our culture may find such attraction, it remains psychologically unilluminating to class it as perverted. Certainly if homosexuality is a perversion, it is so in a very different sense from that in which shoe-fetishism is a perversion, for some version of the full range of interpersonal perceptions seems perfectly possible between two persons of the same sex.

In any case, even if the proposed model is correct, it remains implausible to describe as perverted every deviation from it. For example, if the partners in heterosexual intercourse indulge in private heterosexual fantasies, that obscures the recognition of the real partner and so, on the theory, constitutes a defective sexual relation. It is not, however, generally regarded as a perversion. Such examples suggest that a simple dichotomy between perverted and unperverted sex is too crude to organize the phenomena adequately.

I should like to close with some remarks about the relation of perversion to good, bad, and morality. The concept of perversion can hardly fail to be evaluative in some sense, for it appears to involve the notion of an ideal or at least adequate sexuality which the perversions in some way fail to achieve. So, if the concept is viable, the judgment that a person or practice or desire is perverted will constitute a sexual evaluation, implying that better sex, or a better specimen of sex, is possible. This in itself is a very weak claim, since the evaluation might be in a dimension that is of little interest to us. (Though, if my account is correct, that will not be true.)

Whether it is a moral evaluation, however, is another question entirely—one whose answer would require more understanding of both morality and perversion than can be deployed here. Moral evaluation of acts and of persons is a rather special and very complicated matter, and by no means all our evaluations of persons and their activities are moral evaluations. We make judgments about people's beauty or health or intelligence which are evaluative without being moral. Assessments of their sexuality may be similar in that respect.

Furthermore, moral issues aside, it is not clear that unperverted sex is necessarily *preferable* to the perversions. It may be that sex which receives the highest marks for perfection *as sex* is less enjoyable than certain perversions; and if enjoyment is considered very important, that might outweigh considerations of sexual perfection in determining rational preference.

That raises the question of the relation between the evaluative content of judgments of perversion and the rather common *general* distinction between good and bad sex. The latter distinction is usually confined to sexual acts, and it would seem, within limits, to cut across the other: even someone who believed, for example, that homosexuality was a perversion could admit a distinction between better and worse homosexual sex, and might even allow that good homosexual sex could be better *sex* than not very good unperverted sex. If this is correct, it supports the position that, if judgments of perversion are viable at all, they represent only one aspect of the possible evaluation of sex, even *qua sex*. Moreover, it is not the only important aspect: certainly sexual deficiencies that evidently do not constitute perversions can be the object of great concern.

Finally, even if perverted sex is to that extent not so good as it might be, bad sex is generally better than none at all. This should not be controversial: it seems to hold for other important matters, like food, music, literature, and society. In the end, one must choose from among the available alternatives, whether their availability depends on the environment or on one's own constitution. And the alternatives have to be fairly grim before it becomes rational to opt for nothing.

NOTES

1. Translated by Hazel E. Barnes (New York: Philosophical Library: 1956).
2. "Meaning," *Philosophical Review*, LXVI, 3 (July 1957): 377-388.
3. See Romans, VII, 23; and the *Confessions*, Book 8, v.

BETTER SEX

Sara Ruddick

It might be argued that there is no specifically sexual morality.[1] We have, of course, become accustomed to speaking of sexual morality, but the "morality" of which we speak has a good deal to do with property, the division of labor, and male power, and little to do with our sexual lives. Sexual experiences, like experiences in driving automobiles, render us liable to specific moral situations. As drivers we must guard against infantile desires for revenge and excitement. As lovers we must

From *Philosophy and Sex,* ed. Robert Baker and Frederick Elliston (Buffalo: Prometheus Books, 1975), pp. 83-104. Reprinted by permission of the author and the publisher.

guard against cruelty and betrayal, for we know sexual experiences provide special opportunities for each. We drive soberly because, before we get into a car, we believe that it is wrong to be careless of life. We resist temptations to adultery because we believe it wrong to betray trust, whether it be a parent, a sexual partner, or a political colleague who is betrayed. As lovers and drivers we act on principles that are particular applications of general moral principles. Moreover, given the superstitions from which sexual experience has suffered, it is wise to free ourselves, as lovers, from any moral concerns, other than those we have as human beings. There is no specifically sexual morality, and none should be invented. Or so it might be argued.

When we examine our moral "intuitions," however, the analogy with driving fails us. Unburdened of *sexual* morality, we do not find it easy to apply general moral principles to our sexual lives. "Morally average lovers can be cruel, violate trusts, and neglect social duties with less opprobrium precisely *because* they are lovers. Only political passions and psychological or physical deprivation serve as well as sexual desire to excuse what would otherwise be seriously and clearly immoral acts. (Occasionally, sexual desire is itself conceived of as a deprivation, an involuntary lust. And there is, of course, a tradition that sees sexual morality as a way of controlling those unable to be sexless: "It is better to marry than to burn.") Often, in our sexual lives, we neither flout nor simply apply general moral principles. Rather, the values of sexual experience themselves figure in the construction of moral dilemmas. The conflict between better sex (more complete, natural, and pleasurable sex acts) and, say, social duty is not seen as a conflict between the immoral and compulsive, on one hand, and the morally good, on the other, but as a conflict between alternative moral acts.

Our intuitions vary but at least they suggest we can use "good" sex as a positive weight on some moral balance. What is that weight? Why do we put it there? How do we, in the first place, evaluate sexual experiences? On reflection, should we endorse these evaluations? These are the questions whose answers should constitute a specifically sexual morality.

In answering them, I will first consider three chracteristics that have been used to distinguish some sex acts as better than others—greater pleasure, completeness, and naturalness. Other characteristics may be relevant to evaluating sex acts, but these three are central. If they have *moral* significance, then the sex acts characterized by them will be better than others not so characterized.

After considering those characteristics in virtue of which some sex acts are allegedly better than others, I will ask whether the presence of those characteristics renders the acts *morally* superior. I will not consider here the unclear and overused distinction between the moral and the amoral, nor the illegitimate but familiar distinction between the moral and the prudent. I hope it is sufficient to set out dogmatically and schematically the moral notions I will use. I am confident that better sex is morally preferable to other sex, but I am not at all happy with my characterization of its moral significance. Ultimately, sexual morality cannot be considered apart from a "prudential" morality in which it is shown that what is good is good for us and what is good for us makes us good. In such a morality, not only sex, but art, fantasy, love, and a host of other intellectual and emotional enterprises will regain old moral significances and acquire new ones. My remarks here, then, are partial and provisional.

A characteristic renders a sex act morally preferable to one without that characteristic if it gives, increases, or is instrumental in increasing the "benefit" of the act for the person engaging in it. Benefits can be classified as peremptory or optional. Peremptory benefits are experiences, relations, or objects that anyone who is neither irrational nor anhedonic will want so long as s/he wants anything at all. Optional benefits are experiences, relations, or objects that anyone, neither irrational nor anhedonic, will want so long as s/he will not thereby lose a peremptory benefit. There is widespread disagreement about which benefits are peremptory. Self-respect, love, and health are common examples of peremptory benefits. Arms, legs, and hands are probably optional benefits. A person still wanting a great deal might give up limbs, just as s/he would give up life, when mutilation or death is required by self-respect. As adults we are largely responsible for procuring our own benefits and greatly dependent on good fortune for success in doing so. However, the moral significance of benefits is most clearly seen not from the standpoint of the person procuring and enjoying them but from the standpoint of another *caring* person, for example, a lover, parent, or political leader responsible for procuring benefits for specific others. A benefit may then be described as an experience, relation, or object that anyone who properly cares for another is obliged to attempt to secure for him/her. Criteria for the virtue of care and for benefit are reciprocally determined, the virtue consisting in part in recognizing and attempting to secure benefits for the person cared for, the identification of benefit depending on its recognition by those already seen to be properly caring.

In talking of benefits I shall be looking at our sexual lives from the vantage point of hope, not of fear. The principal interlocutor may be considered to be a child asking what s/he should rightly and reasonably hope for in living, rather than a potential criminal questioning conventional restraints. The specific question the child may be imagined to ask can now be put: In what way is better sex beneficial or conducive to experiences or relations or objects that are beneficial?

A characteristic renders a sex act morally preferable to one without that characteristic if either the act is thereby more just or the act is thereby likely to make the person engaging in it more just. Justice includes giving others what is due them, taking no more than what is one's own, and giving and taking according to prevailing principles of fairness.

A characteristic renders a sex act morally preferable to one without that characteristic if because of the characteristic the act is more virtuous or more likely to lead to virtue. A virtue is a disposition to attempt, and an ability to succeed in, good acts—acts of justice, acts that express or produce excellence, and acts that yield benefits to oneself or others.

Sexual Pleasure

Sensual experiences give rise to sensations and experiences that are paradigms of what is pleasant. Hedonism, in both its psychological and ethical forms, has blinded us to the nature and to the benefits of sensual pleasure by overextending the word "pleasure" to cover anything enjoyable or even agreeable.[2] The paradigmatic type of pleasure is sensual. Pleasure is a temporally extended, more or less intense quality of particular experiences. Pleasure is enjoyable independent of any function pleasurable activity fulfills. The infant who continues to suck well after s/he is nourished, expressing evident pleasure in doing so, gives us a demonstration of the nature of pleasure.[3]

As we learn more about pleasant experiences we not only apply but also extend and attenuate the primary notion of "pleasure." But if pleasure is to have any nonsophistical psychological or moral interest, it must retain its connections with those paradigm instances of sensual pleasure that give rise to it. We may, for example, extend the notion of pleasure so that particular episodes in the care of children give great pleasure; but the long-term caring for children, however intrinsically rewarding, is not an experience of pleasure or unpleasure.

Sexual pleasure is a species of sensual pleasure with its own conditions of arousal and satisfaction. Sexual acts vary considerably in pleasure, the limiting case being a sexual act where no one experiences pleasure even though someone may experience affection or "relief of tension" through orgasm. Sexual pleasure can be considered either in a context of deprivation and its relief or in a context of satisfaction. Psychological theories have tended to emphasize the frustrated state of sexual desire and to construe sexual pleasure as a relief from that state. There are, however, alternative accounts of sexual pleasure that correspond more closely with our experience. Sexual pleasure is "a primary distinctively poignant pleasure experience that manifests itself from early infancy on. . . . Once experienced it continues to be savored. . . ."[4] Sexual desire is not experienced as frustration but as part of sexual pleasure. Normally, sexual desire transforms itself gradually into the pleasure that appears, misleadingly, to be an aim extrinsic to it. The natural structure of desire, not an inherent quality of frustration, accounts for the pain of an aroused but unsatisfied desire.

Sexual desire, like addictive pleasure generally, does not, except very temporarily, result in satiety. Rather, it increases the demand for more of the same while sharply limiting the possibility of substitutes. The experience of sensual pleasures, and particularly of sexual pleasures, has a pervasive effect on our perceptions of the world. We find bodies inviting, social encounters alluring, smells, tastes, and sights resonant because our perception of them includes their sexual significance. Merleau-Ponty has written of a patient for whom "perception had lost its erotic structure, both temporally and physically."[5] As the result of a brain injury the patient's capacity for sexual desire and pleasure (though not his capacity for performing sexual acts) was impaired. He no longer sought sexual intercourse of his own accord, was left indifferent by the sights and smells of available bodies, and if in the midst of sexual intercourse his partner turned away, he showed no signs of displeasure. The capacity for sexual pleasure, upon which the erotic structure of perception depends, can be accidentally damaged. The question that this case raises is whether it would be desirable to interfere with this capacity in a more systematic way than we now do. With greater biochemical and psychiatric knowledge we shall presumably be able to manipulate it at will.[6] And if that becomes possible, toward what end should we interfere? I shall return to this question after describing the other two characteristics of better sex—completeness and naturalness.

Complete Sex Acts

The completeness of a sexual act depends upon the *relation* of the participants to their own and each other's *desire*. A sex act is complete if each partner allows him/herself to be "taken over" by an active desire, which is desire not merely for the other's body but also for his/her active desire. Completeness is hard to characterize, though complete sex acts are at least as natural as any others—especially, it seems, among those people who take them casually and for granted. The notion of "completeness" (as I shall call it) has figured under various guises in the work of Sartre, Merleau-Ponty, and more recently Thomas Nagel. "The being which desires is consciousness making itself body."[7] "What we try to possess, then, is not just a body, but a body brought to life by consciousness."[8] "It is important that the partner be aroused, and not merely aroused, but aroused by the awareness of one's desire."[9]

The precondition of complete sex acts is the "embodiment" of the participants. Each participant submits to sexual desires that take over consciousness and direct action. It is sexual desire and not a separable satisfaction of it (for example, orgasm) that is important here. Indeed, Sartre finds pleasure external to the essence of desire, and Nagel gives an example of embodiment in which the partners do not touch each other. Desire is pervasive and "overwhelming," but it does not make its subject its involuntary victim (as it did the Boston Strangler, we are told), nor does it. except at its climax, alter capacities for ordinary perceptions, memories, and inferences. Nagel's embodied partners can presumably get themselves from bar stools to bed while their consciousness is "clogged" with desire. With what, then, is embodiment contrasted?

Philosophers make statements that when intended literally are evidence of pathology: "Human beings are automata"; "I never really see physical objects"; "I can never know what another person is feeling." The clearest statement of disembodiment that I know of is W. T. Stace's claim: "I become aware of my body in the end chiefly because it insists on accompanying me wherever I go."[10] What "just accompanies me" can also stay away. "When my body leaves me/I'm lonesome for it./ . . . body/goes away I don't know where/ and it's lonesome to drift/ above the space it/fills when it's here."[11] If "the body is felt more as one object among other objects in the world than as the core of the individual's own being,"[12] then what appears to be bodily can be dissociated from the "real self." Both a generalized separation of "self" from body and particular disembodied experiences have had their advocates. The attempt at disembodiment has also been seen as conceptually confused and psychologically disastrous.

We may often experience ourselves as relatively disembodied, observing or "using" our bodies to fulfill our intentions. On some occasions, however, such as in physical combat, sport, physical suffering, or danger, we "become" our bodies; our consciousness becomes bodily experience of bodily activity.[13] Sexual acts are occasions for such embodiment; they may, however, fail for a variety of reasons, for example, because of pretense or an excessive need for self-control. If someone is embodied by sexual desire, s/he submits to its direction. Spontaneous impulses of desire become his/her movements—some involuntary, like gestures of "courting behavior" or physical expressions of intense pleasure, and some deliberate. His/Her consciousness, or "mind," is taken over by desire and the pursuit of its object, in the way that at other times it may be taken over by an intellectual problem or by obsessive fantasies. But unlike the latter takeovers, this one is bodily. A desiring consciousness is flooded with specifically sexual feelings that eroticize all perception and movement. Consciousness "becomes flesh."

Granted the precondition of embodiment, complete sex acts occur when each partner's embodying desire is active and actively responsive to the other's. This second aspect of complete sex constitutes a "reflexive mutual recognition" of desire by desire.[14]

The partner *actively* desires another person's desire. Active desiring includes more than embodiment, which might be achieved in objectless masturbation. It is more, also, than merely being aroused by and then taken over by desire, though it may come about as a result of deliberate arousal. It commits the actively desiring person to his/her desire and requires him/her to identify with it—that is, to recognize herself as a sexual agent as well as respondent. (Active desiring is less encouraged in women, and probably more women than men feel threatened by it.)

The other recognizes and responds to the partner's desire. Merely to recognize the desire as desire, not to reduce it to an itch or to depersonalize it as a "demand," may be threatening. Imperviousness to desire is the deepest defense against it. We have learned from research on families whose members tend to become schizophrenic that such imperviousness, the refusal to recognize a feeling for what it is, can force a vulnerable person to deny or to obscure the real nature of his/her feelings. Imperviousness tends to deprive even a relatively invulnerable person of his efficacy. The demand that our feelings elicit a response appropriate to them is part of a general demand that *we* be recognized, that our feelings be allowed to make a difference.

There are many ways in which sexual desire may be recognized, countless forms of submission and resistance. In complete sex, desire is recognized by a responding and active desire that commits the other, as it committed the partner. Given responding desire, both people identify themselves as sexually desiring the other. They are neither seducer nor seduced, neither suppliant nor benefactress, neither sadist nor victim, but sexual agents acting sexually out of their recognized desire. Indeed, in complete sex one not only welcomes and recognizes active desire, one desires it. Returned and endorsed desire becomes one of the features of an erotically structured perception. Desiring becomes desirable. (Men are less encouraged to desire the other's active and demanding desire, and such desiring is probably threatening to more men than women.)

In sum, in complete sex two persons embodied by sexual desire actively desire and respond to each other's active desire. Although it is difficult to write of complete sex without suggesting that one of the partners is the intitiator, while the other responds, complete sex is reciprocal sex. The partners, whatever the circumstances of their coming together, are equal in activity and responsiveness of desire.

Sexual acts can be partly incomplete. A necrophiliac may be taken over by desire, and a "frigid" woman may respond to her lover's desire without being embodied by her own. Partners whose sexual activities are accompanied by private fantasies engage in an incomplete sex act. Consciousness is used by desire but remains apart from it, providing it with stimulants and controls. Neither partner responds to the other's desire, though each may appear to. Sartre's "dishonest masturbator," for whom masturbation is the sex act of choice, engages in a paradigmatically incomplete sex act: "He asks only to be slightly distanced from his own body, only for there to be a light coating of otherness over his flesh and over his thoughts. His personae are melting sweets. . . . The masturbator is enchanted at never being able to feel himself sufficiently another, and at producing for himself alone the diabolic appearance of a couple that fades away when one touches it. . . . Masturbation is the derealisation of the world and of the masturbator himself."[15]

Completeness is more difficult to describe than incompleteness, for it turns on precise but subtle ways of responding to a particular person's desire with specific expressions of impulse that are both spontaneous and responsive.

There are many possible sex acts that are pleasurable but not complete. Sartre, Nagel, and Merleau-Ponty each suggest that the desire for the responsive desire of one's partner is the "central impulse" of sexual desire.[16] The desire for a sleeping woman, for example, is possible only "in so far as this sleep appears on the ground of consciousness."[17] This seems much too strong. Some lovers desire that their partners resist, others like them coolly controlled, others, prefer them asleep. We would not say that there was anything abnormal or less fully sexual about desire. Whether or not complete sex is preferable to incomplete sex (the question to which I shall turn shortly), incompleteness does not disqualify a sex act from being fully sexual.

Sexual Perversion

The final characteristic of allegedly better sex acts is that they are "natural" rather than "perverted." The ground for classifying sexual acts as either natural or unnatural is that the former type serve or could serve the evolutionary and biological function of sexuality—namely, reproduction. "Natural" sexual desire has as its "object" living persons of the opposite sex, and in particular their postpubertal genitals. The "aim" of natural sexual desire—that is, the act that "naturally" completes it—is genital intercourse. Perverse sex acts are deviations from the natural object (for example, homosexuality, fetishism) or from the standard aim (for example, voyeurism, sadism). Among the variety of objects and aims of sexual desire, I can see no other ground for selecting some as natural, except that they are of the type that can lead to reproduction.[18]

The connection of sexual desire with reproduction gives us the criterion but not the motive of the classification. The concept of perversion depends on a disjointedness between our experience of sexual desire from infancy on and the function of sexual desire—reproduction. In our collective experience of sexuality, perverse desires are as natural as nonperverse ones. The sexual desire of the polymorphously perverse child has many objects—for example, breasts, anus, mouth, genitals—and many aims—for example, autoerotic or other-directed looking, smelling, touching, hurting. From the social and developmental point of view, natural sex is an achievement, partly biological, partly conventional, consisting in a dominant organization of sexual desires in which perverted aims or objects are subordinate to natural ones. The concept of perversion reflects the vulnerability as much as the evolutionary warrant of this organization.

The connection of sexual desire with reproduction is not sufficient to yield the concept of perversion, but it is surely necessary. Nagel, however, thinks otherwise. There are, he points out, many sexual acts that do not lead to reproduction but that we are not even inclined to call perverse—for example, sexual acts between partners who are sterile. Perversion, according to him, is a psychological concept while reproduction is (only?) a physiological one. (Incidentally, this view of reproduction seems to me the clearest instance of male bias in Nagel's paper.)

Nagel is right about our judgments of particular acts, but he draws the wrong conclusions from those judgments. The perversity of sex acts does not depend upon whether they are intended to achieve reproduction. "Natural" sexual desire is for heterosexual genital activity, not for reproduction. The ground for classifying that desire as natural is that it is so organized that it *could* lead to reproduction in normal physiological circumstances. The reproductive organization of sexual desires gives us a *criterion* of naturalness, but the *virtue* of which it is a criterion is the "naturalness" itself, not reproduction. Our vacillating attitude toward the apparently perverse acts of animals reflects our shifting from criterion to virtue. If, when confronted with a perverse act of animals, we withdraw the label "perverted" from our similar acts rather than extend it to theirs, we are relinquishing the reproductive criterion of naturalness, while retaining the virtue. Animals cannot be "unnatural." If, on the other hand, we "discover" that animals can be perverts too, we are maintaining our criterion, but giving a somewhat altered sense to the "naturalness" of which it is a criterion.

Nagel's alternative attempt to classify acts as natural or perverted on the basis of their completeness fails. "Perverted" and "complete" are evaluations of an entirely different order. The completeness of a sex act depends upon qualities of the participants' experience and upon qualities of their relation—qualities of which they are the best judge. To say a sex act is perverted is to pass a conventional judgment about characteristics of the act, which could be evident to any observer. As one can pretend to be angry but not to shout, one can pretend to a complete, but not to a natural, sex act (though one may, of course, conceal desires for perverse sex acts or shout in order to mask one's feelings). As Nagel himself sees, judgments about particular sex acts clearly differentiate between perversion and completeness. Unadorned heterosexual intercourse where each partner has private fantasies is clearly "natural" and clearly "incomplete," but there is nothing prima facie incomplete about exclusive oral-genital intercourse or homosexual acts. If many perverse acts are incomplete, as Nagel claims, this is an important fact *about* perversion, but it is not the basis upon which we judge its occurrence.

Is Better Sex Really Better?

Some sex acts are, allegedly, better than others insofar as they are more pleasurable, complete, and natural. What is the moral significance of this evaluation? In answering this question, official sexual morality sometimes appeals to the social consequences of particular types of better sex acts. For example, since dominantly perverse organizations of sexual impulses limit reproduction, the merits of perversion depend upon the need to limit or increase population. Experience of sexual pleasure may be desirable if it promotes relaxation and communication in an acquisitive society, undesirable if it limits the desire to work or, in armies, to kill. The social consequences of complete sex have not received particular attention, because the quality of sexual experience has been of little interest to moralists. It might be found that those who had complete sexual relations were more cooperative, less amenable to political revolt. If so, complete sexual acts would be desirable in just and peaceable societies, undesirable in unjust societies requiring revolution.

The social desirability of types of sexual acts depends on particular social conditions and independent criteria of social desirability. It may be interesting and important to assess particular claims about the social desirability of sex acts, but this is not my concern. What is my concern is the extent to which we will allow our judgments of sexual worth to be influenced by social considerations. But this issue cannot even be raised until we have a better sense of sexual worth.

The Benefit of Sexual Pleasure

To say that an experience is pleasant is to give a self-evident, terminal reason for seeking it. We can sometimes "see" that an experience is pleasant. When, for example, we observe someone's sensual delight in eating, his/her behavior can expressively characterize pleasure. We can only question the benefit of such an experience by referring to other goods with which it might conflict. Though sensual pleasures may not be sufficient to warrant giving birth or to deter suicide, so long as we live they are self-evidently benefits to us.

The most eloquent detractors of sexual experience have admitted that it provides sensual pleasures so poignant that once experienced they are repeatedly, almost addictively, sought. Yet, unlike other appetites, such as hunger, sexual desire can be permanently resisted, and resistance has been advocated. How can the prima facie benefits of sexual pleasure appear deceptive?

There are several grounds for complaint. Sexual pleasure is ineradicably mixed, frustration being part of every sexual life. The capacity for sexual pleasure is unevenly distributed, cannot be voluntarily acquired, and diminishes through no fault of its subject. If such a pleasure were an intrinsic benefit, benefit would in this case be independent of moral effort. Then again, sexual pleasures are not serious. Enjoyment of them is one of life's greatest recreations, but none of its business. And finally, sexual desire has the defects of its strengths. Before satisfaction, it is, at the least, distracting; in satisfaction, it "makes one little roome, an everywhere." Like psychosis, sexual desire turns us from "reality"—whether the real be God, social justice, children, or intellectual endeavor. This turning away is more than a social consequence of desire, though it is that. Lovers themselves feel that their sexual desires are separate from their "real" political, domestic, ambitious, social selves.

If the plaintiff is taken to argue that sensual pleasures are not peremptory benefits, s/he is probably right. We can still want a good deal and forego sexual pleasures. We often forego pleasure just because we want something incompatible with it, for example, a good marriage. We must distinguish between giving up some occasions for sexual pleasure and giving up sexual pleasure itself. When all circumstances of sexual pleasure seem to threaten a peremptory benefit, such as self-respect, then the hope and the possibility of sexual pleasure may be relinquished. Since sexual pleasure is such a great, though optional, benefit, its loss is a sad one.

In emphasizing the unsocial, private nature of sexual experiences, the plaintiff is emphasizing a morally important characteristic of them. But the case against desire, as I have sketched it, is surely overstated. The mixed, partly frustrated character of any desire is not particularly pronounced for sexual desire, which is in fact especially plastic, or adaptable to changes (provided perverse sex acts have not been ruled out). Inhibition, social deprivation, or disease make our sexual lives unpleasant, but that is because they interfere with sexual desire, not because the desire is by its nature frustrating. More than other well-known desires (for example, desire for knowledge, success, or power), sexual desire is simply and completely satisfied upon attaining its object. Partly for this reason, even if we are overtaken by desire during sexual experience, our sexual experiences do not overtake us. Lovers turn away from the world while loving, but return—sometimes all too easily—when loving is done. The moralist rightly perceives sexual pleasure as a recreation, and those who upon realizing its benefits make a business of its pursuit appear ludicrous. The capacity for recreation, however, is surely a benefit that any human being rightly hopes for who hopes for anything. Indeed, in present social and economic conditions we are more likely to lay waste our powers in work than in play. Thus, though priest, revolutionary, and parent are alike in fearing sexual pleasure, this fear should inspire us to psychological and sociological investigation of the fearing rather than to moral doubt about the benefit of sexual pleasure.

The Moral Significance of Perversion

What is the moral significance of the perversity of a sexual act? Next to none, so far as I can see. Though perverted sex may be "unnatural" both from an evolutionary and developmental perspective, there is no connection, inverse or correlative, between what is natural and what is good. Perverted sex is sometimes said to be less pleasurable than natural sex. We have little reason to believe that this claim is true and no clear idea of the kind of evidence on which it would be based. In any case, to condemn perverse acts for lack of pleasure is to recognize the worth of pleasure, not of naturalness.

There are many other claims about the nature and consequences of perversion. Some merely restate "scientific" facts in morally tinged terminology. Perverse acts are, by definition and according to psychiatric theory, "immature" and "abnormal," since natural sex acts are selected by criteria of "normal" sexual function and "normal" and "mature" psychological development. But there is no greater connection of virtue with maturity and normality than there is of virtue with nature. The elimination of a village by an invading army would be no less evil if it were the expression of controlled, normal, natural, and mature aggression.

Nagel claims that many perverted sex acts are incomplete, and in making his point, gives the most specific arguments that I have read for the inferiority of perverted sex. But as he points out, there is no reason to think an act consisting solely of oral-genital intercourse is incomplete; it is doubtful whether homosexual acts and acts of buggery are especially liable to be incomplete; and the incompleteness of sexual intercourse with animals is a relative matter depending upon their limited consciousness. And again, the alleged inferiority is not a consequence of perversion but of incompleteness, which can afflict natural sex as well.

Perverted acts might be thought to be inferior because they cannot result in children. Whatever the benefits and moral significance of the procreation and care of children (and I believe they are extensive and complicated), the virtue of proper care for children neither requires nor follows from biological parenthood. Even if it did, only a sexual life consisting solely of perverse acts rules out conception.

If perverted sex acts did rule out normal sex acts, if one were *either* perverted *or* natural, then certain kinds of sexual relations would be denied some perverts— relations that are benefits to those who enjoy them. It seems that sexual relations with the living and the human would be of greater benefit than those with the dead or with animals. But there is no reason to think that heterosexual relations are of greater benefit than homosexual ones. It might be that children can only be raised by heterosexual couples who perform an abundance of natural sex acts. If so (though it seems unlikely), perverts will be denied the happiness of parenthood. This would be an *indirect* consequence of perverted sex and might yield a moral dilemma: How is one to choose between the benefits of children and the benefits of more pleasurable, more complete sex acts?

Some perversions are immoral on independent grounds. Sadism is the obvious example, though sadism practiced with a consenting masochist is far less evil than other, more familiar forms of aggression. Voyeurism may seem immoral because, since it must be secret to be satisfying, it violates others' rights to privacy.[19] Various kinds of rape can constitute perversion if rape, rather than genita inter-course, is the aim of desire. Rape is seriously immoral, a vivid violation of respect for persons. Sometimes doubly perverse rape is doubly evil (the rape of a child) but in other cases (the rape of a pig) its evil is halved. In any case, though rape is always wrong, it is only perverse when raping becomes the aim and not the means of desire.

Someone can be dissuaded from acting on his perverse desires either from moral qualms or from social fears. Although there may be ample basis for the latter, I can find none for the former except the possible indirect loss of the benefits of child care. I am puzzled about this since reflective people who do not usually attempt to legislate the preferences of others think differently. There is no doubt that beliefs in these matters involve deep emotions that should be respected. But for those who do in fact have perverted desires, the first concern will be to satisfy them, not to divert or to understand them. For sexual pleasure is intrinsi-cally a benefit, and complete sex acts, which depend upon expressing the desires one in fact has, are both beneficial and conducive to virtue. Therefore, barring extrinsic moral or social considerations, perverted sex acts are preferable to natural ones if the latter are less pleasurable or less complete.

The Moral Significance of Completeness

Complete sex consists in mutually embodied, mutually active, responsive desire. Embodiment, activity, and mutual responsiveness are instrumentally beneficial because they are conducive to our psychological well-being, which is an intrinsic benefit. The alleged pathological consequences of disembodiment are more specific and better documented than those of perversity.[20] To dissociate oneself from one's actual body, either by creating a delusory body or by rejecting the bodily, is to court a variety of ill effects, ranging from self-disgust to diseases of the will, to faulty mental development, to the destruction of a recognizable "self," and finally to madness. It is difficult to assess psychiatric claims outside their theoretical con-texts, but in this case I believe that they are justified. Relative embodiment is a stable, *normal* condition that is not confined to cases of complete embodiment. But psychiatrists tell us that exceptional physical occasions of embodiment seem to be required in order to balance tendencies to reject or to falsify the body. Sexual acts are not the only such occasions, but they do provide an immersion of consciousness in the bodily, which is pleasurable and especially conducive to correcting experi-ences of shame and disgust that work toward disembodiment.

The mutual responsiveness of complete sex is also instrumentally beneficial. It satisfies a general desire to be recognized as a particular "real" person and to make a difference to other particular "real" people. The satisfaction of this desire in sexual experience is especially rewarding, its thwarting especially cruel. Vulner-ability is increased in complete sex by the active desiring of the partners. When betrayal, or for that matter, tenderness or ecstasy, ensues, one cannot dissociate oneself from the desire with which one identified and out of which one acted. The psychic danger is real, as people who attempt to achieve a distance from their desires could tell us. But the cost of distance is as evident as its gains. Passivity in respect to one's own sexual desire not only limits sexual pleasure but, more seriously, limits the extent to which the experience of sexual pleasure can be included as an experience of a coherent person. With passivity comes a kind of irresponsibility in which one can hide from one's desire, even from one's pleasure, "playing" seducer or victim, tease or savior. Active sexual desiring in complete sex acts affords an especially threatening but also especially happy occasion to relinquish these and similar roles. To the extent that the roles confuse and confound our intimate relations, the benefit from relinquishing them in our sexual acts, or the loss from adhering to them then, is especially poignant.

In addition to being beneficial, complete sex acts are morally superior for three reasons. They tend to resolve tensions fundamental to moral life; they are conducive to emotions that, if they become stable and dominant, are in turn conducive to the virtue of loving; and they involve a preeminently moral virtue— respect for persons.

In one of its aspects, morality is opposed to the private and untamed. Morality is "civilization," social and regulating; desire is "discontent" resisting the regulation. Obligation, rather than benefit, is the notion central to morality so conceived, and the virtues required of a moral person are directed to preserving right relations and social order. Both the insistence on natural sex and the encouragement of complete sex can be looked upon as attempts to make sexual desire more amenable to regulation. But whereas the regulation of perverted desires is extrinsic to them, those of completeness modify the desires themselves. The desiring sensual body that in our social lives we may laugh away or disown becomes our "self" and enters into a social relation. Narcissism and altruism are satisfied in complete sex acts in which one gives what one receives by receiving it. Social and private "selves" are unified in an act in which impersonal, spontaneous impulses govern an action that is responsive to a particular person. For this to be true we must surmount our social "roles" as well as our sexual "techniques," though we incorporate rather than surmount our social selves. We must also surmount regulations imposed in the name of naturalness if our desires are to be spontaneously expressed. Honestly spontaneous first love gives us back our private desiring selves while allowing us to see the desiring self of another. Mutually responding partners confirm each others' desires and declare them good. Such occasions, when we are "moral" without cost, help reconcile us to our moral being and to the usual mutual exclusion between our social and private lives.

The connection between sex and certain emotions—particularly love, jealousy, fear, and anger—is as evident as it is obscure. Complete sex acts seem more likely than incomplete pleasurable ones to lead toward affection and away from fear and anger, since any guilt and shame will be extrinsic to the act and meliorated by it. It is clear that we need not feel for someone any affection beyond that required (if any is) simply to participate with him/her in a complete sex act. However, it is equally clear that sexual pleasure, especially as experienced in complete sex acts, is conducive to many feelings—gratitude, tenderness, pride, appreciation, dependency, and others. These feelings magnify their object who occasioned them. When these magnifying feelings become stable and habitual they are conducive to love—not universal love, of course, but love of a particular sexual partner. However, even "selfish" love is a virtue, a disposition to care for someone as her interests and demands would dictate. Neither the best sex nor the best love require each other, but they go together more often than reason would expect—often enough to count the virtue of loving as one of the rewards of the capacity for sexual pleasure exercised in complete sex acts.

It might be argued that the coincidence of sex acts and several valued emotions is a cultural matter. It is notoriously difficult to make judgments about the emotional and, particularly, the sexual lives of others, especially culturally alien others. There is, however, some anthropological evidence that at first glance relativizes the connection between good sex and valued emotion. For example, among the Manus of New Guinea, it seems that relations of affection and love are encouraged primarily among brother and sister, while easy familiarity, joking, and superficial sexual play is expected only between cross-cousins. Sexual intercourse is, however, forbidden between siblings and cross-cousins but required of married men and women, who are as apt to hate as to care for each other and often seem to consider each other strangers. It seems, however, that the Manus do not value or experience complete or even pleasurable sex. Both men and women are described as puritanical, and the sexual life of women seems blatantly unrewarding. Moreover, their emotional life is generally impoverished. This impoverishment, in conjunction with an unappreicated and unrewarding sexual life dissociated from love or affection, would argue for a connection between better sex and valued emotions. If, as Peter Winch suggests, cultures provide their members with particular possibilities of making sense of their lives, and thereby with possibilities of good and evil, the Manus might be said to deny themselves one possibility both of sense and of good—namely the coincidence of good sex and of affection and love. Other cultures, including our own, allow this possibility, whose realization is encouraged in varying degrees by particular groups and members of the culture.[21]

Finally, as Sartre has suggested, complete sex acts preserve a respect for persons. Each person remains conscious and responsible, a "subject" rather than a depersonalized, will-less, or manipulated "object." Each actively desires that the other likewise remain a "subject." Respect for persons is a central virtue when matters of justice and obligation are at issue. Insofar as we can speak of respect for persons in complete sex acts, there are different, often contrary requirements of respect. Respect for persons, typically and in sex acts, requires that *actual present* partners participate, partners whose desires are recognized and endorsed. Respect for persons typically requires taking a distance from both one's own demands and those of others. But in sex acts the demands of desire take over, and equal distance is replaced by mutual responsiveness. Respect typically requires refusing to treat another person merely as a means to fulfilling demands. In sex acts, another person is so clearly a means to satisfaction that s/he is always on the verge of becoming merely a means ("intercourse counterfeits masturbation"). In complete sex acts, instrumentality vanishes only because it is mutual and mutually desired. Respect requires encouraging, or at least protecting, the autonomy of another. In complete sex, autonomy of will is recruited by desire, and freedom from others is replaced by frank dependence on another person's desire. Again the respect consists in the reciprocity of desiring dependence, which bypasses rather than violates autonomy.

Despite the radical differences between respect for persons in the usual moral contexts and respect for persons in sex acts, it is not, I think, a mere play on words to talk of respect in the latter case. When, in any sort of intercourse, persons are respected, their desires are not only, in fair measure, fulfilled. In addition, their desires are active and determine, in fair measure, the form of intercourse and the manner and condition of desire's satisfaction. These conditions are not only met in sexual intercourse when it is characterized by completeness; they come close to defining completeness.

Sartre is not alone in believing that just because the condition of completeness involves respect for persons, complete sex is impossible. Completeness is surely threatened by pervasive tendencies to fantasy, to possessiveness, and to varieties of a sadomasochistic desire. But a complete sex act, as I see it, does not involve an heroic restraint on our sexual impulses. Rather, a complete sex act is a normal mode of sexual activity expressing the natural structure and impulses of sexual desire.

While complete sex is morally superior because it involves respect for persons, incomplete sex acts do not necessarily involve immoral disrespect for persons. They may, depending upon the desires and expectations of the partners; but they may involve neither respect nor disrespect. Masturbation, for example, allows only the limited completeness of embodiment and often fails of that. But masturbation only rarely involves disrespect to anyone. Even the respect of the allegedly desirable sleeping woman may not be violated if she is unknowingly involved in a sex act. Disrespect, though likely, may be obviated by her sensibilities and expectations that she has previously expressed and her partner has understood. Sex acts provide one context in which respect for persons can be expressed. That context is important both because our sexual lives are of such importance to us and because they are so liable to injury because of the experience and the fear of the experience of disrespect. But many complete sex acts in which respect is maintained make other casual and incomplete sex acts unthreatening. In this case a goodly number of swallows can make a summer.

In sum, then, complete sex acts are superior to incomplete ones. First, they are, whatever their effects, better than various kinds of incomplete sex acts because they involve a kind of "respect for persons" in acts that are otherwise prone to violation of respect for, and often to violence to, persons. Second, complete sex acts are good because they are good for us. They are conducive to some fairly clearly defined kinds of psychological well-being that are beneficial. They are conducive to moral well-being because they relieve tensions that arise in our attempts to be moral and because they encourage the development of particular virtues.

To say that complete sex acts are preferable to incomplete ones is not to court a new puritanism. There are many kinds and degrees of incompleteness. Incomplete sex acts may not involve a disrespect for persons. Complete sex acts only *tend* to be good for us, and the realization of these tendencies depends upon individual lives and circumstances of sexual activity. The proper object of sexual desire is sexual pleasure. It would be a foolish ambition indeed to limit one's sexual acts to those in which completeness was likely. Any sexual act that is pleasurable is prima facie good, though the more incomplete it is—the more private, essentially autoerotic, unresponsive, unembodied, passive, or imposed—the more likely it is to be harmful to someone.

On Sexual Morality: Concluding Remarks

There are many questions we have neglected to consider because we have not been sufficiently attentive to the quality of sexual lives. For example, we know little about the ways of achieving better sex. When we must choose between inferior sex and abstinence, how and when will our choice of inferior sex damage our capacity for better sex? Does, for example, the repeated experience of controlled sexual disembodiment ("desire which takes over will take you too far") that we urge (or used to urge) on adolescents damage their capacity for complete sex? The answers to this and similar questions are not obvious, though unfounded opinions are always ready at hand.

Some of the traditional sexual vices might be condemned on the ground that they are inimical to better sex. Obscenity, or repeated public exposure to sexual acts, might impair our capacity for pleasure or for response to desire. Promiscuity might undercut the tendency of complete sex acts to promote emotions that magnify their object. Other of the traditional sexual vices are neither inimical nor conducive to better sex, but are condemned because of conflicting nonsexual benefits and obligations. For example, infidelity qua infidelity neither secures nor prevents better sex. The obligations of fidelity have many sources, one of which may be a past history of shared complete sex acts, a history that included promises of exclusive intimacy. Such past promises are as apt to conflict with as to accord with a current demand for better sex. I have said nothing about how such a conflict would be settled. I hope I have shown that where the possibility of better sex conflicts with obligations and other benefits, we have a *moral dilemma*, not just an occasion for moral self-discipline.

The pursuit of more pleasurable and more complete sex acts is, among many moral activities, distinguished not for its exigencies but for its rewards. Since our sexual lives are so important to us, and since, whatever our history and our hopes, we are sexual beings, this pursuit rightly engages our moral reflection. It should not be relegated to the immoral, nor to the "merely" prudent.

NOTES

1. An earlier version of this paper was published in *Moral Problems,* edited by James Rachels (New York: Harper & Row, 1971). I am grateful to many friends and students for their comments on the earlier version, especially to Bernard Gert, Evelyn Fox Keller, and James Rachels.

2. This may be a consequence of the tepidness of the English "pleasant." It would be better to speak of lust and its satisfaction if our suspicion of pleasure had not been written into that part of our language.

3. The example is from Sigmund Freud, *Three Essays on Sexuality,* standard ed., vol. 7 (London: Hogarth, 1963), p. 182. The concept of pleasure I urge here is narrower but also, I think, more useful than the popular one. It is a concept that, to paraphrase Wittgenstein, we (could) learn when we learn the langauge. The idea of paradigmatic uses and subsequent more-or-less-divergent, more-or-less "normal" uses also is derived from Wittgenstein.

4. George Klein, "Freud's Two Theories of Sexuality," in L. Berger, ed., *Clinical-Cognitive Psychology: Models and Integrations* (Englewood Cliffs, N.J.: Prentice-Hall, 1969), pp. 131-81. This essay gives a clear idea of alternative psychological accounts of sexual pleasure.

5. Maurice Merleau-Ponty, *Phenomenology of Perception,* trans. Colin Smith (London: Routledge & Kegan Paul, 1962), p. 156.

6. See Kurt Vonnegut, Jr., "Welcome to the Monkey House," in *Welcome to the Monkey House* (New York: Dell, 1968), which concerns both the manipulation and the benefit of sexual pleasure.

7. Jean-Paul Sartre, *Being and Nothingness,* trans. Hazel E. Barnes (New York: Philosophical Library, 1956), p. 389.

8. Merleau-Ponty, *Phenomenology of Perception,* p. 167.

9. Thomas Nagel, "Sexual Perversion," *The Journal of Philosophy* 66, no. 1 (January 16, 1969): 13; herein, pp. 255-56. My original discussion of completeness was both greatly indebted to and confused by Nagel's. I have tried here to dispel some of the confusion.

10. W. T. Stace, "Solipsism," from *The Theory of Knowledge and Existence;* reprinted in Tillman, Berofsky, and O'Connor, eds., *Introductory Philosophy* (New York: Harper & Row, 1967), p. 113.

11. Denise Levertov, "Gone Away," in *O Taste and See* (New York: New Directions, 1962), p. 59. Copyright by Denise Levertov Goodman, New Directions Publishing Corporation, New York.

12. R. D. Laing, *The Divided Self* (Baltimore: Pelican Books, 1965), p. 69.

13. We need not become our bodies on such occasions. Pains, muscular feelings, and emotions can be reduced to mere "sensations" that may impinge on "me" but that I attempt to keep at a distance. Laing describes the case of a man who when beaten up felt that any damage to his body could not really hurt *him*. See *The Divided Self,* p. 68.

14. Nagel, "Sexual Perversion," p. 254.

15. Jean-Paul Sartre, *Saint Genet* (New York: Braziller, 1963), p. 398; cited and translated by R. D. Laing, *Self and Others* (New York: Pantheon, 1969), pp. 39-40.

16. Ibid., p. 13.

17. Satre, *Being and Nothingness,* p. 386.

18. See, in support of this point, Sigmund Freud, *Introductory Lectures on Psychoanalysis,* standard ed., vol. 26 (London: Hogarth, 1963), chaps. 20, 21.

19. I am indebted to Dr. Leo Goldberger for this example.

20. See, for example, R. D. Laing, *The Divided Self;* D. W. Winnicott, "Transitional Objects and Transitional Phenomena," *International Journal of Psychoanalysis* 34 (1953): 89-97; Paul Federn, *Ego Psychology and the Psychoses* (New York: Basic Books, 1952); Phyllis Greenacre, *Trauma, Growth, and Personality* (New York: International Universities Press, 1969); Paul Schilder, *The Image and Appearance of the Human Body* (New York: International Universities Press, 1950); Moses Laufer, "Body Image and Masturbation in Adolescence," *The Psychoanalytic Study of the Child* 23 (1968): 114-46. Laing's work is most specific about both

the nature and consequences of disembodiment, but the works cited, and others similar to them, give the clinical evidence upon which much of Laing's work depends.

21. The evidence about the life of the Manus comes from Margaret Mead, *Growing Up in New Guinea* (Harmondsworth, Eng.: Penguin Books, 1942). Peter Winch's dscussion can be found in his "Understanding a Primitive Society," *American Philosophical Quarterly* 1 (1964): 307-34.

MARRIAGE

MONOGAMY: A CRITIQUE

John McMurtry

> *Remove away that black'ning church*
> *Remove away that marriage hearse*
> *Remove away that man of blood*
> *You'll quite remove the ancient curse.*
>
> **William Blake**

Almost all of us have entered or will one day enter a specifically standardized form of monogamous marriage. This cultural requirement is so very basic to our existence that we accept it for most part a kind of intractable given: dictated by the laws of God, Nature, Government, and Good Sense all at once. Though it is perhaps unusual for a social practice to be so promiscuously underwritten, we generally find comfort rather than curiosity in this fact and seldom wonder how something could be divinely inspired, biologically determined, coerced and reasoned out all at the same time. We simply take for granted.

Those in society who are officially charged with the thinking function with regard to such matters are no less responsible for this uncritical acceptance than the man on the street. The psychoanalyst traditionally regards our form of marriage as a necessary restraint on the anarchic id and no more to be queried than civilization itself. The lawyer is as undisposed to questioning the practice as he is to criticizing the principle of private property (this is appropriate, as I shall later point out). The churchman formally perceives the relationship between man and wife to be as inviolable and insusceptible to question as the relationship between the institution he works for and the Christ. The sociologist standardly accepts the formalized bonding of heterosexual pairs as the indispensable basis of social order and perhaps

Reprinted from *The Monist,* 56, no. 4 (1972, 587-99) with the permission of the author and the publisher.

a societal universal. The politician is as incapable of challenging it as he is the virtue of his own continued holding of office. And the philosopher (at least the English-speaking philosopher), as with most issues of socially controversial or sexual dimensions, ignores the question almost altogether.

Even those irreverent adulterers and unmarried couples who would seem to be challenging the institution in the most basic possible way, in practice, tend merely to mimic its basic structure in unofficial form. The coverings of sanctity, taboo and cultural habit continue to hold them with the grip of public clothes.

II

"Monogamy" means, literally, "one marriage." But it would be wrong to suppose that this phrase tells us much about our particular species of official wedlock. The greatest obstacle to the adequate understanding of our monogamy institution has been the failure to identify clearly and systematically the full complex of principles it involves. There are four such principles, each carrying enormous restrictive force and together constituting a massive social control mechanism that has never, so far as I know, been fully schematized.

To come straight to the point, the four principles in question are as follows:

1. *The partners are required to enter a formal contractual relation: (a)* whose establishment demands a specific official participant, certain conditions of the contractors (legal age, no blood ties, etc.) and a standard set of procedures; *(b)* whose governing terms are uniform for all and exactly prescribed by law; and *(c)* whose dissolution may only be legally effected by the decision of state representatives.

The ways in which this elaborate principle of contractual requirement are importantly restrictive are obvious. One may not enter into a marriage union without entering into a contract presided over by a state-investured official.[1] One may not set any of the terms of the contractual relationship by which one is bound for life. And one cannot dissolve the contract without legal action and costs, court proceedings and in many places actual legislation. (The one and only contract in all English-speaking law that is not dissoluble by the consent of the contracting parties.) The extent of control here—over the most intimate and putatively "loving" relationships in all social intercourse—is so great as to be difficult to catalogue without exciting in oneself a sense of disbelief.

Lest it be thought there is always the real option of entering a common law relationship free of such encumbrances, it should be noted that: *(a)* these relationships themselves are subject to state regulation, though of a less imposing sort; and (much more important) *(b)* there are very formidable selective pressures against common law partnerships such as employment and job discrimination, exclusion from housing and lodging facilities, special legal disablements,[2] loss of social and moral status (consider such phrases as "living in sin," "make her an honest woman," etc.), family shame and embarrassment, and so on.

2. *The number of partners involved in the marriage must be two and only two* (as opposed to three, four, five or any of the almost countless other possibilities of intimate union).

This second principle of our specific form of monogamy (the concept of "one marriage," it should be pointed out, is consistent with any number of participating partners) is perhaps the most important and restrictive of the four principles we are considering. Not only does it confine us to just *one* possibility out of an enormous range, but it confines us to that single possibility which involves the *least* number of people, two. It is difficult to conceive of a more thoroughgoing mechanism for limiting extended social union and intimacy. The fact that this monolithic restriction seems so "natural" to us (if it were truly "natural" of course, there would be no need for its rigorous cultural prescription by everything from severe criminal law[3] to ubiquitous housing regulations) simply indicates the extent to which its hold is implanted in our social structure. It is the institutional basis of what I will call the "binary frame of sexual consciousness," a frame through which all our heterosexual relationships are typically viewed ("two's company, three's a crowd") and in light of which all larger circles of intimacy seem almost inconceivable.[4]

3. *No person may participate in more than one marriage at a time or during a lifetime* (unless the previous marriage has been officially dissolved by, normally, one partner's death or successful divorce).

Violation of this principle is, of course, a criminal offence (bigamy) which is punishable by a considerable term in prison. Of various general regulations of our marriage institution it has experienced the most significant modification: not indeed in principle, but in the extent of flexibility of its "escape hatch" of divorce. The case with which this escape hatch is open has increased considerably in the past few years (the grounds for divorce being more permissive than previously) and it is in this regard most of all that the principles of our marriage institution have undergone formal alteration. That is, in plumbing rather than substance.

4. *No married person may engage in any sexual relationship with any person whatever other than the marriage partner.*

Although a consummated sexual act with another person alone constitutes an act of adultery, lesser forms of sexual and erotic relationships[5] may also constitute grounds for divorce (i.e., cruelty) and are generally proscribed as well by informal social convention and taboo. In other words, the fourth and final principle of our marriage institution involves not only a prohibition of sexual intercourse per se outside one's wedlock (this term deserves pause) but a prohibition of all one's erotic relations whatever outside this bond. The penalties for violation here are as various as they are severe, ranging from permanent loss of spouse, children, chattel, and income to job dismissal and social ostracism. In this way, possibly the most compelling natural force towards expanded intimate relations with others[6] is strictly confined within the narrowest possible circle for (barring delinquency) the whole of adult life. The sheer weight and totality of this restriction is surely one of the great wonders of all historical institutional control.

III

,With all established institutions, apologetics for perpetuation are never wanting. Thus it is with our form of monogamous marriage.

Perhaps the most celebrated justification over the years has proceeded from a belief in a Supreme Deity who secretly utters sexual and other commands to privileged human representatives. Almost as well known a line of defence has issued from a conviction, similarly confident, that the need for some social regulation of sexuality demonstrates the need for our specific type of two-person wedlock. Although these have been important justifications in the sense of being very widely supported, they are not—having other grounds than reason—susceptible to treatment here.

If we put aside such arguments, we are left I think with two major claims. The first is that our form of monogamous marriage promotes a profound affection between the partners which is not only of great worth in itself but invaluable as a sanctuary from the pressures of outside society. Since, however, there are no secure grounds whatever for supposing that such "profound affection" is not at least as easily achievable by any number of *other* marriage forms (i.e., forms which differ in one or more of the four principles), this justification conspicuously fails to perform the task required of it.

The second major claim for the defence is that monogamy provides a specially loving context for child upbringing. However here again there are no grounds at all for concluding that it does so as, or any more, effectively than other possible forms of marriage (the only alternative type of upbringing to which it has apparently been shown to be superior is nonfamily institutional upbringing, which of course is not relevant to the present discussion). Furthermore, the fact that at least half the span of a normal monogamous marriage *involves no child-upbringing at all* is disastrously overlooked here, as is the reinforcing fact that there is no reference to or mention of the quality of child-upbringing in any of the prescriptions connected with it.

In brief, the second major justification of our particular type of wedlock scents somewhat too strongly of red herring to pursue further.

There is, it seems, little to recommend the view that monogamy specially promotes "profound affection" between the partners or a "loving context" for child-upbringing. Such claims are simply without force. On the other hand, there are several aspects to the logic and operation of the four principles of this institution which suggest that it actually *inhibits* the achievement of these desiderata. Far from uniquely abetting the latter, it militates against them. In these ways:

(1) Centralized official control of marriage (which the Church gradually achieved through the mechanism of Canon Law after the Fall of the Roman Empire[7] in one of the greatest seizures of social power in history) necessarily alienates the partners from full responsibility for and freedom in their relationship. "Profound closeness" between the partners—or at least an area of it—is thereby expropriated rather than promoted, and "sanctuary" from the pressures of outside society prohibited rather than fostered.

(2) Limitation of the marriage bond to two people necessarily restricts, in perhaps the most unilateral possible way consistent with offspring survival, the number of adult sources of affection, interest, material support and instruction for the young. The "loving context for child-upbringing" is thereby desiccated rather than nourished: providing the structural conditions for such notorious and far-reaching problems as *(a)* sibling rivalry for scarce adult attention,[8] and *(b)* parental oppression through exclusive monopoly of the child's means of life.[9]

(3) Formal exclusion of all others from erotic contact with the marriage partner systematically promotes conjugal insecurity, jealousy and alienation by:

(a) Officially underwriting a literally totalitarian expectation of sexual confinement on the part of one's husband or wife: which expectation is, *ceteris paribus,* inevitably more subject to anxiety and disappointment than one less extreme in its demand and/or cultural-juridical backing;[10]

(b) Requiring so complete a sexual isolation of the marriage partners that should one violate the fidelity code the other is left alone and susceptible to a sense of fundamental deprivation and resentment;

(c) Stipulating such a strict restraint of sexual energies that there are habitual violations of the regulation: which violations *qua* violations are frequently if not always attended by (i) willful deception and reciprocal suspicion about the occurrence or quality of the extramarital relationship, (ii) anxiety and fear on both sides of permanent estrangement from partner and family, and/or (iii) overt and covert antagonism over the prohibited act in both offender (who feels "trapped") and offended (who feels "betrayed").

The disadvantages of the four principles of monogamous marriage do not, however, end with inhibiting the very effects they are said to promote. There are further shortcomings:

(1) The restriction of marriage union to two partners necessarily prevents the strengths of larger groupings. Such advantages as the following are thereby usually ruled out.

(a) The security, range and power of larger socioeconomic units;

(b) The epistemological and emotional substance, variety and scope of more pluralist interactions;

(c) The possibility of extra-domestic freedom founded on more adult providers and upbringers as well as more broadly based circles of intimacy.

(2) The sexual containment and isolation which the four principles together require variously stimulates such social malaises as:

(a) Destructive aggression (which notoriously results from sexual frustration);

(b) Apathy, frustration and dependence within the marriage bond;

(c) Lack of spontaneity, bad faith and distance in relationships without the marriage bond;

(d) Sexual phantasizing, perversion, fetishism, prostitution and pornography in the adult population as a whole.[11]

Taking such things into consideration, it seems difficult to lend credence to the view that the four principles of our form of monogamous marriage constitute a structure beneficial either to the marriage partners themselves or to their offspring (or indeed to anyone else). One is moved to seek for some other ground of the institution, some ground that lurks beneath the reach of our conventional apprehensions.

IV

The ground of our marriage institution, the essential principle that underwrites all four restrictions, is this: *the maintenance by one man or woman of the effective right to exclude indefinitely all other from erotic access to the conjugal partner.*

The first restriction creates, elaborates on, and provides for the enforcement of this right to exclude. And the second, third, and fourth restrictions together ensure that the said right to exclude is—respectively—not cooperative, not simultaneously or sequentially distributed, and not permissive of even casual exception.

In other words, the four restrictions of our form of monogamous marriage together constitute a state-regulated, indefinite and exclusive ownership by two individuals of one another's sexual powers. Marriage is simply a form of private property.[12]

That our form of monogamous marriage is when the confusing layers of sanctity, apologetic and taboo are cleared away another species of private property should not surprise us.[13] The history of the institution is so full of suggestive indicators—dowries, inheritance, property alliances, daughter sales (of which women's wedding rings are a carry-over), bride exchanges, legitimacy and illegitimacy—that it is difficult not to see some intimate connections between marital and ownership ties. We are better able still to apprehend the ownership essence of our marriage institution, when in addition we consider:

(a) That until recently almost the only way to secure official dissolution of consummated marriage was to be able to demonstrate violation of one or both partner's sexual ownership (i.e., adultery);

(b) That the imperative of premarital chasity is tantamount to a demand for retrospective sexual ownership by the eventual marriage partner;

(c) That successful sexual involvement with a married person is prosecutable as an expropriation of ownership—"alienation of affections"—which is restituted by cash payment;

(d) That the incest taboo is an iron mechanism which protects the conjugal ownership of sexual properties: both the husband's and wife's from the access of affectionate offspring and the offsprings' (who themselves are future marriage partners) from access of siblings and parents;[14]

(e) That the language of the marriage ceremony is the language of exclusive possession ("take," "to have and to hold," "forsaking all others and keeping you only unto him/her," etc.), not to mention the proprietary locutions associated with the marital relationship (e.g., "he's mine," "she belongs to him," "keep to your own husband," "wife stealer," "possessive husband," etc.).

V

Of course, it would be remarkable if marriage in our society was not a relationship akin to private property. In our socioeconomic system we relate to virtually everything of value by individual ownership: by, that is, the effective right to exclude others from the thing concerned.[15] That we do so as well with perhaps the most highly valued thing of all—the sexual partners' sexuality—is only to be expected. Indeed it would probably be an intolerable strain on our entire social structure if we did otherwise.

This line of thought deserves pursuit. The real secret of our form of monogamous marriage is not that it functionally provides for the needs of adults who love one another or the children they give birth to, but that it serves the maintenance of our present social system. It is an institution which is indispensable to the persistence of the capitalist order,[16] in the following ways:

(1) A basic principle of current social relations is that some people legally acquire the use of other people's personal powers from which they may exclude other members of society. This system operates in the workplace (owners and hirers of all types contractually acquire for their exclusive use workers' regular labour powers) and in the family (husbands and wives contractually acquire for their exclusive use their partner's sexual properties). A conflict between the structures of these primary relations—as would obtain were there a suspension of the restrictions governing our form of monogamous marriage— might well undermine the systemic coherence of present social intercourse.

(2) The fundamental relation between individuals and things which satisfy their needs is, in our present society, that each individual has or does not have the effective right to exclude other people from the thing in question.[17] A rudimentary need is that for sexual relationship(s). Therefore the object of this need must be related to the one who needs it as owner or not owner (i.e., via marriage or not-marriage, or approximations thereto) if people's present relationship to what they need is to retain—again—systemic coherence.

(3) A necessary condition for the continued existence of the present social formation is that its members feel powerful motivation to gain favorable positions in it. But such social ambition is heavily dependent on the preservation of exclusive monogamy in that:

    (a) The latter confines the discharge of primordial sexual energies to a single unalterable partner and thus typically compels the said energies to seek alternative outlet, such as business or professional success;[18]

    (b) The exclusive marriage necessarily reduces the sexual relationships available to any one person to absolute (nonzero) minimum, a unilateral promotion of sexual shortage which in practice renders hierarchal achievement essential as an economic and "display" means for securing scarce partners.[19]

(4) Because the exclusive marriage necessarily and dramatically reduces the possibilities of sexual-love relationships, it thereby promotes the existing economic system by:

    (a) Rendering extreme economic self-interest—the motivational basis of the capitalistic process—less vulnerable to altruistic subversion;

(b) Disciplining society's members into the habitual repression of natural impulse required for long-term performance of repetitive and arduous work tasks;

(c) Developing a complex of suppressed sexual desires to which sales techniques may effectively apply in creating those new consumer wants which provide indispensable outlets for ever-increasing capital funds.

(5) The present form of marriage is of fundamental importance to:

(a) The continued relative powerlessness of the individual family: which, with larger numbers would constitute a correspondingly increased command of social power;

(b) The continued high demand for homes, commodities and services: which, with the considerable economies of scale that extended unions would permit, would otherwise falter;

(c) The continued strict necessity for adult males to sell their labour power and adult women to remain at home (or vice versa): which strict necessity would diminish as the economic base of the family unit extended;

(d) The continued immense pool of unsatisfied sexual desires and energies in the population at large: without which powerful interests and institutions would lose much of their conventional appeal and force;[20]

(e) The continued profitable involvement of lawyers, priests, and state officials in the jurisdictions of marriage and divorce and the myriad official practices and proceedings connected thereto.[21]

VI

If our marriage institution is a linchpin of our present social structure, then a breakdown in this institution would seem to indicate a breakdown in our social structure. On the face of it, the marriage institution is breaking down—enormously increased divorce rates, nonmarital sexual relationships, wife-swapping, the Playboy philosophy, and communes. Therefore one might be led by the appearance of things to anticipate a profound alteration in the social system.

But it would be a mistake to underestimate the tenacity of an established order or to overestimate the extent of change in our marriage institution. Increased divorce rates merely indicate the widening of a traditional escape hatch. Nonmarital relationships imitate and culminate in the marital mold. Wife-swapping presupposes ownership, as the phrase suggests. The Playboy philosophy is merely the view that if one has the money one has the right to be titillated, the commercial call to more fully exploit a dynamic sector of capital investment. And communes—the most hopeful phenomenon—almost nowhere offer a *praxis* challenge to private property in sexuality. It may be changing. But history, as the old man puts it, weighs like a nightmare on the brains of the living.

NOTES

1. Any person who presides over a marriage and is not authorized by law to do so is guilty of a criminal offense and is subject to several years imprisonment (e.g., Canadian Criminal Code, Sec. 258).

2. For example, offspring are illegitimate, neither wife nor children are legal heirs, and husband has no right of access or custody should separation occur.

3. "Any kind of conjugal union with more than one person at the same time, whether or not it is by law recognized as a binding form of marriage—is guilty of an indictable offence and is liable to imprisonment for five years" (Canadian Criminal Code, Sec. 257, [1] [a] [ii]). Part 2 of the same section adds: "Where an accused is charged with an offence under this section, no averment or proof of the method by which the alleged relationship was entered into, agreed to or consented to is necessary in the indictment or upon the trial of the accused, nor is it necessary upon the trial to prove that the persons who are alleged to have entered into the relationship had or intended to have sexual intercourse."

(Here and elsewhere, I draw examples from Canadian criminal law. There is no reason to suspect the Canadian code is eccentric in these instances.)

4. Even the sexual revolutionary Wilhelm Reich seems constrained within the limits of this "binary frame." Thus he says (my emphasis): "Nobody has the right to prohibit his or her partner from entering a temporary or lasting sexual relationship with someone else. He has only the right *either to withdraw or to win the partner back*." (Wilhelm Reich, *The Sexual Revolution,* trans. by T. P. Wolfe [New York: Farrar, Strauss & Giroux, 1970], p. 28.) The possibility of sexual partners extending their union to include the other loved party as opposed to one partner having either to "win" against this third party or to "withdraw" altogether, does not seem even to occur to Reich.

5. I will be using "sexual" and "erotic" interchangeably throughout the paper.

6. It is worth noting here that: *(a)* man has by nature the most "open" sexual instinct—year-round operativeness and variety of stimuli—of all the species (except perhaps the dolphin); and *(b)* it is a principle of human needs in general that maximum satisfaction involves regular variation in the form of the need-object.

7. "Roman Law had no power of intervening in the formation of marriages and there was no legal form of marriage. . . . Marriage was a matter of simple private agreement and divorce was a private transaction" (Havelock Ellis, *Studies in the Psychology of Sex* [New York: Random House, 1963], Vol. II, Part 3, p. 429).

8. The dramatic reduction of sibling rivalry through an increased number of adults in the house is a phenomenon which is well known in contemporary domestic communes.

9. One of the few other historical social relationships I can think of in which persons hold thoroughly exclusive monopoly over other persons' means of life is slavery. Thus, as with another's slave, it is a criminal offence "to receive" or "harbour" another's child without "right of possession" (Canadian Criminal Code, Sec. 250).

10. Certain cultures, for example, permit extramarital sexuality by married persons with friends, guests, or in-laws with no reported consequences of jealousy. From such evidence, one is led to speculate that the intensity and extent of jealousy at a partner's extramarital sexual involvement is in direct proportion to the severity of the accepted cultural regulations against such involvements. In short such regulations do not prevent jealousy so much as effectively engender it.

11. It should not be forgotten that at the same time marriage excludes marital partners from sexual contact with others, it necessarily excludes those others from sexual contact with marital partners. Walls face two ways.

12. Those aspects of marriage law which seem to fall outside the pale of sexual property holding—for example, provisions for divorce if the husband fails to provide or is convicted of a felony or is an alcoholic—may themselves be seen as simply prescriptive characterizations of the sort of sexual property which the marriage partner must remain to retain satisfactory conjugal status: a kind of permanent warranty of the "good working order" of the sexual possession.

What constitutes the "good working order" of the conjugal possession is, of course, different in the case of the husband and in the case of the wife: an *asymmetry* within the marriage institution which, I gather, women's liberation movements are anxious to eradicate.

13. I think it is instructive to think of even the nonlegal aspects of marriage, for example, its sentiments as essentially private property structured. Thus the preoccupation of those experiencing conjugal sentiments with expressing how much "my very own," "my precious," the other is: with expressing, that is, how valuable and inviolable the ownership is and will remain.

14. I think the secret to the long mysterious incest taboo may well be the fact that in all its forms it protects sexual property: not only conjugal (as indicated above) but paternal and tribal as well. This crucial line of thought, however, requires extended separate treatment.

15. Sometimes—as with political patronage, criminal possession, *de facto* privileges and so forth—a *power* to exclude others exists with no corresponding "right" (just as sometimes a right to exclude exists with no corresponding power). Properly speaking, thus, I should here use the phrase "power to exclude," which covers "effective right to exclude" as well as all non-juridical enablements of this sort.

16. It is no doubt indispensable as well—in some form or other—to any private property order. Probably (if we take the history of Western society as our data base) the more thorough-going and developed the private property formation is, the more total the sexual ownership prescribed by the marriage institution.

17. Things in unlimited supply—like, presently, oxygen—are not of course related to people in this way.

18. This is, of course, a Freudian or quasi-Freudian claim. "Observation of daily life shows us," says Freud, "that most persons direct a very tangible part of their sexual motive powers to their professional or business activities" (Sigmund Freud, *Dictionary of Psychoanalysis*, ed. by Nandor Fodor and Frank Gaynor [New York: Fawcett Publications, Premier Paperbook, 1966], p. 139).

19. It might be argued that exclusive marriage also protects those physically less attractive persons who—in an "open" situation—might be unable to secure any sexual partnership at all. The force of this claim depends, I think, on improperly continuing to posit the very principle of exclusiveness which the "open" situation rules out (e.g., in the latter situation, x might be less attractive to y than z is and yet z not be rejected, any more than at present an intimate friend is rejected who is less talented than another intimate friend).

20. The sexual undercurrents of corporate advertisements, religious systems, racial propaganda and so on is too familiar to dwell on here.

21. It is also possible that exclusive marriage protects the adult youth power structure in the manner outlined on p. 257.

ON THE NATURE
AND VALUE OF MARRIAGE

Lyla H. O'Driscoll

> [Marriage] should be a school of sympathy in equality, of living together in love, without power on one side or obedience on the other.
>
> John Stuart Mill
> *On the Subjection of Women*

> [The married woman] is locked into a relationship which is oppressive politically, exhausting physically, stereotyped emotionally and sexually, and atrophying intellectually.
>
> Judith Brown
> *Toward a Female Liberation Movement*

Marriage—recently condemned as psychologically destructive, as socially pointless or ineffective, as oppressive, sexist, and morally repugnant—is the focus of new and lively scholarly and popular controversy.[1] This paper is an attempt to clarify some

From *Feminism and Philosophy,* ed. Mary Vetterling-Broggin, F. A. Elliston, and Jane English (Totowa, N.J.: Roman and Littlefield, 1977), pp. 249-263.

I would like to thank Robert Hollinger, Gerald P. O'Driscoll, Jr., Warren S. Quinn, Alyce Vrolyk, and Virginia Warren for helpful comments on earlier versions of this paper.

of the issues comprehended in this debate, in particular, certain conceptual issues that seem to have been neglected or misconstrued by both advocates and critics of marriage. The marriage controversy is not merely conceptual, of course; normative issues, including the justifiability of the institution, are familiar themes in the debate. Formulation of normative issues involves conceptual assumptions, however, including assumptions about the kinds of value that institutions and formal relations might have.

This paper does not directly treat the justifiability of marriage. Instead, it attempts to articulate a concept of marriage and suggests that partisans on both sides of controversy, in conceiving of marriage as an instrument, have misjudged its value. The discussion may have some significance for the issue of justification, however: without a clearly formulated concept of marriage and of the kinds of value it might have, attempts to assess its justifiability are likely to be futile.

I

One concept of marriage is the legal concept. Since the Anglo-American institution of heterosexual monogamy is frequently a target of criticism, it will be examined in order to ascertain some of the features of marriage as a legal institution.

According to Anglo-American custom and law, marriage is a social and legal status brought into existence by a civil contract. In the standard case, a marriage originates in a properly witnessed formal contract (distinct from any antenuptial financial contract) entered into by two persons, one male and one female; each party must be of legal age, must possess other requisites of contractual capacity, and must freely consent to the agreement.

The contract initiating a marriage differs in several ways from an ordinary business contract. Contracting a marriage requires the performance of special formalities; the contract cannot be terminated or rendered void except by action of a competent official. Business contractors have considerable leeway in formulating the terms of their agreement; those who contract a marriage are limited to the terms uniformly specified by law. The requirements of contractual capacity are especially stringent for marriage contracts. Marriage contractors are prohibited from having certain degrees of blood kinship and may be required to submit to a physician's examination. Furthermore, marriage contractors may have no prior marital relationships (unless legally dissolved), no concurrent marriages, and must enter the contractual relationship in pairs consisting of one male and one female.[2]

Each party to the marriage contract obtains certain rights and duties, including rights regarding support, fidelity, companionship, sexual congress, inheritance, confidentiality, and protection from interference by third parties.[3] In some cases, spouses choose not to seek enforcement of these rights; persons may even enter the legal relation intending not to seek enforcement—as in the case of a marriage of convenience or marriage to prevent the deportation of one contractor.

In jurisdictions recognizing common-law marriage, mutual rights to support, companionship, sexual congress, inheritance, etc., arise from an overt agreement to become spouses, cohabitation over a legally specified period of time, and public presentation and reputation as spouses.[4]

A leading English case characterizes marriage as "the voluntary union for life of one man and one woman, to the exclusion of all others."[5] The accuracy of the restriction, "for life," is dubious, for even at the time of the decision (1866), divorce was legal in England.[6]

English and American jurists disagree about whether procreation is a principal end of marriage. The leading English case is a 1948 ruling that one spouse's insistence on the use of contraceptives did not constitute willful refusal to consummate the marriage. The judge pointed out that

> the institution of marriage generally is not necessary for the procreation of children; nor does it appear to be a principal end of marriage as understood in Christendom. . . . In any view of Christian marriage, the essence of the matter, as it seems to me, is that the children, *if there be any,* should be born into a family, as that word is understood in Christendom generally, and in the case of a marriage between spouses of a particular faith that they should be brought up and nurtured in that faith. But this is not the same thing as saying that a marriage is not consummated or that procreation is the principal end of marriage.[7]

The judge also noted that it was not alleged in the suit that the sterility of a husband or the barrenness of a wife had some bearing on the question whether a marriage had been consummated.[8]

In the past, American jurists have regarded procreation as "the controlling purpose" of marriage, ruling that a wife's refusal to engage in uncontracepted intercourse constituted desertion of her husband or cruelty to him. In another case, the wife's refusal was adjudged a breach of her marital obligations and resulted in dismissal of her suit for separation and support.[9] Although a few jurisdictions have even ruled that a spouse's premarital sterility renders a marriage void, most have concurred with recent decisions more carefully distinguishing canon law from civil law and rejecting the claim that in civil law procreation is the chief end of marriage.[10]

A recent decision in a suit requesting legal recognition of homosexual alliances was rejected on the grounds that the common usage of the term "marriage" restricted its application to unions of persons of opposite sexes and that marriage is a union "uniquely involving procreation."[11]

The advocacy and existence of deliberately child-free marriages controverts the traditional assumption that the "unique involvement" of procreation in marriage is that it is the *purpose* of marriage. It also controverts the assumption that there is a necessary connection between the intention to become spouses and the intention to become parents. Once those assumptions are discarded, one rationale for nonrecognition of homosexual alliances is weakened.

The characterization of marriage as a legal institution is one concept of marriage; or, to be more precise, it is a concept of a form of marriage. Nonterminable, monogamous heterosexual marriage is one form of marriage. The qualifications can be variously altered to specify other logically possible forms of marriage.

Legal recognition of polyandry, for example, could be accomplished by altering the rules of contractual capacity so that a female could maintain prior or concurrent marital relationships. Legal recognition of homosexual monogamy could be accomplished by abolition of the requirement that persons enter the relationship in pairs consisting of one male and one female.

A multilateral marriage, which consists of three or more partners, "each of whom considers himself/herself to be married (or committed in a functionally analogous way) to more than one of the other partners,"[12] could be legally recognized if the requirement of pairing were deleted and the requirement that spouses have no previous or concurrent marriages were deleted (Multilateral marriage is distinct from polygyny, the marriage of one male to more than one female, and from polyandry. In polygyny, the females are not married to more than one person. It is characteristic of multilateral marriage that each spouse has more than one spouse.)

Successful criticisms of heterosexual monogamy do not suffice to demonstrate the unacceptability of the institution of marriage any more than successful criticism of absolute monarchy demonstrate the unacceptability of the institution of government. The concept of marriage is more abstract and general than the concept of heterosexual monogamy. Thus, for example, John McMurtry's critique of heterosexual monogamy, if well taken, demonstrates at most the unacceptability of that form of marriage (and then only when it has the consequences he attributes to it).[13]

Some constituents of the legal characterization of the institution, including the restriction of entry to male-female pairs, are not part of the concept of marriage. Other features characterize marriage as a legal institution, regardless of form: in law, marriage is a formalized relationship between legal adults, initiated by a more or less explicit agreement, and defined by legally specified rights and duties.

II

Although they are important, the legal aspects of marriage do not exhaust the concept of marriage. A broader conceptual problem remains, and it is one that cannot be resolved by a descriptive study of marriage in various cultures, a study in which common features, if any, are noted and combined as the essence of marriage.

Indeed, resolution of the broader conceptual problem is logically prior to empirical or descriptive study of the institution. The conceptual problem here is one of discerning the characteristics that distinguish a society having an institution of marriage from one lacking it. It is also a problem of determining what features of human association would have to be examined in order to resolve the question whether the institution of marriage exists.

Part of the solution to the broader conceptual problem is evident enough: whatever else it is, marriage is a social institution. The marital relation is not captured in a catalogue of changes in the spatial and temporal locations of human bodies; still less is it comprehended in a list of pieces of behavior. Marriage is a social institution that typically regulates (some) sexual activities and (in some way) the production of offspring. Marriage is of course not the only social institution that serves these functions. In order to determine whether the institution of marriage exists in a society, however, one would examine the social institutions that regulate sexual conduct and procreation.

The difference between a society with marriage and one without it is that in the former the rules constituting an existing social institution distinguish between illegitimate and legitimate progeny and characterize actual or possible instances of sexual congress as conjugal relations. The institution of marriage is partly constituted by rules that structure certain activities and define certain roles. Two-party heterosexual copulation, for example, cannot be adultery unless one of the participants is the spouse of a nonparticipant; it cannot be an instance of conjugal relations unless the participants are married to one another. Other activities structured by the rules constituting marriage include courtship, engagement, payment of dowry, divorce, and bigamy. By reference to the rules defining marriage, the bachelor can be distinguished from the husband, the spinster from the wife, the fiancée from the divorcée, the in-law from the parent, the bastard from the legitimate offspring.

Whatever its form, marriage is a social institution in which sexual intercourse is socially and legally legitimate and in which the production of socially and legally legitimate offspring is possible. Until effective contraception was generally available, it was tempting, in view of the connection between marriage and the production of *legitimate* offspring, to regard procreation as the purpose of marriage. It is important, however, to distinguish the device used to identify an institution as marriage from a specification of the purpose of the institution. The logical connection between marriage and procreation is not that procreation is the purpose of marriage but that it is in marriage that legitimate offspring can be produced.

Social and legal legitimacy are not always all-or-nothing matters. Some societies have not only marriages that confer full legitimacy on sexual intercourse and offspring but also legally recognized systems of concubinage. The legitimacy of sexual congress with a concubine and of the offspring of such a union may be more social than legal, but the relationship is nevertheless distinguished from, and more legitimate than, casual, fleeting sexual encounters or incestuous relationships.[14]

This concept of marriage, an explication by reference to the social functions of the institution, provides a general characterization compatible with the logical possibility of various forms of marriage and usable in deciding whether the institution exists in a particular society. A society lacks the institution if there is no social institution by reference to which one can distinguish conjugal and nonconjugal relations, legitimate offspring and bastards. (Such a society can nevertheless have rules to distinguish rape from consensual intercourse.)

Articulation of this concept of marriage will not end the marriage controversy, but it does indicate that the disputants may share some common ground. Critics of marriage have not generally advocated a society in which marriage does not exist, although some have ventured in the direction of such a proposal.[15] Individuals on both sides of the marriage controversy largely agree that a society will (and perhaps even should) have an institution or institutions to perform these functions.

Part of the marriage controversy is a dispute about whether the institution or institutions performing these functions should be legally defined and should be limited by law to a single form. Another aspect of the dispute focuses on the fact that if spouses become parents, they customarily take on the task of rearing the young. Some, who claim that the additional burden of childrearing inflicts excessive strain on marriages, suggest that this function can and should be separated from the legitimating function of marriage.

The purpose of this paper is not to resolve these disputes, but to formulate the issues more clearly and precisely so that others may approach them with a greater awareness of what is at stake.

III

Participants in the marriage controversy frequently assimilate the question of the justifiability of the institution with the question of the aptness of the institution as a means to the achievement of certain good ends such as human happiness. The issue is then treated as a problem of assessing the costs and benefits of particular arrangements, a problem whose resolution depends essentially on empirical evidence regarding the effects of the arrangements on the psychological, pecuniary, legal, and social well-being of spouses and offspring, and evidence regarding social advantages and disadvantages. Much of the feminist critique of heterosexual monogamy originates in such considerations.

But the issue of the justifiability of the institution is not as simple as this assimilation suggests. Among the complexities is the possibility that a marriage can be good even if its goodness does not lie solely in its aptness as a means of advancing good ends. Not all value is instrumental; the value of marriage, for the spouses, may lie not merely in what it *does* or can do (i.e., the effects it has) but in what it *is* or can be.

I would like to suggest that as an expression of friendship, marriage can have intrinsic value. I do not wish to deny, of course, that marriage can have instrumental value; the suggestion, rather, is that its instrumental value is not its only possible value.[16]

The thesis that marriage can have noninstrumental value for spouses is distinct from the claim that marriage is morally valuable. Something intrinsically valuable is valuable in itself, valuable because of its intrinsic properties, not because of its effects; something morally valuable is good on moral grounds, for example, its aptness as a means to morally praiseworthy ends. Something can be intrinsically good without being morally good; in the view of the hedonistic utilitarian, for example, pleasure is intrinsically and nonmorally good.[17]

It is evident that expressions of friendship can have noninstrumental value. A service performed as a gesture of friendship, for example, can be instrumentally useful, and can also be valuable because it is done by a certain person out of certain motives. In such gestures, friendship can be expressed for its own sake and not for the sake of some external objective. The pledge of marriage can be a gesture of friendship; it creates a public and relatively permanent arrangement that symbolizes the dispositions and attitudes constitutive of friendship.

It might be thought that to characterize the marriage pledge and status as expressions of friendship trivializes the relationship between spouses, reducing it to "mere friendship." To suppose this is to confuse merely being friendly and being friends. Although friendships vary in the degree of affection, intimacy, sharing, and trust involved, these attitudes and behavior are essential to friendship; in the paradigm case—close (but not the closest possible) friendship—the depth of affection amounts to love.

IV

The difference between friendship and ordinary social associations, as described by Kant, is that in ordinary social associations

> we do not enter completely into the social relation. The greater part of our disposition is withheld; there is no immediate outpouring of our feelings, dispositions and judgments. We voice only the judgments that seem advisable in the circumstances. A constraint, a mistrust of others, rests upon all of us, so that we withhold something, concealing our weaknesses to escape contempt, or even withholding our opinions.[18]

If marriage is to express friendship, friendship must exist; if there is to be friendship, certain attitudes must exist and certain kinds of shared activities must occur.[19] Two persons are friends if and only if, first, they regard one another as worthy of respect and trust; second, they are disposed to seek one another's company (for the sake of *that person's* company, not merely for the sake of company); third, they are disposed to seek one another's well-being; and fourth, they have these dispositions because they are fond of one another.

A marriage that expresses friendship reveals and symbolizes attitudes such as affection for and commitment to a particular person. Such a relation is necessarily personal. Affection *for a person* is distinct from regard for someone's virtues and admiration for someone's characteristics, although it may be causally connected with these virtues and characteristics. Admiration and approval of a person's characteristics diminish if the characteristics dwindle; admiration of an artist's ability declines with the artist's declining skill. Affection for a person, on the other hand, does not diminish in the face of diminution of admired and approved qualities in the person. Love of a person, as Shakespeare points out, does not alter when it alteration finds. Affection for a person applies to a particular being; it cannot be automatically transferred to another instantiation of similar characteristics.[20]

Mutual trust and respect underlie the sharing of confidences that is typical of friends. Friendship between two persons entails the existence of durable tendencies; the affection of friends is no transitory fondness or attraction, nor is it unrequited.

Friends do not value one another primarily or merely as means; someone who values another primarily or merely because he has certain instrumentally useful traits values him as an instrument. If customer Jones's association with grocer Smith is primarily or solely instrumentally valuable to both parties, each individual, as far as the other is concerned, is a replaceable component in the arrangement. It is a matter of indifference to Smith whether Jones or some other equally good instrument occupies the role of customer; Jones is indifferent to the particular person occupying the grocer's role, as long as the services are efficiently provided.

In short, if people value one another's characteristics as instruments, their relation is essentially impersonal, not a valuing of a particular person, but an appreciation of the usefulness of certain traits that happen to be embodied in one person but would be equally valuable if found in another. Smith values Jones's patronage, the business he brings to the store; Smith would value equally any other instantiation of the properties that make Jones a good customer. Likewise, Jones values the performance of certain services, and would value equally another instantiation of the characteristics that make Smith a good grocer.

The importance of affection in marriage is often confined to or confused with the importance of erotic love. Although erotic love is one facet of marital affection, others include the tendency to find companionship in one's spouse's company *(philia)* and the tendency to give oneself nonsexually and unselfish—to invest oneself in the relationship.

Activities, including sexual activities, are enhanced in value by being shared with, or done for, the sake of someone of whom the agent is fond. Sexual desire can of course be satisfied in casual encounters. But the mutual respect, trust, and affection that subsist between friends can render sexual activity intrinsically as well as instrumentally valuable—valued because it is shared with a valued individual.[21]

Friends are not necessarily of the same sex; nor are friends necessarily of opposite sexes.

Friendship is neither exclusive nor necessarily transitive. Someone may have several friends, including people who are not mutual friends. It is unlikely, however, that anyone could maintain a large number of close friendships. The problem is not conceptual but empirical: intimacy and intense affection are psychologically demanding and can probably subsist only in small groups.

Not all affectionate relationships are friendships. A parent may be fond of a newborn child. Since the affection is not reciprocated and since mutual trust and respect are not possible, the relationship is not friendship.

Friends need not have made a formal or explicit pledge of friendship. In some cases, one's commitment to a friend is simply a tendency to seek his well-being for his sake. This tendency may exist without having been deliberately cultivated; the principle of action may be unformulated, and the agent may even be unable to formulate it. If the agent's behavior, attitudes, and beliefs are generally consistent with his regarding the other's well-being as a good, and if the agent is disposed to alter his behavior, attitudes, and beliefs to conform to the belief that the other person's well-being is a good, then the person may be characterized as having an inchoate principle of action committing him to seek the other person's good for that person's sake.

Implicit commitment to a friend may consist of a tendency, should the occasion arise, upon reflection to admit the existence of activities, attitudes, and dispositions essential to friendship and to identify the other as a friend.[22] There is a sense, therefore, in which friendship can be initiated and terminated voluntarily. Upon becoming aware of the existence of the relevant attitudes, dispositions, and activities, one can choose to discontinue the activities and seek to eradicate or modify the attitudes and dispositions. Such a choice amounts to refusing to make an explicit commitment to the person, a refusal to affirm the dispositions, attitudes, and activities of friendship, and a refusal to sustain a friendship.

On the other hand, people might choose to affirm the relationship, and furthermore to formalize it in a ceremony such as the ritual of blood brotherhood. Such a public declaration is a fully explicit statement of a willingness to pursue mutual well-being; it is a joint pledge of continuing association, loyalty, and fidelity. A public declaration is not necessary in order to make such a commitment explicit, but it can serve to distinguish an especially serious and significant friendship from other associations.

At any of these levels of explicitness, the commitment of friendship need not be a commitment to the exclusivity of the friendship: even when one has publicly declared the great significance of a particular friendship, it is logically possible to ascribe (and to declare publicly) the equal significance of another friendship.

V

Marriage can single out an especially significant friendship (if monogamous) or especially significant friendships (if multilateral, polygamous, or polyandrous); it can distinguish such relationships from less profound, serious, and durable affections and commitments.

As has been pointed out, friends are disposed to seek one another's company and well-being, and they have these tendencies because they are fond of one another. Between (or among) friends, these dispositions may be manifested in the desire to share domicile and in the desire of each to participate fully in the achievement of the other's aspirations and the execution of the other's plans—the desire to share in the other's life and (good or ill) fortune. Individuals having these desires might reasonably choose a formal declaration to express, affirm, and cement their intentions, and their commitment to, and affection for, one another. They regard their relationship, and its formal expression, as having intrinsic value.

Their willingness to declare their intention to pursue joint well-being openly and in a way that creates legal and moral obligations signifies their confidence in the durability and importance of the relationship. Their willingness to make such a declaration also signifies their willingness to risk censure, from their spouses or from others, should they fail to fulfill their obligations; and it also signifies their willingness to have these obligations enforced. The willingness of friends to make such a declaration and to undertake such obligations signifies their willingness to share in one another's good (or ill) fortune, and to incur the risks inherent in an enduring and legally recognized relationship, including the risk that pursuit of mutual well-being will necessitate some compromise and sacrifice of individual well-being.[23]

No one marries all his friends, not even all his especially significant friends. But considerations of the intrinsic value of the relationship might, in some (rare) cases, account for the decision to marry. Such considerations could provide a satisfactory reason for initiating or continuing a marriage if they were (as they usually are) conjoined with judgments about the instrumental value of a legally recognized bond (for example, the supposition that the special legal and social status accorded to spouses fosters a stable, profound, and enduring affection and enhances the attitudes and commitments of friendship).

Marriage expressive of friendship can be heterosexual, homosexual, multilateral, polygynous, or polyandrous. Thus, this account of the nature and possible value of marriage for spouses is compatible with the conceivability of a variety of forms of marriage.

This discussion is not intended as proof of the justifiability of the institution of marriage. I have considered its possible value for spouses. It may be that the intrinsic value of the relationship for spouses is insufficient to show the institution acceptable from a moral point of view; there may be overriding objections based on other considerations. I have attempted only to outline a different perspective for the assessment of marriage, to suggest that the value of marriage, for spouses, may be intrinsic as well as instrumental.

NOTES

1. Instances of such criticisms can be found in the following: Robin Morgan, ed., *Sisterhood Is Powerful* (New York: Random House, Vintage Books, 1970), pp. 438-54, 514-48; Vivian Gornick and Barbara K. Moran, eds., *Woman In Sexist Society* (New York: New American Library, Mentor Books, 1971), pp. xxvi, 145-86. On the legal effects of marriage on women, see Leo Kanowitz, *Women and the Law* (Albuquerque: University of New Mexico Press, 1969), chap. 3.

2. P. M. Bromley, *Family Law* (London: Butterworth, 1971), pp. 11-12.

3. Morris Ploscowe, Henry H. Foster, Jr., and Doris Jonas Fried, *Family Law* (Boston: Little, Brown, 1972), p. 43.

4. Ibid., pp. 79-81. See also Stuart J. Stein, "Common Law Marriage," *Journal of Family Law* 9 (1970): 271-99.

5. Ploscowe, Foster, and Fried, pp. 16-17. The case is *Hyde* v. *Hyde*.

6. Bromley, p. 12.

7. J. C. Hall, *Sources of Family Law* (Cambridge: Cambridge University Press, 1966), p. 2. The case is *Baxter* v. *Baxter.* Emphasis added.

8. Hall, p. 2.

9. Joseph Goldstein and Jay Katz, *The Family and the Law* (New York: Free Press, 1965), pp. 823-28. The cases are *Raymond* v. *Raymond, Forbes* v. *Forbes,* and *Baretta* v. *Baretta.*

10. Goldstein and Katz, p. 816; Monrad G. Paulsen, Walter Wallington, and Julius Goebel, Jr., *Domestic Relations,* 2d ed. (Mineola, N.Y.: Foundation Press, 1974), p. 155. The cases are *Van Nierke* v. *Van Nierke* and *T.* v. *M.*

11. Paulsen, Wallington, and Goebel, pp. 35-36. The case is *Baker* v. *Nelson.*

12. Larry Constantine and Joan Constantine, *Group Marriage* (New York: Macmillan, 1973), p. 28.

13. John McMurtry, "Monogramy: A Critique," Monist 56 (1972): 587-99; reprinted in *Philosophy and Sex,* ed. Robert Baker and Frederick Elliston (Buffalo, N.Y.: Prometheus Books, 1975). Other relevant essays in the same anthology are David Palmer, "The Consolation of the Wedded," and Michael D. Bayles, "Marriage, Love, and Procreation."

14. See William J. Goode, *World Revolution and Family Patterns* (New York: Free Press, 1963), pp. 282-85, on concubinage in China; and idem. *The Family* (Englewood Cliffs, N.J.: Prentice-Hall, 1964) chap. 3.

15. David E. Engdahl, "Medieval Metaphysics and English Marriage Laws," *Journal of Family Law* 8 (1969): 381-97.

16. The thesis that formalized relationships can be intrinsically valuable is defended in John Rawls, *A Theory of Justice* (Cambridge: Harvard University Press, 1971), pp. 520-29. In *An Anatomy of Values* (Cambridge: Harvard University Press, 1971), pp. 117-21, Charles Fried also defends this claim and applies it to legal institutions in general and to marriage in particular. Fried defines an *expressive* relation as one that has intrinsic value (p. 118n). In this discussion, however, "express" is used in the sense of "serving to manifest, reveal, or symbolize."

17. On the notion of intrinsic value, see William Frankena, *Ethics,* 2d ed. (Englewood Cliffs, N.J.: Prentice-Hall, 1973), p. 82.

18. Immanuel Kant, *Lectures on Ethics* (New York: Harper & Row, Harper Torchbooks, 1963), p. 205.

19. This account of friendship substantially follows Elizabeth Telfer, "Friendship," *Proceedings of the Aristotelian Society* 71 (1970-71): 222-41. The view is rooted in the doctrines of Kant and Aristotle. See especially Immanuel Kant, *The Metaphysical Principles of Virtue* (Indianapolis: Bobbs-Merrill, 1964), and Aristotle, *Nichomachean Ethics* (Indianapolis: Bobbs-Merrill, 1962), book 8.

20. Cf. Gregory Vlastos, "Justice and Equality," in *Social Justice,* ed. Richard B. Brandt (Englewood Cliffs, N.J.: Prentice-Hall, Spectrum Books, 1962), pp. 43-44, and idem, "The Individual As an Object of Love in Plato," in *Platonic Studies* (Princeton: Princeton University Press, 1973), pp. 3-34.

21. Cf. Carl Cohen, "Sex, Birth Control and Human Life," *Ethics* 79 (1969): 257. Cohen argues for the intrinsic worth of sexual passion. In "Marriage, Love, and Procreation" (above, n. 13), pp. 197-98, Michael Bayles argues for the intrinsic value of relationships intentionally of indefinite duration, claiming that they are superior to relationships of intentionally limited duration.

22. See Fried (above, n. 16), pp. 23-24, for a formulation of the distinction between inchoate and implicit principles.

23. Bayles (above, n. 13), p. 198, adduces similar considerations in discussing the value of relationships that are intentionally of indefinite duration.

PARENTS AND CHILDREN

LICENSING PARENTS

Hugh LaFollette

In this essay I shall argue that the state should require all parents to be licensed. My main goal is to demonstrate that the licensing of parents is theoretically desirable, though I shall also argue that a workable and just licensing program actually could be established.

My strategy is simple. After developing the basic rationale for the licensing of parents, I shall consider several objections to the proposal and argue that these objections fail to undermine it. I shall then isolate some striking similarities between this licensing program and our present policies on the adoption of children. If we retain these adoption policies—as we surely should—then, I argue, a general licensing program should also be established. Finally, I shall briefly suggest that the reason many people object to licensing is that they think parents, particularly biological parents, own or have natural sovereignty over their children.

Regulating Potentially Harmful Activities

Our society normally regulates a certain range of activities; it is illegal to perform these activities unless one has received prior permission to do so. We require automobile operators to have licenses. We forbid people from practicing medicine, law, pharmacy, or psychiatry unless they have satisfied certain licensing requirements.

Society's decision to regulate just these activities is not ad hoc. The decision to restrict admission to certain vocations and to forbid some people from driving is based on an eminently plausible, though not often explicitly formulated, rationale. We require drivers to be licensed because driving an auto is an activity which is potentially harmful to others, safe performance of the activity requires a certain competence, and we have a moderately reliable procedure for determining that competence. The potential harm is obvious: incompetent drivers can and do maim and kill people. The best way we have of limiting this harm without sacrificing the benefits of automobile travel is to require that all drivers demonstrate at least minimal competence. We likewise license doctors, lawyers, and psychologists because they perform activities which can harm others. Obviously they must be proficient if they are to perform these activities properly, and we have moderately

From *Philosophy & Public Affairs* 9, no. 2, 1980, pp. 182-197. © 1980 by Princeton University Press.

reliable procedures for determining proficiency.[1] Imagine a world in which everyone could legally drive a car, in which everyone could legally perform surgery, prescribe medications, dispense drugs, or offer legal advice. Such a world would hardly be desirable.

Consequently, any activity that is potentially harmful to others and requires certain demonstrated competence for its safe performance, is subject to regulation—that is, it is theoretically desirable that we regulate it. If we also have a reliable procedure for determining whether someone has the requisite competence, then the action is not only subject to regulation but ought, all things considered, to be regulated.

It is particularly significant that we license these hazardous activities, even though denying a license to someone can severely inconvenience and even harm that person. Furthermore, available competency tests are not 100 percent accurate. Denying someone a driver's license in our society, for example, would inconvenience that person acutely. In effect that person would be prohibited from working, shopping, or visiting in places reachable only by car. Similarly, people denied vocational licenses are inconvenienced, even devastated. We have all heard of individuals who had the "life-long dream" of becoming physicians or lawyers, yet were denied that dream. However, the realization that some people are disappointed or inconvenienced does not diminish our conviction that we must regulate occupations or activities that are potentially dangerous to others. Innocent people must be protected even if it means that others cannot pursue activities they deem highly desirable.

Furthermore, we maintain licensing procedures even though our competency tests are sometimes inaccurate. Some people competent to perform the licensed activity (for example, driving a car) will be unable to demonstrate competence (they freeze up on the driver's test). Others may be incompetent, yet pass the test (they are lucky or certain aspects of competence—for example, the sense of responsibility—are not tested). We recognize clearly—or should recognize clearly—that no test will pick out all and only competent drivers, physicians, lawyers, and so on. Mistakes are inevitable. This does not mean we should forget that innocent people may be harmed by faulty regulatory procedures. In fact, if the procedures are sufficiently faulty, we should cease regulating that activity entirely until more reliable tests are available. I only want to emphasize here that tests need not be perfect. Where moderately reliable tests are available, licensing procedures should be used to protect innocent people from incompetents.[2]

These general criteria for regulatory licensing can certainly be applied to parents. First, parenting is an activity potentially very harmful to children. The potential for harm is apparent: each year more than half a million children are physically abused or neglected by their parents.[3] Many millions more are psychologically abused or neglected—not given love, respect, or a sense of self-worth. The results of this maltreatment are obvious. Abused children bear the physical and psychological scars of maltreatment throughout their lives. Far too often they turn to crime.[4] They are far more likely than others to abuse their own children.[5] Even if these maltreated children never harm anyone, they will probably never be well-adjusted, happy adults. Therefore, parenting clearly satisfies the first criterion of activities subject to regulation.

The second criterion is also incontestably satisfied. A parent must be competent if he is to avoid harming his children; even greater competence is required if he is to do the "job" well. But not everyone has this minimal competence. Many people lack the knowledge needed to rear children adequately. Many others lack the requisite energy, temperament, or stability. Therefore, child-rearing manifestly satisfies both criteria of activities subject to regulation. In fact, I dare say that parenting is a paradigm of such activities since the potential for harm is so great (both in the extent of harm any one person can suffer and in the number of people potentially harmed) and the need for competence is so evident. Consequently, there is good reason to believe that all parents should be licensed. The only ways to avoid this conclusion are to deny the need for licensing *any* potentially harmful activity; to deny that I have identified the standard criteria of activities which should be regulated; to deny that parenting satisfies the standard criteria; to show that even though parenting satisfies the standard criteria there are special reasons why licensing parents is not theoretically desirable; or to show that there is no reliable and just procedure for implementing this program.

While developing my argument for licensing I have already identified the standard criteria for activities that should be regulated, and I have shown that they can properly be applied to parenting. One could deny the legitimacy of regulation by licensing, but in doing so one would condemn not only the regulation of parenting, but also the regulation of drivers, physicians, druggists, and doctors. Furthermore, regulation of hazardous activities appears to be a fundamental task of any stable society.

Thus only two objections remain. In the next section I shall see if there are any special reasons why licensing parents is not theoretically desirable. Then, in the following section, I shall examine several practical objections designed to demonstrate that even if licensing were theoretically desirable, it could not be justly implemented.

Theoretical Objections to Licensing

Licensing is unacceptable, someone might say, since people have a right to have children, just as they have rights to free speech and free religious expression. They do not need a license to speak freely or to worship as they wish. Why? Because they have a right to engage in these activities. Similarly, since people have a right to have children, any attempt to license parents would be unjust.

This is an important objection since many people find it plausible, if not self-evident. However, it is not as convincing as it appears. The specific rights appealed to in this analogy are not without limitations. Both slander and human sacrifice are prohibited by law; both could result from the unrestricted exercise of freedom of speech and freedom of religion. Thus, even if people have these rights, they may sometimes be limited in order to protect innocent people. Consequently, even if people had a right to have children, that right might also be limited in order to protect innocent people, in this case children. Secondly, the phrase "right to have children" is ambiguous; hence, it is important to isolate its most plausible meaning in this context. Two possible interpretations are not credible and can be dismissed summarily. It is implausible to claim either that infertile people have rights to be *given* children or that people have rights to intentionally create children biologically without incurring any subsequent responsibility to them.

A third interpretation, however, is more plausible, particularly when coupled with observations about the degree of intrusion into one's life that the licensing scheme represents. On this interpretation people have a right to rear children if they make good-faith efforts to rear procreated children the best way they see fit. One might defend this claim on the ground that licensing would require too much intrusion into the lives of sincere applicants.

Undoubtedly one should be wary of unnecessary governmental intervention into individuals' lives. In this case, though, the intrusion would not often be substantial, and when it is, it would be warranted. Those granted licenses would face merely minor intervention; only those denied licenses would encounter marked intrusion. This encroachment, however, is a necessary side-effect of licensing parents—just as it is for automobile and vocational licensing. In addition, as I shall argue in more detail later, the degree of intrusion arising from a general licensing program would be no more than, and probably less than, the present (and presumably justifiable) encroachment into the lives of people who apply to adopt children. Furthermore, since some people hold unacceptable views about what is best for children (they think children should be abused regularly), people do not automatically have rights to rear children just because they will rear them in a way they deem appropriate.[6]

Consequently, we come to a somewhat weaker interpretation of this right claim: a person has a right to rear children if he meets certain minimal standards of child rearing. Parents must not abuse or neglect their children and must also provide for the basic needs of the children. This claim of right is certainly more credible than the previously canvassed alternatives, though some people might still reject this claim in situations where exercise of the right would lead to negative consequences, for example, to overpopulation. More to the point, though, this conditional right is compatible with licensing. On this interpretation one has a right to have children only if one is not going to abuse or neglect them. Of course the very purpose of licensing is just to determine whether people *are* going to abuse or neglect their children. If the determination is made that someone will maltreat children, then that person is subject to the limitations of the right to have children and can legitimately be denied a parenting license.

In fact, this conditional way of formulating the right to have children provides a model for formulating all alleged rights to engage in hazardous activities. Consider, for example, the right to drive a car. People do not have an unconditional right to drive, although they do have a right to drive if they are competent.

Similarly, people do not have an unconditional right to practice medicine; they have a right only if they are demonstrably competent. Hence, denying a driver's or physician's license to someone who has not demonstrated the requisite competence does not deny that person's rights. Likewise, on this model, denying a parenting license to someone who is not competent does not violate that person's rights.

Of course someone might object that the right is conditional on actually being a person who will abuse or neglect children, whereas my proposal only picks out those we can reasonably predict will abuse children. Hence, this conditional right *would* be incompatible with licensing.

There are two ways to interpret this objection and it is important to distinguish these divergent formulations. First, the objection could be a way of questioning our ability to predict reasonably and accurately whether people would maltreat their own children. This is an important practical objection, but I will defer discussion of it until the next section. Second, this objection could be a way of expressing doubt about the moral propriety of the prior restraint licensing requires. A parental licensing program would deny licenses to applicants judged to be incompetent even though they had never maltreated any children. This practice would be in tension with our normal skepticism about the propriety of prior restraint.

Despite this healthy skepticism, we do sometimes use prior restraint. In extreme circumstances we may hospitalize or imprison people judged insane, even though they are not legally guilty of any crime, simply because we predict they are likely to harm others. More typically, though prior restraint is used only if the restriction is not terribly onerous and the restricted activity is one which could lead easily to serious harm. Most types of licensing (for example, those for doctors, drivers, and druggists) fall into this latter category. They require prior restraint to prevent serious harm, and generally the restraint is minor—though it is important to remember that some individuals will find it oppressive. The same is true of parental licensing. The purpose of licensing is to prevent serious harm to children. Moreover, the prior restraint required by licensing would not be terribly onerous for many people. Certainly the restraint would be far less extensive than the presumably justifiable prior restraint of, say, insane criminals. Criminals preventively detained and mentally ill people forceably hospitalized are denied most basic liberties, while those denied parental licenses would be denied only that one specific opportunity. They could still vote, work for political candidates, speak on controversial topics, and so on. Doubtless some individuals would find the restraint onerous. But when compared to other types of restraint currently practiced, and when judged in light of the severity of harm maltreated children suffer, the restraint appears *relatively* minor.

Furthermore, we could make certain, as we do with most licensing programs, that individuals denied licenses are given the opportunity to reapply easily and repeatedly for a license. Thus, many people correctly denied licenses (because they are incompetent) would choose (perhaps it would be provided) to take counseling or therapy to improve their chances of passing the next test. On the other hand, most of those mistakenly denied licenses would probably be able to demonstrate in a later test that they would be competent parents.

Consequently, even though one needs to be wary of prior restraint, if the potential for harm is great and the restraint is minor relative to the harm we are trying to prevent—as it would be with parental licensing—then such restraint is justified. This objection, like all the theoretical objections reviewed, has failed.

Practical Objections to Licensing

I shall now consider five practical objections to licensing. Each objection focuses on the problems or difficulties of implementing this proposal. According to these objections, licensing is (or may be) theoretically desirable; nevertheless, it cannot be efficiently and justly implemented.

The first objection is that there may not be, or we may not be able to discover, adequate criteria of "a good parent." We simply do not have the knowledge, and it is unlikely that we could ever obtain the knowledge, that would enable us to distinguish adequate from inadequate parents.

Clearly there is some force to this objection. It is highly improbable that we can formulate criteria that would distinguish precisely between good and less than good parents. There is too much we do not know about child development and adult psychology. My proposal, however, does not demand that we make these fine distinctions. It does not demand that we license only the best parents; rather it is designed to exclude only the very bad ones.[7] This is not just a semantic difference, but a substantive one. Although we do not have infallible criteria for picking out good parents, we undoubtedly can identify bad ones—those who will abuse or neglect their children. Even though we could have a lively debate about the range of freedom a child should be given or the appropriateness of corporal punishment, we do not wonder if a parent who severely beats or neglects a child is adequate. We know that person isn't. Consequently, we do have reliable and useable criteria for determining who is a bad parent; we have the criteria necessary to make a licensing program work.

The second practical objection to licensing is that there is no reliable way to predict who will maltreat their children. Without an accurate predictive test, licensing would be not only unjust, but also a waste of time. Now I recognize that as a philosopher (and not a psychologist, sociologist, or social worker), I am on shaky ground if I make sweeping claims about the present or future abilities of professionals to produce such predictive tests. Nevertheless, there are some relevant observations I can offer.

Initially, we need to be certain that the demands on predictive tests are not unreasonable. For example, it would be improper to require that tests be 100 percent accurate. Procedures for licensing drivers, physicians, lawyers, druggists, etc., plainly are not 100 percent (or anywhere near 100 percent) accurate. Presumably we recognize these deficiencies yet embrace the procedures anyway. Consequently, it would be imprudent to demand considerably more exacting standards for the tests used in licensing parents.

In addition, from what I can piece together, the practical possibilities for constructing a reliable predictive test are not all that gloomy. Since my proposal does not require that we make fine-line distinctions between good and less than good parents, but rather that we weed out those who are potentially very bad, we can use existing tests that claim to isolate relevant predictive characteristics— whether a person is violence-prone, easily frustrated, or unduly self-centered. In fact, researchers at Nashville General Hospital have developed a brief interview questionnaire which seems to have significant predictive value. Based on their data, the researchers identified 20 percent of the interviewees as a "risk group"—those having great potential for serious problems. After one year they found "the incidence of major breakdown in parent-child interaction in the risk group was approximately four to five times as great as in the low risk group."[8] We also know that parents who maltreat children often have certain identifiable experiences; for example, most of them were themselves maltreated as children. Consequently, if we combined our information about these parents with certain psychological test results, we would probably be able to predict with reasonable accuracy which people will maltreat their children.

However, my point is not to argue about the precise reliability of present tests. I cannot say emphatically that we now have accurate predictive tests. Nevertheless, even if such tests are not available, we could undoubtedly develop them. For example, we could begin a longitudinal study in which all potential parents would be required to take a specified battery of tests. Then these parents could be "followed" to discover which ones abused or neglected their children. By correlating test scores with information on maltreatment, a usable, accurate test could be fashioned. Therefore, I do not think that the present unavailability of such tests (if they are unavailable) would count against the legitimacy of licensing parents.

The third practical objection is that even if a reliable test for ascertaining who would be an acceptable parent were available, administrators would unintentionally misuse that test. These unintentional mistakes would clearly harm innocent individuals. Therefore, so the argument goes, this proposal ought to be scrapped. This objection can be dispensed with fairly easily unless one assumes there is some special reason to believe that more mistakes will be made in administering parenting licenses than in other regulatory activities. No matter how reliable our proceedings are, there will always be mistakes. We may license a physician who, through incompetence, would cause the death of a patient; or we may mistakenly deny a physician's license to someone who would be competent. But the fact that mistakes are made does not and should not lead us to abandon attempts to determine competence. The harm done in these cases could be far worse than the harm of mistakenly denying a person a parenting license. As far as I can tell, there is no reason to believe that more mistakes will be made here than elsewhere.

The fourth proposed practical objection claims that any testing procedure will be intentionally abused. People administering the process will disqualify people they dislike, or people who espouse views they dislike, from rearing children.

The response to this objection is parallel to the response to the previous objection, namely, that there is no reason to believe that the licensing of parents is more likely to be abused than driver's license tests or other regulatory procedures. In addition, individuals can be protected from prejudicial treatment by pursuing appeals available to them. Since the licensing test can be taken on numerous occasions, the likelihood of the applicant's working with different administrative personnel increases and therefore the likelihood decreases that intentional abuse could ultimately stop a qualified person from rearing children. Consequently, since the probability of such abuse is not more than, and may even be less than, the intentional abuse of judicial and other regulatory authority, this objection does not give us any reason to reject the licensing of parents.

The fifth objection is that we could never adequately, reasonably, and fairly enforce such a program. That is, even if we could establish a reasonable and fair way of determining which people would be inadequate parents, it would be difficult, if not impossible, to enforce the program. How would one deal with violators and what could we do with babies so conceived? There are difficult problems here, no doubt, but they are not insurmountable. We might not punish parents at all—we might just remove the children and put them up for adoption. However, even if we are presently uncertain about the precise way to establish a just and effective form of enforcement, I do not see why this should undermine my licensing proposal. If it is important enough to protect children from being mal-treated by parents, then surely a reasonable enforcement procedure can be secured. At least we should assume one can be unless someone shows that it cannot.

An Analogy With Adoption

So far I have argued that parents should be licensed. Undoubtedly many readers find this claim extremely radical. It is revealing to notice, however, that this program is not as radical as it seems. Our moral and legal systems already recognize that not everyone is capable of rearing children well. In fact, well-entrenched laws require adoptive parents to be investigated—in much the same ways and for much the same reasons as in the general licensing program advocated here. For example, we do not allow just anyone to adopt a child; nor do we let someone adopt without first estimating the likelihood of the person's being a good parent. In fact, the adoptive process is far more rigorous than the general licensing procedures I envision. Prior to adoption the candidates must first formally apply to adopt a child. The applicants are then subjected to an exacting home study to determine whether they really want to have children and whether they are capable of caring for and rearing them adequately. No one is allowed to adopt a child until the administrators can reasonably predict that the person will be an adequate parent. The results of these procedures are impressive. Despite the trauma children often face before they are finally adopted, they are five times less likely to be abused than children reared by their biological parents.[9]

Nevertheless we recognize, or should recognize, that these demanding procedures exclude some people who would be adequate parents. The selection criteria may be inadequate; the testing procedures may be somewhat unreliable. We may make mistakes. Probably there is some intentional abuse of the system. Adoption procedures intrude directly in the applicants' lives. Yet we continue the present adoption policies because we think it better to mistakenly deny some people the opportunity to adopt than to let just anyone adopt.

Once these features of our adoption policies are clearly identified, it becomes quite apparent that there are striking parallels between the general licensing program I have advocated and our present adoption system. Both programs have the same aim—protecting children. Both have the same drawbacks and are subject to the same abuses. The only obvious dissimilarity is that the adoption requirements are *more* rigorous than those proposed for the general licensing program. Consequently, if we think it is so important to protect adopted children, even though people who want to adopt are less likely than biological parents to maltreat their children, then we should likewise afford the same protection to children reared by their biological parents.

I suspect, though, that many people will think the cases are not analogous. The cases are relevantly different, someone might retort, because biological parents have a natural affection for their children and the strength of this affection makes it unlikely that parents would maltreat their biologically produced children.

Even if it were generally true that parents have special natural affections for their biological offspring, that does not mean that all parents have enough affection to keep them from maltreating their children. This should be apparent given the number of children abused each year by their biological parents. Therefore, even if there is generally such a bond, that does not explain why we should not have licensing procedures to protect children of parents who do not have a sufficiently strong bond. Consequently, if we continue our practice of regulating the adoption of children, and certainly we should, we are rationally compelled to establish a licensing program for all parents.

However, I am not wedded to a strict form of licensing. It may well be that there are alternative ways of regulating parents which would achieve the desired results—the protection of children—without strictly prohibiting nonlicensed people from rearing children. For example, a system of tax incentives for licensed parents, and protective services scrutiny of nonlicensed parents, might adequately protect children. If it would, I would endorse the less drastic measure. My principal concern is to protect children from maltreatment by parents. I begin by advocating the more strict form of licensing since that is the standard method of regulating hazardous activities.

I have argued that all parents should be licensed by the state. This licensing program is attractive, not because state intrusion is inherently judicious and efficacious, but simply because it seems to be the best way to prevent children from being reared by incompetent parents. Nonetheless, even after considering the previous arguments, many people will find the proposal a useful academic exercise, probably silly, and possibly even morally perverse. But why? Why do most of us find this proposal unpalatable, particularly when the arguments supporting it are good and the objections to it are philosophically flimsy?

I suspect the answer is found in a long-held, deeply ingrained attitude toward children, repeatedly reaffirmed in recent court decisons, and present, at least to some degree, in almost all of us. The belief is that parents own, or at least have natural sovereignty over, their children.[10] It does not matter precisely how this belief is described, since on both views parents legitimately exercise extensive and virtually unlimited control over their children. Others can properly interfere with or criticize parental decisions only in unusual and tightly prescribed circumstances—for example, when parents severely and repeatedly abuse their children. In all other cases, the parents reign supreme.

This belief is abhorrent and needs to be supplanted with a more child-centered view. Why? Briefly put, this attitude has adverse effects on children and on the adults these children will become. Parents who hold this view may well maltreat the children. If these parents happen to treat their children well, it is only because they want to, not because they think their children deserve or have a right to good treatment. Moreover, this belief is manifestly at odds with the conviction that parents should prepare children for life as adults. Children subject to parents who perceive children in this way are likely to be adequately prepared for adulthood. Hence, to prepare children for life as adults and to protect them from maltreatment, this attitude toward children must be dislodged. As I have argued, licensing is a viable way to protect children. Furthermore, it would increase the likelihood that more children will be adequately prepared for life as adults than is now the case.

NOTES

For helpful comments and criticisms, I am indebted to Jeffrey Gold, Chris Hackler, James Rachels, and especially to William Aiken, George Graham, and the Editors of the journal. A somewhat different version of this essay will appear in the Proceeding of the Loyola University (Chicago) Symposium, *Justice for the Child within the Family Context.*

Thanks are due to the directors of the symposium for kind permission to publish the essay in *Philosophy & Public Affairs.*

1. When practice of a profession or calling requires special knowledge or skill and intimately affects public health, morals, order or safety, or general welfare, legislature may prescribe reasonable qualifications for persons desiring to pursue such profession or calling and require them to demonstrate possession of such qualifications by examination on subjects with which such profession or calling has to deal as a condition precedent to right to follow that profession or calling." 50 SE 2nd 735 (1949). Also see 199 US 306, 318 (1905) and 123 US 623, 661 (1887).

2. What counts as a moderately reliable test for these purposes will vary from circumstance to circumstance. For example, if the activity could cause a relatively small amount of harm, yet regulating that activity would place extensive constraints on people regulated, then

any tests should be extremely accurate. On the other hand, if the activity could be exceedingly harmful but the constraints on the regulated person are minor, then the test can be considerably less reliable.

3. The statistics on the incidence of child abuse vary. Probably the most recent detailed study (Saad Nagi, *Child Maltreatment in the United States,* Columbia University Press, 1977) suggests that between 400,000 and 1,000,000 children are abused or neglected each year. Other experts claim the incidence is considerably higher.

4. According to the National Committee for the Prevention of Child Abuse, more than 80 percent of incarcerated criminals were, as children, abused by their parents. In addition, a study in the *Journal of the American Medical Association* 168, no. 3: 1755-1758, reported that first-degree murderers from middle-class homes and who have "no history of addiction to drugs, alcoholism, organic disease of the brain, or epilepsy" were frequently found to have been subject to "remorseless physical brutality at the hands of the parents."

5. "A review of the literature points out that abusive parents were raised in the same style that they have recreated in the pattern of rearing children. . . . An individual who was raised by parents who used physical force to train their children and who grew up in a violent household has had as a role model the use of force and violence as a means of family problem solving." R. J. Gelles, "Child Abuse as Psychopathology—a Sociological Critique and Reformulation," *American Journal of Orthopsychiatry* 43, no. 4 (1973): 618-19.

6. Some people might question if any parents actually believe they should beat their children. However, that does appear to be the sincere view of many abusing parents. See, for example, case description in *A Silent Tragedy* by Peter and Judith DeCourcy (Sherman Oaks, CA.: Alfred Publishing Co., 1973).

7. I suppose I might be for licensing only good parents if I knew there were reasonable criteria and some plausible way of deciding if a potential parent satisfied these criteria. However, since I don't think we have those criteria or that method, nor can I seriously envision that we will discover those criteria and that method, I haven't seriously entertained the stronger proposal.

8. The research gathered by Altemeier was reported by Ray Helfer in "Review of the Concepts and a Sampling of the Research Relating to Screening for the Potential to Abuse and/or Neglect One's Child." Helfer's paper was presented at a workshop sponsored by the National Committee for the Prevention of Child Abuse, 3-6 December 1978.

9. According to a study published by the Child Welfare League of America, at least 51 percent of the adopted children had suffered, prior to adoption, more than minimal emotional deprivation. See *A Follow-up Study of Adoptions: Post Placement Functioning of Adoption Families,* Elizabeth A. Lawder et al., New York 1969.

According to a study by David Gil (*Violence Against Children,* Cambridge: Harvard University Press, 1970) only .4 percent of abused children were abused by adoptive parents. Since at least 2 percent of the children in the United States are adopted (*Encyclopedia of Social Work,* National Association of Social Workers, New York, 1977), that means the rate of abuse by biological parents is five times that of adoptive parents.

10. We can see this belief in a court case chronical by DeCourcy and DeCourcy in *A Silent Tragedy.* The judge ruled that three children, severely and regularly beaten, burned, and cut by their father, should be placed back with their father since he was only "trying to do what is right." If the court did not adopt this belief would it even be tempted to so excuse such abusive behavior? This attitude also emerges in the all-too-frequent court rulings (see S. Katz, *When Parents Fail,* Boston: Beacon Press, 1971) giving custody of children back to their biological parents even though the parents had abandoned them for years, and even though the children expressed a strong desire to stay with foster parents.

In "The Child, the Law, and the State" (*Children's Rights: Toward The Liberation of the Child,* Leila Berg et al., New York: Praeger Publishers, 1971), Nan Berger persuasively argues that our adoption and foster care laws are comprehensible only if children are regarded as the property of their parents.

WHAT DO GROWN CHILDREN OWE THEIR PARENTS?

Jane English

What do grown children owe their parents? I will contend that the answer is "nothing." Although I agree that there are many things that children *ought* to do for their parents, I will argue that it is inappropriate and misleading to describe them as things "owed." I will maintain that parents' voluntary sacrifices, rather than creating "debts" to be "repaid," tend to create love or "friendship." The duties of grown children are those of friends and result from love between them and their parents, rather than being things owed in repayment for the parents' earlier sacrifices. Thus, I will oppose those philosophers who use the word "owe" whenever a duty or obligation exists. Although the "debt" metaphor is appropriate in some moral circumstances, my argument is that a love relationship is not such a case.

Misunderstandings about the proper relationship between parents and their grown children have resulted from reliance on the "owing" terminology. For instance, we hear parents complain, "You owe it to us to write home (keep up your piano playing, not adopt a hippie lifestyle), because of all we sacrificed for you (paying for piano lessons, sending you to college)." The child is sometimes even heard to reply, "I didn't ask to be born (to be given piano lessons, to be sent to college)." This inappropriate idiom of ordinary language tends to obscure, or even to undermine, the love that is the correct ground of filial obligation.

1. Favors Create Debts

There are some cases, other than literal debts, in which talk of "owing," though metaphorical, is apt. New to the neighborhood, Max barely knows his neighbor, Nina, but he asks her if she will take in his mail while he is gone for a month's vacation. She agrees. If, subsequently, Nina asks Max to do the same for her, it seems that Max has a moral obligation to agree (greater than the one he would have had if Nina had not done the same for him), unless for some reason it would be a burden far out of proportion to the one Nina bore for him. I will call this a *favor:* when A, at B's request, bears some burden for B, then B incurs an obligation to reciprocate. Here the metaphor of Max's "owing" Nina is appropriate. It is not literally a debt, of course, nor can Nina pass this IOU on to heirs, demand payment in the form of Max's taking out her garbage, or sue Max. Nonetheless, since Max ought to perform one act of similar nature and amount of sacrifice in return, the term is suggestive. Once he reciprocates, the debt is "discharged"—that is, their obligations revert to the condition they were in before Max's initial request.

Contrast a situation in which Max simply goes on vacation and, to his sur-

From *Having Children: Philosophical and Legal Reflections on Parenthood,* ed. Onora O'Neil and William Ruddick (New York: Oxford University Press, 1979), pp. 351-56.

prise, finds upon his return that his neighbor has mowed his grass twice weekly in his absence. This is a voluntary sacrifice rather than a favor, and Max has no duty to reciprocate. It would be nice for him to volunteer to do so, but this would be supererogatory on his part. Rather than a favor, Nina's action is a friendly gesture. As a result, she might expect Max to chat over the back fence, help her catch her straying dog, or something similar—she might expect the development of a friendship. But Max would be chatting (or whatever) out of friendship, rather than in repayment for mown grass. If he did not return her gesture, she might feel rebuffed or miffed, but not unjustly treated or indignant, since Max has not failed to perform a duty. Talk of "owing" would be out of place in this case.

It is sometimes difficult to distinguish between favors and non-favors, because friends tend to do favors for each other, and those who exchange favors tend to become friends. But one test is to ask how Max is motivated. Is it "to be nice to Nina" or "because she did x for me"? Favors are frequently performed by total strangers without any friendship developing. Nevertheless, a temporary obligation is created, even if the chance for repayment never arises. For instance, suppose that Oscar and Matilda, total strangers, are waiting in a long checkout line at the supermarket. Oscar, having forgotten the oregano, asks Matilda to watch his cart for a second. She does. If Matilda now asks Oscar to return the favor while she picks up some tomato sauce, he is obliged to agree. Even if she had not watched his cart, it would be inconsiderate of him to refuse, claiming he was too busy reading the magazines. He may have a duty to help others, but he would not "owe " it to her. But if she has done the same for him, he incurs an additional obligation to help, and talk of "owing" is apt. It suggests an agreement to perform equal, reciprocal, canceling sacrifices.

2. The Duties of Friendship

The terms "owe" and "repay" are helpful in the case of favors, because the sameness of the amount of sacrifice on the two sides is important; the monetary metaphor suggests equal quantities of sacrifice. But friendship ought to be characterized by *mutuality* rather than reciprocity: friends offer what they can give and accept what they need, without regard for the total amounts of benefits exchanged. And friends are motivated by love rather than by the prospect of repayment. Hence, talk of "owing" is singularly out of place in friendship.

For example, suppose Alfred takes Beatrice out for an expensive dinner and a movie. Beatrice incurs no obligation to "repay" him with a goodnight kiss or a return engagement. If Alfred complains that she "owes" him something, he is operating under the assumption that she should repay a favor, but on the contrary his was a generous gesture done in the hopes of developing a friendship. We hope that he would not want her repayment in the form of sex or attention if this was done to discharge a debt rather than from friendship. Since, if Alfred is prone to reasoning in this way, Beatrice may well decline the invitation or request to pay for her own dinner, his attitude of expecting a "return" on his "investment" could hinder the development of a friendship. Beatrice should return the gesture only if she is motivated by friendship.

Another common misuse of the "owing" idiom occurs when the Smiths have dined at the Joneses' four times, but the Joneses at the Smiths' only once. People often say, "We owe them three dinners." This line of thinking may be appropriate between business acquaintances, but not between friends. After all, the Joneses invited the Smiths not in order to feed them or to be fed in turn, but because of the friendly contact presumably enjoyed by all on such occasions. If the Smiths do not feel friendship toward the Joneses, they can decline future invitations and not invite the Joneses; they owe them nothing. Of course, between friends of equal resources and needs, roughly equal sacrifices (though not necessarily roughly equal dinners) will typically occur. If the sacrifices are highly out of proportion to the resources, the relationship is closer to servility than to friendship.[1]

Another difference between favors and friendship is that after a friendship ends, the duties of friendship end. The party that has sacrificed less owes the other nothing. For instance, suppose Elmer donated a pint of blood that his wife Doris needed during an operation. Years after their divorce, Elmer is in an accident and needs one pint of blood. His new wife, Cora, is also of the same blood type. It seems that Doris not only does not "owe" Elmer blood, but that she should actually refrain from coming forward if Cora has volunteered to donate. To insist on donating not only interferes with the newlyweds' friendship, but it belittles Doris and Elmer's former relationship by suggesting that Elmer gave blood in hopes of favors returned instead of simply out of love for Doris. It is one of the heart-rending features of divorce that it attends to quantity in a relationship previously characterized by mutuality. If Cora could not dontate, Doris's obligation is the same as that for any former spouse in need of blood; it is not increased by the fact that Elmer similarly aided her. It *is* affected by the degree to which they are still friends, which in turn may (or may not) have been influenced by Elmer's donation.

In short, unlike the debts created by favors, the duties of friendship do not require equal quantities of sacrifice. Performing equal sacrifices does not cancel the duties of friendship, as it does the debts of favors. Unrequested sacrifices do not themselves create debts, but friends have duties regardless of whether they requested or initiated the friendship. Those who perform favors may be motivated by mutual gain, whereas friends should be motivated by affection. These characteristics of the friendship relation are distorted by talk of "owing."

3. Parents and Children

The relationship between children and their parents should be one of friendship characterized by mutuality rather than one of reciprocal favors. The quantity of parental sacrifice is not relevant in determining what duties the grown child has. The medical assistance grown children ought to offer their ill mothers in old age depends upon the mothers' need, not upon whether they endured a difficult pregnancy, for example. Nor do one's duties to one's parents cease once an equal quantity of sacrifice has been performed, as the phrase "discharging a debt" may lead us to think.

Rather, what children ought to do for their parents (and parents for children) depends upon (1) their respective needs, abilities, and resources and (2) the extent to which there is an ongoing friendship between them. Thus, regardless of the quantity of childhood sacrifices, an able, wealthy child has an obligation to help his needy parents more than does a needy child. To illustrate, suppose sisters Cecile and Dana are equally loved by their parents, even though Cecile was an easy child to care for, seldom ill, while Dana was often sick and caused some trouble as a juvenile delinquent. As adults, Dana is a struggling artist living far away, while Cecile is a wealthy lawyer living nearby. When the parents need visits and financial aid, Cecile has an obligation to bear a higher proportion of these burdens than her sister. This results from her abilities, rather than from the quantities of sacrifice made by the parents earlier.

Sacrifices have an important causal role in creating an ongoing friendship, which may lead us to assume incorrectly that it is the sacrifices that are the source of the obligation. That the source is the friendship instead can be seen by examining cases in which the sacrifices occurred but the friendship, for some reason, did not develop or persist. For example, if a woman gives up her newborn child for adoption, and if no feelings of love ever develop on either side, it seems that the grown child does not have an obligation to "repay" her for her sacrifices in pregnancy. For that matter, if the adopted child has an unimpaired love relationship with the adoptive parents, he or she has the same obligations to help them as a natural child would have.

The filial obligations of grown children are a result of friendship, rather than owed for services rendered. Suppose that Vance married Lola despite his parents' strong wish that he marry within their religion, and that as a result, the parents refuse to speak to him again. As the years pass, the parents are unaware of Vance's problems, his accomplishments, the birth of his children. The love that once existed between them, let us suppose, has been completely destroyed by this event and thirty years of desuetude. At this point, it seems, Vance is under no obligation to pay his parents' medical bills in their old age, beyond his general duty to help those in need. An additional, filial obligation would only arise from whatever love he may still feel for them. It would be irrelevant for his parents to argue, "But look how much we sacrificed for you when you were young," for that sacrifice was not a favor but occurred as part of a friendship which existed at that time but is now, we have supposed, defunct. A more appropriate message would be, "We still love you, and we would like to renew our friendship."

I hope this helps to set the question of what children ought to do for the parents in a new light. The parental argument, "You ought to do x because we did y for you," should be replaced by, "We love you and you will be happier if you do x," or "We believe you love us, and anyone who loved us would do x." If the parents' sacrifice had been a favor, the child's reply, "I never asked you to do y for me," would have been relevant; to the revised parental remarks, this reply is clearly irrelevant. The child can either do *x* or dispute one of the parents' claims: by showing that a love relationship does not exist, or that love for someone does not motivate doing *x,* or that he or she will not be happier doing *x.*

Seen in this light, parental requests for children to write home, visit, and offer them a reasonable amount of emotional and financial support in life's crises are well founded, so long as a friendship still exists. Love for others does call for caring about and caring for them. Some other parental requests, such as for more sweeping changes in the child's lifestyle or life goals, can be seen to be insupportable, once we shift the justification from debts owed to love. The terminology of favors suggests the reasoning, "Since we paid for your college education, you owe it to us to make a career of engineering, rather than becoming a rock musician." This tends to alienate affection even further, since the tuition payments are depicted as investments for a return rather than done from love, as though the child's life goals could be "bought." Basing the argument on love leads to different reasoning patterns. The suppressed premise, "If A loves B, then A follows B's wishes as to A's lifelong career" is simply false. Love does not even dictate that the child adopt the parents' values as to the desirability of alternative life goals. So the parents' strongest available argument here is, "We love you, we are deeply concerned about your happiness, and in the long run you will be happier as an engineer." This makes it clear that an empirical claim is really the subject of the debate.

The function of these examples is to draw out our considered judgments as to the proper relation between parents and their grown children, and to show how poorly they fit the model of favors. What is relevant is the ongoing friendship that exists between parents and children. Although that relationship developed partly as a result of parental sacrifices for the child, the duties that grown children have to their parents result from the friendship rather than from the sacrifices. The idiom of owing favors to one's parents can actually be destructive if it undermines the role of mutuality and leads us to think in terms of quantitative reciprocal favors.

NOTE

1. Cf. Thomas E. Hill, Jr., "Servility and Self-Respect," **Monist** 57 (1973). Thus during childhood, most of the sacrifices will come from the parents, since they have most of the resources and the child has most of the needs. When children are grown, the situation is usually reversed.

CHAPTER FIVE
PHILOSOPHY AND THE CLAIMS OF RELIGION

Socrates is in many ways the paradigm philosopher, not least in his reputation as a dangerous religious heretic. One of the charges that led to his trial and execution was that he did not believe in the traditional gods of his city-state (*Apology* 24b-c). Seeing the way Socrates mercilessly quizzed the fundamentalist religious beliefs of the self-satisfied Euthyphro, one can begin to understand why the good citizens of Athens thought the philosopher lacked proper reverence in theological matters. The popular mind's connection of philosophy and religious heresy has not been broken in the intervening centuries; in fact, it has been strengthened. Many people assume that a commitment to philosophical investigation is necessarily antithetical to faith; that a true philosopher *must* be a skeptic about the claims of religion.

Why should philosophy seen necessarily heretical or atheistic? Part of the reason is a misunderstanding of the nature of Socratic philosophy. It is tempting to believe that philosophy is only a body of doctrine, tempting to assume that a philosopher holds particular substantive beliefs about the nature of reality. On this model, philosophy is an *ideology*—a world-view—of a sort, and as such, it competes with other ideologies. It can seem inevitable that philosophy and Christianity, for example, should conflict with one another. After all, they're both world-views, aren't they? They can't *both* be right, can they?

This conception misconstrues the nature of philosophy. Based on the Socratic model, philosophy is an *activity,* not a body of doctrine. It is not an ideology, so it cannot compete with ideologies. Socratic philosophy is the activity of rational clarification, the search for structures of justification for beliefs, attitudes, and actions, and as such it is not necessarily the enemy of religious commitment. Consider, for example, orthodox Chrisitianity. Philosophical investigation *might* show its beliefs, attitudes, and actions to possess the appropriate structures of justification—to be the *correct* beliefs, attitudes, and injunctions. Socratic philosophy is thus not *inevitably* inconsistent with religious belief.

On the other hand, there is undoubtedly a tension present in the relationship of philosophy to religious belief—a legitimate tension not to be removed by calling attention to philosophy as an activity. This tension is produced by the *kind* of activity Socratic philosophy is. Philosophy insists upon unbiased, open, critical investigation of every claim. It takes nothing for granted; it recognizes no authority outside the self-critical powers of the mind itself. Religious systems, however, present themselves as the fully-present *truth;* they are *proclaimed,* not offered for investigation and cool judgment. The claims of religion deal with ultimate matters: the nature of transcendent reality, the fate of the person after death, the way of virtue. These matters are fundamentally important to us, for we fear death and we want to know virtue and the real. Religion claims to have answers for our deepest questions; it preaches these answers as the only truths and demands our unwavering acceptance of them.

Is it any wonder, then, that philosophy and religion are so often at odds? We hunger for truth, virtue, and immortality. Religion says, "Here they are; take them now, or lose them forever." Philosophy says, "Go slowly, Religion. What are the justifications for your claims? Let us see your arguments." Socrates says to Euthyphro, to Athens, "How do you know? What do you mean?" Is it any wonder that they grew tired of the gadfly's bite?

This tension, the tension between the hungers of our soul and the scruples of our intellect, cannot be removed, and it *ought* not, for it is one of the marks of our humanity. Once the Socratic intellect has awakened, it is fatal to try to lull it back to sleep. The philosopher cannot be a simple believer; he or she cannot fail to pay attention to argument, evidence, and the difference between sense and nonsense. In the same manner, the philosopher examining religion cannot be a mere thinking machine; he or she must pay attention to the promptings of spirit as well as intellect. To do both at once is very difficult; it is no wonder that many of us fail to live with the resultant tension, lapsing into an unthinking (perhaps enthusiastic) fundamentalism or into an arid and dogmatic skepticism. It seems that neither alternative commends itself to a fully realized human being.

Is there another alternative? Can religious belief be compatible with the requirements of Socratic philosophy? In this section we have arranged readings to pose that very question. The reader encounters philosophers' attempts to grasp the essence of religion as a cultural phenomenon and to understand the function and value of religious ideas in social life. We have included philosophers' arguments for the existence of God, as well as arguments that those philosophers fail. Included are accounts of religious experience, along with philosophical reflections on what, if anything, those experiences demonstrate. The problem of evil is explored. Finally, reflections on the relationship of reason to religious faith are discussed.

Encountering the claims of religion give us another important occasion for philosophy. It is, to be sure, an occasion fraught with special tension, inevitable since the passions, hopes, and fears of religious faith seem so hopelessly out of joint with the cool and careful scrutiny demanded of the philosopher. Still, neither religion nor philosophy seems about to disappear. Beliefs about the existence of gods, the fate of the soul, and the conquest of evil have been a part of most of human history; in the West, at least, the questioning, Socratic intellect has become a fundamental ideal of our culture. In this context philosophy plays a crucial rule. It can, through its techniques of self-critical reflection, help us to balance the proper claims of the passionate soul and the rational mind.

WHAT IS RELIGION?

RELIGION AS A CULTURAL SYSTEM

Clifford Geertz

As we are to deal with meaning, let us begin with a paradigm: viz. that sacred symbols function to synthesize a people's ethos—the tone, character, and quality of their life, its moral and aesthetic style and mood—and their world-view—the picture they have of the way things in sheer actuality are, their most comprehensive ideas of order (Geertz, 1958). In religious belief and practice a group's ethos is rendered intellectually reasonable by being shown to represent a way of life ideally adapted to the actual state of affairs the world-view describes, while the world-view is rendered emotionally convincing by being presented as an image of an actual state of affairs peculiarly well arranged to accommodate such a way of life. This confrontation and mutual confirmation has two fundamental effects. On the one hand, it objectivizes moral and aesthetic preferences by depicting them as the imposed conditions of life implicit in a world with a particular structure, as mere common sense given the unalterable shape of reality. On the other, it supports these received beliefs about the world's body by invoking deeply felt moral and aesthetic sentiments as experimental evidence for their truth. Religious symbols formulate a basic congruence between a particular style of life and a specific (if, most often, implicit) metaphysic, and in so doing sustain each with the borrowed authority of the other.

From *Anthropological Approaches to the Study of Religion,* ed. Michael Banton (London: Tavistock Publications, 1965), pp. 3-28, 35-40, 42-46. Reprinted by permission of the publisher.

Phrasing aside, this much may perhaps be granted. The notion that religion tunes human actions to an envisaged cosmic order and projects images of cosmic order onto the plane of human experience is hardly novel. But it is hardly investigated either so, that we have very little idea of how, in empirical terms, this particular miracle is accomplished. We just know that it is done, annually, weekly, daily, for some people almost hourly; and we have an enormous ethnographic literature to demonstrate it. But the theoretical framework which would enable us to provide analytic account of it, an account of the sort we can provide for lineage segmentation political succession, labor exchange, or the socialization of the child does not exist.

Let us, therefore, reduce our paradigm to a definition, for, although it is notorious that definitions establish nothing in themselves, they do, if they are carefully enough constructed, provide a useful orientation, or reorientation, of thought, such that an extended unpacking of them can be an effective way of developing and controlling a novel line of inquiry. They have the useful virtue of explicitness: they commit themselves in a way discursive prose, which in this field especially, is always liable to substitute rhetoric for argument, does not. Without further ado, then, a *religion* is:

(1) a system of symbols which acts to
(2) establish powerful, pervasive, and long-lasting moods and motivations in men by
(3) formulating conceptions of a general order of existence and
(4) clothing these conceptions with such an aura of factuality that
(5) the moods and motivations seem uniquely realistic.

1. a system of symbols which acts to . . .

Such a tremendous weight is being put on the term 'symbol' here that our first move must be to decide with some precision what we are going to mean by it. This is no easy task, for, rather like 'culture', 'symbol' has been used to refer to a great variety of things, often a number of them at the same time. In some hands it is used for anything which signifies something else to someone: dark clouds are the symbolic precursors of an oncoming rain. In others it is used only for explicitly conventional signs of one sort or another: a red flag is a symbol of danger, a white of surrender. In others it is confined to something which expresses in an oblique and figurative manner that which cannot be stated in a direct and literal one, so that there are symbols in poetry but not in science, and symbolic logic is misnamed. In yet others, however (Langer, 1953, 1960, 1962), it is used for any object, act, event, quality, or relation which serves as a vehicle for a conception—the conception is the symbol's 'meaing'—and that is the approach I shall follow here. The number 6, written, imagined, laid out as a row of stones, or even punched into the program tapes of a computer is a symbol. But so also is the Cross, talked about, visualized, shaped worriedly in air or fondly fingered at the neck, the expanse of painted canvas called 'Guernica' or the bit of painted stone called a churinga, the word 'reality', or even the morpheme '-ing.' They are all symbols, or at least symbolic elements, because they are tangible formulations of notions, abstractions from experience fixed in perceptible forms, concrete embodiments of ideas, attitudes, judgments, longings, or beliefs. To undertake the study of cultural activity—activity in which symbolism forms the positive content—is thus not to abandon social analysis for a Platonic cave of shadows, to enter into a mentalistic world of introspective psychology or, worse, speculative philosophy, and wander there forever in a haze of 'Cognitions', 'Affections', 'Conations', and other elusive entities. Cultural acts, the construction, apprehension, and utilization of symbolic forms, are social events like any other; they are as public as marriage and as observable as agriculture.

They are not, however, exactly the same thing; or, more precisely, the symbolic dimension of social events is, like the psychological, itself theoretically abstractable from those events as empirical totalities. There is still, to paraphrase a remark of Kenneth Burke's (1941, p. 9), a difference between building a house and drawing up a plan for building a house, and reading a poem about having children by marriage is not quite the same thing as having children by marriage. Even though the building of the house may proceed under the guidance of the plan or—a less likely occurrence—the having of children may be motivated by a reading of the poem, there is something to be said for not confusing our traffic with symbols with our traffic with objects or human beings, for these latter are not in themselves symbols, however often they may function as such.[1] No matter how deeply interfused the cultural, the social, and the psychological may be in the everyday life of houses, farms, poems, and marriages, it is useful to distinguish them in analysis, and, so doing, to isolate the generic traits of each against the normalized background of the other two (Parsons & Shils, 1951).

So far as culture patterns, i.e., systems or complexes of symbols, are concerned, the generic trait which is of first importance for us here is that they are extrinsic sources of information (Geertz, 1964a). By 'extrinsic', I mean only that—unlike genes, for example—they lie outside the boundaries of the individuals organism as such in that intersubjective world of common understandings into which all human individuals are born, in which they pursue their separate careers, and which they leave persisting behind them after they die (Schutz, 1962). By 'sources of information', I mean only that—like genes—they provide a blueprint or template in terms of which processes external to themselves can be given a definite form (Horowitz, 1956). As the order of bases in a strand of DNA forms a coded program, a set of instructions, or a recipe, for the synthesization of the structurally complex proteins which shape organic functioning, so culture patterns provide such programs for the institution of the social and psychological processes which shape public behavior. Though the sort of information and the mode of its transmission are vastly different in the two cases, this comparison of gene and symbol is more than a strained analogy of the familiar 'social heredity' sort. It is actually a substantial relationship, for it is precisely the fact that genetically programmed processes are so highly generalized in men, as compared with lower animals, that culturally programmed ones are so important, only because human behavior is so loosely determined by intrinsic sources of information that extrinsic sources are so vital (Geertz, 1962). To build a dam a beaver needs only an appropriate site and the proper materials—his mode of procedure is shaped by his physiology. But man, whose genes are silent on the building trades, needs also a conception of what it is to build a dam, a conception he can get only from some symbolic source—a blueprint, a textbook, or a string of speech by someone who already knows how dams are built, or of course, from manipulating graphic or linguistic elements in such a way as to attain for himself a conception of what dams are and how they are built.

This point is sometimes put in the form of an argument that cultural patterns are 'models', that they are sets of symbols whose relations to one another 'model' relations among entities, processes or what-have-you in physical, organic, social, or psychological systems by 'paralleling', 'imitating', or 'simulating' them (Craik, 1952). The term 'model' has, however, two senses—an 'of' and a 'for' sense—and though these are but aspects of the same basic concept they are very much worth distinguishing for analytic purposes. In the first, what is stressed is the manipulation of symbol structures so as to bring them, more or less closely, into parallel with the pre-established non-symbolic system, as when we grasp how dams work by developing a theory of hydraulics or constructing a flow chart. The theory or chart models physical relationships in such a way—i.e., by expressing their structure in synoptic form—as to render them apprehensible: it is a model *of* 'reality'. In the second, what is stressed is the manipulation of the non-symbolic systems in terms of the relationships expressed in the symbolic, as when we construct a dam according to the specifications implied in an hydraulic theory or the conclusions drawn from a flow chart. Here, the theory is a model under whose guidance physical relationships are organized: it is a model *for* 'reality'. For psychological and social systems, and for cultural models that we would not ordinarily refer to as 'theories', but rather as 'doctrines', 'melodies', or 'rites', the case is in no way different. Unlike genes, and other non-symbolic information sources, which are only models *for*, not models *of*, culture patterns have an intrinsic double aspect: they give meaning, i.e., objective conceptual form, to social and psychological reality both by shaping themselves to it and by shaping it to themselves.

It is, in fact, this double aspect which sets true symbols off from other sorts of significative forms. Models *for* are found, as the gene example suggests, through the whole order of nature, for wherever there is a communication of pattern such programs are, in simple logic, required. Among animals, imprint learning is perhaps the most striking example, because what such learning involves is the automatic presentation of an appropriate sequence of behavior by a model animal in the presence of a learning animal which serves, equally automatically, to call out and stabilize a certain set of responses genetically built into the learning animal (Lorenz, 1952). The communicative dance of two bees, one of which has found nectar and the other of which seeks it, is another, somewhat different, more complexly coded, example (von Frisch, 1962). Craik (1952) has even suggested that the thin trickle of water which first finds its way down from a mountain spring to the sea and smooths a little channel for the greater volume of water that follows after it plays a sort of model *for* function. But models *of*—linguistic, graphic, mechanical, natural, etc., processes which function not to provide sources of information in terms of which other processes can be patterned, but to represent those patterned processes as such, to express their structure in an alternative medium—are much rarer and may perhaps be confined, among living animals, to man. The perception of the structural congruence between one set of processes, activities, relations, entities, etc., and another set for which it acts as a program, so that the program can be taken as a representation, or conception—a symbol—of the programmed, is the essence of human thought. The inter-transposability of models *for* and models *of* which symbolic formulation makes possible is the distinctive characteristic of our mentality.

2. . . . to establish powerful, pervasive, and long-lasting moods and motivations in men by . . .

So far as religious symbols and symbol systems are concerned this inter-transposability is clear. The endurance, courage, independence, perseverance, and passionate willfulness in which the vision quest practices the Plains Indian are the same flamboyant virtues by which he attempts to live: while achieving a sense of revelation he stabilizes a sense of direction (Lowie, 1924). The consciousness of defaulted obligation, secreted guilt, and, when a confession is obtained, public shame in which Manus' seance rehearses him are the same sentiments that underlie the sort of duty ethic by which his property-conscious society is maintained: the gaining of an absolution involves the forging of a conscience (Fortune, 1935). And the same self-discipline which rewards a Javanese mystic staring fixedly into the flame of a lamp with what he takes to be an intimation of divinity drills him in that rigorous control of emotional expression which is necessary to a man who would follow a quietistic style of life (Geertz, 1960). Whether one sees the conception of a personal guardian spirit, a family tutelary or an immanent God as synoptic formulations of the character of reality or as templates for producing reality with such a character seems largely arbitrary, a matter of which aspect, the model *of* or model *for,* one wants for the moment to bring into focus. The concrete symbols involved—one or another mythological figure materializing in the wilderness, the skull of the deceased household head hanging censoriously in the rafters, or a disembodied 'voice in the stillness' soundlessly chanting enigmatic classical poetry—point in either direction. They both express the world's climate and shape it.

They shape it by inducing in the worshipper a certain distinctive set of dispositions (tendencies, capacities, propensities, skills, habits, liabilities, proneness) which lend a chronic character to the flow of his activity and the quality of his experience. A disposition describes not an activity or an occurrence but a probability of an activity being performed or an occurrence occurring in certain circumstances: 'When a cow is said to be a ruminant, or a man is said to be a cigarette-smoker, it is not being said that the cow is ruminating now or that the man is smoking a cigarette now. To be a ruminant is to tend to ruminate from time to time, and to be a cigarette-smoker is to be in the habit of smoking cigarettes' (Ryle, 1949, p. 117). Similarly, to be pious is not to be performing something we would call an act of piety, but to be liable to perform such acts. So, too, with the Plains Indian's bravura, the Manus' compunctiousness, or the Javanese's quietism which, in their contexts, form the substance of piety. The virtue of this sort of view of what are usually called 'mental traits' or, if the Cartesianism is unavowed, 'psychological forces' (both unobjectionable enough terms in themselves) is that it gets them out of any dim and inaccessible realm of private sensation into that same well-lit world of observables in which reside the brittleness of glass, the inflammability of paper, and, to return to the metaphor, the dampness of England.

So far as religious activities are concerned (and learning a myth by heart is as much a religious activity as detaching one's finger at the knuckle), two somewhat different sorts of disposition are induced by them: moods and motivations.

A motivation is a persisting tendency, a chronic inclination to perform certain sorts of act and experience certain sorts of feeling in certain sorts of situation, the 'sorts' being commonly very heterogenous and rather ill-defined classes in all three cases:

> '. . . on hearing that a man is vain [i.e. motivated by vanity] we expect him to behave in certain ways, namely to talk a lot about himself, to cleave to the society of the eminent, to reject criticisms, to seek the footlights and to disengage himself from conversations about the merits of others. We expect him to indulge in roseate daydreams about his own successes, to avoid recalling past failures and to plan for his own advancement. To be vain is to tend to act in these and innumerable other kindred ways. Certainly we also expect the vain man to feel certain pangs and flutters in certain situations; we expect him to have an acute sinking feeling when an eminent person forgets his name, and to feel buoyant of heart and light of toe on hearing of the misfortunes of his rivals. But feelings of pique and buoyancy are not more directly indicative of vanity than are public acts of boasting or private acts of daydreaming. . . .' (Ryle, 1949, p. 86).

Similarly for any motivations. As a motive, 'flamboyant courage' consists in such enduring propensities as to fast in the wilderness, to conduct solitary raids on enemy camps, and to thrill to the thought of counting coup. 'Moral circumspection' consists in such ingrained tendencies as to honor onerous promises, to confess secret sins in the face of severe public disapproval, and to feel guilty when vague and generalized accusations are made at seances. And 'dispassionate tranquility' consists in such persistent inclinations as to maintain one's poise come hell or high water, to experience distaste in the presence of even moderate emotional displays, and to indulge in contentless contemplations of featureless objects. Motives are thus neither acts (i.e., intentional behaviors) nor feelings, but liabilities to perform particular classes of act or have particular classes of feeling. And where we say that a man is religious, i.e., motivated by religion, this is at least part—though only part—of what we mean.

Another part of what we mean is that he has, when properly stimulated, a susceptibility to fall into certain moods, moods we sometimes lump together under such covering terms as 'reverential', 'solemn', or 'worshipful'. Such generalized rubrics actually conceal, however, the enormous empirical variousness of the dispositions involved, and, in fact, tend to assimilate them to the unusually grave tone of most of our own religious life. The moods that sacred symbols induce, at different times and in different places, range from exultation to melancholy, from self-confidence to self-pity, from an incorrigible playfulness to a bland listlessness— to say nothing of the erogenous power of so many of the world's myths and rituals. No more than there is a single sort of motivation one can call piety is there a single sort of mood one can call worshipful.

The major difference between moods and motivations is that where the latter are, so to speak, vectorial qualities, the former are merely scalar. Motives have a directional cast, they describe a certain overall course, gravitate toward certain, usually temporary, consummations. But moods vary only as to intensity: they go nowhere. They spring from certain circumstances but they are responsibe to no end. Like fogs, they just settle and lift; like scents, suffuse and evaporate. When present they are totalistic: if one is sad everything and everybody seems dreary; if one is gay, everything and everybody seems splendid. Thus, though a man can be vain, brave, willful and independent at the same time, he can't very well be playful and listless, or exultant and melancholy, at the same time (Ryle, 1949, p. 99). Further, where motives persist for more or less extended periods of time, moods merely recur with greater or lesser frequency, coming and going for what are often quite unfathomable reasons. But perhaps the most important difference, so far as we are concerned, between moods and motivations is that motivations are 'made meaningful' with reference to the ends toward which they are conceived to conduce, whereas moods are 'made meaningful' with reference to the conditions from which they are conceived to spring. We interpret motives in terms of their consummations, but we interpret moods in terms of their sources. We say that a person is industrious because he wishes to succeed, we say that a person is worried because he is conscious of the hanging threat of nuclear holocaust. And this is no less the case when the interpretations invoked are ultimate. Charity becomes Christian charity when it is enclosed in a conception of God's purposes; optimism is Christian optimism when it is grounded in a particular conception of God's nature. The assiduity of the Navaho finds its rationale in a belief that, since 'reality' operates mechanically, it is coercible; their chronic fearfulness finds its rationale in a conviction that, however 'reality' operates, it is both enormously powerful and terribly dangerous (Kluckhohn, 1949).

3. . . . by formulating conceptions
of a general order of existence and . . .

That the symbols or symbol systems which induce and define dispositions we set off as religious and those which place those dispositions in a cosmic framework are the same symbols ought to occasion no surprise. For what else do we mean by saying that a particular mood of awe is religious and not secular except that it springs from entertaining a conception of all-pervading vitality like mana and not from a visit to the Grand Canyon? Or that a particular case of asceticism is an example of a religious motivation except that it is directed toward the achievement of an unconditioned end like nirvana and not a conditioned one like weight-reduction? If sacred symbols did not at one and the same time induce dispositions in human beings and formulate, however obliquely, inarticulately, or unsystematically, general ideas of order, then the empirical differentia of religious activity or religious experience would not exist. A man can indeed be said to be 'religious' about golf, but not merely if he pursues it with passion and plays it on Sundays: he must also see it as symbolic of some transcendent truths. And the pubescent boy gazing soulfully into the eyes of the pubescent girl in a William Steig cartoon and murmuring, 'There is something about you, Ethel, which gives me a sort of religious feeling', is, like most adolescents, confused. What any particular religion affirms about the fundamental nature of reality may be obscure, shallow, or, all too often, perverse, but it must, if it is not to consist of the mere collection of received practices and conventional sentiments we usually refer to as moralism, affirm something. If one were to essay a minimal definition of religion today it would perhaps not be Tylor's famous 'belief in spiritual beings', to which Goody (1961), wearied of theoretical subtleties, has lately urged us to return, but rather what Salvador de Madariaga has called 'the relatively modest dogma that God is not mad'.

Usually, of course, religions affirm very much more than this: we believe, as James (1904, Vol. 2, p. 299) remarked, all that we can and would believe everything if we only could. The thing we seem least able to tolerate is a threat to our powers of conception, a suggestion that our ability to create, grasp, and use symbols may fail us, for were this to happen we would be more helpless, as I have already pointed out, than the beavers. The extreme generality, diffuseness, and variability of man's innate (i.e., genetically programmed) response capacities means that without the assistance of cultural patterns he would be functionally incomplete, not merely a talented ape who had, like some under-privileged child, unfortunately been prevented from realizing his full potentialities, but a kind of formless monster with neither sense of direction nor power of self-control, a chaos of spasmodic impulses and vague emotions (Geertz, 1962). Man depends upon symbols and symbol systems with a dependence so great as to be decisive for his creatural viability and, as a result, his sensitivity to even the remotest indication that they may prove unable to cope with one or another aspect of experience raises within him the gravest sort of anxiety:

'[Man] can adapt himself somehow to anything his imagination can cope with; but he cannot deal with Chaos. Because his characteristic function and highest asset is conception, his greatest fright is to meet what he cannot construe—the "uncanny", as it is popularly called. It need not be a new object; we do meet new things, and "understand" them promptly, if tentatively, by the nearest analog, when our minds are functioning freely; but under mental stress even perfectly familiar things may become suddenly disorganized and give us the horrors. Therefore our most important assets are always the symbols of our general *orientation* in nature, on the earth, in society, and in what we are doing: the symbols of our *Weltanschauung* and *Lebensanschauung.* Consequently, in a primitive society, a daily ritual is incorporated in common activities, in eating, washing, firemaking, etc., as well as in pure ceremonial; because the need of reasserting the tribal morale and recognizing its cosmic conditions is constantly felt. In Christian Europe the Church brought men daily (in some orders even hourly) to their knees, to enact if not to contemplate their assent to the ultimate concepts' (Langer, 1960, p. 287, italics original).

There are at least three points where chaos—a tumult of events which lack not just interpretation but *interpretability*—threatens to break in upon man: at the limits of his analytic capacities, at the limits of his powers of endurance, and at the limits of his moral insight. Bafflement, suffering, and a sense of intractable ethical paradox are all, if they become intense enough or are sustained long enough, radical challenges to the proposition that life is comprehensible and that we can, by taking thought, orient ourselves effectively within it—challenges with which any religion, however 'primitive', which hopes to persist must attempt somehow to cope.

Of the three issues, it is the first which has been least investigated by modern social anthropologists (though Evans-Pritchard's, 1937 classic discussion of why granaries fall on some Azande and not on others, is a notable exception). Even to consider people's religious beliefs as attempts to bring anomalous events or experiences—death, dreams, mental fugues, volcanic eruptions, or marital infidelity—within the circle of the at least potentially explicable seems to smack of Tyloreanism or worse. But it does appear to be a fact that at least some men—in all probability, most men—are unable to leave unclarified problems of analysis merely unclarified, just to look at the stranger features of the world's landscape in dumb astonishment or bland apathy without trying to develop, however fantastic, inconsistent, or simple-minded, some notions as to how such features might be reconciled with the more ordinary deliverances of experience. Any chronic failure of one's explanatory apparatus, the complex of received culture patterns (common sense, science, philosophical speculation, myth) one has for mapping the empirical world, to explain things which cry out for explanation tends to lead to a deep disquiet—a tendency rather more widespread and a disquiet rather deeper than we have sometimes supposed since the pseudo-science view of religious belief was, quite rightfully, deposed. After all, even that high priest of heroic atheism, Lord Russell, once remarked that although the problem of the existence of God had never bothered him, the ambiguity of certain mathematical axioms had threatened to unhinge his mind. And Einstein's profound dissatisfaction with quantum mechanics was based on a—surely religious—inability to believe that, as he put it, God plays dice with the universe.

But this quest for lucidity and the rush of metaphysical anxiety that occurs when empirical phenomena threaten to remain intransigently opaque is found on much humbler intellectual levels. Certainly, I was struck in my own work, much more than I had at all expected to be, by the degree to which my more animistically inclined informants behaved like true Tyloreans. They seemed to be constantly using their beliefs to 'explain' phenomena: or, more accurately, to convince themselves that the phenomena were explainable within the accepted scheme of things, for they commonly had only a minimal attachment to the particular soul possession, emotional disequilibrium, taboo infringement, or bewitchment hypothesis they advanced and were all too ready to abandon it for some other, in the same genre, which struck them as more plausible given the facts of the case. What they were *not* ready to do was abandon it for no other hypothesis at all; to leave events to themselves.

And what is more, they adopted this nervous cognitive stance with respect to phenomena which had no immediate practical bearing on their own lives, or for that matter on anyone's. When a peculiarly shaped, rather large toadstool grew up in a carpenter's house in the short space of a few days (or, some said, a few hours), people came from miles around to see it, and everyone had some sort of explanation—some animist, some animatist, some not quite either—for it. Yet it would be hard to argue that the toadstool had any social value in Radcliffe-Brown's (1952) sense, or was connected in any way with anything which did and for which it could have been standing proxy, like the Andaman cicada. Toadstools play about the same role in Javanese life as they do in ours and in the ordinary course of things Javanese have about as much interest in them as we do. It was just that this one was 'odd', 'strange', 'uncanny'—*aneh*. And the odd, strange, and uncanny simply must be accounted for—or, again, the conviction that it *could be accounted for* sustained. One does not shrug off a toadstool which grows five times as fast as a toadstool has any right to grow. In the broadest sense the 'strange' toadstool did have implications, and critical ones, for those who heard about it. It threatened their most general ability to understand the world, raised the uncomfortable question of whether the beliefs which they held about nature were workable, the standards of truth they used valid.

Nor is this to argue that it is only, or even mainly, sudden eruptions of extraordinary events which engender in man the disquieting sense that his cognitive resources may prove unavailing or that this intuition appears only in its acute form. More commonly it is a persistent, constantly re-experienced difficulty in grasping certain aspects of nature, self, and society, in bringing certain elusive phenomena within the sphere of culturally formulatable fact, which renders man chronically uneasy and toward which a more equable flow of diagnostic symbols is consequently directed. It is what lies beyond a relatively fixed frontier of accredited knowledge that, looming as a constant background to the daily round of practical life, sets ordinary human experience in a permanent context of meta-physical concern and raises the dim, back-of-the-mind suspicion that one may be adrift in an absurd world:

> 'Another subject which is matter for this characteristic intellectual enquiry [among the Iatmul] is the nature of ripples and waves on the surface of water. It is said secretly that men, pigs, trees, grass—all the objects in the world—are only patterns of waves. Indeed there seems to be some agreement about this, although it perhaps conflicts with the theory of reincarnation, according to which the ghost of the dead is blown as a mist by the East Wind up the river and into the womb of the deceased's son's wife. Be that as it may—there is still the question of how ripples and waves are caused. The clan which claims the East Wind as a totem is clear enough about this: the Wind with her mosquito fan causes the waves. But other clans have personified the waves and say that they are a person (Kontummali) independent of the wind. Other clans, again, have other theories. On one occasion I took some Iatmul natives down to the coast and found one of them sitting by himself gazing with rapt attention at the sea. It was a windless day, but a slow swell was breaking on the beach. Among the totemic ancestors of his clan he counted a personified slit gong who had floated down the river to the sea and who was believed to cause the waves. He was gazing at the waves which were heaving and breaking when no wind was blowing, demonstrating the truth of his clan myth' (Bateson, 1958, pp. 130-131).[2]

The second experiential challenge in whose face the meaningfulness of a particular pattern of life threatens to dissolve into a chaos of thingless names and nameless things—the problem of suffering—has been rather more investigated, or at least described, mainly because of the great amount of attention given in works on tribal religion to what are perhaps its two main loci: illness and mourning. Yet for all the fascinated interest in the emotional aura that surrounds these extreme situations, there has been, with a few exceptions such as Lienhardt's recent (1961, pp. 151ff) discussion of Dinka divining, little conceptual advance over the sort of crude confidence-type theory set forth by Malinowski: viz. that religion helps one to endure 'situations of emotional stress' by 'open[ing] up escapes from such situations and such impasses as offer no empirical way out except by ritual and belief into the domain of the supernatural' (1948, p. 67). The inadequacy of this 'theology of optimism', as Nadel (1957) rather drily called it, is, of course, radical. Over its career religion has probably disturbed men as much as it has cheered them; forced them into a head-on, unblinking confrontation of the fact that they are born to trouble as often as it has enabled them to avoid such a confrontation by project-ing them into sort of infantile fairy-tale world where—Malinowski again (1948, p. 67)—'hope cannot fail nor desire deceive'. With the possible exception of Christian Science, there are few if any religious traditions, 'great' or 'little', in which the proposition that life hurts is not strenuously affirmed and in some it is virtually glorified:

> 'She was an old [Ba-Ila] woman of a family with a long genealogy. Leza, "the Besetting-One", stretched out his hand against the family. He slew her mother

and father while she was yet a child, and in the course of years all connected with her perished. She said to herself, "Surely I shall keep those who sit on my thighs." But no, even they, the children of her children, were taken from her. . . . Then came into her heart a desperate resolution to find God and to ask the meaning of it all. . . . So she began to travel, going through country after country, always with the thought in her mind: "I shall come to where the earth ends and there I shall find a road to God and I shall ask him: "What have I done to thee that thou afflictist me in this manner?" She never found where the earth ends, but though disappointed, she did not give up her search, and as she passed through the different countries they asked her, "What have you come for, old woman?" And the answer would be, "I am seeking Leza." "Seeking Leza! For what?" "My brothers, you ask me! Here in the nations is there one who suffers as I have suffered?" And they would ask again, "How have you suffered?" "In this way. I am alone. As you see me, a solitary old woman; that is how I am!" And they answered, "Yes, we see. That is how you are! Bereaved of friends and husband? In what do you differ from others? The Besetting-One sits on the back of every one of us and we cannot shake him off." She never obtained her desire: she died of a broken heart' (Smith & Dale, 1920, II, pp. 197ff; quoted in Radin, 1957, pp. 100-101).

As a religious problem, the problem of suffering is, paradoxically, not how to avoid suffering but how to suffer, how to make of physical pain, personal loss, wordly defeat, or the helpless contemplation of others' agony something bearable, supportable—something, as we say, sufferable. It was in this effort that the Ba-Ila woman-perhaps necessarily, perhaps not—failed and, literally not knowing how to feel about what had happened to her, how to suffer, perished in confusion and despair. Where the more intellective aspects of what Weber called the Problem of Meaning are a matter of affirming the ultimate explicability of experience, the more affective aspects are a matter of affirming its ultimate sufferableness. As religion on one side anchors the power of our symbolic resources for formulating analytic ideas in an authoritative conception of the overall shape of reality, so on another side it anchors the power of our, also symbolic, resources for expressing emotions—moods, sentiments, passions, affections, feelings—in a similar conception of its pervasive tenor, its inherent tone and temper. For those able to embrace them, and for so long as they are able to embrace them, religious symbols provide a cosmic guarantee not only for their ability to comprehend the world, but also, comprehending it, to give a precision to their feeling, a definition to their emotions which enables them, morosely or joyfully, grimly or cavalierly, to endure it.

Consider in this light the well-known Navaho curing rites usually referred to as 'sings' (Kluckhohn & Leighton, 1946; Reichard, 1950). A sing—the Navaho have about sixty different ones for different purposes, but virtually all of them are dedicated to removing some sort of physical or mental illness—is a kind of religious psychodrama in which there are three main actors: the 'singer' or curer, the patient, and, as a kind of antiphonal chorus, the patient's family and friends. The structure of all the sings, the drama's plot, is quite similar. There are three main acts: a purification of the patient and audience; a statement, by means of repetitive chants and ritual manipulations, of the wish to restore well-being ('harmony') in the patient; an identification of the patient with the Holy People and his consequent 'cure'. The purification rites involved forced sweating, induced vomiting, etc. to expel the sickness from the patient physically. The chants, which are numberless, consist mainly of simple optative phrases ('may the patient be well', 'I am getting better all over', etc.). And, finally, the identification of the patient with the Holy People, and thus with cosmic order generally, is accomplished through the agency of a sand painting depicting the Holy People in one or another appropriate mythic setting. The singer places the patient on the painting, touching the feet, hands, knees, shoulders, breast, back, and head of the divine figures and then the corresponding parts of the patient, performing thus what is essentially a communion rite between the patient and the Holy People, a bodily identification of the human and the divine (Reichard, 1950). This is the climax of the sing: the whole curing process may be likened, Reichard says, to a spiritual osmosis in which the illness in man and the power of the deity penetrate the ceremonial membrane in both directions, the former being neutralized by the latter. Sickness seeps out in the sweat, vomit, and other purification rites; health seeps in as the Navaho patient touches, through the medium of the singer, the sacred sand painting. Clearly, the symbolism of the sing focuses upon the problem of human suffering and attempts to cope with it by placing it in a meaningful context, providing a mode of action through which it can be expressed, being expressed understood, and being understood, endured. The sustaining effect of the sing (and since the commonest disease is tuberculosis, it can in most cases be only sustaining), rest ultimately on its ability to give the stricken person a vocabulary in terms of which to grasp the nature of his distress and relate it to the wider world. Like a calvary, a recitation of Buddha's emergence from his father's palace or a performance of *Oedipus Tyrannos* in other religious traditions, a sing is mainly concerned with the presentation of a specific and concrete image of truly human, and so endurable, suffering powerful enough to resist the challenge of emotional meaninglessness raised by the existence of intense and unremovable brute pain.

The problem of suffering passes easily into the problem of evil, for if suffering is severe enough it usually, though not always, seems morally undeserved as well, at least to the sufferer. But they are not, however, exactly the same thing—a fact I think Weber, too influenced by the biases of a monotheistic tradition in which, as the various aspects of human experience must be conceived to proceed from a single, voluntaristic source, man's pain reflects directly on God's goodness, did not fully recognize in his generalization of the dilemmas of Christian theodicy Eastward. For where the problem of suffering is concerned with threats to our ability to put our 'undisciplined squads of emotion' into some sort of soldierly order, the problem of evil is concerned with threats to our ability to make sound moral judgments. What is involved in the problem of evil is not the adequacy of our symbolic resources to govern our affective life, but the adequacy of those resources to provide a workable set of ethical criteria, normative guides to govern our action. The vexation here is the gap between things as they are and as they ought to be if our conceptions of right and wrong make sense, the gap between what we deem various individuals deserve and what we see that they get—a phenomenon summed up in that profound quatrain:

> The rain falls on the just
> And on the unjust fella;
> But mainly upon the just,
> Because the unjust has the just's umbrella.

Or if this seems too flippant an expression of an issue that, in somewhat different form, animates the Book of Job and the *Baghavad Gita,* the following classical Javanese poem, known, sung, and repeatedly quoted in Java by virtually everyone over the age of six, puts the point—the discrepancy between moral prescriptions and material rewards, the seeming inconsistency of 'is' and 'ought'—rather more elegantly:

> We have lived to see a time without order
> In which everyone is confused in his mind.
> One cannot bear to join in the madness,
> But if he does not do so
> He will not share in the spoils,
> And will starve as a result.
> Yes, God; wrong is wrong:
> Happy are those who forget,
> Happier yet those who remember and have deep insight.

Nor is it necessary to be theologically self-conscious to be religiously sophisticated. The concern with intractable ethical paradox, the disquieting sense that one's moral insight is inadequate to one's moral experience, is as alive on the level of so-called 'primitive' religion as it is on that of the so-called 'civilized'. The set of notions about 'division in the world' that Lienhardt describes (1961, pp. 28-55) for the Dinka is a useful case in point. Like so many peoples, the Dinka believe that the sky, where 'Divinity' is located, and earth, where man dwells, were at one time contiguous, the sky lying just above the earth and being connected to it by a rope, so that men could move at will between the two realms. There was no death and the first man and woman were permitted but a single grain of millet a day, which was all that they at that time required. One day, the woman—of course—decided, out of greed, to plant more than the permitted grain of millet and in her avid haste and industry accidentally struck Divinity with the handle of the hoe. Offended, he severed the rope, withdrew into the distant sky of today, and left man to labor for his food, to suffer sickness and death, and to experience separation from the source of his being, his Creator. Yet the meaning of this strangely familiar story to the Dinka is, as indeed is Genesis to Jews and Christians, not homiletic but descriptive:

> 'Those [Dinka] who have commented on these stories have sometimes made
> it clear that their sympathies lie with Man in his plight, and draw attention to

the smallness of the fault for which Divinity withdrew the benefits of his closeness. The image of striking Divinity with a hole . . . often evokes a certain amusement, almost as though the story were indulgently being treated as too childish to explain the consequences attributed to the event. But it is clear that the point of the story of Divinity's withdrawal from men is not to suggest an improving moral judgement on human behaviour. It is to represent a total situation known to the Dinka today. Men now are—as the first man and woman then became—active, self-assertive, inquiring, acquisitive. Yet they are also subject to suffering and death, ineffective, ignorant and poor. Life is insecure; human calculations often prove erroneous, and men must often learn by experience that the consequences of their acts are quite other than they may have anticipated or consider equitable. Divinity's withdrawal from Man as the result of a comparatively trifling offence, by human standards, presents the contrast between equitable human judgements and the action of the Power which are held ultimately to control what happens in Dinka life. . . . To the Dinka, the moral order is ultimately constituted according to principles which often elude men, which experience and tradition in part reveal, and which human action cannot change. . . . The myth of Divinity's withdrawal then reflects the facts of existence as they are known. The Dinka are in a universe which is largely beyond their control, and where events may contradict the most reasonable human expectations' (Lienhardt, 1961, pp. 53-54).

Thus the problem of evil, or perhaps one should say the problem *about* evil, is in essence the same sort of problem of or about bafflement and the problem of or about suffering. The strange opacity of certain empirical events, the dumb senselessness of intense of inexorable pain, and the enigmatic unaccountability of gross iniquity all raise the uncomfortable suspicion that perhaps the world, and hence man's life in the world, has no genuine order at all—no empirical regularity, no emotional form, no moral coherence. And the religious response to this suspicion is in each case the same: the formulation, by means of symbols, of an image of such a genuine order of the world which will account for, and even celebrate, the perceived ambiguities, puzzles, and paradoxes in human experience. The effort is not to deny the undeniable—that there are unexplained events, that life hurts, or that rain falls upon the just—but to deny that there are inexplicable events, that life is unendurable, and that justice is a mirage. The pinciples which constitute the moral order may indeed often elude men, as Lienhardt puts it, in the same way as fully satisfactory explanations of anomalous events or effective forms for the expression of feeling often elude them. What is important, to a religious man at least, is that this elusiveness be accounted for, that it be not the result of the fact that there are no such principles, explanations, or forms, that life is absurd and the attempt to make moral, intellectual or emotional sense out of experience is bootless. The Dinka can admit, in fact insist upon, the moral ambiguities and contradictions of life as they live it because these ambiguities and contradictions are seen not as ultimate, but as the 'rational', 'natural', 'logical' (one may choose one's own adjective here, for none of them is truly adequate) outcome of the moral structure of reality which the myth of the withdrawn 'Divinity' depicts, or as Lienhardt says, 'images'.

The Problem of Meaning in each of its intergrading aspects (how these aspects in fact intergrade in each particular case, what sort of interplay there is between the sense of analytic, emotional, and moral impotence, seems to me one of the outstanding, and except for Weber untouched, problems for comparative research in this whole field) is a matter of affirming, or at least recognizing, the inescapability of ignorance, pain, and injustice on the human plane while simultaneously denying that these irrationalities are characteristic of the world as a whole. And it is in terms of religious symbolism, a symbolism relating man's sphere of existence to a wider sphere within which it is conceived to rest, that both the affirmation and the denial are made.[3]

4. . . . and clothing those conceptions with such an aura of factuality that . . .

There arises here, however, a profounder question: how is it that this denial comes to be believed? how is it that the religious man moves from a troubled perception of experienced disorder to a more or less settled conviction of fundamental order? just what does 'belief' mean in a religious context? Of all the problems surrounding attempts to conduct anthropological analysis of religion this is the one that has perhaps been most troublesome and therefore the most often avoided, usually by relegating it to psychology, that raffish outcast discipline to which social anthropologists are forever consigning phenomena they are unable to deal with within the framework of a denatured Durkheimianism. But the problem will not go away, it is not 'merely' psychological (nothing social is), and no anthropoligical theory of religion which fails to attack it is worthy of the name. We have been trying to stage Hamlet without the Prince quite long enough.

It seems to me that it is best to begin any approach to this issue with frank recognition that religious belief involves not a Baconian induction from everyday experience—for then we should all be agnostics—but rather a prior acceptance of authority which transforms that experience. The existence of bafflement, pain, and moral paradox—of The Problem of Meaning—is one of the things that drive men toward belief in gods, devils, spirits, totemic principles, or the spiritual efficacy of cannibalism (an enfolding sense of beauty or a dazzling perception of power are others), but it is not the basis upon which those beliefs rest, but rather their most important field of application:

> 'We point to the state of the world as illustrative of doctrine, but never as evidence for it. So Belsen illustrates a world of original sin, but original sin is not an hypothesis to account for happenings like Belsen. We justify a particular religious belief by showing its place in the total religious conception; we justify a religious belief as a whole by referring to authority. We accept authority because we discover it at some point in the world at which we worship, at which we accept the lordship of something not ourselves. We do not worship authority, but we accept authority as defining the worshipful. So someone may discover the possibility of worship in the life of the

Reformed Churches and accept the Bible as authoritative; or in the Roman Church and accept papal authority' (MacIntyre, 1957, pp. 201-202).

This is, of course, a Christian statement of the matter; but it is not to be despised on that account. In tribal religions authority lies in the persuasive power of traditional imagery; in mystical ones in the apodictic force of supersensible experience; in charismatic ones in the hypnotic attraction of an extraordinary personality. But the priority of the acceptance of an authoritative criterion in religious matters over the revelation which is conceived to flow from that acceptance is not less complete than in scriptural or hieratic ones. The basic axiom underlying what we may perhaps call 'the religious perspective' is everywhere the same: he who would know must first believe.

But to speak of 'the religious perspective' is, by implication, to speak of one perspective among others. A perspective is a mode of seeing, in that extended sense of 'see' in which it means 'discern', 'apprehend', 'understand', or 'grasp'. It is a particular way of looking at life, a particular manner of construing the world, as when we speak of an historical perspective, a scientific perspective, an aesthetic perspective, a common-sense perspective, or even the bizarre perspective embodied in dreams and in hallucinations.[4] The question then comes down to, first, what is 'the religious perspective' generically considered, as differentiated from other perspectives; and second, how do men come to adopt it.

If we place the religious perspective against the background of three of the other major perspectives in terms of which men construe the world—the commonsensical, the scientific, and the aesthetic—its special character emerges more sharply. What distinguishes common sense as a mode of 'seeing' is, as Schutz (1962) has pointed out, a simple acceptance of the world, its objects, and its processes as being just what they seem to be—what is sometimes called naive realism—and the pragmatic motive, the wish to act upon that world so as to bend it to one's practical purposes, to master it, or so far as that proves impossible, to adjust to it. The world of everyday life, itself, of course, a cultural product, for it is framed in terms of the symbolic conceptions of 'stubborn fact' handed down from generation to generation, is the established scene and given object of our actions. Like Mt. Everest it is just there and the thing to do with it, if one feels the need to do anything with it at all, is to climb it. In the scientific perspective it is precisely this givenness which disappears (Schutz, 1962). Deliberate doubt and systematic inquiry, the suspension of the pragmatic motive in favor of disinterested observation, the attempt to analyze the world in terms of formal concepts whose relationship to the informal conceptions of common sense become increasingly problematic—these are the hallmarks of the attempts to grasp the world scientifically. And as for the aesthetic perspective, which under the rubric of 'the aesthetic attitude' has been perhaps most exquisitely examined, it involves a different sort of suspension of naive realism and practical interest, in that instead of questioning the credentials of everyday experience that experience is merely ignored in favor of an eager dwelling upon appearances, an engrossment in surfaces, an absorption in things, as we say, 'in themselves': 'The function of artistic illusion is not "make-believe" . . . but the very opposite, disengagement from belief—the contemplation of sensory qualities without their usual meanings of "here's that chair", "That's my telephone" . . . etc. The knowledge that what is before us has no practical significance in the world is what enables us to give attention to its appearance as such' (Langer, 1953, p. 49). And like the common-sensical and the scientific (or the historical, the philosophical, and the autistic), this perspective, this 'way of seeing' is not the product of some mysterious Cartesian chemistry, but is induced, mediated, and in fact created by means of symbols. It is the artist's skill which can produce those curious quasi-objects—poems, dramas, sculptures, symphonies—which, dissociating themselves from the solid world of common sense, take on the special sort of eloquence only sheer appearances can achieve.

The religious perspective differs from the common-sensical in that, as already pointed out, it moves beyond the realities of everyday life to wider ones which correct and complete them, and its defining concerns is not action upon those wider realities but acceptance of them, faith in them. It differs from the scientific perspective in that it questions the realities of everyday life not out of an institutionalized scepticism which dissolves the world's givenness into a swirl of probabilistic hypotheses, but in terms of what it takes to be wider, nonhypothetical truths. Rather than detachment, its watchword is commitment; rather than analysis, encounter. And it differs from art in that instead of effecting a disengagement from the whole question of factuality, deliberately manufacturing an air of semblance and illusion, it deepens the concern with fact and seeks to create an aura of utter actuality. It is this sense of the 'really real' upon which the religious perspective rests and which the symbolic activities of religion as a cultural system are devoted to producing, intensifying, and, so far as possible, rendering inviolable by the discordant revelations of secular experience. It is, again, the imbuing of a certain specific complex of symbols—of the metaphysic they formulate and the style of life they recommend—with a persuasive authority which, from an analytic point of view is the essence of religious action.

Which brings us, at length, to ritual. For it is in ritual—i.e., consecrated behavior—that this conviction that religious conceptions are veridical and that religious directives are sound is somehow generated. It is in some sort of ceremonial form—even if that form be hardly more than the recitation of a myth, the consultation of an oracle, or the decoration of a grave—that the moods and motivations which sacred symbols induce in men and the general conceptions of the order of existence which they formulate for men meet and reinforce one another. In a ritual, the world as lived and the world as imagined, fused under the agency of a single set of symbolic forms, turn out to be the same world, producing thus that idiosyncratic transformation in one's sense of reality to which Santayana refers in my epigraph.[5] Whatever role divine intervention may or may not play in the creation of faith—and it is not the business of the scientist to pronounce upon such matters one way or the other—it is, primarily at least, out of the context of concrete acts of religious observance that religious conviction emerges on the human plane.

5. . . . that the moods and motivations seem uniquely realistic.

But no one, not even a saint, lives in the world religious symbols formulate all of the time, and the majority of men live in it only at moments. The everyday world of common-sense objects and practical acts is, as Schutz (1962, pp. 226ff.) says, the paramount reality in human experience—paramount in the sense that it is the world in which we are most solidly rooted, whose inherent actuality we can hardly question (however much we may question certain portions of it), and from whose pressures and requirements we can least escape. A man, even large groups of men, may be aesthetically insensitive, religiously unconcerned, and unequipped to pursue formal scientific analysis, but he cannot be completely lacking in common sense and survive. The dispositions which religious rituals induce thus have their most important impact—from a human point of view—outside the boundaries of the ritual itself as they reflect back to color the individual's conception of the established world of bare fact. The peculiar tone that marks the Plains vision quest, the Manus confession, or the Javanese mystical exercise pervades areas of the life of these peoples far beyond the immediately religious, impressing upon them a distinctive style in the sense both of a dominant mood and a characteristic movement. The interweaving of the malignant and the comic, which the Rangda-Barong combat depicts, animates a very wide range of everyday Balinese behavior, much of which, like the ritual itself, has an air of candid fear narrowly contained by obsessive playfulness. Religion is sociologically interesting not because, as vulgar positivism would have it (Leach, 1954, pp. 10ff.), it describes the social order (which, in so far as it does, it does not only very obliquely but very incompletely), but because, like environment, political power, wealth, jural obligation, personal affection, and a sense of beauty, it shapes it.

The movement back and forth between the religious perspective and the common-sense perspective is actually one of the more obvious empirical occurrences on the social scene, though, again, one of the most neglected by social anthropologists, virtually all of whom have seen it happen countless times. Religious belief has usually been presented as an homogeneous characteristic of an individual, like his place of residence, his occupational role, his kinship position, and so on. But religious belief in the midst of ritual, where it engulfs the total person, transporting him, so far as he is concerned, into another mode of existence, and religious belief as the pale, remembered reflection of that experience in the midst of everyday life are not precisely the same thing, and the failure to realize this has led to some confusion, most especially in connection with the so-called 'primitive mentality' problem. Much of the difficulty between Lévy-Bruhl (1926) and Malinowski (1948) on the nature of 'native thought', for example, arises from a lack of full recognition of this distinction; for where the French philosopher was concerned with the view of reality savages adopted when taking a specifically religious perspective, the Polish-English ethnographer was concerned with that which they adopted when taking a strictly common-sense one. Both perhaps vaguely sensed that they were not talking about exactly the same thing, but where they went astray was in failing to give a specific accounting of the way in which these two forms of 'thought'—or, as I would rather say, these two modes of symbolic formulation—interacted, so that when Lévy-Bruhl's savages tended to live, despite his postludial disclaimers, in a world composed entirely of mystical encounters, Malinowski's tended to live, despite his stress on the functional importance of religion, in a world composed entirely of practical actions. They became reductionists (an idealist is as much of a reductionist as a materialist) in spite of themselves because they failed to see man as moving more or less easily, and very frequently, between radically contrasting ways of looking at the world, ways which are not continuous with one another but separated by cultural gaps across which Kierkegaardian leaps must be made in both directions:

> 'There are as many innumerable kinds of different shock experiences as there are different finite provinces of meaning upon which I may bestow the accent of reality. Some instances are: the shock of falling asleep as the leap into the world of dreams; the inner transformation we endure if the curtain in the theatre rises as the transition to the world of the stageplay; the radical change in our attitude if, before a painting, we permit our visual field to be limited by what is within the frame as the passage into the pictorial world; our quandary relaxing into laughter, if, in listening to a joke, we are for a short time ready to accept the fictitious world of the jest as a reality in relation to which the world of our daily life takes on the character of foolishness; the child's turning toward his toy as the transition into the play-world; and so on. But also the religious experiences in all their varieties—for instance, Kierkegaard's experience of the "instant" as the leap into the religious sphere—are examples of such a shock, as well as the decision of the scientist to replace all passionate participation in the affairs of "this world" by a disinterested [analytical] attitude' (Schutz, 1962, p. 231).

The recognition and exploration of the qualitative difference—an empirical, not a transcendental difference—between religion pure and religion applied, between an encounter with the supposedly 'really real' and a viewing of ordinary experience in light of what that encounter seems to reveal, will, therefore, take us further toward an understanding of what a Bororo means when he says 'I am a parakeet', or a Christian when he says 'I am a sinner', than either a theory of primitive mysticism in which the commonplace world disappears into a cloud of curious ideas or of a primitive pragmatism in which religion disintegrates into a collection of useful fictions. The parakeet example, which I take from Percy (1961), is a good one. For, as he points out, it is unsatisfactory to say either that the Bororo thinks he is literally a parakeet (for he does not try to mate with other parakeets), that his statement is false or nonsense (for, clearly, he is not offering—or at least not only offering—the sort of class-membership argument which can be confirmed or refuted as, say, 'I am a Bororo' can be confirmed or refuted), or yet again that it is false scientifically but true mythically (because that leads immediately to the pragmatic fiction notion which, as it denies the accolade of truth to 'myth' in the very act of bestowing it, is internally self-contradictory). More coherently it would seem to be necessary to see the sentence as having a different sense in the context of the 'finite province of meaning' which makes up the religious perspective and of that which makes up the common-sensical. In the religious, our Bororo is 'really' a 'parakeet', and given the proper ritual context might well 'mate' with other 'parakeets'—with metaphysical ones like himself not commonplace ones such as those which fly bodily about in ordinary trees. In the common-sensical perspective he is a parakeet in the sense—I assume—that he belongs to a clan whose members regard the parakeet as their totem, a membership from which, given the fundamental nature of reality as the religious perspective reveals it, certain moral and practical consequences flow. A man who says he is a parakeet is, if he says it in normal conversation, saying that, as myth and ritual demonstrate, he is shot through with parakeetness, and that this religious fact has some crucial social implications—we parakeets must stick together, not marry one another, not eat mundane parakeets, and so on, for to do otherwise is to act against the grain of the whole universe. It is this placing of proximate acts in ultimate contexts that makes religion, frequently at least, socially so powerful. It alters, often radically, the whole landscape presented to common sense, alters it in such a way that the moods and motivations induced by religious practice seem themselves supremely practical, the only sensible ones to adopt given the way things 'really' are.

Having ritually 'leapt' (the image is perhaps a bit too athletic for the actual facts—'slipped' might be more accurate) into the framework of meaning which religious conceptions define and, the ritual ended, returned again to the common-sense world, a man is—unless, as sometimes happens, the experience fails to register—changed. And as he is changed so also is the common-sense world, for it is now seen as but the partial form of a wider reality which corrects and completes it. But this correction and completion is not, as some students of 'comparative religion' (e.g. Campbell, 1949, pp. 236-237) would have it, everywhere the same in content. The nature of the bias religion gives to ordinary life varies with the religion involved, with the particular dispositions induced in the believer by the specific conceptions of cosmic order he has come to accept. On the level of the 'great' religions, organic distinctiveness is usually recognized, at times insisted upon to the point of zealotry. But even at its simplest folk and tribal levels—where the individuality of religious traditions has so often been dissolved into such desiccated types as 'animism', 'animatism', 'totemism', 'shamanism', 'ancestor worship', and all the other insipid categories by means of which ethnographers of religion devitalize their data—the idiosyncartic character of how various groups of men behave because of what they believe they have experienced is clear. A tranquil Javanese would be no more at home in guilt-ridden Manus than an activist Crow would be in passion-less Java. And for all the witches and ritual clowns in the world, Rangda and Barong are not generalized but thoroughly singular figurations of fear and gaiety. What men believe is as various as what they are—a proposition that holds with equal force when it is inverted.

It is this particularity of the impact of religious systems upon social systems (and upon personality systems) which renders general assessments of the value of religion in either moral or functional terms impossible. The sorts of moods and motivations which characterize a man who has just come from an Aztec human sacrifice are rather different from those of one who has just put off his Kachina mask. Even within the same society, what one 'learns' about the essential pattern of life from a sorcery rite and from a commensal meal will have rather diverse effects on social and psychological functioning. One of the main methodological problems in writing about religion scientifically is to put aside at once the tone of the village atheist and that of the village preacher, as well as their more sophisticated equivalents, so that the social and psychological implications of particular religious beliefs can emerge in a clear and neutral light. And when that is done, overall questions about whether religion is 'good' or 'bad', 'functional' or 'dysfunctional', 'ego strengthening' or 'anxiety producing' disappear like the chimeras they are, and one is left with particular evaluations, assessments, and diagnoses in particular cases. There remain, of course, the hardly unimportant questions of whether this or that religious assertion is true, this or that religious experience genuine, or whether true religious assertions and genuine religious experiences are possible at all. But such questions cannot even be asked, much less answered, within the self-imposed limitations of the scientific perspective.

NOTES

1. The reverse mistake, especially common among neo-Kantians such as Cassirer (1953-57), of taking symbols to be identical with, or 'constitutive of,' their referents is equally pernicious. 'One can point to the moon with one's finger,' some, probably well-invented, Zen Master is supposed to have said, 'but to take one's finger for the moon is to be a fool.'

2. That the chronic and acute forms of this sort of cognitive concern are closely interrelated, and that responses to the more unusual occasions of it are patterned on responses established in coping with the more usual is also clear from Bateson's description, however, as he goes on to say: 'On another occasion I invited one of my informants to witness the development of photographic plates. I first desensitised the plates and then developed them in an open dish in moderate light, so that my informant was able to see the gradual appearance of the images. He was much interested, and some days later made me promise never to show this process to members of other clans. Kontum-mali was one of his ancestors, and he saw in the process of photographic development the actual embodiment of ripples into images, and regarded this as a demonstration of the clan's secret' (Bateson, 1958).

3. This is *not*, however, to say that everyone in every society does this; for as the immortal Don Marquis once remarked, you don't have to have a soul unless you really want one. The oft-heard generalization (e.g. Kluckhohn, 1953) that religion is a human universal embodies a confusion between the probably true (though on present evidence unprovable) proposition that there is no human society in which cultural patterns that we can, under the present definition or one like it, call religious are totally lacking, and the surely untrue proposition that all men in all societies are, in any meaningful sense of the term, religious. But if the anthropological study of religious commitment is underdeveloped, the anthropological study of religious non-commitment is non-existent. The anthropology of religion will have come of age when

some more subtle Malinowski writes a book called 'Belief and Unbelief (or even "Faith and Hypocrisy") in a Savage Society'.

4. The term 'attitude' as in 'aesthetic attitude' (Bell, 1914) or 'natural attitude' (Schutz, 1962; the phrase is originally Husserl's) is another, perhaps more common term for what I have here called 'perspective'. But I have avoided it because of its strong subjectivist connotations, its tendency to place the stress upon a supposed inner state of an actor rather than on a certain sort of relation—a symbolically mediated one—between an actor and a situation. This is not to say, of course, that a phenomenological analysis of religious experience, if cast in inter-subjective, non-transcendental, genuinely scientific terms (see Percy, 1958) is not essential to a full understanding of religious belief, but merely that that is not the focus of my concern here. 'Outlook', 'frame of reference', 'frame of mind', 'orientation', 'stance', 'mental set', etc. are other terms sometimes employed, depending upon whether the analyst wishes to stress the social, psychological, or cultural aspects of the matter.

5. Any attempt to speak without speaking any particular language is not more hopeless than the attempt to have a religion that shall be no religion in particular. . . . Thus every living and healthy religion has a marked idiosyncrasy, its power consists in its special and surprising message and in the bias which that revelation gives to life. The vistas it opens and the mysteries it propounds are another world to live in; and another world to live in—whether we expect ever to pass wholly over into it or no—is what we mean by having a religion. Santayana: *Reason in Religion* (1906).

REFERENCES

BATESON, G., 1958.   *Naven.* Stanford: Stanford University Press, 2nd ed.
BATESON, G. & MEAD, M. 1942.   *Balinese Character.* New York: N.Y. Academy of Sciences.
BELL, C. 1914.   *Art.* London: Chatto & Windus.
BELO, J. 1949.   *Bali: Rangda and Barong.* New York: J. J. Augustin.
—— 1960.   *Trance in Bali.* New York: Columbia University Press.
BURKE, K. 1941.   *The Philosophy of Literary Form.* n.p.: Louisiana State University Press.
CAMPBELL, J. 1949.   *The Hero with a Thousand Faces.* New York: Pantheon.
CASSIRIR, E. 1953-57.   *ThePhilosophy of Symbolic Forms* (trans. R. Mannheim). New Haven: Yale University Press. 3 vols.
COVARRUBIAS, M. 1937.   *The Island of Bali.* New York: Knopf.
CRAIK, K. 1952.   *The Nature of Explanation.* Cambridge: Cambridge University Press.
EVANS-PRITCHARD, E. E. 1937.   *Witchcraft, Oracles and Magic Among the Azande.* Oxford: Clarendon Press.
FIRTH, R. 1951.   *Elements of Social Organization.* London: Watts; New York: Philosophical Library.
FORTUNE, R. F. 1935.   *Manus Religion.* Philadelphia: American Philosophical Society.
VON FRISCH, K. 1962.   Dialects in the Language of the Bees. *Scientific American,* August.
GEERTZ, C. 1958.   Ethos, World-View and the Analysis of Sacred Symbols. *Antioch Review,* Winter (1957-58): 421-437.
—— 1960.   *The Religion of Java.* Glencoe, Ill.: The Free Press.
—— 1962.   The Growth of Culture and the Evolution of Mind. In J. Scher (ed.), *Theories of the Mind.* New York: The Free Press, pp. 713-740.
—— 1964a.   Ideology as a Cultural System. In D. Apter (ed.), *Ideology of Discontent.* New York: The Free Press.

—— 1964b. 'Internal Conversion' in Contemporary Bali. In J. Bastin & R. Roolvink (eds.), *Malayan and Indonesian Studies.* Oxford: Oxford University Press, pp. 282-302.

GOODY, J. 1961. Religion and Ritual: The Definition Problem. *British Journal of Sociology* **12**: 143-164.

HOROWITZ, N. H. 1956. The Gene. *Scientific American,* February.

JAMES, WILLIAM. 1904. *The Principles of Psychology.* New York: Henry Holt, 2 vols.

JANOWITZ, M. 1963. Anthropology and the Social Sciences. *Current Anthropology* **4**: 139, 146-154.

KLUCKHOHN, C. 1949. The Philosophy of the Navaho Indians. In F. S. C. Northrop (ed.), *Ideological Differences and World Order.* New Haven: Yale University Press, pp. 356-384.

—— 1953. Universal Categories of Culture. In A. L. Kroeber (ed.), *Anthropology Today.* Chicago: University of Chicago Press, pp. 507-523.

KLUCKHOHN, C. & LEIGHTON, D. 1946. *The Navaho.* Cambridge, Mass.: Harvard University Press.

LANGER, S. 1953. *Feeling and Form.* New York: Scribner's.

—— 1960. *Philosophy in a New Key.* Fourth Edition. Cambridge, Mass.: Harvard University Press.

—— 1962. *Philosophical Sketches.* Baltimore: Johns Hopkins.

LEACH, E. R. 1954. *Political Systems of Highland Burma.* London: Bell; Cambridge, Mass.: Harvard University Press.

LÉVY-BRUHL, L. 1926. *How Natives Think.* New York: Knopf.

LIENHARDT, G. 1961. *Divinity and Experience.* Oxford: Clarendon Press.

LORENZ, K. 1952. *King Solomon's Ring.* London: Methuen.

LOWIE, R. H. 1924. *Primitive Religion.* New York: Boni and Liveright.

MACINTYRE, A. 1957. The Logical Status of Religious Belief. In A. MacIntyre (ed.), *Metaphysical Beliefs.* London: SCM Press, pp. 167-211.

MALINOWSKI, B. 1948. *Magic, Science and Religion.* Boston: Beacon Press.

NADEL, S. F. 1957. Malinowski on Magic and Religion. In R. Firth (ed.), *Man and Culture.* London: Routledge & Kegan Paul, pp. 189-208.

PARSONS, T. & SHILS, E. 1951. *Toward a General Theory of Action.* Cambridge, Mass.: Harvard University Press.

PERCY, W. 1958. Symbol, Consciousness and Intersubjectivity. *Journal of Philosophy* **15**: 631-641.

—— 1961. The Symbolic Structure of Interpersonal Process. *Psychiatry* **24**: 39-52.

RADCLIFFE-BROWN, A. R. 1952. *Structure and Function in Primitive Society.* Glencoe, Ill.: Free Press.

RADIN, P. 1957. *Primitive Man as a Philosopher.* New York: Dover.

REICHARD, G. 1950. *Navaho Religion.* New York: Pantheon, 2 vols.

RYLE, G. 1949. *The Concept of Mind.* London: Hutchinson; New York: Barnes & Noble.

SANTAYANA, G. 1905-1906. *Reason in Religion.* Vol. 2 of *The Life of Reason, or The Phases of Human Progress.* London: Constable; New York: Scribner's.

SCHUTZ, A. 1962. *The Problem of Social Reality* (vol. I. of *Collected Papers*). The Hague: Martinus Nijhoff.

SINGER, M. 1955. The Cultural Pattern of Indian Civilization. *Far Eastern Quarterly* **15**: 23-36.

—— 1958. The Great Tradition in a Metropolitan Center: Madras. In M. Singer (ed.), *Traditional India.* Philadelphia: American Folklore Society, pp. 140-82.

SMITH, C. W. & DALE, A. M. 1920.   *The Ila-Speaking Peoples of Northern Rhodesia.* London: Macmillan.
DE ZOETE, B. & SPIES, W. 1938.   *Dance and Drama in Bali.* London: Faber & Faber.

RELIGION VERSUS THE RELIGIOUS

John Dewey

Never before in history has mankind been so much of two minds, so divided into two camps, as it is today. Religions have traditionally been allied with ideas of the supernatural, and often have been based upon explicit beliefs about it. Today there are many who hold that nothing worthy of being called religious is possible apart from the supernatural. Those who hold this belief differ in many respects. They range from those who accept the dogmas and sacraments of the Greek and Roman Catholic church as the only sure means of access to the supernatural to the theist or mild deist. Between them are the many Protestant denominations who think the Scriptures, aided by a pure conscience, are adequate avenues to supernatural truth and power. But they agree in one point: the necessity for a Supernatural Being and for an immortality that is beyond the power of nature.

The opposed group consists of those who think the advance of culture and science has completely discredited the supernatural and with it all religions that are allied with belief in it. But they go beyond this point. The extremists in this group believe that with elimination of the supernatural not only must historic religions be dismissed but with them everything of a religious nature. When historical knowledge has discredited the claims made for the supernatural character of the persons said to have founded historic religions; when the supernatural inspiration attributed to the literatures held sacred has been riddled, and when anthropological and psychological knowledge has disclosed the all-too-human source from which religious beliefs and practices have sprung, everything religious must, they say, also go.

There is one idea held in common by these two opposite groups: identification of the religious with the supernatural. The question I shall raise in these chapters concerns the ground for and the consequences of this identification: its reasons and its value. In the discussion I shall develop another conception of the nature of the religious phase of experience, one that separates it from the supernatural and the things that have grown up about it. I shall try to show that these derivations are encumbrances and that what is genuinely religious will undergo an emancipation when it is relieved from them; that then, for the first time, the religious aspect of experience will be free to develop freely on its own account.

This view is exposed to attack from both the other camps. It goes contrary

From *A Common Faith* (New Haven: Yale University Press, 1934), pp. 2-28. Reprinted by permission of the publisher.

to traditional religions, including those that have the greatest hold upon the religiously minded today. The view announced will seem to them to cut the vital nerve of the religious element itself in taking away the basis upon which traditional religions and institutions have been founded. From the other side, the position I am taking seems like a timid halfway position, a concession and compromise unworthy of thought that is thoroughgoing. It is regarded as a view entertained from mere tendermindedness, as an emotional hangover from childhood indoctrination, or even as a manifestation of a desire to avoid disapproval and curry favor.

The heart of my point, as far as I shall develop it in this first section, is that there is a difference between religion, *a* religion, and the religious; between anything that may be denoted by a noun substantive and the quality of experience that is designated by an adjective. It is not easy to find a definition of religion in the substantive sense that wins general acceptance. However, in the *Oxford Dictionary* I find the following: "Recognition on the part of man of some unseen higher power as having control of his destiny and as being entitled to obedience, reverence and worship."

This particular definition is less explicit in assertion of the supernatural character of the higher unseen power than are others that might be cited. It is, however, surcharged with implications having their source in ideas connected with the belief in the supernatural, characteristic of historic religions. Let us suppose that one familiar with the history of religions, including those called primitive, compares the definition with the variety of known facts and by means of the comparison sets out to determine just what the definition means. I think he will be struck by three facts that reduce the terms of the definition to such a low common denominator that little meaning is left.

He will note that the "unseen powers" referred to have been conceived in a multitude of incompatible ways. Eliminating the differences, nothing is left beyond the bare reference to something unseen and powerful. This has been conceived as the vague and undefined Mana of the Melanesians; the Kami of primitive Shintoism; the fetish of the Africans; spirits, having some human properties, that pervade natural places and animate natural forces; the ultimate and impersonal principle of Buddhism; the unmoved mover of Greek thought; the gods and semi-divine heroes of the Greek and Roman Pantheons; the personal and loving Providence of Christianity, omnipotent, and limited by a corresponding evil power; the arbitrary Will of Moslemism; the supreme legislator and judge of deism. And these are but a few of the outstanding varieties of ways in which the invisible power has been conceived.

There is no greater similarity in the ways in which obedience and reverence have been expressed. There has been worship of animals, of ghosts, of ancestors, phallic worship, as well as of a Being of dread power and of love and wisdom. Reverence has been expressed in the human sacrifices of the Peruvians and Aztecs; the sexual orgies of some Oriental religions; exorcisms and ablutions; the offering of the humble and contrite mind of the Hebrew prophet, the elaborate rituals of the Greek and Roman Churches. Not even sacrifice has been uniform; it is highly sublimated in Protestant denominations and in Moslemism. Where it has existed it has taken all kinds of forms and been directed to a great variety of powers and spirits. It has been used for expiation, for propitiation and for buying special favors. There is no conceivable purpose for which rites have not been employed.

Finally, there is no discernible unity in the moral motivations appealed to and utilized. They have been as far apart as fear of lasting torture, hope of enduring bliss in which sexual enjoyment has sometimes been a conspicuous element; mortification of the flesh and extreme asceticism; prostitution and chasity; wars to extirpate the unbeliever, and philanthropic zeal; servile acceptance of imposed dogma, along with brotherly love and aspiration for a reign of justice among men.

I have, of course, mentioned only a sparse number of the facts which fill volumes in any well-stocked library. It may be asked by those who do not like to look upon the darker side of the history of religions why the darker facts should be brought up. We all know that civilized man has a background of bestiality and superstition and that these elements are still with us. Indeed, have not some religions, including the most influential forms of Christianity, taught that the heart of man is totally corrupt? How could the course of religion in its entire sweep not be marked by practices that are shameful in their cruelty and lustfulness, and by beliefs that are degraded and intellectually incredible? What else than what we find could be expected, in the case of people having little knowledge and no secure method of knowing; with primitive institutions, and with so little control of natural forces that they lived in a constant state of fear?

I gladly admit that historic religions have been relative to the conditions of social culture in which peoples lived. Indeed, what I am concerned with is to press home the logic of this method of disposal of outgrown traits of past religions. Beliefs and practices in a religion that now prevails are by this logic relative to the present state of culture. If so much flexibility has obtained in the past regarding an unseen power, the way it affects human destiny, and the attitudes we are to take toward it, why should it be assumed that change in conception and action has now come to an end? The logic involved in getting rid of inconvenient aspects of past religions compels us to inquire how much in religions now accepted are survivals from outgrown cultures. It compels us to ask what conception of unseen powers and our relations to them would be consonant with the best achievements and aspirations of the present. It demands that in imagination we wipe the slate clean and start afresh by asking what would be the idea of the unseen, of the manner of its control over us and the ways in which reverence and obedience would be manifested, if whatever is basically religious in experience had the opportunity to express itself free from all historic encumbrances.

So we return to the elements of the definition that has been given. What boots it to accept, in defense of the universality of religion, a definition that applies equally to the most savage and degraded beliefs and practices that have related to unseen powers and to noble ideals of a religion having the greatest share of moral content? There are two points involved. One of them is that there is nothing left worth preserving in the notions of unseen powers, controlling human destiny to which obedience, reverence and worship are due, if we glide silently over the nature that has been attributed to the powers, the radically diverse ways in which they have been supposed to control human destiny, and in which submission and awe have been manifested. The other point is that when we begin to select, to choose, and say that some present ways of thinking about the unseen powers are better than others; that the reverence shown by a free and self-respecting human being is better than the servile obedience rendered to an arbitrary power by frightened men; that we should believe that control of human destiny is exercised by a wise and loving spirit rather than by madcap ghosts or sheer force—when I say, we begin to choose, we have entered upon a road that has not yet come to an end. We have reached a point that invites us to proceed further.

For we are forced to acknowledge that concretely there is no such thing as religion in the singular. There is only a multitude of religions. "Religion" is a strictly collective term and the collection it stands for is not even of the kind illustrated in textbooks of logic. It has not the unity of a regiment or assembly but that of any miscellaneous aggregate. Attempts to prove the universality prove too much or too little. It is probable that religions have been universal in the sense that all the peoples we know anything about have had *a* religion. But the differences among them are so great and so shocking that any common element that can be extracted is meaningless. The idea that religion is universal proves too little in that the older apologists for Christianity seem to have been better advised than some modern ones in condemning every religion but one as an impostor, as at bottom some kind of demon worship or at any rate a superstitious figment. Choice among religions is imperative, and the necessity for choice leaves nothing of any force in the argument from universality. Moreover, when once we enter upon the road of choice, there is at once presented a possibility not yet generally realized.

For the historic increase of the ethical and ideal content of religions suggests that the process of purification may be carried further. It indicates that further choice is imminent in which certain values and functions in experience may be selected. This possibility is what I had in mind in speaking of the difference between the religious and a religion. I am not proposing a religion, but rather the emancipation of elements and outlooks that may be called religious. For the moment we have a religion, whether that of the Sioux Indian or of Judaism or of Christianity, that moment the ideal factors in experience that may be called religious take on a load that is not inherent in them, a load of current beliefs and of institutional practices that are irrelevant to them.

I can illustrate what I mean by a common phenomenon in contemporary life. It is widely supposed that a person who does not accept any religion is thereby shown to be a non-religious person. Yet it is conceivable that the present depression in religion is closely connected with the fact that religions now prevent, because of their weight of historic encumbrances, the religious quality of experience from coming to consciousness and finding the expression that is appropriate to present conditions, intellectual and moral. I believe that such is the case. I believe that many persons are so repelled from what exists as a religion by its intellectual and moral implications, that they are not even aware of attitudes in themselves that if they came to fruition would be genuinely religious. I hope that this remark may help make clear what I mean by the distinction between "religion" as a noun substantive and "religious" as adjectival.

To be somewhat more explicit, a religion (and as I have just said there is no such thing as religion in general) always signifies a special body of beliefs and practices having some kind of institutional organization, loose or tight. In contrast, the adjective "religious" denotes nothing in the way of a specifiable entity, either institutional or as a system of beliefs. It does not denote anything to which one can specifically point as one can point to this and that historic religion or existing church. For it does not denote anything that can exist by itself or that can be organized into a particular and distinctive form of existence. It denotes attitudes that may be taken toward every object and every proposed end or ideal.

Before, however, I develop my suggestion that realization of the distinction just made would operate to emancipate the religious quality from encumbrances that now smother or limit it, I must refer to a position that in some respects is similar in words to the position I have taken, but that in fact is a whole world removed from it. I have several times used the phrase "religious elements of experience." Now at present there is much talk, especially in liberal circles, of religious experience as vouching for the authenticity of certain beliefs and the desirability of certain practices, such as particular forms of prayer and worship. It is even asserted that religious experience is the ultimate basis of religion itself. The gulf between this position and that which I have taken is what I am now concerned to point out.

Those who hold to the notion that there is a definite kind of experience which is itself religious, by that very fact make out of it something specific, as a kind of experience that is marked off from experience as aesthetic, scientific, moral, political; from experience as companionship and friendship. But "religious" as a quality of experience signifies something that may belong to all these experiences. It is the polar opposite of some type of experience that can exist by itself. The distinction comes out clearly when it is noted that the concept of this distinct kind of experience is used to validate a belief in some special kind of object and also to justify some special kind of practice.

For there are many religionists who are now dissatisfied with the older "proofs" of the existence of God, those that go by the name of ontological, cosmological, and telological. The cause of the dissatisfaction is perhaps not so much the arguments that Kant used to show the insufficiency of these alleged proofs, as it is the growing feeling that they are too formal to offer any support to religion in action. Anyway, the dissatisfaction exists. Moreover, these religionists are moved by the rise of the experimental method in other fields. What is more natural and proper, accordingly, than that they should affirm they are just as good empiricists as anybody else—indeed, as good as the scientists themselves? As the latter rely upon certain kinds of experience to prove the existence of certain kinds of objects, so the religionists rely upon a certain kind of experience to prove the existence of the object of religion, especially the supreme object, God.

This discussion may be made more definite by introducing, at this point, a particular illustration of this type of reasoning. A writer says: "I broke down from overwork and soon came to the verge of nervous prostration. One morning after a long and sleepless night . . . I resolved to stop drawing upon myself so continuously and begin drawing upon God. I determined to set apart a quiet time every day in which I could relate my life to its ultimate source, regain the consciousness that in God I live, move and have my being. That was thirty years ago. Since then I have had literally not one hour of darkness or despair."

This an impressive record. I do not doubt its authenticity nor that of the experience related. It illustrates a religious aspect of experience. But it illustrates also the use of that quality to carry a superimposed load of a particular religion. For having been brought up in the Christian religion, its subject interprets it in the terms of the personal God characteristic of that religion. Taoists, Buddhists, Moslems, persons of no religion including those who reject all supernatural influence and power, have had experiences similar in their effect. Yet another author commenting upon the passage says: "The religious expert can be more sure that this God exists than he can of either the cosmological God of speculative surmise or the Christlike God involved in the validity of moral optimism," and goes on to add that such experiences "mean that God the savior, the power that gives victory over sin on certain conditions that man can fulfill, is an existent, accessible and scientifically knowable reality." It should be clear that this inference is sound only if the conditions, of whatever sort, that produce the effect are called "God." But most readers will take the inference to mean that the existence of a particular Being, of the type called "God" in the Christian religion, is proved by a method akin to that of experimental science.

In reality, the only thing that can be said to be "proved" is the existence of some complex of conditions that have operated to effect an adjustment in life, an orientation, that brings with it a sense of security and peace. The particular interpretation given to this complex of conditions is not inherent in the experience itself. It is derived from the culture with which a particular person has been imbued. A fatalist will give one name to it; a Christian Scientist another, and the one who rejects all supernatural being still another. The determining factor in the interpretation of the experience is the particular doctrinal apparatus into which a person has been inducted. The emotional deposit connected with prior teaching floods the whole situation. It may readily confer upon the experience such a peculiarly sacred preciousness that all inquiry into its causation is barred. The stable outcome is so invaluable that the cause to which it is referred is usually nothing but a reduplication of the thing that has occurred, plus some name that has acquired a deeply emotional quality.

The intent of this discussion is not to deny the genuiness of the result nor its importance in life. It is not, save incidentally, to point out the possibility of a purely naturalistic explanation of the event. My purpose is to indicate what happens when religious experience is already set aside as something *sui generis*. The actual religious quality in the experience described is the *effect* produced, the better adjustment in life and its conditions, not the manner and cause of its production. The way in which the experience operated, its function, determines its religious value. If the reorientation actually occurs, it, and the sense of security and stability accompanying it, are forces on their own account. It takes place in different persons in a multitude of ways. It is sometimes brought about by devotion to a cause; sometimes by a passage of poetry that opens a new perspective; sometimes as was the case with Spinoza—deemed an atheist in his day—through philosophical reflection.

The difference between an experience having a religious force because of what it does in and to the processes of living and religious experience as a separate kind of thing gives me occasion to refer to a previous remark. If this function were rescued through emancipation from dependence upon specific types of beliefs and practices, from those elements that constitute a religion, many individuals would find that experiences having the force of bringing about a better, deeper and enduring adjustment in life are not so rare and infrequent as they are commonly supposed to be. They occur frequently in connection with many significant moments of living. The idea of invisible powers would take on the meaning of all the conditions of nature and human association that support and deepen the sense of values which carry one through periods of darkness and despair to such an extent that they lose their usual depressive character.

I do not suppose for many minds the dislocation of the religious from a religion is easy to effect. Tradition and custom, especially when emotionally charged, are a part of the habits that have become one with our very being. But the possibility of the transfer is demonstrated by its actuality. Let us then for the moment drop the term "religious," and ask what are the attitudes that lend deep and enduring support to the process of living. I have, for example, used the words "adjustment" and "orientation." What do they signify?

While the words "accommodation," "adaptation," and "adjustment" are frequently employed as synonyms, attitudes exist that are so different that for the sake of clear thought they should be discriminated. There are conditions we meet that cannot be changed. If they are particular and limited, we modify our own particular attitudes in accordance with them. Thus we accommodate ourselves to changes in weather, to alterations in income when we have no other recourse. When the external conditions are lasting we become inured, habituated, or, as the process is now often called, conditioned. The two main traits of this attitude, which I should like to call accommodation, are that it affects *particular* modes of conduct, not the entire self, and that the process is mainly *passive*. It may, however, become general and then it becomes fatalistic resignation or submission. There are other attitudes toward the environment that are also particular but that are more active. We re-act against conditions and endeavor to change them to meet our wants and demands. Plays in a foreign language are "adapted" to meet the needs of an

American audience. A house is rebuilt to suit changed conditions of the household; the telephone is invented to serve the demand for speedy communication at a distance; dry soils are irrigated so that they may bear abundant crops. Instead of accommodating ourselves to conditions, we modify conditions so that they will be accommodated to our wants and purposes. This process may be called adaptation.

Now both of these processes are often called by the more general name of adjustment. But there are also changes in ourselves in relation to the world in which we live that are much more inclusive and deep seated. They relate not to this and that want in relation to this and that condition of our surroundings, but pertain to our being in its entirety. Because of their scope, this modification of ourselves is enduring. It lasts through any amount of vicissitude of circumstances, internal and external. There is a composing and harmonizing of the various elements of our being such that, in spite of changes in the special conditions that surround us, these conditions are also arranged, settled, in relation to us. This attitude includes a note of submission. But it is voluntary, not externally imposed; and as voluntary it is something more than a mere Stoical resolution to endure unperturbed throughout the buffetings of fortune. It is more outgoing, more ready and glad, than the latter attitude, and it is more active than the former. And in calling it voluntary, it is not meant that it depends upon a particular resolve or volition. It is a change *of* will conceived as the organic plenitude of our being, rather than any special change *in* will.

It is the claim of religions that they effect this generic and enduring change in attitude. I should like to turn the statement around and say that whenever this change takes place there is a definitely religious attitude. It is not *a* religion that brings it about, but when it occurs, from whatever cause and by whatever means, there is a religious outlook and function. As I have said before, the doctrinal or intellectual apparatus and the institutional accretions that grow up are, in a strict sense, adventitious to the intrinsic quality of such experiences. For they are affairs of the traditions of the culture with which individuals are inoculated. Mr. Santayana has connected the religious quality of experience with the imaginative, as that is expressed in poetry. "Religion and poetry," he says, "are identical in essence, and differ merely in the way in which they are attached to practical affairs. Poetry is called religion when it intervenes in life, and religion, when it merely supervenes upon life, is seen to be nothing but poetry." The difference between intervening *in* and supervening *upon* is as important as is the identity set forth. Imagination may play upon life or it may enter profoundly into it. As Mr. Santayana puts it, "poetry has a universal and a moral function," for "its highest power lies in its relevance to the ideals and purposes of life." Except as it intervenes, "all observation is observation of brute fact, all discipline is mere repression, until these facts digested and this discipline embodied in humane impulses become the starting point for a creative movement of the imagination, the firm basis for ideal constructions in society, religion, and art."

If I may make a comment upon this penetrating insight of Mr. Santayana, I would say that the difference between imagination that only supervenes and imagination that intervenes is the difference between one that completely inter-penetrates all the elements of our being and one that is interwoven with only special and partial factors. There actually occurs extremely little observation of brute facts merely for the sake of the facts, just as there is little discipline that is repression and nothing but repression. Facts are usually observed with reference to some practical end and purpose, and that end is presented only imaginatively. The most repressive discipline has some end in view to which there is at least imputed an ideal quality; otherwise it is purely sadistic. But in such cases of observation and discipline imagination is limited and partial. It does not extend far; it does not permeate deeply and widely.

The connection between imagination and the harmonizing of the self is closer than is usually thought. The idea of a whole, whether of the whole personal being or of the world, is an imaginative, not a literal, idea. The limited world of our observation and reflection becomes the Universe only through imaginative exten-sion. It cannot be apprehended in knowledge nor realized in reflection. Neither observation, thought, nor practical activity can attain that complete unification of the self which is called a whole. The *whole* self is an ideal, an imaginative projec-tion. Hence the idea of a thoroughgoing and deep-seated harmonizing of the self with the Universe (as a name for the totality of conditions with which the self is connected) operates only through imagination—which is one reason why this composing of the self is not voluntary in the sense of an act of special volition or resolution. An "adjustment" possesses the will rather than is its express product. Religionists have been right in thinking of it as an influx from sources beyond conscious deliberation and purpose—a fact that helps explain, psychologically, why it has so generally been attributed to a supernatural source and that, perhaps, throws some light upon the reference of it by William James to unconscious factors. And it is pertinent to note that the unification of the self throughout the ceaseless flux of what it does, suffers, and achieves, cannot be attained in terms of itself. The self is always directed toward something beyond itself and so its own unifica-tion depends upon the idea of the integration of the shifting scenes of the world into that imaginative totality we call the Universe.

The intimate connection of imagination with ideal elements in experience is generally recognized. Such is not the case with respect to its connection with faith. The latter has been regarded as a substitute for knowledge, for sight. It is defined, in the Christian religion, as *evidence* of things not seen. The implication is that faith is a kind of anticipatory vision of things that are now invisible because of the limita-tions of our finite and erring nature. Because it is a substitute for knowledge, its material and object are intellectual in quality. As John Locke summed up the matter, faith is "assent to a proposition . . . on the credit of its proposer." Religious faith is then given to a body of propositions as true on the credit of their supernatural author, reason coming in to demonstrate the reasonableness of giving such credit. Of necessity there results the development of theologies, or bodies of systematic propositions, to make explicit in organized form the content of the propositions to which belief is attached and assent given. Given the point of view, those who hold that religion necessarily implies a theology are correct.

But belief or faith has also a moral and practical import. Even devils, according to the older theologians, believe—and tremble. A distinction was made, therefore, between "speculative" or intellectual belief and an act called "justifying" faith. Apart from any theological context, there is a difference between belief that is a conviction that some end should be supreme over conduct, and belief that some object or being exists as a truth for the intellect. Conviction in the moral sense signifies being conquered, vanquished, in our active nature by an ideal end; it signifies acknowledgment of its rightful claim over our desires and purposes. Such acknowledgment is practical, not primarily intellectual. It goes beyond evidence that can be presented to *any* possible observer. Reflection, often long and arduous, may be involved in arriving at the conviction, but the import of thought is not exhausted in discovery of evidence that can justify intellectual assent. The authority of an ideal over choice and conduct is the authority of an ideal, not of a fact, of a truth guaranteed to intellect, not of the status of the one who propounds the truth.

Such moral faith is not easy. It was questioned of old whether the Son of Man should find faith on the earth in his coming. Moral faith has been bolstered by all sorts of arguments intended to prove that its object is not ideal and that its claim upon us is not primarily moral or practical, since the ideal in question is already embedded in the existent frame of things. It is argued that the ideal is already the final reality at the heart of things that exist, and that only our senses or the corruption of our natures prevent us from apprehending its prior existential being. Starting, say, from such an idea as that justice is more than a moral ideal because it is embedded in the very make-up of the actually existent world, men have gone on to build up vast intellectual schemes, philosophies, and theologies, to prove that ideals are real not as ideals but as antecedently existing actualities. They have failed to see that in converting moral realities into matters of intellectual assent they have evinced lack of *moral* faith. Faith that something should be in existence as far as lies in our power is changed into the intellectual belief that it is already in existence. When physical existence does not bear out the assertion, the physical is subtly changed into the metaphysical. In this way, moral faith has been inextricably tied up with intellectual beliefs about the supernatural.

The tendency to convert ends of moral faith and action into articles of an intellectual creed has been furthered by a tendency of which psychologists are well aware. What we ardently desire to have thus and so, we tend to believe is already so. Desire has a powerful influence upon intellectual beliefs. Moreover, when conditions are adverse to realization of the objects of our desire—and in the case of significant ideals they are extremely adverse—it is an easy way out to assume that after all they are already embodied in the ultimate structure of what is, and that appearances to the contrary are *merely* appearances. Imagination then merely supervenes and is freed from the responsibility for intervening. Weak natures take to reverie as a refuge as strong ones do to fanaticism. Those who dissent are mourned over by the first class and converted through the use of force by the second.

What has been said does not imply that all moral faith in ideal ends is by virtue of that fact religious in quality. The religious is "morality touched by emotion" only when the ends of moral conviction arouse emotions that are not only intense but are actuated and supported by ends so inclusive that they unify the self. The inclusiveness of the end in relation to both self and the "universe" to which an inclusive self is related is indispensable. According to the best authorities, "religion" comes from a root that means being bound or tied. Originally, it meant being bound by vows to a particular way of life—as *les religieux* were monks and nuns who had assumed certain vows. The religious attitude signifies something that is bound through imagination to a *general* attitude. This comprehensive attitude, moreover, is much broader than anything indicated by "moral" in its usual sense. The quality of attitude is displayed in art, science, and good citizenship.

If we apply the conception set forth to the terms of the definition earlier quoted, these terms take on a new significance. An unseen power controlling our destiny becomes the power of an ideal. All possibilities, as possibilities, are ideal in character. The artist, scientist, citizen, parent, as far as they are actuated by the spirit of their callings, are controlled by the unseen. For all endeavor for the better is moved by faith in what is possible, not by adherence to the actual. Nor does this faith depend for its moving power upon intellectual assurance or belief that the things worked for must surely prevail and come into embodied existence. For the authority of the object to determine our attitude and conduct, the right that is given it to claim our allegiance and devotion is based on the intrinsic nature of the ideal. The outcome, given our best endeavor, is not with us. The inherent vice of all intellectual schemes of idealism is that they convert the idealism of action into a system of beliefs about antecedent reality. The character assigned this reality is so different from that which observation and reflection lead to and support that these schemes inevitably glide into alliance with the supernatural.

All religions, marked by elevated ideal quality, have dwelt upon the power of religion to introduce perspective into the piecemeal and shifting episodes of existence. Here too we need to reverse the ordinary statement and say that whatever introduces genuine perspective is religious, not that religion is something that introduces it. There can be no doubt (referring to the second element of the definition) of our dependence upon forces beyond our control. Primitive man was so impotent in the face of these forces that, especially in an unfavorable natural environment, fear became a dominant attitude, and, as the old saying goes, fear created the gods.

With increase of mechanisms of control, the element of fear has, relatively speaking, subsided. Some optimistic souls have even concluded that the forces about us are on the whole essentially benign. But every crisis, whether of the individual or of the community, reminds man of the precarious and partial nature of the control he exercises. When man, individually and collectively, has done his uttermost, conditions that at different times and places have given rise to the ideas of Fate and Fortune, of Chance and Providence, remain. It is the part of manliness to insist upon the capacity of mankind to strive to direct natural and social forces to humane ends. But unqualified absolutistic statements about the omnipotence of such endeavors reflect egoism rather than intelligent courage.

The fact that human destiny is so interwoven with forces beyond human control renders it unnecessary to suppose that dependence and the humility that accompanies it have to find the particular channel that is prescribed by traditional doctrines. What is especially significant is rather the form which the sense of dependence takes. Fear never gave stable perspective in the life of anyone. It is dispersive and withdrawing. Most religions have in fact added rites of communion to those of expiation and propitiation. For our dependence is manifested in those relations to the environment that support our undertakings and aspirations as much as it is in the defeats inflicted upon us. The essentially unreligious attitude is that which attributed human achievement and purpose to man in isolation from the world of physical nature and his fellows. Our successes are dependent upon the cooperation of nature. The sense of the dignity of human nature is as religious as is the sense of awe and reverence when it rests upon a sense of human nature as a cooperating part of a larger whole. Natural piety is not of necessity either a fatalistc acquiescence in natural happenings or a romantic idealization of the world. It may rest upon a just sense of nature as the whole of which we are parts, while it also recognizes that we are parts that are marked by intelligence and purpose, having the capacity to strive by their aid to bring conditions into greater consonance with what is humanly desirable. Such piety is an inherent constituent of a just perspective in life.

Understanding and knowledge also enter into a perspective that is religious in quality. Faith in the continued disclosing of truth through directed cooperative human endeavor is more religious in quality than is any faith in a completed revelation. It is of course now usual to hold that revelation is not completed in the sense of being ended. But religions hold that the essential framework is settled in its significant moral features at least, and that new elements that are offered must be judged by conformity to this framework. Some fixed doctrinal apparatus is necessary for *a* religion. But faith in the possibilities of continued and rigorous inquiry does not limit access to truth to any channel or scheme of things. It does not first say that truth is universal and then add there is but one road to it. It does not depend for assurance upon subjection to any dogma or item of doctrine. It trusts that the natural interactions between man and his environment will breed more intelligence and generate more knowledge provided the scientific methods that define intelligence in operation are pushed further into the mysteries of the world, being themselves promoted and improved in the operation. There is such a thing as faith in intelligence becoming religious in quality—a fact that perhaps explains the efforts of some religionists to disparage the possibilities of intelligence as a force. They properly feel such faith to be a dangerous rival.

Lives that are consciously inspired by loyalty to such ideals as have been mentioned are still comparatively infrequent to the extent of that comprehensiveness and intensity which arouse an ardor religious in function. But before we infer the incompetency of such ideals and of the actions they inspire, we should at least ask ourselves how much of the existing situation is due to the fact that the religious factors of experience have been drafted into supernatural channels and thereby loaded with irrelevant encumbrances. A body of beliefs and practices that are apart from the common and natural relations of mankind must, in the degree in which it is influential, weaken and sap the force of the possibilities inherent in such relations. Here lies one aspect of the emancipation of the religious from religion.

Any activity pursued in behalf of an ideal end against obstacles and in spite of threats of personal loss because of conviction of its general and enduring value is religious in quality. Many a person, inquirer, artist, philanthropist, citizen, men, and women in the humblest walks of life, have achieved, without presumption and without display, such unification of themselves and of their relations to the conditions of existence. It remains to extend their spirit and inspiration to ever wider numbers. If I have said anything about religions and religion that seems harsh, I have said those things because of a firm belief that the claim on the part of religions to possess a monopoly of ideals and of the supernatural means by which alone, it is alleged, they can be furthered, stands, in the way of the realization of distinctively religious values inherent in natural experience. For that reason, if for no other, I should be sorry if any were misled by the frequency with which I have employed the adjective "religious" to conceive of what I have said as a disguised apology for what have passed as religions. The opposition between religious values as I conceive them and religions is not to be bridged. Just because the release of the values is so important, their identification with the creeds and cults of religions must be dissolved.

RELIGIOUS EPISTEMOLOGY: REASON

THE ONTOLOGICAL ARGUMENT

St. Anselm

Chapter II

Truly there is a God, although the fool hath said in his heart, There is no God.

And so, Lord, do thou, who dost give understanding to faith, give me, so far as thou knowest it to be profitable, to understand that thou art as we believe; and that thou

Reprinted from *Basic Writings* by St. Anselm, by permission of The Open Court Publishing Company, La Salle, Illinois. Copyright © 1910.

art that which we believe. And, indeed, we believe that thou art a being than which nothing greater can be conceived. Or is there no such nature, since the fool hath said in his heart, there is no God (Psalms xiv. 1). But, at any rate, this very fool, when he hears of this being of which I speak—a being than which nothing greater can be conceived—understands what he hears, and what he understands is in his understanding; although he does not understand it to exist.

For, it is one thing for an object to be in the understanding, and another to understand that the object exists. When a painter first conceives of what he will afterwards perform, he has it in his understanding, but he does not yet understand it to be, because he has not yet performed it. But after he has made the painting, he both has it in his understanding, and he understands that it exists, because he has made it.

Hence, even the fool is convinced that something exists in the understanding, at least, than which nothing greater can be conceived. For, when he hears of this, he understands it. And whatever is understood, exists in the understanding. And assuredly that, than which nothing greater can be conceived, cannot exist in the understanding alone. For, suppose it exists in the understanding alone: then it can be conceived to exist in reality; which is greater.

Therefore, if that, than which nothing greater can be conceived, exists in the understanding alone, the very being, than which nothing greater can be conceived, is one, than which a greater can be conceived. But obviously this is impossible. Hence, there is no doubt that there exists a being, than which nothing greater can be conceived, and it exists both in the understanding and in reality.

Chapter III

God cannot be conceived not to exist.—God is that, than which nothing greater can be conceived.—That which can be conceived not to exist is not God.

And it assuredly exists so truly, that it cannot be conceived not to exist. For, it is possible to conceive of a being which cannot be conceived not to exist; and this is greater than one which can be conceived not to exist. Hence, if that, than which nothing greater can be conceived, can be conceived not to exist, it is not that, than which nothing greater can be conceived. But this is an irreconcilable contradiction. There is, then, so truly a being than which nothing greater can be conceived to exist, that it cannot even be conceived not to exist; and this being thou art, O Lord, our God.

So truly, therefore, dost thou exist, O Lord, my God, that thou canst not be conceived not to exist; and rightly. For, if a mind could conceive of a being better than thee, the creature would rise above the Creator; and this is most absurd. And, indeed, whatever else there is, except thee alone, can be conceived not to exist. To thee alone, therefore, it belongs to exist more truly than all other beings, and hence in a higher degree than all others. For, whatever else exists does not exist so truly, and hence in a less degree it belongs to it to exist. Why, then, has the fool said in his heart, there is no God (Psalms xiv. 1), since it is so evident, to a rational mind, that thou dost exist in the highest degree of all? Why, except that he is dull and a fool?

Chapter IV

How the fool has said in his heart what cannot be conceived.—A thing may be conceived in two ways: (1) when the word signifying it is conceived; (2) when the thing itself is understood. As far as the word goes, God can be conceived not to exist; in reality he cannot.

But how has the fool said in his heart what he could not conceive; or how is it that he could not conceive what he said in his heart? since it is the same to say in the heart, and to conceive.

But, if really, nay, since really, he both conceived, because he said in his heart; and did not say in his heart, because he could not conceive; there is more than one way in which a think is said in the heart or conceived. For, in one sense, an object is conceived, when the word signifying it is conceived; and in another, when the very entity, which the object is, is understood.

In the former sense, then, God can be conceived not to exist; but in the latter, not at all. For no one who understands what fire and water are can conceive fire to be water, in accordance with the nature of the facts themselves, although this is possible according to the words. So, then, no one who understands what God is can conceive that God does not exist; although he says these words in his heart, either without any or with some foreign, signification. For, God is that than which a greater cannot be conceived. And he who thoroughly understands this, assuredly understands that this being so truly exists, that not even in concept can it be nonexistent. Therefore, he who understands that God so exists, cannot conceive that he does not exist.

I thank thee, gracious Lord, I thank thee; because what I formerly believed by thy bounty, I now so understand by thine illumination, that if I were unwilling to believe that thou dost exist, I should not be able not to understand this to be true.

THE FIVE WAYS

St. Thomas Aquinas

The existence of God can be proved in five ways.

The first and more manifest way is the argument from motion. It is certain, and evident to our senses, that in the world some things are in motion. Now whatever is moved is moved by another, for nothing can be moved except it is in poten-

From *Introduction to St. Thomas Aquinas,* ed. Anton C. Pegis (New York: The Modern Library, 1948), pp. 25-27. Reprinted by permission of the editor.

tiality to that towards which it is moved; whereas a thing moves inasmuch as it is in act. For motion is nothing else than the reduction of something from potentiality to actuality. But nothing can be reduced from potentiality to actuality, except by something in a state of actuality. Thus that which is actually hot, as fire, makes wood, which is potentially hot, to be actually hot, and thereby moves and changes it. Now it is not possible that the same thing should be at once in actuality and potentiality in the same respect, but only in different respects. For what is actually hot cannot simultaneously be potentially hot; but it is simultaneously potentially cold. It is therefore impossible that in the same respect and in the same way a thing should be both mover and moved, *i.e.,* that it should move itself. Therefore, whatever is moved must be moved by another. If that by which it is moved be itself moved, then this also must needs be moved by another, and that by another again. But this cannot go on to infinity, because then there would be no first mover, and, consequently, no other mover, seeing that subsequent movers move only inasmuch as they are moved by the first mover; as the staff moves only because it is moved by the hand. Therefore it is necessary to arrive at a first mover, moved by no other; and this everyone understands to be God.

The second way is from the nature of efficient cause. In the world of sensible things we find there is an order of efficient causes. There is no case known (neither is it, indeed, possible) in which a thing is found to be the efficient cause of itself; for so it would be prior to itself, which is impossible. Now in efficient causes it is not possible to go on to infinity, because in all efficient causes following in order, the first is the cause of the intermediate cause, and the intermediate is the cause of the ultimate cause, whether the intermediate cause be several, or one only. Now to take away the cause is to take away the effect. Therefore, if there be no first cause among efficient causes, there will be no ultimate, nor any intermediate, cause. But if in efficient causes it is possible to go on to infinity, there will be no first efficient cause, neither will there be an ultimate effect, nor any intermediate efficient causes; all of which is plainly false. Therefore it is necessary to admit a first efficient cause, to which everyone gives the name of God.

The third way is taken from possibility and necessity, and runs thus. We find in nature things that are possible to be and not to be, since they are found to be generated, and to be corrupted, and consequently, it is possible for them to be and not to be. But it is impossible for these always to exist, for that which can not-be at some time is not. Therefore, if everything can not-be, then at one time there was nothing in existence. Now if this were true, even now there would be nothing in existence, because that which does not exist begins to exist only through something already existing. Therefore, if at one time nothing was in existence, it would have been impossible for anything to have begun to exist; and thus even now nothing would be in existence—which is absurd. Therefore, not all beings are merely possible, but there must exist something the existence of which is necessary. But every necessary thing either has its necessity caused by another, or not. Now it is impossible to go on to infinity in necessary things which have their necessity caused by another, as has been already proved in regard to efficient causes. Therefore we cannot but admit the existence of some being having of itself its own necessity, and not receiving it from another, but rather causing in others their necessity. This all men speak of as God.

The fourth way is taken from the gradation to be found in things. Among beings there are some more and some less good, true, noble, and the like. But *more* and *less* are predicted of different things according as they resemble in their different ways something which is the maximum, as a thing is said to be hotter according as it more nearly resembles that which is hottest; so that there is something which is truest, something best, something noblest, and, consequently, something which is most being, for those things that are greatest in truth are greatest in being, as it is written in *Metaph.* ii.[1] Now the maximum in any genus is the cause of all in that genus, as fire, which is the maximum of heat, is the cause of all hot things, as is said in the same book.[2] Therefore there must also be something which is to all beings the cause of their being, goodness, and every other perfection; and this we call God.

The fifth way is taken from the governance of the world. We see that things which lack knowledge, such as natural bodies, act for an end, and this is evident from their acting always, or nearly always, in the same way, so as to obtain the best result. Hence it is plain that they achieve their end, not fortuitously, but designedly. Now whatever lacks knowledge cannot move towards an end, unless it be directed by some being endowed with knowledge and intelligence; as the arrow is directed by the archer. Therefore some intelligent being exists by whom all natural things are directed to their end; and this being we call God.

NOTES

1. Metaph. Ia I (993b 30).
2. Ibid. (993b 25).

RELIGIOUS EPISTEMOLOGY: EXPERIENCE

THE ASCENT TO MOUNT CARMEL

St. John of the Cross

The main theme and final goal: the soul's union with God.

This treatise deals with the manner in which a soul may prepare itself to attain to union with God. It gives useful advice and instruction, both to beginners and to those more advanced in the spiritual life, so that they may learn how to free them-

From *The Dark Night of the Soul,* trans. Kurt F. Reinhardt (New York: Frederick Ungar Publishing Co., 1957), pp. 1-3, 32-44, 51-53. Reprinted by permission of the publisher.

selves from all that is temporal and not weigh themselves down with the spiritual, and remain in that complete nakedness and freedom of the spirit which are necessary for union with God.

The entire doctrine which I intend to discuss in the Ascent to Mount Carmel is contained in the following stanzas, and they describe also the manner of ascending to the peak of the mountan, that is, that high state of perfection which we here designate as the union of the soul with God. The poem reads as follows:

1

In a dark night,
My longing heart aglow with love,
—Oh, blessed lot!—
I went forth unseen
From my house that was at last in deepest rest.

2

Secure and protected by darkness,
I climbed the secret ladder, in disguise,
—Oh, blessed lot!—
In darkness, veiled and concealed I went
Leaving behind my house in deepest rest.

3

Oh, blissful night!
Oh, secret night, when I remained unseeing and unseen,
When the flame burning in my heart
Was my only light and guide.

4

This inward light,
A safer guide than noonday's brightness,
Showed me the place where He awaited me
—My soul's Beloved—
A place of solitude.

5

Oh, night that guided me!
Oh, night more lovely than the rosy dawn!
Oh, night whose darkness guided me
To that sweet union,
In which the lover and Beloved are made one.

6

Upon the flower of my breast,
Kept undefiled for Him alone,
He fell asleep,
While I was waking,
Caressing Him with gentle cedars' breeze.

7

And when Aurora's breath
Began to spread His curled hair,
His gentle hand
He placed upon my neck,
And all my senses were in bliss suspended.

8

Forgetful of myself,
My head reclined on my Beloved,
The world was gone
And all my cares at rest,
Forgotten all my grief among the lilies.

Chapter IV

To be guided by faith, the soul must be in darkness.

It seems to be appropriate at this juncture to describe in greater detail the darkness that must be in the soul if it wishes to enter into this abyss of faith. If a soul aspires to supernatural transformation, it is clear that it must be far removed from all that is contained in its sensual and rational nature. For we call supernatural that which transcends nature, so that the natural is left behind. The soul must completely and by its own will empty itself of everything that can be contained in it with respect to affection and volition, in such a way that, regardless of how many supernatural gifts it may receive, it will remain detached from them and in darkness. It must be like a blind man, finding its only support in dark faith, taking it as its guide and light, and leaning upon none of the things which it understands, enjoys, feels, and imagines. And if the soul does not make itself blind in this manner, remaining in total darkness, it will not attain to those greater things which are taught by faith.

When St. Paul said: "He who would come into the presence of God, must first believe that God exists" (Heb. 11:6), he meant by this that he who aspires to being joined with God in perfect union must not walk by the way of understanding, nor lean on either joyful sensations, or inner feelings, or imagination, but he must believe in God's Being, which is hidden as much from the understanding as from desire, imagination and any other sensory apperception, nor can it be known at all in this life in its essential nature. Even the highest concerning God that can be felt and perceived in this life is infinitely remote from Him and from the pure possession of Him. The goal which the soul pursues is thus beyond even the highest things that can be known or perceived. And the soul must therefore pass beyond everything to a state of unknowing.

The soul which attains to this state makes no longer use of any particular ways or methods—whether they relate to understanding, apperception, or feeling— although it bears within itself all possible ways, after the manner of one who owns nothing, yet possesses all things.

On this road, then, the soul, by becoming blind in its faculties, will see the light, as Our Saviour says in the Gospel: "I have come into this world for judgment, that those who are blind should see, and those who see should become blind" (John 9:39). This saying evidently applies to this spiritual road, where the soul which has entered into darkness and has become blind in all its natural lights, will learn to see supernaturally.

And in order that we may proceed from here on with less confusion, it appears necessary to describe in the following chapter what we mean when we speak of the union of the soul with God. For, once this is clearly understood, what we shall have to say in subsequent chapters will become a great deal more intelligible.

Chapter V

The union of the soul with God is a union of love and of likeness, not division of substance.

To understand, then, the nature of this union, it must be known that God dwells or is present sybstantially *[per essentiam]* in every soul, even in the soul of the greatest sinner. This kind of union between God and all His creatures is never lacking, since it is in and by this union that He sustains their being; and if it were ever lacking, these creatures would immediately cease to be and would fall back into nothingness. Thus, if we here speak of the union of the soul with God, we do not have in mind this ever-present substantial union, but we do mean that union of the soul with God which is consummated in the soul's transformation in God—a union which can come about only when the soul attains to a likeness with God by virtue of love. We shall therefore call this the union of likeness, to distinguish it from the union of substance or essence. The former is supernatural, the latter natural. And the supernatural union comes about when the two wills—that of the soul and that of God— are conformed in one, so that there is nothing in the one that is repugnant to the other. Thus, when the soul rids itself totally of that which is repugnant to and not in conformity with the Divine will, it is transformed in God through love.

This applies not only to whatever is repugnant to God in human action, but also in habit, so that the soul must not only desist from all voluntary acts of imperfection but must also completely overcome the acquired habits of these imperfections. And since no creature nor the actions or capabilities of any creature can ever measure up or attain to that which is God, the soul must be stripped of all creaturely attachments as well as of its own activities and capabilities—that is to say, of its understanding, its likings, and its feelings—so that, when all that which is unlike God and unconformed to Him is cast out, the soul may then receive the likeness of God.

Supernatural being is communicated only by love and grace. Not all souls, however, abide in God's love and grace, and those who do abide in them do not possess them in the same degree; for some attain higher degrees of love than others. And thus, God communicates Himself most to that soul which has progressed farthest in love and has most conformed its will to God's will. And that soul which has attained to a total conformity and likeness of its will and God's will is totally united with Him and supernaturally transformed in Him.

Let me clarify [the nature of this union] by a simile. Picture a ray of sunlight that is striking a window. Now if the window is coated with stains or vapors, the ray will be unable to illumine it and transform it into its own light; this it could do only if the window were stainless and pure. And the greater or lesser degree of illumination will be strictly in proportion to the window's greater or lesser purity; and this will be so, not because of the ray of sunlight but because of the condition of the window. Thus, if the window were entirely clean and pure, the ray would transform and illumine it in such a way that it would become almost undistinguishable from the brightness of the ray and would diffuse the same light as the ray. And yet, however much the window may resemble the ray of sunlight, it actually retains its own distinct nature. But this does not prevent us from saying that this window is luminous as a ray of the sun or is sunlight by participation. Now the soul is like this window: the Divine light of the Being of God is unceasingly beating upon it, or, to use a better expression, the Divine light is ever dwelling in it.

When the soul thus allows God to work in it, it will soon be transformed and transfigured in God, and God will communicate to it His supernatural Being in such a way that the soul appears to be God Himself, and it will indeed be God by participation. Yet it remains true nevertheless that the soul's natural being—notwithstanding the soul's supernatural transformation—remains as distinct from the Being of God as it was before, even as the window has and retains a nature of its own, distinct from the nature of the ray, although it owes its luminosity to the light of the sun.

This consideration should make it clearer why a soul can not dispose itself for this union by either understanding, or sensory apperception, or inner feelings and imaginings, or by any other experiences relating either to God or to anything else, but only by purity and love, that is, by perfect resignation and total detachment from all things for the sake of God alone. And as there can be no perfect transformation unless there be perfect purity, the soul will not be perfect unless it be totally cleansed and wholly pure.

Those souls [who attain to Divine union] do so according to their greater or smaller capacity and thus not in the same degree; and the degree of union depends also on what the Lord wishes to grant to each soul. And it is similar in the beatific vision: though some souls will have a more perfect vision of God in Heaven than others, they all see God, and all are content, since their capacity is satisfied. And in this life, too, all souls [who have attained to the state of perfection] will be equally satisfied, each one according to its knowledge of God and thus according to its capacity. A soul, on the other hand, that does not attain to a degree of purity corresponding to its capacity, will never find true peace and contentment.

Chapter VI

The three theological virtues perfect the three faculties of the soul.

We shall now endeavor to show how the three faculties of the soul—understanding, memory, and will—are brought into this spiritual night, which is the means leading to the end of Divine union. To do this, it is necessary first of all to explain in this chapter how the three theological virtues—faith, hope, and love [*caritas*]—by means of which the soul is united with God according to its faculties, produce an identical emptiness and darkness, each one with respect to its corresponding faculty. Thus, faith produces darkness in the understanding; hope, in the memory; love, in the will. Subsequently, we shall describe how the understanding is perfected in the darkness of faith, and memory in the emptiness of hope; and we shall then show how the will must be voided and stripped of all affection in order to move toward God. For, as we have pointed out, the soul is united with God in this life not through the understanding, nor through joyous feelings, nor through imagination, nor through any other sensory experience; but only through faith, which perfects the understanding; through hope, which perfects the memory; and through love, which perfects the will.

Faith, then, tells us what cannot be comprehended with the [natural] *understanding.* According to St. Paul, "Faith is the substance of our hopes; it convinces us of things we cannot see" (Heb. 11:1). Although the understanding may give its consent with a firm and perfect assurance, the things of faith are not revealed to the understanding; for, if they were revealed to it, there would be no need for faith. Wherefore, though faith gives certainty to the understanding, it does not illumine it, but leaves it in darkness.

As to *hope,* there is no doubt it in its turn plunges the *memory* into emptiness and darkness with respect to both things here below and things above. For hope has always to do with that which is not yet in our possession, since, if we already possessed it, there would no longer be room for hope. This is what St. Paul means when he says: "Hope would no longer be hope if its object were in plain view; for how could a man still hope for something that is fully seen [that is, fully possessed]?" (Rom. 8:24).

And, similarly, *love* empties the *will* of all things, since it obliges us to love God above them all; this, however, we cannot do unless we detach our affection from all of them in order to attach it wholly to God. Wherefore, Christ tells us through the mouth of St. Luke: "No one can be My disciple who does not detach himself from all that he [wilfully] possesses." (Luke, 14:33). All three of these virtues, then, plunge the soul into darkness and emptiness with respect to all things.

This, then, is the spiritual night which we have called *active;* for all the soul is able to do to enter into this night, it does by its own power. And as, when we were speaking of the night of sense, we described a method of emptying the faculties of sense of all the objects of sense—so that the soul might advance from its point of departure to the intermediate state of faith—so also, in this spiritual night, we shall, with Divine aid, describe a method whereby the spiritual faculties are emptied and purified of all that is not God. As a result, the spiritual faculties will then be placed in the darkness of the three [theological] virtues, which, as we have seen, are the means that dispose the soul for its union with God. And it should be noted that I am now speaking in particular to those who have begun to enter the state of contemplation.

Chapter VII

The narrow road; detachment of the understanding; spiritual poverty.

Speaking of the road [that leads to eternal life], Our Saviour said: "How small is the gate and how narrow the road that leads to Life; and there are few who find it" (Matt. 7:14). Now what Christ says of the small gate, we may understand in relation to the sensual part of man; and what He says of the narrow road, may be understood in relation to the spiritual or rational part. And the reason for His saying that "there are few who find it" is that there are few who know how to enter and who actually desire to enter into this total nakedness and emptiness of the spirit. For this path that leads to the high mountain of perfection is steep and narrow and therefore requires travellers who are not weighed down and encumbered by any cares for either the lower things of sense or the higher things of the spirit. Since this is an undertaking in which the prize of our search is God alone. He alone must be the object of our striving and our victory.

Hence we can see clearly that the soul which travels on this road must not only be free from all creaturely attachments but must also be spiritually poor and as dead to its own self. This is why Our Lord taught us through the mouth of St. Mark that priceless doctrine which, because of its great importance and because it specifically applies to our purpose, I shall quote here in full and then explain in its true spiritual meaning.

Our Lord says: "If any man wishes to go My way, let him deny his own self, and take up his cross, and follow Me. He who tries to save his life will lose it; but he who loses his life for My sake will save it" (Mark 8:34—35).

I wish someone would properly teach us how to understand, practise, and inwardly grasp the true meaning and significance of this counsel, so that spiritual persons would see how different is the method they should employ on this road from what many of them regard as proper. While some believe that any kind of withdrawal from the world and any external reform suffice, others are content with practising the virtues and continuing in prayer and penance; but neither attain to that nakedness, self-denial, and spiritual poverty which the Lord here commends to us; for they prefer feeding and clothing their natural selves with spiritual feelings and consolations to emptying themselves of all things and renouncing their natural selves for God's sake. Or they think that it suffices to strip their natural selves of worldly things, without purifying themselves by the total renunciation also of spiritual attachments. Thus, when they get a glimpse of this concrete and perfect life of the spirit—which manifests itself in the complete absence of all sweetness, in aridity, distaste, and in the many trials that are the true spiritual cross—they flee from it as from death. What they seek in their communion with God is sweet and delectable feelings; but this is a sort of spiritual gluttony rather than self-denial and spiritual poverty. As far as their spirituality is concerned, they become enemies of Christ. They seek themselves in God, which is the very opposite of love; for to seek oneself in God is to seek the favors and refreshing delights of God, whereas to seek God in oneself is to incline oneself to choose, for Christ's sake, all that is most distasteful; and this is love of God.

And when Our Lord said that he who tries to save his life will lose it, He meant that he who desires to possess anything for himself will lose it; whereas he who for Christ's sake renounces all that his will can desire and enjoy, and chooses that which is most like to the Cross, will save his life. This is precisely what His Majesty taught to those two disciples [the sons of Zebedee] who asked that they be allowed a place on His right and on His left. He answered their request for such glory by offering them the cup of which He had to drink, as a thing more precious and more secure on this earth than any joy of possession.

To drink of this cup, however, is to die to the natural self by detachment and self-annihilation, so that the soul may be able to travel by this narrow path unimpeded, since there remains to it nothing but self-denial and the Cross. And this Cross is the pilgrim's staff on which the soul may lean on its way to God and which greatly eases its burden and travail. Wherefore Our Lord said through the mouth of St. Matthew: "My yoke is easy, and My burden is light" (Matt. 11:30). For if a man resolves to carry this cross willingly, that is, if he is truly determined to undergo and bear hardships and trials for God's sake, he will find in them great solace and sweetness. If, on the other hand, he desires to possess anything or remains attached to anything whatsoever, his self is not totally stripped and emptied of all things, and he will not be able to continue his upward journey on this narrow path. For progress [in the spiritual life] can be made only by imitating Christ, Who is the Way, the Truth and the Life; and no one can come to the Father, except through Christ (cf. John 14:6).

Christ, then, is the Way, and this way is death to the natural self in both sense and spirit. And I shall now try to explain how we must die [to our natural selves], following the example of Christ, Who is our guiding light.

First, it is certain that, as far as the senses are concerned, He died (spiritually) in His life and (naturally) in His death. For, as He said, He had not in His life where to lay His head, and in His death He had even less.

Second, it is equally certain that in the hour of His death He felt annihilated and abandoned also in His soul, deprived of all consolation and help, since His Father left His humanity in a state of such complete aridity that the cry "My God, My God, why hast Thou forsaken Me?" (Matt. 27:46) forced itself upon His lips. This was, with respect to His sensory nature, the greatest desolation He had suffered in His life. And yet, it was then that He wrought the greatest work of His entire life, greater than any of His miracles and other mighty deeds—the reconciliation and union of the human race with God, through grace.

The words of David, "I was reduced to nothingness and unknowning," (Ps. 72:22), point to the mystery of the small gate and the narrow way, so that the truly spiritual man may learn to understand the way of Christ, the way of union with God. He will learn from these words that the more he becomes as nothing, the more intimately he is united with God and the greater is the work that he accomplishes. This union, then, consists not in delights, consolations, and sweet spiritual feelings, but in a living sensual and spiritual, internal and external, death of the cross.

MYSTICISM

William James

Over and over again in these lectures I have raised points and left them open and unfinished until we should have come to the subject of Mysticism. Some of you, I fear, may have smiled as you noted my reiterated postponements. But now the hour has come when mysticism must be faced in good earnest, and those broken threads wound up together. One may say truly, I think, that personal religious experience has its root and centre in mystical states of consciousness; so for us, who in these lectures are treating personal experience as the exclusive subject of our study, such states of consciousness ought to form the vital chapter from which the other chapters get their light. Whether my treatment of mystical states will shed more light or darkness, I do not know, for my own constitution shuts me out from their enjoyment almost entirely, and I can speak of them only at second hand. But though forced to look upon the subject so externally, I will be as objective and receptive as I can; and I think I shall at least succeed in convincing you of the reality of the states in question, and of the paramount importance of their function.

First of all, then I ask, What does the expression "mystical states of consciousness" mean? How do we part off mystical states from other states?

From *The Varieties of Religious Experience.* Reprinted by persmission of the David McKay Company, Inc.

The words "mysticism" and "mystical" are often used as terms of mere reproach, to throw at any opinion which we regard as vague and vast and sentimental, and without a base in either facts or logic. For some writers a "mystic" is any person who believes in thought-transference, or spirit-return. Employed in this way the word has little value: there are too many less ambiguous synonyms. So, to keep it useful by restricting it, I will do what I did in the case of the word "religion," and simply propose to you four marks which, when an experience has them, may justify us in calling it mystical for the purpose of the present lectures. In this way we shall save verbal disputation, and the recriminations that generally go therewith.

1. *Ineffability.*—The handiest of the marks by which I classify a state of mind as mystical is negative. The subject of it immediately says that it defies expression, that no adequate report of its contents can be given in words. It follows from this that its quality must be directly experience; it cannot be imparted or transferred to others. In this peculiarity mystical states are more like states of feeling than like states of intellect. No one can make clear to another who has never had a certain feeling, in what the quality or worth of it consists. One must have musical ears to know the value of a symphony; one must have been in love one's self to understand a lover's state of mind. Lacking the heart or ear, we cannot interpret the musician or the lover justly, and are even likely to consider him weak minded or absurd. The mystic finds that most of us accord to his experiences and equally incompetent treatment.

2. *Noetic quality.*—Although so similar to states of feeling, mystical states seem to those who experience them to be also states of knowledge. They are states of insight into depths of truth unplumbed by the discursive intellect. They are illuminations, revelations, full of significance and importance, all inarticulate though they remain; and as a rule they carry with them a curious sense of authority for aftertime.

These two characters will entitle any state to be called mystical, in the sense in which I use the word. Two other qualities are less sharply marked, but are usually found. These are:—

3. *Transiency.*—Mystical states cannot be sustained for long. Except in rare instances, half an hour, or at most an hour or two, seems to be the limit beyond which they fade into the light of common day. Often, when faded, their quality can but imperfectly be reproduced in memory; but when they recur it is recognized; and from one recurrence to another it is susceptible of continuous development in what is felt as inner richness and importance.

4. *Passivity.*—Although the oncoming of mystical states may be facilitated by preliminary voluntary operations, as by fixing the attention, or going through certain bodily performances, or in other ways which manuals of mysticism prescribe; yet when the characteristic sort of consciousness once has set in, the mystic feels as if his own will were in abeyance, and indeed sometimes as if he were grasped and held by a superior power. This latter peculiarity connects mystical

states with certain definite phenomena of secondary or alternative personality, such as prophetic speech, automatic writing, or the mediumistic trance. When these latter conditions are well pronounced, however, there may be no recollection whatever of the phenomenon, and it may have no significance for the subject's usual inner life, to which, as it were, it makes a mere interruption. Mystical states, strictly so-called, are never merely interruptive. Some memory of their content always remains, and a profound sense of their importance. They modify the inner life of the subject between the times of their recurrence. Sharp divisions in this region are, however, difficult to make, and we find all sorts of gradations and mixtures.

These four characteristics are sufficient to mark out a group of states of consciousness peculiar enough to deserve a special name and to call for careful study. Let it then be called the mystical group.

Our next step should be to gain acquaintance with some typical examples. Professional mystics at the height of their development have often elaborately organized experiences and a philosophy based thereupon. But you remember what I said in my first lecture: phenomena are best understood when placed within their series, studied in their germ and in their over-ripe decay, and compared with their exaggerated and degenerated kindred. The range of mystical experience is very wide, much too wide for us to cover in the time at our disposal. Yet the method of serial study is so essential for interpretation that if we really wish to reach conclusions we must use it. I will begin, therefore, with phenomena which claim no special religious significance, and end with those of which the religious pretensions are extreme.

The simplest rudiment of mystical experience would seem to be that deepened sense of the significance of a maxim or formula which occasionally sweeps over one. "I've heard that said all my life," we exclaim, "but I never realized its full meaning until now." "When a fellow-monk," said Luther, "one day repeated the words of the Creed: 'I believe in the forgiveness of sins,' I saw the Scripture in an entirely new light; and straightway I felt as if I were born anew. It was as if I had found the door of paradise thrown wide open."[1] This sense of deeper significance is not confined to rational propositions. Single words,[2] and conjunctions of words, effects of light on land and sea, odors and musical sounds, all bring it when the mind is tuned aright. Most of us can remember the strangely moving power of passages in certain poems read when we were young, irrational doorways as they were through which the mystery of fact, the wildness and the pang of life, stole into our hearts and thrilled them. The words have now perhaps become mere polished surfaces for us; but lyric poetry and music are alive and significant only in proportion as they fetch these vague vistas of a life continuous with our own, beckoning and inviting, yet ever eluding our pursuit. We are alive or dead to the eternal inner message of the arts according as we have kept or lost this mystical susceptibility.

A more pronounced step forward on the mystical ladder is found in an extremely frequent phenomenon, that sudden feeling, namely, which sometimes sweeps over us, of having "been here before," as if at some indefinite past time, in just this place, with just these people, we were already saying just these things. As Tennyson writes:

"Moreover, something is or seems
That touches me with mystic gleams,
Like glimpses of forgotten dreams—

"Of something felt, like something here;
Of something done, I know not where;
Such as no language may declare."[3]

Sir James Crichton-Browne has given the technical name of "dreamy states" to these sudden invasion of vaguely reminiscent consciousness.[4] They bring a sense of mystery and of the metaphysical duality of things, and the feeling of an enlargement of perception which seems imminent but which never completes itself. In Dr. Crichton-Browne's opinion they connect themselves with the perplexed and scared disturbances of self-consciousness which occasionally precede epileptic attacks. I think that this learned alienist takes a rather absurdly alarmist view of an intrinsically insignificant phenomenon. He follows it along the downward ladder, to insanity; our path pursues the upward ladder chiefly. The divergence shows how important it is to neglect no part of a phenomenon's connections, for we make it appear admirable or dreadful according to the context by which we set it off.

The next step into mystical states carries us into a realm that public opinion and ethical philosophy have long since branded as pathological, though private practice and certain lyric strains of poetry seem still to bear witness to its ideality. I refer to the consciousness produced by intoxicants and anaesthetics, especially by alcohol. The sway of alcohol over mankind is unquestionably due to its power to stimulate the mystical faculties of human nature, usually crushed to earth by the cold facts and dry criticisms of the sober hour. Sobriety diminishes, discriminates, and says no; drunkenness expands, unites, and says yes. It is in fact the great exciter of the *Yes* function in man. It brings its votary from the chill periphery of things to the radiant core. It makes him for the moment one with truth. Not through mere perversity do men run after it. To the poor and the unlettered it stands in the place of symphony concerts and of literature; and it is part of the deeper mystery and tragedy of life that whiffs and gleams of something that we immediately recognize as excellent should be vouchsafed to so many of us only in the fleeting earlier phases of what in its totality is so degrading a poisoning. The drunken consciousness is one bit of the mystic consciousness, and our total opinion of it must find its place in our opinion of that larger whole.

Nitrous oxide and ether, especially nitrous oxide, when sufficiently diluted with air, stimulate the mystical consciousness in an extraordinary degree. Depth beyond depth of truth seems revealed to the inhaler. This truth fades out, however, or escapes, at the moment of coming to; and if any words remain over in which it seemed to clothe itself, they prove to be the veriest nonsense. Nevertheless, the sense of a profound meaning having been there persists; and I know more than one person who is persuaded that in the nitrous oxide trance we have a genuine metaphysical revelation.

Some years ago I myself made some observations on this aspect of nitrous oxide intoxication, and reported them in print. One conclusion was forced upon my mind at that time, and my impression of its truth has ever since remained unshaken. It is that our normal waking consciousness, rational consciousness as we call it, is but one special type of consciousness, whilst all about it, parted from it by the filmiest of screens, there lie potential forms of consciousness entirely different. We may go through life without suspecting their existence; but apply the requisite stimulus, and at a touch they are there in all their completeness, definite types of mentality which probably somewhere have their field of application and adaptation. No account of the universe in its totality can be final which leaves these other forms of consciousness quite disregarded. How to regard them is the question—for they are so discontinuous with ordinary consciousness. Yet they may determine attitudes though they cannot furnish formulas, and open a region though they fail to give a map. At any rate, they forbid a premature closing of our accounts with reality. Looking back on my own experiences, they all converge towards a kind of insight to which I cannot help ascribing some metaphysical significance. The keynote of it is invariably a reconciliation. It is as if the opposites of the world, whose contradictoriness and conflict make all our difficulties and troubles, were melted into unity. Not only do they, as contrasted species, belong to one and the same genus, but *one of the species,* the nobler and better one, *is itself the genus, and so soaks up and absorbs its opposite into itself.* This is a dark saying, I know, when thus expressed in terms of common logic, but I cannot wholly escape from its authority. I feel as if it must mean something, something like what the hegelian philosophy means, if one could only lay hold of it more clearly. Those who have ears to hear, let them hear; to me the living sense of its reality only comes in the artificial mystic state of mind.[5]

Certain aspects of nature seem to have a peculiar power of awakening such mystical moods. Most of the striking cases which I have collected have occurred out of doors. Literature has commemorated this fact in many passages of great beauty—this extract, for example, from Amiel's Journal Intime:—

Shall I ever again have any of those prodigious reveries which sometimes came to me in former days? One day, in youth, at sunrise, sitting in the ruins of the castle of Faucigny; and again in the mountains, under the noonday sun, above Lavey, lying at the foot of a tree and visited by three butterflies; once more at night upon the shingly shore of the Northern Ocean, my back upon the sand and my vision ranging through the milky way;—such grand and spacious, immortal, cosmogonic reveries, when one reaches to the stars, when one owns the infinite! Moments divine, ecstatic hours; in which our thought flies from world to world, pierces the great enigma, breathes with a respiration broad, tranquil, and deep as the respiration of the ocean, serene and limitless as the blue firmament; . . . instants of irresistible intuition in which one feels one's self great as the universe, and calm as a god. . . . What hours, what memories!

The vestiges they leave behind are enough to fill us with belief and enthusiasm, as if they were visits of the Holy Ghost.

Even the least mystical of you must by this time be convinced of the existence of mystical moments as states of consciousness of an entirely specific quality, and of the deep impression which they make on those who have them. A Canadian psychiatrist, Dr. R. M. Bucke, gives to the more distinctly characterized of these phenomena the name of cosmic consciousness. "Cosmic consciousness in its more striking instances is not," Dr. Bucke says, "simply an expansion or extension of the self-conscious mind with which we are all familiar, but the superaddition of a function as distinct from any possessed by the average man as *self*-consciousness is distinct from any function possessed by one of the higher animals."

> The prime characteristic of cosmic consciousness is a consciousness of the cosmos, that is, of the life and order of the universe. Along with the consciousness of the cosmos there occurs an intellectual enlightenment which alone would place the individual on a new plane of existence—would make him almost a member of a new species. To this is added a state of moral exaltation, an indescribable feeling of elevation, elation, and joyousness, and a quickening of the moral sense, which is fully as striking, and more important than is the enhanced intellectual power. With these come what may be called a sense of immortality, a consciousness of eternal life, not a conviction that he shall have this, but the consciousness that he has it already.[6]

We have now seen enough of this cosmic or mystic consciousness, as it comes sporadically. We must next pass to its methodical cultivation as an element of the religious life. Hindus, Buddhists, Mohammedans, and Christians all have cultivated it methodically.

In India, training in mystical insight has been known from time immemorial under the name of yoga. Yoga means the experimental union of the individual with the divine. It is based on persevering exercise; and the diet, posture, breathing, intellectual concentration, and moral discipline vary slightly in the different systems which teach it. The yogi, or disciple, who has by these means overcome the obscurations of his lower nature sufficiently, enters into the condition termed *samādhi*, "and comes face to face with facts which no instinct or reason can ever know." He learns—

> That the mind itself has a higher state of existence, beyond reason, a superconscious state, and that when the mind gets to that higher state, then this knowledge beyond reasoning comes. . . . All the different steps in yoga are intended to bring us scientifically to the superconscious state or Samādhi. . . . Just as unconscious work is beneath consciousness, so there is another work which is above consciousness, and which, also, is not accompanied with the feeling of egoism. . . . There is not feeling of *I*, and yet the mind works, desireless, free from restlessness, objectless, bodiless. Then the Truth shines in its full effulgence, and we know ourselves—for Samādhi lies potential in us all—for what we truly are, free, immortal, omnipotent, loosed from the

finite, and its contrasts of good and evil altogether, and identical with the Atman or Universal Soul.[7]

The Vedantists say that one may stumble into superconsciousness sporadically, without the previous discipline, but it is then impure. Their test of its purity, like our test of religion's value, is empirical: its fruits must be good for life. When a man comes out of Samâdhi, they assure us that he remains "enlightened, a sage, a prophet, a saint, his whole character changed, his life changed, illumined."[8]

The Buddhists used the word "samâdhi" as well as the Hindus; but "dhyâna" is their special word for higher states of contemplation. There seem to be four stages recognized in dhyâna. The first stage comes through concentration of the mind upon one point. It excludes desire, but not discernment or judgment: it is still intellectual. In the second stage the intellectual functions drop off, and the satisfied sense of unity remains. In the third stage the satisfaction departs, and indifference begins, along with memory and self-consciousness. In the fourth stage the indifference, memory, and self-consciousness are perfected. [Just what "memory" and "self-consciousness" mean in this connection is doubtful. They cannot be the faculties familiar to us in the lower life.] Higher stages still of contemplation are mentioned—a region where there exists nothing, and where the mediator says: "There exists absolutely nothing," and stops. Then he reaches another region where he says: "There are neither ideas nor absence of ideas," and stops again. Then another region where, "having reached the end of both idea and perception, he stops finally." This would seem to be, not yet Nirvâna, but as close an approach to it as this life affords.[9]

In the Mohammedan world the Sufi sect and various dervish bodies are the possessors of the mystical tradition. The Sufis have existed in Persia from the earliest times, and as their pantheism is so at variance with the hot and rigid monotheism of the Arab mind, it has been suggested that Sufism must have been inoculated into Islam by Hindu influences. We Christians know little of Sufism, for its secrets are disclosed only to those initiated. To give its existence a certain liveliness in your minds, I will quote a Moslem document, and pass away from the subject.

Al-Ghazzali, a Persian philosopher and theologian, who flourished in the eleventh century, and ranks as one of the greatest doctors of the Moslem church, has left us one of the few autobiographies to be found outside of Christian literature. Strange that a species of book so abundant among ourselves should be so little represented elsewhere—the absence of strictly personal confessions is the chief difficulty to the purely literary student who would like to become acquainted with the inwardness of religions other than the Christian.

M. Schmölders has translated a part of Al-Ghazzali's autobiography into French:[10] —

"The Science of the Sufis," says the Moslem author, "aims at detaching the heart from all that is not God, and at giving to it for sole occupation the meditation of the divine being. Theory being more easy for me than practice, I read [certain books] until I understood all that can be learned by study and hearsay. Then I recognized that what pertains most exclusively to their method is just what no study can grasp, but only transport, ecstasy, and the transformation of the soul. How great, for example, is the difference between knowing the definitions of health, of satiety, with their causes and conditions, and being really healthy or filled. How different to know in what drunkenness consists—as being a state occasioned by a vapor that rises from the stomach—and *being* drunk effectively. Without doubt, the drunken man knows neither the definition of drunkenness nor what makes it interesting for science. Being drunk, he knows nothing; whilst the physician, although not drunk, knows well in what drunkenness consists, and what are its predisposing conditions. Similarly there is a difference between knowing that nature of abstinence, and *being* abstinent or having one's soul detached from the world.—Thus I had learned what words could teach of Sufism, but what was left could be learned neither by study nor through the ears, but solely by giving one's self up to ecstasy and leading a pious life.

"Reflecting on my situation, I found myself tied down by a multitude of bonds—temptations on every side. Considering my teaching, I found it was impure before God. I saw myself struggling with all my might to achieve glory and to spread my name. [Here follows an account of his six months' hesitation to break away from the conditions of his life at Bagdad, at the end of which he fell ill with a paralysis of the tongue.] Then, feeling my own weakness, and having entirely given up my own will, I repaired to God like a man in distress who has no more resources. He answered, as he answers the wretch who invokes him. My heart no longer felt any difficulty in renouncing glory, wealth, and my children. So I quitted Bagdad, and reserving from my fortune only what was indispensable for my subsistence, I distributed the rest. I went to Syria, where I remained about two years, with no other occupation than living in retreat and solitude, conquering my desires, combating my passions, training myself to purify my soul, to make my character perfect, to prepare my heart for meditating on God—all according to the methods of the Sufis, as I had read of them.

"This retreat only increased my desire to live in solitude, and to complete the purification of my heart and fit it for meditation. But the vicissitudes of the times, the affairs of the family, the need of subsistence, changed in some respects my primitive resolve, and interfered with my plans for a purely solitary life. I had never yet found myself completely in ecstasy, save in a few single hours; nevertheless, I kept the hope of attaining this state. Every time that the accidents led me astray, I sought to return; and in this situation I spent ten years. During this solitary state things were revealed to me which it is impossible either to describe or to point out. I recognized for certain that the Sufis are assuredly walking in the path of God. Both in their acts and in their inaction, whether internal or external, they are illumined by the light which proceeds from the prophetic source. The first condition for a Sufi is to purge his heart entirely of all that is not God. The next key of the contemplative life consists in the humble prayers which escape from the fervent soul, and in the meditations on God in which the heart is swallowed up entirely. But in reality this is only the beginning of the Sufi life, the end of Sufism being total absorption in God. The intuitions and all that precede are, so to speak, only the threshold for those who enter. From the beginning, revelations take place in so flagrant a shape that the Sufis see before them, whilst wide awake, the angels and the souls of the prophets. They hear their voices and obtain their favors. Then the transport rises from the perception of forms and figures to a degree which escapes all expression, and which no man may seek to give an account of without his words involving sin.

"Whosoever has had no experience of the transport knows of the true nature of prophetism nothing but the name. He may meanwhile be sure of its existence, both by experience and by what he hears the Sufis say. As there are men endowed only with the sensitive faculty who reject what is offered them in the way of objects of the pure understanding, so there are intellectual men who reject and avoid the things perceived by the prophetic faculty. A blind man can understand nothing of colors save what he has learned by narration and hearsay. Yet God has brought prophetism near to men in giving them all a state analogous to it in its principal characters. This state is sleep. If you were to tell a man who was himself without experience of such a phenomenon that there are people who at times swoon away so as to resemble dead men, and who [in dreams] yet perceive things that are hidden, he would deny it [and give his reasons]. Nevertheless, his arguments would be refuted by actual experience. Wherefore, just as the understanding is a stage of human life in which an eye opens to discern various intellectual objects uncomprehended by sensation; just so in the prophetic the sight is illumined by a light which uncovers hidden things and objects which the intellect fails to reach. The chief properties of prophetism are perceptible only during the transport, by those who embrace the Sufi life. The prophet is endowed with qualities to which you possess nothing analogous, and which consequently you cannot possibly understand. How should you know their true nature, since one knows only what one can comprehend? But the transport which one attains by the method of the Sufis is like an immediate perception, as if one touched the objects with one's hand."[11]

This incommunicableness of the transport is the keynote of all mysticism. Mystical truth exists for the individual who has the transport, but for no one else. In this, as I have said, it resembles the knowledge given to us in sensations more than that given by conceptual thought. Thought, with its remoteness and abstractness, has often enough in the history of philosophy been contrasted unfavorably with sensation. It is a commonplace of metaphysics that God's knowledge cannot be discursive but must be intuitive, that is, must be constructed more after the pattern of what in ourselves is called immediate feeling, than after that of proposition and judgment. But *our* immediate feelings have no content but what the five senses supply; and we have seen and shall see again that mystics may emphatically deny that the senses play any part in the very highest type of knowledge which their transports yield.

In the Christian church there have always been mystics. Although many of them have been viewed with suspicion some have gained favor in the eyes of the authorities. The experiences of these have been treated as precedents, and a codified system of mystical theology has been based upon them, in which everything legitimate finds its place.[12] The basis of the system is "orison" or meditation, the methodical elevation of the soul towards God. Through the practice of orison the higher levels of mystical experience may be attained. It is odd that Protestantism, especially evangelical Protestantism, should seemingly have abandoned everything methodical in this line. Apart from what prayer may lead to, Protestant mystical experience appears to have been almost exclusively sporadic. It has been left to our mind-curers to reintroduce methodical meditation into our religious life.

The first thing to be aimed at in orison is the mind's detachment from outer sensations, for these interfere with its concentration upon ideal things. Such manuals as Saint Ignatius's Spiritual Exercises recommend the disciple to expel sensation by a graduated series of efforts to imagine holy scenes. The acme of this kind of discipline would be a semi-hallucinatory mono-ideism—an imaginary figure of Christ, for example, coming fully to occupy the mind. Sensorial images of this sort, whether literal or symbolic, play an enormous part in mysticism.[13] But in certain cases imagery may fall away entirely, and in the very highest raptures it tends to do so. The state of consciousness becomes then insusceptible of any verbal description. Mystical teachers are unanimous as to this. Saint John of the Cross, for instance, one of the best of them, thus describes the condition called the "union of love," which, he says, is reached by "dark contemplation." In this the Deity compenetrates the soul, but in such a hidden way that the soul—

> finds no terms, no means, no comparison whereby to render the sublimity of the wisdom and the delicacy of the spiritual feeling with which she is filled. . . . We receive this mystical knowledge of God clothed in none of the kinds of images, in none of the sensible representations, which our mind makes use of in other circumstances. Accordingly in this knowledge, since the senses and the imagination are not employed, we get neither form nor impression, nor can we give any account or furnish any likeness, although the mysterious and sweet-tasting wisdom comes home so clearly to the inmost parts of our soul. Fancy a man seeing a certain kind of thing for the first time in his life. He can understand it, use and enjoy it, but he cannot apply a name to it, nor communicate any idea of it, even though all the while it be a mere thing of sense. How much greater will be his powerlessness when it goes beyond the senses! This is the peculiarity of the divine language. The more infused, intimate, spiritual, and supersensible it is, the more does it exceed the senses, both inner and outer, and impose silence upon them. . . . The soul then feels as if placed in a vast and profound solitude, to which no created thing has access, in an immense and boundless desert, desert the more delicious the more solitary it is. There, in this abyss of wisdom, the soul grows by what it drinks in from the well-springs of the comprehension of love, . . . and recognizes, however sublime and learned may be the terms we employ, how utterly vile, insignificant, and improper they are when we seek to discover of divine things by their means.[14]

I cannot pretend to detail to you the sundry stages of the Christian mystical life.[15] Our time would not suffice, for one thing; and moreover, I confess that the subdivisions and names which we find in the Catholic books seem to me to represent nothing objectively distinct. So many men, so many minds: I imagine that these experiences can be as infinitely varied as are the idiosyncrasies of individuals.

To the medical mind these ecstasies signify nothing but suggested and imitated hypnoid states, on an intellectual basis of superstition, and a corporeal one of degeneration and hysteria. Undoubtedly these pathological conditions have existed in many and possibly in all the cases, but that fact tells us nothing about the value for knowledge of the consciousness which they induce. To pass a spiritual judgment upon these states, we must not content ourselves with superficial medical talk, but inquire into their fruits for life.

Their fruits appear to have been various. Stupefaction, for one thing, seems not to have been altogether absent as a result. You may remember the helplessness in the kitchen and schoolroom of poor Margaret Mary Alacoque. Many other ecstatics would have perished but for the care taken of them by admiring followers. The "other-worldliness" encouraged by the mystical consciousness makes this over-abstraction from practical life peculiarly liable to befall mystics in whom the character is naturally passive and the intellect feeble; but in natively strong minds and characters we find quite opposite results. The great Spanish mystics, who carried the habit of ecstasy as far as it has often been carried, appear for the most part to have shown indomitable spirit and energy, and all the more so for the trances in which they indulged.

Saint Ignatius was a mystic, but his mysticism made him assuredly one of the most powerfully practical human engines that ever lived. Saint John of the Cross, writing of the intuitions and "touches" by which God reaches the substance of the soul, tells us that—

> They enrich it marvelously. A single one of them may be sufficient to abolish at a stroke certain imperfections of which the soul during its whole life had vainly tried to rid itself, and to leave it adorned with virtues and loaded with supernatural gifts. A single one of these intoxicating consolations may reward it for all the labors undergone in its life—even were they numberless. Invested with an invincible courage, filled with an impassioned desire to suffer for its God, the soul then is seized with a strange torment—that of not being allowed to suffer enough.[16]

Saint Teresa is as emphatic, and much more detailed. You may perhaps remember a passage I quoted from her in my first lecture.[17] There are many similar pages in her autobiography. Where in literature is a more evidently veracious account of the formation of a new centre of spiritual energy, than is given in her description of the effects of certain ecstasies which in departing leave the soul upon a higher level of emotional excitement?

> Often, infirm and wrought upon with dreadful pains before the ecstasy, the soul emerges from it full of health and admirably disposed for action . . . as if God had willed that the body itself, already obedient to the soul's desires, should share in the soul's happiness. . . . The soul after such a favor is animated with a degree of courage so great that if at that moment its body should be torn to pieces for the cause of God, it would feel nothing but the liveliest comfort. Then it is that promises and heroic resolutions spring up in profusion in us, soaring desires, horror of the world, and the clear perception of our proper nothingness. . . . What empire is comparable to that of a soul who, from this sublime summit to which God has raised her, sees all the things of earth beneath her feet, and is captivated by no one of them? How ashamed she is of her former attachments! How amazed at her blindness!

What lively pity she feels for those whom she recognizes still shrouded in the darkness! ... She groans at having ever been sensitive to points of honor, at the illusion that made her ever see as honor what the world calls by that name. Now she sees in this name nothing more than an immense lie of which the world remains a victim. She discovers, in the new light from above, that in genuine honor there is nothing spurious, that to be faithful to this honor is to give our respect to what deserves to be respected really, and to consider as nothing, or as less than nothing, whatsoever perishes and is not agreeable to God. ... She laughs when she sees grave persons, persons of orison, caring for points of honor for which she now feels profoundest contempt. It is suitable to the dignity of their rank to act thus, they pretend, and it makes them more useful to others. But she knows that in despising the dignity of their rank for the pure love of God they would do more good in a single day than they would effect in ten years by preserving it. ... She laughs at herself that there should ever have been a time in her life when she made any case of money, when she ever desired it. ... Oh! if human beings might only agree together to regard it as so much useless mud, what harmony would then reign in the world! With what friendship we would all treat each other if our interest in honor and in money could not disappear from earth! For my own part, I feel as if it would be a remedy for all our ills.[18]

Mystical conditions may, therefore, render the soul more energetic in the lines which their inspiration favors. But this could be reckoned an advantage only in case the inspiration where a true one. If the inspiration were erroneous, the energy would be all the more mistaken and misbegotten. So we stand once more before that problem of truth which confronted us at the end of the lectures on saintliness. You will remember that we turned to mysticism precisely to get some light on truth. Do mystical states establish the truth of those theological affections in which the saintly life has its root?

In spite of their repudiation of articulate self-description, mystical states in general assert a pretty distinct theoretic drift. It is possible to give the outcome of the majority of them in terms that point in definite philosophical directions. One of these directions is optimism, and the other is monism. We pass into mystical states from out of ordinary consciousness as from a less into a more, as from a smallness into a vastness, and at the same time as from an unrest to a rest. We feel them as reconciling, unifying states. They appeal to the yes-function more than to the no-function in us. In them the unlimited absorbs the limits and peacefully closes the account. Their very denial of every adjective you may propose as applicable to the ultimate truth—He, the Self, the Atman, is to be described by "No! no!" only, say the Upanishads[19]—though it seems on the surface to be a no-function, is a denial made on behalf of a deeper yes. Whoso calls the Absolute anything in particular, or says that it is *this,* seems implicitly to shut it off from being *that*—it is as if he lessened it. So we deny the "this," negating the negation which it seems to us to imply, in the interests of the higher affirmative attitude by which we are possessed. The fountain-head of Christian mysticism is Dionysius the Areopagite. He describes the absolute truth by negatives exclusively.

"The cause of all things is neither soul nor intellect; nor has it imagination, opinion, or reason, or intelligence; nor is it reason or intelligence; nor is it spoken or thought. It is neither number, nor order, nor magnitude, nor little-ness, nor equality, nor inequality, nor similarity, nor dissimilarity. It neither stands, nor moves, nor rests. . . . It is neither essence, nor eternity, nor time. Even intellectual contact does not belong to it. It is neither science nor truth. It is not even royalty or wisdom; not one; not unity; not divinity or goodness; nor even spirit as we know it," etc., *ad libitum.*[20]

But these qualifications are denied by Dionysius, not because the truth falls short of them, but because it so infinitely excels them. It is above them. It is *super*-lucent, *super*-splendent, *super*-essential, *super*-sublime, *super everything* that can be named. Like Hegel in his logic, mystics journey towards the positive pole of truth only by the "Methode der Absoluten Negativität."[21]

This overcoming of all the usual barriers between the individual and the Absolute is the great mystic achievement. In mystic states we both become one with the Absolute and we become aware of our oneness. This is the everlasting and triumphant mystical tradition, hardly altered by differences of clime or creed. In Hinduism, in Neoplatonism, in Sufism, in Christian mysticism, in Whitmanism, we find the same recurring note, so that there is about mystical utterances an eternal unanimity which ought to make a critic stop and think, and which brings it about that the mystical classics have, as has been said, neither birthday nor native land. Perpetually telling of the unity of man with God, their speech antedates languages, and they do not grow old.[22]

I have now sketched with extreme brevity and insufficiency, but as fairly as I am able in the time allowed, the general traits of the mystic range of consciousness. *It is on the whole pantheistic and optimistic, or at least the opposite of pessimistic. It is anti-naturalistic, and harmonizes best with twice-bornness and so-called other-worldly states of mind.*

My next task is to inquire whether we can invoke it as authoritative. Does it furnish any *warrant for the truth* of the twice-bornness and supernaturality and pantheism which it favors? I must give my answer to this question as concisely as I can.

In brief my answer is this—and I will divide it into three parts: —

(1) Mystical states, when well developed, usually are, and have the right to be, absolutely authoritative over the individuals to whom they come.

(2) No authority emanates from them which should make it a duty for those who stand outside of them to accept their revelations uncritically.

(3) They break down the authority of the non-mystical or rationalistic con-sciousness, based upon the understanding and the senses alone. They show it to be only one kind of consciousness. They open out the possibility of other

orders of truth, in which, so far as anything in us vitally responds to them, we may freely continue to have faith.

I will take up these points one by one.

1

As a matter of psychological fact, mystical states of a well-pronounced and emphatic sort *are* usually authoritative over those who have them.[23] They have been "there," and know. It is vain for rationalism to grumble about this. If the mystical truth that comes to a man proves to be a force that he can live by, what mandate have we of the majority to order him to live in another way? We can throw him into a prison or a madhouse, but we cannot change his mind—we commonly attach it only the more stubbornly to its beliefs.[24] It mocks our utmost efforts, as a matter of fact, and in point of logic it absolutely escapes our jurisdiction. Our own more "rational" beliefs are based on evidence exactly similar in nature to that which mystics quote for theirs. Our senses, namely, have assured us of certain states of fact; but mystical experiences are as direct perceptions of fact for those who have them as any sensations ever were for us. The records show that even though the five senses be in abeyance in them, they are absolutely sensational in their epistemological quality, if I may be pardoned the barbarous expression—that is, they are face to face presentations of what seems immediately to exist.

The mystic is, in short, *invulnerable,* and must be left whether we relish it or not, in undisturbed enjoyment of his creed. Faith, says Tolstoy, is that by which men live. And faith-state and mystic state are practically convertible terms.

2

But I now proceed to add that mystics have no right to claim that we ought to accept the deliverance of their peculiar experiences, if we are ourselves outsiders and feel no private call thereto. The utmost they can ever ask of us in this life is to admit that they establish a presumption. They form a consensus and have an unequivocal outcome; and it would be odd, mystics might say, if such a unanimous type of experience should prove to be altogether wrong. At bottom, however, this would only be an appeal to numbers like the appeal of rationalism the other way; and the appeal to numbers has no logical force. If we acknowledge it, it is for "suggestive," not for logical reasons: we follow the majority because to do so suits life.

But even this presumption from the unanimity of mystics is far from being strong. In characterizing mystic states as pantheistic, optimistic, etc., I am afraid I over-simplified the truth. I did so for expository reasons, and to keep the closer to the classic mystical tradition. The classic religious mysticism, it now must be confessed, is only a "privileged case." It is an *extract*, kept true to type by the selection of the fittest specimens and their preservation in "schools." It is carved out from a much larger mass; and if we take the larger mass as seriously as religious mysticism has historically taken itself, we find that the supposed unanimity largely disappears. To begin with, even religious mysticism itself, the kind that accumulates traditions and makes schools, is much less unanimous than I have allowed. It has been both ascetic and antinomianly self-indulgent within the Christian church.[25] It is dualistic in Sankhya, and monistic in Vedanta philosophy. I called it pantheistic; but the great Spanish mystics are anything but pantheists. They are with few exceptions non-metaphysical minds, for whom "the category of personality" is absolute. The "union" of man with God is for them much more like an occasional miracle than like an original identity.[26] How different again, apart from the happiness common to all, is the mysticism of Walt Whitman, Edward Carpenter, Richard Jefferies, and other naturalistic pantheists, from the more distinctively Christian sort.[27] The fact is that the mystical feeling of enlargement, union, and emancipation has no specific intellectual content whatever of its own. It is capable of forming matrimonial alliances with material furnished by the most diverse philosophies and theologies, provided only they can find a place in their framework for its peculiar emotional mood. We have no right, therefore, to invoke its prestige as distinctively in favor of any special belief, such as that in absolute idealism, or in the absolute monistic identity, or in the absolute goodness of the world. It is only relatively in favor of all these things—it passes out of common human consciousness in the direction in which they lie.

So much for religious mysticism proper. But more remains to be told, for religious mysticism is only one half of mysticism. The other half has no accumulated traditions except those which the text-books on insanity supply. Open any one of these, and you will find abundant cases in which "mystical ideas" are cited as characteristic symptoms of enfeebled or deluded states of mind. In delusional insanity, paranoia, as they sometimes call it, we may have a *diabolical* mysticism, a sort of religious mysticism turned upside down. The same sense of ineffable importance in the smallest events, the same texts and words coming with new meanings, the same voices and visions and leadings and missions, the same controlling by extraneous powers; only this time the emotion is pessimistic: instead of consolations we have desolations; the meanings are dreadful; and the powers are enemies to life. It is evident that from the point of view of their psychological mechanism, the classic mysticism and these lower mysticisms spring from the same mental level, from that great subliminal or transmarginal region of which science is beginning to admit the existence, but of which so little is really known. That region contains every kind of matter: "seraph and snake" abide there side by side. To come from thence is no infallible credential. What comes must be sifted and tested, and run the gauntlet of confrontation with the total context of experience, just like what comes from the outer world of sense. Its value must be ascertained by empirical methods, so long as we are not mystics ourselves.

Once more, then, I repeat that non-mystics are under no obligation to acknowledge in mystical states a superior authority conferred on them by their intrinsic nature.[28]

Yet, I repeat once more, the existence of mystical states absolutely overthrows the pretension of non-mystical states to be the sole and ultimate dictators of what we may believe. As a rule, mystical states merely add a supersensuous meaning to the ordinary outward data of consciousness. They are excitements like the emotions of love or ambition, gifts to our spirit by means of which facts already objectively before us fall into a new expressiveness and make a new connection with our active life. They do not contradict these facts as such, or deny anything that our senses have immediately seized.[29] It is the rationalistic critic rather who plays the part of denier in the controversy, and his denials have no strength, for there never can be a state of facts to which new meaning may not truthfully be added, provided the mind ascend to a more enveloping point of view. It must always remain an open question whether mystical states may not possibly be such superior points of view, windows through which the mind looks out upon a more extensive and inclusive world. The difference of the views seen from the different mystical windows need not prevent us from entertaining this supposition. The wider world would in that case prove to have a mixed constitution like that of this world, that is all. It would have its celestial and its infernal regions, its tempting and its saving moments, its valid experiences and its counterfeit ones, just as our world has them; but it would be a wider world all the same. We should have to use its experiences by selecting and subordinating and substituting just as is our custom in this ordinary naturalistic world; we should be liable to error just as we are now; yet the counting in of that wider world of meanings, and the serious dealing with it, might, in spite of all the perplexity, be indispensable stages in our approach to the final fullness of the truth.

In this shape, I think, we have to leave the subject. Mystical states indeed wield no authority due simply to their being mystical states. But the higher ones among them point in directions to which the religious sentiments even of non-mystical men incline. They tell of the supremacy of the ideal, of vastness, of union, of safety, and of rest. They offer us *hypotheses,* hypotheses which we may voluntarily ignore, but which as thinkers we cannot possibly upset. The supernaturalism and optimism to which they would persuade us may, interpreted in one way or another, be after all the truest of insights into the meaning of this life.

"Oh, the little more, and how much it is; and the little less, and what worlds away!" It may be that possibility and permission of this sort are all that our religious consciousness requires to live on. In my last lecture I shall have to try to persuade you that this is the case. Meanwhile, however, I am sure that for many of my readers this diet is too slender. If supernaturalism and inner union with the divine are true, you think, then not so much permission, as compulsion to believe, ought to be found. Philosophy has always professed to prove religious truth by coercive argument; and the construction of philosophies of this kind has always been one favorite function of the religious life, if we use this term in the large historic sense. But religious philosophy is an enormous subject, and in my next lecture I can only give that brief glance at it which my limits will allow.

1. Newman's *Securus judicat orbis terrarum* is another instance.

2. "Mesopotamia" is the stock comic instance.–An excellent old German lady, who had done some traveling in her day, used to describe to me her *Sehnsucht* that she might yet visit "Philadelphia," whose wondrous name had always haunted her imagination. Of John Foster it is said that "single words (as *chalcedony*), or the names of ancient heroes, had a mighty fascination over him. 'At any time the word *hermit* was enough to transport him.' The words *woods* and *forests* would produce the most powerful emotion." Foster's Life, by Ryland, New York, 1846, p. 3.

3. The Two Voices. In a letter to Mr. B. P. Blood, Tennyson reports of himself as follows:–

"I have never had any revelation through anaesthetics, but a kind of waking trance–this for lack of a better word–I have frequently had, quite up from boyhood, when I have been all alone. This has come upon me through repeating my own name to myself silently, till all at once, as it were out of the intensity of the consciousness of individuality, individuality itself seemed to dissolve and fade away into boundless being, and this not a confused state but the clearest, the surest of the surest, utterly beyond words–where death was an almost laughable impossibility–the loss of personality (if so it were) seeming no extinction, but the only true life. I am ashamed of my feeble description. Have I not said the state is utterly beyond words?"

Professor Tyndall, in a letter, recalls Tennyson saying of this condition: "By God Almighty! there is no delusion in the matter! It is no nebulous ecstasy, but a state of transcendent wonder, asociated with absolute clearness of mind." Memoris of Alfred Tennyson, ii. 473.

4. The Lancet, July 6 and 13, 1895, reprinted as the Cavendish Lecture, on Dreamy Mental States, London, Baillière, 1895. They have been a good deal discussed of late by psychologists. See, for example, Bernard-Leroy: L'Illusion de Fausse Reconnaissance, Paris, 1898.

5. What reader of Hegel can doubt that that sense of a perfected Being with all its otherness soaked up into itself, which dominates his whole philosophy, must have come from the prominence in his consciousness of mystical moods like this, in most persons kept subliminal? The notion is thoroughly characteristic of the mystical level, and the *Aufgabe* of making it articulare was surely set to Hegel's intellect by mystical feeling.

6. Cosmic Consciousness: a study in the evolution of the human Mind, Philadelphia, 1901, p. 2.

7. My quotations are from Vivekananda, Raja Yoga, London, 1896. The completest source of information on Yoga is the work translated by Vhiari Lala Mitra: Yoga Vasishta Maha Ramayana, 4 vols. Calcutta, 1891-99.

8. A European witness, after carefully comparing the results of Yoga with those of the hypnotic or dreamy states artificially producible by us, says: "It makes of its true disciples good, healthy, and happy men.... Through the mastery which the yogi attains over his thoughts and his body, he grows into a 'character.' By the subjection of his impulses and propensities to his will, and the fixing of the latter upon the ideal of goodness, he becomes a 'personality' hard to influence by others, and thus almost the opposite of what we usually imagine a 'medium' so-called, or 'psychic subject' to be." Karl Kellner: Yoga: Eine Skizze, Müchen, 1896, p. 21.

9. I follow the account of C. F. Koeppen: Die Religion des Buddha, Berlin, 1857, i, 585ff.

10. For a full account for him, see D. B. MacDonald: The Life of Al-Ghazzali, in the Journal of the American Oriental Society, 1899, vol. ix, p. 71.

11. A. Schmölders: Essai sur les écoles philosophiques chez les Arabes, Paris, 1842, pp. 54-68, abridged.

12. Görres's Christliche Mystik gives a full account of the facts. So does Ribet's Mystique Divine, 2 vols., Paris, 1890. A still more methodical modern work is the Mystica Theologia of Vallcornera, 2 vols., Turin, 1890.

13. M. Récéjac, in a recent volume, makes them essential. Mysticism he defines as "the tendency to draw near to the Absolute morally, *and by the aid of Symbols.*" See his

Fondements de la Connaissance Mystique, Paris, 1897, p. 66. But there are unquestionably mystical conditions in which sensible symbols play no part.

14. Saint John of the Cross: The Dark Night of the Soul, book ii, ch. xvii, in Vie et Œuvres, 3me édition, Paris, 1893, iii, 428-432. Chapter xi, of book ii, of Saint John's Ascent of Carmel is devoted to showing the harmfulness for the mystical life of the use of sensible imagery.

15. In particular I omit mention of visual and auditory hallucinations, verbal and graphic automatisms, and such marvels as "levitation," stigmatization, and the healing of disease. These phenomena, which mystics have often presented (or are believed to have presented), have no essential mystical significance, for they occur with no consciousness of illumination whatever, when they occur, as they often do, in persons of non-mystical mind. Consciousness of illumination is for us the essential mark of "mystical" states.

16. Œuvres, ii, 320.

17. Ibid., p. 22.

18. Autobiography, pp. 229, 200, 231-233, 243.

19. Müller's translation, part ii, p. 180.

20. T. Davidson's translation, in Journal of Speculative Philosophy, 1893, vol. xxii, p. 399.

21. "Deus propter excellentiam non immerito Nihil vocatur." Scotus Erigena, quoted by Andrew Seth: Two Lectures on Theism, New York, 1897, p. 55.

22. Compare M. Maeterlinck: L'Ornement des Noces spirituelles de Ruysbroeck, Bruxelles, 1891, Introduction, p. xix.

23. I abstract from weaker states, and from those cases of which the books are full, where the director (but usually not the subject) remains in doubt whether the experience may not have proceeded from the demon.

24. Example: Mr. John Nelson writes of his imprisonment for preaching Methodism: "My soul was as a watered garden, and I could sing praises to God all day long; for he turned my captivity into joy, and gave me to rest as well on the boards, as if I had been on a bed of down. Now could I say, 'God's service is perfect freedom,' and I was carried out much in prayer that my enemies might drink of the same river of peace which my God gave so largely to me." Journal, London, no date, p. 172.

25. Ruysbroeck, in the work which Maeterlinck has translated, has a chapter against the antinomianism of disciples. H. Delacroix's book (Essai sur le mysticisme spéculatif en Allemagne au XIVme Siècle, Paris, 1900) is full of antinomain material. Compare also A. Jundt: Les Amis de Dieu au XIV Siècle, Thèse de Strasbourg, 1879.

26. Compare Paul Rousselot: Les Mystiques Espagnols, Paris, 1869, ch. xii.

27. See Carpenter's Towards Democracy, especially the latter parts, and Jefferies's wonderful and splendid mystic rhapsody, The Story of my Heart.

28. In chapter i of book ii, of his work Degeneration, "Max Nordau" seeks to undermine all mysticism by exposing the weakness of the lower kinds. Mysticism for him means any sudden perception of hidden significance in things. He explains such perception by the abundant uncompleted associations which experiences may rouse in a degenerate brain. These give to him who has the experience a vague and vast sense of its leading further, yet they awaken no definite or useful consequent in his thought. The explanation is a plausible one for certain sorts of feeling of significance; and other alienists (Wernicke, for example, in his Grundriss der Psychiatrie, Theil ii, Leipzig, 1896) have explained "paranoiac" conditions by a laming of the association organ. But the higher mystical flights, with their positiveness and abruptness, are surely products of no such merely negative condition. It seems far more reasonable to ascribe them to inroads from the subconscious life, of the cerebral activity correlative to which we as yet know nothing.

29. They sometimes add subjective *audita et visa* to the facts, but as these are usually interpreted as transmundane, they oblige no alteration in the facts of sense.

RELIGIOUS EPISTEMOLOGY:
FAITH

REASON AND REVELATION

St. Thomas Aquinas

Chapter 3

On the Way in Which Divine Truth Is to Be Made Known

[1] The way of making truth known is not always the same, and, as the Philosopher has very well said, "it belongs to an educated man to seek such certitude in each thing as the nature of that thing allows."[1] The remark is also introduced by Boethius.[2] But, since such is the case, we must first show what way is open to us in order that we may make known the truth which is our object.

[2] There is a twofold mode of truth in what we profess about God. Some truths about God exceed all the ability of the human reason. Such is the truth that God is triune. But there are some truths which the natural reason also is able to reach. Such are that God exists, that He is one, and the like. In fact, such truths about God have been proved demonstratively by the philosophers, guided by the light of the natural reason.

[3] That there are certain truths about God that totally surpass man's ability appears with the greatest evidence. Since, indeed, the principle of all knowledge that the reason perceives about some thing is the understanding of the very substance of that being (for according to Aristotle "what a thing is" is the principle of demonstration),[3] it is necessary that the way in which we understand the substance of a thing determines the way in which we know what belongs to it. Hence, if the human intellect comprehends the substance of some thing, for example, that of a stone or of a triangle, no intelligible characteristic belonging to that thing surpasses the grasp of the human reason. But this does not happen to us in the case of God. For the human intellect is not able to reach a comprehension of the divine substance through its natural power. For, according to its manner of knowing in the present life, the intellect depends on the sense for the origin of knowledge; and so those things that do not fall under the senses cannot be grasped by the human intellect except in so far as the knowledge of them is gathered from sensible things. Now, sensible things cannot lead the human intellect

to the point of seeing in them the nature of the divine substance; for sensible things are effects that fall short of the power of their cause. Yet, beginning with sensible things, our intellect is led to the point of knowing about God that He exists, and other such characteristics that must be attributed to the First Principle. There are, consequently, some intelligible truths about God that are open to the human reason; but there are others that absolutely surpass its power.

[4] We may easily see the same point from the gradation of intellects. Consider the case of two persons of whom one has a more penetrating grasp of a thing by his intellect than does the other. He who has the superior intellect understands many things that the other cannot grasp at all. Such is the case with a very simple person who cannot at all grasp the subtle speculations of philosophy. But the intellect of an angel surpasses the human intellect much more than the intellect of the greatest philosopher surpasses the intellect of the most uncultivated simple person; for the distance between the best philosopher and a simple person is contained within the limits of the human species, which the angelic intellect surpasses. For the angel knows God on the basis of a more noble effect than does man; and this by as much as the substance of an angel, through which the angel in his natural knowledge is led to the knowledge of God, is nobler than sensible things and even than the soul itself, through which the human intellect mounts to the knowledge of God. The divine intellect surpasses the angelic intellect much more than the angelic surpasses the human. For the divine intellect is in its capacity equal to its substance, and therefore it understands fully what it is, including all its intelligible attributes. But by his natural knowledge the angel does not know what God is, since the substance itself of the angel, through which he is led to the knowledge of God, is an effect that is not equal to the power of its cause. Hence, the angel is not able, by means of his natural knowledge, to grasp all the things that God understands in Himself; nor is the human reason sufficient to grasp all the things that the angel understands through his own natural power. Just as, therefore, it would be the height of folly for a simple person to assert that what a philosopher proposes is false on the ground that he himself cannot understand it, so (and even more so) it is the acme of stupidity for a man to suspect as false what is divinely revealed through the ministry of the angels simply because it cannot be investigated by reason.

[5] The same thing, moreover, appears quite clearly from the defect that we experience every day in our knowledge of things. We do not know a great many of the properties of sensible things, and in most cases we are not able to discover fully the natures of those properties that we apprehend by the sense. Much more is it the case, therefore, that the human reason is not equal to the task of investigating all the intelligible characteristics of that most excellent substance.

[6] The remark of Aristotle likewise agrees with this conclusion. He says that "our intellect is related to the prime beings, which are most evident in their nature, as the eye of an owl is related to the sun."[4]

[7] Sacred Scripture also gives testimony to this truth. We read in Job: "Peradventure thou wilt comprehend the steps of God, and wilt find out the

Almighty perfectly?" (11:7). And again: "Behold, God is great, exceeding our knowledge" (Job 36:26). And St. Paul: "We know in part" (I Cor.13:9).

[8] We should not, therefore, immediately reject as false, following the opinion of the Manicheans and many unbelievers, everything that is said about God even though it cannot be investigated by reason.

Chapter 4

That the Truth About God to Which the Natural Reason Reaches Is Fittingly Proposed to Men for Belief

[1] Since, therefore, there exists a twofold truth concerning the divine being, one to which the inquiry of the reason can reach, the other which surpasses the whole ability of the human reason, it is fitting that both of these truths be proposed to man divinely for belief. This point must first be shown concerning the truth that is open to the inquiry of the reason; otherwise, it might perhaps seem to someone that, since such a truth can be known by the reason, it was uselessly given to men through a supernatural inspiration as an object of belief.

[2] Yet, if this truth were left solely as a matter of inquiry for the human reason, three awkward consequences would follow.

[3] The first is that few men would possess the knowledge of God. For there are three reasons why most men are cut off from the fruit of diligent inquiry which is the discovery of truth. Some do not have the physical disposition for such work. As a result, there are many who are naturally not fitted to pursue knowledge; and so, however much they tried, they would be unable to reach the highest level of human knowledge which consists in knowing God. Others are cut off from pursuing this truth by the necessities imposed upon them by their daily lives. For some men must devote themselves to taking care of temporal matters. Such men would not be able to give so much time to the leisure of contemplative inquiry as to reach the highest peak at which human investigation can arrive, namely, the knowledge of God. Finally, there are some who are cut off by indolence. In order to know the things that the reason can investigate concerning God, a knowledge of many things must already be possessed. For almost all of philosophy is directed towards the knowledge of God, and that is why metaphysics, which deals with divine things, is the last part of philosophy to be learned. This means that we are able to arrive at the inquiry concerning the aforementioned truth only on the basis of a great deal of labor spent in study. Now, those who wish to undergo such a labor for the mere love of knowledge are few, even though God has inserted into the minds of men a natural appetite for knowledge.

[4] The second awkward effect is that those who would come to discover the abovementioned truth would barely reach it after a great deal of time. The reasons are several. There is the profundity of this truth, which the human intellect is made capable of grasping by natural inquiry only after a long training. Then, there are many things that must be presupposed, as we have said. There is also the

fact that, in youth, when the soul is swayed by the various movements of the passions, it is not in a suitable state for the knowledge of such lofty truth. On the contrary, "one becomes wise and knowing in repose," as it is said in the *Physics*.[5] The result is this. If the only way open to us for the knowledge of God were solely that of the reason, the human race would remain in the blackest shadows of ignorance. For then the knowledge of God, which especially renders men perfect and good, would come to be possessed only by a few, and these few would require a great deal of time in order to reach it.

[5] The third awkward effect is this. The investigation of the human reason for the most part has falsity present within it, and this is due partly to the weakness of our intellect in judgment, and partly to the admixture of images. The result is that many, remaining ignorant of the power of demonstration, would hold in doubt those things that have been most truly demonstrated. This would be particularly the case since they see that, among those who are reputed to be wise men, each one teaches his own brand of doctrine. Furthermore, with the many truths that are demonstrated, there sometimes is mingled something that is false, which is not demonstrated but rather asserted on the basis of some probable or sophistical argument, which yet has the credit of being a demonstration. That is why it was necessary that the unshakeable certitude and pure truth concerning divine things should be presented to men by way of faith.

[6] Beneficially, therefore, did the divine Mercy provide that it should instruct us to hold by faith even those truths that the human reason is able to investigate. In this way, all men would easily be able to have a share in the knowledge of God, and this without uncertainty and error.

[7] Hence it is written: "Henceforward you walk not as also the Gentiles walk in the vanity of their mind, having their understanding darkened" (Eph. 4:17-18). And again: "All thy children shall be taught of the Lord" (Isa. 54:13).

Chapter 5

That the Truths the Human Reason Is Not Able to Investigate Are Fittingly Proposed to Men for Belief

[1] Now, perhaps some will think that men should not be asked to believe what the reason is not adequate to investigate, since the divine Wisdom provides in the case of each thing according to the mode of its nature. We must therefore prove that it is necessary for man to receive from God as objects of belief even those truths that are above the human reason.

[2] No one tends with desire and zeal towards something that is not already known to him. But, as we shall examine later on in this work, men are ordained by the divine Providence towards a higher good than human fragility can experience in the present life.[6] That is why it was necessary for the human mind to be called to something higher than the human reason here and now can reach, so that it would thus learn to desire something and with zeal tend towards something that

surpasses the whole state of the present life. This belongs especially to the Christian religion, which in a unique way promises spiritual and eternal goods. And so there are many things proposed to men in it that transcend human sense. The Old Law, on the other hand, whose promises were a temporal character, contained very few proposals that transcended the inquiry of the human reason. Following this same direction, the philosophers themselves, in order that they might lead men from the pleasure of sensible things to virtue, were concerned to show that there were in existence other goods of a higher nature than these things of sense, and that those who gave themselves to the active or contemplative virtues would find much sweeter enjoyment in the taste of these higher goods.

[3] It is also necessary that such truth be proposed to men for belief so that they may have a truer knowledge of God. For then only do we know God truly when we believe Him to be above everything that it is possible for man to think about Him; for, as we have shown,[7] the divine substance surpasses the natural knowledge of which man is capable. Hence, by the fact that some things about God are proposed to man that surpass his reason, there is strengthened in man the view that God is something above what he can think.

[4] Another benefit that comes from the revelation to men of truths that exceed the reason is the curbing of presumption, which is the mother of error. For there are some who have such a presumptuous opinion of their own ability that they deem themselves able to measure the nature of everything; I mean to say that, in their estimation, everything is true that seems to them so, and everything is false that does not. So that the human mind, therefore, might be freed from this presumption and come to a humble inquiry after truth, it was necessary that some things should be proposed to man by God that would completely surpass his intellect.

[5] A still further benefit may also be seen in what Aristotle says in the *Ethics*.[8] There was a certain Simonides who exhorted people to put aside the knowledge of divine things and to apply their talents to human occupations. He said that "he who is a man should know human things, and he who is mortal, things that are mortal." Against Simonides Aristotle says that "man should draw himself towards what is immortal and divine as much as he can." And so he says in the *De animalibus* that, although what we know of the higher substances is very little, yet that little is loved and desired more than all the knowledge that we have about less noble substances.[9] He also says in the *De caelo et mundo* that when questions about the heavenly bodies can be given even a modest and merely plausible solution, he who hears this experiences intense joy.[10] From all these considerations it is clear that even the most imperfect knowledge about the most noble realities brings the greatest perfection to the soul. Therefore, although the human reason cannot grasp fully the truths that are above it, yet, if it somehow holds these truths at least by faith, it acquires great perfection for itself.

[6] Therefore it is written: "For many things are shown to thee above the understanding of men" (Eccles. 3:25). Again: "So the things that are of God no

man knoweth but the Spirit of God. But to us God hath revealed them by His Spirit" (I Cor. 2:11, 10).

Chapter 6

That to Give Assent to the Truths of Faith Is Not Foolishness Even Though They Are Above Reason

[1]　Those who place their faith in this truth, however, "for which the human reason offers no experimental evidence,"[11] do not believe foolishly, as though "following artificial fables" (II Peter 1:16). For these "secrets of divine Wisdom" (Job 11:6) the divine Wisdom itself, which knows all things to the full, has deigned to reveal to men. It reveals its own presence, as well as the truth of its teaching and inspiration, by fitting arguments; and in order to confirm those truths that exceed natural knowledge, it gives visible manifestation to works that surpass the ability of all nature. Thus, there are the wonderful cures of illnesses, there is the raising of the dead, and the wonderful immutation in the heavenly bodies; and what is more wonderful, there is the inspiration given to human minds, so that simple and untutored persons, filled with the gift of the Holy Spirit, come to possess instantaneously the highest wisdom and the readiest eloquence. When these arguments were examined, through the efficacy of the abovementioned proof, and not the violent assault of arms or the promise of pleasures, and (what is most wonderful of all), in the midst of the tyranny of the persecutors, an innumerable throng of people, both simple and most learned, flocked to the Christian faith. In this faith there are truths preached that surpass every human intellect; the pleasures of the flesh are curbed; it is taught that the things of the world should be spurned. Now, for the minds of mortal men to assent to these things is the greatest of miracles, just as it is a manifest work of divine inspiration that, spurning visible things, men should seek only what is invisible. Now, that this has happened neither without preparation nor by chance, but as a result of the disposition of God, is clear from the fact that through many pronouncements of the ancient prophets God had foretold that He would do this. The books of these prophets are held in veneration among us Christians, since they give witness to our faith.

[2]　The manner of this confirmation is touched on by St. Paul: "Which," that is, human salvation, "having begun to be declared by the Lord, was confirmed unto us by them that hear Him: God also bearing them witness of signs, and wonders, and divers miracles, and distributions of the Holy Ghost" (Heb. 2:3-4).

[3]　This wonderful conversion of the world to the Christian faith is the clearest witness of the signs given in the past; so that it is not necessary that they should be further repeated, since they appear most clearly in their effect. For it would be truly more wonderful than all signs if the world had been led by simple and humble men to believe such lofty truths, to accomplish such difficult actions, and to have such high hopes. Yet it is also a fact that, even in our own time, God does not cease to work miracles through His saints for the confirmation of the faith.

[4] On the other hand, those who founded sects committed to erroneous doctrines proceeded in a way that is opposite to this. The point is clear in the case of Mohammed. He seduced the people by promises of carnal pleasure to which the concupiscence of the flesh goads us. His teaching also contained precepts that were in conformity with his promises, and he gave free rein to carnal pleasure. In all this, as is not unexpected, he was obeyed by carnal men. As for proofs of the truth of his doctrine, he brought forward only such as cold be grasped by the natural ability of anyone with a very modest wisdom. Indeed, the truths that he taught he mingled with many fables and with doctrines of the greatest falsity. He did not bring forth any signs produced in a supernatural way, which alone fittingly gives witness to divine inspiration; for a visible action that can be only divine reveals an invisibly inspired teacher of truth. On the contrary, Mohammed said that he was sent in the power of his arms—which are signs not lacking even to robbers and tyrants. What is more, no wise men, men trained in things divine and human, believed in him from the beginning. Those who believed in him were brutal men and desert wanderers, utterly ignorant of all divine teaching, through whose numbers Mohammed forced others to become his followers by the violence of his arms. Nor do divine pronouncements on the part of preceding prophets offer him any witness. On the contrary, he perverts almost all the testimonies of the Old and New Testaments by making them into fabrications of his own, as can be seen by anyone who examines his law. It was, therefore, a shrewd decision on his part to forbid his followers to read the Old and New Testaments, lest these books convict him of falsity. It is thus clear that those who place any faith in his words believe foolishly.

Chapter 7

That the Truth of Reason Is Not Opposed to the Truth of the Christian Faith

[1] Now, although the truth of the Christian faith which we have discussed surpasses the capacity of the reason, nevertheless that truth that the human reason is naturally endowed to know cannot be opposed to the truth of the Christian faith. For that with which the human reason is naturally endowed is clearly most true; so much so, that it is impossible for us to think of such truths as false. Nor is it permissible to believe as false that which we hold by faith, since this is confirmed in a way that is so clearly divine. Since, therefore, only the false is opposed to the true, as is clearly evident from an examination of their definitions, it is impossible that the truth of faith should be opposed to those principles that the human reason knows naturally.

[2] Furthermore, that which is introduced into the soul of the student by the teacher is contained in the knowledge of the teacher—unless his teaching is fictitious, which is improper to say of God. Now, the knowledge of the principles that are known to us naturally has been implanted in us by God; for God is the Author of our nature. These principles, therefore, are also contained by the divine Wisdom. Hence, whatever is opposed to them is opposed to the divine Wisdom, and,

therefore, cannot come from God. That which we hold by faith as divinely revealed, therefore, cannot be contrary to our natural knowledge.

[3] Again. In the presence of contrary arguments our intellect is chained, so that it cannot proceed to the knowledge of the truth. If, therefore, contrary knowledges were implanted in us by God, our intellect would be hindered from knowing truth by this very fact. Now, such an effect cannot come from God.

[4] And again. What is natural cannot change as long as nature does not. Now, it is impossible that contrary opinions should exist in the same knowing subject at the same time. No opinion or belief, therefore, is implanted in man by God which is contrary to man's natural knowledge.

[5] Therefore, the Apostle says: "The word is nigh thee, even in thy mouth and in thy heart. This is the word of faith, which we preach" (Rom. 10:8). But because it overcomes reason, there are some who think that it is opposed to it: which is impossible.

[6] The authority of St. Augustine also agrees with this. He writes as follows: "That which truth will reveal cannot in any way be opposed to the sacred books of the Old and the New Testament."[12]

[7] From this we evidently gather the following conclusion: whatever arguments are brought forward against the doctrines of faith are conclusions incorrectly derived from the first and self-evident principles imbedded in nature. Such conclusions do not have the force of demonstration; they are arguments that are either probable or sophistical. And so, there exists the possibility to answer them.

Chapter 8

How the Human Reason Is Related to the Truth of Faith

[1] There is also a further consideration. Sensible things, from which the human reason takes the origin of its knowledge, retain within themselves some sort of trace of a likeness to God. This is so imperfect, however, that it is absolutely inadequate to manifest the substance of God. For effects bear within themselves, in their own way, the likeness of their causes, since an agent produces its like; yet an effect does not always reach to the full likeness of its cause. Now, the human reason is related to the knowledge of the truth of faith (a truth which can be most evident only to those who see the divine substance) in such a way that it can gather certain likenesses of it, which are yet not sufficient so that the truth of faith may be comprehended as being understood demonstratively or through itself. Yet it is useful for the human reason to exercise itself in such arguments, however weak they may be, provided only that there be present no presumption to comprehend or to demonstrate. For to be able to see something of the loftiest realities, however thin and weak the sight may be, is, as our previous remarks indicate, a cause of the greatest joy.

[2] The testimony of Hilary agrees with this. Speaking of this same truth, he writes as follows in his *De Trinitate*: "Enter these truths by believing, press

forward, persevere. And though I may know that you will not arrive at an end, yet I will congratulate you in your progress. For, though he who pursues the infinite with reverence will never finally reach the end, yet he will always progress by pressing onward. But do not intrude yourself into the divine secret, do not, presuming to comprehend the sum total of intelligence, plunge yourself into the mystery of the unending nativity; rather, understand that these things are incomprehensible."[13]

NOTES

1. Aristotle, *Nicomachean Ethics*, I, 3 (1094b 24).
2. Boethius, *De Trinitate*, II (*PL*, 64, col. 1250)
3. Aristotle, *Posterior Analytics*, II, 3 (90b 31).
4. Aristotle, *Metaphysics*, Ia, 1 (993b 9).
5. Aristotle, *Physics, VII*, 3 (247b 9).
6. *SCG*, III, ch. 48.
7. Ibid., ch. 3.
8. Aristotle, *Nicomachean Ethics*, X, 7 (1177b 31).
9. Aristotle, *De partibus animalium*, I, 5 (644b 32).
10. Aristotle, *De Caelo et mundo*, II, 12 (291b 26).
11. St. Greogry, *Homilae in evangelia*, II, hom. 26, i (*PL*, 76, col. 1197).
12. St. Augustine, *De genesi ad litteram*, II, c. 18 (*PL*, 34, col. 280).
13. St. Hilary, *De Trinitate*, II, 10, ii (*PL*, 10, coll. 58-59).

TRUTH AS SUBJECTIVITY

Soren Kierkegaard

All essential knowledge relates to existence, or only such knowledge as has an essential relationship to existence is essential knowledge. All knowledge which does not inwardly relate itself to existence, in the reflection of inwardness, is, essentially viewed, accidental knowledge; its degree and scope is essentially indifferent. That essential knowledge is essentially related to existence does not mean the above-mentioned identity which abstract thought postulates between thought and being; nor does it signify objectivity, that knowledge corresponds to some thing existent as its object. But it means that knowledge has a relationship to the knower, who is essentially an existing individual, and that for this reason all essential knowledge

From "The Subjective Truth, Inwardness; Truth is Subjectivity," in *Concluding Unscientific Postscript,* trans. David F. Swenson and Walter Lowrie (copyright 1941 © 1969 by Princeton University Press; Princeton Paperback, 1968), pp. 176-88. Reprinted by permission of Princeton University Press and the American Scandinavian Foundation.

is essentially related to existence. Only ethical and ethico-religious knowledge has an essential relationship to the existence of the knower.

Mediation is a mirage, like the I-am-I. From the abstract point of view everything is and nothing comes into being. Mediation can therefore have no place in abstract thought, because it presupposes *movement*. Objective knowledge may indeed have the existent for its object; but since the knowing subject is an existing individual, and through the fact of his existence in process of becoming, philosophy must first explain how a particular existing subject is related to a knowledge of mediation. It must explain what he is in such a moment, if not pretty nearly *distrait;* where he is, if not in the moon? There is constant talk of mediation and mediation; is mediation then a man, as Peter Deacon believes that *Imprimatur* is a man? How does a human being manage to become something of this kind? Is this dignity, this great *philosophicum,* the fruit of study, or does the magistrate give it away, like the office of deacon or grave-digger? Try merely to enter into these and other such plain questions of a plain man, who would gladly become mediation if it could be done in some lawful and honest manner, and not either by saying *ein zwei drei kokolorum,* or by forgetting that he is himself an existing human being, for whom existence is therefore something essential, and an ethico-religious existence a suitable *quantum satis.* A speculative philosopher may perhaps find it in bad taste to ask such questions. But it is important not to direct the polemic to the wrong point, and hence not to begin in a fantastic objective manner to discuss *pro* and *contra* whether there is a mediation or not, but to hold fast what it means to be a human being.

In an attempt to make clear the difference of way that exists between an objective and a subjective reflection, I shall now proceed to show how a subjective reflection makes its way inwardly in inwardness. Inwardness in an existing subject culminates in passion; corresponding to passion in the subject the truth becomes a paradox; and the fact that the truth becomes a paradox is rooted precisely in its having a relationship to an existing subject. Thus the one corresponds to the other. By forgetting that one is an existing subject, passion goes by the board and the truth is no longer a paradox; the knowing subject becomes a fantastic entity rather than a human being, and the truth becomes a fantastic object for the knowledge of this fantastic entity.

When the question of truth is raised in an objective manner, reflection is directed objectively to the truth, as an object to which the knower is related. Reflection is not focussed upon the relationship, however, but upon the question of whether it is the truth to which the knower is related. If only the object to which he is related is the truth, the subject is accounted to be in the truth. When the question of the truth is raised subjectively, reflection is directed subjectively to the nature of the individual's relationship; if only the mode of this relationship is in the truth, the individual is in the truth even if he should happen to be thus related to what is not true.[1] Let us take as an example the knowledge of God. Objectively, reflection is directed to the problem of whether this object is the true God; subjectively, reflection is directed to the question whether the individual is related to a something *in such a manner* that his relationship is in truth a God-relationship. On which side is the truth now to be found? Ah, may we not here resort to a mediation, and say: It is on neither side, but in the mediation of both? Excellently well said, provided we might have it explained how an existing individual manages to be in a state of mediation. For to be in a state of mediation is to be finished, while to exist is to become. Nor can an existing individual be in two places at the same time—he cannot be an identity of subject and object. When he is nearest to being in two places at the same time he is in passion; but passion is momentary, and passion is also the highest expression of subjectivity.

The existing individual who chooses to pursue the objective way enters upon the entire approximation-process by which it is proposed to bring God to light objectively. But this is in all eternity impossible, because God is a subject, and therefore exists only for subjectivity in inwardness. The existing individual who chooses the subjective way apprehends instantly the entire dialectical difficulty involved in having to use some time, perhaps a long time, in finding God objectively; and he feels this dialectical difficulty in all its painfulness, because every moment is wasted in which he does not have God.[2] That very instant he has God, not by virtue of any objective deliberation, but by virtue of the infinite passion of inwardness. The objective inquirer, on the other hand, is not embarrassed by such dialectical difficulties as are involved in devoting an entire period of investigation to finding God— since it is possible that the inquirer may die tomorrow; and if he lives he can scarcely regard God as something to be taken along if convenient, since God is precisely that which one takes *a tout prix,* which in the understanding of passion constitutes the true inward relationship to God.

It is at this point, so difficult dialectically, that the way swings off for every-one who knows what it means to think, and to think existentially; which is some-thing very different from sitting at a desk and writing about what one has never done, something very different from writing *de omnibus dubitandum* and at the same time being as credulous existentially as the most sensuous of men. Here is where the way swings off, and the change is marked by the fact that while objective knowledge rambles comfortably on by way of the long road of approximation without being impelled by the urge of passion, subjective knowledge counts every delay a deadly peril, and the decision so infinitely important and so instantly pressing that it is as if the opportunity had already passed.

Now when the problem is to reckon up on which side there is most truth, whether on the side of one who seeks the true God objectively, and pursues the approximate truth of the God-idea; or on the side of one who, driven by the infinite passion of his need of God, feels an infinite concern for his own relation-ship to God in truth (and to be at one and the same time on both sides equally, is as we have noted not possible for an existing individual, but is merely the happy delusion of an imaginary I-am-I): the answer cannot be in doubt for anyone who has not been demoralized with the aid of science. If one who lives in the midst of Christendom goes up to the house of God, the house of the true God, with the true conception of God in his knowledge, and prays, but prays in a false spirit; and one who lives in an idolatrous community prays with the entire passion of the infinite, although his eyes rest upon the image of an idol: where is there most truth? The one prays in truth to God though he worships an idol; the other prays falsely to the true God, and hence worships in fact an idol.

When one man investigates objectively the problem of immortality, and another embraces an uncertainty with the passion of the infinite: where is there most truth, and who has the greater certainty? The one has entered upon a never-ending approximation, for the certainty of immortality lies precisely in the subjectivity of the individual; the other is immortal, and fights for his immortality by struggling with the uncertainty. Let us consider Socrates. Nowadays everyone dabbles in a few proofs; some have several such proofs, others fewer. But Socrates! He puts the question objectively in a problematic manner: *if* there is an immortality. He must therefore be accounted a doubter in comparison with one of our modern thinkers with the three proofs? By no means. On this "if" he risks his entire life, he has the courage to meet death, and he has with the passion of the infinite so determined the pattern of his life that it must be found acceptable—*if* there is an immortality. Is any better proof capable of being given for the immortality of the soul? But those who have the three proofs do not at all determine their lives in conformity therewith; if there is an immortality it must feel disgust over their manner of life: can any better refutation be given of the three proofs? The bit of uncertainty that Socrates had, helped him because he himself contributed the passion of the infinite; the three proofs that the others have do not profit them at all, because they are dead to spirit and enthusiasm, and their three proofs, in lieu of proving anything else, prove just this. A young girl may enjoy all the sweetness of love on the basis of what is merely a weak hope that she is beloved, because she rests everything on this weak hope; but many a wedded matron more than once subjected to the strongest expressions of love, has in so far indeed had proofs, but strangely enough has not enjoyed *quod erat demonstrandum.* The Socratic ignorance, which Socrates held fast with the entire passion of his inwardness, was thus an expression for the principle that the eternal truth is related to an existing individual, and that this truth must therefore be a paradox for him as long as he exists; and yet it is possible that there was more truth in the Socratic ignorance as it was in him, than in the entire objective truth of the System, which flirts what the times demand and accommodates itself to *Privatdocents.*

The objective accent falls on WHAT is said, the subjective accent on HOW it is said. This distinction holds even in the aesthetic realm, and receives definite expression in the principle that what is in itself true may in the month of such and such a person become untrue. In these times this distinction is particularly worthy of notice, for if we wish to express in a single sentence the difference between ancient times and our own, we should doubtless have to say: "In ancient times only an individual here and there knew the truth; now all know it, except that the inwardness of its appropriation stands in an inverse relationship to the extent of its dissemination."[3] Aesthetically the contradiction that truth becomes untruth in this or that person's mouth, is best construed comically: In the ethico-religious sphere, accent is again on the "how." But this is not to be understood as referring to demeanor, expression, or the like; rather it refers to the relationship sustained by the existing individual, in his own existence, to the content of his utterance. Objectively the interest is focussed merely on the thought-content, subjectively on the inwardness. At its maximum this inward "how" is the passion of the infinite, and the passion of the infinite is the truth. But the passion of the infinite is precisely subjectivity, and thus subjectivity becomes the truth. Objectively there is no infinite decisiveness, and hence it is objectively in order to annual the difference between good and evil, together with the principle of contradiction, and therewith also the infinite difference between the true and the false. Only in subjectivity is there decisiveness, to seek objectivity is to be in error. It is the passion of the infinite that is the decisive factor and not its content, for its content is precisely itself. In this manner subjectivity and the subjective "how" constitute the truth.

But the "how" which is thus subjectively accentuated precisely because the subject is an existing individual, is also subject to a dialectic with respect to time. In the passionate moment of decision, where the road swings away from objective knowledge, it seems as if the infinite decision were thereby realized. But in the same moment the existing individual finds himself in the temporal order, and the subjective "how" is transformed into a striving, a striving which receives indeed its impulse and a repeated renewal from the decisive passion of the infinite, but is nevertheless a striving.

When subjectivity is the truth, the conceptual determination of the truth must include an expression for the antithesis to objectivity, a memento of the fork in the road where the way swings off; this expression will at the same time serve as an indication of the tension of the subjective inwardness. Here is such a definition of truth: *An objective uncertainty held fast in an appropriation-process of the most passionate inwardness is the truth,* the highest truth attainable for an *existing* individual. At the point where the way swings off (and where this is cannot be specified objectively, since it is a matter of subjectivity), there objective knowledge is placed in abeyance. Thus the subject merely has, objectively, the uncertainty; but it is this which precisely increases the tension of that infinite passion which constitutes his inwardness. The truth is precisely the venture which chooses an objective uncertainty with the passion of the infinite. I contemplate the order of nature in the hope of finding God, and I see omnipotence and wisdom; but I also see much else that disturbs my mind and excites anxiety. The sum of all this is an objective uncertainty. But it is for this very reason that the inwardness becomes as intense as it is, for it embraces this objective uncertainty with the entire passion of the infinite. In the case of a mathematical proposition the objectivity is given, but for this reason the truth of such a proposition is also an indifferent truth.

But the above definition of truth is an equivalent expression for faith. Without risk there is no faith. Faith is precisely the contradiction between the infinite passion of the individual's inwardness and the objective uncertainty. If I am capable of grasping God objectively, I do not believe, but precisely because I cannot do this

I must believe. If I wish to preserve myself in faith I must constantly be intent upon holding fast the objective uncertainty, so as to remain out upon the deep, over seventy thousand fathoms of water, still preserving my faith.

In the principle that subjectivity, inwardness, is the truth, there is comprehended the Socratic wisdom, whose everlasting merit it was to have become aware of the essential significance of existence, of the fact that the knower is an existing individual. For this reason Socrates was in the truth by virtue of his ignorance, in the highest sense in which this was possible within paganism. To attain to an understanding of this, to comprehend that the misfortune of speculative philosophy is again and again to have forgotten that the knower is an existing individual, is in our objective age difficult enough. But to have made an advance upon Socrates without even having understood what he understood, is at any rate not "Socratic." Compare the "Moral" of the *Fragments*.

Let us now start from this point, and as was attempted in the *Fragments,* seek a determination of thought which will really carry us further. I have nothing here to do with the question of whether this proposed thought-determination is true or not, since I am merely experimenting; but it must at any rate be clearly manifest that the Socratic thought is understood within the new proposal, so that at least I do not come out behind Socrates.

When subjectivity, inwardness, is the truth, the truth becomes objectively a paradox; and the fact that the truth is objectively a paradox shows in its turn that subjectivity is the truth. For the objective situation is repellent; and the expression for the objective repulsion constitutes the tension and the measure of the corresponding inwardness. The paradoxical character of the truth is its objective uncertainty; this uncertainty is an expression for the passionate inwardness, and this passion is precisely the truth. So far the Socratic principle. The eternal and essential truth, the truth which has an essential relationship to an existing individual because it pertains essentially to existence (all other knowledge being from the Socratic point of view accidental, its scope and degree a matter of indifference), is a paradox. But the eternal essential truth is by no means in itself a paradox; but it becomes paradoxical by virtue of its relationship to an existing individual. The Socratic ignorance gives expression to the objective uncertainty attaching to the truth, while his inwardness in existing is the truth. To anticipate here what will be developed later, let me make the following remark. The Socratic ignorance is an analogue to the category of the absurd, only that there is still less of objective certainty in the absurd, and in the repellent effect that the absurd exercises. It is certain only that it is absurd, and precisely on that account it incites to an infinitely greater tension in the corresponding inwardness. The Socratic inwardness in existing is an analogue to faith; only that the inwardness faith, corresponding as it does, not to the repulsion of the Socratic ignorance, but to the repulsion exerted by the absurd, is infinitely more profound.

Socratically the eternal essential truth is by no means in its own nature paradoxical, but only in its relationship to an existing individual. This finds expression in another Socratic proposition, namely, that all knowledge is recollection. This proposition is not for Socrates a cue to the speculative enterprise, and hence he does not follow it up; essentially it becomes a Platonic principle. Here the way swings off; Socrates concentrates essentially upon accentuating existence, while Plato forgets this and loses himself in speculation. Socrates' infinite merit is to have been an *existing* thinker, not a speculative philosopher who forgets what it means to exist. For Socrates therefore the principle that all knowledge is recollection has at the moment of his leave-taking and as the constantly rejected possibility of engaging in speculation, the following two-fold significance: (1) that the knower is essentially *integer,* and that with respect to the knowledge of the eternal truth he is confronted with no other difficulty than the circumstances that he exists; which difficulty, however, is so essential and decisive for him that it means that existing, the process of transformation to inwardness in and by existing, is the truth; (2) that existence in time does not have any decisive significance, because the possibility of taking oneself back into eternity through recollection is always there, though this possibility is constantly nullified by utilizing the time, not for speculation, but for the transformation to inwardness in existing.[4]

The infinite merit of the Socratic position was precisely to accentuate the fact that the knower is an existing individual, and that the task of existing is his essential task. Making an advance upon Socrates by failing to understand this, is quite a mediocre achievement. This Socratic principle we must therefore bear in mind, and then inquire whether the formula may not be so altered as really to make an advance beyond the Socratic position.

Subjectivity, inwardness, has been posited as the truth; can any expression for the truth be found which has a still higher degree of inwardness? Aye, there is such an expression, provided the principle that subjectivity or inwardness is the truth begins by positing the opposite principle: that subjectivity is untruth. Let us not at this point succumb to such haste as to fail in making the necessary distinctions. Speculative philosophy also says that subjectivity is untruth, but says it in order to stimulate a movement in precisely the opposite direction, namely, in the direction of the principle that objectivity is the truth. Speculative philosophy determines subjectivity negatively as tending toward objectivity. This second determination of ours, however, places a hindrance in its own way while proposing to begin, which has the effect of making the inwardness far more intensive. Socratically speaking, subjectivity is untruth if it refuses to understand that subjectivity is truth, but, for example, desires to become objective. Here, on the other hand, subjectivity in beginning upon the task of becoming the truth through a subjectifying process, is in the difficulty that it is already untruth. Thus, the labor of the task is thrust backward, backward, that is, in inwardness. So far is it from being the case that the way tends in the direction of objectivity, that the beginning merely lies still deeper in subjectivity.

But the subject cannot be untruth eternally, or eternally be presupposed as having been untruth; it must have been brought to this condition in time, or here become untruth in time. The Socratic paradox consisted in the fact that the eternal was related to an existing individual, but now existence has stamped itself upon the existing individual a second time. There has taken place so essential an alteration in him that he cannot now possibly take himself back into the eternal by way of recollection. To do this is to speculate; to be able to do this, but to reject the possibility by apprehending the task of life as a realization of inwardness in existing, is the Socratic position. But now the difficulty is that what followed Socrates on his way as a rejected possibility, has become an impossibility. If engaging in speculation was a dubious merit even from the point of view of the Socratic, it is now neither more nor less than confusion.

The paradox emerges when the eternal truth and existence are placed in juxtaposition with one another; each time the stamp of existence is brought to bear, the paradox becomes more clearly evident. Viewed Socratically the knower was simply an existing individual, but now the existing individual bears the stamp of having been essentially altered by existence.

Let us now call the untruth of the individual *Sin.* Viewed eternally he cannot be sin, nor can he be eternally presupposed as having been in sin. By coming into existence therefore (for the beginning was that subjectivity is untruth), he becomes a sinner. He is not born as a sinner in the sense that he is presupposed as being a sinner before he is born, but he is born in sin and as a sinner. This we might call *Original Sin.* But if existence has in this manner acquired a power over him, he is prevented from taking himself back into the eternal by way of recollection. If it was paradoxical to posit the eternal truth in relationship to an existing individual, it is now absolutely paradoxical to posit it in relationship to such an individual as we have here defined. But the more difficult it is made for him to take himself out of existence by way of recollection, the more profound is the inwardness that his existence may have in existence; and when it is made impossible for him, when he is held so fast in existence that the back door of recollection is forever closed to him, then his inwardness will be the most profound possible. But let us never forget that the Socratic merit was to stress the fact that the knower is an existing individual; for the more difficult the matter becomes, the greater the temptation to hasten along the easy road of speculation, away from fearful dangers and crucial decisions, to the winning of renown and honors and property, and so forth. If even Socrates understood the dubiety of taking himself speculatively out of existence back into the eternal, although no other difficulty confronted the existing individual except that he existed, and that existing was his essential task, now it is impossible. Forward he must, backward he cannot go.

Subjectivity is the truth. By virtue of the relationship subsisting between the eternal truth and the existing individual, the paradox came into being. Let us now go further, let us suppose that the eternal essential truth is itself a paradox. How does the paradox come into being? By putting the eternal essential truth into juxtaposition with existence. Hence when we posit such a conjunction within the truth itself, the truth becomes a paradox. The eternal truth has come into being in time: this is the paradox. If in accordance with the determinations just posited, the subject is prevented by sin from taking himself back into the eternal, now he need not trouble himself about this; for now the eternal essential truth is not behind him but in front of him, through its being in existence or having existed, so that if the individual does not existentially and in existence lay hold of the truth, he will never lay hold of it.

Existence can never be more sharply accentuated than by means of these determinations. The evasion by which speculative philosophy attempts to recollect itself out of existence has been made impossible. With reference to this, there is nothing for speculation to do except to arrive at an understanding of this impossibility; every speculative attempt which insists on being speculative shows *eo ipso* that it has not understood it. The individual may thrust all this away from him, and take refuge in speculation; but it is impossible first to accept it, and then to revoke it by means of speculation, since it is definitely calculated to prevent speculation.

When the eternal truth is related to an existing individual it becomes a paradox. The paradox repels in the inwardness of the existing individual, through the objective uncertainty and the corresponding Socratic ignorance. But since the paradox is not in the first instance itself paradoxical (but only in its relationship to the existing individual), it does not repel with a sufficient intensive inwardness. For without risk there is no faith, and the greater the risk the greater the faith; the more objective security the less inwardness (for inwardness is precisely subjectivity), and the less objective security the more profound the possible inwardness. When the paradox is paradoxical in itself, it repels the individual by virtue of its absurdity, and the corresponding passion of inwardness is faith. But subjectivity, inwardness, is the truth; for otherwise we have forgotten what the merit of the Socratic position is. But there can be no stronger expression for inwardness than when the retreat out of existence into the eternal by way of recollection is impossible; and when, with truth confronting the individual as a paradox, gripped in the anguish and pain of sin, facing the tremendous risk of the objective insecurity, the individual believes. But without risk no faith, not even the Socratic form of faith, much less the form of which we here speak.

When Socrates believed that there was a God, he held fast to the objective uncertainty with the whole passion of his inwardness, and it is precisely in this contradiction and in this risk, that faith is rooted. Now it is otherwise. Instead of the objective uncertainty, there is here a certainty, namely, that objectively it is absurd; and this absurdity, held fast in the passion of inwardness, is faith. The Socratic ignorance is as a witty jest in comparison with the earnestness of facing the absurd; and the Socratic existential inwardness is as Greek light-mindedness in comparison with the grave strenuosity of faith.

What now is the absurd? The absurd is—that the eternal truth has come into being in time, that God has come into being, has been born, has grown up, and so forth, precisely like any other individual human being, quite indistinguishable from other individuals.

NOTES

1. The reader will observe that the question here is about essential truth or about the truth which is essentially related to existence, and that it is precisely for the sake of clarifying it as inwardness or as subjectivity that this contrast is drawn.

2. In this manner God certainly becomes a postulate, but not in the otiose manner in which this word is commonly understood. It becomes clear rather that the only way in which an existing individual comes into relation with God, is when the dialectical contradiction brings his passion to the point of despair, and helps him to embrace God with the "category of despair" (faith). Then the postulate is so far from being arbitrary that it is precisely a life-necessity. It is then not so much that God is a postulate, as that the existing individual's postulation of God is a necessity.

3. *Stages on Life's Way.* Though ordinarily not wishing an expression of opinion on the part of reviewers, I might at this point almost desire it, provided such opinions, so far from flattering me, amounted to an assertion of the daring truth that what I say is something that everybody knows, even every child, and that the cultured know infinitely much better. If it only stands fast that everyone knows it, my standpoint is in order, and I shall doubtless make shift to manage with the unity of the comic and the tragic. If there were anyone who did not know it I might perhaps be in danger of being dislodged from my position of equilibrium by the thought that I might be in a position to communicate to someone the needful preliminary knowledge. It is just this which engages my interest so much, this that the cultured are accustomed to say: that everyone knows what the highest is. This was not the case in paganism, nor in Judaism, nor in the seventeen centuries of Christianity. Hail to the nineteenth century! Everyone knows it. What progress has been made since the time when only a few knew it. To make up for this, perhaps, we must assume that no one nowadays does it.

4. This will perhaps be the proper place to offer an explanation with respect to a difficulty in the plan of the *Fragments,* which had its ground in the fact that I did not wish at once to make the case as difficult dialectically as it is, because in our age terminologies and the like are turned so topsy-turvy that it is almost impossible to secure oneself against confusion. In order if possible clearly to exhibit the difference between the Socratic position (which was supposed to be the philosophical, the pagan-philosophical position) and the experimentally evoked thought-determination which really makes an advance beyond the Socratic, I carried the Socratic back to the principle that all knowledge is recollection. This is, in a way, commonly assumed, and only one who with a specialized interest concerns himself with the Socratic, returning again and again to the sources, only for him would it be of importance on this point to distinguish between Socrates and Plato. The proposition does indeed belong to both, only that Socrates is always departing from it, in order to exist. By holding Socrates down to the proposition that all knowledge is recollection, he becomes a speculative philosopher instead of an existential thinker, for whom existence is the essential thing. The recollection-principle belongs to speculative philosophy, and recollection is immanence, and speculatively and eternally there is no paradox. But the difficulty is that no human being is speculative philosophy; the speculative philosopher himself is an existing individual, subject to the claims that existence makes upon him. There is no merit in forgetting this, but a great merit in holding it fast, and this is precisely what Socrates did. To accentuate existence, which also involves the qualification of inwardness, is the Socratic position; the Platonic tendency, on the other hand, is to pursue the lure of recollections and immanence. This puts Socrates fundamentally in advance of speculative philosophy; he does not have a fantastic beginning, in which the speculative philosopher first disguises himself, and then goes on to speculate, forgetting the most important thing of all, which is to exist. But precisely because Socrates is thus in advance of speculation, he presents, when properly delineated, a certain analogous resemblance to that which the experiment described as in truth going beyond the Socratic. The truth as paradox in the Socratic sense becomes analogous to the paradox *sensu eminentiori,* the passion of inwardness in existing becomes an analogue to faith *sensu eminentiori.* That the difference is none the less infinite, that the characterization which the *Fragments* made of that which in truth goes beyond the Socratic remains unchanged, it will be easy to show; but by using at once apparently the same determination, or at any rate the same words, about these two different things, I feared to cause a misunderstanding. Now I think there can be no objection to speaking of the paradoxical and of faith in reference to Socrates, since it is quite correct to do so when

properly understood. Besides, the old Greeks also used the word *pistis,* though not by any means in the sense of the experiments; and they used it in such a manner that, especially with reference to a work of Aristotle where the term is employed, it would be possible to set forth some very enlightening considerations bearing upon its difference from faith *sensu eminentiori.*

GOD AND EVIL

THE MANY FACES OF EVIL

Edward H. Madden

1

The formal way of presenting the problem of evil is this: If God is all-powerful and all-good, why is there so much *prima facie* gratuitous and unnecessary evil in the world? If he is all-powerful he should be able to remove unnecessary evil, and if he is all-good he should want to remove it; but he does not. Why? Must we assume that he is either not all-powerful or not all-good? Theists want to avoid this conclusion at all costs; they see the problem as one of logical compatibility: they must have an answer which squares God's all-powerfulness, all-goodness, and the existence, *prima facie* at least, of gratuitous evil. The qualification *"prima facie"* is important and not to be taken lightly, for to speak of evil as absolutely unnecessary would beg the question at issue and rule out in advance certain attempted solutions to the problem as inadequate.

Theists offer numerous solutions to their problem of evil, and I cannot hope to attend exhaustively to each one. I shall make every effort, however, to analyze carefully the most significant and historically influential ones. In two of them, the free will and ultimate harmony views, I shall be most interested, and to them I shall devote most analysis. However, I shall be explicit enough about the other alleged solutions also, so that it should be quite clear why I think none of them succeeds. I shall conclude, then, that the problem of evil is insoluble and that this insolubility is a sufficient reason for not believing in any type of theistic god whatever.

2

(i) Theistic solutions to the problem vary a great deal in merit. Two terribly flimsy ones, yet ones that are prevalent in the literature and in everyday life, are

From "The Many Faces of Evil," *Philosophy and Phenomenological Research* 24:4 (June 1964), pp. 481-92. Reprinted by permission of *Philosophy and Phenomenological Research.* This paper was read at the Brown University Philosophy Colloquium, November 30, 1962.

the "contrast" and the "nonintervention" solutions. Evil, so the first argument goes, is necessary as a contrast so that we shall be able properly to understand and appreciate the good of life. Evil, according to the second argument, is a by-product of the operation of the laws of the universe. Evil events like earthquakes, floods, famines, and plagues are simply natural events in a world which is, overall, a good one. One can look elsewhere for detailed criticisms of these views.[1] I shall be content with one simple criticism of each. (a) We need little evil by way of contrast to get the point: one should be allowed to bite his lip rather than go through life with a harelip. (b) Even if acceptable, which it is not, the second "solution" would account only for physical evil and leave moral evil untouched.

(ii) For a better try at the problem there is a cluster of related scriptural views. To the question "What does God have in mind by allowing gratuitous evil in his world?" students of Christian Scripture have replied variously: (a) evil is punishment for sin; (b) evil tests man's faith; and (c) evil is God's warning to man.

(a) Job's comforters, it is well-known, held this view. We know, of course, from the very structure of the Book of Job that this interpretation of evil is wrong from the Christian standpoint. Job, as God knew, had *not* done anything to merit his misery; the point of his suffering lay elsewhere. Indeed, Christ himself apparently rejected this view.[2] Scriptural argument aside, this retribution solution is quite untenable on any ground, Christian or otherwise. Consider the Peru landslides which annihilated many men, women, and children of several valley villages. If evil is punishment for sin, it is difficult to believe that only the inhabitants of these villages deserved such reprimands. Moreover, as Voltaire said, it is difficult to believe that just the sinners get singled out for destruction in such catastrophes.

(b) The notion that evil tests man's faith is not entirely clear. What precisely does it mean? It might mean that God inflicts pain on man to discover whether he will keep his faith in time of adversity or whether he is simply a summer Christian or a fair-weather believer. This interpretation will not do, however, for if God is all-powerful and hence all-knowing, he should already know the outcome.

However, this view might be interpreted quite differently. God tests people like Job, it is said, precisely because he knows they will be steadfast in their faith and thus act as a salutary example to other people. Unfortunately, this interpretation is even more vulnerable than the first one. Not everyone is a Job, and when affliction causes renunciation of God this makes a very bad example for fellow Christians. Moreover, such an interpretation could not account for mass disasters and catastrophes; the price would be too high to pay for an example, even if it were effective.

(c) The view that evil is God's "warning" to man is a clear and straightforward one, and it is particularly dear to the heart of a practical theist. Men are sunk, he says, in religious indifference and they need to be shocked into realization of God's presence by some awesome display of his power. When natural catastrophes like earthquakes, floods, and tornadoes occur, men become aware of God's great power, and their own littleness in the face of it, and they take on, as a result, the proper reverential awe of the Creator and a fear of violating his laws. These moral and religious results, in short, justify the physical pain resulting from natural causes. But do they? I think it is clear enough to anyone except a practical theist that they do not. Even if there were no objections to this view whatever, it would account for physical evil only and not moral evil, and hence leave the problem half-unsolved. Moreover, the demonstration of power need not be so deadly to achieve its aim, if this aim could be achieved at all. But it is certain that its aim, in fact, is not achieved. Indeed, rather than bringing man to God, these natural calamities frequently turn men against him. Such calamities forcefully bring to man's attention the whole problem of evil, and this problem, so difficult to solve, causes many people to give up their religious beliefs rather than strengthening them. According to a recent commentator, ". . . if God's object in bringing about natural calamities is to inspire reverence and awe, He is a bungler." Moreover,

> . . . the use of physical evil to achieve this object is hardly the course one would expect a benevolent God to adopt when other, more effective, less evil methods are available to Him, for example, miracles, special revelation, etc.[3]

(iii) An even stronger try at solving the problem is the character-building theory. On this view evil is a necessary part of our world because the experience of it yields such virtues as courage, endurance, charity, and sympathy. People are born into the world as base metal, which has many impurities. The experience of evil is the fire that burns away the impurities and leaves the base metal, the spiritually significant self, free and unencumbered.

One must admit that this view is an attractive one. Who has not had the experience of wishing fervently to avoid some painful or even harrowing event and yet, after the event, having to admit that he is better person for having undergone it? The difficulty with this view, of course, is clear and utterly damaging: it could only account for a small amount of evil, in any case, and could not account at all for the maiming of character which too much evil often produces (consider the brainwashing cases) or the mass annihilation of character (recall the Peru landslides). And it is difficult to see how the knowledge of such events could have an uplifting influence on people who witness or hear about them. Even if there were such an influence, the price would be much too high to pay for it. I would be the first one to insist on having *some* evil in the world for I, too, believe, it is impossible that a race "ignorant of suffering and unacquainted with grief should also achieve the heights and sound the depths of intellectual and spiritual life."[4] But this view of spiritual ennoblement is not only deficient in ways already pointed out, but also cannot account for any moral evil at all. If someone does me a cruel wrong I may grow spiritually through the agony, but the evildoer's character is thereby being depraved at the expense of my spiritual growth. Moreover, it is not clear why God, if he is all-powerful, could not have created spiritually significant people in the first place. Finally, this solution is simply inapplicable to some physical evils, insanity being perhaps the best example.

(iv) The philosophical optimist claims that this is the best of all possible worlds even though evil is a necessary ingredient of it. The world, it is claimed, has just the right amount of pain to cultivate patience, the right amount of danger to cultivate courage, *etc.* "If there were any less evil, it would be a worse world, rather than a better one."[5] Optimists like Leibniz did not claim that evil was only an appearance or illusion, as he is so often interpreted. He readily admitted that the world contained evil in a positive, real way, but his point was that it contained just exactly the right amount of evil. Hence it is the best of all possible worlds.

Arguments against this view are rather obvious. It seems oddly omniscient to announce that we have precisely the right amount of evil in the world. Much of it seems utterly gratuitous and does not lead to patience, courage, or anything else desirable; rather it crushes, shrivels, and annihilates the hapless ones it falls upon. Moreover, the distribution of evil presents a difficulty for the Optimist. That some people live in daily agony while others prosper hardly seems like just the right amount of evil to achieve the highest good. Indeed, "the theory seems to be most earnestly espoused by fairly comfortable people who point out to others how much worse their lives would be if they had less to combat."[6] Finally, it seems that God, if he were all-powerful, ought to be able to achieve the desirable ends without the evil means.

Leibniz, of course, had an answer to the last criticism.[7] Only God is infinite and perfect. Anything other than God of necessity is limited, imperfect, or—what is the same—evil. Hence, if God were to create anything at all, it had to exhibit some evil. God created the world which had the least amount; hence it is the best of all possible worlds. Leibniz called the imperfection inherent in all created things "metaphysical evil." However, this reply will not do. One willingly admits that the orthodox theistic God is not all-powerful in the sense that he can do what is logically self-contradictory. Such a limitation on omnipotence is not damaging. But Leibniz insisted that God could not create a finite thing that was perfect. But why not? The theistic God, after all, is supposed to be omnipotent not only *within* nature but over nature as well. *Thus,* God could have created *any world* he pleased—and he could have pleased to create a perfect one, or at least a better one! Moreover—and this point is fundamental—if metaphysical evil *were* ineluctable, then he should not have created any world at all, as any moral god would have refrained from doing.

The remaining two efforts to solve the problem, I believe, are the strongest ones—the most difficult ones to criticize effectively—and also the most influential ones historically. They are the free-will solution and the ultimate harmony viewpoint. Theism, I believe, depends for its very life on the success of one or the other of these notions.

(v) The free-will argument often is presented in the following way. God granted men free will, and man, unhappily, frequently misuses this gift, producing evil. Thus man, not God, is responsible for evil. This formulation is not satisfactory, however, because God, since he is all-knowing, would have foreseen this evil consequence of granting men free will and hence avoided it. It must be shown, therefore, why God gave man free will, even though he knew evil consequences would occur.

Theists have refurbished the argument in the following way. Free will is an inestimably important gift. Without it man would be a mere automation, marching through life without significance or dignity, It is free will which makes him a human being and thus set apart from all the other creatures in the world. But it is not only the intrinsic value of free will which justifies God's granting it, but also its consequences; the claim being, that it leads more often than not to good works, moral endeavor, and beatitude. After these deliberations, God granted man free will, in spite of certain evil consequences, for not to do so would have been far more evil.

There are still numerous difficulties with this strengthened view. (a) Even if there were no objections whatever to this solution, it would explain the occurrence only of moral evil and would leave the problem of physical evil untouched. Man's free will had nothing to do with the Lisbon earthquake, the Peru landslides, the China famines, or with leprosy, cancer, and muscular dystrophy. To be sure, if one believes that free will accounts for moral evil, then he need only to find another solution for physical evil, and the whole problem will be solved. However, we have not yet encountered an adequate solution to the problem of physical evil, nor will we encounter one.

(b) God could have granted men free will but nevertheless still have prevented or avoided some of the moral evil in the world. He could do this in various ways: being all-powerful, God could have created man with a *disposition* to act decently, even though, to account for freedom, he *could* choose to do evil; God could have created a world in which men's wrong choices did not lead to quite such disastrous consequences; and God could, upon occasion, intervene to prevent a particularly hideous result.

The theist counterargues in the following way. God should *not* reduce the amount of evil in the world by giving men a disposition to do good, intervening, *etc.*, because the proper use of free will has moral significance only if it is done in the face of great odds and is the result of strenuous effort and struggle. However, this view leads to odd consequences.[8] On this view it becomes my duty to throw evil in the paths of my fellow men so that their struggle, and hence their beatitude, may grow! Unhappily, however, great evil, rather than causing growth, often stunts and destroys the free human soul. God, on this view, is doing this dreadful thing apparently: He creates human beings with free will, some of whom will grow spiritually through great evil, and some of whom will be destroyed completely. How can the former justify God's way in view of the latter? The price is too high to pay. Indeed, this whole view goes contrary to ordinary moral standards. We would consider it brazenly immoral to tempt a reformed alcoholic by drinking in his presence or by daring a person we know to be reckless to do some impossible feat. Such behavior would increase their struggle, to be sure, but might well cause their utter downfall. A human being who acted in such a way would be called immoral; if God acts that way, why should we call his behavior a "higher" morality?

(c) The claim is made that more often than not free will results in desirable consequences rather than undesirable ones. But this claim is an empirical one, and it is difficult indeed to see how anyone could have adequate evidence to establish its truth. It might *possibly* be the case, but we do not know that it is. Hence it might be a possible justification for God's granting free will, but we do not know that it is.

(d) This traditional criticism is well-known: God's omniscience and man's free will are incompatible notions. Jonathan Edwards was a brilliant advocate of this criticism. This question is fantastically complicated in its own right, and I could not hope to do justice to it within the scope of this paper. Suffice it to say here that if one means by 'free will' an 'uncaused will', then I think one can show that the concepts of omniscience and free will are incompatible. However, if one carefully analyzes the notion of free will and concludes that it is not only compatible with determinism but in some sense implies it, then he may be able to show the consistency of omniscience and free will. In this case, however, one still has sufficient grounds in the previous criticisms to reject the free will solution to the problem of evil.

3

(vi) The ultimate harmony solution has been, perhaps, the most historically influential one of all, and many theists believe it to be their soundest answer. The view is usually presented in a metaphorical way, and the favorite metaphor is a musical one. A chord heard in isolation may sound dissonant and ugly, but when heard in context blends into a perfect whole or an ultimate harmony. So it is with evil. What human beings call evil is an event seen out of context, in isolation, and since man has only a fragmentary view of events, this is the only way he can see it. God, however, who has an overall view of events, sees how such events are good in the long run or good from an overall viewpoint. (For our purposes the notions of "good in the long run" and "good from an overall viewpoint" need not be separated, because any criticisms of the ultimate harmony view will apply equally well to both.) The ultimate harmony view has the important consequence that evil is only an appearance, an illusion; what appears to be evil is, after all, good.

What can be said against this view? There are numerous objections, as we shall see, but we might well begin by asking for an example of how apparent evil is really an ultimate good. I have been astounded through the years by the examples I have been offered: indeed, I have become convinced there is nothing that someone cannot find to be a good in disguise. I once mentioned Buchenwald as an example of great moral evil. But it was not really an evil, someone suggested, because it had helped immeasurably in solving the problem of population explosion. I confess that I was greatly agitated: I offered to shovel the speaker into my furnace as an added good. The important point here is this: if one holds the ultimate harmony view and honestly goes into detail trying to discover the ultimate good, he gets really bizarre results. Hence, the person who holds this view wisely refrains from offering detailed analyses. He contents himself by saying simply that in all cases there is an ultimate good, known to God, which human beings, with their limited powers, are unable to fathom. They say, in effect, that the ways of God pass understanding.

There are at least four serious objections to the present view. (a) To be sure, we are all aware of cases in our own experience where an apparent evil led to good. But what right do I have to assert that they always do, when I am equally aware of cases of apparent good leading to evil? If it be asserted that in the latter case I have not waited long enough for ultimate consequences, I must inquire how long the "long run" must be and must further inquire why the same argument does not apply equally well to the former case: perhaps I have not waited long enough either in cases where apparent evil leads to good consequences. In any case, even if apparent evil sometimes leads to good, and we neglect the opposite circumstances, it does not follow that we have proved it always will do so. This fact would only establish that it is *possible* that all cases of apparent evil lead to good, not that it is *probable*. But many events are possible for which we have, however, no warrant whatever to believe likely to happen. Moreover, in view of the enormous amount of apparent evil in the world, it seems *prima facie* unlikely that it could all be explained away as leading to good.[9]

(b) The ultimate harmony view has this outlandish consequence: if evil is really good in disguise, then we are wrong in thinking it is our moral duty to eliminate or mitigate evil circumstances. Rather, it apparently becomes our duty to aid and abet them. Moreover, if whatever is, is right, then we should not interfere in the slightest with the way things are in our world. Reform movements, on this view, must be viewed as positively immoral and pernicious. They are a kind of practical atheism which, in effect, say to the creation fresh from God's hands, "Lo,—you are a miserable business; I will make you fairer!"[10]

(c) The price that is paid for ultimate harmony is too great; ultimate harmony is not worth its cost in human misery. The end does not justify the means. The notion "all's well that ends well" is too simple-minded, particularly in this case, where we do not even know what the end is. Ivan makes this point forcefully in *The Brothers Karamazov,* in the section "Pro and Contra," where Ivan and Alyosha are discussing the problem of evil. The way he makes the point carries a person far beyond a simple understanding of it to a profound *feeling* for it. Let me paraphrase Ivan's great speech, however imperfectly, since it is too long to quote in full.

Take the suffering of children, Ivan tells Alyosha; there the point becomes very clear. Here is one example: a Russian general, retired on his great estate, treats his serfs like fools and buffons, He is a great hunter and has many fine dogs. One day a serf boy of eight throws a stone in play and hurts the paw of the general's favorite dog. The general asks about his dog—what happened? After he is told, he has the boy locked in a shed overnight. Early the next morning the serfs, including the child's mother, are assembled for their edification. The child is stripped naked and told to run. The general sets the hounds after him, shouting "Get him, get him!" The dogs quickly overtake the boy and tear him to pieces in front of his mother's eyes. Did the general deserve to be shot? No doubt, but the atrocity already had been committed. If such an atrocity is needed to manure the soil for some future harmony, Ivan says, then such harmony is not worth the price. Then he asks, if *you* were God, Alyosha, could *you* consent to create a world in which everything turned out well in the end, but to achieve this end you had to see just one child tortured to death, beating its breast in a stinking outhouse, crying to "dear, kind God." No, it is not worth it. No doubt, God sees things differently from men. No doubt, on the day of resurrection, Ivan says, I too will join in the chorus, "Hallelujah, God, thy ways are just!" I too shall sing, as the mother embraces her son's murderer, "Praise God, I see why it had to be!" But, he concludes, I loathe myself now for the very thought of doing that then. I renounce the "higher" morality, the ultimate harmony, altogether, while I still can, while there is still time. For the love of humanity I now renounce it altogether.

(d) The renunciation of the "higher" morality implied by the ultimate harmony theory requires further comment. J. S. Mill renounced it in the following way. He said, in effect: In everyday life I know what to call right or wrong, because I can plainly see its rightness or its wrongness. Now if a god requires that what I ordinarily call wrong in human behavior I must call right when he does it; or that what I ordinarily call wrong I must call right because he does, even though I do not see the point of it; and if by refusing to do so, he can sentence me to hell, to hell I will gladly go.

Theists have argued against Mill in the following way. Consider the moral relations between a father and son. Certainly a father knows moral principles of action that are unknown to his son. Now would it not be presumptuous for a son to say to his father that he could not accept as right anything of which he did not plainly see the rightness. Would it not be presumptuous to say, "Father, rather than call right what you call right—which I cannot, since this is not what I mean by right—I would be willing to go to—" —but theists do not repeat Mr. Mill's alternative. They ask, however, is it not just possible that there may be as much difference between man and God as there is between a child and his father.

This analogy, I believe, is not very convincing. We need to make the parallel more exact.[11] The child rightly has faith in his father's wisdom about things unknown to him. But the point is this: the child infers this wisdom from the wisdom and goodness of his father which he has seen and understood. He is, in short, as in all areas of thught, reasoning from the known to the unknown. With God, however, the case is quite otherwise. We are asked to accept a "higher" morality out of devotion and total ignorance. Indeed, the only thing we do know about it is that it runs counter to all that we *have* seen and understood about right and wrong. We are asked, in effect, to forget the little we know of right and wrong, abdicate our intelligence, submit ourselves to something we know not of, and all this out of blind devotion to the God about whom we wish to raise serious questions! If a child followed such a course of action toward his father, we would not think it an act of deep filial piety at all, but one of abject submission. The same attitude ought to exist, I submit, in the case of God and man.

At this point, the theist introduces a new gambit that is designed to cut off philosophical argument and discussion altogether. Belief in God, a higher morality, and ultimate harmony, they tell us, is a matter of faith—not blind faith, to be sure, but faith built on deep feeling and mystical experience.[12] About mystical experience and faith, presumably, there can be no philosophical argument. We have come, they say, to the moment of silence where nothing more can be said. I profoundly dislike this manuever, so I have constructed a whimsical argument which staves off the moment of silence a while longer. That it is a whimisical argument will become evident by and by, but this quality, I hope, will not obscure the dead earnestness and significant points it contains.

The usual naturalistic way of explaining mystical experiences is well known. They are explained away by the concepts of abnormal psychology; they are results, some say, of hallucination, delusion, hypnosis, paranoia, *etc.* Indeed, if Saint Joan were alive today, hearing voices as she did, she would be committed immediately to a state mental hospital. However, I find it difficult to look at Saint Joan, Saint Therese, and Saint John of the Cross in this way. Rather, I shall accept all Christian mystical experiences at face value—assuming that they have significant religious meaning for those who experience them. Christian mysticism, however, is not the only kind. I have a friend who reported having a mystical experience with an all-powerful, all-evil god—"It was ghastly," he said, shaking even at the recollection of it. (If you do not choose to believe this, no matter; just consider that it is still a logical possibility.)

What, now, can the theists say to my friend? How can they show him to be wrong, for his sake and for their own peace of mind? They might, of course, explain the experience away by various hypotheses: he was drunk, he has a persecution complex, or whatever. But this tactic will not do; we have agreed that we would not explain away the Christian mystic's experience in such ways, but would accept it at face value. So, too, must the Christian accept my friend's experience at face value.

The theists, of course, still want mightily to show that my friend is mistaken. What can they say by way of rational argument to show that he is wrong? Why, they can point out to him that he has an insoluble problem of good on his hands. If God is all-powerful and all-evil, how can you explain the enormous amount of apparently unnecessary physical and moral good in the world? Consider, *e.g.,* how the soil, rain, and sunshine produce our crops and how many men have sacrificed themselves for the good of others. My friend sees that he has a problem but replies in the following way: yes, but I can square God's character with good by a contrast theory. Good is necessary as a contrast so that we shall be able properly to understand and feel the horror of evil. The theist objects that we do not need so much good to achieve this goal. My friend agrees, but offers another theory: it is man's free will, he says, which solves his problem. God granted man free will, knowing full well how he would use it to produce enormous evil. Unhappily, of course, if he is to have free will, he must be capable of doing good also. The theist objects that God's omniscience and man's free will are incompatible concepts. My friend is forced to agree, but offers another theory: it is, he says, the ultimate disharmony theory.

What human beings call good is an event seen out of context, in isolation, and since man has only a fragmentary view of events, this is the only way he can see it. God, however, who has an overall view of events, sees how such events are evil in the long run or evil from an overall viewpoint. The theist objects that if one is not competent to know how good leads to evil, then he is not competent to judge evil either; for all he knows it might lead to good eventually. My friend retreats before this argument, but he has another—but it is not necessary to go further! The point should be perfectly clear by now that the problems of evil and good are completely isomorphic; what can be said about the one can be said about the other in reverse. For any solution to one problem, there is a parallel solution to the other, and for every counterargument in the one there is a parallel counterargument in the other.

There are two conclusions, or morals, to be drawn from my whimsical discussion of the problem of good. (a) All I ask the theist is to let others do unto him as he would do unto them. If people hold a position opposed to him and buttressed on the same ground of mysticism, he would wish to dissuade them from their view by rational argument in spite of their basing it on mystical experience. I simply wish to do the same to the theist. I do not say that he should ignore his mysticism and rely on rational argument alone, but I do suggest that he temper his mystical thought with a good dose of thought about his problem of evil, and check finally to see which way it goes.

(b) It is an interesting and ironic consequence of the problem of good that the theist cannot have what he wants both ways. He would like the problem of evil to be soluble, since he would dispose of the strongest antitheistic argument thereby. On the other hand, he would like the problem of good to be insoluble, because this insolubility would be the best reason possible for giving up belief in an all-powerful, all-evil god. (By the way, the notion of an evil god is not all whimsy. It is difficult indeed to dispose of such a concept.) Unfortunately for the theist, he cannot have it both ways. Since the two problems are entirely isomorphic, if one is soluble so is the other, and if one is insoluble so is the other. The theist must choose one way or the other and lose something important either way he chooses.

NOTES

1. Cf. H. J. McCloskey, "God and Evil," in *The Philosophical Quarterly*, Vol. 10 (1960), pp. 102, 103-04.

2. Luke, 13:1-5.

3. McCloskey, *op. cit.*, p. 103.

4. Alfred Noyes in *The Unknown God.*

5. David Elton Trueblood, *The Logic of Belief,* p. 288.

6. *Ibid.*, p. 289.

7. Cf. C. J. Ducasse, *A Philosophical Scrutiny of Religion*, pp. 357-61.

8. Cf. McCloskey, *op. cit.*, p. 113.

9. *Ibid.*, p. 105.

10. Cf. E. H. Madden, "G. W. Curtis: Practical Transcendentalist," *The Personalist,* Vol. XL (1959), p. 373.

11. Cf. Chauncey Wright, *Philosophical Discussions,* pp. 358-59.

12. At this point the ultimate harmony view and the notion that God's ways simply "pass understanding" are indistinguishable.

EVIL AND THE FINAL HARMONY

Feodor Dostoyevsky

"A well-educated, cultured gentleman and his wife beat their own child with a birch-rod, a girl of seven. I have an exact account of it. The papa was glad that the birch was covered with twigs. 'It stings more,' said he, and so he began stinging his daughter. I know for a fact there are people who at every blow are worked up to sensuality, to literal sensuality, which increases progressively at every blow they inflict. They beat for a minute, for five minutes, for ten minutes, more often and more savagely. The child screams. At last the child cannot scream, it gasps, 'Daddy! daddy!' By some diabolical unseemly chance the case was brought into court. A counsel is engaged. The Russian people have long called a barrister 'a conscience for hire.' The counsel protests in his client's defence. 'It's such a simple thing,' he says, 'an everyday domestic event. A father corrects the child. To our shame be it said, it is brought into court.' The jury, convinced by him, give a favourable verdict. The public roars with delight that the torturer is acquitted. Ah, pity I wasn't there! I would have proposed to raise a subscription in his honour! . . . Charming pictures.

"But I've still better things about children. I've collected a great, great deal about Russian children, Alyosha. There was a little girl of five who was hated by her father and mother, 'most worthy and respectable people, of good education and breeding.' You see, I must repeat again, it is a peculiar characteristic of many people, this love of torturing children, and children only. To all other types of humanity these torturers behave mildly and benevolently, like cultivated and humane Europeans; but they are very fond of tormenting children, even fond of children themselves in that sense. It's just their defencelessness that tempts the tormentor, just the angelic confidence of the child who has no refuge and no appeal, that sets his vile blood on fire. In every man, of course, a demon lies hidden—the demon of rage, the demon of lustful heat at the screams of the tortured victim, the demon of lawlessness let off the chain, the demon of diseases that follow on vice, gout, kidney disease, and so on.

"This poor child of five was subjected to every possible torture by those cultivated parents. They beat her, thrashed her, kicked her for no reason till her body was one bruise. Then, they went to greater refinements of cruelty—shut her up all night in the cold and frost in a privy, and because she didn't ask to be taken

From *The Brothers Karamazov,* trans. Constance Garnett (New York: Random House, Inc., 1950), pp. 286-290.

up at night (as though a child of five sleeping its angelic, sound sleep could be trained to wake and ask), they smeared her face and filled her mouth with excrement, and it was her mother, her mother did this. And that mother could sleep, hearing the poor child's groans! Can you understand why a little creature, who can't even undersand what's done to her, should beat her little aching heart with her tiny fist in the dark and the cold, and weep her meek unresentful tears to dear, kind God to protect her? Do you understand that, friend and brother, you pious and humble novice? Do you understand why this infamy must be and is permitted? Without it, I am told, man could not have existed on earth, for he could not have known good and evil. Why should he know that diabolical good and evil when it costs so much? Why, the whole world of knowledge is not worth that child's prayer to 'dear, kind God'! I say nothing of the sufferings of grown-up people, they have eaten the apple, damn them, and the devil take them all! But these little ones! I am making you suffer, Alyosha, you are not yourself. I'll leave off if you like."

"Never mind, I want to suffer too," muttered Alyosha.

"One picture, only one more, because it's so curious, so characteristic, and I have only just read it in some collection of Russian antiquities. I've forgotten the name. I must look it up. It was in the darkest days of serfdom at the beginning of the century, and long live the Liberator of the People! There was in those days a general of aristocratic connections, the owner of great estates, one of those men— somewhat exceptional, I believe, even then—who, retiring from the service into a life of leisure, are convinced that they've earned absolute power over the lives of their subjects. There were such men then. So our general, settled on his property of two thousand souls, lives in pomp, and domineers over his poor neighbours as though they were dependents and buffoons. He has kennels of hundreds of hounds and nearly a hundred dog-boys—all mounted, and in uniform. One day a serf boy, a little child of eight, threw a stone in play and hurt the paw of the general's favourite hound. 'Why is my favourite dog lame?' He is told that the boy threw a stone that hurt the dog's paw. 'So you did it.' The general looked the child up and down. 'Take him.' He was taken—taken from his mother and kept shut up all night. Early that morning the general comes out on horseback, with the hounds, his dependents, dog-boys, and huntsmen, all mounted around him in full hunting parade. The servents are summoned for their education, and in front of them all stands the mother of the child. The child is brought from the lock-up. It's a gloomy cold, foggy autumn day, a capital day for hunting. The general orders the child to be undressed; the child is stripped naked. He shivers, numb with terror, not daring to cry. . . . 'Make him run,' commands the general. 'Run! run!' shout the dog-boys. The boy runs. . . . 'At him!' yells the general, and he sets the whole pack of hounds on the child. The hounds catch him, and tear him to pieces before his mother's eyes! . . . I believe the general was afterwards declared incapable of administering his estates. Well—what did he deserve? To be shot? To be shot for the satisfaction of our moral feelings? Speak, Alyosha!"

"To be shot," murmured Alyosha, lifting his eyes to Ivan with a pale, twisted smile.

"Bravo!" cried Ivan delighted. "If even you say so . . . You're a pretty monk! So there is a little devil sitting in your heart, Aloysha Karamazov!"

"What I said was absurd, but—"

"That's just the point, that 'but'!" cried Ivan. "Let me tell you, novice, that the absurd is only too necessary on earth. The world stands on absurdities, and perhaps nothing would have come to pass in it without them. We know what we know!"

"What do you know?"

"I understand nothing," Ivan went on, as though in delirium. "I don't want to understand anything now. I want to stick to the fact. I made up my mind long ago not to understand. If I try to understand anything, I shall be false to the fact and I have determined to stick to the fact."

"Why are you trying me?" Alyosha cried, with sudden distress. "Will you say what you mean at last?"

"Of course, I will; that's what I've been leading up to. You are dear to me, I don't want to let you go, and I won't give you up to your Zossima."

Ivan for a minute was silent, his face became all at once very sad.

"Listen! I took the case of children only to make my case clearer. Of the other tears of humanity with which the earth is soaked from its crust to its centre, I will say nothing. I have narrowed my subject on purpose. I am a bug, and I recognise in all humility that I cannot understand why the world is arranged as it is. Men are themselves to blame, I suppose; they were given paradise, they wanted freedom, and stole fire from heaven, though they knew they would become unhappy, so there is no need to pity them. With my pitiful, earthly, Euclidian understanding, all I know is that there is suffering and that there are none guilty; that cause follows effect, simply and directly; that everything flows and finds its level— but that's only Euclidian nonsense, I know that, and I can't consent to live by it! What comfort is to me that there are none guilty and that cause follows effect simply and directly, and that I know it—I must have justice, or I will destroy myself. And not justice in some remote infinite time and space, but here on earth, and that I could see myself. I have believed in it. I want to see it, and if I am dead by then, let me rise again, for if it all happens without me, it will be too unfair. Surely I haven't suffered, simply that I, my crimes and my sufferings, may manure the soil of the future harmony for somebody else. I want to see with my own eyes the hind lie down with the lion and the victim rise up and embrace his murderer. I want to be there when every one suddenly understands what it has all been for. All the religions of the world are built on this longing, and I am a believer. But then there are the children, and what am I to do about them? That's a question I can't answer. For the hundredth time I repeat, there are numbers of questions, but I've only taken the children, because in their case what I mean is so unanswerably clear. Listen! If all must suffer to pay for the eternal harmony, what have children to do with it, tell me, please? It's beyond all comprehension why they should suffer, and why they should pay for the harmony. Why should they, too, furnish material to enrich the soil for the harmony of the future? I understand solidarity in sin among men. I understand solidarity in retribution, too; but there can be no such solidarity with children. And if it is really true that they must share responsibility for all their fathers' crimes, such a truth is not of this world and is beyond my comprehension. Some jester will say, perhaps, that the child would have grown up and have sinned, but you see he didn't grow up, he was torn to pieces by the dogs, at eight years old. Oh, Alyosha, I am not blaspheming! I understand, of course, what an upheaval of the universe it will be, when everything in heaven and earth blends in one hymn of praise and everything that lives and has lived cries aloud: 'Thou art just, O Lord, for Thy ways are revealed.' When the mother embraces the fiend who threw her child to the dogs, and all three cry aloud with tears, 'Thou art just, O Lord!' then, of course, the crown of knowledge will be reached and all will be made clear. But what pulls me up here is that I can't accept that harmony. And while I am on earth, I make haste to take my own measures. You see Alyosha, perhaps it really may happen that if I live to that moment, or rise again to see it, I, too, perhaps, may cry aloud with the rest, looking at the mother embracing the child's torturer, 'Thou art just, O Lord!' but I don't want to cry aloud then. While there is still time, I hasten to protect myself and so I renounce the higher harmony altogether. It's not worth the tears of that one tortured child who beat itself on the breast with its little fist and prayed in its stinking outhouse, with its unexpiated tears to 'dear, kind God'! It's not worth it, because those tears are unatoned for. They must be atoned for, or there can be no harmony. But how? How are you going to atone for them? Is it possible? By their being avenged? But what do I care for avenging them? What do I care for a hell for oppressors? What good can hell do, since those children have already been tortured? And what becomes of harmony, if there is hell? I want to forgive. I want to embrace. I don't want more suffering. And if the sufferings of children go to swell the sum of sufferings which was necessary to pay for truth, then I protest that the truth is not worth such a price. I don't want the mother to embrace the oppressor who threw her son to the dogs! She dare not forgive him! Let her forgive him for herself, if she will, let her forgive the torturer for the immeasurable suffering of her mother's heart. But the sufferings of her tortured child she has no right to forgive; she dare not forgive the turturer, even if the child were to forgive him! And if that is so, if they dare not forgive, what becomes of harmony? Is there in the whole world a being who would have the right to forgive and could forgive? I don't want harmony. From love for humanity I don't want it. I would rather be left with the unavenged suffering. I would rather remain with my unavenged suffering and unsatisfied indignation, *even if I were wrong.* Besides, too high a price is asked for harmony; it's beyond our means to pay so much to enter on it. And so I hasten to give back my entrance ticket, and if I am an honest man I am bound to give it back as soon as possible. And that I am doing. It's not God that I don't accept, Alyosha, only I most respectfully return Him the ticket."

"That's rebellion," murmured Alyosha, looking down.

"Rebellion? I am sorry you call it that," said Ivan earnestly. "One can hardly live in rebellion, and I want to live. Tell me yourself, I challenge you—answer.

Imagine that you are creating a fabric of human destiny with the object of making men happy in the end, giving them peace and rest at last, but it was essential and inevitable to torture to death only one tiny creature—that baby beating its breast with its fist, for instance—and to found that edifice on its unavenged tears, would you consent to be the architect on those conditions? Tell me, and tell the truth."

"No, I wouldn't consent," said Alyosha softly.

"And can you admit the idea that men for whom you are building it would agree to accept their happiness on the foundation of the unexpiated blood of a little victim? And accepting it would remain happy for ever?"

CHAPTER SIX
DEATH
AND THE
MEANING OF LIFE

Buckdancer's Choice

So I would hear out those lungs,
The air split into nine levels,
Some gift of tongues of the whistler

In the invalid's bed: my mother,
Warbling all day to herself
The thousand variations of one song;

It is called Buckdancer's Choice.
For years, they have all been dying
Out, the classic buck-and-wing men

Of traveling minstrel shows;
With them also an old woman
Was dying of breathless angina,

Yet still found breath enough
To whistle up in my head
A sight like a one-man band,

Freed black, with cymbals at heel,
An ex-slave who thrivingly danced
To the ring of his own clashing light

Through the thousand variations of one song
All day to my mother's prone music,
The invalid's warbler's note,

While I crept close to the wall
Sock-footed, to hear the sounds alter,
Her tongue like a mockingbird's break

Through stratum after stratum of a tone
Proclaiming what choices there are
For the last dancers of their kind,

For ill women and for all slaves
Of death, and children enchanted at walls
With a brass-beating glow underfoot,

Not dancing but nearly risen
Through barnlike, theatrelike houses
On the wings of the buck and wing.

James Dickey

In James Dickey's splendid poem, most of us can readily identify with the child, now grown up to be the poem's narrator. We too have known people about to die, "slaves of death" like the invalid mother and the black buckdancers; and, like the child, we have sometimes been mystified that these dying persons are able to go on doing such normal, everyday things—whistling, earning a living—while they wait for their end. How can they? Shouldn't they be doing something *extraordinary,* making preparations, at least *raging* against their doom? How could one give over one's last hours to "warbling . . . all day the thousand variations of one song"?

A moment's thought reveals the self-indulgence and myopia of such an attitude; for we too, all of us without exception, are the slaves of death. Dickey's child, standing in stocking-feet, is just as much death's prisoner as is his bedridden mother. He too will surely die, perhaps without the grace of a warning. As I write, and as you read, our own deaths approach, inexorably; yet we whistle on—reading philosophy, making love, making money, making children—"the thousand variations of one song."

How can we do it? Ordinarily, of course, we camouflage the reality to make it bearable. We make ourselves forget how fragile we are, how powerless we are to alter the natural laws which have dominion over us and which are blind to our cherished desires.

> Our personality is entirely dependent upon external circumstances which have unlimited power to crush it. But we would rather die than admit this. From our point of view the equilibrium of the world is a combination of circumstances so ordered that our personality remains intact and seems to belong to us. All the circumstances of the past that have wounded our

personality appear to us to be disturbances of balance which should infallibly be made up for one day or another by phenomena having a contrary
effect. The near approach of death is horrible chiefly because it forces the
knowledge upon us that these compensations will never come.[1]

In addition, we make ourselves forget how trivial and temporary are the activities
which consume the greatest part of our energies. Over some of these routines—
eating and sleeping, for instance—we have no real control; they are rooted in our
physiology. What of the routines we *have* chosen? How do they look to us—what
sense do they have—face-to-face with death? For a single sort of example, consider
all our enormously powerful desires to "succeed": we want so much to be popular,
to be rich, to be a member of Phi Beta Kappa, to be loved. Think of the hours we
devote to such pursuits. What's the point? Even if—as is not likely—all our dreams
come true, what do we have? Money, a few pleasant hours, a few initials after our
name. There are, as the proverb says, no pockets in a shroud—and no place to hang
a ϕBK key either. Viewed from the grave, all is vanity.

What happens to our lives when this reality is acknowledged? Many people,
some philosophers among them, have argued that once we clearly see that we are
death's permanent slaves, once we *feel* this as well as assent to it intellectually, then
our daily routines necessarily lose their sense and become insupportable. In his
Confession, Tolstoy tells of the despair and anger which can paralyze the person
who has perceived death's threat to his life's meaning.

> I could give no reasonable meaning to any single action or to my whole life.
> I was only surprised that I could have avoided understanding this from the
> very beginning—it has been so long known to all. Today or tomorrow sickness
> and death will come (they had come already) to those I love or me; nothing
> will remain but stench and worms. Sooner or later my affairs, whatever they
> be, will be forgotten, and I shall not exist. Then why go on making any
> effort? . . . How can man fail to see this? And how go on living? . . . One can
> only live while one is intoxicated with life; as soon as one is sober it is impos-
> sible not to see that it is all a mere fraud and a stupid fraud. That is precisely
> what it is: there is nothing either amusing or witty about it, it is simply cruel
> and stupid.[2]

Is Tolstoy's an extreme reaction? The facts are not, it seems, in dispute: we *will* all
die, we *will* all be forgotten, any effort to which we set our hands *will* someday go
to dust. Do these putative facts necessarily rob life of its ordinary meaning? If they
do, could there be some extraordinary meaning to a person's life that even annihilation cannot menace? In this section we have arranged several responses to these
fundamental philosophical questions, ranging from the Christian denial of death's
finality to Tom Nagel's attempt to draw the venom from the recognition of life's
absurdity.

NOTES

1. Simone Weil, *Waiting for God* (New York: Harper and Row, 1973), p. 224.
2. Leo Tolstoy, *A Confession,* trans. Aylmer Maude (London: Oxford University Press,
1974), pp. 19-20.

STATEMENT OF THE PROBLEM

MY CONFESSION

Leo Tolstoy

Chapter I

I was christened and educated in the Orthodox Christian Faith; I was taught it in my childhood, and in my boyhood and youth. Nevertheless, when, at eighteen years of age, I left the university in the second year, I had discarded all belief in anything I had been taught.

To judge by what I can now remember, I never had a serious belief; I merely trusted in what my elders made their profession of faith, but even this trust was very precarious.

I remember once in my twelfth year, a boy, now long since dead, Volodinka M——, a pupil in the gymnasium, spent a Sunday with us, and brought us the news of the last discovery in the gymnasium. This discovery was that there was no God, and that all we were taught on the subject was a mere invention (this was in 1838). I remember well how interested my elder brothers were in this news; I was admitted to their deliberations, and we all eagerly accepted the theory as something particularly attractive and possibly quite true.

I remember, also, that when my elder brother, Dmitri, then at the university, with the impulsiveness natural to his character, gave himself up to a passionate faith, began to attend the church services regularly, to fast, and to lead a pure and moral life, we all of us, and some older than ourselves, never ceased to hold him up to ridicule, and for some incomprehensible reason gave him the nickname of Noah. I remember that Musin-Pushkin, then curator of the University of Kazan, having invited us to a ball, tried to persuade my brother, who had refused the invitation, by the jeering argument that even David danced before the Ark.

I sympathized then with these jokes of my elders, and drew from them this conclusion,—that I was bound to learn my catechism, and go to church, but that it was not necessary to take all this too seriously.

I also remember that I read Voltaire when I was very young, and that his tone of mockery amused without disgusting me.

This estrangement from all belief went on in me, as it does now, and always has done, in those of the same social position and culture. This falling off, as it seems to me, for the most part goes on thus: people live as others live, and their lives are guided, not by the principles of the faith that is taught them, but by their very opposite; belief has no influence on life, nor on the relations among men—it is relegated to some other sphere apart from life and independent of it; if the two

From *The Works of Leo N. Tolstoy* (New York: T. Y. Crowell, 1917).

ever come into contact at all, belief is only one of the outward phenomena, and not one of the constituent parts of life.

By a man's life, by his acts, it was then, as it is now, impossible to know whether he was a believer or not. If there be a difference between one who openly professes the doctrines of the Orthodox Church, and one who denies them, the difference is to the advantage of the former. Then, as now, the open profession of the Orthodox doctrines was found mostly among dull, stern, immoral men, and those who think much of their own importance. Intellect, honor, frankness, good nature, and morality are oftener met with among those who call themselves disbelievers.

The school-boy is taught his catechism and sent to church; chinovniks, or functionaries, are required to show a certificate of having taken the holy communion. But the man belonging to our class, who is done with school and does not enter the public service, may now live a dozen years—still more was this the case formerly—without being once reminded of the fact that he lives among Christians, and is reckoned as a member of the Orthodox Christian Church.

Thus it happens that now, as formerly, the influence of early religious teaching, accepted merely on trust and upheld by authority, gradually fades away under the knowledge and practical experience of life, which is opposed to all its principles, and that a man often believes for years that his early faith is still intact, while all the time not a trace of it remains in him.

A certain S——, a clever and veracious man, once related to me how he came to give up his belief.

Twenty-six years ago, while he was off on a hunting expedition, he knelt down to pray before he lay down to rest, according to a habit of his from childhood. His elder brother, who was of the party, lay on some straw and watched him. When S—— had finished, and was preparing to lie down, his brother said to him:—

"Ah, so you still keep that up?"

Nothing more passed between them, but from that day S—— ceased to pray and to go to church. For thirty years S—— has not said a prayer, has not taken the communion, has not been in a church,—not because he shared the convictions of his brother, or even knew them,—not because he had come to any conclusions of his own,—but because his brother's words were like the push of a finger against a wall ready to tumble over with its own weight; they proved to him that what he had taken for belief was an empty form, and that consequently every word he uttered, every sign of the cross he made, every time he bowed his head during his prayers, his act was unmeaning. When he once admitted to himself that such acts had no meaning in them, he could not continue them.

Thus it has been, and is, I believe, with the large majority of men. I am speaking of men of our class, I am speaking of men who are true to themselves, and not of those who make of religion a means of obtaining some temporal advantage. (These men are truly absolute unbelievers; for if faith be to them a means of obtaining any wordly end, it is most certainly not faith at all.) Such men of our own class are in this position: the light of knowledge and life has melted the artificially constructed edifice of belief within, and they have either observed that and cleared away the superincumbent ruins, or they have remained unconscious of it.

The belief instilled from childhood in me, as in so many others, gradually disappeared, but with this difference; that as from fifteen years of age I had begun to read philosophical works, I became very early conscious of my own disbelief. From the age of sixteen I ceased to pray, and ceased, from conviction, to attend the services of the church and to fast. I no longer accepted the faith of my childhood, but I believed in something, though I could not exactly explain in what. I believed in a God,—or rather, I did not deny the existence of a God,—but what kind of God I could not have told; I denied neither Christ nor His teaching, but in what the teaching consisted I could not have said.

Now, when I think over that time, I see clearly that all the faith I had, the only belief which, apart from mere animal instinct, swayed my life, was a belief in the possibility of perfection, though what it was in itself, or what would be its results, I could not have said.

I tried to reach intellectual perfection; my studies were extended in every direction of which my life afforded me a chance; I strove to strengthen my will, forming for myself rules which I forced myself to follow; I did my best to develop my physical powers by every exercise calculated to give strength and agility, and by way of accustoming myself to patient endurance; I subjected myself to many voluntary hardships and trials of privation. All this I looked on as necessary to obtain the perfection at which I aimed.

At first, of course, moral perfection seemed to me the main end, but I soon found myself contemplating in its stead an ideal of general perfectibility; in other words, I wished to be better, not in my own eyes nor in God's, but in the sight of other men. And very soon this striving to be better in the sight of men feeling again changed into another,—the desire to have more power than others, to secure for myself a greater share of fame, of social distinction, and of wealth.

Chapter II

At some future time I may relate the story of my life, and dwell in detail on the pathetic and instructive incidents of my youth. I think that many and many have had the same experiences as I did. I desired with all my soul to be good; but I was young, I had passions, and I was alone, wholly alone, in my search after goodness. Every time I tried to express the longings of my heart to be morally good, I was met with contempt and ridicule, but as soon as I gave way to low passions, I was praised and encouraged.

Ambition, love of power, love of gain, lechery, pride, anger, vengeance, were held in high esteem.

As I gave way to these passions, I became like my elders and I felt that they were satisfied with me. A kind-hearted aunt of mine, a really good woman with whom I lived, used to say to me that there was one thing above all others which she wished for me—an intrigue with a married woman: *"Rien ne forme un jeune homme, comme une liaison avec une femme comme il faut."* Another of her wishes for my happiness was that I should become an adjutant, and, if possible to the Emperor; the greatest piece of good fortune of all she thought would be that I should find a very wealthy bride, who would bring me as her dowry as many slaves as could be.

I cannot now recall those years without a painful feeling of horror and loathing.

I put men to death in war. I fought duels to slay others, I lost at cards, wasted my substance wrung from the sweat of peasants, punished the latter cruelly, rioted with loose women, and deceived men. Lying, robbery, adultery of all kinds, drunkenness, violence, murder. There was not one crime which I did not commit, and yet I was not the less considered by my equals a comparatively moral man.

Such was my life during ten years.

During that time I began to write, out of vanity, love of gain, and pride. I followed as a writer the same path which I had chosen as a man. In order to obtain the fame and the money for which I wrote, I was obliged to hide what was good and to say what was evil. Thus I did. How often while writing have I cudgeled my brains to conceal under the mask of indifference or pleasantry those yearnings for something better which formed the real thought of my life. I succeeded in this also, and was praised.

At twenty-six years of age, on the close of the war, I came to Petersburg and made the acquaintance of the authors of the day. I met with a healthy reception and much flattery.

Before I had time to look around, the prejudices and views of life common to the writers of the class with which I associated became my own, and completely put an end to all my former struggles after a better life. These views, under the influence of the dissipation of my life, supplied a theory which justified it.

The view of life taken by these my fellow-writers was that life is a development, and the principal part in that development is played by ourselves, the thinkers, while among the thinkers the chief influence is again due to us, the artists, the poets. Our vocation is to teach men.

In order to avoid answering the very natural question, "What do I know, and what can I teach?" the theory in question is made to contain the formula that it is not necessary to know this, but that the artist and the poet teach unconsciously.

I was myself considered a marvelous artist and poet, and I therefore very naturally adopted this theory. I, an artist and poet, wrote and taught I knew not what. For doing this I received money; I kept a splendid table, had excellent lodgings, women, society; I had fame. Naturally what I taught was very good.

The faith in poetry and the development of life was a true faith, and I was one of its priests. To be one of its priests was very advantageous and agreeable. I long remained in this belief, and never once doubted its truth.

But in the second, and especially in the third year of this way of life, I began to doubt the infallibility of the doctrine, and to examine it more closely. What first led me to doubt was the fact that I began to notice the priests of this belief did not agree among themselves. Some said:—

"We are the best and most useful teachers; we teach what is needful, and all others teach wrong."

They disputed, quarreled, abused, deceived, and cheated one another. Moreover, there were many among us who, quite indifferent to the question who was right or who was wrong, advanced only their own private interests by the aid of our activity. All this forced on me doubts as to the truth of our belief.

Again, having begun to doubt the truth of our literary faith, I began to study its priests more closely, and became convinced that almost all the priests of this faith were immoral men, most of them worthless and insignificant, and beneath the moral level of those with whom I associated during my former dissipated and military career; but conceited and self-satisfied as only those can be who are wholly saints, or those who know not what holiness is.

I grew disgusted with mankind and with myself, and I understood that this belief was a delusion. The strangest thing in all this was that, though I soon saw the falseness of this belief and renounced it, I did not renounce the rank given me by these men,—the rank of artist, poet, teacher. I was simple enough to imagine that I was a poet and artist, and could teach all men without knowing what I was teaching. But so I did.

By my companionship with these men I had gained a new vice,—a pride developed to a morbid extreme, and an insane self-confidence in teaching men what I myself did not know.

When I now think over that time, and remember my own state of mind and that of these men (a state of mind common enough among thousands still), it seems to my pitiful, terrible, and ridiculous; it excites the feelings which overcome us as we pass through a madhouse.

We were all then convinced that it behooved us to speak, to write, and to print as fast as we could, as much as we could, and that on this depended the welfare of the human race. And thousands of us wrote, printed, and taught, and all the while confuted and abused one another. Quite unconscious that we ourselves knew nothing, that to the simplest of all problems in life—what is right and what is wrong—we had no answer, we all went on talking together without one to listen, at times abetting and praising one another on condition that we were abetted and praised in turn, and again turning upon one another in wrath—in short, we reproduced the scenes in a madhouse.

Thousands of laborers worked day and night, to the limit of their strength, setting up the type and printing millions of words to be spread by the post all over Russia, and still we continued to teach, unable to teach enough, angrily complaining the while that we were not much listened to.

A strange state of things indeed, but now it is comprehensible to me. The real motive that inspired all our reasoning was the desire for money and praise, to obtain which we knew of no other means than writing books and newspapers, and so we did. But in order to hold fast to the conviction that while thus uselessly employed we were very important men, it was necessary to justify our occupation to ourselves by another theory, and the following was the one we adopted: —

Whatever is, is right; everything that is, is due to development; development comes from civilization; the measure of civilization is the diffusion of books and newspapers; we are paid and honored for the books and newspapers which we write, and we are therefore the most useful and best of men!

This reasoning might have been conclusive had we all been agreed; but, as for every opinion expressed by one of us there instantly appeared from another one diametrically opposite, we had to hesitate before accepting it. But we did not notice this; we received money, and were praised by those of our party, consequently we—each one of us—considered that we were in the right.

It is now clear to me that between ourselves and the inhabitants of a madhouse there was no difference: at the time I only vaguely suspected this, and, like all madmen, thought all were mad except myself.

Chapter III

I lived in this senseless manner another six years, up to the time of my marriage. During this time I went abroad. My life in Europe, and my acquaintance with many eminent and learned foreigners, confirmed my belief in the doctrine of general perfectibility, as I found the same theory prevailed among them. This belief took the form which is common among most of the cultivated men of our day. This belief was expressed in the word "progress." It then appeared to me this word had a real meaning. I did not as yet understand that, tormented like every other man by the question, "How was I to live better?" when I answered that I must live for progress, I was only repeating the answer of a man carried away in a boat by the waves and the wind, who to the one important question for him, "Where are we to steer?" should answer, "We are being carried somewhere."

I did not see this then; only at rare intervals my feelings, and not my reason, were roused against the common superstition of our age, which leads men to ignore their own ignorance of life.

Thus, during my stay in Paris, the sight of a public execution revealed to me the weakness of my superstitious belief in progress. When I saw the head divided from the body, and heard the sound with which they fell separately into the box, I understood, not with my reason, but with my whole being, that no theory of the wisdom of all established things, nor of progress, could justify such an act; and that if all the men in the world from the day of creation, by whatever theory, had found this thing necessary, I knew it was not necessary, it was a bad thing, and that therefore I must judge of what was right and necessary, not by what men said and did, not by progress, but what I felt to be true in my heart.

Another instance of the insufficiency of this superstition of progress as a rule for life was the death of my brother. He fell ill while still young, suffered much during a whole year, and died in great pain. He was a man of good abilities, of a kind heart, and of a serious temper, but he died without understanding why he had lived, and still less what his death meant for him. No theories could give an answer to these questions, either to him or to me, during the whole period of his long and painful lingering.

But these occasions for doubt were few and far between; on the whole, I continued to live in the profession of the faith of progress. "Everything develops, and I myself am developing; and why this is so will one day be apparent," was the formula I was obliged to adopt.

On my return from abroad I settled in the country, and occupied myself with the organization of schools for the peasantry. This occupation was especially dear to my heart, because it was free from the spirit of falseness so evident to me in the career of a literary teacher.

Here again I acted in the name of progress, but this time I brought a spirit of critical inquiry to the system on which the progress rested. I said to myself that progress was often attempted in an irrational manner, and that it was necessary to leave a primitive people and the children of peasants perfectly free to choose the way of progress which they thought best. In reality I was still bent on the solution of the same impossible problem,—how to teach without knowing what I had to teach. In the highest spheres of literature I had understood that it was impossible to do this because I had seen that each taught differently, and that the teachers quarreled among themselves, and scarcely succeeded in concealing their ignorance from one another. Having now to deal with peasants' children, I thought that I could get over this difficulty by allowing the children to learn what they liked. It seems now absurd when I remember the expedients by which I carried out this whim of mine to teach, though I knew in my heart that I could teach nothing useful, because I myself did not know what was necessary.[1]

After a year spent in this employment with the school I again went abroad, for the purpose of finding out how I was to teach without knowing anything.

I believed that I had found a solution abroad, and, armed with all that essence of wisdom, I returned to Russia, the same year in which the peasants were freed from serfdom; and, accepting the office of arbitrator,[2] I began to teach the uneducated people in the schools, and the educated classes in the journal which I began to publish. Things seemed to be going on well, but I felt that my mind was not in a normal state and that a change was near. I might even then, perhaps, have come to that state of despair to which I was brought fifteen years later, if it had not been for a new experience in life which promised me safety—family life.

For a year I was occupied with arbitration, with the schools and with my newspaper, and got so involved that I was harrassed to death; the struggle over the arbitration was so hard for me, my activity in the schools was so dubious to me, my shuffling in the newspaper became so repugnant to me, consisting as it did in forever the same thing,—in the desire to teach all people and to hide the fact that I did not know how or what to teach,—that I fell ill, more with a mental than physical sickness, gave up everything, and started for the steppes to the Bashkirs to breathe a fresher air, to drink kumiss, and live an animal life.

After I returned I married. The new circumstances of a happy family life completely led me away from the search after the meaning of life as a whole. My life was concentrated at this time in my family, my wife and children, and consequently in the care for increasing the means of life. The effort to effect my own individual perfection, already replaced by the striving after general progress, was again changed into an effort to secure the particular happiness of my family.

In this way fifteen years passed.

Notwithstanding that during these fifteen years I looked upon the craft of authorship as a very trifling thing, I continued all the time to write. I had experienced the seductions of authorship, the temptations of an enormous pecuniary reward and of great applause for valueless work, and gave myself up to it as a means of improving my material position, and of stifling in my soul all questions regarding my own life and life in general. In my writing I taught what for me was the only truth,—that the object of life should be our highest happiness and that of our family.

Thus I lived; but, five years ago, a strange state of mind began to grow upon me: I had moments of perplexity, of a stoppage, as it were, of life, as if I did not know how I was to live, what I was to do, and I began to wander, and was a victim to low spirit. But this passed, and I continued to live as before. Later, these periods of perplexity began to return more and more frequently, and invariably took the same form. These stoppages of life always presented themselves to me with the same questions: "Why?" and "What after?"

At first it seemed to me that these were aimless, unmeaning questions; it seemed to me that all they asked about was well known, and that if at any time when I wished to find answers to them I could do so without much trouble—that just at that time I could not be bothered with this, but whenever I should stop to think them over I should find an answer. But these questions presented themselves to my mind with ever increasing frequency, demanding an answer with still greater and greater persistence, and like dots grouped themselves into one black spot.

It was with me as it happens in the case of every mortal internal ailment—at first appear the insignificant symptoms of indisposition, disregarded by the patient; then these symptoms are repeated more and more frequently, till they merge in uninterrupted suffering. The sufferings increase, and the patient, before he has time to look around, is confronted with the fact that what he took for a mere indisposition has become more important to him than anything else on earth, that it is death!

This is exactly what happened to me. I became aware that this was not a chance indisposition, but something very serious, and that if all these questions continued to recur, I should have to find an answer to them. And I tried to answer them. The questions seemed so foolish, so simple, so childish; but no sooner had I taken hold of them and attempted to decide them than I was convinced, first, that they were neither childish nor silly, but were concerned with the deepest problems of life; and, in the second place, that I could not decide them—could not decide them, however I put my mind upon them.

Before occupying myself with my Samara estate, with the education of my son, with the writing of books, I was bound to know why I did these things. As long as I do not know the reason "why" I cannot do anything. I cannot live. While thinking about the management of my household and estate, which in these days occupied much of my time, suddenly this question came into my head:—

"Well and good, I have now six thousand desyatins in the government of Samara, and three hundred horses—what then?"

I was perfectly disconcerted, and knew not what to think. Another time, dwelling on the thought of how I should educate my children, I asked myself, *"Why?"* Again, when considering by what means the well-being of the people might best be promoted, I suddenly exclaimed, "But what concern have I with it?" When I thought of the fame which my works were gaining me, I said to myself:—

"Well, what if I should be more famous than Gogol, Pushkin, Shakespeare, Molière—than all the writers of the world—well, and what then?"

I could find no reply. Such questions will not wait; they demand an immediate answer; without one it is impossible to live; but answer there was none.

I felt that the ground on which I stood was crumbling, that there was nothing for me to stand on, that what I had been living for was nothing, that I had no reason for living.

Chapter IV

My life had come to a stop. I was able to breathe, to eat, to drink, to sleep, and I could not help breathing, eating, drinking, sleeping; but there was no real life in me because I had not a single desire, the fulfillment of which I could feel to be reasonable. If I wished for anything, I knew beforehand that, were I to satisfy the wish, or were I knot to satisfy it, nothing would come of it. Had a fairy appeared and offered me all I desired, I should not have known what to say. If I had, in moments of excitement, I will not say wishes, but the habits of former wishes, at calmer moments I knew that it was a delusion, that I really wished for nothing. I could not even wish to know the truth, because I guessed in what it consisted.

The truth was, that life was meaningless. Every day of life, every step in it, brought me, as it were, nearer the precipice, and I saw clearly that before me there was nothing but ruin. And to stop was impossible; to go back was impossible; and it was impossible to shut my eyes so as not to see that there was nothing before me but suffering and actual death, absolute annihilation.

Thus I, a healthy and a happy man, was brought to feel that I could live no longer,—some irresistible force was dragging me onward to escape from life. I do not mean that I wanted to kill myself.

The force that drew me away from life was stronger, fuller, and more universal than any wish; it was a force like that of my previous attachment to life, only in a contrary direction. With all my force I struggled away from life. The idea of suicide came as naturally to me as formerly that of bettering my life. This thought was so attractive to me that I was compelled to practise upon myself a species of self-deception in order to avoid carrying it out too hastily. I was unwilling to act hastily, only because I wanted to employ all my powers in clearing away the confusion of my thoughts; if I should not clear them away, I could at any time kill myself. And here was I, a man fortunately situated, hiding away a cord, to avoid being tempted to hang myself by it to the transom between the closets of my room, where I undressed alone every evening; and I ceased to go hunting with a gun because it offered too easy a way of getting rid of life. I knew not what I wanted; I was afraid of life; I struggled to get away from it, and yet there *was* something I hoped for from it.

Such was the condition I had to come to, at a time when all the circumstances of my life were preeminently happy ones, and when I had not reached my fiftieth year. I had a good, loving, and beloved wife, good children, and a large estate, which, without much trouble on my part, was growing and increasing; I was more than ever respected by my friends and acquaintances; I was praised by strangers, and could lay claim to having made my name famous without much self-deception. Moreover, I was not mad or in an unhealthy mental state; on the contrary, I enjoyed a mental and physical strength which I have seldom found in men of my class and pursuits; I could keep up with a peasant in mowing, and could continue mental labor for eight or ten hours at a stretch, without any evil consequences. And in this state of things it came to this,—that I could not live, and as I feared death I was obliged to employ ruses against myself so as not to put an end to my life.

The mental state in which I then was seemed to me summed up in the following: My life was a foolish and wicked joke played on me by some one. Notwithstanding that fact that I did not recognize a "Someone," who may have created me, this conclusion that some one had wickedly and foolishly made a joke of me in bringing me into the world seemed to me the most natural of all conclusions.

I could not help reasoning that *there,* somewhere, is some one who is now diverting himself at my expense, as he watches me, as after from thirty to forty years of a life of study and development, of mental and bodily growth with all my powers matured and having reached that summit of life from which it is seen in its completeness, I stand like a fool on this height, understanding clearly that there is nothing in life, that there never was anything, and never will be. To him it must seem ridiculous.

But whether there is, or is not, such a being, in either case it did not help me. I could not attribute a reasonable motive to any single act in my whole life. I was only astonished that I could not have realized this at the very beginning. All this had so long been known to me! Illness and death would come (indeed, they had come), if not to-day, then tomorrow, to those whom I loved, to myself, and nothing remains but stench and worms. All my acts, whatever I did, would sooner or later be forgotten, and I myself be nowhere. Why, then, busy one's self with anything? How could men fail to see this, and live? How wonderful this is! It is possible to live only as long as life intoxicates us; as soon as we are sober again we see that it is all a delusion, and a stupid delusion! In this, indeed, there is nothing either ludicrous or amusing; it is only cruel and stupid!

There is an old Eastern fable about a traveler in the steppes who is attacked by a furious wild beast. To save himself the traveler gets into a waterless well; but at the bottom of it he sees a dragon with its jaws wide open to devour him. The unhappy man dares not get out for fear of the wild beast, and dares not descend for fear of the dragon, so he catches hold of the branch of a wild plant growing in a crevice of the well. His arms grow tired, and he feels that he must soon perish, death awaiting him on either side, but he still holds on; and he sees two mice, one black and one white, gradually making their way round the stem of the wild plant on which he is hanging, nibbling it through. The plant will soon give way and break off, and he will fall into the jaws of the dragon. The traveler sees this, and knows that he must inevitably perish; but, while still hanging, he looks around him, and, finding some drops of honey on the leaves of the wild plant, he stretches out his tongue and licks them.

Thus do I cling to the branch of life, knowing that the dragon of death inevitably awaits me, ready to tear me to pieces, and I cannot understand why such tortures have fallen to my lot. I also strive to suck the honey which once comforted me, but this honey no longer rejoices me, while the white mouse and the black, day and night, gnaw through the branch to which I cling. I see the dragon plainly, and the honey is no longer sweet. I see the dragon, from which there is no escape, and the mice, and I cannot turn my eyes away from them. It is no fable, but a living, undeniable truth, to be understood of all men.

The former delusion of happiness in life which hid from me the horror of the dragon no longer deceives me. However I may reason with myself that I cannot understand the meaning of life, that I must live without thinking, I cannot do this, because I have done so too long already. Now I cannot help seeing the days and nights hurrying by and bringing me nearer to death. I can see but this, because this alone is true—all the rest is a lie. The two drops of honey, which more than anything else drew my eyes away from the cruel truth, my love for my family and for my writings, to which later I gave the name of art, were no longer sweet to me.

"My family," I said to myself; "but a family—a wife and children—are also human beings, and subject to the same conditions as I myself; they must either be living in a lie, or they must see the terrible truth. Why should they live? Why should I love them, care for them, bring them up, and watch over them? To bring them to the despair which fills myself, or to make dolts of them? As I love them, I cannot conceal from them the truth—every step they take in knowledge leads them to it, and that truth is death."

"Art, poetry?" . . . .

Under the influence of success, and flattered by praise, I had long been persuading myself that this was a work which must be done notwithstanding the approach of death, which would destroy everything—my writings, and the memory of them; but I soon saw that this was only another delusion, I saw clearly that art is only the ornament and charm of life. Life having lost its charm for me, how could I make others see a charm in it? While I was not living my own life, but one that was external to me was bearing me away on its billows, while I believed that life had a meaning, though I could not say what it was, the reflections of life of every kind in poetry and art gave me delight, it was pleasant to me to look at life in the mirror of art; but when I tried to discover the meaning of life, when I felt the necessity of living myself, the mirror became either unnecessary, superfluous, and ridiculous, or painful. I could no longer take comfort from what I saw in the mirror—that my position was stupid and desperate.

It was a genuine cause of rejoicing when in the depths of my soul I believed that my life had a meaning. Then this play of lights, the comic, the tragic, the pathetic, the beautiful, and the terrible in life, amused me. But when I knew that life was meaningless and terrible, the play in the mirror could no longer entertain me. No sweetness could be sweet to me when I saw the dragon, and the mice nibbling away my support.

Nor was that all. Had I simply come to know that life has no meaning, I might have quietly accepted it, might have known that was my allotted portion. But I could not rest calmly on this. Had I been like a man living in a forest, out of which he knows that there is no issue, I could have lived on; but I was like a man lost in a forest, and who, terrified by the thought that he is lost, rushes about trying to find a way out, and though he knows each step leads him still further astray, cannot help rushing about.

It was this that was terrible! And to get free from this horror, I was ready to kill myself. I felt a horror of what awaited me; I knew that this horror was more horrible than the position itself, but I could not patiently await the end. However persuasive the argument might be that all the same a blood-vessel in the heart would be ruptured or something would burst and all be over, still I could not patiently await the end. The horror of the darkness was too great to bear, and I longed to free myself from it as speedily as possible by a rope or a pistol ball. This was the feeling that, above all, drew me to think of suicide.

NOTES

1. See "School Scenes from Yasnaya Polyana," Vol. XV.
2. *Posrednik,* sometimes translated Justice of the Peace.

DEATH

Thomas Nagel

"The syllogism he had learnt from Kiesewetter's logic: 'Caius is a man, men are mortal, therefore Caius is mortal,' had always seemed to him correct as

From NOUS, 4 no. 1 (1970), pp. 73-80. Reprinted by permission of publisher and author.

applied to Caius, but certainly not as applied to himself. . . . What did Caius know of the smell of that striped leather ball Vanya had been so fond of?"

Tolstoy, *The Death of Ivan Ilyich*

If, as many people believe, death is the unequivocal and permanent end of our existence, the question arises whether it is a bad thing to die. There is conspicuous disagreement about the matter: some people think death is dreadful; others have no objection to death *per se,* though they hope their own will be neither premature nor painful.

Those in the former category tend to think those in the latter are blind to the obvious, while the latter suppose the former to be prey to some sort of confusion. On the one hand it can be said that life is all one has, and the loss of it is the greatest loss one can sustain. On the other hand it may be objected that death deprives this supposed loss of its subject, and that if one realizes that death is not an unimaginable condition of the persisting person, but a mere blank, one will see that it can have no value whatever, positive or negative.

Since I want to leave aside the question whether we are, or might be, immortal in some form, I shall simply use the word "death" and its cognates in this discussion to mean *permanent* death, unsupplemented by any form of conscious survival. I wish to consider whether death is in itself an evil, and how great an evil, and of what kind, it might be. This question should be of interest even to those who believe that we do not die permanently, for one's attitude toward immortality must depend in part on one's attitude toward death.

Clearly if death is an evil at all, it cannot be because of its positive features, but only because of what it deprives us of. I shall try to deal with the difficulties surrounding the natural view that death is an evil because it brings to an end all the goods that life contains.[1] An account of these goods need not occupy us here, except to observe that some of them, like perception, desire, activity, and thought, are so general as to be constitutive of human life. They are widely regarded as formidable benefits in themselves, despite the fact that they are conditions of misery as well as of happiness, and that a sufficient quantity of more particular evils can perhaps outweigh them. That is what is meant, I think, by the allegation that it is good simply to be alive, even if one is undergoing terrible experiences. The situation is roughly this: There are elements which, if added to one's experience, make life better; there are other elements which, if added to one's experience, make life worse. But what remains when these are set aside is not merely *neutral*: it is emphatically positive. Therefore life is worth living even when the bad elements of experience are plentiful, and the good ones too meager to outweigh the bad ones on their own. The additional positive weight is supplied by experience itself, rather than by any of its contents.

I shall not discuss the value that one person's life or death may have for others, or its objective value, but only the value it has for the person who is its subject. That seems to me the primary case, and the case which presents the greatest difficulties. Let me add only two observations. First, the value of life and its contents does not attach to mere organic survival: almost everyone would be indifferent (other things equal) between immediate death and immediate coma followed by death twenty years later without reawakening. And second, like most goods, this can be multiplied by time: more is better than less. The added quantities need not be temporarily continuous (though continuity has its social advantages). People are attracted to the possibility of long-term suspended animation or freezing, followed by the resumption of conscious life, because they can regard it from within simply as a *continuation* of their present life. If these techniques are ever perfected, what from outside appeared as a dormant interval of three hundred years could be experienced by the subject as nothing more than a sharp discontinuity in the character of his experiences. I do not deny, of course, that this has its own disadvantages. Family and friends may have died in the meantime; the language may have changed; the comforts of social, geographical, and cultural familiarity would be lacking. Nevertheless these inconveniences would not obliterate the basic advantage of continued, though discontinuous, existence.

If we turn from what is good about life to what is bad about death, the case is completely different. Essentially, though there may be problems about their specification, what we find desirable in life are certain states, conditions, or types of activity. It is *being* alive, *doing* certain things, having certain experiences, that we consider good. But if death is an evil, it is the *loss of life,* rather than the state of being dead, or nonexistent, or unconscious, that is objectionable.[2] This asymmetry is important. If it is good to be alive, that advantage can be attributed to a person at each point of his life. It is a good of which Bach had more than Schubert, simply because he lived longer. Death, however, is not an evil of which Shakespeare has so far received a larger portion than Proust. If death is a disadvantage, it is not easy to say when a man suffers it.

There are two other indications that we do not object to death merely because it involves long periods of nonexistence. First, as has been mentioned, most of us would not regard the *temporary* suspension of life, even for substantial intervals, as in itself a misfortune. If it develops that people can be frozen without reduction of the conscious lifespan, it will be inappropriate to pity those who are temporarily out of circulation. Second, none of us existed before we were born (or conceived), but few regard that as a misfortune. I shall have more to say about this later.

The point that death is not regarded as an unfortunate state enables us to refute a curious but very common suggestion about the origin of the fear of death. It is often said that those who object to death have made the mistake of trying to imagine what it is like to *be* dead. It is alleged that the failure to realize that this task is logically impossible (for the banal reason that there is nothing to imagine) leads to the conviction that death is a mysterious and therefore terrifying prospective state. But this diagnosis is evidently false, for it is just as impossible to imagine being totally unconscious as to imagine being dead (though it is easy enough to imagine oneself, from the outside, in either of those conditions). Yet people who are averse to death are not usually averse to unconsciousness (so long as it does not entail a substantial cut in the total duration of waking life).

If we are to make sense of the view that to die is bad, it must be on the ground that life is a good and death is the corresponding deprivation or loss, bad not because of any positive features but because of the desirability of what it removes. We must now turn to the serious difficulties which this hypothesis raises, difficulties about loss and privation in general, and about death in particular.

Essentially, there are three types of problem. First, doubt may be raised whether *anything* can be bad for a man without being positively unpleasant to him: specifically, it may be doubted that there are any evils which consist merely in the deprivation or absence of possible goods, and which do not depend on someone's *minding* that deprivation. Second, there are special difficulties, in the case of death, about how the supposed misfortune is to be assigned to a subject at all. There is doubt both as to who its subject is, and as to *when* he undergoes it. So long as a person exists, he has not yet died, and once he has died, he no longer exists; so there seems to be no time when death, if it is a misfortune, can be ascribed to its unfortunate subject. The third type of difficulty concerns the asymmetry, mentioned above, between our attitudes to posthumous and prenatal nonexistence. How can the former be bad if the latter is not?

It should be recognized that if these are valid objections to counting death as an evil, they will apply to many other supposed evils as well. The first type of objection is expressed in general form by the common remark that what you don't know can't hurt you. It means that even if a man is betrayed by his friends, ridiculed behind his back, and despised by people who treat him politely to his face, none of it can be counted as a misfortune for him so long as he does not suffer as a result. It means that a man is not injured if his wishes are ignored by the executor of his will, or if, after his death, the belief becomes current that all the literary works on which his fame rests were really written by his brother, who died in Mexico at the age of 28. It seems to me worth asking what assumptions about good and evil lead to these drastic restrictions.

All the questions have something to do with time. There certainly are goods and evils of a simple kind (including some pleasures and pains) which a person possesses at a given time simply in virtue of his condition at that time. But this is not true of all the things we regard as good or bad for a man. Often we need to know his history to tell whether something is a misfortune or not; this applies to ills like deterioration, deprivation, and damage. Sometimes his experiential state is relatively unimportant—as in the case of a man who wastes his life in the cheerful pursuit of a method of communicating with asparagus plants. Someone who holds that all goods and evils must be temporarily assignable states of the person may of course try to bring difficult cases into line by pointing to the pleasure or pain that more complicated goods and evils cause. Loss, betrayal, deception, and ridicule are on this view bad because people suffer when they learn of them. But it should be asked how our ideas of human value would have to be constituted to accommodate these cases directly instead. One advantage of such an account might be that it would enable us to explain why the discovery of these misfortunes causes suffering—in a way that makes it reasonable. For the natural view is that the discovery of betrayal makes us unhappy because it is bad to be betrayed—not that betrayal is bad because its discovery makes us unhappy.

It therefore seems to me worth exploring the position that most good and ill fortune has as its subject a person identified by his history and his possibilities, rather than merely by his categorical state of the moment—and that while this subject can be exactly located in a sequence of places and times, the same is not necessarily true of the goods and ills that befall him.[3]

These ideas can be illustrated by an example of deprivation whose severity approaches that of death. Suppose an intelligent person receives a brain injury that reduces him to the mental condition of a contented infant, and that such desires as remain to him can be satisfied by a custodian, so that he is free from care. Such a development would be widely regarded as a severe misfortune, not only for his friends and relations, or for society, but also, and primarily, for the person himself. This does not mean that a contented infant is unfortunate. The intelligent adult who has been *reduced* to this condition is the subject of the misfortune. He is the one we pity, though of course he does not mind his condition—there is some doubt, in fact, whether he can be said to exist any longer.

The view that such a man has suffered a misfortune is open to the same objections which have been raised in regard to death. He does not mind his condition. It is in fact the same condition he was in at the age of three months, except that he is bigger. If we did not pity him then, why pity him now; in any case, who is there to pity? The intelligent adult has disappeared, and for a creature like the one before us, happiness consists in a full stomach and a dry diaper.

If these objections are invalid, it must be because they rest on a mistaken assumption about the temporal relation between the subject of a misfortune and the circumstances which constitute it. If, instead of concentrating exclusively on the oversized baby before us, we consider the person he was, and the person he *could* be now, then his reduction to this state and the cancellation of his natural adult development constitute a perfectly intelligible catastrophe.

This case should convince us that it is arbitrary to restrict the goods and evils that can befall a man to nonrelational properties ascribable to him at particular times. As it stands, that restriction excludes not only such cases of gross degeneration, but also a good deal of what is important about success and failure, and other features of a life that have the character of processes. I believe we can go further, however. There are goods and evils which are irreducibly relational; they are features of the relations between a person, with spatial and temporal boundaries of the usual sort, and circumstances which may not coincide with him either in space or in time. A man's life includes much that does not take place within the boundaries of his body and his mind, and what happens to him can include much that does not take place within the boundaries of his life. These boundaries are commonly crossed by the misfortunes of being deceived, or despised, or betrayed. (If this is correct, there is a simple account of what is wrong with breaking a deathbed promise. It is an injury to the dead man. For certain purposes it is possible to regard time as just another type of distance.) The case of mental degeneration shows us an evil that depends on a contrast between the reality and the possible alternatives. A man is the subject of good and evil as much because he has hopes which may or may not be fulfilled, or possibilities which may or may not be realized, as because of his capacity to suffer and enjoy. If death is an evil, it must be accounted for in these terms, and the impossibility of locating it within life should not trouble us.

When a man dies we are left with his corpse, and while a corpse can suffer the kind of mishap that may occur to an article of furniture, it is not a suitable object for pity. The man, however, is. He has lost his life, and if he had not died, he would have continued to live it, and to possess whatever good there is in living. If we apply to death the account suggested for the case of dementia, we shall say that although the spatial and temporal locations of the individual who suffered the loss are clear enough, the misfortune itself cannot be so easily located. One must be content just to state that his life is over and there will never be any more it. That *fact,* rather than his past or present condition, constitutes his misfortune, if it is one. Nevertheless if there is a loss, someone must suffer it, and *he* must have existence and specific spatial and temporal location even if the loss itself does not. The fact that Beethoven had no children may have been a cause of regret to him, or a sad thing for the world, but it cannot be described as a misfortune for the children that he never had. All of us, I believe, are fortunate to have been born. But unless good and ill can be assigned to an embryo, or even to an unconnected pair of gametes, it cannot be said that not to be born is a misfortune. (That is a factor to be considered in deciding whether abortion and contraception are akin to murder.)

This approach also provides a solution to the problem of temporal asymmetry, pointed out by Lucretius. He observed that no one finds it disturbing to contemplate the eternity preceding his own birth, and he took this to show that it must be irrational to fear death, since death is simply the mirror image of the prior abyss. That is not true, however, and the difference between the two explains why it is reasonable to regard them differently. It is true that both the time before a man's birth and time after his death are times when he does not exist. But the time after his death is time of which his death deprives him. It is time in which, had he not died then, he would be alive. Therefore any death entails the loss of some life that its victim would have led had he not died at that or any earlier point. We know perfectly well what it would be for him to have had it instead of losing it, and there is no difficulty in identifying the loser.

But we cannot say that the time prior to a man's birth is time in which he would have lived had he been born not then but earlier. For aside from the brief margin permitted by premature labor, he *could* not have been born earlier: anyone born substantially earlier than he was would have been someone else. Therefore the time prior to his birth is not time in which his subsequent birth prevents him from living. His birth, when it occurs, does not entail the loss to him of any life whatever.

The direction of time is crucial in assigning possibilities to people or other individuals. Distinct possible lives of a single person can diverge from a common beginning, but they cannot converge to a common conclusion from diverse beginnings. (The latter would represent not a set of different possible lives of one individual, but a set of distinct possible individuals, whose lives have identical conclusions.) Given an identifiable individual, countless possibilities for his continued existence are imaginable, and we can clearly conceive of what it would be for him to go on existing indefinitely. However inevitable it is that this will not come about, its possibility is still that of the continuation of a good for him, if life is the good we take it to be.[4]

We are left, therefore, with the question whether the nonrealization of this possibility is in every case a misfortune, or whether it depends on what can naturally be hoped for. This seems to me the most serious difficulty with the view that death is always an evil. Even if we can dispose of the objections against admitting misfortune that is not experienced, or cannot be assigned to a definite time in the person's life, we still have to set some limits on *how* possible a possibility must be for its nonrealization to be a misfortune (or good fortune, should the possibility be a bad one). The death of Keats at 24 is generally regarded as tragic; that of Tolstoy at 82 is not. Although they will both be dead forever, Keats's death deprived him of many years of life which were allowed to Tolstoy; so in a clear sense Keats's loss was greater (though not in the sense standardly employed in mathematical comparison between infinite quantities). However, this does not prove that Tolstoy's loss was insignificant. Perhaps we record an objection only to evils which are gratuitously added to the inevitable; the fact that it is worse to die at 24 than at 82 does not imply that it is not a terrible thing to die at 82, or even at 806. The question is whether we can regard as a misfortune any limitation, like mortality, that is normal to the species. Blindness or near-blindness is not a misfortune for a mole, nor would it be for a man, if that were the natural condition of the human race

The trouble is that life familiarizes us with the goods of which death deprives us. We are already able to appreciate them, as a mole is not able to appreciate vision. If we put aside doubts about their status as goods and grant that their quantity is in part a function of their duration, the question remains whether death, no matter when it occurs, can be said to deprive its victim of what is in the relevant sense a possible continuation of life.

The situation is an ambiguous one. Observed from without, human beings obviously have a natural lifespan and cannot live much longer than a hundred years. A man's sense of his own experience, on the other hand, does not embody this idea of a natural limit. His existence defines for him an essentially open-ended possible future, containing the usual mixture of goods and evils that he has found so tolerable in the past. Having been gratuitously introduced to the world by a collection of natural, historical, and social accidents, he finds himself the subject of a *life,* with an indeterminate and not essentially limited future. Viewed in this way, death, no matter how inevitable, is an abrupt cancellation of indefinitely extensive possible goods. Normality seems to have nothing to do with it, for the fact that we will all inevitably die in a few score years cannot by itself imply that it would not be good to live longer. Suppose that we were all inevitably going to die in *agony*—

physical agony lasting six months. Would inevitability make *that* prospect any less unpleasant? And why should it be different for a deprivation? If the normal lifespan were a thousand years, death at 80 would be a tragedy. As things are, it may just be a more widespread tragedy. If there is no limit to the amount of life that it would be good to have, then it may be that a bad end is in store for us all.

NOTES

1. As we shall see, this does not mean that it brings to an end all the goods that a man can possess.

2. It is sometimes suggested that what we really mind is the process of *dying*. But I should not really object to dying if it were not followed by death.

3. It is certainly not true in general of the things that can be said of him. For example, Abraham Lincoln was taller than Louis XIV. But when?

4. I confess to being troubled by the above argument, on the ground that it is too sophisticated to explain the simple difference between our attitudes to prenatal and post-humous nonexistence. For this reason I suspect that something essential is omitted from the account of the badness of death by an analysis which treats it as a deprivation of possibilities. My suspicion is supported by the following suggestion of Robert Nozick. We could imagine discovering that people developed from individual spores that had existed indefinitely far in advance of their birth. In this fantasy, birth never occurs naturally more than 100 years before the permanent end of the spore's existence. But then we discover a way to trigger the premature hatching of these spores, and people born who have thousands of years of active life before them. Given such a situation, it would be possible to imagine *oneself* having come into existence thousands of years previously. If we put aside the question whether this would really be the same person, even given the identity of the spore, then the consequence appears to be that a person's birth at a given time could deprive him of many earlier years of possible life. Now while it would be cause for regret that one had been deprived of all those possible years of life by being born too late, the feeling would differ from that which many people have about death. I conclude that something about the future prospect of permanent nothingness is not captured by the analysis in terms of denied possiblities. If so, then Lucretius's argument still awaits an answer.

THE AESTHETIC RESPONSE

THE ROTATION METHOD

Soren Kierkegaard

CHREMYLOS: You get too much at last of everything.
                       Of love,
       KARION: of bread,

From *Either/Or,* Vol. I, trans. David F. Swenson and Lillian Marvin Swenson (copyright 1944 © 1959 by Princeton Unviersity Press; Princeton Paperback, 1971), pp. 281-96. Reprinted by permission of Princeton University Press.

CHREMYLOS:	of music,	
KARION:		and of sweetmeats.
CHREMYLOS:	Of honor,	
KARION:	cakes,	
CHREMYLOS:	of courage,	
KARION:		and of figs.
CHREMYLOS:	Ambition,	
KARION:	barley-cakes,	
CHREMYLOS:	high office,	
KARION:	lentils.	

(Aristophanes' *Plutus*, v. 189ff.)

Starting from a principle is affirmed by people of experience to be a very reasonable procedure; I am willing to humor them, and so begin with the principle that all men are bores. Surely no one will prove himself so great a bore as to contradict me in this. This principle possesses the quality of being in the highest degree repellent, an essential requirement in the case of negative principles, which are in the last analysis the principles of all motion. It is not merely repellent, but infinitely forbidding; and whoever has this principle back of him cannot but receive an infinite impetus forward, to help him make new discoveries. For if my principle is true, one need only consider how ruinous boredom is for humanity, and by properly adjusting the intensity of one's concentration upon this fundamental truth, attain any desired degree of momentum. Should one wish to attain the maximum momentum, even to the point of almost endangering the driving power, one need only say to oneself: Boredom is the root of all evil. Strange that boredom, in itself so staid and stolid, should have such power to set in motion. The influence it exerts is altogether magical, except that it is not the influence of attraction, but of repulsion.

In the case of children, the ruinous character of boredom is universally acknowledged. Children are always well-behaved as long as they are enjoying themselves. This is true in the strictest sense; for if they sometimes become unruly in their play, it is because they are already beginning to be bored—boredom is already approaching, though from a different direction. In choosing a governess one, therefore, takes into account not only her sobriety, her faithfulness, and her competence, but also her aesthetic qualifications for amusing the children; and there would be no hesitancy in dismissing a governess who was lacking in this respect, even if she had all the other desirable virtues. Here, then, the principle is clearly acknowledged; but so strange is the way of the world, so pervasive the influence of habit and boredom, that this is practically the only case in which the science of aesthetics receives its just dues. If one were to ask for a divorce because his wife was tiresome, or demand the abdication of a king because he was boring to look at, or the banishment of a preacher because he was tiresome to listen to, or the dismissal of a prime minister, or the execution of a journalist, because he was terribly tiresome, one would find it impossible to force it through. What wonder, then, that the world goes from bad to worse, and that its evils increase more and more, as boredom increases, and boredom is the root of all evil.

The history of this can be traced from the very beginning of the world. The gods were bored, and so they created man. Adam was bored because he was alone, and so Eve was created. Thus boredom entered the world, and increased in proportion to the increase of population. Adam was bored alone; then Adam and Eve were bored together; then Adam and Eve and Cain and Abel were bored *en famille;* then the population of the world increased, and the people were bored *en masse.* To divert themselves they conceived the idea of constructing a tower high enough to reach the heavens. This idea is itself as boring as the tower was high, and constitutes a terrible proof of how boredom gained the upper hand. The nations were scattered over the earth, just as people now travel abroad, but they continued to be bored. Consider the consequences of this boredom. Humanity fell from its lofty height, first because of Eve, and then from the Tower of Babel. What was it, on the other hand, that delayed the all of Rome, was it not *panis* and *circenses*? And is anything being done now? Is anyone concerned about planning some means of diversion? Quite the contrary, the impending ruin is being accelerated. It is proposed to call a constitutional assembly. Can anything more tiresome be imagined, both for the participants themselves, and for those who have to hear and read about it? It is proposed to improve the financial condition of the state by practicing economy. What could be more tiresome? Intstead of increasing the national debt, it is proposed to pay it off. As I understand the political situation, it would be an easy matter for Denmark to negotiate a loan of fifteen million dollars. Why not consider this plan? Every once in a while we hear of a man who is a genius, and therefore neglects to pay his debts—why should not a nation do the same, if we were all agreed? Let us then borrow fifteen millions, and let us use the proceeds, not to pay our debts, but for public entertainment. Let us celebrate the millennium in a riot of merriment. Let us place boxes everywhere, not, as at present, for the deposit of money, but for the free distribution of money. Everything would become gratis; theaters gratis, women of easy virtue gratis, one would drive to the park gratis, be buried gratis, one's eulogy would be gratis; I say gratis, for when one always has money at hand, everything is in a certain sense free. No one should be permitted to own any property. Only in my own case would there be an exception. I reserve to myself securities in the Bank of London to the value of one hundred dollars a day, partly because I cannot do with less, partly because the idea is mine, and finally because I may not be able to hit upon a new idea when the fifteen millions are gone.

What would be the consequences of all this prosperity? Everything great would gravitate toward Copenhagen, the greatest artists, the greatest dancers, the greatest actors. Copenhagen would become a second Athens. What then? All rich men would establish their homes in this city. Among others would come the Shah of Persia, and the King of England would also come. Here is my second idea. Let us kidnap the Shah of Persia. Perhaps you say an insurrection might take place in Persia and a new ruler be placed on the throne, as has often happened before, the consequence being a fall in price for the old Shah. Very well then, I propose that we sell him to the Turks; they will doubtless know how to turn him into money. Then there is another circumstance which our politicians seem entirely to have overlooked. Denmark holds the balance of power in Europe. It is impossible to imagine a more fortunate lot. I know that from my own experience; I once held the balance of power in a family and could do as I pleased; the blame never fell on me, but always on the others. O that my words might reach your ears, all you who sit in high places to advise and rule, you king's men and men of the people, wise and understanding citizens of all classes! Consider the crisis! Old Denmark is on the brink of ruin; what a calamity! It will be destroyed by boredom. Of all calamities the most calamitous! In ancient times they made him king who extolled most beautifully the praises of the deceased king; in our times we ought to make him king who utters the best witticism, and make him crown prince who gives occasion for the utterance of the best witticism.

O beautiful, emotional sentimentality, how you carry me away! Should I trouble to speak to my contemporaries, to initiate them into my wisdom? By no means. My wisdom is not exactly *zum Gebrauch für Jedermann,*[1] and it is always more prudent to keep one's maxims of prudence to onself. I desire no disciples; but if there happened to be someone present at my deathbed, and I was sure that the end had come, then I might in an attack of philanthropic delirium, whisper my theory in his ear, uncertain whether I had done him a service or not. People talk so much about man being a social animal; at bottom, he is a beast of prey, and the evidence for this is not confined to the shape of his teeth. All this talk about society and the social is partly inherited hypocrisy, partly calculated cunning.

All men are bores. The world itself suggests the possibility of a subdivision. It may just as well indicate a man who bores others as one who bores himself. Those who bore others are the mob, the crowd, the infinite multitude of men in general. Those who bore themselves are the elect, the aristocracy; and it is a curious fact that those who do not bore themselves usually bore others, while those who bore themselves entertain others. Those who do not bore themselves are generally people who, in one way or another, keep themselves extremely busy; these people are precisely on this account the most tiresome, the most utterly unendurable. This species of animal life is surely not the fruit of man's desire and woman's lust. Like all lower forms of life, it is marked by a high degree of fertility, and multiplies endlessly. It is inconceivable that nature should require nine months to produce such beings; they ought rather to be turned out by the score. The second class, the aristocrats, are those who bore themselves. As noted above, they generally entertain others—in a certain external sense sometimes the mob, in a deeper sense only their fellow initiates. The more profoundly they bore themselves, the more powerfully do they serve to divert these latter, even when their boredom reaches its zenith, as when they either die of boredom (the passive form) or shoot themselves out of curiosity (the active form).

It is usual to say that idleness is a root of all evil. To prevent this evil one is advised to work. However, it is easy to see, both from the nature of the evil that is feared and the remedy proposed, that this entire view is of a very plebeian extraction. Idleness is by no means as such a root of evil; on the contrary, it is a truly divine life, provided one is not himself bored. Idleness may indeed cause the loss of one's fortune, and so on, but the high-minded man does not fear such dangers; he fears only boredom. The Olympian gods were not bored, they lived happily in happy idleness. A beautiful woman, who neither sews nor spins nor bakes nor reads nor plays the piano, is happy in her idleness, for she is not bored. So far from idleness being the root of all evil, it is rather the only true good. Boredom is the root of all evil, and it is this which must be kept at a distance. Idleness is not an evil; indeed one may say that every human being who lacks a sense for idleness proves that his consciousness has not yet been elevated to the level of the humane. There is a restless activity which excludes a man from the world of the spirit, setting him in a class with the brutes, whose instincts impel them always to be on the move. There are men who have an extraordinary talent for transforming everything into a matter of business, whose whole life is business, who fall in love, marry, listen to a joke, and admire a picture with the same industrious zeal with which they labor during business hours. The Latin proverb, *otium est pulvinar diaboli,*[2] is true enough, but the devil gets not time to lay his head on this pillow when one is not bored. But since some people believe that the end and aim of life is work, the disjunction, idleness-work, is quite correct. I assume that it is the end and aim of every man to enjoy himself, and hence my disjunction is no less correct.

Boredom is the daemonic side of pantheism. If we remain in boredom as such, it becomes the evil principle; if we annul it, we posit it in its truth; but we can only annul boredom by enjoying ourselves—*ergo,* it is our duty to enjoy ourselves. To say that boredom is annulled by work betrays a confusion of thought; for idleness can certainly be annulled by work, since it is its opposite, but not boredom, and experience shows that the busiest workers, whose constant buzzing most resembles an insect's hum, are the most tiresome of creatures; if they do not bore themselves, it is because they have no true conception of what boredom is; but then it can scarcely be said that they have overcome boredom.

Boredom is partly an inborn talent, partly an acquired immediacy. The English are in general the paradigmatic nation. A true talent for indolence is very rare; it is never met with in nature, but belongs to the world of the spirit. Occasionally, however, you meet a traveling Englishman who is, as it were, the incarnation of this talent—a heavy, immovable animal, whose entire language exhausts its riches in a single word of one syllable, an interjection by which he signifies his deepest admiration and his supreme indifference, admiration and indifference having been neutralized in the unity of boredom. No other nation produces such miracles of nature; every other national will always show himself a little more vivacious, not so absolutely still-born. The only analogy I know of is the apostle of the empty enthusiasm, who also makes his way through life on an interjection. This is the man who everywhere makes a profession of enthusiasm, who cries Ah! or Oh! whether the event be significant or insignificant, the difference having been lost for him in the emptiness of a blind and noisy enthuasism. The second form of boredom is usually the result of a mistaken effort to find diversion. The fact that the remedy against boredom may also serve to produce boredom, might appear to be a suspicious circumstance; but it has this effect only in so far as it is incorrectly employed. A misdirected search for diversion, one which is eccentric in its direction, conceals boredom within its own depths and gradually works it out toward the surface, thus revealing itself as that which it immediately is. In the case of horses, we distinguish between blind staggers and sleepy staggers, but call both staggers; and so we can also make a distinction between two kinds of boredom, though uniting both under the common designation of being tiresome.

Pantheism is, in general, characterized by fullness; in the case of boredom we find the precise opposite, since it is characterized by emptiness; but it is just this which makes boredom a pantheistic conception. Boredom depends on the nothingness which pervades reality; it causes a dizziness like that produced by looking down into a yawning chasm, and this dizziness is infinite. The eccentric form of diversion noted above sounds forth without producing an echo, which proves it to be based on boredom; for in nothingness not even an echo can be produced.

Now since boredom as shown above is the root of all evil, what can be more natural than the effort to overcome it? Here, as everywhere, however, it is necessary to give the problem calm consideration; otherwise one may find oneself driven by the daemonic spirit of boredom deeper and deeper into the mire in the very effort to escape. Everyone who feels bored cries out for change. With this demand I am in complete sympathy, but it is necessary to act in accordance with some settled principle.

My own dissent from the ordinary view is sufficiently expressed in the use I make of the word, "rotation." This word might seem to conceal an ambiguity, and if I wished to use it so as to find room in it for the ordinary method, I should have to define it as a change of field. But the farmer does not use the word in this sense. I shall, however, adopt this meaning for a moment, in order to speak of the rotation which depends on change in its boundless infinity, its extensive dimension, so to speak.

This is the vulgar and inartistic method, and needs to be supported by illusion. One tires of living in the country, and moves to the city; one tires of one's native land, and travels abroad; one is *europamüde*,[3] and goes to America, and so on; finally one indulges in a sentimental hope of endless journeyings from star to star. Or the movement is different but still extensive. One tires of porcelain dishes and eats on silver; one tires of silver and turns to gold; one burns half of Rome to get an idea of the burning of Troy. This method defeats itself; it is plain endlessness. And what did Nero gain by it? Antonine was wiser; he says: "It is in your power to review your life, to look at things you saw before, from another point of view."

My method does not consist in change of field, but resembles the true rotation method in changing the crop and the mode of cultivation. Here we have at once the principle of limitation, the only saving principle in the world. The more you limit yourself, the more fertile you become in invention. A prisoner in solitary confinement for life becomes very inventive, and a spider may furnish him with much entertainment. One need only hark back to one's schooldays. We were at an age when aesthetic considerations were ignored in the choice of one's instructors,

417 *The Rotation Method*

most of whom were for that reason very tiresome; how fertile in invention one then proved to be! How entertaining to catch a fly and hold it imprisoned under a nut shell and to watch how it pushed the shell around; what pleasure from cutting a hole in the desk, putting a fly in it, and then peeping down at it through a piece of paper! How entertaining sometimes to listen to the monotonous drip of water from the roof! How close an observer one becomes under such circumstances, when not the least noise nor movement escapes one's attention! Here we have the extreme application of the method which seeks to achieve results intensively, not extensively.

The more resourceful in changing the mode of cultivation one can be, the better; but every particular change will always come under the general categories of *remembering* and *forgetting*. Life in its entirety moves in these two currents, and hence it is essential to have them under control. It is impossible to live artistically before one has made up one's mind to abandon hope; for hope precludes self-limitation. It is a very beautiful sight to see a man put out to sea with the fair wind of hope, and one may even use the opportunity to be taken in tow; but one should never permit hope to be taken aboard one's own ship, least of all as a pilot; for hope is a faithless shipmaster. Hope was one of the dubious gifts of Prometheus; instead of giving men the foreknowledge of the immortals, he gave them hope.

To forget—all men wish to forget, and when something unpleasant happens, they always say: Oh, that one might forget! But forgetting is an art that must be practiced beforehand. The ability to forget is conditioned upon the method of remembering, but this again depends upon the mode of experiencing reality. Whoever plunges into his experiences with the momentum of hope will remember in such wise that he is unable to forget. *Nil admirari* is therefore the real philosophy.[4] No moment must be permitted so great a significance that it cannot be forgotten when convenient; each moment ought, however, to have so much significance that it can be recollected at will. Childhood, which is the age which remembers best, is at the same time the most forgetful. The more poetically one remembers, the more easily one forgets; for remembering poetically is really only another expression for forgetting. In a poetic memory the experience has undergone a transformation, by which it has lost all its painful aspects. To remember in this manner, one must be careful how one lives, how one enjoys. Enjoying an experience to its full intensity to the last minute will make it impossible either to remember or to forget. For there is then nothing to remember except a certain satiety, which one desires to forget, but which now comes back to plague the mind with an involuntary remembrance. Hence, when you begin to notice that a certain pleasure or experience is acquiring too strong a hold upon the mind, you stop a moment for the purpose of remembering. No other method can better create a distaste for continuing the experience too long. From the beginning one should keep the enjoyment under control, never spreading every sail to the wind in any resolve; one ought to devote oneself to pleasure with a certain suspicion, a certain wariness, if one desires to give the lie to the proverb which says that no one can have his cake and eat it too. The carrying of concealed weapons is usually forbidden, but no weapon is so dangerous as the art of remembering. It gives one a very peculiar feeling in the midst of one's enjoyment to look back upon it for the purpose of remembering it.

One who has perfected himself in the twin arts of remembering and forgetting is in a position to play at battledore and shuttlecock with the whole of existence.

The extent of one's power to forget is the final measure of one's elasticity of spirit. If a man cannot forget, he will never amount to much. Whether there be somewhere a Lethe gushing forth, I do not know; but this I know, that the art of forgetting can be developed. However, this art does not consist in permitting the impressions to vanish completely; forgetfulness is one thing, and the art of forgetting is something quite different. It is easy to see that most people have a very meager understanding of this art, for they ordinarily wish to forget only what is unpleasant, not what is pleasant. This betrays a complete one-sidedness. Forgetting is the true expression for an ideal process of assimilation by which the experience is reduced to a sounding-board for the soul's own music. Nature is great because it has forgotten that it was chaos; but this thought is subject to revival at any time. As a result of attempting to forget only what is unpleasant, most people have a conception of oblivion as an untamable force which drowns out the past. But forgetting is really a tranquil and quiet occupation, and one which should be exercised quite as much in connection with the pleasant as with the unpleasant. A pleasant experience has as past something unpleasant about it, by which it stirs a sense of privation; this unpleasantness is taken away by an act of forgetfulness. The unpleasant has a sting, as all admit. This, too, can be removed by the art of forgetting. But if one attempts to dismiss the unpleasant absolutely from mind, as many do who dabble in the art of forgetting, one soon learns how little that helps. In an unguarded moment it pays a surprise visit, and it is then invested with all the forcibleness of the unexpected. This is absolutely contrary to every orderly arrangement in a reasonable mind. No misfortune or difficulty is so devoid of affability, so deaf to all appeals, but that it may be flattered a little; even Cerberus accepted bribes of honey-cakes, and it is not only the lassies who are beguiled. The art in dealing with such experiences consists in talking them over, thereby depriving them of their bitterness; not forgetting them absolutely, but forgetting them for the sake of remembering them. Even in the case of memories such that one might suppose an eternal oblivion to be the only safeguard, one need permit oneself only a little trickery, and the deception will succeed for the skillful. Forgetting is the shears with which you cut away what you cannot use, doing it under the supreme direction of memory. Forgetting and remembering are thus identical arts, and the artistic achievement of this identity is the Archimedean point from which one lifts the whole world. When we say that we *consign* something to oblivion, we suggest simultaneously that it is to be forgotten and yet also remembered.

The art of remembering and forgetting will also ensure against sticking fast in some relationship of life, and make possible the realization of a complete freedom.

One must guard against *friendship*. How is a friend defined? He is not what philosophy calls the necessary other, but the superfluous third. What are friendship's ceremonies? You drink each other's health, you open an artery and mingle your blood with that of the friend. It is difficult to say when the proper moment for this arrives, but it announces itself mysteriously; you feel some way that you can no longer address one another formally. When once you have had this feeling, then it can never appear that you have made a mistake, like Geert Vestphaler, who discovered that he had been drinking to friendship with the public hangman. What are the infallible marks of friendship? Let antiquity answer: *idem velle, idem nolle, ea demum firma amicitia,*[5] and also extremely tiresome. What are the infallible marks of friendship? Mutual assistance in word and deed. Two friends form a close association in order to be everything to one another, and that although it is impossible for one human being to be anything to another human being except to be in his way. To be sure one may help him with money, assist him in and out of his coat, be his humble servant, and tender him congratulations on New Year's Day, on the day of his wedding, on the birth of a child, on the occasion of a funeral.

But because you abstain from friendshp it does not follow that you abstain from social contacts. On the contrary, these social relationships may at times be permitted to take on a deeper character, provided you always have so much more momentum in yourself that you can sheer off at will, in spite of sharing for a time in the momentum of the common movement. It is believed that such conduct leaves unpleasant memories, the unpleasantness being due to the fact that a relationship which has meant something now vanishes and becomes as nothing. But this is a misunderstanding. The unpleasant is merely a piquant ingredient in the sullenness of life. Besides, it is possible for the same relationship again to play a significant role, though in another manner. The essential thing is never to stick fast, and for this it is necessary to have oblivion back of one. The experienced farmer lets his land lie fallow now and then, and the theory of social prudence recommends the same. Everything will doubtless return, though in a different form; that which has once been present in the rotation will remain in it, but the mode of cultivation will be varied. You therefore quite consciously hope to meet your friends and acquaintances in a better world, but you do not share the fear of the crowd that they will be altered so that you cannot recognize them; your fear is rather lest they be wholly unaltered. It is remarkable how much significance even the most insignificant person can gain from a rational mode of cultivation.

One must never enter into the relation of *marriage.* Husband and wife promise to love one another for eternity. This is all very fine, but it does not mean very much; for if their love comes to an end in time, it will surely be ended in eternity. If, instead of promising forever, the parties would say: until Easter, or until May-day comes, there might be some meaning in what they say; for then they would have said something definite, and also something that they might be able to keep. And how does a marriage usually work out? In a little while one party begins to perceive that there is something wrong, then the other party complains, and cries to heaven: faithless! faithless! A little later the second party reaches the same standpoint, and a neutrality is established in which the mutual faithlessness is mutually canceled, to the satisfaction and contentment of both parties. But it is now too late, for there are great difficulties connected with divorce.

Such being the case with marriage, it is not surprising that the attempt should be made in so many ways to bolster it up with moral supports. When a man seeks separation from his wife, the cry is at once raised that he is depraved, a scoundrel, etc. How silly, and what an indirect attack upon marriage! If marriage has reality, then he is sufficiently punished by forfeiting this happiness; if it has no reality, it is absurd to abuse him because he is wiser than the rest. When a man grows tired of his money and throws it out of the window, we do not call him a scoundrel; for either money has reality, and so he is sufficiently punished by depriving himself of it, or it has none, and then he is, of course, a wise man.

One must always take care not to enter into any relationship in which there is a possibility of many members. For this reason friendship is dangerous, to say nothing of marriage. Husband and wife are indeed said to become one, but this is a very dark and mystic saying. When you are one of several, then you have lost your freedom; you cannot send for your traveling boots whenever you wish, you cannot move aimlessly about in the world. If you have a wife it is difficult; if you have a wife and perhaps a child, it is troublesome; if you have a wife and children, it is impossible. True, it has happened that a gypsy woman has carried her husband through life on her back, but for one thing this is very rare, and for another, it is likely to be tiresome in the long run—for the husband. Marriage brings one into fatal connection with custom and tradition, and tradition and customs are like the wind and weather, altogether incalculable. In Japan, I have been told, it is the custom for husbands to lie in childbed. Who knows but the time will come when the customs of foreign countries will obtain a foothold in Europe?

Friendship is dangerous, marriage still more so; for woman is and ever will be the ruin of a man, as soon as he contracts a permanent relation with her. Take a young man who is fiery as an Arabian courser, let him marry, he is lost. Woman is first proud, then is she weak, then she swoons, then he swoons, then the whole family swoons. A woman's love is nothing but dissimulation and weakness.

But because a man does not marry, it does not follow that his life need be wholly deprived of the erotic element. And the erotic ought also to have infinitude; but poetic infinitude, which can just as well be limited to an hour as to a month. When two beings fall in love with one another and begin to suspect that they were made for each other, it is time to have the courage to break it off; for by going on they have everything to lose and nothing to gain. This seems a paradox, and it is so for the feeling, but not for the understanding. In this sphere it is particularly necessary that one should make use of one's moods; through them one may realize an inexhaustible variety of combinations.

One should never accept appointment to an official position. If you do, you will become a mere Richard Roe, a tiny little cog in the machinery of the body politic; you even cease to be master of your own conduct, and in that case your theories are of little help. You receive a title, and this brings in its train every sin and evil. The law under which you have become a slave is equally tiresome, whether your advancement is fast or slow. A title can never be got rid of except by the commission of some crime which draws down on you a public whipping; even then you are not certain, for you may have it restored to you by royal pardon.

Even if one abstains from involvement in official business, one ought not to be inactive, but should pursue such occupations as are compatible with a sort of leisure; one should engage in all sorts of breadless arts. In this connection the self-development should be intensive rather than extensive, and one should, in spite of mature years, be able to prove the truth of the proverb that children are pleased with a rattle and tickled with a straw.

If one now, according to the theory of social jurisprudence, varies the soil—for if he had contact with one person only, the rotation method would fail as badly as if a farmer had only one acre of land, which would make it impossible for him to fallow, something which is of extreme importance—then one must also constantly vary himself, and this is the essential secret. For this purpose one must necesarily have control over one's moods. To control them in the sense of producing them at will is impossible, but prudence teaches how to utilize the moment. As an experienced sailor always looks out over the water and sees a squall coming from far away, so one ought always to see the mood a little in advance. One should know how the mood affects one's own mind and the mind of others, before putting it on. You first strike a note or two to evoke pure tones, and see what there is in a man; the intermediate tones follow later. The more experience you have, the more readily you will be convinced that there is often much in a man which is not suspected. When sentimental people, who as such are extremely tiresome, become angry, they are often very entertaining. Badgering a man is a particular effective method of exploration.

The whole secret lies in arbitrariness. People usually think it easy to be arbitrary, but it requires much study to succeed in being arbitrary so as not to lose oneself in it, but so as to derive satisfaction from it. One does not enjoy the immediate but something quite different which he arbitrarily imports into it. You go to see the middle of a play, you read the third part of a book. By this means you ensure yourself a very different kind of enjoyment from that which the author has been so kind as to plan for you. You enjoy something entirely accidental; you consider the whole of existence from this standpoint; let its reality be stranded thereon. I will cite an example. There was a man whose chatter certain circumstances made it necessary for me to listen to. At every opportunity he was ready with a little philosophical lecture, a very tiresome harangue. Almost in despair, I suddenly discovered that he perspired copiously when talking. I saw the pearls of sweat gather on his brow, unite to form a stream, glide down his nose, and hang at the extreme point of his nose in a drop-shaped body. From the moment of making this discovery, all was changed. I even took pleasure in inciting him to begin his philosophical instruction, merely to observe the perspiration on his brow and at the end of his nose.

The poet Baggesen says somewhere of someone that he was doubtless a good man, but that there was one insuperable objection against him, that there was no word that rhymed with his name. It is extremely wholesome thus to let the realities of life split upon an arbitrary interest. You transform something accidental into the absolute, and, as such, into the object of your admiration. This has an excellent effect, especially when one is excited. This method is an excellent stimulus for many persons. You look at everything in life from the standpoint of a wager, and so forth. The more rigidly consistent you are in holding fast to your arbitrariness, the more amusing the ensuing combinations will be. The degree of consistency shows whether you are an artist or a bungler; for to a certain extent all men do the same. The eye with which you look at reality must constantly be changed. The Neo-Platonists assumed that human beings who had been less perfect on earth became after death more or less perfect animals, all according to their deserts. For example, those who had exercised the civic virtues on a lower scale (retail dealers) were transformed into busy animals, like bees. Such a view of life, which here in this world sees all men transformed into animals or plants (Plotinus also thought that some would become plants), suggests rich and varied possibilities. The painter Tischbein sought to idealize every human being into an animal. His method has the fault of being too serious, in that it endeavors to discover a real resemblance.

The arbitrariness in oneself corresponds to the accidental in the external world. One should therefore always have an eye open for the accidental, always be *expeditus*,[6] if anything should offer. The so-called social pleasures for which we prepare a week or two in advance amount to so little; on the other hand, even the most insignificant thing may accidentally offer rich material for amusement. It is impossible here to go into detail, for no theory can adequately embrace the concrete. Even the most completely developed theory is poverty-stricken compared with the fullness which the man of genius easily discovers in his ubiquity.

NOTES

1. For use of everyone.
2. Idleness is the Devil's pillow.
3. Tired of Europe.
4. To wonder at nothing.
5. To want the same thing and not to want the same thing, this finally is a firm friendship.
6. Ready to go.

THE CHRISTIAN RESPONSE

THE CHRISTIAN VIEW
OF DEATH

John Calvin

But, most strange to say, many who boast of being Christians, instead of thus longing for death, are so afraid of it that they tremble at the very mention of it as a thing ominous and dreadful. We cannot wonder, indeed, that our natural feelings

From *The Institute of the Christian Religion,* (London: James Clarke and Co., Ltd., 1957). Reprinted by permission of the publisher.

should be somewhat shocked at the mention of our dissolution. But it is altogether intolerable that the light of piety should not be so powerful in a Christian breast as with greater consolation to overcome and suppress that fear. For if we reflect that this our tabernacle, unstable, defective, corruptible, fading, pining, and putrid, is dissolved, in order that it may forthwith be renewed in sure, perfect, incorruptible, in fine, in heavenly glory, will not faith compel us eagerly to desire what nature dreads? If we reflect that by death we are recalled from exile to inhabit our native country, a heavenly country, shall this give us no comfort? But everything longs for permanent existence. I admit this, and therefore contend that we ought to look to future immortality, where we may obtain that fixed condition which nowhere appears on the earth. For Paul admirably enjoins believers to hasten cheerfully to death, not because they "would be unclothed, but clothed upon" (2 Cor. v. 2). Shall the lower animals, and inanimate creatures themselves, even wood and stone, as conscious of their present vanity, long for the final resurrection, that they may with the sons of God be delivered from vanity (Rom. viii, 19); and shall we, endued with the light of intellect, and more than intellect, enlightened by the Spirit of God, when our essence is in question, rise no higher than the corruption of this earth? But it is not my purpose, nor is this the place, to plead against this great perverseness. At the outset, I declared that I had no wish to engage in a diffuse discussion of common-places. My advice to those whose minds are thus timid is to read the short treatise of Cyprian, De Mortalitate, unless it be more accordant with their deserts to send them to the philosophers, that by inspecting what they say on the contempt of death, they may begin to blush. This, however, let us hold as fixed, that no man has made much progress in the school of Christ who does not look forward with joy to the day of death and final resurrection (2 Tim. iv. 18; Tit. ii. 13); for Paul distinguishes all believers by this mark; and the usual course of Scripture is to direct us thither whenever it would furnish us with an argument for substantial joy. "Look up," says our Lord, "and lift up your heads: for your redemption draweth nigh" (Luke xxi. 28). Is it reasonable, I ask, that what he intended to have a powerful effect in stirring us up to alacrity and exultation should produce nothing but sadness and consternation? If it is so, why do we still glory in him as our Master? Therefore, let us come to a sounder mind, and how repugnant so ever the blind and stupid longing of the flesh may be, let us doubt not to desire the advent of the Lord not in wish only, but with earnest sighs, as the most propitious of all events. He will come as a Redeemer to deliver us from an immense abyss of evil and misery, and lead us to the blessed inheritance of his life and glory.

Thus, indeed, it is; the whole body of the faithful, so long as they live on the earth, must be like sheep for the slaughter, in order that they may be conformed to Christ their head (Rom. viii. 36). Most deplorable, therefore, would their situation be did they not, by raising their mind to heaven, become superior to all that is in the world, and rise above the present aspect of affairs (1 Cor. xv. 19). On the other hand, when once they have raised their head above all earthly objects, though they see the wicked flourishing in wealth and honour, and enjoying profound peace, indulging in luxury and splendour, and revelling in all kinds of delights, though they should moreover be wickedly assailed by them, suffer insult from their pride, be robbed by their avarice or assailed by any other passion, they will have no difficulty in bearing up under these evils. They will turn their eye to that day (Isaiah xxv. 8: Rev. vii. 17) on which the Lord will receive his faithful servants, wipe away all tears from their eyes, clothe them in a robe of glory and joy, feed them with the ineffable sweetness of his pleasures, exalt them to share with him in his greatness; in fine, admit them to a participation in his happiness. But the wicked who may have flourished on the earth, he will cast forth in extreme ignomiy, will change their delights into torments, their laughter and joy into wailing and gnashing of teeth, their peace into the gnawing of conscience, and punish their luxury with unquenchable fire. He will also place their necks under the feet of the godly, whose patience they abused. For, as Paul declares, "it is a righteous thing with God to recompense tribulation to them that trouble you; and to you who are troubled rest with us, when the Lord Jesus shall be revealed from heaven" (2 Thess. i. 6, 7). This, indeed, is our consolation; deprived of it, we must either give way to despondency, or resort to our destruction to the vain solace of the world. The Psalmist confesses, "My feet were almost gone, by steps had well nigh slipt: for I was envious at the foolish when I saw the prosperity of the wicked" (Psalm lxxiii. 3, 4); and he found no resting-place until he entered the sanctuary, and considered the latter end of the righteous and the wicked. To conclude in one word, the cross of Christ then only triumphs in the breasts of believers over the devil and the flesh, sin and sinners, when their eyes are directed to the power of his resurrection.

Chapter XXV: Of the Last Resurrection

1. Although Christ, the Sun of righteousness, shining upon us through the gospel, hath, as Paul declares, after conquering death, given us the light of life; and hence on believing we are said to have passed from "death unto life," being no longer strangers and pilgrims, but fellow-citizens with the saints, and of the household of God, who has made us sit with his only begotten Son in heavenly places, so that nothing is wanting to our complete felicity; yet, lest we should feel it grievous to be exercised under a hard warfare, as if the victory obtained by Christ has produced no fruit, we must attend to what is elsewhere taught concerning the nature of hope. For since we hope for what we see not, and faith, as is said in another passage, is "the evidence of things not seen," so long as we are imprisoned in the body we are absent from the Lord. For which reason Paul says, "Ye are dead, and your life is hid with Christ in God. When Christ, who is our life, shall appear, then shall ye also appear with him in glory." Our present condition, therefore, requires us to "live soberly, righteously, and godly;" ' looking for that blessed hope. and the glorious appearing of the great God and our Saviour Jesus Christ." Here there is no need of no ordinary patience, lest, worn out with fatigue, we either turn backwards or abandon our post. Wherefore, all that has hitherto been said of our salvation calls upon us to raise our minds towards heaven, that, as Peter exhorts, though we now see not Christ, "yet believing," we may "rejoice with joy unspeakable and full of glory," receiving the end of our faith, even the salvation of our

souls.[1] For this reason Paul says, that the faith and charity of the saints have respect to the faith and hope which is laid up for them in heaven (Col. i. 5). When we thus keep our eyes fixed upon Christ in heaven, and nothing on earth prevents us from directing them to the promised blessedness, there is a true fulfilment of the saying, "where your treasure is, there will your heart be also" (Matth. vi. 21). Hence the reason why faith is so rare in the world; nothing being more difficult for our sluggishness than to surmount innumerable obstacles in striving for the prize of our high calling. To the immense load of miseries which almost overwhelm us, are added the jeers of profane men, who assail us for our simplicity, when spontaneously renouncing the allurements of the present life we seem, in seeking a happiness which lies hid from us, to catch at a fleeting shadow. In short, we are beset above and below, behind and before, with violent temptations, which our minds would be altogether unable to withstand, were they not set free from earthly objects, and devoted to the heavenly life, though apparently remote from us. Wherefore, he alone has made solid progress in the gospel who has acquired the habit of meditating continually on a blessed resurrection.

2.   In ancient times philosophers discoursed, and even debated with each other, concerning the chief good: none however, except Plato, acknowledged that it consisted in union with God. He could not, however, form even an imperfect idea of its true nature; nor is this strange, as he had learned nothing of the sacred bond of that union. We even in this our earthly pilgrimage know wherein our perfect and only felicity consists,—a felicity which, while we long for it, daily inflames our hearts more and more, until we attain to full fruition. Therefore I said, that none participate in the benefits of Christ save those who raise their minds to the resurrection. This, accordingly, is the mark which Paul sets before believers, and at which he says they are to aim, forgetting everything until they reach it (Phil. iii. 8). The more strenuously, therefore, must we contend for it, lest if the world engross us we be severely punished for our sloth.[2] Accordingly, he in another passage distinguishes believers by this mark, that their conversation is in heaven, from whence they look for the Saviour (Phil. iii. 20). And that they may not faint in their course, he associates all the other creatures with them. As shapeless ruins are everywhere seen, he says, that all things in heaven and earth struggle for renovation. For since Adam by his fall destroyed the proper order of nature, the creatures groan under the servitude to which they have been subjected through his sin; not that they are at all endued with sense, but that they naturally long for the state of perfection from which they have fallen. Paul therefore describes them as groaning and travailing in pain (Rom. viii. 19); so that we who have received the first-fruits of the Spirit may be ashamed to grovel in our corruption, instead of at least imitating the inanimate elements which are bearing the punishment of another's sin. And in order that he may stimulate us the more powerfully, he terms the final advent of Christ *our redemption*. It is true, indeed, that all the parts of our redemption are already accomplished; but as Christ was once offered for sins (Heb. ix. 28), so he shall again appear without sin unto salvation. Whatever, then, be the afflictions by which we are pressed, let this redemption sustain us until its final accomplishment.

3. The very importance of the subject ought to increase our ardour. Paul justly contends, that if Christ rise not the whole gospel is delusive and vain (1 Cor. xv. 13-17); for our condition would be more miserable than that of other mortals, because we are exposed to much hatred and insult, and incur danger every hour; nay, are like sheep destined for slaughter; and hence the authority of the gospel would fail, not in one part merely, but in its very essence, including both our adoption and the accomplishment of our salvation. Let us, therefore, give heed to a matter of all others the most serious, so that no length of time may produce weariness. I have deferred the brief consideration to be given of it to this place, that my readers may learn, when they have received Christ, the author of perfect salvation, to rise higher, and know that he is clothed with heavenly immortality and glory, in order that the whole body may be rendered conformable to the Head. For thus the Holy Spirit is ever setting before us in his person an example of the resurrection. It is difficult to believe that after our bodies have been consumed with rottenness, they will rise again at their appointed time. And hence, while many of the philosophers maintained the immortality of the soul, few of them assented to the resurrection of the body. Although in this they were inexcusable, we are thereby reminded that the subject is too difficult for human apprehension to reach it. To enable faith to surmount the great difficulty, Scripture furnishes two auxiliary proofs, the one the likeness of Christ's resurrection, and the other the omnipotence of God. Therefore, whenever the subject of the resurrection is considered, let us think of the case of our Saviour, who, having completed his mortal course in our nature which he had assumed, obtained immortality, and is now the pledge of our future resurrection. For in the miseries by which we are beset, we always bear "about in the body the dying of the Lord Jesus, that the life also of Jesus might be made manifest in our mortal flesh" (2 Cor. iv. 10). It is not lawful, it is not even possible, to separate him from us, without dividing him. Hence Paul's argument, "If there be no resurrection of the dead, then is Christ not risen" (1 Cor. xv. 13); for he assumes it as an acknowledged principle, that when Christ was subjected to death, and by rising gained a victory over death, it was not on his own account, but in the Head was begun what must necessarily be fulfilled in all the members, according to the degree and order of each. For it would not be proper to be made equal to him in all respects. It is said in the psalm, "Neither wilt thou suffer thine Holy One to see corruption" (Ps. xvi. 10). Although a portion of this confidence appertain to us according to the measure bestowed on us, yet the full effect appeared only in Christ, who, free from all corruption, resumed a spotless body. Then, that there may be no doubt as to our fellowship with Christ in a blessed resurrection, and that we may be contented with this pledge, Paul distinctly affirms that he sits in the heavens, and will come as a judge on the last day for the express purpose of changing our vile body, "that it may be fashioned like unto his glorious body" (Phil. iii. 21). For he elsewhere says that God did not raise up his Son from death to give an isolated specimen of his mighty power, but that the Spirit exerts the same efficacy in regard to them that believe; and accordingly he says, that the Spirit when he dwells in us is life, because the end for which he was given is to quicken our mortal

body (Rom. viii. 10, 11; Col. iii. 4). I briefly glance at subjects which might be treated more copiously, and deserve to be adorned more splendidly, and yet in the little I have said I trust pious readers will find sufficient materials for building up their faith. Christ rose again, that he might have us as partakers with him of future life. He was raised up by the Father, inasmuch as he was the Head of the Church, from which he cannot possibly be dissevered. He was raised up by the power of the Spirit, who also in us performs the office of quickening. In fine, he was raised up to be the resurrection and the life. But as we have said, that in this mirror we behold a living image of the resurrection, so it furnishes a sure evidence to support our minds, provided we faint not, nor grow weary at the long delay, because it is not ours to measure the periods of time at our own pleasure; but to rest patiently till God in his own time renew his kingdom. To this Paul refers when he says, "But every man in his own order: Christ the first-fruits; afterward they that are Christ's at his coming" (1 Cor. xv. 23).

But lest any question should be raised as to the resurrection of Christ on which ours is founded, we see how often and in what various ways he has borne testimony to it. Scoffing men will deride the narrative which is given by the Evangelist as a childish fable. For what importance will they attach to a message which timid women bring, and the disciples, almost dead with fear, afterwards confirm? Why does not Christ rather place the illustrious trophies of his victory in the midst of the temple and the forum? Why does he not come forth, and in the presence of Pilate strike terror? Why does he not show himself alive again to the priests and all Jerusalem? Profane men will scarcely admit that the witnesses whom he selects are well qualified. I answer, that though at the commencement their infirmity was contemptible, yet the whole was directed by the admirable providence of God, so that partly from love to Christ and religious zeal, partly from incredulity, those who were lately overcome with fear now hurry to the sepulchre, not only that they might be eyewitnesses of the fact, but that they might hear angels announce what they actually saw. How can we question the veracity of those who regarded what the women told them as a fable, until they saw the reality? It is not strange that the whole people and also the governor, after they were furnished with sufficient evidence for conviction, were not allowed to see Christ or the other signs (Matth. xxvii. 66; xxviii. 11). The sepulchre is sealed, sentinels keep watch, on the third day the body is not found. The soldiers are bribed to spread the report that his disciples had stolen the body. As if they had had the means of deforcing a band of soldiers, or been supplied with weapons, or been trained so as to make such a daring attempt. But if the soldiers had not courage enough to repel them, why did they not follow and apprehend some of them by the aid of the populace? Pilate, therefore, in fact, put his signet to the resurrection of Christ, and the guards who were placed at the sepulchre by their silence or falsehood also became heralds of his resurrection. Meanwhile, the voice of angels was heard, "He is not here, but is risen" (Luke xxiv. 6). The celestial splendour plainly shows that they were not men but angels. Afterwards, if any doubt still remained, Christ himself removed it. The disciples saw him frequently; they even touched his hands and his feet, and their unbelief is of no little avail in confirming our faith. He discoursed to them of the mysteries of the kingdom of God, and at length, while they beheld, ascended to heaven. This spectacle was exhibited not to eleven apostles only, but was seen by more than five hundred brethren at once (1 Cor. xv. 6). Then by sending the Holy Spirit he gave a proof not only of life but also of supreme power, as he had fore- told, "It is expedient for you that I go away: for if I go not away, the Comforter will not come unto you" (John xvi. 7). Paul was not thrown down on the way by the power of a dead man, but felt that he whom he was opposing was possessed of sovereign authority. To Stephen he appeared for another purpose—viz. that the might overcome the fear of death by the certainty of life. To refuse assent to these numerous and authentic proofs is not diffidence, but depraved and therefore infatuated obstinacy.

But a more difficult question here arises. How can the resurrection, which is a special benefit of Christ, be common to the ungodly, who are lying under the curse of God? We know that in Adam all died. Christ has come to be the resurrection and the life (John xi. 25). Is it to revive the whole human race indiscriminately? But what more incongruous than that the ungodly in their obstinate blindness should obtain what the pious worshippers of God receive by faith only? It is certain, there- fore, that there will be one resurrection to judgment, and another to life, and that Christ will come to separate the kids from the goats (Matth. xxv. 32). I observe, that this ought not to seem very strange, seeing something resembling it occurs every day. We know that in Adam we were deprived of the inheritance of the whole world, and that the same reason which excludes us from eating of the tree of life, excludes us also from common food. How comes it, then, that God not only makes his sun to rise on the evil and on the good, but that, in regard to the uses of the present life, his inestimable liberality is constantly flowing forth in rich abundance? Hence we certainly perceive, that things which are proper to Christ and his members, abound to the wicked also: not that their possession is legitimate, but that they may thus be rendered more inexcusable. Thus the wicked often experi- ence the beneficence of God, not in ordinary measures, but such as sometimes throw all the blessings of the godly into the shade, though they eventually lead to greater damnation. Should it be objected, that the resurrection is not properly compared to fading and earthly blessings, I again answer, that when the devils were first alienated from God, the fountain of life, they deserved to be utterly destroyed; yet, by the admirable counsel of God, an intermediate state was prepared, where without life they might live in death. It ought not to seem in any respect more absurd that there is to be an adventitious resurrection of the ungodly which will drag them against their will before the tribunal of Christ, whom they now refuse to receive as their master and teacher. To be consumed by death would be a light punishment were they not, in order to the punishment of their rebellion, to be sisted before the Judge whom they have provoked to a vengeance without measure and without end. But although we are to hold, as already observed, and as is con- tained in the celebrated confession of Paul to Felix, "That there shall be a resurrec- tion of the dead, both of the just and unjust" (Acts xxiv. 15); yet Scripture more frequently sets forth the resurrection as intended, along with celestial glory, for the children of God only: because, properly speaking, Christ comes not for the destruction, but for the salvation of the world; and, therefore, in the Creed the life of blessedness only is mentioned.

10. But since the prophecy, that death shall be swallowed up in victory (Hosea xiii. 14), will then only be completed, let us always remember that the end of the resurrection is eternal happiness, of whose excellence scarcely the minutest part can be described by all that human tongues can say. For though we are truly told that the kingdom of God will be full of light, and gladness, and felicity, and glory, yet the things meant by these words remain most remote from sense, and as it were involved in enigma, until the day arrive on which he will manifest his glory to us face to face (1 Cor. xv. 54). "Now," says John, "are we the sons of God; and it doth not yet appear what we shall be: but we know that, when he shall appear, we shall be like him; for we shall see him as he is" (1 John iii. 2). Hence, as the prophets were unable to give a verbal description of that spiritual blessedness, they usually delineated it by corporeal objects. On the other hand, because the fervour of desire must be kindled in us by some taste of its sweetness, let us specially dwell upon this thought, If God contains in himself as an inexhaustible fountain all fulness of blessing, those who aspire to the supreme good and perfect happiness must not long for anything beyond him. This we are taught in several passages, "Fear not, Abraham; I am thy shield, and thy exceeding great reward" (Gen. xv. 1). With this accords David's sentiment, "The Lord is the portion of mine inheritance, and of my cup; thou maintainest my lot. The lines are fallen unto me in pleasant places" (Ps. xvi. 5, 6). Again, "I shall be satisfied when I awake with thy likeness" (Ps. xvii. 15). Peter declares that the purpose for which believers are called is, that they may be "partakers of the divine nature" (2 Pet. i. 4). How so? Because "he shall come to be glorified in his saints, and to be admired in all them that believe" (2 Thess. i. 10). If our Lord will share his glory, power, and righteousness with the elect, nay, will give himself to be enjoyed by them; and what is better still, will, in a manner, become one with them, let us remember that every kind of happiness is herein included. But when we have made great progress in thus meditating, let us understand that if the conceptions of our minds be contrasted with the sublimity of the mystery, we are still halting at the very entrance.[3] The more necessary is it for us to cultivate sobriety in this matter, lest, unmindful of our feeble capacity, we presume to take too lofty a flight, and be overwhelmed by the brightness of the celestial glory. We feel how much we are stimulated by an excessive desire of knowing more than is given us to know, and hence frivolous and noxious questions are ever and anon springing forth: by frivolous, I mean questions from which no advantage can be extracted. But there is a second class which is worse than frivolous; because those who indulge in them involve themselves in hurtful speculations. Hence I call them noxious. The doctrine of Scripture on the subject ought not to be made the ground of any controversy, and it is that as God, in the varied distribution of gifts to his saints in this world, gives them unequal degrees of light, so when he

shall crown his gifts, their degrees of glory in heaven will also be unequal. When Paul says, "Ye are our glory and our joy" (2 Thess. ii. 19), his words do not apply indiscriminately to all; nor do those of our Saviour to his apostles, "Ye also shall sit on twelve thrones judging the twelve tribes of Israel" (Matth. xix. 28). But Paul, who knew that as God enriches the saints with spiritual gifts in this world, he will in like manner adorn them with glory in heaven, hesitates not to say, that a special crown is laid up for him in proportion to his labours. Our Saviour, also, to commend the dignity of the office which he had conferred on the apostles, reminds them that the fruit of it is laid up in heaven. This, too, Daniel says, "They that be wise shall shine as the brightness of the firmament; and they that turn many to righeousness as the stars for ever and ever" (Dan. xii. 3). Any one who attentively considers the Scriptures will see not only that they promise eternal life to believers, but a special reward to each. Hence the expression of Paul, "The Lord grant unto him that he may find mercy of the Lord in that day" (2 Tim. i. 18; iv. 14). This is confirmed by our Saviour's promise, that they "shall receive an hundredfold, and shall inherit everlasting life" (Matth. xix. 29). In short, as Christ, by the manifold variety of his gifts, begins the glory of his body in this world, and gradually increases it, so he will complete it in heaven.

11. While all the godly with one consent will admit this, because it is sufficiently attested by the word of God, they will, on the other hand, avoid perplexing questions which they feel to be a hindrance in their way, and thus keep within the prescribed limits. In regard to myself, I not only individually refrain from a superfluous investigation of useless matters, but also think myself bound to take care that I do not encourage the levity of others by answering them. Men puffed up with vain science are often inquiring how great the difference will be between prophets and apostles, and again, between apostles and martyrs; by how many degrees virgins will surpass those who are married; in short, they leave not a corner of heaven untouched by their speculations. Next it occurs to them to inquire to what end the world is to be repaired, since the children of God will not be in want of any part of this great and incomparable abundance, but will be like the angels, whose abstinence from food is a symbol of eternal blessedness. I answer, that independent of use, there will be so much pleasantness in the very sight, so much delight in the very knowledge, that this happiness will far surpass all the means of enjoyment which are now afforded. Let us suppose ourselves placed in the richest quarter of the globe, where no kind of pleasure is wanting, who is there that is not ever and anon hindered and exluded by disease from enjoying the gifts of God? who does not oftentimes interrupt the course of enjoyment by intemperance? Hence it follows, that fruition, pure and free from all defect, though it be of no use to a corruptible life, is the summit of happiness. Others go further, and ask whether dross and other impurities in metals will have no existence at the restitution, and are inconsistent with it. Though I should go so far as concede this to them, yet I expect with Paul a reparation of those defects which first began with sin, and on account of which the whole creation groaneth and travaileth with pain (Rom. viii. 22). Others go a step further, and ask, What better condition can await the human

race, since the blessing of offspring shall then have an end? The solution of this difficulty also is easy. When Scripture so highly extols the blessing of offspring, it refers to the progress by which God is constantly urging nature forward to its goal; in perfection itself we know that the case is different. But as such alluring speculations instantly captivate the unwary, who are afterwards led farther into the labyrinth, until at length, every one becoming pleased with his own view, there is no limit to disputation, the best and shortest course for us will be to rest contented with seeing through a glass darkly until we shall see face to face. Few out of the vast multitude of mankind feel concerned how they are to get to heaven; all would fain know before the time what is done in heaven. Almost all, while slow and sluggish in entering upon the contest, are already depicting to themselves imaginary triumphs.

12. Moreover, as language cannot describe the severity of the divine vengeance on the reprobate, their pains and torments are figured to us by corporeal things, such as darkness, wailing and gnashing of teeth, unextinguishable fire, the ever-gnawing worm (Matth. viii. 12; xxii. 13; Mark ix. 43; Isa. lxvi. 21). It is certain that by such modes of expression the Holy Spirit designed to impress all our senses with dread, as when it is said, "Tophet is ordained of old; yea, for the king it is prepared: he hath made it deep and large; the pile thereof is fire and much wood; the breath of the Lord, like a stream of brimstone, doth kindle it" (Isa. xxx. 33). As we thus require to be assisted to conceive the miserable doom of the reprobate, so the consideration on which we ought chiefly to dwell is the fearful consequence of being estranged from all fellowship with God, and not only so, but of feeling that his majesty is adverse to us, while we cannot possibly escape from it. For, first, his indignation is like a raging fire, by whose touch all things are devoured and annihilated. Next, all the creatures are the instruments of his judgment, so that those to whom the Lord will thus publicly manifest his anger will feel that heaven, and earth, and sea, all beings, animate and inanimate, are, as it were, inflamed with dire indignation against them, and armed for their destruction. Wherefore, the Apostle made no trivial declaration, when he said that unbelievers shall be "punished with everlasting destruction from the presence of the Lord, and from the glory of his power" (2 Thess. i. 9). And whenever the prophets strike terror by means of corporeal figures, although in respect of our dull understanding there is no extravagance in their language, yet they give preludes of the future judgment in the sun and the moon, and the whole fabric of the world. Hence unhappy consciences find no rest, but are vexed and driven about by a dire whirlwind, feeling as if torn by any angry God, pierced through with deadly darts, terrified by his thunderbolt, and crushed by the weight of his hand; so that it were easier to plunge into abysses and whirlpools than endure these terrors for a moment. How fearful, then, must it be to be thus beset throughout eternity! On this subject there is a memorable passage in the ninetieth Psalm: Although God by a mere look scatters all mortals, and brings them to nought, yet as his worshippers are more timid in this world, he urges them the more, that he may stimulate them, while burdened with the cross, to press onward until he himself shall be all in all.

NOTES

1. 2 Tim. i. 10; John v. 24; Eph. ii. 6, 19; Rom. viii. 16-18; Heb. xi. 1; 2 Cor. v. 6; Col. iii. 8; Titus ii. 12.

2. French, "nous receovions un povre salaire de nostre lacheté et paresse;"—we receive a poor salary for our carelessness and sloth.

3. French, Et encore quand nons aurons bien profité en cette mediation, si nous faut il entendre que nous sommes encoure tout au bas et à la premiere entree, et que jamais nous n'approcherons durant cette vie à la hautesse de ce mystere."—And still, when we shall have profitted much by thus meditating, we must understand that we are still far beneath it, and at the very threshold, and that never during this life shall we approach the height of this mystery.

THE EXISTENTIALIST RESPONSE

EXISTENTIALISM AND THE FEAR OF DYING

Michael A. Slote

In this paper I shall present a fairly systematic "existentialist" view of human anxiety about death and human responses to that anxiety, based on the work of Pascal, Kierkegaard, Heidegger, and Sartre. My main purpose is constructive, rather than exegetical. What seems to me most distinctive and important about the work of these existentialist authors is their approach to the fear of dying—or at least the relevance of what they say to that subject, for sometimes, when they deal with other topics, what they say can (I shall attempt to show) be used to illuminate the nature of human responses to the fear of death. But I think that much of what these authors say about the fear of dying is inchoate, confusing, or incomplete, and requires supplementation, clarification and systematization of the kind I shall be attempting to provide here.[1]

I

Perhaps the central locus of discussion by an Existentialist, of human attitudes toward and responses to death is the section of Kierkegaard's *Concluding Unscientific Postscript* called "The Task of Becoming Subjective." According to Kierkegaard, becoming subjective is "the most difficult of all tasks in fact, precisely because every human being has a strong natural bent and passion to become something more and different."[2] But what is it to be subjective or to be objective, and why is the former so difficult and the latter so tempting? Part of Kierkegaard's explana-

From *American Philosophical Quarterly*, 12, no. 1 (January 1975), pp. 17-28. Reprinted by permission of the author and the editor.

tion involves him in a contrast between the subjective and objective acceptance of Christianity. But Kierkegaard also applies the subjective/objective distinction to attitudes toward life and death generally. And what unites Kierkegaard in the "Becoming Subjective" section of the *Postscript* with such non-religious Existentialists as Heidegger and Sartre is the fact that he has something to say about human attitudes toward life and death that presupposes no particular form of religiosity and that has not, I think, been said by anyone outside the existentialist tradition. And it is this aspect of Kierkegaard's work that I shall be examining.

According to Kierkegaard, to have an objective attitude toward one's life is to have the kind of attitude toward one's life encouraged by an Hegelian view of the world. On such a view, one is part of a larger "world-historical" process of the self-realization of Reason or Spirit, and one's life takes on significance if one plays a role, however minor, in that world-historical process. One does not have to be an Hegelian to think in this kind of way. One can be thinking in a similar way if, as a scientist or philosopher, e.g., one devotes oneself to one's field in the belief or hope that one's life gains significance through one's contribution to something "bigger."

Kierkegaard says that people with such an attitude have an objective attitude toward their lives; and he wants each of us to dare to become subjective and renounce this "loftily pretentious and yet delusive intercourse" with the world-historical.[3] Those who live objectively are, according to Kierkegaard, under a delusion or illusion, and if so, then surely he has a real argument in favor of being subjective. For Kierkegaard, at least part of the illusion is, I think, the belief that by living objectively, one's dividend, what (good) one gets from life, is greater.[4] In the first place even if a certain world-historical process of development is a great good, it is a good that is divided up among those participating in that development into many parts, none of which, presumably, is large in relation to the whole, and so perhaps the good to be derived from participating in that development will be less than the good to be gained by living subjectively. But Kierkegaard then seems to question whether indeed there is *any* good to be gained from living for some world-historical process, since one who does so may not be around when it comes to fruition. But it is not clear that the good of such a process of development must all come at the end of that development, so I think Kierkegaard has still not given us any very strong reason for believing that one who lives objectively is under some kind of illusion that his life is better.

However, in the *Postscript* Kierkegaard attempts to tie up his discussion of living objectively, i.e., of living for the world-historical, with certain illusory "objective" attitudes towards death. One who lives world-historically will sometimes say: "What does it matter whether I die or not; the work is what is important, and others will be able to carry it forward." But this is to think of one's death as nothing special, as just one death among others, as a "something in general." And Kierkegaard seems to believe that one who thinks this way is under an illusion, the illusion that his own death has no more significance *for him* than the death of (random) others, or, to put it slightly differently, that he *should be* no more concerned about his own death than about that of others. However, various Stoic philosophers would, I think, tend to argue that it is Kierkegaard's belief that one should be especially concerned about one's own death that is an illusion, an illusion born of irrational self-centeredness. So it is not obvious that Kierkegaard is correct about the illusory nature of objective living, or about the advisability of living subjectively. In any case, the attitude of people who live for the world-historical toward their own deaths is of some interest: they are, at least at some level, not as afraid of dying as they might be or as some people are. And I think there are interesting implications to be drawn from this fact that have some of the spirit of what Kierkegaard says in the *Postscript*.

II

Those who live world-historically for some enterprise like science or philosophy seem not to be very anxious about dying. And I would like to suggest, what Kierkegaard never actually says, that we may be able to *explain* the tendency to live for the world historical as resulting from our characteristically human fear of dying. For no one wants to live in fear, and since one who lives objectively, for the world-historical, does not feel the fear or dying that some of us do, there is reason and motive for people who have experienced anxiety or fear at the prospect of dying to (try to) adopt an objective existence, including an objective attitude toward their own deaths. But what are the psychological mechanisms by which living world-historically assuages someone's fear of death? Here I can only suggest, not establish, an answer, and what I shall say is intended as exploratory and somewhat speculative.

Consider the claim that people who live for the world-historical sometimes make that they will *be or become immortal through their works,* or that they will *live on through their works.* Why do people ever say such things; if what they are saying is just metaphorical, why do they use *that* metaphor and why do they seem to take the metaphor seriously?[5] It seems to me that such claims of immortality or living on are not (if there is no afterlife along traditional religious lines) literally true. It is not even literally true to say that part of one lives on in one's works, for books, e.g., are not literally parts of those who write them. Moreover, even if there is a traditional religious type of afterlife, one presumably does not live on *through one's works.*[6]

When we say that we shall live on or be immortal through our writings, e.g., I think we sometimes make that claim in a serious spirit. We are not just joking or deliberately speaking loosely. But when someone points out that what we are saying is not literally true, I think that most of us are willing to admit that what we have said is not literally true. How is this possible? It is my conjecture that someone who says he will live on, at least unconsciously believes that what he has said is (literally) true. Part of the evidence for the *unconsciousness* of the belief, if it exists, is the fact that when someone brings it to our attention that it cannot literally be true, we are ready, at least on a conscious level, to admit that this is so. What (further) supports the idea that the belief exists on some unconscious level is the fact that we at first express it in a serious vein and are not fully conscious that what we are saying is not literally true. We have to be reminded that what we have said is not literally true and in this respect are not like someone who says that a certain person has a heart of gold. In the latter case, one is quite clear in one's mind *ab initio* that what one is saying is not the literal truth. One is, I think, often less clear, and in some sense more confused, about the literal falsehood of what one says when one says that one will live on in one's works. And this unclarity or confusion, as compared with the "heart of gold" case, is some evidence that one who speaks of living on in his works unconsciously believes that he will do so, inasmuch as the existence of such an unconscious belief is one very obvious possible explanation of that unclarity or confusion.[7] But what lends the greatest support to the view that such an unconscious belief exists in those who live world-historically and say they will live on in their works is the generally accepted fact that human beings naturally tend to fear dying. It is to be expected that men will try to avoid that fear and repress it, if possible. One way of doing this would be to convince oneself that one was immortal through one's works, so that death was not really or fully the end of one's existence. It would be hard to convince oneself of such a claim on a conscious level, just because of its literal falseness. But such belief in one's immortality could perhaps survive on an unconscious level where it would be less subject to rational scrutiny, and perhaps be capable of counteracting one's fear of death. The unconscious delusion of one's immortality (or living on) through one's works can, if we adopt Freudian terminology, be thought of as an unconscous defense mechanism of the ego that protects us from conscious fear about death by repressing that fear and counterbalancing it in such a way that it for the most part remains unconscious.[8] And this would explain why people who live for the world historical are not consciously afraid of dying much of the time, and, in effect, why people so often live for the world-historical.[9]

Let me carry my speuclation further. At one point in the *Postscript* (p. 274) Kierkegaard says that to live for the world-historical is to forget that one exists. This curious claim is, I think, more plausible or forceful than it may seem at first. Consider a person who lives objectively and unconsciously believes that he will live on through his books. Such a belief is not just false, but necessarily false, since it involves both the idea that one is alive and the idea that the existence of certain works like books is sufficient for one's continued existence; and nothing whose continued existence is entailed by the existence of such works can be *alive*. Moreover, the belief that one's books' existence is sufficient for one's continued existence seems to involve the idea that one has roughly the same kind of being as a book or series of books. So I think there is something to the idea that one who lives objectively somehow thinks of himself as not existing as a person, and as not being alive. But he presumably does not think this on a conscious level, for much the same reason that one does not on a conscious level think that one is going to live on through one's works. On the other hand, the *unconscious* delusion that one is not alive (or is of the same kind as a series of books) would seem capable of counteracting and allaying anxiety about dying just as easily as the unconscious belief that one is immortal through one's works does so. If one is going to live on in books, one is not going to lose one's life and there is nothing to fear from death, so that fears about dying may be prevented from becoming conscious by being allayed on an unconscious level. Similarly, if one is not really alive, or is of the same "stuff" as books, then one also has nothing to fear from dying; and one's ceasing to be, if it occurs, will be no more tragic than the ceasing to be of a book.[10] So if one believes this kind of thing on an unconscious level, it is again not hard to see how one's fear of death may be allayed and kept unconscious.[11] Thus it would seem that people so often live for the world-historical because such living involves unconscious beliefs (delusions) that help them, more or less successfully, to avoid conscious fears about dying.[12]

According to Kierkegaard, however, not only does one who lives for the world historical forget that he exists, but such a person at least to some extent ceases to exist as a person, ceases to live.[13] For if we use our lives as a means to the existence of certain works and/or to be mentioned in some paragraph of footnote of some authoritative history of our field of endeavor, then we are valuing our lives no more than we value the existence of certain works or our being mentioned in paragraphs or footnotes. And when we unconsciously think of ourselves as immortal through our works, we are in effect thinking that what we lose when we die cannot be that important or valuable. And to do and think in this way is to put a low value on one's living. But if one places a low value on actual living, one will not take full advantage of one's life (living) and that is a bit like already being dead, or not alive. So I think there really is something to Kierkegaard's claim that to live world-historically is to some extent to cease to exist as a person, to cease to be alive. The claim constitutes not literal truth, but a forceful and penetrating metaphor.

It is well known that the fear of dying is a prime source of much of human religiosity. Belief in an afterlife of the traditional religious sort is one way that men can assuage their anxiety about dying. What is perhaps not so well known is how the fear of dying can give rise to (and explain) certain attitudes and activities of people who are not in any ordinary way religious and perhaps also certain attitudes and activities of religious people that are not generally associated with religion. What I have tried to show here is that there are in Kierkegaard's *Concluding Unscientific Postscript* insights about our attitudes toward life and death that can be used to help us understand how certain non-religious aspects of human life result from the fear of dying.

In doing so, I have assumed that people who live objectively and say that they are not terribly anxious about dying are nonetheless afraid of dying at some level. And this may seem high-handed. However, I am inclined to think that in general people living world-historically (who do not believe in some traditional religious type of life after death) continue to be subject to a certain welling-up of death anxiety that can overtake them in the midst of their daily lives.[14] Despite my own tendencies toward the world-historical, I have often experienced this sudden welling-up of death anxiety, and I think that the fact that this phenomenon is widespread among non-religious world-historical people (and indeed among people in general) is evidence that fear of dying never entirely ceases to exist in (such) people, but always continues to exist at least on an unconscious plane. For it is easier to imagine such a sudden welling-up of fear as the "return of the repressed" and as indicating a certain inefficiency of one's repressive mechanisms than to think of it as resulting from the sudden regeneration of death fears within one. What could plausibly explain such a sudden rebirth of death anxiety *in medias res?* Moreover, the earlier-mentioned fact that world-historical people (people who live for the world-historical) sometimes seriously say that they will be immortal through their works, without being clear in their own minds that this is just a metaphor, is, as I have already argued, evidence that such people unconsciously believe that they are immortal through their works (or that they are not alive). But why should they have such unconscious beliefs, except as part of a mechanism to relieve and keep repressed their fear of dying? So even such seemingly innocuous locutions as that we shall be immortal through our works indicate the existence of death fears even on the part of people who live for the world historical and claim not be afraid of dying. Let us now turn to Pascal's *Pensées* to see how the fear of dying affects other aspects of human life.

III

There is a famous long passage in the *Pensées* where Pascal talks about diversion, its role in human life and its sources. Men "cannot stay quietly in their own chamber" alone and meditating, for any length of time.[15] We need or think we need diversion and activity and cannot be happy without diverting ourselves from ourselves because of the "natural poverty of our feeble and mortal condition, so miserable that nothing can comfort us when we think of it closely."[16] Now Pascal does not go on to decry the vanity of human diversion and claim that life would be less vain if we thought more about ourselves and our mortality. He is not arguing for the vanity of worldly human concerns in the time-worn manner of *Ecclesiastes*. He has an entirely new perspective on where the vanity of human life really lies. The vanity of our lives consists, for Pascal, in the fact that when we divert ourselves (from ourselves), we typically deceive ourselves about our motives for behaving as we do.[17] For example, a man who gambles often convinces himself that obtaining the money he is gambling for would make him happy (at least for a while). He focuses on the getting of the money and forgets that his real or main purpose is to divert himself. Thus if he were offered the money on condition that he does not gamble, he would be (at least temporarily) unhappy, because he seeks diversion. On the other hand, if he were offered the diversion, say, of playing cards without being able to gamble for money, he would also be unhappy. For it is not just diversion he seeks; he must also have some imagined goal that he focuses on in such a way that he does not see that diversion is his real or main goal. Pascal does not, however, explain why men cannot simply seek diversion without fooling themselves about their goal. But an explanation can be given along lines that Pascal might have approved. Imagine that we divert ourselves in order not to have to think of ourselves and also realize that this is so. Shall we not *ipso facto* be thrust back into that very awareness of self that we sought to avoid through diversion? To realize that one wants not to think of oneself because it is unpleasant to dwell on one's feeble and mortal condition is *ipso facto* to be thinking of oneself and opening oneself up to the very unpleasantness one wishes to avoid. And if those who want to avoid thinking of themselves must remain ignorant of that fact if they are to succeed in not thinking of themselves, how better to accomplish this than by focusing on something outside themselves and thinking of it as their goal?

This explanation of human striving and activity applies not just to gambling, but, as Pascal says, to the waging of campaigns in love or in war and to many other human activities. Many of us fool ourselves about our motives much of the time when engaged in such activities. One objection to this analysis, however, would be that to explain so much human activity in terms of the fear of, or desire not to be, thinking of oneself is to offer a gratuitous explanation of our behavior. Why not just say that as animals we have an instinctive desire for certain activities that typically involve a lack of self-consciousness and that are called "diversions"? But the instinct theory of the origin of our diversions has, as it stands, no obvious way of explaining the self-deception Pascal points out. If we simply have an instinct for certain activities, activities that in fact tend to divert us from ourselves, why do some of us much of the time and many of us some of the time deceive ourselves into thinking that it is winning a certain victory or honor or woman that is our main goal, when it is the diverting activity leading up to that winning that is our main goal? On the theory that we do not like thinking about ourselves, however, the fact of self-deception can be explained along the above lines; so the assumption of a desire not to think of oneself is not gratuitous.

Furthermore, there is good independent evidence that people do not like to think about themselves. There is, for example, an experience that I have sometimes had, and that I think the reader will probably also have had; in the middle of thinking about something else I have all of a sudden thought to myself: "All this is being done by *me* and all these people are talking about *me*." I hope this description will suffice to convey the kind of experience I have in mind. What is interesting, but also perplexing and distressing to me, are the following facts. When I have this experience of myself, there seems to me to be something precious about it; and I think: "This is the moment when I am most alive; it is very good to have this experience." (There is, after all, a long tradition in which self-consciousness is a great, or the greatest, good.) I usually also think that though I am at that moment too busy to prolong the self-consciousness, I shall definitely set aside a good deal of time in the future to take full advantage of this kind of experience of self-awareness. But somehow that never happens. And when I am again momentarily self-conscious in the way I have been describing, I again put off a long bout of such self-consciousness to the future, despite my typical accompanying conviction that the experience of being self-conscious is a wonderful one that I really should and shall take greater advantage of. All this needs explaining, and the obvious explanation, I think, is that I really do not like the experience of self-consciousness, as Pascal suggests.

But why, in the end, should we not want to think about ourselves? Pascal suggests that the reason is that thinking about ourselves makes us think of our feeble and mortal condition. He also says about man: "to be happy, he would have to make himself immortal; but, not being able to do so, it has occurred to him to prevent himself from thinking of death."[18] Presumably, then, Pascal thinks there is a connection between thinking about oneself and thinking unpleasant thoughts about one's death; and this seems to me to be quite plausible. For at least while we are absorbed in things outside us, we do not think of ourselves, or thus, it would seem, of our death; whereas if and when one does think about oneself, one might very easily think about one's death. It would seem, then, that the explanation of our diverting ourselves from (thinking about) ourselves is that this at least to some degree enables us to avoid thinking anxiously about our mortality. And so we have now clarified two general areas or aspects of human life in terms of the fear of dying. Let us turn next to Heidegger.

IV

Men's attitudes toward death are a major theme in Heidegger's *Being and Time*.[19] For Heidegger, in everyday life we exist in a mode that Heidegger calls the "they" (German: "das Man"). Heidegger characterizes this mode of existence as inauthentic, at least in part because in it, one is forgetful of the fact that death is one's ownmost possibility and cannot be outstripped. By this he means something close to the Kierkegaardian idea that one's own death has greater significance for one than does the death of others. Heidegger says that such a mode of existence is tempting because it tranquilizes one's anxiety in the face of death.[20] So it would seem that Heidegger can be thought of as providing a psychological explanation of certain aspects of human life, which he calls collectively "(being lost in) the 'they'," and thus that Heidegger is doing something similar to what we have seen Kierkegaard doing in the *Postscript* and Pascal doing in the *Pensées*.[21]

According to Heidegger, one important aspect of our average everyday lostness in the "they" is its typical modes of discourse, chatter, and idle talk, and the busy-body curiosity that characterizes such discourse. Heidegger points out that when people are idly and curiously talking about whether John and Mary will get divorced, the actual event, the divorce, if it occurs, actually disappoints the idle talkers; for then they are no longer able to conjecture about and be in on the thing in advance. The curiosity of everyday idle talk is concerned with the very latest thing(s), with novelty; and what interests in anticipation may be "old hat" or out of date when it occurs. Horse races and even pennant races in baseball seem to me to be good examples of this tendency. We have the keenest interest in who will win, but it is hard to maintain much interest in such races once we know their outcome; there is even a certain disappointment or "let-down" sometimes when the results of such things finally do become known.[22] Heidegger's discussion here seems to have a good deal in common with what Pascal says about diversion, for one way of diverting ourselves from ourselves would be to be constantly curious about the latest things. But why not be interested in things that are not new and be diverted by them? The answer here—though it is not one that Heidegger actually gives— seems to me to lie precisely in the desire not to think of oneself that Pascal lays such emphasis on. What is newer is less well known, and the more there is to learn about something, the less likely one is to get bored with it or to cease being absorbed in it, and so be thrust back into thoughts about oneself. Furthermore, our earlier discussion of Pascal can help us explain why we are sometimes let down when a certain event we have (only) conjectured about occurs, even though in advance we thought that "nothing would make us happier" than to know exactly when and how the event would occur. For if our goal is distraction from ourselves through conjecturing, we cannot very well admit this to ourselves without (running a grave risk of) defeating that goal; so we somehow fool ourselves into thinking that what we want is to know for sure about the character of the event we are conjecturing about, as a means to our real goal of diverting ourselves through conjecturing about something or someone outside ourselves; and when we cannot conjecture anymore, then of course we are let down.

There may be a further reason why the desire for novelty is so pervasive in human life—though what I shall now be saying is perhaps more speculative than anything else I have to say here. As Heidegger says (p. 217), when one has the desire for novelty, it is as if one's motive were to have known (seen) rather than to know (see); for as soon as one has known (seen) something, one no longer wants to know (see) it. And there seems to be a certain vanity in such a way of dealing with things. Now consider what is implicitly involved in wanting, say, to have seen Rome, but not to see (keep seeing) Rome. There are tours whose advertising has the feeling of: "Come to Europe with us and you will see 8—count 'em—8 countries in 8 days"; and such advertising and such tours appeal to many people who want to (say they) have been, e.g., in Rome, but who do not much want to *be* in Rome. When one makes such a tour, one often even wishes the tour were already over so that one (could say that one) had already been to Rome in Italy (and to the other seven countries). The actual touring, with its "inconveniences," is often not desired or enjoyed. But to want the eight days and the trip to be already over with is in a certain sense to want a part of one's life over with in exchange for a being able to say one has been. This desire is in many cases unconscious. Sometimes some of us say, with an air of seriousness, that we wish that a certain trip or period of time were already over. But when confronted with the implications of what we have said, we almost inevitably recoil from what we have said and say that of course we do not *really* want a certain part of our life to be already over, perhaps adding that we were only speaking loosely or jokingly in making our original remark. In that case our desire to have a certain part of our life over with exists, if at all, only on an unconscious level. Evidence that there *is* such an unconscious desire comes from the fact of our original seriousness in saying that we wished a certain trip over with and from the fact that we are by no means clear in our own minds that we do not mean our statement literally, the way a hungry man is, for example, when he says that he could eat a mountain of flapjacks. I think this initial unclarity is best explained by (and thus evidence for) the existence of an unconscious desire to have a certain part of our life over with.[23] And perhaps for the very purpose of keeping this desire out of consciousness, we convince ourselves at least temporarily that we really want to *be* in Rome, or *feel* its living antiquity, etc. But then, after we have spent the tour rushing about, impatient with tarrying in one place too long, we *may,* upon reflection, recognize that we wanted the having seen more than the seeing of the places, like Rome, that we visited.

The logical extension of the wish to have a certain portion of one's life already over with is the wish to have one's whole life over with, and I would like now very tentatively to argue that at some deep level many of us have this latter wish, and so want not to be alive. Part of the reason for thinking so consists in the way we deceive ourselves about the extent of our desires to have portions of our lives over with. We sometimes think: if only it were a week from now so that I knew whether *p*, everything would be all right. But then when the time comes at which everything is supposed to be going to be all right, we soon find another reason for thinking things are not all right and for wishing other parts of our lives over with. I think that the initially implausible assumption that some people unconsciously wish their whole lives over with, wish not to be alive, provides the best explanation of this whole perplexing phenomenon. For if one has the unconscious desire to have one's whole life over with, there will be mechanisms in force to prevent it from becoming conscious. If one were conscious that one wanted *many different parts* of one's life over with *seriatim,* one would be dangerously close to being conscious that one wanted one's *whole life* over with. So it might reasonably be expected that someone with the unconscious wish or desire that his whole life was over with would be (made to be) unaware of the extent to which he wanted particular portions of his life over with before they were lived. Thus I think there is reason to believe that people who deceive themselves in this way unconsciously wish not to be alive.[24]

It will perhaps seem more plausible to hold that such a wish exists if I can show how it is explained by our fear of dying. One way of allaying fear of the loss of something is a kind of denial that one might call the technique of "sour grapes in advance." We can convince ourselves that the thing we may lose is not worth having or that we do not really want it. (This recalls the studies psychologists have done on the resolution of "cognitive dissonance.") An unconscious desire not to be alive might, then, help us counterbalance or keep repressed our fear of dying. The existence of such a desire can thus be supported in various ways and fits well into the kind of theory about our attitudes toward death so far proposed. But there is no time to speculate further in its favor.[25]

We argued earlier that if someone thinks of himself as not alive, he will not take full advantage of his life and it will be as if he not (fully) alive. The same can be said for someone who wants not to be alive. We saw earlier the force of the metaphor that some of us are dead. Since it is as if some of us are dead because of what we have, unconsciously, done to ourselves, there is also force to the metaphor that some of us have killed ourselves. To live for the having seen and known of things is, metaphorically speaking, not to be alive, and to have killed onself.[26] And one can also say this about those who live for the world-historical. I have a tendency to put myself entirely into my work and to live for something "bigger," philosophy. But sometimes I recoil from such an existence and from myself, and I feel that I have really just thrown my life away, have been personally emptied, through world-historical living. At such a time the metaphor of killing oneself seems particularly compelling.

We have thus far characterized those who live world-historically as assuaging the fear of dying via the *beliefs* that they are immortal and/or that they are not alive. But I think such people also sometimes unconsciously wish not to be alive in the manner of those who divert temselves the novelties.[27] (Of course, those who live world-historically can be diverting themselves as well, e.g., with busy research or advocacy of causes.) For one thing, as we have already seen, people who live world-historically unconsciously think that they are not alive. And they want to think this, at least unconsciously, as a means to less fear or anxiety. But presumably if one wants to think one is not alive, that is because one wants not to be alive. This kind of inference from what one wants to think to what one wants is surely *usually* in order. Secondly, there is evidence that world-historical people tend to want parts of their lives over with in much the same way that seekers after novelty do. Someone writing a book that is intended to advance some field in the long run will often wish that the next six months of his life were already over so that he could see the book in finished form and have the writing of it over with. If only this were possible, everything would start being all right, he thinks, and he would be ready really to live his life again. Such a person, however, will, in many cases, be fooling himself about the extent to which he wants to "put off living" by missing parts of his life. As soon as there is another book to write, or academic appointment in the offering, he may very well once again want some part of his life already over with. Saying that such a man really wants to live, but only wants to avoid certain tense or burdensome parts of life, does not really allow us to understand why he so often on such slight pretexts (is writing a book really so unpleasant and tense, considering the rest of the things that can be going on in one's life at the same time?) thinks up reasons for wanting to postpone living by omitting some part of his life. Just as a man who is always *just about* to take a vacation and really live (it up) for a change, but who never does, can be plausibly suspected of preferring his work to a vacation or to "life" despite his protestations to the contrary, the perplexing behavior of one who lives world-historically and keeps wanting parts of his life over with while remaining unconscious or unaware of the extent to which this is so can, I think, only be made sense of in terms of an unconscious desire not to be alive.[28] Such a desire is strange and perplexing, perhaps, but no more so than the behavior it is supposed to explain.

Heidegger says many more interesting things about the "they." Idle talk and curiosity seem to be interested in anything and everything, though in fact, unbeknownst to us, limits have been set on what we are to be interested in. For example, one is not, in the midst of curious talk, supposed to bring up the tragedy of life or the inevitability of death. Anyone who brings up such things is told not to be "morbid." Heidegger suggests that idle talk and curiosity function as a way of keeping us from thinking of our own death. For one thing—if I may borrow again from our discussion of Pascal to supplement what Heidegger is saying here—the illusion of interest in everything is an excellent means for blocking off thought about dying and its consequent anxiety, since if we believed, while we were engaged in idle talk, that we were not supposed to be deeply talking about death, we might very easily be thrust back into the very anxiety that idle talk was supposed to avoid. Moreover, the very self-assurance and harshness with which someone who brings up death in the midst of idle talk is branded as morbid tends to encourage and rationalize our avoidance of the topic of death.

Another device by which everyday living in the "they" keeps us from fears of death is by branding such fears as cowardly. Heidegger, however, thinks that it is more cowardly *not* to face death anxiously. Now there certainly seems to be room for disagreement on this issue. Some of the Stoics seem to have thought that it was irrational, rather than courageous, to be anxious about one's own death because death was a matter of indifference. And this latter philosophy of death may be correct; but it might be interesting at this point to make some educated guesses about the psychology of those who have advocated the "Stoic" view of death. For to my mind there is something strange and suspicious about (holding) the view that one's own death is not an evil. I have already discussed the fact that despite our best repressive mechanisms, the fear of dying sometimes comes upon (some of) us suddenly in the midst of life. When others tell us that it is morbid or cowardly to worry about death, we are given an excuse or motive not to worry about death, and such advice may help us to get rid of the conscious fear of death at least temporarily. The philosophical view that it is irrational to worry about death because death is a matter of indifference may have a similar function to play in the psychic lives of those who propound it. Philosophers pride themselves on being rational, and by branding the fear of dying as "irrational," they may give themselves a motive for ceasing consciously to worry about death and actually help themselves get rid of the conscious fear of dying. I am inclined to think, then, that the view that it is irrational, and not courageous, to fear death, because death is no evil, may well be motivated, in many of those who propound it, by the fear of death itself, a fear that they are consequently able to repress, but not to get rid of. If so, then those who are helped to repress their fear of dying by holding a "Stoic" view of death are under an illusion when they claim as rational philosophers to be totally indifferent to death. But it might be better to live under such an illusion without consciously worring about death than to know that one was not indifferent to death because one *was* consciously afraid of death. In the light of these complexities, it would seem hard to decide between Heidegger, on the one hand, and the Stoics and the "they," on the other, as to whether it is courageous to be (consciously) anxious in the face of dying.

Heidegger suggests yet further ways in which existence in the "they" tranquilizes our anxiety about dying. In the "they" there is an emphasis on keeping busy doing things, as the means to, or sign of, a full and good life. When someone suggests that one might do better to be more reflective and less busy, the response of the "they" is that by keeping busy, one is living "concretely" and avoiding self-defeating and morbid self-consciousness; this encourages the person who hears this to keep busy and not reflect on himself, and thus functions as a means to keeping us from the conscious fear of dying. (Consider, in particular, how the old, who are especially subject to fears of death, are told to keep busy and active.)

Heidegger points out that someone lost in the "they" will *admit* that death is certain and that one (everyone) dies in the end. According to Heidegger, in speaking of what happens to "everyone" or to "one" eventually, we "depersonalize" and "intellectualize" death. In this depersonalizing death, it is as if the person were saying that death has nothing to do with *him right now,* and this enables him to talk about death without focusing on himself or having that particularly intimate experience of self-awareness described earlier or, thus, having fearful thoughts about death. Also talk about the inevitability or certainty of death, etc., may be part of a process of "isolation of affect" in which one intellectualizes (about) a certain phenomenon to keep away from (consciousness of) certain related feelings.[29] Heidegger also points out that social scientists often seek to create "typologies" and systematic theories about humanity in the belief that they are thereby penetrating to the deepest level on which one can understand humanity and oneself, but that such intellectual "hustle and bustle" may entirely ignore the question of the significance for men of their own death and death anxiety; such intellectualization, he suggests, may serve to keep one from anxious thoughts about death by convincing one that one has reflected as deeply as it is possible to do. And the very stuffiness and detachment with which some sociologists, psychologists, etc., sometimes declare their desire to plumb the depths of the human spirit is, I would think, some evidence that they have a deeper need to avoid the *feeling* of their own mortality.

An important further point that is due to Kierkegaard rather than to Heidegger is that one can even overintellectualize one's response to a work, like that of Kierkegaard or Heidegger, that attempts to reveal in an "existential" manner the importance of our attitudes toward dying.[30] Spinoza has said that "passive" feelings like fear tend to dissipate when we scrutinize them, and this may well mean that it is difficult at one and the same time both intellectually to focus on and learn the significance of death anxiety and to *feel* that significance. And so there seems to be a real danger that someone who reads the writings of Existentialists will only intellectually understand and agree with what they say, and thus fail to derive all the benefit one could or should get from reading them. Of course, Spinoza's dictum also implies that it is difficult to think intellectually about death anxiety while feeling such anxiety. And one reason why I and others may be interested in thinking and writing about death anxiety is that such thinking and writing may, in effect, involve an isolation of affect about death.[31]

In discussing Heidegger, we have brought in Kierkegaard and Pascal to help "deepen" his analysis of how death anxiety affects large portions of human life. I would like now to make use of certain ideas of Sartre's (in ways that Sartre undoubtedly would not approve) to point out yet another aspect of human life that can be explained in terms of the fear of dying. (However, I shall not discuss Sartre's own views on death, which in fact run counter to much of what we have to say on that subject.)

V

Being and Nothingness is perhaps most famous for its discussion of what Sartre calls "bad faith," which consists in being or putting oneself under the illusion that one is not free and cannot do other than what one in fact does.[32] For Sartre, one is in bad faith when one says: I have to get up and get to work; I can't stay in bed, I have a family to feed. Bad faith is involved because one does not *have* to get up and go to work.

Some people will immediately object to what Sartre is saying on the grounds that if determinism about human behavior is true and a certain person in fact will not stay in bed, then he is under no illusion when he says that he cannot stay in bed. Since, despite anything Sartre says, it is by no means obvious to me that such determinism is not (approximately) true or that human beings possess free will, I would like now to (re)interpret Sartre's "bad faith" in such a way as to avoid assuming either human indeterminism or human free will.

Someone who says he has to go to work in the morning will sometimes say: "I have no choice in the matter." But I think that he does have a choice, even if a determined and unfree one, and that if he cannot stay at home, that is in part *because* of his (perhaps determined and unfree) choice. Moreover, I think that someone who is reminded of these facts will typically be willing to take back his original claim to have no choice in some matter, will grant that he had been speaking loosely or metaphorically. But it seems to me that such a person will typically not have been clear in his own mind about all this at the time when he originally claimed to have "no choice." And for reasons we have already gone into at length, I think this indicates that the person making such a claim unconsciously believes that he has no choice in a certain matter, even though he really does have a (possibly determined and unfree) choice in that matter and can be brought to conscious awareness of that fact. Such a person is under an illusion about the part he (and his choosing or deciding) plays in certain events or situations, and it is *this kind* of illusion that *I* shall call "bad faith."

Bad faith in this new sense is clearly related to bad faith in Sartre's sense.

And, assuming that the new kind of bad faith does exist, it would be good if we could give some sort of explanation of it. Sartre's explanation of bad faith in the old sense will not be of much help to us here, since it assumes not only that human behavior is undetermined but also (implausibly enough) that human beings basically realize (believe) that this is so. My suggestion is that we explain bad faith in my new sense in much the same way that we have been explaining various other phenomena, namely, in terms of the fear of dying. (Indeed, Heidegger hints at this idea in *Being and Time*, p. 239.) I think that we can explain bad faith in terms of the fear of dying, if we suppose that the illusion of bad faith helps to repress such fear and if we borrow one further idea of Sartre's. According to Sartre, someone in bad faith (in his sense) who denies his own freedom is, in effect, thinking of himself as a thing or object, since things and objects are unfree, etc. I would like tentatively to claim that people who unconsciously believe that they have no choice, say, about getting up in the morning are, in effect, thinking of themselves as things or objects,[33] since things and objects really do lack choice. If we make this assumption, we can explain how bad faith in my sense enables one to relieve or repress death fears. For objects cannot die, and so unconsciously thinking of oneself as an object is unconsciously to think that one has nothing to fear from death.[34] (And if one passes away but is a mere object, then that is no more tragic than the passing away of a rock.)

Bad faith in the new sense seems to have much in common with living for the world-historical. In the latter case, one thinks of oneself as not alive; in the former, one thinks of oneself as a mere thing; and one might wonder whether there is much difference here either in the content of these unconscious beliefs or in the way they act on the fear of dying. Furthermore, just as one who lives for the world-historical can aptly be described metaphorically as not alive[35] and as having killed himself, one who lives in bad faith is, metaphorically speaking, a mere thing and not alive, and since he has (unconsciously) done this to himself, he has, metaphorically speaking, turned himself into a thing. And given the fact that the only way a person really can turn himself into a thing is by turning himself into a corpse, it is perhaps metaphorically appropriate to describe someone who is (constantly) in bad faith as having killed himself. Sartre holds that someone who thinks of himself as a mere thing wants (among other things) to *be* a mere thing. And I think we could argue that people in bad faith in my sense sometimes unconsciously want to be things in something like the way we earlier argued that people living for the world historical want not to be alive. Furthermore, the unconscious desire to be an object would seem capable of countering the fear of dying in much the same way that the unconscious desire not to be alive does so, and so there is this further similarity between living in bad faith and living for the world-historical.

VI

If what has been said here is on the right track, then it would seem that Pascal, Kierkegaard, Heidegger, and Sartre all describe phenomena that pervade our lives and that are best explained in terms of their efficacy in relieving or repressing the fear of dying. Our explanation has made use of a Freudian type of view of repression and of the unconscious. This will certainly make our arguments here suspect in the eyes of some people. I have in effect been "practicing" a kind of "existential psychoanalysis," and though this term is one that was originally used by Sartre in *Being and Nothingness* to describe some of his own procedures, it may well apply more accurately to the kinds of things I have been doing here. For Sartre does not posit an unconscious, but I have followed Freud in doing just that.[36] In any case, I hope that this paper may bring to light an area, or areas, where Existentialism and Psychoanalysis can be mutually enlightening.

Of course, in addition to using psychoanalytic ideas, I have also frequently appealed to my own experience and intuitions, to how things strike me and to the "feel" of certain ideas. Though some things, I trust, will strike readers the way they have struck me, this will no doubt not always be the case; and when it is not, my appeals to how things feel to me, etc., are bound to seem like special pleading. Perhaps I *am* guilty of this, but I do not know how to avoid it in a paper like this when personal experience may be more relevant to seeing certain points than abstract arguments. And perhaps some of the ideas or intuitions I have relied on will seem more palatable to the reader if he "lives with them" and takes the time to see whether they do not, perhaps, make sense in and of his experience of himself and the world. For it is in something like this way that many of the ideas and intuitions of this paper have become acceptable to me.

In this paper, I have pieced together various ideas from Pascal, Heidegger, Sartre, and Kierkegaard, as well as extrapolated beyond what any of them has said, to provide a fairly general picture of how the fear of dying accounts for many aspects of human life. The explanatory "theory" we have presented links together phenomena that the various Existentialists discussed separately, and as such should, given any standard account of scientific method, be more plausible than the accounts of the various Existentialists taken seperately. So I hope I have helped to support and fill out the basically existentialist notion that the equality of a (non-religious) man's life greatly depends on his attitude toward his own death. And even if this idea is not particularly prevalent in Sartre, we can use things Sartre says to substantiate it.

Some people will complain that I have only been doing psychology, not philosophy. But it may not be important whether this accusation is true. And I also think that when psychology is general enough and speaks directly to the human condition, it can also count as philosophy. If, as we have argued, the main motive for world-historical (or busily self-distractive) participation in certain enterprises comes from (desire to avoid) the fear of dying, then a good many intellectuals, scientists, and others may be less pure in motive, less selfless, than they are often thought to be.[37] And this fact, if it is one, is surely very relevant to our understanding of the human condition, and so counts in favor of calling what we have been doing philosophy.[38]

1. I shall by no means, however, be discussing all the things these authors say on the topic of death.

2. *Concluding Unscientific Postscript* (Princeton, 1960), p. 116.

3. *Ibid.,* p. 133.

4. *Ibid.,* p. 130ff.

5. Horace in the *Odes* (3, XXX) seems to be an example of someone who takes the metaphor seriously.

6. I think that people who talk of gaining immortality through their children also say what is literally false, and their psychology is, I think, significantly similar to the psychology of those who talk of living on through their books.

7. Kierkegaard hints at the idea that world-historical people believe they live on through their works when he implies (*Postscript,* p. 140) that such people need to be reminded that "in the world-historical process the dead are not recalled to life."

8. For examples of reasoning similar to that just used that appear in the psychoanalytic literature, see, e.g., S. Freud's "Splitting of the Ego in the Defensive Process" (in his *Collected Papers* [London, 1956], vol. 5, pp. 372-375) and Otto Fenichel's *The Psychoanalytic Theory of Neurosis* (New York, 1945, pp. 479-484). For another *philosophical* use of an argument like mine above, see M. Lazerowitz' *The Structure of Metaphysics* (London, 1955, p. 69ff.) and *Studies in Metaphilosophy* (London, 1964, pp. 225ff., 251). I am indebted to Lazerowitz' account for some of the structure of my own analysis.

9. J. P. Sartre (in *Being and Nothingness* [New York, 1956], p. 543) says that "to be dead is to be a prey for the living." And Thomas Nagel (in "Death," *Noûs,* vol. 4 [1970], p. 78) has tentatively claimed that a man can be harmed or unfortunate as a result of things that happen after his death, e.g., if his reputation suffers posthumously. I wonder whether these views are not, perhaps, indicative of some sort of unconscious belief that people live on in their works.

10. The unconscious belief that one is going to live on and the unconscous belief that one is not alive seem to counteract the unconscious belief or fear that one is going to die in contradictory ways, the former with the "message" that we are not really going to lose what we have, the latter with the "message" that we really have nothing to lose. But we have already seen that the unconscious belief that one lives on in books is itself contradictory or necessarily false, so it should not, perhaps, be so surprising that the unconscious uses mutually contradictory means to repress death-fears. On this see Freud's *The Interpretation of Dreams,* ch. 2. For similar use of the (metaphorical?) notion of unconscious "messages," see Otto Fenichel's *Outline of Clinical Psychoanalysis* (New York, 1934), esp. pp. 13, 30, 33, 52, 250, 260, 275f.

11. In "A Lecture on Ethics," *The Philosophical Review,* vol. 74 (1965), pp. 8ff. Ludwig Wittgenstein speaks of the feeling people sometimes have of being safe whatever happens. He claims that such a feeling or belief is nonsensical; but perhaps this occasional feeling is better thought of as the expression of a meaningful, but necessarily or clearly false, unconscious belief that we are safe whatever happens, a belief that counteracts the fear of dying and that is roughly equivalent to the unconscious belief that one is not alive. For one is absolutely safe (from death) if and only if one is not alive.

12. I do not want to claim that everyone dedicated to some "cause," to something "bigger" than himself is living world-historically. Such dedication may result from altruism or "conviction" and may not involve the world-historical psychology if it is not accompanied by delusions of immortality through one's works or actions, or the view that one's own death is unimportant.

13. *Ibid.,* pp. 118, 175, 271, 273.

14. See Heidegger's *Being and Time* (New York, 1962), p. 233f.

15. New York, 1958, p. 39.

16. *Ibid.*

17. *Ibid.,* p. 40.

18. *Ibid.,* p. 49.

19. Our discussion here will be based on sections 27, 35-42, and 47-53 of *Being and Time* (New York, 1962).

20. Heidegger uses "fear" only with respect to things in the world. For death "anxiety" is reserved; but this is not necessarily dictated by ordinary usage.

21. Of course, some philosophers will say that by treating Heidegger as an explanatory psychologist, I am treating him as if he were operating on the "ontic" level, whereas Heidegger thinks of himself as operating on an "ontological" level deeper than the "ontic" level on which science, psychology, and most pre-Heideggerian philosophy typically function. However, despite many efforts, I myself have never been able to make satisfactory sense of the ontic/ontological distinction. If the distinction is viable, Heidegger may have a good deal more to say than I shall be giving him credit for; but we can at least credit him with insights on a level with those of a Pascal or a Kierkegaard.

22. Of course, some people constantly dwell on past (sporting) events (and their part in them), but I do not think this is incompatible with the general tendency I am describing.

23. Compare here our earlier argument for the existence, in world-historical people, of an unconscious belief in their immortality through their works.

24. Our earlier argument that we do not like thinking about ourselves can be strengthened along the lines of our present argument for the existence of an unconscious wish not to be alive. Similar self-deception occurs in the two cases.

25. I have posited the wish not to be alive as an unconscious defense mechanism of the ego that responds to (prior) fear of dying. Freud, on the other hand, late in his career posited a basic (id-based) death instinct to account for various phenomena. See *Beyond the Pleasure Principle* (New York, 1950). The two sorts of views are incompatible, and so the explanation given just now in the text may be mistaken. However, there is some reason to prefer it. Our ego-theory of the death wish fits in better with our earlier-discussed theories about the ego's unconscious handling of the fear of dying. Moreover, other things being equal, it is better to treat a phenomenon as a derived phenomenon, within a theory, than to treat it as basic, within that theory. In addition, there is the sheer unintuitiveness of supposing that we have death wishes *ab initio,* rather than acquiring such (irrational) wishes in the *neurotic* process of repression. Finally, it is by no means clear that a basic death instinct is needed to account for clinical phenomena. On this see Otto Fenichel's "A Critique of the Death Instinct" in *The Collected Papers of Otto Fenichel,* first series (New York, 1953), pp. 363-372.

26. I think we have some inkling of this metaphorical killing when we speak of "killing time" at moments when we want to have something over with, want a certain (perhaps boring) part of our lives over with. Use of that phrase may be a disguised conscious expression of the unconscious desire not to be alive.

27. Kierkegaard's claim in the *Postscript* (p. 137) that one whose eye is on world-historical things has perhaps found "a highly significant way of . . . killing time" seems to indicate some awareness on his part that world-historical people want not to be alive and have, metaphorically speaking, killed themselves. Whose time, after all, does one kill except one's own? And one's time is one's life. Incidentally, it is natural to say that world-historical people "bury themselves in their work," and this metaphor seems to suggest the very same things that our use of the metaphor of killing time does.

28. Cf. Emerson's remark in his *Journals* (13 April, 1834) that "we are always getting ready to live, but never living."

29. Cf. O. Fenichel's *Outline of Clinical Psychoanalysis, op. cit.,* p. 190f., for ideas about "isolation of affect" that are related to some of the things we have said here and earlier in the paper.

30. *Postscript,* p. 166f.

31. Heidegger also points out that the force of living in the "they" is such as to make people lost in the "they" scoff at his analysis of such lostness. Once one is aware of one's tendencies to cover up certain anxieties, it may be harder to use the mechanisms one has previously used in doing so; so one who wishes at some level to keep covering up his anxiety has a motive to reject Heidegger's analysis and, indeed, our analysis here.

32. See *Being and Nothingness* (New York, 1956), Pt. 1.

33. I hope I shall be forgiven for ignoring plants.

34. This recalls the Simon and Garfunkel song that goes: "I am a rock, I am an island; and a rock feels no pain and an island never cries." The idea that we sometimes want to think of ourselves as things to avoid the pain of life or of facing death is not new or silly. Moreover, even if people in bad faith only think of themselves, unconsciously, as *similar* to mere things, that thought may itself be capable of relieving the fear of death.

35. Kierkegaard says that such a person is also a "walking stick," which suggests the similarity of such a person to someone in bad faith who exists as a mere object.

36. Sartre rejects the unconscious for reasons that seem to me to be interesting, but ultimately unacceptable.

37. This is not to say that such people should stop doing science, etc., with their present motives. They may be happier than they are otherwise likely to be, and may be contributing to the intellectual or practical good of other people. Also see footnote 12, above.

38. I am indebted to G. Boolos, E. Erwin, B. Jacobs, D. Lewin, S. Ogilvy, and M. Wilson for helpful comments on earlier drafts of this paper.

THE HUMANIST RESPONSE

TO HAVE AND TO BE

John Lachs

In an incident Aesop did not record, three animals were lamenting their fate. "If only I had more to eat," said the pig, and he imagined himself buried under an avalanche of fragrant victuals. "If only I had shorter hours and less work," complained the ass as he rubbed his aching back. "If only people had more things and I greater skill to steal them." whispered the fox, for he did not want to be found out.

The God Zeus, known for his cruel sense of humor, heard their complaints and decided to grant the animals what they desired. The pig's larder was overflowing with food: he had so much that he had to ask the fox to store some of it for him. But soon the pig could no longer enjoy these good things. Eating too much had caused indigestion and he could not even think of cooking or of food. The ass's workday was reduced; his master bought a small truck to do his heavy work. But soon, instead of concentrating on all the important things he had said he would do, the ass fell asleep and spent his day in a stupor. The fox did not fall asleep, but once the initial glory and excitement of plucking defenseless chickens had abated, he grew indifferent to the charm of pillage. He was bored.

The fable has of course, no moral for anyone who thinks that boredom, stupor, and the glut that comes of overconsumption are integral parts of a good and human life. No good has ever come of the fanatic claim that only one's own ideas are right and only one's own values authentic: if there is anyone who wishes to

From *The Personalist,* 45 no. 1 (Winter 1964), pp. 5-14. Reprinted by permission of the author and the editor.

adopt the fabled pig's desires or share the fox's fate, I will be glad to have him try. The ultimate test of living by the right values is satisfaction or equilibrium, and satisfaction is an individual matter. It is possible that undisciplined consumption is the good of some, while others find happiness in the indulgence of their orgiastic passions. Nothing could be farther from my intention than to censure such behavior. Nature continues to laugh in the face of those stern moralists who strain to set bounds to the plasticity of man.

I will, then, not condemn a way of life, and I will not categorically reject the set of values which in embodies. Nor will I recommend the universal acceptance of another, possibly quite dissimilar, set of principles or aims. I will restrict myself to a critical appraisal of some of the values by which some men in our society live, and for which too many may be willing to die. A critical approach need not lead to criticism: it is merely the dispassionate attitude of the investigator who attempts, in this instance, to determine the value of certain values. As sympathy can only be aroused in men who share a certain concern and possess imagination, values can only be discerned by persons whose nature coincide and who are endowed with sagacity and insight. For this reason, my conclusions will have no validity at all save for those whose nature—being similar to mine—prescribes for them a similar way of life, who are able to achieve the self-knowledge that is required to recognize this, and eventually perhaps to muster the courage to carry it out.

If the values of the pig, the fox, or the ass satisfy you, I will not argue: surely, nature will out. Your satisfaction implies that in truth you are a human pig, or a human fox, or an ass. But what of the rest of us who live amidst the ruins of values that were our fathers'? Tossed in an ocean of conflicting obligations and alien pressures, many of us survive by makeshift, impermanent adjustments: we live without settled principles, without a private attitude to life, without a planned pattern to our being. We are not trained to divine the demands of our individual nature, and as a consequence many of us lack the inner unity that is the unmistakable feature of a *person*. There is nothing mysterious about this inner unity. Morality is a kind of hygiene: it is a cleanliness and unpromiscuity of mind. As the child learns the simple facts of animal hygiene—to eat only that which nourishes and to reject whatever does not agree with his nature—the adult has to learn, sometimes through tragic experiences, the importance of acting by a single principle and living by a single plan, assimilating and dismissing as his nature commands. A healthy conscience is but the inner demand for consistency which makes one's life the history of a person instead of a disconnected series of events.

There is a current fallacy whose prevalence I do not feel called upon to discuss. This specious but unuttered principle is best expressed in the phrase "To live is to make a living." All the values of our Consumer Age are implicit in this phrase. "To make a living," of course, means to earn enough to be able to purchase the goods necessary for life. But what are the goods necessary for life? According to what I shall, for short, call the Consumer's Fallacy about the Ends of Human Life, enough food to avoid hunger, and enough shelter and clothing to keep warm, are not enough to *live* in the full sense of that word. Implicit in the Consumer's Fallacy is the claim that we do not even begin to *live* until we have the right or approved kind of food bought in a good store, fashionable clothing, and a cave as good as our neighbors'. This, of course, is only the beginning. For there are characteristically human needs, such as the need for fast cars, the need for heartshaped bathtubs, and the need for the envy of one's fellows. We *live* when we have as many of these and other goods as our fortune will allow or our stratagems create.

The possession and the use of manufactured physical objects have become primary and fundamental facts in our culture and in our lives. They have penetrated our thought to such an extent that the attitudes appropriate to ownership and use have come to serve as the model for our attitudes to the world at large and to other human beings in it. Our attitude to almost every thing we have or wish for is the attitude of a consumer. We use not only cars and washing machines, but also reputation and the goodwill of our neighbors. We possess not only typewriters and television sets, but also security and the loyalty of our children. It is, of course, natural for the human mind to reify the intangible: to substitute images for attitudes and concrete objects for abstract relations. But when such conceptual aids cease to be merely that and begin to penetrate our mental life and to govern our actions, when human beings begin to be considered physical objects and human feelings things to be consumed, the result is that the good life becomes a life filled with goods, and our attempt to live it culminates in a rage of possessiveness.

At the basis of the Consumer's Fallacy is the supposition that a man is what he has: that happiness is a function of the goods we possess and the things we consume, that it is the result of urges satisfied. Thus Hobbes, an early exponent of the Consumer's Fallacy, writes:

> Continual success in obtaining those things which a man from time to time desires, that is to say, continual prospering, is what men called *felicity*.[1]

If this is true, the introduction of mass advertising and of credit buying are the two greatest steps ever taken to promote the happiness of man. Advertisers create new desires, and consumer credit makes it possible for these desires to be readily satisfied. The unbroken cycle of desires and satisfactions guaranteed amounts to that "continual prospering" which men call "felicity." Continual success, which is happiness, is the share of the American who desires, purchases and consumes in proportion to the installment payments he can meet. And lest my point be misunderstood: what is purchased need not be a manufactured object, it may be love, and the installment payment need not be a sum of money, it may be time to listen to a woman's troubles, or a promise of security.

If Hobbes and his contemporary soul-mates are right and happiness is but the satisfaction of desires on the basis of wisdom in trading, I wonder why so many Americans, shrewd businessmen at work as well as in their private life, remain unhappy. If Hobbes's analysis were correct, the successful consumption of physical objects and of human emotions should suffice to make us happy. How is it then, that so many of us are successful as owners and consumers, even as consumers of human feelings, but unsuccessful as men? The answer to this question is not to be found by an examination of the means we utilize to achieve our ends: it resides, instead, in the nature and inadequacy of our current ends. Similarly, the cure for human dissatisfaction is not by concentrating or increasing our possessions, nor again by concentrating on combating the natural urge to have, but by relegating possession and consumption to their rightful and limited place in a comprehensive scheme of human values.

The Consumer's Fallacy and the accompanying tendency to treat human feelings as commodities and human beings as serviceable objects, is closely connected with our current veneration of progress. Progress is a kind of motion: it is motion in the direction of some desirable goal. What differentiates progress from mere movement or change is its directionality. Direction, in turn, implies a fixed point of reference: some state of affairs for which we strive, an objective that is deemed worthwhile. I do not wish to assail the apologists of progress on the issue of mistaken standards: that some of the objectives in terms of which we measure our "progress" are insignificant or worthless is too obvious to require emphasis. It is as easy to suppose as it is barbarous to assert that the possession of two radios per family or the development of wash-and-wear, warm-yet-light, no-ironing-needed underwear is the yardstick by which human advance is to be judged. My immediate concern here is not with such mistakes, but with two even more fundamental errors which the indiscriminate veneration of progress promotes.

The first blunder is best expressed in the scandalous slogan "Progress is our most important product." Progress, in fact, is a movement not a product, and its sole importance derives from the importance and the value of its goal. No progress is valuable in and of itself: only the end of progress is of any worth, and it is only by reference to this end that a change may be called "progressive." The value of progress is, in this way, entirely derivative: it is wholly dependent on the value of the fixed objective at which progress aims. This single reflection should eliminate the mistake of supposing that progress can or ought to go on indefinitely or, in other words, that progress can be its own end. Like all forms of transit, progress aims at a destination not at its own self-propagation: its object is a state where progress will no longer be because its goal will have been achieved. I am, of course, not denying that progress is a "good thing" in some sense of that ambiguous phrase. But good things are of two sorts: those which we want for their own sake or as ends, and those which we want for the sake of other things or as means. Comfort and pleasure may be things we want in and of themselves: if they are such *ends,* they are valuable. Coal and electrical generators are a *means* to these ends. They help to bring about our comfort and pleasure and while not intrinsically valuable, they are at least useful. Now progress is at best useful; it is not intrinsically valuable. It is good as a means but not as an end: it must have an end or objective other than itself. Hence progress can never be the goal of progress and no progress can be indefinitely sustained. Progress makes no sense at all without the possibility of fulfillment or attainment, and the more fervently we desire the attainment of our goals, the more we look forward to the time when progress, having got us our aim, will have ceased to be.

The sharp separation of progress from its goal is the source of the second mistake to which I alluded. We believe that it is important to progress and pride ourselves on being a "progressive" nation. We tend to overlook the fact that progress is not a term of unqualified commendation. Progress is movement in the direction of that which we do not have and which, at the same time, it would be good to have. Its existence implies a current lack along with the hope of future consummation. For this reason, any society committed to progress is at once also committed to the future, and whoever is committed to the future ceases to live in the present. But it is impossible to live in anything but the present. The person who attempts to live in the future ends up by not living at all: his present is saturated with a heavy sense of impermanence, worthlessness and longing for the morrow. His concentration on what is yet to come blinds him to the satisfactions that are possible now. His desire to come closer to his goal makes his present a chamber of horrors: by hastening the passage of the days he wishes his life away. And not only is his longing agonized, after such fierce desire each attainment is an anticlimax. Unreleased emotion paints in hues reality can never match. The object of desire once possessed is only a pale replica of what it was to be.

The meaning of life is not to be found in the future and the characteristically human malady of trying to find it there leads only to disappointment and despair. Caught between the incompleteness of striving and the essential insufficiency of the possessions which flow from desire and hard work, the future-directed man lives with a pervasive sense of insecurity, anxiety, defeat. The paradigm is the grotesque figure of the man who works so hard to provide for his retirement that he dies of a heart-attack when he is forty-two. I will call the belief, fostered by our veneration of progress, that the means and the end must be distinct and separated by time, the Fallacy of Separation. The combination of the attitudes of ownership and use implicit in the Consumer's Fallacy with this Fallacy of Separation issues in disastrous effects on the attempt to lead the good life.

The Fallacy of Separation is so deep-seated in our thinking that it is difficult for us to conceive and almost impossible to admit that means and end may coincide. But this admission is the foundation of all sound ethics and, accordingly, it is found on the first page of Aristotle's great work on the subject. There Aristotle says:

> A certain difference is found among ends; some are activities, others are products apart from the actions that produce them.[2]

As a result of our commitment to the future and of our interest in "products apart from the actions that produce them," the concept of *activity* has been virtually lost to Western civilization. An activity is a deed, any deed, that is performed for its own sake. It is an action done not as a means to obtaining some ulterior end or producing some product. Let me make my point with unceremonious simplicity: to engage in activity is to keep doing things without getting anywhere. But why should we wish to get anywhere if we are satisfied with whatever we are doing? The desire to get somewhere, our everlasting restlessness, betrays a sense of dissatisfaction with what we have and what we do and what we are. If we find something worth doing, it is reasonable to enjoy doing it and to ask for no more. If we are satisfied with what we do and are, it becomes unnecessary to look to the future and hope for improvement and progress.

Because the concept of activity is alien to us today, we tend to think that whenever change ceases, stagnation sets in. If this were true, no one would be more stagnant than the Christian God, who is free of desire and eternally changeless. However, to be without the striving that characterizes the infantile romantic mind is not necessarily to be static or inert. Striving might come to an end not only out of exhaustion or disgust, but also because the condition of all striving, the separation of means and end, of creative act and created product, is eliminated. Activity is not the sequestered sleep of the impotent: it is, instead, achievement unfailing and instantaneous, because in it alone the human act is its own reason for existence. I readily admit that all activity is useless, and hasten to add that this uselessness of activity is the best indication of its great value. The useful merely *produces* good things without being one. Activity, on the other hand, is good in and of itself. Too often our actions are useful to bring about ends that are worthless. When these actions cease to point beyond themselves, like poisoned arrows, when they begin to function as ultimate ends, they acquire a worth that places them in the category of what is useless but because of its intrinsic value also priceless.

If the good life is a happy life, the pig, the fox, and the ass are guilty of two fundamental errors. The first is an error of attitudes, the second an error of aims. The Consumer's Fallacy prompted the animals to extend the attitudes of ownership, use and consumption to areas, such as leisure, happiness and the emotions of human persons, in which they are inappropriate. The Fallacy of Separation prompted the unfelicitous beasts to look for aims and goals that are other than activities, for products of the human act instead of the enjoyment of the act for what it is. In short, the pig, the fox, and the ass all wished to *have* and not to *do*. But human beings are built to be bustling engines: they are agents and only action can satisfy them. Possession is not action, it is a passive state and as such at best a substitute for activity.

There is no clearer instance of a possession that functions as an activity-substitute than what is now commonly called a "status-symbol." To *be* a developed person is to engage in characteristic activity. Nothing is more difficult than this, since it involves self-knowledge, spontaneous action and self-control. Thus the majority of us settle for less, while we wish to appear as if we had not compromised. If we cannot *be* someone, we can do the next best and *appear to be*: and this is done by acquiring the possessions that seem to go with being a man of distinction or a developed individual. On the level of the popular mind the confusion is even clearer. Each status symbol reveals an attempt to substitute having for being, ownership for activity, possessions for character: each is a visible manifestation of our endeavor to be someone by having what he has.

A question spontaneously arises in my mind, and I am sure it has already arisen in yours. What cure can we prescribe for the three beasts? My answer to this is as simple as it is disarming. I cannot prescribe a cure for animals. If satisfaction attends their life, I congratulate them: if they do not interfere with mine, I will at least tolerate them. But how could I prescribe a mode of life for forms of life that are as alien from mine as oysters are from migratory mice? I can only speak for myself and for anyone else whose similar nature demands a similar fulfilment.

For us my counsel is to be. Life itself is an activity, and we should not approach it with the attitude of the devourer of experiences or with a possessive violence. We must develop attitudes appropriate to activity, to self-contained, self-validating human action: nothing short of this can make a life happy, spontaneous, and free. Finally, we must engage in appropriate activity. Which activities are appropriate for us is determined by our nature and may be discovered by self-knowledge. The two rules of the personal hygiene of the mind are to know oneself and to concentrate on the exercise of human powers for its own sake and not for its products or its usefulness. By knowing ourselves we will do the right things, by concentrating on the exercise of human powers for its own sake we will do them for the right reason. In this way, each moment of life acquires meaning and inalienable value. In this way, death cannot cut us off or leave our lives dismembered. For under these conditions each moment of existence shines like a total crystal: each is an appropriate, meaningful, and completed human act.

NOTES

1. Thomas Hobbes, *Leviathan* (London, 1943), p. 30.
2. Aristotle, *Nicomachean Ethics,* 1094a 3-5.

A FiNAL REJOINDER

THE ABSURD

Thomas Nagel

Most people feel on occasion that life is absurd, and some feel it vividly and continually. Yet the reasons usually offered in defense of this conviction are patently

From *Journal of Philosophy,* 58, no. 20 (October 21, 1971), pp. 716-27. Reprinted by permission of the author and the editor. Presented in an APA symposium on The Meaning of Life, December 29, 1971.

inadequate: they *could* not really explain why life is absurd. Why then do they provide a natural expression for the sense that it is?

I

Consider some examples. It is often remarked that nothing we do now will matter in a million years. But if that is true, then by the same token, nothing that will be the case in a million years matters now. In particular, it does not matter now that in a million years nothing we do now will matter. Moreover, even if what we did now *were* going to matter in a million years, how could that keep our present concerns from being absurd? If their mattering now is not enough to accomplish that, how would it help if they mattered a million years from now?

Whether what we do now will matter in a million years could make the crucial difference only if its mattering in a million years depended on its mattering, period. But then to deny that whatever happens now will matter in a million years is to beg the question against its mattering, period; for in that sense one cannot know that it will not matter in a million years whether (for example) someone now is happy or miserable, without knowing that it does not matter, period.

What we say to convey the absurdity of our lives often has to do with space or time: we are tiny specks in the infinite vastness of the universe; our lives are mere instants even on a geological time scale, let alone a cosmic one; we will all be dead any minute. But of course none of these evident facts can be what *makes* life absurd, if it is absurd. For suppose we lived forever; would not a life that is absurd if it lasts seventy years be infinitely absurd if it lasted through eternity? And if our lives are absurd given our present size, why would they be any less absurd if we filled the universe (either because we were larger or because the universe was smaller)? Reflection on our minuteness and brevity appears to be intimately connected with the sense that life is meaningless; but it is not clear what the connection is.

Another inadequate argument is that because we are going to die, all chains of justification must leave off in mid-air: one studies and works to earn money to pay for clothing, housing, entertainment, food, to sustain oneself from year to year, perhaps to support a family and pursue a career—but to what final end? All of it is an elaborate journey leading nowhere. (One will also have some effect on other people's lives, but that simply reproduces the problem, for they will die too.)

There are several replies to this argument. First, life does not consist of a sequence of activities each of which has as its purpose some later member of the sequence. Chains of justification come repeatedly to an end within life, and whether the process as a whole can be justified has no bearing on the finality of these end-points. No further justification is needed to make it reasonable to take aspirin for a headache, attend an exhibit of the work of a painter one admires, or stop a child from putting his hand on a hot stove. No larger context or further purpose is needed to prevent these acts from being pointless.

Even if someone wished to supply a further justification for pursuing all the things in life that are commonly regarded as self-justifying, that justification would have to end somewhere too. If *nothing* can justify unless it is justified in terms of something outside itself, which is also justified, then an infinite regress results, and no chain of justification can be complete. Moreover, if a finite chain of reasons cannot justify anything, what could be accomplished by an infinite chain, each link of which must be justified by something outside itself?

Since justifications must come to an end somewhere, nothing is gained by denying that they end where they appear to, within life—or by trying to subsume the multiple, often trivial ordinary justifications of action under a single, controlling life scheme. We can be satisfied more easily than that. In fact, through its misrepresentation of the process of justification, the argument makes a vacuous demand. It insists that the reasons available within life are incomplete, but suggests thereby that all reasons that come to an end are incomplete. This makes it impossible to supply any reasons at all.

The standard arguments for absurdity appear therefore to fail as arguments. Yet I believe they attempt to express something that is difficult to state, but fundamentally correct.

II

In ordinary life a situation is absurd when it includes a conspicuous discrepancy between pretension or aspiration and reality: someone gives a complicated speech in support of a motion that has already been passed; a notorious criminal is made president of a major philanthropic foundation; you declare your love over the telephone to a recorded announcement; as you are being knighted, your pants fall down.

When a person finds himself in an absurd situation, he will usually attempt to change it, by modifying his aspirations, or by trying to bring reality into better accord with them, or by removing himself from the situation entirely. We are not always willing or able to extricate ourselves from a position whose absurdity has become clear to us. Nevertheless, it is usually possible to imagine some change that would remove the absurdity—whether or not we can or will implement it. The sense that life as a whole is absurd arises when we perceive, perhaps dimly, an inflated pretension or aspiration which is inseparable from the continuation of human life and which makes its absurdity inescapable, short of escape from life itself.

Many people's lives are absurd, temporarily or permanently, for conventional reasons having to do with their particular ambitions, circumstances, and personal relations. If there is a philosophical sense of absurdity, however, it must arise from the perception of something universal—some respect in which pretension and reality inevitably clash for us all. This condition is supplied, I shall argue, by the collision between the seriousness with which we take our lives and the perpetual possibility of regarding everything about which we are serious as arbitrary, or open to doubt.

We cannot live human lives without energy and attention, nor without making choices which show that we take some things more seriously than others. Yet we have always available a point of view outside the particular form of our lives, from which the seriousness appears gratuitous. These two inescapable view-points collide in us, and that is what makes life absurd. It is absurd because we ignore the doubts that we know cannot be settled, continuing to live with nearly undiminished seriousness in spite of them.

This analysis requires defense in two respects: first as regards the unavoid-ability of seriousness; second as regards the inescapability of doubt.

We take ourselves seriously whether we lead serious lives or not and whether we are concerned primarily with fame, pleasure, virtue, luxury, triumph, beauty, justice, knowledge, salvation, or mere survival. If we take other people seriously and devote ourselves to them, that only multiplies the problem. Human life is full of effort, plans, calculation, success and failure: we *pursue* our lives, with varying degrees of sloth and energy.

It would be different if we could not step back and reflect on the process, but were merely led from impulse to impulse without self-consciousness. But human beings do not act solely on impulse. They are prudent, they reflect, they weigh consequences, they ask whether what they are doing is worthwhile. Not only are their lives full of particular choices that hang together in larger activities with temporal structure: they also decide in the broadest terms what to pursue and what to avoid, what the priorities among their various aims should be, and what kind of people they want to be or become. Some men are faced with such choices by the large decisions they make from time to time; some merely by reflection on the course their lives are taking as the product of countless small decisions. They decide whom to marry, what profession to follow, whether to join the Country Club, or the Resistance; or they may just wonder why they go on being salesmen or academics or taxi drivers, and then stop thinking about it after a certain period of inconclusive reflection.

Although they may be motivated from act to act by those immediate needs with which life presents them, they allow the process to continue by adhering to the general system of habits and the form of life in which such motives have their place—or perhaps only by clinging to life itself. They spend enormous quantities of energy, risk, and calculation on the details. Think of how an ordinary individual sweats over his appearance, his health, his sex life, his emotional honesty, his social utility, his self-knowledge, the quality of his ties with family, colleagues, and friends, how well he does his job, whether he understands the world and what is going on in it. Leading a human life is a full-time occupation, to which everyone devotes decades of intense concern.

This fact is so obvious that it is hard to find it extraordinary and important. Each of us lives his own life—lives with himself twenty-four hours a day. What else is he supposed to do—live someone else's life? Yet humans have the special capacity to step back and survey themselves, and the lives to which they are committed, with that detached amazement which comes from watching an ant struggle up a heap of sand. Without developing the illusion that they are able to escape from their highly specific and idiosyncratic position, they can view it *sub specie aeter-nitatis*—and the view is at once sobering and comical.

The crucial backward step is not taken by asking for still another justification in the chain, and failing to get it. The objections to that line of attack have already been stated; justifications come to an end. But this is precisely what provides universal doubt with its object. We step back to find that the whole system of justification and criticism, which controls our choices and supports our claims to rationality, rests on responses and habits that we never question, that we should not know how to defend without circularity, and to which we shall continue to adhere even after they are called into question.

The things we do or want without reasons, and without requiring reasons—the things that define what is a reason for us and what is not—are the starting points of our skepticism. We see ourselves from outside, and all the contingency and specificity of our aims and pursuits become clear. Yet when we take this view and recognize what we do as arbitrary, it does not disengage us from life, and there lies our absurdity: not in the fact that such an external view can be taken of us, but in the fact that we ourselves can take it, without ceasing to be the persons whose ultimate concerns are so coolly regarded.

III

One may try to escape the position by seeking broader ultimate concerns, from which it is impossible to step back—the idea being that absurdity results because what we take seriously is something small and insignificant and individual. Those seeking to supply their lives with meaning usually envision a role or function in something larger than themselves. They therefore seek fulfillment in service to society, the state, the revolution, the progress of history, the advance of science, or religion and the glory of God.

But a role in some larger enterprise cannot confer significance unless that enterprise is itself significant. And its significance must come back to what we can understand, or it will not even appear to give us what we are seeking. If we learned that we were being raised to provide food for other creatures fond of human flesh, who planned to turn us into cutlets before we got too stringy—even if we learned that the human race had been developed by animal breeders precisely for this purpose—that would still not give our lives meaning, for two reasons. First, we would still be in the dark as to the significance of the lives of those other beings; second, although we might acknowledge that this culinary role would make our lives meaningful to them, it is not clear how it would make them meaningful to us.

Admittedly, the usual form of service to a higher being is different from this. One is supposed to behold and partake of the glory of God, for example, in a way in which chickens do not share in the glory of coq au vin. The same is true of service to a state, a movement, or a revolution. People can come to feel, when they are part of something bigger, that it is part of them too. They worry less about what is peculiar to themselves, but identify enough with the larger enterprise to find their role in it fulfilling.

However, any such larger purpose can be put in doubt in the same way that the aims of an individual life can be, and for the same reasons. It is as legitimate to find ultimate justification there as to find it earlier, among the details of individual life. But this does not alter the fact that justifications come to an end when we are content to have them end—when we do not find it necessary to look any further. If we can step back from the purposes of individual life and doubt their point, we can step back also from the progress of human history, or of science, or the success of a society, or the kingdom, power, and glory of God,[1] and pull all these things into question in the same way. What seems to us to confer meaning, justification, significance, does so in virtue of the fact that we need no more reasons after a certain point.

What makes doubt inescapable with regard to the limited aims of individual life also makes it inescapable with regard to any larger purpose that encourages the sense that life is meaningful. Once the fundamental doubt has begun, it cannot be laid to rest.

Camus maintains in *The Myth of Sisyphus* that the absurd arises because the world fails to meet our demands for meaning. This suggests that the world might satisfy those demands if it were different. But now we can see that this is not the case. There does not appear to be any conceivable world (containing us) about which unsettled doubts could not arise. Consequently the absurdity of our situation derives not from a collison between our expectations and the world, but from a collision within ourselves.

IV

It may be objected that the standpoint from which these doubts are supposed to be felt does not exist—that if we take the recommended backward step we will land on thin air, without any basis for judgment about the natural responses we are supposed to be surveying. If we retain our usual standards of what is important, then questions about the significance of what we are doing with our lives will be answerable in the usual way. But if we do not, then those questions can mean nothing to us, since there is no longer any content to the idea of what matters, and hence no content to the idea that nothing does.

But this objection misconceives the nature of the backward step. It is not supposed to give us an understanding of what is *really* important, so that we see by contrast that our lives are insignificant. We never, in the course of these reflections, abandon the ordinary standards that guide our lives. We merely observe them in operation, and recognize that if they are called into question we can justify them only by reference to themselves, uselessly. We adhere to them because of the way we are put together; what seems to us important or serious or valuable would not seem so if we were differently constituted.

In ordinary life, to be sure, we do not judge a situation absurd unless we have in mind some standards of seriousness, significance, or harmony with which the absurd can be contrasted. This contrast is not implied by the philosophical judgment of absurdity, and that might be thought to make the concept unsuitable for the expression of such judgments. This is not so, however, for the philosophical judgment depends on another contrast which makes it a natural extension from more ordinary cases. It departs from them only in contrasting the pretensions of life with a large context in which *no* standards can be discovered, rather than with a context from which alternative, overriding standards may be applied.

V

In this respect, as in others, philosophical perception of the absurd resembles epistemological skepticism. In both cases the final philosophical doubt is not contrasted with any unchallenged certainties, though it is arrived at by extrapolation from examples of doubt within the system of evidence or justification, where a contrast with other certainties *is* implied. In both cases our limitedness joins with a capacity to transcend those limitations in thought (thus seeing them as limitations, and as inescapable).

Skepticism begins when we include ourselves in the world about which we claim knowledge. We notice that certain types of evidence convince us, that we are content to allow justifications of belief to come to an end at certain points, that we feel we know many things even without knowing or having grounds for believing the denial of others which, if true, would make what we claim to know false.

For example, I know that I am looking at a piece of paper, although I have no adequate grounds to claim I know that I am not dreaming; and if I am dreaming then I am not looking at a piece of paper. Here an ordinary conception of how appearance may diverge from reality is employed to show that we take our world largely for granted; the certainty that we are not dreaming cannot be justified except circularly, in terms of those very appearances which are being put in doubt. It is somewhat far-fetched to suggest I may be dreaming; but the possibility is only illustrative. It reveals that our claims to knowledge depend on our not feeling it necessary to exclude certain incompatible alternatives, and the dreaming possibility or the total hallucination possibility are just representatives for limitless possibilities most of which we cannot even conceive.[2]

Once we have taken the backward step to an abstract view of our whole system of beliefs, evidence, and justification, and seen that it works only, despite its pretensions, by taking the world largely for granted, we are *not* in a position to contrast all these appearances with an alternative reality. We cannot shed our ordinary responses, and if we could it would leave us with no means of conceiving a reality of any kind.

It is the same in the practical domain. We do not step outside our lives to a new vantage point from which we see what is really, objectively significant. We continue to take life largely for granted while seeing that all our decisions and certainties are possible only because there is a great deal we do not bother to rule out.

Both epistemological skepticism and a sense of the absurd can be reached via initial doubts posed within systems of evidence and justification that we accept, and can be stated without violence to our ordinary concepts. We can ask not only why we should believe there is a floor under us, but also why we should believe the evidence of our senses at all—and at some point the framable questions will have outlasted the answers. Similarly, we can ask not only why we should take aspirin, but why we should take trouble over our own comfort at all. The fact that we shall take the aspirin without waiting for an answer to this last question does not show that it is an unreal question. We shall continue to believe there is a floor under us without waiting for an answer to the other question. In both cases it is this unsupported natural confidence that generates skeptical doubts; so it cannot be used to settle them.

Philosophical skepticism does not cause us to abandon our ordinary beliefs, but it lends them a peculiar flavor. After acknowledging that their truth is incompatible with possibilities that we have no grounds for believing do not obtain— apart from grounds in those very beliefs which we have called into question—we return to our familiar convictions with a certain irony and resignation. Unable to abandon the natural responses on which they depend, we take them back, like a spouse who has run off with someone else and then decided to return; but we regard them differently (not that the new attitude is necessarily inferior to the old, in either case).

The same situation obtains after we have put in question the seriousness with which we take our lives and human life in general and have looked at ourselves without presuppositions. We then return to our lives, as we must, but our seriousness is laced with irony. Not that irony enables us to escape the absurd. It is useless to mutter: "Life is meaningless; life is meaningless . . ." as an accompaniment to everything we do. In continuing to live and work and strive, we take ourselves seriously in action no matter what we say.

What sustains us, in belief as in action, is not reason or justification, but something more basic than these—for we go on in the same way even after we are convinced that the reasons have given out.[3] If we tried to rely entirely on reason, and pressed it hard, our lives and beliefs would collapse—a form of madness that may actually occur if the inertial force of taking the world and life for granted is somehow lost. If we lose our grip on that, reason will not give it back to us.

VI

In viewing ourselves from a perspective broader than we can occupy in the flesh, we become spectators of our own lives. We cannot do very much as pure spectators of our own lives, so we continue to lead them, and devote ourselves to what we are able at the same time to view as no more than a curiosity, like the ritual of an alien religion.

This explains why the sense of absurdity finds its natural expression in those bad arguments with which the discussion began. Reference to our small size and short lifespan and to the fact that all of mankind will eventually vanish without a trace are metaphors for the backward step which permits us to regard ourselves from without and to find the particular form of our lives curious and slightly surprising. By feigning a nebula's-eye view, we illustrate the capacity to see ourselves without presuppositions, as arbitrary, idiosyncratic, highly specific occupants of the world, one of countless possible forms of life.

Before turning to the question whether the absurdity of our lives is something to be regretted and if possible escaped, let me consider what would have to be given up in order to avoid it.

Why is the life of a mouse not absurd? The orbit of the moon is not absurd either, but that involves no strivings or aims at all. A mouse, however, has to work to stay alive. Yet he is not absurd, because he lacks the capacities for self-consciousness and self-transcendence that would enable him to see that he is only a mouse. If that *did* happen, his life would become absurd, since self-awareness would not make him cease to be a mouse and would not enable him to rise above his mousely strivings. Bringing his new-found self-consciousness with him, he would have to return to his meagre yet frantic life, full of doubts that he was unable to answer, but also full of purposes that he was unable to abandon.

Given that the transcendental step is natural to us humans, can we avoid absurdity by refusing to take that step and remaining entirely within our sublunar lives? Well, we cannot refuse consciously, for to do that we would have to be aware of the viewpoint we were refusing to adopt. The only way to avoid the relevant self-consciousness would be either never to attain it or to forget it—neither of which can be achieved by the will.

On the other hand, it is possible to expend effort on an attempt to destroy the other component of the absurd—abandoning one's earthly, individual, human life in order to identify as completely as possible with that universal viewpoint from which human life seems arbitrary and trivial. (This appears to be the ideal of certain Oriental religions.) If one succeeds, then one will not have to drag the superior awareness through a strenuous mundane life, and absurdity will be diminished.

However, insofar as this self-etiolation is the result of effort, willpower, asceticism, and so forth, it requires that one take oneself seriously as an individual—that one be willing to take considerable trouble to avoid being creaturely and absurd. Thus one may undermine the aim of unworldliness by pursuing it too vigorously. Still, if someone simply allowed his individual, animal nature to drift and respond to impulse, without making the pursuit of its needs a central conscious aim, then he might, at considerable dissociative cost, achieve a life that was less absurd than most. It would not be a meaningful life either, of course; but it would not involve the engagement of a transcendent awareness in the assiduous pursuit of mundane goals. And that is the main condition of absurdity—the dragooning of an unconvinced transcendent consciousness into the service of an immanent, limited enterprise like a human life.

The final escape is suicide; but before adopting any hasty solutions, it would be wise to consider carefully whether the absurdity of our existence truly presents us with a *problem,* to which some solution must be found—a way of dealing with *prima facie* disaster. That is certainly the attitude with which Camus approaches the issue, and it gains support from the fact that we are all eager to escape from absurd situations on a smaller scale.

Camus—not on uniformly good grounds—rejects suicide that the other solutions he regards as escapist. What he recommends is defiance or scorn. We can salvage our dignity, he appears to believe, by shaking a fist at the world which is deaf to our pleas, and continuing to live in spite of it. This will not make our lives un-absurd, but it will lend them a certain nobility.[4]

This seems to me romantic and slightly self-pitying. Our absurdity warrants neither that much distress nor that much defiance. At the risk of falling into romanticism by a different route, I would argue that absurdity is one of the most human things about us: a manifestation of our most advanced and interesting characteristics. Like skepticism in epistemology, it is possible only because we possess a certain kind of insight—the capacity to transcend ourselves in thought.

If a sense of the absurd is a way of perceiving our true situation (even though the situation is not absurd until the perception arises), then what reason can we have to resent or escape it? Like the capacity for epistemological skepticism, it results from the ability to understand our human limitations. It need not be a matter for agony unless we make it so. Nor need it evoke a defiant contempt of fate that allows us to feel brave or proud. Such dramatics, even if carried on in private, betray a failure to appreciate the cosmic unimportance of the situation. If *sub specie aeternitatis* there is no reason to believe that anything matters, then that doesn't matter either, and we can approach our absurd lives with irony instead of heroism or despair.

NOTES

1. Cf. Robert Nozick, "Teleology," *Mosaic,* XII, 1 (Spring 1971): 27/8.

2. I am aware that skepticism about the external world is widely thought to have been refuted, but I have remained convinced of its irrefutability since being exposed at Berkeley to Thompson Clarke's largely unpublished ideas on the subject.

3. As Hume says in a famous passage of the *Treatise:* "Most fortunately it happens, that since reason is incapable of dispelling these clouds, nature herself suffices to that purpose, and cures me of this philosophical melancholy and delirium, either by relaxing this bent of mind, or by some avocation, and lively impression of my senses, which obliterate all these chimeras. I dine, I play a game of backgammon, I converse, and am merry with my friends; and when after three or four hours' amusement, I would return to these speculations, they appear so cold, and strain'd, and ridiculous, that I cannot find in my heart to enter into them any farther" (Book 1, Part 4, Section 7; Selby-Bigge, p. 269).

4. "Sisyphus, proletarian of the gods, powerless and rebellious, knows the whole extent of his wretched condition: it is what he thinks of during his descent. The lucidity that was to constitute his torture at the same time crowns his victory. There is no fate that cannot be surmounted by scorn" (*The Myth of Sisyphus,* Vintage edition, p. 90).